HELL'S
HIGHWAY

Also by George E. Koskimaki

D-Day with the Screaming Eagles
The Battered Bastards of Bastogne

HELL'S
HIGHWAY

A CHRONICLE OF THE 101ST AIRBORNE IN THE HOLLAND CAMPAIGN,
September–November 1944

George E. Koskimaki

PRESIDIO PRESS

BALLANTINE BOOKS • NEW YORK

2007 Presidio Press Mass Market Edition

Published in the United States by Presidio Press, an imprint of The Random House Publishing Group, a division of Random House, Inc., New York.

PRESIDIO PRESS and colophon are registered trademarks of Random House, Inc.

Originally published in hardcover in the United States by George E. Koskimaki in 1989. Subsequently published in 2003 by Casemate Publishing, Havertown, PA.

Map illustrations by Peter Barnette

ISBN 978-0-89141-893-1

Cover photograph: Corbis

Printed in the United States of America

This edition published by arrangement with Casemate Publishing.

www.presidiopress.com

OPM   9 8 7 6 5 4 3 2 1

Dedicated to the paratroopers and glidermen of the 101st Airborne Division as well as the brave pilots and crews who delivered them to participate in the Market-Garden campaign along Hell's Highway.

It is dedicated, also, to the brave men and women of the underground movement in the Netherlands during World War II.

Foreword

Hell's Highway as a historical work will make you feel as if you were there! My first encounter with the book was on an airplane, on the way to Holland in September of 1988, when George Koskimaki asked me to read a chapter of his original manuscript. After one chapter I was addicted. I wanted to read one more chapter, and then one more. My first reading of *Hell's Highway* was disjointed because chapters arrived singly and in small multiples, until I had the whole book. I have read *Hell's Highway* twice in its complete form and have reached the conclusion that it is the best story of a military action I have read.

George Koskimaki is a master at weaving the individual stories of the airborne soldiers with personal accounts of Dutch civilians to produce a story that could not be improved by the embellishments of a writer of fiction. This is high adventure that could not be imagined. It is told by those who experienced the airborne assault into Holland, kept the highway open for the British armored drive toward Arnhem, and the Dutch people who were liberated from years of occupation by the Nazi German forces.

If you liked *A Bridge Too Far,* you will love *Hell's Highway.* This book tells how the "Screaming Eagles" of the 101st Airborne Division accomplished their mission by securing their assigned section of the highway to Arnhem. You will also learn from firsthand observations why this airborne force, surrounded by the German army of occupation, found the task of keeping the road open so difficult that they named their objective Hell's Highway.

Hell's Highway is a history, most of which has never before been written. It is adventure recorded by those who lived it and put in perspective by an author who was also there and saw and wrote accounts about actions of the entire 101st Airborne Division. It is human drama on a scale that could not be produced by an author without the 612 contributors of written and oral accounts of the Screaming Eagles' part in liberating a part of Holland.

The objective of Operation Market-Garden, to cross the Rhine at Arnhem, was not achieved. Ask any of the citizens of the Netherlands who were liberated from the German occupation by the airborne troops and they will tell you it succeeded for them. They prove it every year, in September, by celebrating their liberation and serving as perfect hosts to veterans and active-duty members of the 101st Airborne Division who travel to Holland to be a part of the celebration of the anniversary of their regained freedom.

Hell's Highway is a true story of liberators who dropped from the sky and those on the ground who were liberated and have never forgotten the bravery of airborne soldiers who survived and of those who made the supreme sacrifice for freedom.

Ivan G. Worrell
Executive Secretary
101st Airborne Division Association

Acknowledgments

I wish to first acknowledge the assistance of the 612 individuals, former comrades of the 101st Airborne Division; troop carrier pilots and crew members; glider pilots; as well as the ninety Dutch citizens who responded to a newspaper request in the corridor town publications by Peter Hendrikx in my behalf. This narrative would never have been completed without the help of all these people.

I thank the members of the Dutch Airborne Friends Society and especially Frans Kortie and Abraham Bom for providing the opportunity to visit the corridor towns and interview individuals during the 1987 and 1988 "Remember September" celebrations.

Heartfelt thanks go to my drivers on various research missions in the Netherlands: Pierre Cuijpers, Peter Hendrikx, Mia v.d. Linden-deGreef, Lisa van Overveld, Pete Pulles, Tony Rijkers, and Christ van Rooy. Also for my guides who led me to specific battle sites: Bernie Florissen, Guert deHartog, Mia v.d. Linden-deGreef, Albert Marinus, Pete Pulles, and Jan Tornga.

My translators: Micky Bokker, Peter Hendrikx, Andre Van Bergeijk, Ernst Van Bergeijk, Arie Van Dort, William Van Wely, and Tony Wernaart.

Photographs used in the account came from the collections of: Mark Bando, Roger Bell, Glenn Braddock, John E. Fitzgerald, James Haslam, Robert E. Jones, Lisa van Overveld, John Van Geffen, and Ivan Worrell, national secretary of the 101st Airborne Division Association, who allowed use of any appropriate photos in the association collection.

Diaries and unit logs provided by Bruce M. Beyer, Earl L. Cox, Edward Jurecko, William Knickerbocker, George Koskimaki, Joke van Hapert-Lathouwers, Jacoba (Koos van Schaik) Milovich, Charles Ritzler, Bert Sanders, Peter Santini, Harry Tinkcom, Gerald Van Boeckel, and Gerald Zimmerman.

Extensive narratives came from Henry Barnes, Harold Spence, and Harry Tinkcom. All three accounts did much to tie in the stories of others. Kees Wittebrood sent a short history of the North Brabant Sanitarium (Zonhove), which became the division hospital. I am so grateful to them.

I thank David Galarneau and Bill Wedeking, former platoon leaders who sent their wartime maps for my use. These helped Peter Barnette in preparing many of the maps used with the text of *Hell's Highway.*

I want to thank Paul Lawson at the Pratt Museum at Fort Campbell for copies of the unit histories of the 81st Airborne Anti-Aircraft and Anti-Tank Battalion and the 326th Airborne Medical Company. I thank Harold E. Young and "Stub" Storeby for copies of the *326th Airborne Engineer Battalion Unit History,* which helped much in getting the actions of those units into proper perspective. I thank Fred Patheiger for a copy of the 502nd Regimental Action Report for Holland. To Charles McCallister I owe a debt of gratitude for the copy of the 506th After-Action Report for Holland; to the Eisenhower Library at Fort Leavenworth for reports on the 501st Parachute Infantry Regiment and the 327th Glider Infantry Regiment.

And thanks to my wife, Eva, for the many hours she spent going through my copy, checking proper usage and making changes when necessary; to Jack Taylor, eldest son of our wartime commanding general, for an interesting anecdote on his father. He also provided sound advice as an experienced author himself; to Darlyle Watters for checking my materials on the glider phase of the Holland operation; to Joe Ludwig, Robert E. Jones, and John Fitzgerald for critical reading of chapters concerning their regiment; to Robert O'Connell, George Rosie, and Ivan Worrell for their assistance and suggestions.

I was so pleased to work with Mrs. Sonia Kurtyka of Graphic Touch and appreciate the many, many hours of work she spent at typesetting and getting the text of *Hell's Highway* camera-ready.

I may have missed others who had a hand in the preparation of this book and I am truly sorry. The omission was unintended.

George Koskimaki
Northville, Michigan
June 28, 1989

Contents

Contents

Maps

Drawn by Peter Barnette

.

Illustration

Glossary

AA	Anti-aircraft
AT	Anti-tank
AWOL	Absent without official leave
BAR	Browning automatic rifle
CG	Commanding general
CO	Commanding officer
CP	Collecting point
DZ	Drop zone
EM	Enlisted men
F/O	Flight officer
GI	Government issue; enlisted man
IP	Initial point
LD	Line of departure
LMG	Light (.30-caliber) machine gun
LZ	Landing zone
MLR	Main line of resistance
MP	Military police
NCO	Non-commissioned officer
OP	Observation post
Stick	Group of paratroopers jumping from same plane
Streamer	Parachute that failed to open properly
TCC	Troop Carrier Command
TCG	Troop Carrier Group
TCS	Troop Carrier Squadron
TO	Table of organization

U.S. Army Rankings

Pvt.	Private
PFC	Private first class (one stripe)
Cpl.	Corporal (two stripes)
T/5	Technician 5th grade (two stripes)
Sgt.	Sergeant (three stripes)
T/4	Technician 4th grade (three stripes)
S/Sgt.	Staff sergeant (four stripes)
T/3	Technician 3rd grade (four stripes)
T/Sgt.	Technical sergeant (five stripes)
M/Sgt.	Master sergeant (six stripes)
1/Sgt.	First sergeant (six stripes with diamond insert)
WOJG	Warrant officer junior grade
CWO	Chief warrant officer
2Lt.	Second lieutenant (one brass bar)
1Lt.	First lieutenant (one silver bar)
Capt.	Captain (two silver bars)
Maj.	Major (one bronze leaf)
LTC	Lieutenant colonel (one silver leaf)
Col.	Colonel (silver eagle)
BG	Brigadier general (one star)
MG	Major general (two stars)
LTG	Lieutenant general (three stars)
Gen.	General (four stars)

ONE

Introductory Review

This is history as witnessed by participants in the greatest airborne operation of the entire war. The Market-Garden operation covered a period of a week, interrupted by bad weather during three days of the campaign.

The narrative includes the stories of pilots and crew members of the C-47 troop carrier transport planes, glider pilots, glider troops and paratroopers of the 101st Airborne Division, and one glider trooper from the British 1st Airborne Corps who was part of the 101st operation. The stories of former Dutch underground resistance fighters as well as Dutch citizens are included in the account.

The narrative takes the reader from the return of the bloodied but now veteran 101st Airborne Division from Normandy to England where they prepare for the second airborne operation after several aborted missions.

The pathfinder mission, the paratroop flights, and the glider lifts over several days are described by the participants. Descriptions of the operations to seize the objectives assigned to the Screaming Eagles are provided by the men with their little human interest tales.

No attempt is made to analyze the soundness of various moves but the tales unfold as they happened. *Hell's Highway* has much that has not appeared in previous historical accounts of the Market-Garden campaign.

The actions of the 82nd and 101st Airborne Divisions received very little attention from the media during or since the war's end. The focus was concentrated on the plight of the gallant British 1st Airborne Division and the Polish Airborne Brigade in their losing battle in and around Arnhem. LTG Lewis H. Brereton, commander of the 1st Allied Airborne Army, stated that the

101st and 82nd American Airborne Divisions had fought their hearts out and whipped the hell out of the Germans and got very little credit for their efforts.

The corridor leading from Eindhoven to Arnhem needed to be kept open so the British 2nd Army, and particularly 30th Corps, could move quickly northward to relieve the beleaguered British sky troopers. This was a continuing assignment of both the 82nd and 101st Airborne Divisions.

Hell's Highway concentrates on the efforts of the 101st Airborne Division during the first two weeks of the operation in the area between Eindhoven and Uden, and then again when the 101st is involved in a defensive struggle on the island (Betuwe) between Arnhem and Nijmegen for a period of almost two months. Their responsibility during that time was to keep the enemy from attacking the Nijmegen bridge from the west and away from the one highway open to the British leading to the south bank of the Neder Rijn near Arnhem.

I have made considerable use of small-unit after-action reports for the Holland campaign. These reports covered actions of the 327th Glider Infantry Regiment, the 502nd and 506th Parachute Infantry Regiments, the 81st Anti-Tank and Anti-Aircraft Battalion, and the 326th Engineer Battalion. An unpublished narrative by BG S.L.A. Marshall and his assistant, Lieutenant Westover, concerning the first-day moves of LTC Harry W. O. Kinnard's 1st Battalion of the 501st Parachute Infantry Regiment was also used. Extensive use was made of an after-action report for the first ten days in Holland. It was prepared by BG Gerald J. Higgins and his staff. This report helped place the actions into the proper time sequence.

Diaries of individual soldiers play a key role in this book as it kept stories fresh in the minds of those who kept records of their days in combat in Holland. Where others may have forgotten the names of participants in specific actions, the diary notations brought the long-forgotten soldiers back into memory.

Because of my knowledge of the makeup of the entire 101st Airborne Division, unit by unit (company and battery), I was able to assist the men with their recall by providing company or battery rosters along with news about surviving members. Many of the men had been out of touch since the end of the war forty-five years ago. Many who had been wounded and never returned after the Holland campaign said they cried when they saw the names of close buddies as having been killed later in the Holland campaign, which extended over a period of seventy-two days, or later at or near Bastogne during the Battle of the Bulge.

Many happy reunions of long-lost buddies have resulted from the five years of extensive research done in writing to, and interviewing 1,382 former members of the 101st Airborne Division, troop carrier pilots and crew members, glider pilots, Dutch underground, some of whom now live in Canada and the United States. Dutch citizen participation in this project has been great. Many have sent descriptions of the airborne landings when the troops of the 101st descended from the sky by parachute and glider near their homes, or who came to their small Dutch towns and cities, pushing the enemy out ahead of them. They greeted us with a lot of pent-up emotion. We felt like heroes.

The Dutch in the corridor towns are an unusual people. They have not allowed their children to forget the sacrifices made on their behalf by soldiers who came thousands of miles from across the wide expanse of the Atlantic Ocean. As Mrs. C. Cornuijt-Gosen of Eindhoven wrote in *Static Line,* an airborne newspaper published by Don Lassen in College Park, Georgia, "This gives me an opportunity to pronounce my gratitude to America, to the American people, especially to all those men who were willing to fight in another part of the world for countries and people they did not know. I thank all those men who were prepared to fight and, if necessary, to die, to sacrifice their lives for letting us live in peace. Thanks to these men for letting me live my life in freedom. God bless you all."

The ceremonies each year at the U.S. Military Cemetery at Margraten are most impressive. Dutch children by the thousands file into the cemetery to place flowers on each of the 8,301 graves of our military dead. The gravestones are set in long graceful curves. On each side of the Court of Honor are two walls on which are recorded the names of 1,722 men who gave their lives in the service of their country but who sleep in unknown graves. Many Dutch people have written to me to relate how they have tended specific graves over four decades since the end of World War II. While the temporary cemetery was near Son, the family of Mrs. C. Boonman-Lammers tended the grave of 1Lt. Fred Gibbs on a weekly basis. She and her husband continue to visit his grave at Margraten each year. Rita van Loon of Eindhoven wrote: "My sister Oddy, now 64 years old, still tends the grave of S/Sgt. George S. Hunter of the 327th Glider Infantry Regiment. He was from Minneapolis. We will never forget the boys who fought for our freedom!" Her family adopted the graves of four 101st soldiers who were buried in the temporary cemetery near Son. The remains of some of those soldiers were sent back home to the States after the war.

In September of 1988, I stopped in the cemetery in the village of St. Oedenrode to pay homage to some of the local members of the underground who were executed by the enemy for their efforts in freeing their fellow countrymen from the yoke of an oppressive conqueror. I have learned from former resistance fighters that thousands of their fellows and women died for their efforts and beliefs. I choke up now as I write these lines about a Dutch girl whose story was related by PFC George K. Mullins: "One evening a Dutch girl came riding her bicycle through our outposts along a country road and headed through the German lines. It was related to us a few days later when that enemy territory was occupied that she was found dead in a barn hung by the neck." Undoubtedly the young lady was suspected of being a courier for the Allied cause. Many women risked their lives during the war and particularly during the Market-Garden campaign, and many died at the hands of the enemy.

As related in the story, the youngsters took to the friendly airborne soldiers. Some of them were caught up in the fierce battles and died with their newfound friends. Former medic Paul R. Miller still thinks of fourteen-year-old Jac Wynen, who led Miller to avoid Germans and "Quislings" to tend to wounded, both military and civilian. The boy died during a heavy shelling.

Perhaps Wynen was the same lad described by PFC Leonard T. Schmidt of the same regiment who wrote: "We had a little Dutch boy of 14, an orphan, who followed us all around in combat and he finally got killed."

This, then, is the story of airmen, soldiers, underground, Dutch men and women, told collectively in remembering those days of the war in Holland. A total of 612 participants sent me their recollections and I have pieced them together like a giant jigsaw puzzle.

As written in the introduction of our first book, *D-Day with the Screaming Eagles,* former mortar sergeant John Urbank said, "I feel I'm holding faith with some of the boys who didn't make it. I remember more than once hearing Buford Perry and David Mythaler say, 'If anyone asks what war is like—we're going to tell them in the best way we know how—none of this crap that War is Hell and we can't talk about it!' So be it. So keep their faith."

The feats of the airborne soldiers as we knew them have faded into legend as the helicopter has been replacing the parachute and glider. Now the extensive use of the helicopter as an airborne weapon may be questioned with the development of the heat-seeking missile, fired from a simple launcher from the shoulder of an individual soldier. It may alter the use of the modern means of moving the present-day airborne soldier to a quickly developing battle situation.

TWO

English Summer

The shipping lanes were filled with traffic headed for the invasion beaches of Normandy when the 101st Airborne Division set off for their return to England on the twelfth of July on board LSTs. The Screaming Eagles were the first division-sized unit to be removed from the combat zone after their successful June 6 drop and subsequent five weeks in combat.

The division band was on hand to serenade the troops as they marched off the landing ships in Southampton Harbor on the afternoon of July 13. There was "ole Moe" to greet his troopers. Col. George Van Horn Moseley had suffered a broken leg in landing in France and was destined to lose his beloved 502nd Parachute Infantry Regiment to his successor, LTC John Michaelis.

After picking up coffee and doughnuts passed out by the American Red Cross "doughnut dollies," the troops filed onto the waiting trains to be whisked off to their former training areas to once more begin the preparation for a future combat mission.

But first there was time for rest and relaxation. Most headed for their favorite pubs that evening to relate hair-raising tales to their British friends. The next day, after receiving their pay, which had accumulated for two months, the men headed for London, nearby weekend haunts, or parts unknown in Scotland for a much-needed seven-day furlough.

One who delayed his departure was 1Lt. Sumpter Blackmon, executive officer of "A" Company of the 501st Parachute Infantry Regiment. He decided to complete a letter-writing mission to the many families of men from his unit who had lost their sons in the Company "A" combat actions in Normandy. They were many. Some had drowned in the flooded swamps and fields as they floundered in chin-deep water, loaded down with

heavy equipment. Others had dropped far to the south of designated drop zones. Some survived to spend the rest of the war in
POW camps. Others died in short, fierce battles that were
fought by small groups against better-equipped enemy forces.
Those not accounted for had to be counted as possible KIAs.
Blackmon wrote: "I felt every one of the families needed to be
notified by someone who knew about their sons. (PFC Charles
Emerson of Derby, CT was one. Sgt. Leonard A. Davis of Louisiana was another.)"

After the furloughs were over, additional replacements arrived on the scene. Others had arrived in the English training
camps while the men fought in Normandy.

How had the 101st Airborne Division fared in Normandy?
They had suffered a total of 3,836 casualties during the month
of June with 868 being listed as killed in action.

The drop of the parachute segment of the division had been
badly scattered over much of the Cherbourg Peninsula. The
drop pattern covered an area of twenty-five by fifteen miles.
Seventy percent of the men had landed within an eight-mile-
square area. Of the fifteen hundred dropped outside this area,
most were killed or captured.

A total of forty-six planes of the 1,656 night and day sorties
were shot down. Glider losses were less because of predawn
flights. It had been an amazing accomplishment that the pilots
of the fifty-two predawn gliders had brought their craft into the
small gridiron-sized fields in the predawn hours. The fields had
been rimmed with forty- to fifty-foot-tall trees and interspersed
throughout the fields were "Rommel's Asparagus," anti-glider
poles that had been installed to discourage airborne operations.
During the evening of D-Day the larger plywood Horsa gliders
had arrived in the same small areas but they had light by which
to steer away from obstacles.

The division had sent fourteen thousand men into combat in
France of which sixty-six hundred had gone via parachute. A
total of eighty-four gliders had carried 101st troops into France.
The rest of the men had come in over the beaches because of the
limited number of gliders. One would wonder how the glider infantry regiment and the artillery battalions would have fared if
ample aircraft had been available to them.

Because of the scattered drops, assembly had been a terrible
problem. On D-Day, only eleven hundred men of the sixty-six

hundred dropped were with their units by H-Hour when the invasion forces began landing on beaches along the Normandy coast. By 1800 hours, twenty-five hundred men had assembled with their units which meant only 38 percent of the men in on the initial airborne assault got together with their units the first day. Future airborne operations would have to be much improved or this mode of combat would be dropped as too costly.[1]

Many of the soldiers who had shown their mettle in Normandy would now be in positions of leadership as platoon sergeants and several had received battlefield commissions.

Leaders who were lost as the result of the first combat mission included a regimental commander who was evacuated with a severe leg fracture. Another was shipped out in the early stages for being too cautious. Three battalion commanders had died in action. Ten company commanders were gone. Four had been killed. Battalion staffs had been decimated and needed reorganization.

A large number of replacements had arrived on the training camp scene on D-Day in anticipation of expected heavy losses to the regiments and battalions in combat. These men had to be worked into the squads, platoons, and battery formations so they would become integral parts of fighting units. In the last week of July and the early part of August, training at the platoon and company level went on in earnest.

During August the 1st Allied Airborne Army came into being with LTG Lewis H. Brereton being selected as its commander. MG Matthew P. Ridgway, former head of the 82nd Airborne Division, was chosen to head the U.S. XVIII Airborne Corps, one segment of that new army. The British had their 1st Airborne Corps as their part of 1st Allied Airborne Army.

Long before the decision to drop an airborne carpet over which the British 2nd Army and particularly the XXX Corps would move north through Holland was made, military planners decided there would be no further large-scale night operations for paratroops and glidermen. The Allies now had almost total superiority in the skies. Large flights of troop carrier

---

1. For a detailed account of how the 101st Airborne Division fared in Normandy on D-Day, the reader is encouraged to read Koskimaki's *D-Day with the Screaming Eagles*.

planes could be protected adequately by the many squadrons of fighter planes. Bombers, and particularly fighter-bombers, could take out known flak batteries. The airborne army was ready for a large-scale, daylight operation.

After Normandy, a total of sixteen Allied airborne operations got to the paper-planning stage and several came close enough to send troops to the marshaling areas.

The code name for the first aborted operation was Transfigure. It was scheduled for August 17th and was to destroy a large part of the German 7th Army by trapping it south of Paris. As Gen. George S. Patton approached Orléans, airborne troops would spring the trap by blocking the roads over which the enemy intended to retreat. In its final form the plan called for parachute and glider troops of the 101st Airborne Division to land near St-Arnolult-en-Yvelines and for the British 1st Airborne Division and the Polish Parachute Brigade to drop in the vicinity of Rambouillet. By the sixteenth almost every usable troop carrier plane was marshaled and ready.

The personal diary of T/4 George E. Koskimaki of the 101st Signal Company illustrates the fast-moving events that were suddenly thrust upon the airborne divisions.

> August 12, 1944—Got fifty more replacements in the company. We started getting our new equipment this morning. We're hot again so it is combat again soon.
>
> August 14, 1944—Really busy today. The seaborne troops left. We got our chutes again. Our second combat jump is coming soon.
>
> August 16, 1944—We were at Aldermaston Airbase but were transferred to Welford Park Aerodrome. We had our briefings tonight.
>
> We are scheduled to jump near Paris tomorrow morning for our second D-Day.

On the sixteenth, Patton's tanks moved faster than anticipated and approached Rambouillet. Next morning Transfigure was postponed and later canceled.

Linnet was the next airborne operation that was given serious consideration. It would have involved the 82nd and 101st Airborne Divisions, the 1st British Airborne Division, and the Polish Brigade. It was scheduled for September 3.

Again there was a flurry of activity at the 101st Airborne Division bases around Newbury. T/4 George Koskimaki described the rapid changes involving his company.

August 30—Had a company dance in town. A formation was called at midnight. Had to pack our bags and prepared to leave for the marshaling area at 0800.

August 31—We arrived at the marshaling area this morning. Our company was the first to make its appearance this time. We get foreign money again tomorrow after the briefings. It isn't France this time.

September 1—We helped the glider boys load up. I found out we are scheduled to jump in Belgium, just behind the Maginot Line. We will be briefed tomorrow.

September 2—Had our briefing today. This should be our toughest mission. I'm jumping a 45-pound radio in a leg pack. We take off at 0702 tomorrow morning.

September 3—Our mission was called off at midnight because the British Guards Armored Division reached our objective. We shall wait here until we get a new mission.

The same units were to have jumped north of Liège in Operation Linnet II to secure crossings over the Meuse River on September 4. Field Marshal Bernard Montgomery ruled against it on September 3. Had the operation taken place, it would have been seriously disrupted for lack of maps, photographs, and other information.

Of the 2,303 men of the 101st who had been wounded or injured in Normandy, some were ready to return to their units. Others had been captured when they landed on German fortifications. They were to be repatriated to the States. Many showed up at their home bases just before departure for the marshaling areas the third time, or caught up with their units in the staging areas.

T/5 Leonard F. Hicks had been wounded in Normandy. He was still "officially" a patient in a military hospital from which he had not been discharged. He wrote: "I just left. When I arrived back in 'F' Company of the 506th Regiment, they dressed me in borrowed clothing, took me to Division headquarters for back pay and sent me on a furlough to Scotland. Two or three days later MP's picked me up with no explanation. They took me back to the division by train. Everyone who knew anything was gone. That was three months lost for me. I joined the paratroops for other reasons."

PFC Robert "Buck" Barger was one of those "lucky" ones who talked his way into going on the mission. He wrote: "After Normandy, I was grounded by our executive officer, Captain Edwin C. Yeary." Barger had been badly injured on the Normandy jump and was not fully recovered. He had caused his parachute to streamer to get out of the line of tracer bullets streaking up to meet him and a bad landing was the result with numerous fractures and dislocations. Barger had lain in the field for two and a half days, dosing himself with morphine ampules when the pain became unbearable. He was later found by a patrol and taken to the division hospital, which was operated by his company.

When his company was ready for another mission, Barger wanted to be in on it. "When the Holland campaign became reality, I went over Captain Yeary's head to our company commander, Major William Barfield and convinced him I should go. Captain Yeary assigned me to the third glider."

Sgt. Chester Pentz remembered his pal, Pvt. Redmond Wells. "He was in the hospital recovering from his D-Day wounds when he heard that we were going on another mission. He went AWOL from the hospital and found us in the marshaling area the day before the jump. He didn't have a thing with him in the way of a combat uniform or a weapon so we fixed him up and talked the 'Doc' into letting him go."

Pvt. William J. Houston had suffered a broken leg on the D-Day jump in Normandy and had his moments in and out of the hands of the enemy but he made it back to England. Now, with his leg heavily taped, he was ready for the Holland mission.

The moment he had set foot on French soil, Cpl. Martin W. Clark was in enemy hands along with many of his friends. They had landed directly in a fortified German position. After weeks of captivity, he finally escaped and returned to England where he was supposed to be repatriated back to the United States. However, he and buddy PFC Joseph Gorenc decided to make one last visit to their old outfit in Ramsbury. When they got there, they discovered their unit was on alert. He wrote: "The 506th Regiment was on alert when we got there and your two stupid heroes had to volunteer to go along."

When the 101st Division returned from the marshaling areas

for the Linnet I and Linnet II "dry runs," the 81st Anti-Aircraft and Anti-Tank Battalion left their area for a training mission to Kimmeridge for range firing of all batteries. The whole battalion moved out on the twelfth of September to their new locations. While the firing was in progress, an alert order was received and all men and equipment were returned to the home base at Basildon on the fourteenth of September.

Taking part in a rather unique operation, Cpls. F. J. Sellers and Harold Spence, members of the 1st British Airborne Corps, were to join the 101st Airborne Division for the Market-Garden operation as cipher specialists. They were assigned to the message center section of the 101st Signal Company. Harold Spence has chronicled those experiences in a booklet called *Experiences of an Airborne Cipher Operator.* Part of those experiences are included here. Spence wrote: "On September 14th, Cpl. F. J. Sellers and I left the 1st British Airborne Corps and joined the 101st Airborne Division as 'attached' liaison personnel. After establishing contact with their cipher officer, Sellers and I settled down with the signalmen and very quickly were quite at home in their company. Everything was new and very interesting, and this helped us to forget the object of our visit.

"During the next day (Friday) we moved over to the Transit Camp adjoining the airfield from which we were to take off. Here we would have the briefing, a final check on equipment, and then await 'H' hour. Not unnaturally, the chief topic of conversation was 'where do we go from here?' Speculation was rife. That U.S. division went all over Europe by the hour, but the popular vote easily went to Germany. In spite of the belief that a really tough job faced them, morale ran very high. Indeed, the greatest fear was that this Op would develop into another 'dry run'—the fate of so many of its predecessors.

"The camp was sealed thoroughly. Naturally, we were not allowed outside the camp boundary but I was rather surprised to find ourselves conducted everywhere. We paraded for washing, meals, cinema shows—in fact, everything. This was to avoid our conversing with those troops who had already been briefed or those not 'going in'. Security was certainly the order of the day and no risks were being taken.

"During the evening we went to a film shown in the camp which had been 'laid on' for our entertainment. Going to the pictures with the Yanks is an interesting experience. Mugs are taken along and before going in everyone draws a pint of hot coffee and three or four doughnuts as refreshment during the show. We two British corporals discovered during those few days that our American friends have some habits we could well emulate."

S/Sgt. Edward Jurecko received his briefing a day early as a platoon leader. He was also serving as jumpmaster for his stick of "D" Company jumpers. In a diary he kept in Holland, until wounded along the dike in October, he recorded his actions whenever combat situations permitted it. Jurecko describes the events taking place in the marshaling area:

> Sept. 14—We were just now briefed and we are going for sure—Holland! Just in front of the Siegfried Line to make way for the advancing British armor. It looks like a good job and we should make it. All currency will be exchanged for Dutch money today. Each man will carry his own map of our drop sector. It's funny, but I'm ready to go and don't regret it.
>
> Sept. 16—We take off tomorrow. It will be a daylight jump. Jumpmaster notes: Station time: 0920, Engine 10:05, Taxi 10:15, Takeoff 10:26, Coast of France 1212, Drop time 1305. I'm sitting here taking notes of the operation which is slated for tomorrow. A huge map of Holland stands before the jumpmasters. Without a doubt, each man has his own thoughts and they are numerous. This will be the biggest airborne operation in history.

British cipher specialist Harold Spence described his experience with an American briefing: "On Saturday, about 11 A.M., we were summoned for the briefing. This was it. We trooped along, most of us silent and apparently unmoved, but I am sure the hearts of most of us were beating a little faster than normal. I know mine was. So much depended on where the 'Op' was to take place. In Germany, everyone was your avowed enemy whereas, if we were going to an occupied country, there was always the Underground to assist.

"The Signal Company gradually filled the tent and all eyes instantly went to the table which filled the center of the tent. On this was a large-scale map of the theater of operations. The first place name I saw was Eindhoven. So it was not to be Germany after all, but HOLLAND!

"Relief was obvious but the briefing officer cut short our sub-dued whispers and commenced to brief.

"The 'Op' was considered to be a typical 'Airborne' job. It had been well planned but was daring and would require the best from everyone to make it a success. The aim was to cap-ture, intact, certain bridges and hold them, in order to allow the British 2nd Army to go right through Holland as far as Arnhem. The officer explained the presence of the two British cipher op-erators. Questions were finally called for and Sellers and I were able to clear up one or two matters affecting British formations. The briefing was very thorough and lasted 90 minutes.

"Another cinema show was provided in the evening. At 11 P.M. we were preparing for bed when an orderly summoned Sellers and myself to a last minute cipher briefing. We swore, but really were glad, because there were quite a number of technical points we wanted cleared up and we welcomed this opportunity of getting some 'griff.' Two hours with them settled everything to our satisfaction and we came away with a clear picture of the operation and the part we were to play.

"After a final check on our equipment, personal and opera-tional, we went to bed at 1:30 A.M. wondering if, and where, we should sleep on the morrow."

Operation Market-Garden was to provide an airborne carpet for British forces so they could race to outflank the Germans who were in retreat to northern Germany. The British and Pol-ish airborne units were to be concentrated in the Arnhem area while the 82nd Airborne Division was to cover the Nijmegen-Grave area and the 101st Airborne Division was spread out be-tween Veghel and Eindhoven.

Field Marshal Bernard Montgomery had proposed to drop the 101st over an area spanning thirty miles. This had upset division commander MG Maxwell D. Taylor. LTG Miles C. Dempsey of the British forces and Major General Taylor had consulted about this and modified the plan so the Screaming Eagles were not overextended. No drops were to be made near Eindhoven but were concentrated in the broad flat fields be-tween Son and Veghel.

The time for H-Hour was set for 1300. The 82nd and the British used a northern route of approach to Arnhem and Nij-megen while the 101st traveled a southern route to their DZs.

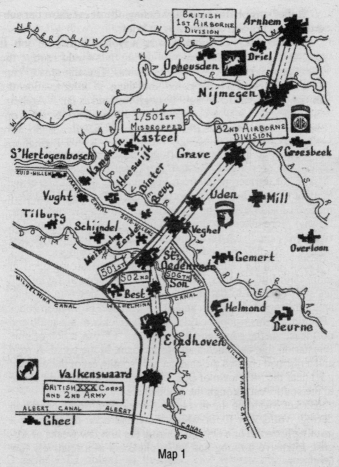

Map 1

The Troop Carrier Command had spaced the American parachute serials at four-minute intervals and the glider serials at
seven-minute intervals. Hoping to improve on the June 6, 1944,
procedure the TCC groups planned to deliver 1,055 planeloads
of paratroopers and 478 gliders within sixty-five minutes. It
took that much time to bring in 369 sticks of paratroops for the
82nd Airborne Division in Normandy.

It is likely the 101st may have chosen the desired drop zones even before Major General Taylor's meeting with Lieutenant General Dempsey. Detailed descriptions of the DZs were already in the field orders issued on the thirteenth of September. The initial tasks of the 101st were to seize the span over the Wilhelmina Canal at Son, two shorter spans over branches of the Dommel River in St. Oedenrode and four bridges over the Zuid-Willems-Vaart Canal and the Aa River in Veghel. The distance from the Son drop zone to Eindhoven was five air miles; the Dommel River passed through St. Oedenrode, four miles from the drop zone. The Veghel bridges were approximately two miles from drop zones "A" and "A-1" near Eerde. It would be a distance of thirteen miles from Veghel to the nearest DZ of the 82nd at Grave. The most important objectives for the 101st were the two canal bridges, which were twenty yards wide and the waterways were much too deep for tanks to cross by fording. The rivers were much narrower and, in Eindhoven, the Dommel was a mere creek flowing under the four secondary bridges.

Faced with the challenge of taking objectives strung out over more than fifteen miles of highway, Major General Taylor and his staff decided to put most of his division down in a single area midway between Son and St. Oedenrode. From drop zones "B" and "C" his troops could strike out quickly to the south and northeast. At the south end of drop zone "C" was a belt of pine forestation that extended south to the bank of the canal. A road and a railroad crossed the canal, a mile southwest of the wooded tract near the little town of Best. The distance to Best was a mile to the southwest through the wooded area.

Market was to be the first large American airborne operation during World War II for which there had been no time for a training program or a dry run. During the first few weeks of August, intensive training had taken place but at a relatively low level.

The night before the invasion RAF bombers attacked airfields that were within fighter range of the Market objectives. On the morning of the airborne landings, B-17s were sent in to attack anti-aircraft gun positions along the troop carrier routes. Fighter planes made sweeps near the drop zones between Son and Veghel. Suspected gun positions and suspected barracks were attacked again just before the arrival of the pathfinder planes.

THREE

Occupation

The Dutch Have Been Waiting

The German invasion of the lowlands of Belgium, Denmark, and Holland had taken place in the early weeks of May 1940. The Germans had struck quickly in Holland, seizing key bridges and strategic points to enable their "blitzkrieg" forces to overwhelm the undermanned security troops. All communications centers were quickly seized and the Germans were in full control. A full four years under the Nazi yoke had then begun.

At the time of the German invasion of Holland in 1940, Mrs. Joke van Hapert-Lathouwers and her sister were telephone operators in the Eindhoven exchange. On the day of the capitulation, May 10, German soldiers entered the exchange with guns in their hands, telling the operators to leave and that they were taking over. The women were replaced by older Germans. A few days later, the civilian staff was allowed to return. Life had to go on under the Germans. In 1943, the younger sister, Bets, joined her sisters as an operator.

While working as a cashier in the distribution office, her fiancé had forged ID documents which were used by downed Allied airmen. The Germans became aware of his activities. Her fiancé had to flee. His father, sister, and Joke were taken to prison. Joke was held for a week before being released. The Germans expected her to lead them to their prey. She was tailed for six weeks. (The father died in a concentration camp and his sister was liberated by the Americans in May 1945.)

In 1944, Joke was an operator, again, in the telephone exchange in Eindhoven. For a time she couldn't be hired as she had served time in prison. However, Seyss-Inquart (Dutch Quisling) provided a paper entitling her to return to her old job.

Joke didn't know why. By the time the Germans were pushed out of Normandy and northern France and into Belgium, the Dutch had a very small group of operators who helped the underground with its calls. Sister Gon organized the group.

Bert Pulles was six years old when the family moved to Prince Albert in Saskatchewan in Canada. With the coming of the Depression in the early 1930s, the family returned to Eindhoven to reestablish a family-operated bakery, which had first been set up by his grandfather.

After serving in the Dutch infantry, Pulles was discharged from the army in May 1940 when Holland capitulated and he went back to work in the bakery. Later, an order from the Germans directed that all ex-military men were to report and be put up as prisoners of war. Pulles went to work for the Philips factory to get an exemption. He worked there in name only, reporting for work when there was danger of being picked up.

At the age of fourteen, Gerard van Boeckel had already experienced four years of war. He remembered Allied bombing missions on objectives in the Eindhoven area. He listed in chronological order the air raids which affected his home city.

"On March 3, 1941, at 2300 hours, the RAF bombed the gas storage tank near our home. The big gas holder, 80 meters high, burned out. You could read a newspaper by its light that night, there was so much light from the fire. We also had a 500-pound bomb land in our house but it did not explode—lucky for us.

"On the 6th of December, 1942, we had an RAF bombardment of the Philips Works. One hundred British Ventura and Mosquito aircraft bombed for a quarter of an hour. One hundred eighty civilians were killed by misplaced bombs. On the 3rd of March, there was an attack by ten Mosquitoes on Philips resulting in 30 civilians being killed. In August, 1944, heavy bombing on the Welschap airfield near Eindhoven took place. It was in use by the German (Luftwaffe) Air Force."

Work in the resistance started early for Peter van Breevoort, who was arrested for the first time as a seventeen-year-old for helping Jewish people in Amsterdam. With the intercession of his father, he was released.

During those years, young van Breevoort was studying ship engineering in Amsterdam. At school, there was some activity of resistance going on. Breevoort recalled, "One morning, in the early hours, I was aroused from my bed by the police and brought to the headquarters of the S.D. They held me for the day for interrogation but they could not prove anything against me and I was released.

"A month later, I was ordered to go to Germany for forced labor. Instead I went into hiding, leaving Amsterdam as nothing was as yet organized there. Through the pastor of a Reformed church, I was brought into contact with a farmer named Burkink in Wichmond; here, I stayed in hiding for one and a half years, working on his farm.

"I belonged to the first group of men to go into hiding and, through contact with other farmers, a network of hiding places was organized to help other men in need to go underground. Some months later, my brother, Tom, also went into hiding with a farmer nearby and together we were able to help more Amsterdamers. In our district that blossomed into about 600 men.

"My father was able, through contact with the resistance in Amsterdam, to get us both a false Ausweis and we were able to move around more freely. However, in July of 1944, while traveling by train from Vugt to s'Hertogenbosch, we encountered a German S.D. control of papers and because they suspected that ours were false, we were taken to the Gestapo headquarters in Den Bosch. We were put in prison and, under pressure, each of us was questioned separately to reveal the origin of our false Ausweis. We both stuck to the same story without revealing where it came from.

"In August of 1944, they put us with 30 other prisoners under 15 guards on a bus for transport by train to an undisclosed concentration camp in Germany. The train was delayed because of heavy Spitfire strafings and we were returning to jail on the same bus.

"On the way back, my brother and I were sitting in the rear of the bus, next to an exit door. Tom discovered that the door was unlocked and with one look at each other we knew what we had to do. Now, to wait for the right moment to jump out. With a turn into a side street, the bus slowed down and Tom opened the door and one after the other we jumped out under the noses of the 15 guards who were positioned throughout the bus. We ran for our lives, while the guards yelled stop, stop and started shooting.

"Unfortunately, we ended up in a dead-end street. On the right stood a freight building with two big doors, which we opened. Inside were empty boxes stacked against a wall with only a window high on the far wall. We quickly stacked the boxes to reach the window, only to find this enmeshed with wire. With both hands and great force, I managed to break it resulting in two big cuts on my wrists. We looked down and called for help. People came running and, with a ladder, managed to help us out and they hid us in the sewer system that ran under the city. Tom even fell into it but I managed to pull him out. The Germans searched for us unsuccessfully and when it was dark the good burghers of Den Bosch took us out, bandaged my cuts and gave Tom dry clothes. They led us to the outskirts of the city and we started walking through the fields. We did not know which direction to go in the dark and for some time we stretched out on our backs in the grass and just drank in deeply our returned freedom.

"In the half darkness, we saw a farmer in his field. We went up to him and, not risking anything, we asked him straight out if he was an N.S.B.'er (traitor). The farmer gave us a disgusted look and we were satisfied. We told him that we had just escaped from the Germans and he took us home with him. His name was farmer Voets of Den Dungen. We both went into hiding on his farm.

"Because the Allied troops were closing in, more German soldiers were stationed in Den Dungen on different farms. We soon found out, through contact with these soldiers, that they were never used on the front line. Hitler did not trust them. They were usually older men from annexed countries and afraid to desert. Some of them offered to go into hiding and ten of them responded. Two came from the Alsace, one Polish, one Austrian and the rest from Rhineland. We managed to get ten overalls to put over their uniforms. At night, they slept in an underground dug-out hut, and in the daytime they helped pick corn. The one from Austria wove baskets from the husks."

One of the members of the resistance, Hans Kropman, is now a citizen of the United States. During the Market-Garden operation, he gave valuable assistance to the men of "A" Company of the 501st Parachute Infantry Regiment. He describes some of his activities while his native land was under the occupation of the Germans.

"At the time of the airborne invasion, I was hiding from the

German occupation in the Netherlands because they were looking for me since I was involved in several acts of sabotage.

"I had just completed my study in mechanical engineering and had obtained a job with a company that was producing parts and sub-assemblies, which were critical for the German military, and I had the confidence of the management of that organization. During many months I was able to make sketches and take photographs of secret documents and drawings and forward this information to the Dutch intelligence.

"Later, I made different essential tools and test equipment disappear, which turned out to be very effective in slowing down production and even stopped for some time the fabrication of certain parts, etc. However, I became careless and was caught and, after some very unpleasant interrogations, I was put on transport to Germany, for I presumed, forced labor, utilizing my engineering know-how.

"I escaped before we crossed the German border and was hiding on a farm in the southern part of Holland where I was helping with the work and at night I was assisting a doctor in writing a thesis about 'premature birth.' "

In the part of Holland that is situated between the lower Rhine (Neder Rijn) and the Waal River, Bill van Wely was destined to be much involved with the 101st Airborne Division in October and November. He describes what it was like in his home area, which which would witness the arrival of the British airborne forces scheduled to seize Arnhem and its key bridge.

Van Wely wrote: "There were not many German soldiers on the Island in the weeks before the airborne invasion. As a resident of Dodewaard, it wasn't considered important. Only a few soldiers looked after the communications lines. Activity began to develop in August and, as the Allies moved up around Antwerp, they started building machine gun nests and foxholes along our side of the dike along the Waal River facing Nijmegen. The enemy soldiers were older, not really interested in the fighting. They wanted the civilians to help dig those holes but most of us disappeared."

In describing some of the changes taking place on the battlefields to the west and the anticipations of the German defenders in the Eindhoven-Son area, Kees Wittebrood described actions in a pamphlet he had prepared on the occasion of visits by American veterans to Holland in 1979:

The weeks preceding D-Day, September 17, 1944, had been nerve-wracking ones for the Germans. Now the British 2nd Army was advancing through northern France and had taken the Belgian town of Tornai. The airfield at Eindhoven had been bombed heavily on August 15 and 27. There were repeated reconnaissance flights by the Allies, a constant source of irritation to the occupying forces.

The Germans were not expecting a mass invasion by air-landing troops. A fast thrust through Belgium seemed more probable. They were mainly concerned (in our area) with the bridge over the Wilhelmina Canal. On September 11, it was rumored that the bridge would be blown up at 10:00 hours next day. The windows and doors of the sanitarium were opened wide but after hours of tense waiting it became apparent that it was a false alarm.

On Tuesday, September 12, people living near the bridge started moving out to places offering more safety and the Germans began placing heavy artillery on the north side of the bridge. These were the dreaded 88mm guns.

On Friday, September 15, the Germans ordered the evacuation of everyone living in the vicinity of the bridge. Some of the people of Son took their belongings to the basement of the sanitarium.[2]

Changes were taking place in the communications system. Just before the liberation of Eindhoven, only telephone numbers for those friendly to the enemy, hospitals, German military numbers, and food supply service numbers were being honored. Since the German women operators brought in from Munchen-Gladbach were unfamiliar with procedures, they asked for assistance from the Dutch women, who would listen in on the conversations.

In the diary that Joke van Hapert-Lathouwers kept during the war she provided this information:

Sept. 7, 1944—The German operators are gone. They have been relieved by soldiers. There are few lines left for us. The suspense is growing. We see the Germans going back to their country, a tired, poor army in retreat. The underground is working hard. Everywhere railroad lines are being blown up. All traffic is in disorder.

Sept. 10—I was on duty today. Not all telephone offices can be reached. Venlo and Maastricht fell already. The big offices like Amsterdam and Rotterdam have a single line. S'Hertogenbosch has

2. Wittebrood, Kees. *History of Zonhove*. Son, Holland, 1979, 2.

only six girls friendly to the enemy to take only German army calls. The whole country is experiencing phone line problems.

Sept. 11—At 0300, the Dutch operators were sent home. The German soldiers stay. The position feels very critical.

Sept. 13—The time we are not allowed to work in the office we do courier service for the underground.

Gerard van Boeckel remembered that on Sunday, the tenth of September, the Germans destroyed the railways and station with explosives and also blew up the bomb and ammunition dump at the airfield.

Joop (Joe) van der Linden remembered what happened on his nineteenth birthday, the sixth of September. "A band of fleeing Germans, mostly young SS soldiers of the Hitler Youth Division, burst into our home, which was the local post office and had the telephone center for the village. They demanded possession of the telephone exchange and billeted about 15 of their men in our home. We were eight kids plus my parents, so we didn't have much room left. The Germans had all sorts of loot with them, such as big flasks of French cognac, sugar, cigarettes, coffee and offered some to my parents so that my mother would cook for them. She refused, and, luckily, they did not harm us. They also installed some of the 4-barrelled rapid fire anti-aircraft guns around the house and I do remember all sorts of hand weapons, bazookas and heavy machine guns lying around. It was very interesting to me and my brothers, of course."

As a thirteen-year-old, Mia v.d. Linden-deGreef remembered watching many retreating German soldiers passing through her village of St. Oedenrode during the week prior to the airborne drop. "They would stop and ask for water. The only cruel ones were the Hitler Youth (Jugens), 14 to 16 year olds, some of them in short trousers. They robbed us at pistol point. I remember one soldier who had a canteen which he wanted filled with water. It contained a large number of gold rings which he had stolen elsewhere. The Dommel River was near our home. There was a lane that led to the river. The Germans would drive their horses and stolen carts down there and dump whatever they were carrying, into the river.

"I remember the older Germans who would stop to rest in front of our house. One in particular was very old and he was crying. He had walked his way from France, through Belgium and now into Holland. I remember him saying, 'I wish it was over. It is enough!' "

In the city of Eindhoven, Bert Pulles observed: "All of a sudden the roads were full of retreating Germans. They came through Eindhoven on bicycles, with hand carts, with push carts, horse-drawn vehicles of every description and with fear written all over their faces. They were a scared but very mean bunch and nothing could stand in their way to get back to Germany."

Nurse Koos van Schaik of the Dutch Red Cross was on temporary duty at the evacuation hospital for old and infirm people in the village of St. Oedenrode. During her stay there she kept a daily diary of the events unfolding during the middle of September 1944. On the thirteenth of September, her diary entry included the following:

Last night the minister and nine nurses climbed the tower of the Protestant church to see if we could notice something on the horizon. Far away we could hear the guns. We were peeking through the slit windows of the steeple, when we suddenly saw fire and smoke north of Eindhoven. A few seconds later we did hear the boom, but the air pressure was not very strong so high up. At least we did not feel it. Later we heard that downstairs everything had rattled. The bridge between Eindhoven and some small village had been blown up and we had seen it from the top of the steeple. (This was probably one of the side bridges along the Wilhelmina Canal, either to the right or left of the main bridge at Son.)

There is a lot of activity in the air. For three days we have heard the planes fire at the troops on the highway. This afternoon I was still in bed (I am on night duty) and Willy was resting because she did not sleep last night. She worries herself to death about home. So, while still in bed, we heard the whistling of bombs. We almost fell out of our beds and rushed over to the inner wall to protect ourselves. Two terrific explosions followed and then only dust and the smell of powder. Nobody had heard the plane diving down towards the village to drop its bombs in front of the retreating German troops. However, the bombs fell on the Catholic church instead of on the road. The damage is severe. Several blind (duds) bombs have been found around the church and the area has been roped off. We hope the rest will not explode. In the village, the damage to windows and roofs is enormous. Homes were moved from their foundations. The canal of Son is being defended. Here the bridges over the River Dommel have been charged (explosives put into place).

The bombing incident involving the Catholic church was witnessed by Christ van Rooy. He wrote: "About three or four days before the landing, I was in a field near the village of St. Oedenrode. Two days before, the Germans brought much ammunition into the school. I looked up into the sky and saw two bombers. I saw four bombs fall from the sky. One of the bombs went through the roof of the church. Three bombs went into a field. None of the bombs hit the school, where all of the ammunition was stored."

Nurse Koos van Schaik provided information for the following day, after which she added her recollections of activities at the hospital where she and her Dutch Red Cross companion, Willy Ogg, had been assigned to duty.

September 14—It is coming closer, unmistakable, it is louder than yesterday. I am standing very protected in the backyard on the west side of the kindergarten building. The wind is east so it is not due to the wind that I can hear the noise better. I see lightning on the southern horizon. The rumble of artillery is like a faraway thunderstorm approaching slowly. But there is no thunderstorm in the sky on this nice September night. One can notice that the summer is gone. It is getting chilly at night. I shiver and go inside. When I have closed the door I feel with my finger tips at the glass. I can feel the constant vibrations caused by the heavy guns.

Nurse van Schaik adds to her diary notation: "Miss Miep Kosterman is in charge of this hospital. We do not have a resident doctor. The village doctor comes in the morning to make his daily visit.

"We have had an eventful day. At four o'clock a few Germans came to requisition two rooms for a field dressing station for the German Red Cross. The head nurse has given them the community hall and the stage. Tomorrow they will bring their material and supplies. Tonight the German guard is sleeping in the hall already. We moved the radio to the kindergarten building. No strangers are allowed in the hospital. We locked the doors and posted a lookout at the connecting door between the school and the community building so we can listen to the news. We have heard the report of the liberation of the city of Maastricht by American troops, broadcasted from England by Radio Oranje.

"At a quarter till twelve, I turned on the radio as low as possible and listened to the news. A repeat account of the liberation of Maastricht. The 2nd British Army, after heavy fighting, had broken the defense line at Bourg Leopold in Belgium and is pushing north to Hechtel and the Dutch border. Walkenswaard is under artillery fire. *They Are Coming!*"

Up on the island in the little town of Dodewaard, situated between the Neder Rijn on the north and the Waal River on the south, Bill van Wely remembered keeping posted on the war news through an illegally kept radio. He said, "One of the neighbors had a radio and I used to sneak through the orchard at night to listen to Radio Oranje over the BBC. The signal was weak and there was much jamming. The lady kept the radio behind clothes in the closet. Radio Oranje did keep our spirits up."

German Red Cross personnel now took over part of the building in which the nurses had their quarters in St. Oedenrode. Nurse Koos van Schaik continues her story in the diary for September 15:

> Willy and I clear out the stageroom which until now has been our sleeping quarters. We will now have to sleep on mattresses on the floor upstairs with the other nurses. There is not enough room. We have to give the Germans every bed and stretcher we can spare and put them on the stage and in the hall. We clean out the shelves and cupboards and made room for medical supplies and bandages. In the afternoon, the big German ambulance pulls up in front. Two German medics are carrying big cases inside marked "Luftwaffe Sanitatskasten" (Air Force medical supplies).

Severe tension developed within the staff as local nurses and trainees didn't want to be helpful to the Germans. However, the head nurse and Koos van Schaik and Willy Ogg, both Dutch Red Cross personnel, felt that Red Cross nurses come to the aid of anyone in time of need. There was bickering about accepting tea and coffee and German bread from the German medical corpsmen. Some didn't want to get hot water from the kitchen for the German surgeon and his small staff. Nurse van Schaik recorded in her diary:

> This evening all the nurses are in the room of nurse Vogelaar. The head nurse had made real tea. Nurses Verstappen, Truus and Rietje Hoonhout are coming upstairs.
> "Boy, what is this—real tea? Wow!"

"From the German ambulance," one of the other nurses remarks. As in one movement, they put down their cups. "Thank you, but we do not drink that!"

I move two of the cups to the other side of the table and take the third cup myself. "Take it or leave it," I say, "most likely it came special now that I am on night duty. Good night, I am going to work on the floor."

Downstairs I stop in amazement in the front hall. The Germans are listening to the British broadcast with their own radio. I can hear the German interference on the same wave lengths to garble the spoken words.

In Son, the Germans had ordered the Dutch people living near the Wilhelmina Canal bridge to move away. Some had gone to the North Brabant Sanitarium or Zonhove, as it was also called, where they sought shelter in the basement. According to Kees Wittebrood, their troubles did not end:

> The evacuation was not the end of the trouble for Son. On Friday, September 15, men were summarily rounded up on the streets of the town and made to dig fire trenches and a few tank traps. One of the diggers was Hub Bakens, then still a youth of 18, who lived near the bridge. He had been evacuated a few days earlier, on orders of the Germans. The next day he and his father went back to their smithy to collect their tools and hid them from the Germans, who had displayed an interest in them. The invitation to participate in digging was repeated on Saturday at the point of a rifle.

Some of the nurses ventured forth to observe from the church steeple once more. Enemy traffic fleeing north is increasing. Nurse van Schaik chronicles her observations for Saturday, September 16:

> The tension is increasing by the day. Again we climb the tower of the Dutch Reformed Church and see a big explosion in the southeast. Flames are shooting up in the sky and there are enormous smoke clouds. We hurry down when we see British planes approaching. At the crossroad, we see a German tank stop under some trees. Retreating, motorized troops follow the road to Veghel, in the direction of Nijmegen.

> The German surgeon has arrived at our hospital. He tells the head nurse that he will go to Nijmegen tomorrow morning to pick up more supplies and food.

The civilian switchboard operators were no longer on duty at the telephone exchange in Eindhoven. The girls had been busy running courier missions. Joke van Hapert-Lathouwers added a brief notation to her diary:

> Sept. 16—Today we heard the Germans left the office. The troops in the south should have crossed the border.

The real action for Joop v.d. Linden started on Saturday the sixteenth. "Masses of Typhoons, Mustangs and Hurricanes started to strafe the woods between the border and our village. This was in the afternoon and it went on for hours. I remember sitting with brothers and friends on the flat roof on the back of the house having a front row view of the actions.

"The Germans left on the night of the 16th, leaving behind most of the heavy weapons in the room they had occupied. We heard the most incredible stories, rumors from Germans that still fled along the small forest roads, some with bikes, some with small carts, but all anxious to head for the roads to the Heimat! They told stories about the masses of armored vehicles they had seen."

FOUR

Liberation

Liberation at Hand

The day bloomed bright and sunny with little portent of things to come. In those days, Dutch-Canadian Pierre Drenters lived in the area between St. Oedenrode and Son. He remembered: "Sunday began as a very quiet, beautiful, summer day with no wind and a cloudless sky. The people living in the area near the bridges of Son, St. Oedenrode and Veghel, the towns on the main highway in this placid central part of southern Holland, began the day in their usual Sunday church-going routine, unaware that in just a few hours they would be witness to the greatest airborne spectacle they will ever have seen."

A few miles farther south, on a large farm just to the north of Son, Lisa van Overveld, a fourteen-year-old, lived with her family on a farm that was to be right in the middle of one of the drop zones. She wrote: "You could tell from the bright sky that it was going to be beautiful weather that day. That morning my mother decided to take me and my twelve-year-old sister, Adrie, to church in Son. We went by foot to the 9:30 service. Usually we traveled by bike but the Germans had been picking up all bicycles with good tires in recent days. We did not want to take the risk of losing them.

"Before our departure, mother gave dad instructions, as he had to take care of my five-year-old brother, Wan, and my little one-year-old sister, Lia. My fifteen-year-old brother, Paul, also stayed home.

"It was an hour-long walk to church and we chatted all the way. I remember the service was shorter than usual. After twenty minutes, the priest went to the pulpit and told the congregation he had some unpleasant news.

"On the outside of the church were Germans and NSB-ers waiting to pick up men who were inside. They were to be taken to dig fortifications alongside the canal at Son. The priest advised all men to leave the church by the back door as quickly as possible. After this incident, those who were left behind were very tense but the men were saved."

Other menfolk of Son were less fortunate, according to Kees Wittebrood. "On D-Day, some thirty men had to report for duty with spades and handed in their identity cards at the bridge. Among them was Hub Baatsen, normally a member of the kitchen staff at the sanitarium. There was little chance to escape and any attempt to do so would have meant death on the spot."

Farther to the north in the little town of Eerde, which would see much activity in just a few hours, John H. van Geffen was in church with his family. The fourteen-year-old admired the parish priest and was assisting with the Mass on that Sunday morning. Van Geffen wrote: "Father Joseph Willenborg read Holy Mass and told the people in church, 'Today parents, keep awake, keep your children at home because great things are coming.' On the morning of the 17th, I was an altar boy. Father Willenborg was an outstanding man. He was also a member of the Dutch resistance."

The mother of Lisa van Overveld had been very frightened when the menfolk of the church had been directed to leave by the back door to avoid the distasteful chore of digging foxholes and gun emplacements near the canal for the Germans. Lisa wrote: "If it had been physically possible, my mother would have had us run all the way home to which we had a one-hour return journey. She considered, after fifteen minutes of walking, to take a short cut through the forest. On second thought, she decided not to leave the main road, sensing there were probably Germans in the forest. Thank God we did not take the forest route. Some time later the strafing and bombing began. It was called the 'clearance of the invasion territory.'

"When we were halfway home, my sister noticed two men on bicycles. This was strange. We hadn't seen a single cyclist up to that moment.

" 'They're Germans! Look ahead of you,' said my mother in a hushed voice. 'Move quickly!'

"The cyclists reached us. We moved over to one side of the narrow bike path to let them pass. They said nothing. I don't suppose they were over 16 years old—greenhorns. Some one hundred meters ahead of us they stopped, looked around, and then threw a grenade into the field. They scared the hell out of us. Just a boyish trick! Then they cycled on.

"My mother was becoming more and more nervous. She had a red face from the hard running and fear. She complained of having a painful hunch. Because my mother always had strong intuitions, my sister and I thought, 'Is something really about to happen?'

"When we neared our home, airplanes came over. They made the same noise as those machines you heard sometimes at night. They are English, as we used to say then. They were flying rather high. From the sounds you knew they were not German planes. There were more and more of them. Mother urged us on. 'Children, move on for heavens' sake. Something is going to happen!' "

Writing in her diary for Sunday, September 17, Dutch Red Cross nurse Koos van Schaik provided this description:

At six in the morning, we were awakened by the drone of many Allied planes. It seems they do not care anymore if it is day or night. They come over in big formations and also as single planes flying in all directions.

At ten o'clock we are in church. Halfway through the sermon, the minister has to stop. We cannot understand him anymore due to the rattle of the windows. It is like one big earthquake. Bombs drop everywhere. Plaster is falling from the ceiling and the walls. People want to go outside. However, they are reminded to remain calm and stay where they are. The church is very old and relatively safe. The enormous thick walls can stand the compression and the windows are stained glass in lead frames and bend without being shattered. Willy and I sit motionless. I look at her. She is very pale. I put my hand on her folded hands—"Will, we are together!" Thankfully, she nods.

We are singing Psalm 27, "Zoo ik nist had geloofd det in dit Levan, mijn ziel Gods gunst en hulp genieten zou . . . (The Lord is my light and my salvation, whom shall I fear? The Lord is the stronghold of my life, of whom shall I be afraid?)"

With the memories kept fresh by her diary notations, Nurse Koos van Schaik continued: "Most of the people cannot sing. The organ has a difficult time competing with the drone of the planes. 'Sing, Will, Sing, the only way to keep the people quiet!'

"I sang as I have never sung before. One of our patients is an invalid and in a wheelchair and with us in church. A twenty-year-old boy, lame and blind. He is very afraid. The organ music has a calming influence and I notice he is relaxing a bit. Also, the children are quieter now. One little one is still sobbing in the arms of a bigger sister.

"After a serious prayer by the minister, we leave the church. The planes have disappeared. Two German cars pass the crossroad at high speed. One almost loses control and is now weaving from side to side on the road, missing our wheelchair by inches. With three people, we are holding on. We are trembling but our patient hasn't noticed the danger. He did not see it. The nurses look at each other. Thank heaven we make it back to the hospital. The head nurse orders that nobody is allowed to leave the building unless on official duty. Our lives are at stake now."

The three van Overvelds were nearing home. Lisa van Overveld continued her story: "When we reached the Theresia Hoeve (our neighbor) everyone was standing outside looking up at the sky. 'Come here with the girls. Don't walk on. You'll never know what's going to happen!' Mrs. Sweere told us. But mother told her that she had to take the baby out of the crib and we had already been gone three hours from home and we were only fifteen minutes away now. Mrs. Sweere told us some Germans had just arrived and had taken up quarters in an upstairs room with a balcony. Normally, mother had always stopped in for a chat, but not this morning. She was afraid and her fear appeared to be well founded.

"As we continued on toward home, we heard a strange, heavy, roaring sound in the distance, of approaching planes from the southern direction. Suddenly, dozens of airplanes, terrifying, low, strafing as they thundered over the woods, adjoining meadows and fields, roared over head. In the meantime, we found ourselves a hiding place in a drainage ditch and we escaped, suffering only shock and shaking with fear. We were lucky.

"The whole scene was repeated twice before we reached home. When we arrived at our drive, we saw two heavily wounded horses. One of them was missing an entire leg. It had been ripped off. I was sick at the sight. We were helpless. At that very moment the planes came over, once more strafing and dropping bombs.

"We reached the house in the nick of time. The sight of that poor horse was etched in my mind."

In an interview with Marienus de Visser, eighty-eight-year-old brother of Piet de Visser, who died on September 17, 1944, Lisa van Overveld sent this information: "On Saturday, 16 of September, 1944, the Dutch police got instructions from the Germans to post all houses in Son and Bruegel and order the men to come to the canal to dig foxholes. Most of them refused to work for the enemy and hid in the woods. This was repeated again on Sunday, the 17th of September. So, when the bombardment started on the morning of the 17th, many Dutchmen were hidden in the woods, including Piet de Visser and his comrade Henk Scheepens. During one of the bombing and strafing runs, Piet de Visser was hit on the side of the head near the brain by shrapnel. He fell to the ground. He was seriously wounded. His friend, Henk Scheepens, who was unhurt, hastened back to the home of the Vissers in Son and told Piet's wife what had happened to her husband. She was terribly frightened but knew that she had to do something quickly. She went to Nell Peynburg and these two women went to the Germans and managed to get a Red Cross car. A younger brother of policeman Baak accompanied the two women in the car with three German soldiers. One soldier rode on the side of the car with his gun, ready in anticipation of an attack. They sped along the woods in the direction to which Scheepens guided them. Just as they reached the spot where de Visser lay wounded, another strafing run started. An incendiary bomb hit the ambulance. It started burning. The three Dutch people and two of the German Red Cross soldiers burned and died instantly. Piet de Visser died that evening. A daughter and a son were left without mother or father."

When the van Overvelds reached home they found the other family members safe. Lisa wrote: "What a relief! We were all together and unharmed. Mother went first to the baby to get her from her crib. My little brother, Wan, had hidden under the table in fear and prayed his little child's prayer, 'Holy Maria, Amen!' My father had probably prayed out loud with my brother, Paul, and the little ones. They were exceedingly worried as we had not reached home.

"After a while, it was quiet again. The neighbors who lived opposite our farm and the sons of the Merks family, along with some evacuees, went out to check the wounded cattle.

"My brother, Paul, said, 'I want to take a look, too,' and he left quickly.

"Mr. Coppelmans was there with his two sons and little daughter, looking at the badly wounded cattle in the meadow. The whole bunch stood there, dismayed, talking about what had happened.

"Suddenly, the planes appeared once again, strafing and dropping bombs. Everybody ran for cover, dropping to the ground, except for Kees Coppelmans. He ran toward a distant drainage ditch. He didn't make it. He was totally ripped apart. His father and little sister were wounded. My brother, Paul, had a slight grazing wound in the shoulder and came home pale as death. 'It was terrible, terrible!' he said.

"When my mother went to the baby's room, she saw that there was a hole in the window and another one in the closet, just above the head of the cradle. Mother opened the closet and noticed three hats with burn holes in them. She also found a shell fragment.

"We didn't feel safe in the house any longer. My parents decided to move to the deep cellar under the house as quickly as possible. Nobody knew how long this situation would last. Father took a hacksaw with him in case he had to break out through the barred window. Within our concealment we missed out on the actions taking place above ground."

The strafing had caught Germans in the open, also. The staff at the hospital in St. Oedenrode was in the midst of eating lunch. Nurse Koos van Schaik relates what happened. "We had almost finished eating when we heard a motorcycle stop in front of the building. One of the girls could see outside from her place at the table. She put her hands to her mouth and cried out, 'Look, how terrible, they are bringing in a wounded one. His arm is dangling—blood all over!'

"We looked through the window and saw the German motorcycle with a stretcher alongside with a seriously wounded German soldier. At the same moment, the car of the German surgeon pulled up from the other direction. He was back from Nijmegen."

Albert Marinus was a member of the underground in the

Eerde area. He wrote: "Together, with a man who had been in hiding, I walked to St. Oedenrode via the sand dunes of Eerde to the Koevering. We also passed the Genoveva farm of the van Genuchten family, which was well known as a place for members of the Dutch underground. It was about 1230 hours when we heard the sounds of aircraft. We got the impression an air battle was taking place near Eindhoven.

"We passed the Genoveva farm at the very moment, when above Eerde, an aircraft dropped about eight paratroopers (pathfinder team). Many people were watching this at the farmyard and one of them yelled to me, 'Don't walk too far—it won't be necessary anymore!'

"After walking another kilometer, we stopped and watched toward the sky since 'hundreds' of aircraft flew over, heading east (1st Battalion of the 501st Parachute Infantry Regiment). A few minutes later huge aircraft flew over very low, with the doors open. We could see paratroopers standing in the openings. Suddenly, hundreds of paratroopers jumped down—a sight I will never forget. The man who had been in hiding, whom I was escorting, disappeared. I lost track of him so I ran back to Eerde and passed the Genoveva farm again. Everyone was gone from there, too."

For fourteen-year-old Joseph Verstappen,[3] Sunday, September 17, will be a day never to be forgotten. He wrote: "I was in an open field, quite a ways from home and close to the village of Eerde, when the first plane came over and dropped its load of paratroopers, when it was almost overhead. Soon, there were more planes and pretty soon the sky was full of paratroopers. It was such a beautiful sight, especially since there wasn't a German in sight. They had been retreating for several days and we were delighted for that."

With his home situated near the fringe of drop zones "B" and "C," north of Son, Pierre Drenters was in position to view the arrival of the paratroops and gliders on the afternoon of September 17. He has this description of the momentous occasion: "It was 1300 hours in the afternoon. A faint drone seemed to fill the sky. Although there had been bombing runs by low flying aircraft over the Zonsche Forest, along the canal between Best

3. Joseph Verstappen is now a tailor in Grants Pass, Oregon, and is a member of the Oregon National Guard.

and Son, and on German positions in the forest, there was nothing to indicate that something big was under way. As the sound grew louder, it was not the same sound we were used to hearing. We looked up. An armada of planes appeared over our area. They came in quite low. We feared for an air strike and headed for the shelter. But these were not bombers. They were transport planes on some kind of a mission. Then a beautiful sight—literally hundreds of paratroopers spilled out from the planes. We could see the paratroopers jump, one after another, evenly spaced. They were quite low but they seemed to have ample time to get set for a landing."

Joseph Verstappen added to his story: "For me, being just 14 years old, it was an exciting time and we wanted to help wherever we could but I think it was turned around. The soldiers did the helping. I remember they had printed lists of questions. 'Have the Germans big guns? Are there many? Where?, etc. Do you have coffee?' I went home and got a pot of our substitute coffee. When I brought it to the trooper he tried it and you should have seen his face! Then he gave me a little package of real instant coffee which we drank that night at home.

"When the paratroopers had completed their jumps, they all went to different colored smoke flares. Nobody spoke as I remember and I thought that was kind of strange. I found a half-pack of Lucky Strikes and held it up and one soldier nodded his head as if he wanted to say, 'It's yours, now.'"

Joe Luyk, a seventeen-year-old, had been sent by his father out into the country to see if he could buy some food from the farmers. With a younger friend, he happened to be crossing the fields that became the drop zone for the paratroops north of Son. Luyk wrote: "We found ourselves in the fields and all of a sudden 'all hell broke loose.' Though we had experienced war for nearly five years, this was really scary stuff.

"Here we were, a nice sunny day, minding our own business, when all of a sudden there were aircraft all around above us. Parachutists were coming down. Aircraft, without engines, were descending. We did not know about gliders.

"I recall we stood transfixed, but then realized the danger we were in. We jumped into a ditch and decided to wait for things to happen. I remember saying to my young friend, who was 14 years old, that we should make our presence known to whoever it was that had come down. At that time we didn't know it was the 101st Airborne, though we realized it was an Allied drop because the Germans were shooting at them. We stripped to the waist and used a white undershirt stuck on a pole and waved it above the ditch. After a while we heard rustling in the grass and all of a sudden there were six paratroopers on elbows and knees pointing six rifles at us. We raised our hands and I said, in English, 'Don't shoot, we're civilians!'

"These soldiers were rather rough. They pulled us out of the ditch by the scruff of the neck. Then they said my English was very good and told me to stay with them. (I had studied English for 6½ years.)

"I was taken to the commander who asked if I also spoke German, which I did. He asked me to stay with them as an interpreter."

On the island, not far from Arnhem, Dutch underground fighter Bill van Wely was made aware of the invasion in a surprising fashion. At a later time he would spend much time joining forces with the men of the 101st. Van Wely wrote: "It was about one o'clock on Sunday afternoon as we came home from church in Zetten, about seven kilometers from Dodewaard, where I lived with my parents and four sisters. We heard a droning sound and, in looking in that direction, we could not believe our eyes. There were hundreds of planes, big ones pulling smaller ones, surrounded by fighter planes. They were flying so low that we saw men standing in the doorways. We waved and they waved back to us. They started jumping out just across the Rhine River, approximately 12 kilometers from our place. Different colored parachutes—it was a fantastic sight! Then we realized it was the beginning of our liberation. We didn't know at that time that they were British paras and part of the Market-Garden operation."

In the drop zone areas, the enemy soldiers began to make their presence known. Pierre Drenters added to his story: "On the descent, small, thick black clouds appeared among the paratroopers and planes from bursting shells. A panzer unit fired at them from concealment in an orchard next to the highway at Wolfswinkel. They had moved there, along with other troops, a week before, awaiting ground forces. The soldiers were dressed in black. They were panzer troops belonging to the Herman Goering Panzer Kampfwagons.

"More planes were flying in. They flew right through the

puffs of black smoke and exploding flak, but they didn't take evasive action to avoid it. The formations remained steady on course until all the paratroopers had left the planes. Then the planes turned west and away from the landing zone. Some of the planes caught fire while over the drop zone and crashed. We did not see anyone get out. There was too much going on.

"When the parachutists landed, there was another surprise as gliders came on the scene. They slowly separated from the planes that had them in tow and started landing all over the area. They tried to avoid the obstacles on the ground. Some gliders ripped through the fences that lined the pastures. Others smashed their huge wings and some landed with their tails high in the air. One stayed upright and one glider nearly twisted right around before coming to rest. There was instant chaos. A horse stampeded past us, covered with blood. The noise was deafening as the tow planes, now without the gliders, passed overhead, their tow cables still sweeping behind them. The pilots released them just beyond the houses at the highway.

"The gliders on the ground seemed to open up at the front. The nose was raised showing an open vehicle coming out with soldiers already sitting in them in full battle dress. They drove out of them in full view of the enemy, who was under cover on the other side of the highway. The soldiers quickly drove away from the gliders.

"Just as the last of the tow planes crossed the landing zone, it became quiet again. Fighter planes appeared over the drop zone. They looked brand new, gleaming in the sun. They had been circling high above the airborne drop in progress and were coming down for a closer look. They went into a wide diving curve. Their targets seemed to be the panzers in the orchard that were shooting at the paratroopers and planes. They roared low over the orchard again and again with a terrifying noise as they fired their guns. Three of the panzers came out onto the highway but two of them didn't get very far. They were immediately attacked and started burning near the town of St. Oedenrode. The third tank drove off the highway and escaped over a dirt road. The tank approached a wooden bridge at the Dommel River by the old mill at Wolfswinkel. The panzer, a Mark III, weighed 20 tons. The bridge was too weak. The capacity was only about eight tons. In their hurry to get away, the tank crew drove on without stopping and broke off the right railing in the process. Incredibly, the bridge held and they made it across."[4]

From the windows of the hospital in St. Oedenrode, the staff and some of the patients were able to witness the airborne landings. A few of the patients panicked, thinking the gliders were going to land right in the building, as they barely missed the treetops. A short time later, the fighters made their presence known once more.

Nurse Koos van Schaik relates: "After one o'clock, fighter planes came back. A terrific explosion in the neighborhood made us realize the seriousness of the moment. Nobody said a word. We tried to calm the patients. Suddenly, the fighter planes were attacking our town. This was so terrible; no description could even come close. One after another they were diving, strafing the crossroad in front of the school, pulling up again over the gardens and fields behind the house and dived a second time over the road where the Germans were retreating. Two patients became hysterical. Henk, our blind patient, screamed, 'Take me outside, the roof will fall in, I want to go outside!' It was impossible to take him outside. The bullets were raining on the village."

More closely involved personally in the strafing and bombing of St. Oedenrode, the story of Mia v.d. Linden-deGreef fits with the account of Red Cross nurse Koos van Schaik. Linden describes the harrowing experiences of her family: "The fighter planes that were strafing would sweep in low, rise over our house, which was in their path, and then dip back down on the other side. A large German car was strafed and burning and a little further north were two German tanks that had been knocked out. Beside the road were hedges about six feet high. Two soldiers jumped from one of the tanks and climbed over a tall hedge and came tumbling into our bomb shelter. This happened soon after the paratroopers and gliders had landed to the south and west. One of the enemy soldiers was an officer who had a bullet hole through his helmet. The bullet had creased his skull with little bleeding. The other one had his whole back open. Though he was badly wounded, he was cursing the English. The officer ordered father to go into the house to get them

4. Pierre Drenters was fourteen years old and lived in the Wolfswinkel area as a boy. He became a Canadian citizen after the war.

water to wash out the wound. The planes were still circling overhead looking for targets and shooting at any thing that moved. Father was pushed out of the shelter with a rifle pointed at him. After he returned, mother did the best she could to cleanse the wounds and bandage them with the few remaining diapers of my four-month-old brother.

"Then it got real quiet. The planes disappeared. No Germans were visible. There were some Germans in the two church steeples we had in St. Oedenrode. The two Germans climbed out of our bomb shelter and headed for the hospital. The badly wounded man was still angry but managed to walk. Close to the hospital he collapsed, probably from loss of blood.

"After the Germans left, our family—my father, mother and four children—went across the road and through the bush to the shelter of the Fathers of the Holy Heart. They were using a factory for their work. The convent was on the way to Schijndel. One of the fathers died at Buchenwald. He was a member of the resistance. Their bomb shelter was metal over the earthen cover. The firing started as the Americans approached St. Oedenrode. You could hear the bullets ricocheting off the metal cover. We were very frightened."

In the town of Schijndel, Mike Nooijen had observed the air activity and landing of airborne troops to the south and east. He set off in the direction of Eerde to offer his assistance. In a dry ditch, he had come upon four paratroopers with the American flag on their sleeves. He wrote: "I jumped into the ditch and shook hands and said, 'Velkom to Holland!'" After being offered his first (Lucky Strike) cigarette and chocolate, Nooijen was impressed with the novel means of communication carried by the soldiers. "Then came my first surprise. One of them took a piece of paper from his helmet which had a few simple sentences on it, in Dutch and English. I thought it invaluable for both the Allies and me. They pointed to 'Go back home—Ga naar huis!' I thought, not on my life—these people are my age. They came from a foreign land to liberate us. We talked to each other with the help of the little paper, as my English was limited to 'Yes, No and OK.' One thing was clear to them—I wanted to do anything to help them. Eight months as a German prisoner had hardened me.

"One of them started talking into a rectangular box with an antenna. They called it a 'Walkie-Talkie.' An officer appeared from somewhere and he spoke German, which I understood. The usual shaking of the head and saying that I was crazy, but how do you explain the meaning of being liberated to foreign people who had been free all along. The officer brought out a map and asked where the Germans were in Veghel. 'There are Germans in the Farmers Union Hall, or they were,' I replied. He marked it on the map and started to talk into the little box. He said I was to go with him. I saw an ever-increasing number of paratroopers. He asked if I wanted a German rifle and I said yes. There was one for me with ammunition. With the aid of the map he asked me the way to Veghel. I showed him the main road and a short cut through 'Den Beemd' and along the canal. In the meantime, it had become evening and rations were consumed and I shared with the men.

"With about twenty people, we went on our way through 'Den Beemd.' I took the point as guide. (Beemd was half-swamp with small paths and was overgrown with poplar trees.) We arrived in Veghel and went to the Farmers Union but the Germans had fled. There were two German army trucks with the fuel tanks drained."

Having been on the way to escort another underground member to St. Oedenrode, Albert Marinus had witnessed the dropping of the 501st pathfinder team near Eerde and shortly after had witnessed the dropping of the multitude of paratroopers in the area so he headed back toward Eerde. Marinus wrote: "When I got back to Eerde, I saw the first Americans. Gijs, the assumed name of Gerrit Bossert, who was also with the Eerde resistance group, was already in contact with the paratroopers. A few Americans and Gijs were studying a map when Gijs asked me whether I knew the Dalen Street and Broe Alley in Veghel. These names were unknown in Eerde but we found out, with the help of the map. Gijs gave me instructions to get the weapons of the Eerde-Veghel resistance group which were hidden in the Eerde cemetery."

Noting the frantic flight of enemy soldiers in the vicinity of Wolfswinkel, Pierre Drenters wrote: "The hasty retreat of German soldiers on foot was observed heading for the Dommel River, showing how completely they had been surprised, as we were, by the airborne assault. Getting caught between the river and the paratroopers with no way out, the soldiers swam the river and those who couldn't swim were pulled across with ropes. Much of their equipment was left on the opposite bank."

Known by the code name of "John the Baptist" to his friends in the Dutch resistance movement, Johan Scheutjens remembered, "We, of the underground, helped unload jeeps and trailers from the gliders. It was a formidable sight to see the paratroopers on both sides of the road neatly marching along in silence. One group of paratroopers was able to communicate to us by maps and signs that their objective was Wolfswinkel."

Lisa van Overveld and her family had missed the landings of the paratroopers but they did see the gliders come in. She wrote: "It was beautiful to see the gliders landing. You could see the gliders opening their fronts and all of a sudden a jeep would dart out at full speed and head into the meadows. Those Yankees were so quick!

"When we had the opportunity to meet them, we were impressed by their extreme politeness as well as their love for children. They were so relaxed seeing my five-year-old brother and my little baby sister. I still can remember that American paratrooper who was badly wounded. He was sitting outside of our house waiting for transportation. Some jeeps were already driving by with medical soldiers who drove the badly wounded to a first aid station. This paratrooper had been hit in the throat while coming down in his parachute. The fingers of his right hand were also hurt. He suffered intense pain and blood came out of his throat and mouth. We really didn't know what we could do for him. We gave him water and a towel so he could refresh himself. He was so grateful. In fact, because we took notice of him, little Wan followed me and sat on his heels near the man. It did the American good and, though he must have felt miserable, he searched with his good hand through his pockets to give sweets to my brother. That is something you don't forget."

Albert Marinus had contacted his friend Albert Mobers, and the two had gone to the hidden cache of weapons in the Eerde cemetery. Now armed, the men headed for Veghel. Marinus wrote: "We had to go to the crossroads of Dalen Street and Broe Alley. When we arrived, we requisitioned some bikes for the Americans. Six of them went to the Veghel bridge, across the Zuid-Willems-Vaart Canal. Large groups of Americans headed for Veghel. Mobers went back to the landing zone in Eerde.

"Usually a very quiet village, Eerde was now crowded with

people carrying chutes of many different colors. You also felt some tension. The Dutch flag was streaming in front of some houses, since we had been liberated. The older people knew it wouldn't remain that way. Some farmers were busy with horse carts which were loaded with equipment and sent to Veghel.

"Frans van de Pol was transporting five or six injured Americans in a horse cart. I joined him. When we were on the Veghel–St. Oedenrode highway, it was completely deserted; no civilians, no Germans and no Americans could be seen or heard. Frans, who had been a soldier in 1940, didn't like this at all. One of the injured Americans also noticed the silence and concluded the area wasn't in American hands yet. He handed me a rifle so I could escort the cart. When we reached Veghel, an American sent us to the nun's house where the injured were cared for. I saw lots of equipment coming in from the drop zone at Eerde.

"When I came back home, two Americans were questioning a German soldier who had been captured just outside of Eerde. All the Dutch flags had been taken away, since everyone felt the 'party was over and that we were now the front line.' "

As a twenty-year-old, Mrs. Josephine van Herpen-Hout lived in the center of Veghel. She had witnessed the appearance of many planes passing over the town. "We were crying for joy but the few Germans who were in Veghel started shooting at the planes and ordered us to go indoors.

"After some time, we heard no more shooting so we came out and looked into the street. What we saw! I'll never forget for the rest of my life. American parachutists were sitting and standing before each house."

Fate would make him a principal in events that would take place in Eindhoven on the eighteenth, but on Sunday, Bert Pulles was an excited onlooker like so many others in the city. "With all the air activity and bombing on the outskirts of the city, I hurried over to Coby's home to be of comfort to her. She was very scared of the shooting and bombing, as her father had been killed in the Allied bombing of December 6, 1942. We were in the house, together with her mother, sister and brothers, discussing the course of the war. Suddenly, a neighbor came dashing in and yelled, 'Come quick, see the planes!' We dashed outside and there they came—planes by the hundreds. We climbed on a neighbor's roof to better view the spectacle. The street was crowded with people who cheered and waved. We saw thousands of parachutists drop just a little north and north-east of Eindhoven. Then came the planes towing gliders. We were being shown the first phase of Operation Market-Garden."

Jan Hurks, a member of the underground, was in hiding on the Woenselschestraat at the time of the parachute and glider landings, near Son. From his location at the north end of Eind-hoven, he had a great view of the airborne operation, but at a distance.

Many of the enemy fled from the scene of the fighting around the canal bridge at Son. Hurks recalled: "I was very nervous, since I knew the fighting was just beginning. We saw Germans coming from the direction of Son, asking the way to Helmond, which was eastward toward Germany. They weren't carrying weapons anymore. Near the school, right behind our home, those Germans were stopped and given weapons and ammuni-tion. About 100 meters from our garden, they began digging foxholes. They said the Americans would not attack at night so they expected the area between Son and Eindhoven would be a no-man's land."

Little did Johan Evers, of the Dutch resistance group, realize as he watched the paratroopers jumping in the distance that his street in Eindhoven would be the scene of a fierce, short battle the next day. He wrote: "Everywhere the people were watching the sky, many with tears in their eyes. After the paratroopers were dropped and the Dakotas disappeared, it became fright-fully quiet.

"At about 2000 hours, we heard small arms fire on the Woen-selstraat. Half an hour later we got a message from the HQ of the BS (Interior Forces) to prepare for action. Then, at 2230, a group of Germans knocked on our door and we were just putting away our armbands and weapons. The Germans placed an 88mm gun under the trees in front of our house. All doors and windows had to be opened. In a very short period of time, we were surrounded by Germans wearing all kinds of uniforms and varying in age from 15 to 50. Some were still wet from crossing the canal near Son. The younger soldiers were very frightened, since they had been told that the American para-troopers do not take prisoners. A ray of hope for them was that they were also told the SS was on its way to help them."

Jan Hurks continued his story: "During the night, the Germans were pulling a big gun to the crossroads of Woenselsche-straat and Niewediyk. They forced a farmer to get his horse to pull the gun. He had to do it quickly, otherwise they threatened to burn his farm. It was ridiculous. The night was very quiet and tension ran high. My father wondered what would happen if they hit our house. It was decided to dig a big hole, with doors and dirt on top of it, to use as a family shelter when the actual fighting started. We dug from 0200 hours until dawn of the 18th."

FIVE

Pathfinders

The Pathfinder Mission

For the Normandy campaign, the 101st Airborne Division had used eleven sticks of pathfinders to cover the three drop zones and one glider landing area.[5]

Because the Holland jump was a daylight mission, the number of pathfinder teams was reduced to four, with one stick being assigned for each drop zone. The 501st Parachute Infantry Regiment had drop zone "A" in the Eerde area, west of Veghel, and drop zone "A-1" just to the northwest of Veghel between the Aa River and the Zuid-Willems-Vaart Canal on the north side of the railroad track. The 502nd was assigned DZ "B" which would put the regiment in close proximity to both Best and St. Oedenrode. The 506th would land on DZ "C." Its southern boundary was the northern edge of the Zonsche Forest. The glider landing zone extended beyond the boundaries of both DZs "B" and "C" and provided a huge area in which to land hundreds of CG-4A gliders.

In Normandy, the serials of troop-carrying planes had relied heavily on the Eureka-Rebecca radar sets and the T's formed with Halifane lights angled in such a way that they could be seen only from the approaching aircraft.

For the Holland mission, the paratroopers relied on the radar sets to home in the planes from a distance of twenty miles. Once the planes came into view, orange smoke bombs were set off to provide visual sightings. The pathfinders also laid out panels in the form of a large "T" to further direct the incoming planes.

5. See *Rendezvous with Destiny* or *D-Day with the Screaming Eagles* for Normandy drop zone assignments and locations.

The soldier who packed all the parachutes for the pathfinder teams was T/5 Glenn E. Braddock. His recollections of the preparations after the Normandy campaign had been completed are as follows: "Shortly after the Normandy mission, after we had received our recuperation furloughs (during this time I was transferred from the Rigger Section of Service Company to the 502nd Regimental Headquarters Company) we were organized again and moved in to an air base outside of Oxford, England—Chalgrove Airbase, I believe.

"We received a new group of men to train as replacements; also, we were resupplied on equipment, some of which had just arrived from the States and required our own rigid type of testing. The men we selected for the pathfinder training remained and the others went back to their original companies. We then continued more rigid sessions of renewed training.

"On the 15th of September, some of our men were granted passes, I being one of the luckier ones, having a high old time in Nottingham when (Thomas G.) 'Glider-Flaps' Walton caught up with me and said we were to report back to the base—that we were designated for possibly another mission.

"On the night of the 16th we were under quarters and area arrest. This time there were no barbed wire enclosures around us and our only guards were at the supply room and my parachute shed. (The MPs maintained a constant dog patrol on my parachute packing shed unless I was present and at work.) 1Lt. (Robert) Smith of the 377th Parachute Field Artillery was my parachute supply officer."

First Lieutenant Gordon DeRamus Jr. had been a mortar platoon officer in Normandy. He found himself in charge of one of the four pathfinder teams. He listed the direction equipment carried by the team as: "2 Eureka sets, one CRN-4, 7 green lights, 7 orange panels, 7 white panels and 5 cases of orange smoke grenades."

There was a mission but the pathfinders didn't know where they were going. T/5 Glenn Braddock continued his narrative: "We went to breakfast more or less as a group and when we returned, received orders to prepare for combat—supplies and chutes were issued and much excitement prevailed. Where were we going? Nobody knew—but we were told we'd receive our flight plans and orders of action at the planes."

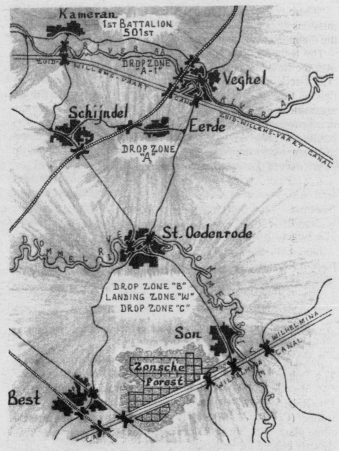

Drop Zones—Map 2

Drop zone "A"—501st Parachute Infantry Regiment less 1st Battalion plus two platoons of engineers from "A" and "B" Companies. *Drop zone "A-1"*—Not used. *Drop zone "B"*—502nd Regiment and two platoons of engineers from "C" Company. *Drop zone "C"*—506th Regiment and 1st Platoon of "C" Company of the 326th Engineer Battalion. 1st Battalion of the 501st Parachute Infantry Regiment landed near Kameran without pathfinder guidance. Landing zone "W"—All gliders.

"There really hadn't been time for rehearsals. Three earlier missions had been cancelled. The stay at the marshaling area for the regiments and battalions had only been two days duration."

The two serials of two planes each made landfall together over the Belgian coast. The rear pair (headed for DZs "B" and "C") circled to reestablish its time interval while the lead pair flew on toward DZs "A" and "A-1." Both pairs sighted the orange smoke set out near Gheel to mark the front, and both ran into heavy fire over the German lines. Evasive action was forbidden. All the pilots could do was speed their lumbering planes to 180 miles per hour or alter the altitude on approach. The drop zones were now twenty-five miles away.

Near Ratie, one of the pair bound for the Veghel area (DZ "A-1") was hit in the left engine and wing tank and crashed in flames. The ill-fated plane, nicknamed "Chevelet," belonged to the 9th Troop Carrier Pathfinder Group. It was piloted by 1Lt. Eugene Shauvin. It was hit by 20mm anti-aircraft fire.

First Lieutenant Robert Centers, flying one of the other planes, reported: "Lt. Shauvin flew in the second position on our right wing and stayed with us till about 1230 hours at about 1400 feet when we started our run. We had just passed the front line when we were shot at by very accurate anti-aircraft gunners. As we had lots to do in controlling our plane, we did not check on Lt. Shauvin's plane. When it was quiet, we did not see any plane in the far surroundings."[6]

T/5 Glenn Braddock was on board the plane piloted by 1Lt. Robert Centers and the team assignment was to mark DZ "A." Braddock wrote: "I was jumping last as clean-up man in Lt. (Robert) Smith's plane. I had drawn straws with another trooper (Cpl. Roy L.) Stephens and had lost so I would be in the same plane with Sgt. John O'Shaughnessey, who was jumping directly behind the lieutenant.

"Lt. Charles Faith (Stephens was in his stick) and his pathfinders were in the second 501st plane. Although I was a 502nd man, I went in with the 501st team. We were all trained in the duties required of pathfinders, regardless of which company or regiment we came from and any man could replace any position on the team.

"We were joking above the roar of the engines on the plane to

6. From a report sent by Dutch researcher Piet Pulles.

our left and the Canadian fighter escort that accompanied us. 1Lt. Faith's plane was flying just to the left and a little behind and below us. A voice over the intercom said, 'Don't you love me anymore?' and damn if the pilot of the second plane didn't fly and put his wing tip right in the door of our plane—Christ! I thought we would crash. The pilot had barely dropped off and as I was watching the other plane, I heard loud explosions and rattle like heavy hail on the roof. Lt. Faith's plane started smoking and the left front end went down with smoke spewing out behind.

"The Canadian escort—up to this time playing 'ring around the rosie' with us—seemed to have disappeared and, as I looked out the window of our plane, a huge hole appeared just off the leading edge of the wing and about six feet back. I quit looking out that window as I was too damned busy thinking when that next slug was coming up through the bottom of the plane between me and the navigator's compartment and hitting me in the butt—holes were coming through the bottom and going out through the roof with little streamers of fire attached to some of them—TRACERS!!! Up to this time the navigator's door had been open but when the barrage started it was closed.

"Then we heard the heavy, sharp whine of diving planes— 'Flak tower to the left and firing at us,' someone shouted. The diving aircraft screamed past us and I saw it firing tracers at the top of the tower and then a fiery jettison of what appeared to be a rocket—the tower went up in dust and smoke—boy! Were we relieved. There was no more flak but I knew we had lost one of our planes and the entire pathfinder stick going in to the 501st DZ with us. Bastards!"

Four crew members and four pathfinders, including Cpl. Roy L. Stephens, died in that crash. The pilot, Lieutenant Shauvin, badly injured, and several pathfinders were taken prisoners. First Lieutenant Charles M. Faith was found by the Belgian underground, hidden from the enemy until they retreated from the area and then sent back to England.

Fortunately, the surviving craft flew safely and accurately to Veghel, sighted the railway that bounded the zone on the north, turned parallel to the tracks and made its run right over the zone. At 1247 hours, it dropped its troops on DZ "A" from standard altitude, at minimum speed. The paratroops met no resistance and were able to put the Eureka in operation in a minute and to lay out the panels in two and a half minutes. They had trouble with the radio antenna but had that set working within five minutes. The smoke signals were not set off until the main serials were sighted.

T/5 Glenn Braddock continued his story: "We had slipped down to low-level flying when the firing started and Lt. Smith called back, 'Stand up, hook up and check equipment!' which we did, hurriedly. We were ready to jump on a second order if we were lucky enough to clear the plane.

"After the flak tower was knocked out, we flew low for a short period of time, maybe five minutes, and someone said, 'Red light, recheck hookup and equipment.'

"The plane started a slight climb and banked to the left sharply. In looking out of the window, I could see the end of a canal and what appeared to be a series of cross or intermingled roads. In the middle of this was an old man and a little girl holding his hand and waving at us. The plane straightened out, leveled off and the green light came on. I came down through the top of a barbed wire fence which tumbled me rather roughly on the soft dirt."

There were anxious moments on drop zone "A." Having jumped as the last man in the stick, Braddock had this recollection: "After struggling out of my harness and still trying to clear my head from that tumble I got after hitting the barbed wire fencing, I tried to line up just where the rest of the stick had landed on the other side of the trees.

" 'They're over here!' I heard Ernest Stene yell. He added, 'Hold it, there's someone spotted us and coming down the road toward us.'

"I waited until a soldier in a kind of bluish uniform was right across the road from me—a distance of about fifteen yards. I called out 'Halt!' The safety was off on my Thompson sub and I knew that one bad move would have been his last. Although he was armed with a pistol, he made no effort to draw it, and said 'Take me to your commandant.' I said, 'Ah, you speak English.' He nodded and said 'Yes' and raised his hand above his shoulders and up both sides of the ditches men in different attire rose up, each armed with a weapon. I kept my Thompson sub machine gun trained on him and said, 'Tell your men not to move or I'll kill you!' Meanwhile, I heard someone say, 'Where in hell is Braddock with the rest of the equipment?'

" 'Stene—Stene—Come over here!' I yelled. 'Come over here quick!' Stene came over on the double and I quickly explained—'This soldier claims to be a Dutch underground officer but as far as I am concerned he is still enemy.'

" 'Take my equipment, and with him in front of you, take him to Lt. Robert Smith. If he makes a bad move, kill him. If I hear a shot I'll start shooting likewise. If you hear a shot from this direction—let the rest of the stick know someone is with you or they might start shooting at you.

" 'I will stay here and act as security for the rest of the team so they can take whatever precautions are necessary.'

" 'Have you heard and understood what we have just been talking about?' I asked the officer and he replied that he did. 'OK then, instruct your men to stay as they are until I walk out to the middle of the road.'

"He spoke to them in Dutch and Stene ushered him to the rest of the stick and Lt. Smith.

"The others were busy getting the Eureka in operation and had set out the panels. The smoke grenades were ready to be exploded just as soon as the planes came into view.

"There were some very tense and nervous moments from the time I first saw the underground men until after our troops started dropping from the skies. The Dutch never made a move to take their weapons off their shoulders where they were slung and when the first parachutes opened and started drifting earthward they cheered and gave light claps with their hands. I was still very nervous and doubtful until I saw one of our troopers coming around a bend in the road and I stepped out in the middle of the road to wave him on. It was Lt. Smith and the underground officer already shaking hands with the point echelon of parachutists from the 501st going toward Veghel."

The pair of planes slated for DZs "B" and "C" dropped their teams side by side with pinpoint accuracy at 1254. They had slowed to less than ninety miles per hour for the jump, and the men landed so close together that no assembly was necessary. The Eureka was in operation in less than a minute, and the panels and radio were ready within four minutes. Although a few enemy troops were in the vicinity, they were readily disposed of without affecting the pathfinders' work.

First Lieutenant DeRamus provided a brief description of his landing on drop zone "C." "After a very uneventful flight (the last two planes were not in the vicinity when Lt. Shauvin's plane was shot down), we were dropped at 600 feet over the DZ near Son. There was no opposition on the field."

Serving as medic for the pathfinder teams, Pvt. Raymond D. Smith noted: "Before my feet touched the ground, I could see a German soldier fleeing the drop zone on a motorcycle. There were no other enemy soldiers near our area at Son."

"We got there about 30 minutes ahead of the main body of troops," added First Lieutenant DeRamus. "We were met by several Dutch underground boys who told us of locations of Krauts near the DZ. We set up our equipment and formed protection around it."

The Dutch underground also had been preparing for the invasion by the Allies.

Johannes J. van Gorkum was twenty-three years old at the time of the airborne operation in Holland. During the war years, he was a member of the LKP group of St. Oedenrode under the command of Sjef De Groot. Since September of 1943, they had worked together with Theo van Schijndel, M. Boere, M. Bouwman, and M. Van Aken, all from the St. Oedenrode area. The last four had all been captured and executed by the Germans during the past year.

Describing his part in the airborne landings, van Gorkum related: "My code name was 'Joe' and, together with Piet J. Jeuke in the underground HQ in Nijmegen, orders came from Sjef De Groot to go to the Zonsche heath fields. Sjef De Groot and his colleagues would go to a field between Schijndel and St. Oedenrode (501st DZ 'A').

"Our instructions were to be alert and ready to help and provide information, if necessary. Nothing was mentioned to us of a landing and nobody knew what was going on. As we rode our bicycles toward the fields, we heard the sound of planes. We saw a German plane being pursued by an English fighter. These planes were flying very low and making a lot of noise. We could clearly see their markings.

"After that a scouting plane (pathfinders) came and several parachutists came down. My colleague, who was riding up front, pedaled his bike so fast I was unable to keep up with him as he rode toward the landing place. I left my bike at farmer Sanders' and started running toward the paratroopers. When I was within 30 meters one of them shouted, 'Hands-up!!' I quickly put my hands up as weapons were pointed at me. At this time I wished I could go back as I was scared. Piet, in the meantime, had informed them who we were."

Pvt. Raymond Smith, who had suffered a broken ankle on the Normandy pathfinder jump, described some of the actions of the team members. "The mission for this pathfinder team was to mark the drop zone with 4' x 8' identifying panels placed in a 'T' shape and to guide the planes in with the Eureka radar set."

PFC Fred A. Wilhelm, a member of the same stick, said: "The Air Force assured us that nothing would move (against us) on the field. My job was to lay out the panels in the form of a 'T' and to use the orange smoke bombs."

No individual German soldiers threatened their presence. However, this didn't prevent enemy soldiers from firing light artillery and mortars at the men from a distance. Some time later, mortar shells began to land on the Son DZ.

Private First Class Wilhelm added, "After we had set up our navigation aids, Zamanakos, Smith and I were standing together talking, as we were good buddies from way back. A shell hit near us and Zamanakos was struck in the chest."

"I was hit about a half hour after landing and setting up panels—it was just before the arrival of the planes," said Cpl. John Zamanakos. "I was the radar operator."

Zamanakos' mission ended abruptly. He said, "Medic Ray Smith patched me up and I was treated at a civilian hospital in Son."

This was the end of the Holland campaign for Zamanakos.

From his vantage point on drop zone "C," First Lieutenant DeRamus had this to add: "The main body of troops came in around 30 minutes later, and it seems as though the Krauts must have known something because I saw around 17 C-47s shot down on the fields around us."

Johannes van Gorkum continued his assistance at the Son drop zone. He added: "The landing went really well but from the direction of Best, light German cannons were shooting at the planes. Suddenly, I noticed an orange parachute. I rushed toward the parachutist and he spoke to me in perfect Dutch. He said he was a radio man and asked for directions to Son. Together we went to a captain who had all his men assembled. I told him how many German soldiers were in Best and Son. The captain was heading in another direction and the information did not pertain to him. He suggested I give that information to others. We wished him success and, together with the radio man, we started toward Son. Near the farm of H. Van Gerven, we met two old Jewish people that I helped to hide on the farm. They gave me a big hug and thanked me for what I had done for them. Then I sent the radio man to Son and never heard from him again. The next day we set up panels and radio equipment for resupply. We stayed there for a couple days, directing other serials until the missions were completed and then moved north to regimental headquarters of the 502nd where I was assigned as 1st Battalion mortar platoon leader."

Commenting on his part in later pathfinder actions, Raymond Smith wrote: "The next two or three days, following the invasion on the 17th of September, brought very sad memories for me. We pathfinders continued the procedure of marking drop zones for glider troops and supplies but the German Air Force still had plenty of fighting planes to shoot down our transport planes and I witnessed dozens of dog fights between Allied and German pilots. In France we didn't encounter this kind of action. We lost planes and gliders to anti-aircraft artillery."

Even though 1st Battalion of the 501st Regiment wasn't directed to the proper drop zone, forty-two planes of the forty-five-plane serial managed to land its troopers in a very compact pattern despite the fact that it meant a double-time march of three miles from the Heeswijk-Dinter castle area near Kameran. Opposition was almost nonexistent and much help was provided by the local residents.

SIX

Parachute Drops

Parachute Flights and Landings

Late summer often brought early-morning fog throughout the countryside in England. Such was the case on the morning of September 17, 1944, when the men of the 101st Airborne Division moved out to the airfields from which they would shortly emplane for the parachute drop into Holland.

Air force weathermen said not to worry. The fog would lift by nine in the morning.

Five airfields were used for the parachute operation. The 501st Parachute Infantry Regiment, less its 3rd Battalion, would take off from Aldermaston. They would be accompanied and supported by a parachute platoon from each of "A" and "B" Companies of the 326th Airborne Engineer Battalion. Third Battalion of the 501st plus 3rd Battalion of the 506th plus 1st Platoon of "C" Company of the 326th Engineers would depart from Chilbolton. Membury Air Base would see the departure of the remainder of the 506th Parachute Regiment. Welford Air Base would be the starting point of 1st Battalion of the 502nd plus nine planes carrying the Division Headquarters parachute echelon and three planes of Division Artillery and eight planeloads of men from 2nd and 3rd Platoons of "C" Company of the engineer battalion. The remainder of the 502nd Regiment would emplane from Greenham Common.

The aircrews had been bloodied in the Normandy invasion. They had carried gasoline and other critical supplies to the forward elements of Gen. George S. Patton's rapidly advancing armored units. Many had participated in the airborne invasion of southern France on August 15, 1944.

For the most part, the same troop carrier groups and squadrons that carried the 101st regiments to Normandy were on hand to take them on their second parachute drop and their continuing rendezvous with destiny.

From a journal he kept during the war as a member of the 82nd Troop Carrier Squadron, T/Sgt. Harry M. Tinkcom wrote: "On the morning of the 17th of September, a tenseness as heavy as the thick haze that covered the ground seemed to pervade the entire base. The men knew full well that the impending series of missions into Holland were of grave importance and fraught with danger. The group was scheduled to drop paratroopers in the vicinity of Eindhoven, Nijmegen and Arnhem. One didn't need prophetic sense to visualize the difficulties involved in operations so large and so far behind enemy lines.

"The air crewmen scanned the sky anxiously as they rode in trucks down to the field where all available aircraft in the group were lined up in the fog in ghostly array. The base was completely closed in at this early hour."

At an air base where the fog was already dissipating that morning, a surprising encounter provided a lasting memory for Cpl. Charles Shoemaker. "When we were walking out to the planes—ours being stuck way out on the edge of the field, we stopped to rest half way across as we were heavily loaded down with equipment. We took a short break. We were sitting on top of our equipment when we saw two guys walking across the field toward us. One looked familiar and sure enough it was my brother Bob. He was with another glider pilot, a man named Bob Gilman. They came up and we talked. Dave Clark, one of our medics, called out, 'I'll be damned!' He recognized Gilman. They had gone to school together and had lost track of each other when they went into service. Of course, we had a quick reunion and talked for a few minutes and then it was time to move out again. We all wished each other good luck."

As commander of the airborne troopers taking part in the Market-Garden operation, LTG Lewis H. Brereton visited the airfields from which troops of his 1st Allied Airborne Army would emplane in a few hours for Holland.

At Aldermaston Air Base, W. B. Courtney, one of a group of war correspondents accompanying Lieutenant General Brereton, took in the scene. "Already long files of the fighting skymen are waddling in their grotesque clothes, and with packs and weapons of all sizes carried on their shoulders, out to the planes.

You are not prepared for their happy-go-lucky mood at such a moment, so unlike the quiet grimness of land infantry. They shout and wise crack and catcall. They see a handful of U.S. nurses, trim in blue fatigue coveralls, watching them from beside the control tower, and immediately there is an outburst of whistling all over the field.

"The General orders his driver to put down the car top, then calls to the nurses: 'Get in and ride up and down those lines. Sass the boys and let them sass you. It will do them good.' The whistling becomes monumental as the girls drive by."[7]

One of the soldiers in the group marching toward the planes was 1Lt. William G. Sefton, intelligence officer for his battalion. He wrote: "Just prior to departure from the marshaling area, some nurses came along in a jeep and told us 'Monty' had already jumped off with his drive and we wondered if this mission would also be scrubbed." This bit of news would have a bearing on Sefton's actions later in the day.

But the operation was not to be scrubbed. In T/Sgt. Harry Tinkcom's recollection: "At 0845, all crew members were called to the control tower for final instructions. None of the enlisted men knew the exact nature of the mission, for in the briefing the preceding day they were told that the drop zones would remain secret to them for security reasons until the time of take-off. Search as they might, the crewmen could read little reassurance in the facial expressions of the pilots, who has been told the ultimate destination.

"Major Bryant spoke little and, for once, without humor. This in itself boded no good. The men were informed that much time would be spent over German-held territory and that they could reasonably expect considerable ground fire.

"As usual, the weather was not good, said the meteorologist, but should clear up. 'It certainly should!' muttered the listening men. When the chaplain had spoken, the meeting was dissolved and the men went to their respective aircraft through the haze.

Technical Sergeant Tinkcom strolled out to the *Clay Pigeon,* which was number 45, the last plane in the first serial, or serial A12. He wrote: "Such a position in flight is known as 'Purple Heart Corner,' so called because the enemy gunners can, by the time the leading elements pass by, get the last planes accurately

7. Courtney, W. B. "Army in the Sky." *Colliers,* November 11, 1944.

zeroed in their sights. However, there were forty-five more ships behind the second serial, which could also expect heavy fire."[8]

Most of the final preparations went smoothly, but there were some disruptive incidents.

According to 2Lt. Robert P. O'Connell: "I had two men from the intelligence section put in my stick at the last minute. I didn't even know their names. One of these men refused to get in the plane. I talked to him and shook his shoulders but he wouldn't budge. The pilot radioed the tower and an MP jeep came out and took him away."[9]

First Lieutenant Sefton recalls another incident on the same airfield. "One of the battalion aidmen came limping up to me with blood oozing from his boot as the result of a bullet wound. 'What do you think I should do?' he asked. He was everything but convincing about his accident, and I gave him what I thought was pretty good advice. 'If I were you, trooper, I'd get on the plane, make the jump and then report to the aid station with the other casualties. I doubt that a court-martial here in England will buy your story.' He didn't take the advice. Later, I heard that he had, indeed, been court-martialed and sentenced to hard labor."

In an incident in the marshaling area, Pvt. C. D. Kreider[10] had a feeling of impending doom. Sgt. James D. Edgar related the incident: "C. D. Kreider gave me his watch and wedding band and told me to send them home to his wife as he wasn't going to make it. I told him 'If you don't make it, I'll be with you and I won't make it either.' Kreider responded, 'Sarge—you're too mean to die!' "

A typical takeoff saga was that of the *Clay Pigeon*. Technical Sergeant Tinkcom wrote: "With the rear four parapacks attached to the fuselage, plus the eighteen troopers and their heavy equipment, the *Pigeon* was quite heavily loaded. When all the men were seated, I walked out of the flight cabin down between the two rows of tense men, one of whom said dryly, 'Say pal, I hope this *Clay Pigeon* doesn't live up to its name!'

" 'Don't worry,' I replied, 'this old girl will get you there and land you smack on the DZ.' "

8. Technical Sergeant Tinkcom's narrative was also used by the Air Force Historical Section.
9. In December, at Mourmelon, he was court-martialed and sentenced to eight years. O'Connell was one of the witnesses.
10. Pvt. C. D. Kreider survived Holland but died at Bastogne.

Then Tinkcom returned to his radio table, checked the required frequencies, the Colors of the Day, and the interphone system between the pilot's jackbox and the one used by the crew chief at the back of the plane for oral instructions at jump time. Satisfied that all was in order, he put on his Mae West, flak suit, flak helmet, and, for the first time on an operational flight, or any other kind of flight in a C-47, his parachute. It was the backpack type, just issued to him, which fitted snugly enough to allow the flak suit to be tied over it.

S/Sgt. Joseph Curreri, the crew chief, also adjusted his parachute, but the pilots, issued chest packs, didn't wear theirs as it would have interfered with their work. Then the engines were started, the magnetos and propeller pitch checked. With ease and their usual savoir faire, "Basso and Profundo" reached twenty-five hundred rpm in perfect harmony. True, their voices had grown a bit hoarser with the number of miles covered, but they were still powerful and sturdy.

The takeoff by the *Clay Pigeon* was one that gave the crew tense moments. In Technical Sergeant Tinkcom's words, "That take-off was the shakiest and most uncertain that the *Pigeon* had ever made. As she started down the runway, 1Lt. Guido Brassesco, her regular pilot and one of the steadiest men that ever held a stick, found that she wanted to take to the air prematurely because of the confused air currents caused by propeller wash. As he held her to the runway she jumped first to one side, then to the other. Then, down on the grass at the end of the strip, with the bordering trees looming larger and taller, she made one last desperate jump and climbed roughly and waveringly into the air. It was a very close thing, and the men in the other planes marveled that she had ever gotten into the air at all."

Takeoff and assembly had gone smoothly and swiftly. One serial got its forty-five planes off the ground in five minutes and a quarter of an hour later swept over the field in formation on its way to Hatfield, the wing assembly point. The 435th got a thirty-two-plane serial into the air and in formation in fifteen minutes.

The weather was almost exactly as promised. Fog, present in the early morning, had cleared by 0900. A little thin, low stratus persisted longer but had dissipated by takeoff time. Over the channel, the weather was excellent, and over Belgium and Holland it was generally good with visibility of from three to seven miles. In some places, masses of cumulus clouds were present.

Having been assigned to plane 2 of the division parachute echelon so he could jump at the front of the stick, T/4 George E. Koskimaki remembered his takeoff and flight. "The takeoff was much like the one on our first D-Day. It was an impressive sight to watch the planes behind us take off. Air corps personnel stood on both sides of the runway, waving as each plane roared into the air."

Capt. Robert E. Jones remembered: "A beautiful day. Amazing sight—planes could be seen forward and backward as far as the eye could see. The front of the air column was over Holland while the rear was over England."

Koskimaki added: "As we flew across the channel, I watched the shadows of the planes in their formations on an almost placid sea. Air-sea rescue craft were everywhere, just in case planes ran into trouble. We picked up our fighter escort at midchannel. We crossed into Belgium. We got our first bird's-eye view of the effects of Allied bombing as we passed over leveled factory buildings. The landscape of Belgium was very lovely with large green fields cut by small canals. Now and then we'd pass one of the large ones such as the Albert Canal, which was bordered by tall Lombardy poplar trees. People could be seen below, pedaling along on their bicycles."

S/Sgt. Charles A. Mitchell recalled, "In the plane, on the way over, we passed the bucket for that last relief. PFC Bill Barclay was last and it fell to him to throw the contents out the door. My position was just to the rear of the open door and the prop-blast blew it back all over me. When we reached the drop zone every man went out of the ship still laughing, at my expense."

Communications corporal Sam R. Pope stewed about a particular challenge his commander had given him—and didn't relish it one bit. He wrote: "Captain Edmund Rhett, our company commander, was in charge of the stick in the plane and would be lead man out. He told me we were to guide on the railroad track going into Veghel. He didn't know which side of the railroad bridge I would land on but there was a machine gun nest there and if I knocked it out he would give me a three-day pass to London. I will not try to describe how that made me feel."

Tinkcom was entirely ignorant as to their destination. He sat at the radio table listening to the assigned frequency. The ground station identified itself at regular intervals but other than that it was no transmissions. All he knew about the mission was that the stick of troopers in the *Pigeon* would jump over the DZ at 1320. At 1300, S/Sgt. Joe Curreri walked back to his station at the parapack release buttons, and shortly after that the troopers were given their commands from the jumpmaster: "Stand up and hook up."

The jump into Holland was a new experience for Pvt. Gerald B. Johnston: "After all the training in jump procedures we were given, I managed to get the static line the wrong way around my left arm. Lt. Troy D. Wall (my jumpmaster) checked us out after we hooked up and rearranged the static line with a somewhat disgusted look. My only excuse was that I just couldn't believe I was doing what I was doing. Here I was, a year and a half out of high school, never had traveled out of the state of Virginia, flying across the English Channel to jump into Holland, by God, with a parachute and a load of ammunition and grenades."

A veteran of the earlier Normandy jump, Cpl. Glen A. Derber had this observation: "The actual jump was more serene, but the anticipation was more harrowing because experience taught me what to expect. The most frightening experience on the flight was that my static line was under my belly band and Cpl. Fletcher P. Cranford did not discover it until we were hooked up and waiting for the green light. I had to unhook my static line and he untangled my line so I could hook up again, properly. I kept praying that the green light wouldn't go on while we were in the process. I can only imagine what might have happened had I tried to jump with a tangled static line, but it would probably have been a miracle to survive."

Having served two years with an anti-aircraft unit before he volunteered for the paratroops, PFC Robert Marohn knew what easy targets we must have been. As jump time approached, he became more and more nervous and anxious to get out. "First Sergeant Jay Shenk got the stick ready. I was number 12 of 18 men. At the last moment, I could see that Sergeant Shenk was digging around in some gear and then he came up with a bottle of whiskey, which he tucked behind his reserve chute. At that, I nearly laughed and much of the tenseness left me."

According to T/4 Earl H. Tyndall Jr., there was one unusual occurrence during his flight. "One member of our stick became quite upset and all of a sudden his reserve chute spilled onto the floor. Obviously, this meant that he had to return to England."

"The front lines were rapidly approaching as we neared the

Dutch border," wrote T/4 George Koskimaki. "The front lines were separated by bright panels to show strafing pilots which troops were friend and foe. We began to hear small-arms fire, as was heard over France on D-Day. I looked down and saw a burning C-47 on the ground. How its occupants made out, I do not know."

The plane on the ground was most likely the *Clay Pigeon.* T/Sgt. Harry M. Tinkcom describes the jump and its sequel: "The parachute static cords were attached to the static line, all equipment given a last inspection, and the men were ready to jump on signal. It was only a minute or so after that when puff balls of flak began to appear in the sky around the aircraft ahead—inoffensive looking little puffs, but each burst carried destruction to any plane that received a hit in a vulnerable spot.

"Then something hit our right wing with three sharp spats which I, from the sound, recognized as bullets. Two flak bursts came dangerously close. Then came a terrific explosion under the left wing that threw the aircraft to the side, out of formation. When the pilot had her back on even keel, I realized that the flight cabin had suddenly become quite hot. The feeling was similar to that experienced when one walks from cold air into a warm, heated room."

While conversing with a bomber pilot several weeks earlier, 1Lt. Guido Brassesco, the pilot of *Clay Pigeon,* learned that those pilots made use of the automatic pilot on bombing runs and, sensing he might experience difficulties on a paratroop drop mission, had been making the preliminary adjustments a few minutes before the flak started. "What are you doing?" asked co-pilot 1Lt. Joe P. Andrews. "I explained that I was making some adjustments in case it became necessary," said Brassesco. "A few minutes later the plane was hit amidships, cutting the control cables and puncturing the gas tanks. Both engines were dead and the plane was sinking fast. During those few minutes, I switched to the settings and the plane made its own flight adjustments, angle of descent, wing flaps, etc. Visibility was bad in the plane due to smoke and flame."

Technical Sergeant Tinkcom continued his story: "It was then approximately 1310, just ten minutes from DZ time. I stood up and looked inquiringly at the pilots who were calmly flying ahead. The shell had broken some of the main control cables, burst the left auxiliary tank and fuel lines and stopped both engines. Brassesco, with great presence of mind, had shifted to automatic pilot. Had he not done that at the right moment, it is likely that the craft would have gone completely out of control. Instead, it maintained a slow descent on a true course, permitting the men in the main cabin to get out.

"I opened the door into the passenger cabin to find it full of smoke and flames. Flames were licking up at the main bulkhead and at midship. There was a large hole, about the size of a bass drum, in the left side of the fuselage.

"I saw at a glance that the cabin was empty except for one paratrooper and Joe Curreri, who had already told the trooper to jump. Two of his companions had been killed, or so badly wounded as to be helpless. They had been taken out by the others to prevent fouling of the static lines and also to keep them from burning. Had the two men been alive at the time it is almost certain that they would have died in the plane before reaching the ground, so rapidly were the flames spreading. Several of the men had jumped with their clothing on fire.

"While unsnapping my flak suit, I jumped over the two rows of flame and walked back to the cargo door to see if the plane was high enough off the ground to permit a safe jump. The earth seemed dangerously close."

PFC George D. Doxzen was the last paratrooper on board the *Clay Pigeon.* He wrote: "When the aircraft was over Belgium, 1Lt. Tom Seibel had us 'Stand up and hook up,' which we did in a very orderly, well disciplined, manner. We then took a heading toward the drop zone. We were only minutes from the DZ when a burst of flak hit our aircraft under my feet, causing me to fall to the seat. When the flak burst hit, Lt. Seibel was struck in the chest. The rest of the stick exited the aircraft as though it was a routine jump. As they were going out, they played out my static line. In fact, Cpl. Harvey White asked me if I was 'okay.' I nodded yes and he went on his way.

"I decided then and there I was quitting the war. I even imagined what it would be like when the plane hit the ground with me in it. I was not going to jump."

Tinkcom and Curreri were undecided what to do. They wanted to see what the pilots were going to do.

Tinkcom related, "Curreri and I both started to walk to the cockpit but the walls of fire amidships and at the bulkhead had now leaped so high that it was impossible for us to go forward.

Choking in the acrid smoke, we were forced to turn back. Through that blazing inferno, we could barely see the pilots who were still sitting in their seats, trying to keep the plane steady. Then the co-pilot, Joe Andrews, turned around and shouted and waved the three men out.

"As I took off my flak helmet, fearing the shock of the opening parachute would break my neck, Joe said, 'Go ahead!'

" 'O.K.' I said, as I stepped toward the door. The paratrooper who had been hesitating now decided to jump, too. Both he and I left the plane at almost the same time. As he leaped, my right arm hooked around the trooper's static line and I went out sidewise, out and back, instead of out and down. I was just barely conscious of the horizontal stabilizer passing close to my face when I pulled the ripcord."

Doxzen remembered: "The plane was on fire. I could not see the cockpit for smoke and the crew chief was yelling at me to jump. The radio operator of the plane yelled, 'What do we do?' The pilot yelled 'Jump!' As the radio operator jumped, he caught his arm on my played-out static line and would have hit the plane if I hadn't jumped as an automatic reflex."

As the plane settled toward earth on its automatic pilot settings, pilots Brassesco and Andrews struggled with their flak jackets. Lieutenant Brassesco added: "It was too late to jump. As the plane plowed through trees and underbrush and farmers' fences at two hundred miles per hour, Lt. Andrews had opened a side window and was part way out when the plane came to an abrupt halt. This threw Andrews out of the window and clear of the plane. With both legs fractured, I managed to crawl through a window and dropped clear of the flaming inferno. I dragged myself, using my hands and arms, to get away from the heat."

Radio operator Tinkcom, crew chief Curreri, and paratrooper Doxzen survived their parachute jumps. Brassesco and Andrews were found by the Dutch underground a short time later and were moved to a place of hiding. They were joined later by occupants of several gliders that were forced down when the towplanes were hit by the same battery of anti-aircraft guns and crashed.[11]

11. Six of the paratroopers died, including Lieutenant Seibel and Corporal White. The experiences of PFC George Doxzen, T/Sgt. Harry Tinkcom, S/Sgt. Joe Curreri, and the pilots appear in a later chapter with their Dutch resistance helpers.

PFC Hugh A. Kiser of "A" Company of the 502nd Parachute Infantry Regiment was a survivor of the other troop carrier plane that was shot down before it reached the DZ. He said, "Our plane was shot down as it passed over the German lines at the Belgian-Dutch border but most of us got back to our company."[12]

When troopers in nearby planes witnessed men jumping from *Clay Pigeon,* they may well have been tempted to jump, thinking the flight had reached the drop zone.

PFC Giles M. Thurman wrote: "At least two nearby planes were hit and one was on fire. Sgt. Bill King stood up and was going to jump. I told him this was not the drop zone and that those people were jumping because their plane was on fire."

For PFC Leonard T. Schmidt, flying into Holland was his first taste of combat. He wrote: "It didn't seem like combat until all the flak started up and the fighter planes were buzzing around us and the plane was bobbing up and down every once in a while. When the red light came on, Lt. Robert Pennell got up and walked the full length of the plane, wishing everybody good luck and happy landings."

Being assigned as the jumpmaster of the stick gave Sgt. Chester L. Brooks an opportunity to instill confidence in the others waiting in the plane. He said, "I believe we were in the lead plane of our serial for the jump. I was jumpmaster and stood in the door and waved at the people in their doorways down below. As we neared the jump field, I stood back from the door and put on my best 'John Wayne' manner. I saw myself as instilling confidence in those who couldn't see out. Much later, S/Sgt. George Caloger, who was battalion sergeant major, said that I turned and faced the group with sweat pouring down my face and shouted in a pipsqueak voice, 'It's going to be a parade ground jump, men!' So much for heroics."

Pvt. Henry A. DeSimone had his own story. "When we were given the order to stand up, the trooper in front of me was hit by flak that came up through the body of the plane. He unhooked his static line from the cable and sat down in his seat for the ride back to England."

12. Kiser's plane was shot down four miles behind the German lines. Eleven of the troopers got together with the Belgian underground and reached the 101st Division twelve days later.

For Sgt. James D. Edgar, the pre-jump problem was more complicated. "We were standing up and word came up the line that a man was down in back. S/Sgt. Frank Sciaccotti told me to check. I went back about half way down the stick. There lay a man named Jackson. I couldn't find any blood but his eyes were going round and round. I unhooked him and rolled him to the side—closed up the men—found the crew chief and told him to return Jackson to England. By this time I heard the lines hitting against the plane. I hitched up at the rear and went out of the door."

The 3rd Battalion serial of the 506th Parachute Infantry Regiment was the first to arrive over drop zone "C." The serial in which regimental commander Col. Robert F. Sink and his executive officer, LTC Charles H. Chase, were traveling began getting light flak about ten minutes before drop time. Then a tremendous increase in the volume of fire came up at the five-minute mark. Most of the ack-ack was coming from the left of the forty-plane formation. Many ships were hit. Chase, in plane 2, was watching for the green light and looking at the 3 craft as they came on toward the DZ. When he figured they were two minutes out, he told the stick to stand up. At that moment, he noticed 3 blazing fiercely from the left engine but steady on course. Glancing at the wing of his own plane, he saw a hole appear and looked at the wing again to see that two feet of the wingtip had been sheared away. The green light appeared and Chase led his men out over drop zone "C."

"Colonel Sink, who was in plane 1, had been looking out of the door when something shook the body of the plane and he saw a part of the wing whip loose and dangle in the breeze. He turned and said, 'Well, there goes the wing' but nobody seemed to think much about it as they figured by now they were practically 'in.' It is known that in the first group (3rd Battalion), numbers 2, 3 and 12 were shot down and that they burned on the ground, but the parachutists who were in them had a chance to get away. They did not know if the crews escaped."[13]

Cpl. Steve Kovacs, of the demolitions section, may have been one of the troopers on board plane 3 as described by Lieutenant Colonel Chase. Kovacs wrote: "Our plane was hit by flak and

---

13. 506th Unit After-Action Report for Holland. See also story of PFC George D. Doxzen on page 64.

caught fire a minute or so out of the DZ. We jumped with the smoke choking us. I hit the ground hard. Heard later the pilot and crew chief died in the crash."

Colonel Sink and Lieutenant Colonel Chase also reported that two 506th parachutists were killed over the DZ as they were descending when a disabled plane struck them as it passed through the stick of men as they floated to earth.

Reporting on the D-Day activities of the 79th Troop Carrier Squadron, 1Lt. Roger Airgood[14] described what happened to a C-47A piloted by 1Lt. Robert S. Stoddard Jr. "The plane was hit hard by flak with the left engine burning. Stoddard kept his plane on course until all paratroopers were out. He then ordered the rest of the crew, co-pilot 2Lt. Raymond L. Blowers, crew chief T/Sgt. Ivan W. Thede and radio operator T/Sgt. Howard G. Wilson to bail out, which they did. Lt. Stoddard brought the plane down in a smooth glide, but, upon landing, it burst into flames and Lt. Stoddard was lost. T/Sgt. Thede was found later; his chute had failed to open. Lt. Blowers and T/Sgt. Wilson survived, with injuries."

Jumping from a plane that had a hit through the floor near the pilot's compartment, T/5 Edward R. Vetch of "G" Company was near the impact area. "The last man in the stick was hooking up behind me and took the full blast and lay on the floor with part of one leg on the seat, with smoke all around him. I realized they were jumping already and it was up hill to get to the door. I crawled to the door and rolled out. The plane was on fire and the flames singed my hair and eyelashes. I can remember one plane coming in on fire with troopers dangling from both wings as it came down through the sky full of troopers and hit the ground and exploded, not far from where I lay."

PFC John Vlachos was a member of the ill-fated stick Vetch had seen. He recalled, "As the green light came on and we jumped, a disabled plane veered in below and behind us. The 5 and 6 men of my stick were hit by the wing of the crippled plane."

Maj. Harold W. Hannah, of the G-3 section of Division Headquarters, never forgot his jump from a burning plane. "The plane was hit and on fire when we jumped. One lad spilled his

14. Roger Airgood, historian for the 79th Troop Carrier Squadron.

reserve chute and had the sergeant cut it off. The guy was happy to jump when he saw fire and smoke. I remember watching the plane from which I jumped, smoke, climb, turn and dive into the ground and burst into flames."

On board the same plane carrying members of the division parachute echelon was PFC William K. Crews. He wrote: "South of the drop zone, the plane was hit by flak. While I tried to stand up, my reserve chute popped open. Smoke was coming up through the floor of the plane. I was the last trooper to leave the plane."

T/Sgt. George L. Ritter was crew chief on aircraft 3 of the division parachute echelon. He wrote:[15] "On the approach leg, our plane burst into flames, after being hit several times by German anti-aircraft fire. With the left engine on fire, the tail section partly shot away, and the entire left side of the aircraft in flames, the pilot, Major Dan Elam, nevertheless continued on in formation. By the time the drop zone was reached, the fire had increased to great proportions. After seeing that his paratroopers had jumped safely, Major Elam[16] ordered the radio operator and me to bail out. He attempted to crash-land in a small, inadequate, field but in doing so, the plane crashed into a wooded area and exploded killing Major Elam and the co-pilot."

Paratroopers on the ground came upon plane crew members. Some were ready to join the fight. Others had paid the supreme sacrifice.

"For the first time in 22 jumps, I had bad body position and, as the result, lost my weapon," wrote PFC James G. McCann. "All I had was a trench knife strapped to my ankle. I headed for a ditch and a guy there in officer's pinks and a leather jacket had a .45 pistol. It was one of the pilots who had been shot down. I asked him, 'How are you gonna fight a war with a .45?' He replied, 'I've got more than you do!' I had to wait until an equipment bundle dropped and I picked up a 60mm mortar barrel and then I joined in the war effort."

After parachuting safely as a member of the advance party for the Division Artillery, Sgt. Arthur Parker related a recurring memory of the war: "We recovered our survey gear and headed

---

15. From *435th Troop Carrier Group History*. The posthumous award of the Distinguished Service Cross, the first such decoration within the 53rd Wing, was given to Maj. Dan Elam of Duncan, Oklahoma.
16. From *435th Troop Carrier Group History*.

for St. Oedenrode. A C-47 crashed right in front of us. We rushed over to it and entered the plane but it was empty except for the pilot and co-pilot, both dead. We tried to get the bodies out but gas fumes forced us out of the plane. I will never forget that co-pilot. He had the bluest eyes and flaming red hair. Even though he was dead, his eyes seemed to follow our every move as we tried to get him out. I still see his face from time to time."

S/Sgt. William F. McAllister,[17] radio operator on board a 435th Troop Carrier transport, described his experience: "As we approached the drop zone, we heard a loud explosion that sounded very close. I happened to look down at my feet and saw flames coming up through the floor. By the time I got the fire extinguisher that hangs behind the pilot's head, the flames were too intense for me to handle. I looked toward the back of the plane and saw the paratroopers bailing out. So I started to take off my flak suit and get into my parachute. By the time I did, the plane was too low for me to jump, so I sat down and waited for the crash. The next thing I knew, I was being revived in a hospital."

"Don't worry about me!" the pilot of another burning plane, 2Lt. Herbert E. Shulman, told his flight leader. "I'm going to drop these troops on the DZ!" He kept his word—and immediately crashed in flames after the drop. At least three other pilots stayed at the controls of burning aircraft and gave their lives to give their paratroopers an accurate drop. Every one of the 424 sticks was dropped, and, except for those of two planes shot down near Rethy, not one was dropped prematurely.[18]

One stick of jumpers had to deal with the shock of losing their platoon leader, even before the jump. S/Sgt. Clive Barney wrote: "The first shock was 1Lt. Edward Jansen being hit in the aircraft. He called me up to jump the stick but when I got there, he had balanced himself against the wall and proceeded to direct the men out. I helped him to the bulkhead and hooked up and went out. I realized that I had not checked my equipment when my carbine hit me in the mouth when the chute opened. My second shock came when, on looking up to check my chute, I saw the aircraft I had just left burst into flames. Watching and praying, I saw two chutes blossom just before it hit. I found out much later that one was Lt. Jansen."

17. From *435th Troop Carrier Group History.*
18. *Operation Market-Garden, An Air Force Study.*

Sgt. Joseph P. Powers remembers that his plane was called *Round Trip Ticket.* "After 'stand up and hook up,' I stood in the door and when I jumped I somehow was hooked to something outside the door and found myself flying along, upside down, looking up at Don Brininstool standing in the door. He immediately sensed what was wrong and kicked me loose and went out after me. Don saved my life."

Sgt. Donald W. Brininstool recalled the incident. He wrote: "Over the drop zone, with the green light on, Joe Powers got caught in the door of the plane. Somehow his chute was caught inside the door with Joe's body outside. With the help of the crew chief, I was able to free Joe."

Most troopers carried their M-1 rifles in Griswold bags strapped vertically under the reserve chute, and the result was many dental problems. First Lieutenant William G. Sefton remembered: "Too many troopers had lost teeth when their knees buckled on landing, driving the top of the Griswold bag into their lower jaws. In considering this hazard, I had mentally rehearsed holding the rifle in both hands. Unfortunately, a suspension line managed to wrap itself around the front sight of my rifle as my chute opened, jerking it out of my hands."

Recalling the same problem from the Normandy jump, Cpl. Henry Gogola made a change: "After the Normandy foul-up with the Griswold canvas bag in which our rifles were carried, most of us discarded the bags and jumped with our rifles cradled in our arms. Because I was carrying a walkie-talkie (SCR-536) radio into Holland, I elected to jump with my M-1 slung on my shoulder, butt up. As I went out of the door, the barrel swung out and somehow got tangled in the lines and caused me to streamer. Looking up at my chute, I saw what happened and remember calling out, 'Oh my God!' I guess he heard me because the next thing I knew, I had the D ring of the reserve in my hand and the beautiful sight of that white mushroom above my head. I must have been no more than fifty feet off the ground when it opened. I still have the D ring. I keep it for sentimental reasons, or as a reminder of an answered prayer."

Pvt. Emil Zorich also had to resort to his reserve parachute. "I was carrying a .30 caliber machine gun, secured with rope to my right pant leg, when I jumped. My main chute did not open so I let go of the gun and opened my reserve. The machine gun tore off a hole in the pant leg and was lost in a soft, plowed field near Eerde."

For some like PFC Emmert O. Parmley, "The jump was routine. I left my reserve chute in the plane, as I did in France."

Having arrived on the 101st scene a week after the Normandy D-Day, 2Lt. David H. Forney was assigned as an assistant platoon leader of "H" Company of the 506th Regiment. Recalling his first and only combat jump, Forney said, "The pilot had said, as the plane was approaching the DZ, 'We're gonna be hitting a lot of flak up here.' He advised me to stand in the door early in case the plane was hit. Just as we neared the drop zone the pilot yelled, 'I'm hit! I don't know how long I can hold my altitude!' I said, 'Let's go!' and went out with the rest of the stick following."

"We were over heavy flak for about five minutes," remembered T/4 George Koskimaki. "I was second man this time because of a cumbersome load I was carrying. We stood up—four minutes out from the DZ. The plane bounced as a sister ship was hit and caught fire. Cattle and chickens were scurrying around on the ground, disturbed by the terrific bombardment coming up at us.

"I stood with the heavy leg pack in the doorway, just behind the jumpmaster. He shouted, 'Let's go!' and out we went. My chute opened with that pleasant jerk that almost tore my shoulders loose. The radio bag was ripped loose from my gloved grasp by the shock and now dangled on the toe of my boot. My folding stock carbine had been ripped from its canvas holster and hung loosely, attached to me only by its front sight, which was caught in the untorn portion of the holster.

"I tried to draw my right foot up so I could release the radio equipment bundle but forty-five pounds was too much to draw to a suitable height. With my left foot, I finally managed to push the bundle off the toe of the boot and then pulled the little ripcord that enabled the bundle to be lowered about twenty feet below me where it swung like a pendulum still attached to my parachute harness. I didn't have to guide my chute as I was headed for a large plowed field. I hit the loosely tilled soil and made the softest landing I had ever experienced."

Another radioman had to jump with an SCR-300 radio strapped to his leg and unfortunately he became entangled with a trooper. In the recollection of T/5 Charles McCallister, "After my chute opened, I was slipping to the rear to avoid another trooper in front of me when I tangled with still another trooper who apparently was doing the same thing behind me. Our chutes became entwined and one of them collapsed. In addition to my normal load, I was carrying a 45-pound radio and when I landed on top of the other trooper he got much the worst of it. All I remember is that he was a medic and I was unable to revive him immediately."

Jumping from General Taylor's plane as his radio operator, T/4 James F. Kennedy recalled, "I was third or fourth in the stick, and had a radio attached to my leg. The general asked me two or three times if I could make it. I told him I was okay. After going out and the chute opening, I proceeded to pull the pins to swing the radio below me on a pendulum-like line. I was oscillating so much I couldn't hang on to it while lowering the line to the end. I had to let go at about 200 feet. The line snapped. Even so, it scorched the gloves I was wearing."

Cpl. Howard J. Matthews remembered, "In Normandy, we had lost our machine gun so we decided to do it better this time. In Holland, I moved to the end of the stick with Sgt. George Spear. We put the machine gun bundle by the door. Then we started forward when the stick members started jumping. We got to the door and Spears and I pushed the bundle out and I held it all the way down. We had the only machine gun in 'F' Company."

In describing the actions of his company commander in the company log while the impressions were fresh in his mind, Cpl. Peter Santini wrote: "Some flak burst beneath the plane and she lurched quite a bit. Captain Martin's voice rolled back to us above the din and roar of the motors, telling us that we were about thirty seconds from the drop zone. About that time some 20mm shells whizzed right by his face. Luckily he wasn't hit. It was time for the jump now. The men in the other planes began to bail out. We still didn't have a green light or verbal 'go' signal. We waited for a few seconds, which seemed an eternity, then jumped without ever getting the green light. All the men in our plane landed right on the field. It was a good thing Captain Martin jumped us when he did, because if he had waited a few seconds longer, the end of the stick would have landed in the woods."

Santini continued: "The Air Corps did a wonderful job on this drop. A repetition of the Normandy jump would have proven very costly. We saw wave after wave of planes come in right behind us. They were all in formation. They even slowed down while the men were bailing out."

Farther back in the same serial, Pvt. Gerald Johnston came down on the same drop zone. He wrote: "I was bazooka man for the 2nd Platoon on the jump. The bazooka and ammunition were in a bundle to be dropped from the plane with a blue parachute. Parker, who was just ahead of me in the stick, was to work with me.

"I saw several blue chutes on the way down but lost them in the huge crowd of chutes. I had never jumped with such a large group before. The sky was literally full of parachutes and people were headed in all directions on the ground."

For Sgt. Russell Schwenk, the Holland jump resulted in the loss of a valuable piece of equipment as well as a surprise on landing. He had this recollection: "Our plane was hit by shrapnel and our #1 man, PFC Arthur Peterson, was wounded in the butt—very bloody. I told him to stay with the plane. Going out of the door, I got my first surprise—some cord broke, and the land mine I had attached to the belt took off and spiraled earthward. Then, upon landing, who greeted me first—Art Peterson. He said he wasn't staying with the plane—too much flak. It sounded like rain on the roof."

Having alerted his jumpmaster earlier not to jump when he saw men bailing out of a burning aircraft that was shot down before reaching the drop zone, PFC Giles Thurman now exited the plane over drop zone "C." "I looked down and saw tracers below me. I pulled out my .45 caliber pistol, checked it, threw a round in the chamber and held it ready in my right hand while grasping my risers. Tracers continued to reach skyward. I then pulled down on my risers trying to slip into some trees on the edge of the drop zone and at the same time I kept hearing shots. When I landed, I stuck the pistol barrel into the ground. On shaking the dirt out of the barrel, I found I had emptied the full clip through my chute, firing every time I pulled down on the risers as I tried to slip into the trees at the edge of the drop zone."

For those going into combat for the first time, there were invariably some raw nerves. First Lieutenant Robert Stroud recalled, "When I landed, I saw three German soldiers coming out with white flags. They were trying to surrender, but I was trying to pull my folding stock carbine from its canvas holster and shot the damn thing, almost hitting my foot. I think I was more nervous than the Germans."

As a green replacement, Pvt. William N. Chivvis was somewhat nervous after landing in enemy-held territory. He said, "I landed in the rear of a farmyard. The farmer ran toward me in a very excited manner. He just about got himself shot as we had been warned to be very careful and not trust anyone. Fortunately, he stopped and I settled down and everything was all right."

PFC Leonard T. Schmidt remembered: "Shortly after landing, I saw a little farmer wearing wooden shoes. He had a beard and a little skull cap on his head and he was dancing up and down and crying for joy at being liberated. This really impressed me."

A total of 6,641 Screaming Eagles had been dropped during a forty-minute time period.

The first three serials dropped the 501st Parachute Infantry Regiment and two platoons of engineers totaling 2,050 troops on drop zone "A" and a compact mis-drop area near the Heeswijk-Dinter castle. The mis-drop was probably the result of the assigned pathfinder plane being shot down a half hour earlier, leaving no Eureka set to home in on. As a result, the lead serial swerved west of its true course and dropped forty-two sticks in fields three miles northwest of the proper drop zone. This setback, however, was offset by an excellent drop pattern. First Battalion was able to assemble 90 percent of its men and material within forty-five minutes. It then marched directly to Veghel, preceded by an advance guard on requisitioned trucks and bicycles. The paratroopers overcame token resistance by about thirty rear-echelon troops and by 1600 hours had taken their objectives, the two bridges over the Aa River within the town limits.

The second serial, consisting of the 2nd Battalion and Regimental Headquarters, was dropped in an excellent pattern several hundred yards short at the western boundary of the drop zone at 1306; at 1311 the third serial made up of 3rd Battalion made its drop in a fine pattern centered about fifteen hundred yards west of the zone. A few stragglers from the first serial also dropped near DZ "A." The 501st Regiment assembled 95 percent of its men and materials within forty-five minutes without any opposition and dispatched its battalions to their assigned objectives. By 1515, the 2nd Battalion had secured the road and railroad bridges over the Willems-Vaart Canal on the west and southwest ends of Veghel. The 3rd Battalion had taken Eerde and set up roadblocks south of the drop zone on the Eindhoven–Arnhem highway. Within another hour, contact was established with the 1st Battalion and Veghel was occupied. At about 1800 hours the 3rd Battalion made contact with the 502nd.[19]

The 501st had taken all its Holland D-Day objectives intact and thirty-two prisoners at the cost of ten jump casualties and only two battle casualties (Capt. William Burd and Pvt. Robert Peninger). It was in touch with airborne units dropped south of it and had encountered very few of the enemy.

The next three serials, forty-five planes of the 442nd Troop Carrier Group and ninety from the 436th TCG, delivered the 506th Regiment and 1st Platoon of "C" Company of the 326th Engineer Battalion, about twenty-two hundred men on drop zone "C." Except for one aircraft that was shot down early, those serials dropped their parachutists with great accuracy from tight formations at 1312, 1315, and 1324.

The regimental assembly point was set up at 1345 and, within an hour after the jump, assembly was 80 percent complete. Only twenty-four men of the 506th were hurt in the drop. As described by T/5 Edward R. Vetch and PFC John Vlachos, two troopers were killed when a badly disabled plane came down through the stick of men as they were descending.

The 1st Battalion had the urgent task of taking the highway bridge and two smaller spans approximately fourteen hundred yards east and west of the main canal span before they could be blown. To reach their objectives as quickly as possible, the troops took a shortcut through the woods. Most of the battalion was on its way within forty-five minutes. The first troops were observed and came under fire of two 88mm guns and mortars positioned near the main bridge.

Second Battalion assembled at the east end of the drop zone and was a half hour late getting off the drop zone as some of its troops were confused by 502nd assembly signals on neighboring drop zone "B." They also became intent on helping with glider landings and extricating men and materials from crashed gliders. The 506th met no opposition in its southward march

19. See comments of S/Sgt. Robert J. Houston and PFC Richard M. Ladd.

until it reached the outskirts of Son. Resistance was broken by 1600, but as the two battalions converged on the bridge, the span blew up in their faces. The other smaller crossings had been destroyed several days earlier.

The last parachute serials flown by the 53rd Wing were two of 36 and 28 planes respectively from the 435th TCG and two of 45 each from the 438th bearing the 502nd, the advance echelon of the 101st Division Headquarters and 2nd and 3rd Platoons of "C" Company of the 326th Engineers, a total of 2,434 men to be dropped on DZ "B." The lead plane of the 435th was flown by Col. Frank J. MacNees, the group commander, with MG Maxwell D. Taylor and 1st Battalion commander LTC Patrick Cassidy as passengers.

These serials kept the prescribed formation, route, and timing all the way to the drop zone. When they were between ten and twenty miles from the drop zone, they picked up the signals of the pathfinders' Eureka beacon. As the first serial of the 435th approached the DZ, the last of the 436th, slightly off course and four minutes late, cut across its path, forcing the 435th to climb to avoid a collision. As a result, these paratroopers had a somewhat higher drop than normal—nine hundred to twelve hundred feet. Between 1324 and 1338 the four serials dropped 2,391 of their paratroopers on or near DZ "B." As narrated by PFC Hugh A. Kiser, one stick had been dropped near Rethy when its plane was fatally hit.

The 502nd Regiment considered its jump fully as good as that of the 506th. It assembled within an hour.

The 502nd served as a connecting link between the 501st on the north and the 506th on the south; 2nd Battalion served as the division reserve on D-Day. The 1st Battalion easily captured St. Oedenrode, seizing two small bridges over the Dommel River in the town. "H" Company of the 3rd Battalion was sent on a hurried mission to seize the highway bridge near Best, a mile southwest of the drop zone.

Of the 424 planes carrying 101st troops on D-Day, 16 C-47s were shot down, 14 were badly damaged and 84 received moderate or light damage. Of the badly damaged aircraft, four made emergency landings in Belgium and several barely reached England. The 53rd Wing had twenty-six men dead or missing and fifteen wounded.

Enemy fire had almost no effect on the delivery of the paratroops. The formations held tightly together, and the pilots of damaged planes coaxed them along with a skill and a courage that won the admiration of the paratroops. One officer, Lieutenant Colonel Cassidy, was so absorbed in watching the struggle of a badly damaged plane that he almost forgot to jump. It was left to the division commander, MG Maxwell Taylor, to remind Cassidy of the business at hand.

SEVEN

Glider Lifts

The First Glider Lifts

Following the paratroop formations to the Son area came two serials from the 437th Troop Carrier Group with thirty-five planes each, towing CG-4A Waco gliders.

In Normandy, the 101st Airborne Division had used both the CG-4A Waco glider and the British-built Horsa. For the Holland operation the division relied entirely on the Waco for its glider operations. The Waco CG-4A was an American-built glider. It had a tubular steel framework covered with canvas. It was smaller than the Horsa, more maneuverable, and could be landed on smaller fields. The payload was limited to 3,750 pounds. It could carry thirteen combat-equipped soldiers plus a crew of two, or it might carry a jeep or a quarter-ton trailer with a crew of three to six. Another type of load was a 57mm anti-tank gun with its handlers, a 75mm pack howitzer, or a 105mm snub-nosed howitzer. On almost every glider flying into Holland for the Market-Garden mission, one of the airborne soldiers served as co-pilot, thereby increasing the load by one glider trooper. The co-pilot was usually someone who had some knowledge of flying a light plane, or he received some very hasty instructions prior to take-off.

Equipment was moved into the glider through a hinged nose section, which served as the pilot's compartment. The hinged nose was raised and a jeep was backed in. Soldiers entered the craft through a side door. The tubular steel framework provided considerable safety during a crash landing.[20]

20. Koskimaki, George. *D-Day with the Screaming Eagles* (3rd ed). 101st Airborne Division Association, Sweetwater, TN, 1970.

The gliders contained forty-three jeeps, eighteen trailers, and 311 airborne troops, mainly from the 101st Signal Company, medical personnel, the Reconnaissance Platoon, plus Division Artillery Headquarters and a Phantom detachment (British liaison and combat communications unit). The large number of vehicles and the complete lack of artillery pieces shows that the 101st expected to need mobility more than firepower. Also, its planners had supposed the British artillery would very quickly come within supporting distance.

These are the recollections of glidermen who participated in the first-day operations.

First Lieutenant Henry Barnes served as one of the medical evacuation officers for the 326th Airborne Medical Company. He has written a lengthy narrative of his combat experiences. Part of his Holland adventure follows: "A curious throng of Air Force G.I.'s watched a long line of glidermen walk out on to the roaring propeller-swept field. It was in the gray chill of an English morn at Ramsbury Airfield in southern England.

"Row after row of C-47s were lined along the runways in tightly packed rows. On each side of the runway were the gliders sitting quietly, motorless, vibrationless in their brooding manner. Folded in accordion fashion in front of each glider was a white nylon rope.

"These silent gliders would later attain their grace, their airy sweep, their majestic individuality after they were detached from these tow-ropes binding them to their tow-planes in some hostile country miles behind enemy lines."

Cpl. Harold Spence, one of two cipher experts, joined members of the 101st Airborne Signal Company on the flight. He wrote: "A newsreel cameraman took shots of us as we marched off to the airfield about half a mile away. Arriving there we found the tug-planes and gliders all lined up like troops on parade. Certainly an impressive sight if one hadn't seen anything like it before. As we passed the gliders the crews would drop out of the column as they identified their particular Waco. I dropped out on sighting No. 21 and saw for the first time my companions for the journey. There were six of us, and the glider pilot to come, making seven in all. No one had much to say, each obviously rather nervous as we once again checked items of equipment, paying particular attention to life-belts and speculating on the possibility of them being used. Air-sickness pills were handed round and we each took one right away. Someone started a small fire as wallets were being cleaned out of anything which might assist the enemy to identify the body—other than number and name."

When Cpl. James L. Evans loaded up for the trip and fastened his seat belt, he noted that there weren't enough seats for everyone so he unfastened his belt and got up on the machine-gun cart's load of radio batteries. It was tied down behind the pilot's seat.

This was a vantage point that gave him a bird's-eye view over the pilot and through the windshield. The glider had small angle-irons[21] welded to the bottom and top, and they came to a point in front of the windshield. He wondered what they were for but forgot to ask.

There was an intercom between the towplane and glider. A communications wire was attached to the towrope. He thought that was a good idea. There was a real surprise when the pilot and co-pilot climbed in. The glider troopers had been told in training not to expect a co-pilot as one of our men would serve in that capacity. The reason for the two-man air force crew was most likely due to the fact they were carrying Col. Thomas L. Sherburne, one of the top artillery officers in the division.

Cpl. Harold Spence, the English liaison cipher expert, had never flown in a glider, nor was he familiar with American equipment. He added to his account: "Just now our glider pilot turned up and I'm afraid he was subjected to rather a keen scrutiny from me. I realized that in a tight corner so much would depend on him and I was curiously relieved to see that he was an officer. I began to wonder what would happen if he 'stopped one.' However, he soon chose one of the crew and proceeded to give some sort of elementary instruction in case of emergency, saying he would hand over the glider to him for half an hour during the trip. Having criticized the pilot, the glider was next subjected to my attention. The tubular steel frame was reassuring. On the outside someone had chalked the prayer, 'I hope to God the crew of this glider land safely,' to which I mentally added my name."

First Lieutenant Henry Barnes continued his story: "With the

21. According to historian Roger Airgood, this was called the Griswold nose. It was used after Normandy to help protect glider pilots.

gliders already loaded with the heavy equipment, it was now time to load the personnel. The troops filed into the gliders, shook hands with their pilots, gulped down their anti-motion tablets and then tightened their safety belts."

Barnes continued: "The blast from the two engines grew louder shaking our glider even more. Seven hearts skipped a beat. A moment later the cement runway was sliding by below us. All eyes focused on our tow rope and our tow plane. Our rope was intact, our plane was dead ahead. Then, we realized we were in the air. For us, the invasion of Holland had begun.

"As our glider slowly circled the field, it gradually found its place with the other sixty-nine tow planes and gliders and we all settled back for the ride.

"It was the 17th day of September, 1944, in the morning and the early sunlight reflected from the plastic canopies and windows of assorted aircraft which were gradually forming into a huge armada."

Cpl. Harold Spence worried about the secret cipher equipment that was being carried on the mission. He wrote: "We were airborne at 10:30. Thus started my first Op and my first trip in a glider. Immediately in front of us was No. 18 carrying Cpl. Sellers and to our right, slightly in the rear, I noticed No. 22 in which the American sergeant Cy O'Connell carried the third installment of our British cipher equipment. This in case neither Sellers or I got down safely."

Corporal Spence soon found out that the structure of the glider made conversation impossible. "I was surprised to find conversation impossible, even with my immediate neighbor. The noise of the wind on the canvas sides of the glider was terrific and, after a time, I gave up all attempt at conversation. Over the channel we suffered our first casualty. I noticed the acting co-pilot gesticulating to us to the effect that the glider in front had gone down into the sea. Thinking that my friend Sellers was on board I felt sickened and prayed he would be picked up by the sea rescue people."

The downed glider was from another unit. PFC John B. Moore of the Recon Platoon remembered: "During the flight over the Channel, Sgt. Roland Hyde, who was seated in the front with the glider pilot, Lt. Bennett, turned to Chuck Taylor and myself seated in the jeep behind them and pointed down.

There, on the top of the water, was a glider which we later found to be one of ours."[22]

Barnes continued his story: "Then we were over the land mass that was Fortress Europa. This is more like it I thought to myself and watched the flooded, marshy, brown, desolate land slide by. Sitting in the co-pilot's seat with my lap crammed with maps, I suddenly became air-sick and vomited. My maps now resembled the area below.

"But I was undismayed. This was more like it, I thought again as I settled back in my seat.

"The pilot looked lazily comfortable as he sat slouched with his eyes glued on a tow rope that could be seen out of the window—our life line.

"My flak jacket had been taken off and my 'Mae West' was on the floor. I had put my flak jacket under me because I felt more shooting would be coming from below than ack-ack explosions from above."

Riding in the command B-17 of LTG Lewis H. Brereton as the 1st Allied Airborne Army commander flew along beside, over, and below the giant armada headed for Holland, war correspondent W. B. Courtney moved about the giant bomber looking for the best viewing spot to watch the progress of the seemingly endless skytrain. He wrote: "We are beside one of the towing groups as it turns the corner. The nylon ropes catch the fitful sun and glisten across the width of the column like a spider web on a June hedge. Suddenly the towline of the glider nearest us snaps. The broken ends of the line rear up, and there is a frozen moment like an arrested motion picture while they face each other in midair like snakes in a fight. Then they coil and writhe away. The glider slides downward, and you think at first that the pilot has it under control and will manage a landing. Abruptly, the glide becomes a dive.

" 'Goddamn!' our waist gunner yells. 'The cargo's shifted.'

"The glider flips over on its back, lurches right side up once more and finally plunges like a shot arrow to the ground. It hits nose first in a field beside a road, losing all definition in a sickening eruption of dirt and fragments. Its C-47 tow plane peels out of formation and returns to circle the spot, like an eagle

22. Unfortunately, the air-sea rescue people did not get there in time and Cpl. Chad B. Lewis, PFC Russell M. Pike, and T/5 Alonzo Whitfield drowned.

mourning a broken fledgling. The dust cloud slowly blows away, and you can see there will be no one to save from that crash and nothing for anyone to do but carry on."[23]

"Now we were above the Guards Armored Division," related 1Lt. Henry Barnes. "Stretched out for miles are large and medium tanks with their supporting paraphernalia strung out behind. Look ahead, I can see the orange panels atop them. Hey, that is to be our signal of the forward line of the British. All beyond that orange line is enemy. Orange was the color of the day. It is Holland's national color. It was the color of the luminous panels atop the British tanks. It was the color of the smoke from the flares set off by our brave pathfinders who had parachuted earlier to mark out the drop and landing zones."

As an occupant of one of the Signal Company gliders that would later be listed as missing, T/4 Melvin Arthur "Artie" Kitterman wrote: "We were told we would see a railroad track with orange panels placed between the rails and that, in effect, would be the front line or as far north as the British had advanced. We were in a flight of several planes pulling gliders.

"It was a smooth ride until we crossed the railroad tracks. I don't believe the tracks were out of sight when we were being shot at from three small towns located in a triangle. Tracer bullets from the guns were aimed at the tow plane but the gunner would get behind and two shells went through the right wing and two more through the tail of our glider. We were lucky none hit our control wires. The shells were 20mm that made a ⅝ inch hole when they went in the wing and 6 to 8 inch holes when they came out. In a short time they had our tow plane on fire but they never cut us loose from the plane. We cut loose at our end after the plane really began to burn and when we did the plane went over on its left wing and nosed straight into the ground. No one jumped from the plane. By now we had passed the guns on the ground and our pilot decided to land in what turned out to be a potato patch behind a house. We came to a stop with the nose of the glider buried in a haystack."[24]

Barnes added to his account: "To the left of us I saw a C-47 go down in flames, still pulling the intact nylon tow rope

23. Courtney, W. B., "Army in the Sky." Colliers.
24. The experiences of T/4 Melvin Arthur Kitterman, T/4 Mike H. Lewis, and PFC John "Jack" Kessel in the days to come will be related in a later chapter.

onto which was attached a glider. A feeling of revulsion welled up in me as I riveted my gaze on the glider to see if any troops would get out. Then it passed from sight below us."

There was plenty of excitement in the glider carrying Col. Tom Sherburne and Cpl. Jim Evans. There was a loud noise in the glider. Evans thought at first a 20mm shell had hit the glider. It turned out to be a large part of an anti-aircraft shell. It came up through the plywood floor between the co-pilot's feet, cutting his left calf completely in two, except for the shinbone. Having observed this, Evans noted the pilot fell over at the same time. Evans didn't know what was wrong with him but he knew the co-pilot couldn't fly the glider so he jumped between them from his perch on top of the ammunition cart and shifted the steering wheel over to the pilot. Evans then shook the pilot with one hand while steering the glider. The pilot recovered his senses and grabbed the wheel. The plane was still pulling the glider. As soon as the pilot looked able, Evans put a tourniquet on the co-pilot, then a large British shell bandage, pulling the muscles and tendons in place.

After that Evans checked the pilot and found the same piece of shrapnel that passed through the co-pilot's calf was now lodged in the right thigh of the pilot. He didn't need a tourniquet and no major blood vessel had been severed.

The pilot asked Evans to use the intercom and tell the tow-plane that they had been hit. The pilot then added, "Tell them not to turn us loose." They towed the glider to the right LZ. Both pilot and co-pilot coordinated in a good landing. The angle-irons knocked down the four barbed-wire fences when the glider landed.

Col. Tom Sherburne remembered the incident. "One of our artillery corporals took over for a while when the pilot and co-pilot were hit. The glider took down several fences before it came to a stop."[25]

In a similar incident, F/O Lawrence W. Kubale was painfully wounded when enemy flak tore through the nose of the glider. Momentarily stunned by the explosion, he recovered sufficiently to retrieve the controls from an airborne soldier who had meanwhile kept the glider in level flight. Although his vision was impaired by blood streaming from his right temple, and in

25. Cpl. James Evans was awarded the Silver Star for his actions.

spite of shrapnel fragments in his arms, Flight Officer Kubale piloted his craft to the designated landing zone where he was released from the towplane, skillfully bringing the glider to rest without injury to passengers or damage to the equipment.[26]

Sgt. Elmer Weber of the Recon Platoon remembered, "One of our squad leaders (Ted Klann), who was riding in the co-pilot seat, was wounded when a bullet came up through the seat and entered his body."[27]

The heavy concentration of anti-aircraft and small-arms fire had been passed. Now it was time to find a landing spot. Barnes wrote: "The pilot mumbled something and pointed ahead. There were the parachute covered fields that outlined our landing zone. Then we passed over the Wilhelmina Canal. We were right on target.

"The pilot reached up and tapped the release and then there was silence, at least comparative silence from the roar of planes and the explosions of anti-aircraft fire.

"The air armada swept by above us.

"We were still gliding on in the same direction. The wind could be heard humming softly as we glided over the landing zone and then banked to the left to circle back to our field.

"It was a long, steep, banking turn and we were on a severe angle, leaning to the left, holding on to any support. The ropes holding our jeep in position groaned and stretched and the jeep shifted slightly. I was hoping it wouldn't rip loose.

"As we leveled out I glanced hurriedly at the map, the last map, and saw a little triangular point of a forest mimicking the real triangular forest now looming menacingly ahead. We were right on target. I muttered, 'God Bless the Air Force!' The pilot smiled as he clenched tightly the wheel awaiting the shock of the landing.

"Looking for a way to get out of this damn coffin, I swung around and looked behind me. The picture of the burning towplane still pulling its glider had affected me finally. My men were all sitting in a forward leaning position, straining at their

---

26. Material from the *History of the 435th Troop Carrier Group.*
27. Thought to be dead, Klann was placed with the rest of the soldiers killed in action. Later that night, as a Catholic chaplain was going around giving last rites, he noticed the eyelids move and Klann was taken to the hospital. He is still alive today.

safety belts, as though preparing for the shock of the landing. There was no sound from any of them.

"I turned forward to see our glider knock down the first of four barbed wire fences. Our speed seemed to increase as we watched the grass field streak by below us. The singing voice of the glider grew louder and the fences were now ahead of us instead of below us, and the forest began to loom over us.

"The pilot dragged first the right wing and then the left as we swung around viciously away from the oncoming forest. The dirt piled up to my seat and I raised my legs to brace myself for the end. I managed to bless my foresight for putting the flak jacket under my seat."

First Lieutenant Henry Barnes continued his story: "One wing buckled and with one final lunge the glider skidded to a halt and the pilot and I swung up while the jeep broke loose of the restraints and bindings and rolled out onto terra firma. The men scrambled out after loosening their seat belts. One climbed up and released us and, in a moment, we were all out of the glider."

PFC Robert "Buck" Barger had parachuted into Normandy as aidman for MG Maxwell D. Taylor. Barger had slipped his chute too much to get out of the line of fire and had suffered numerous fractures and dislocations on landing. He had lain in the field for two and a half days before being discovered. The ampules of morphine he carried were used to relieve the pain when it became too intense. In spite of his harrowing experience and incomplete healing, Barger begged to be allowed to take part in the Holland mission. He may well have been in Barnes' glider. He wrote: "Our glider came in minus part of its tail. We hit like a ton of bricks and skidded across our LZ and down into a ditch. The jeep I was in tore loose and went forward, throwing the pilot's compartment up in the air."

"I heard some shots ring out," added First Lieutenant Barnes. "I ran forward, dropping near a bundle on the ground. I hid behind it trying to figure where the shots were coming from.

"I couldn't believe it. We had arrived safely. It felt like a great weight had been lifted off my shoulders. Just then a loud voice cut through my thoughts.

"A major walking by on the way to his assembly area shouted, 'Damn it, Barnes, you haven't been here five minutes and already you got yourself a girl!' Puzzled, I followed his wave and looked at the bundle I was lying near. Sure enough, it was the remains of a Dutch girl, almost unrecognizable, almost blown apart.

"Near us could be discerned the remains of a small German car with a tiny Red Cross on the windshield. Also, there were the bodies of two German soldiers and another Dutch girl. It seems they were parked here in the same woods, about 1300 P.M. sitting in the car, when their 'necking' was ended with the anti-personnel bombs and machine gun bullets that the Air Corps used to clean out our landing zone—and I had chosen a corpse to hide behind."[28]

The collision of two gliders over the Son landing zone on D-Day was witnessed by many paratroopers as they moved off the field to their assembly areas. Some had stopped to offer assistance. All felt there could be few, if any, survivors from the resulting crashes on the ground. Two survivors from the glider that was damaged most heavily relate their experiences.

F/O Thornton C. Schofield was at the controls of the glider shown in the insert. His recollections of the incident are as follows: "The crash was caused by a freak mid-air collision occurring at an altitude of approximately 50 feet. The other glider involved came at me from above and to the rear so that I, unaware of my danger, had no opportunity to get out of the way. The other pilot was apparently not aware of my position and thus failed to take preventive measures. Suddenly, his glider slammed into my tail surfaces from the port side, completely demolishing all the rudder controls. All I saw of the other glider, after the collision, was the left wing sweeping over the top of my disabled craft.

"My glider shuddered violently, after being hit, hovered momentarily, then nosed over and plunged toward the earth at an angle of about 70 degrees. First there was the terrific shock—enveloping my entire body—when the jeep we were carrying slammed down on my back.

"During moments of consciousness—thankfully, few—I was aware that I had nearly been catapulted out of the glider. My head and left arm had punched a hole in the Plexiglas windshield.

"My three passengers and I were extremely fortunate to have

28. Read the story of Lisa van Overveld on page 29.

survived the crash, considering the force of the impact, and I am not hesitant in calling it a miracle."

PFC Anthony Wysocki had parachuted into Normandy but rode a glider into Holland. A parachute lieutenant[29] rode the co-pilot seat while Wysocki had been joined by a "hitchhiker," Davis Hart, from 501st Regimental Headquarters. Wysocki wrote: "As we were approaching the landing zone, we cut loose from our plane and came in for a landing. Another glider took our tail off. The only thing I could do in the driver's seat of the jeep was jam my foot on the brakes. Fortunately, we had a good pilot. He was able to bring the glider in in such a way that we didn't come straight down. The chain binders holding the jeep and the seat belt I was wearing saved the lives of the lieutenant, Hart, and myself cuz all we could see was our helmets coming forward as we crashed. A colonel came up to me, after I got out of that glider and said, 'Soldier, I want that jeep!' I said, 'Sir, you can have that jeep!' It was no good to anybody. The whole front end was pushed in because of the impact."

In describing the success or failure of the glider operations for their units on D-Day, T/4 George Koskimaki and Sgt. Elmer Weber had the statistics for their units.

T/4 George E. Koskimaki had this notation in his diary for September 17: "Our Signal Company lost five of fifteen gliders. One had crashed near the front lines. The six signalmen and the pilot perished."

Sgt. Elmer Weber, of the Recon Platoon, related: "We had loaded 14 gliders, four men to a jeep in each glider. Only seven of the fourteen reached the designated landing zone. One crash-landed near London, one went down in the Channel and five were forced to land in enemy territory when their tow planes were shot down. The men in four of the gliders were later returned to us. The occupants of the fifth were captured."

As part of the summary of the Market-Garden operation, BG Gerald J. Higgins, assistant division commander of the 101st Airborne Division, wrote the following for Major General Taylor: "Of the 70 gliders and tow planes which took off in two serials of 35 each, three of the gliders aborted over England, one

---

29. Former lieutenant Bill Sefton remembers seeing 1Lt. Laurence Critchell in the 501st command post in Veghel with a heavily bandaged head. When questioned, Critchell mentioned being involved in a midair glider collision.

ditched in the Channel, two broke loose and were released over friendly Belgium. The Germans found the glider formations a splendid target, brought down 6 of the 64 planes which crossed their lines and damaged 46 others, 6 so badly they were fit for nothing more than salvage. The troop carriers had 19 men missing and 3 wounded. Aircraft losses of 9 percent and a damage rate of 70 percent contrasted painfully with the corresponding ratios of 4 and 23 percent in the paratroop serials. Glider missions had flown in daylight with impunity on D-Day plus 1 in Normandy. Market (Garden) was a different story.

"Seven gliders came down between the IP and Landing Zone 'W' near Son. At least 3 and perhaps 5 of these premature releases were made because the tug ship was hit and about to crash. One of the gliders plummeted into the ground.[30]

"One was unaccounted for. The rest landed safely and all the men and material aboard then reached the division in a day or two with the help of friendly Belgians and Hollanders.

"The first serial released its gliders at 1348, less than half an hour after the parachute landings. The second did so at 1355. Three Wacos, two of which collided in flight, crash-landed on the LZ, killing a pilot, injuring five men and damaging the cargoes. The remaining 53 gliders found ample room on the zone and landed safely with 252 troops, 32 jeeps and 13 trailers. In one instance, a soldier took the controls after the pilot was wounded and steered the glider until the pilot regained consciousness and was able to steer the glider down. The glider operation had been costly, but it had successfully delivered to the landing zone about 80 percent of the personnel and about 75 percent of the heavy equipment and vehicles carried."[31]

Second-Day Glider Lifts

As a result of the losses to equipment and personnel suffered by the troop carrier wings on D-Day, it was decided to switch the approach on Monday, September 18.

"The flight paths of the planes carrying parachutists and planes towing gliders on Sunday, September 17, 1944, had pro-

30. The glider carried six 101st Signal Company men, a British liaison soldier and the glider pilot to their deaths.
31. Brigadier General Higgins wrote a summary of the first ten days in Holland for the commanding general. This was part of that summary.

vided an approach from behind Allied lines and over the heaviest fighting—probably the cause of severe damage to planes in that operation. The route for the September 18 glider serials was switched to the north, coming in over the Scheldt River Estuary behind German lines."[32]

There were no paratroop operations for the 101st Airborne Division on D plus 1. The glider serials had been limited to seventy gliders the day previous. Monday would see the largest lift of gliders into a combat mission for the Screaming Eagles.

Departing from numerous airfields in England were some 428 gliders carrying 2nd and 3rd Battalions of the 327th Glider Infantry Regiment, 327th Glider Infantry Regimental Headquarters Company, the 326th Engineer Battalion, the remainder of the 101st Signal and 326th Medical Companies. Elements of the 377th Parachute Field Artillery Battalion and additional supply and administrative vehicles and the flight leader, BG Anthony C. McAuliffe, would eventually arrive in the landing zone "W" area.

"There weren't enough planes available for the parachute regiments and glider tows the first day so more gliders were used on Monday," wrote Sgt. Ben L. "Doc" Ottinger. "I was in on the first group on the 18th. Our group was made up of 178 gliders."

T/5 Jack E. Millman, radioman for his company commander, remembered the preparations and departure from England: "Bright and early on the 18th of September, we began to check our equipment and walked a half mile to the gliders which had been loaded previously with extra food, water and ammunition. The planes, tow ropes, and gliders were getting their final check before the takeoff. There was a tense feeling about the whole place, but everyone was boisterous and happy-go-lucky in appearance.

"We signed on as 'Hell's Angels.' Our signatures accompanied the many decorations. I remember a small drawing of Coney Island that radioman Pescia put on the nose. Word came to load up. We were the fifth glider to leave that field."[33]

32. From copy of a letter from troop carrier historian Roger Airgood to Fr. Gerald Thuring in Groesbeck, Holland, November 17, 1982.
33. Jack Millman wrote a long letter to his parents on September 17, 1945, relating his experience in the Holland campaign. His comments are from a copy of that letter.

Though the glider troops hadn't been told about the severe beating the flights took from the flak the day before, at least a few had been told of a change in flight path. PFC Charles Kocourek said, "I heard our pilot say 'We're gonna try a different route because we're taking a beating out there.' "

Sgt. Ben Ottinger said, "General McAuliffe, though a qualified parachutist, chose to ride in a glider to show his support for the glider troops."

At age thirty-three, T/5 Charles H. Laden was one of the older enlisted men in his company. He had been assigned as radio operator for BG A. C. McAuliffe for the Holland mission. He remembered, "In addition to the general, the load included a war correspondent and some MPs. Our glider was number 1 on D plus 1."

Sgt. Gerald A. Zimmerman was part of a radio team accompanying a powerful SCR-499 transmitter-receiver that had been installed in a quarter-ton trailer. It was vital to long-distance communication. He recalled, "The radio trailer didn't leave much room to move around in the glider."

An echelon of forty parachuting medics had participated in the D-Day jump in Normandy as part of the 326th Medical Company. It had been the hope of Capt. Willis P. McKee to perform in the same fashion in Holland. He wrote: "I had hoped to be used in a similar manner in Holland, but, at the last minute a field hospital was assigned to us and it fell my lot to take them in by glider. None of them had ever seen a glider and you can imagine the conferences I had in the days preceding the take-off. I commanded sixty glider loads and we went in on D plus 1."

"I was part of a glider load that consisted of six or seven G.I.'s, our company chain saw, which was in a box about the size of a coffin," wrote T/5 Paul J. Quaiver. "It was big enough to hold fifty or more land mines."

Cpl. "Brownie" Rusin was anxious to get the flight over. He wrote: "At least as a paratrooper you could jump out when your plane was hit. In a glider, you were a sitting duck."

"The captain (Hugh Evans) was acting as co-pilot," said Jack Millman. "I was in the seat right behind him. I was his SCR-536 'walkie-talkie' radio operator. The hookup from plane to glider was made and we were off down the runway. It took about thirty minutes for the group to form."

"We circled once or twice to move into formation," wrote Corporal Rusin. "That's when I saw a glider banking on the right front with its left wing close to the tree tops and in a split second it hit the tops of the trees and toppled into them. It looked like the trees swallowed the whole glider. That glider carried men from our weapons platoon."

PFC Charles Kocourek remembers they took off while the air corps personnel were lined up for chow at the mess tent. "One of the 'F' Company gliders went down and crashed. The airmen all broke ranks and headed for the wounded glider in the woods. Three of our men were killed and five injured in that one."[34]

Glider pilot F/O Edward L. Hillyard of the 80th Troop Carrier Squadron wrote: "We took off at Membury and flew a staggered formation from left to right in rows of four. My glider was number 2 in the second row and the jeep that was to pull the trailer I had was in another glider in the number 1 position in the second row."

Hillyard continued his narrative: "The trip after takeoff was routine until we were about half way to the coast. At that time the lead glider flown by F/O Ford cut loose from the formation. That was upsetting, for he was our glider officer. As we neared the coast we hit cloud cover at our flight altitude and that was terrifying for we couldn't see our tow plane. I just had to fly by the 'angle of the dangle' of the rope. Thank goodness we were not in it very long. My manifest for this trip was a trailer loaded with medical supplies and four airborne personnel. We had no co-pilot. One of the airborne troops sat in that seat. I told him if anything happened to me to just fly straight ahead at 80 miles per hour."

Cpl. Michael J. Friel, medic for the 327th Glider Infantry Regiment, was in the co-pilot's seat of Hillyard's glider. He wrote: "The pilot gave me instructions on how to land the glider in case he, the pilot, was disabled. This lesson occurred while in flight to Holland."

Flight Officer Hillyard continued: "Our next exciting moment was over the North Sea. There in the water was an English

---

34. According to historian Roger Airgood, F/O Robert Gilman lost his life on September 18. His towrope broke on takeoff. He didn't have sufficient altitude and speed to maneuver so he crashed into the trees at the edge of the field.

Horsa glider and no rescue ships were near it. We saw only one soldier out towards the end of the wing. How many were lost? We looked in the distance and saw a rescue ship coming toward it.

"I had communications with the tow pilot by a coil of wire interwoven in the tow rope. However, I didn't use it much. We were too busy trying to keep a good tow position. I do remember letting the airborne soldier fly so he would be a little familiar in case we had to cut loose. As I remember, he didn't do too badly. I believe he could have saved himself and his friends."

Cpl. Arie Van Dort was headed back to the land of his birth when the mission of the 101st became part of the Market-Garden operation. He had left Holland with his parents when he was a small boy. He remembered, "We lost our companion load with trailer when it went down in the English Channel."

From a report sent by Dutch historical researcher Piet Pulles in which he reported that the people of Oisterwijk, which was on the approach run for the troop carrier planes and glider tows, had noted the appearance of fifteen German soldiers who dug deep holes in a meadow near a farm in Oisterwijk in the southern part of the Netherlands: "Just after the anti-aircraft guns were mounted, but before they could be camouflaged, some English fighter planes discovered the enemy and the guns and started shooting at them. Some moments later, four American Thunderbolts (P-47s) turned up and bombed the guns with good results. The guns were rendered useless and several soldiers were brought to a first aid station in town.

"The next day new flak was installed and they started shooting immediately at the many low flying Skytrains towing supply gliders for the 101st Airborne Division."

Pilot Hillyard continued: "Finally the tow pilot called back and told me that in about five minutes we would be over Holland and he was right. The next report I didn't like. He stated that in five minutes we would be in the flak zone. Before we hit it I could hear something that sounded like popcorn being popped way off in another room. I found out later from one of the old troopers that it was small arms fire coming up from the ground. Just as well I didn't know. I knew what the next noise was—FLAK! The flak helmet I was wearing shrank to tea-cup size. The flak came in bursts of about five and some had black smoke and others a gray color. Seems like we were in the flak area for about twenty minutes."

Sgt. Alvin H. Kargas remembered: "During the flight the glider pilot didn't wear his helmet until the ack-ack suddenly burst around us. Then he very casually reached for it and put it on his head."

Piet Pulles continued his report: "One of the gliders was knocked down. Captain Ardell C. Tiedeman, who flew close to the unlucky craft reported afterwards that the left wing broke off and the glider went straight down from 500 feet. The pilot, F/O Noel C. McCann, 1Lt. Ray J. Hiltunen, T/5 Robert J. LeMay and Pvt. Raymond L. Carson plunged to their deaths in the crash."

Cpl. Courtney H. Boom remembered, "that Lt. Hiltunen's glider was immediately to our right when he was shot down."

Sgt. Ben Ottinger reported: "There was some air sickness but the flak was zipping through the tails, wings and floors of the gliders. This cured most of it and we were anxious to get on the ground."

Cpl. Brownie Rusin was in a glider in which one of the men was killed by anti-aircraft fire. He related: "As we passed over enemy held territory all of a sudden German anti-aircraft batteries were in full blast. Flak was all over.

"This is when PFC Warren Mills was hit in the back of the head. He was sitting third to my left. I could see blood trickling on the side of the ear and face. Mills didn't know what hit him. The men were tense and hoping we would land before anything else happened."

"Our glider was struck by small arms fire, narrowly missing my head," wrote Sgt. Robert M. Bowen. "Captain Preston Towns' glider was aborted. He later reached the LZ through the efforts of the Dutch Underground."

Flying with Captain Towns was S/Sgt. Grayson A. Davis, who wrote: "Our tow plane was shot down. It had been hit hard by flak from 88s. Capt. Towns had to knock out the Plexiglas windshield to cut the tow rope from the glider. We landed safely."

Sgts. Willie R. Hiney and J. Herschel Morgan had aborted flights far behind the enemy lines.

Sergeant Hiney had his glider shot down at Boxtel. He wrote: "We were flying to the right and lower than the rest of the planes and gliders. It sounded like someone typing on loose paper from the sound of the small arms bullets in the wings and fuselage. Then the tow plane was hit in the rudder and cut us loose."

Sgt. J. Herschel Morgan, a thirty-year-old at the time of the Holland invasion, remembered, "The glider was hit and we floundered down near Echloo, Belgium."

Flight Officer Hillyard described his landing: "Now the tow pilot informed us that we were approaching the landing zone but we already had it in view. Our map was very accurate. The tow pilot wished us a safe landing and we thanked him for the tow and as soon as the glider on my left cut loose we followed suit.

"In our briefing the night before, we were told that the wind would be coming from the south and west. It was just the opposite and made pin-point landings more difficult. The load I had on, which was 3,600 pounds, caused me to have to fly a little faster, which put me at 80 miles per hour and, with the wind helping me along, gave me a ground speed of 90 mph. I tried to get into two fields before it was do or die for the one I landed in. At the other end of the field was a road with a six foot ditch. Had to make it. I saw another glider ahead of me trying for the same field. The field had a fence at the end of entry so I thought I would try an aircraft carrier landing—I would fly low by nosing down just over it then dip the tail wheel down and catch the wire fence. It worked—didn't roll but 50 feet.

"Now the amusing part—we had been trained to knock out the side door (escape panel) of the glider and jump, then hit the dirt. I did but soon heard people talking and even some whistling. I looked up and no one seemed to be excited and I said to myself, 'Get up, you fool!' "

Medical officer Capt. Willis McKee said, "My glider pilot, a major, command pilot, and I picked out from aerial photographs, the corner of a field beside a gate as the spot that we were going to stop the glider. When we landed, the nose was twenty feet from the gate."

S/Sgt. Grayson Davis' glider settled to the ground after standing on its nose momentarily. He relates: "I released my safety belt and hit the door with my M-1 rifle butt. I was running in mid-air; hit the ground with one foot and the butt of my M-1 and kept running for cover in a canal ditch. Everyone in the glider followed me."

Sgt. Willie R. Hiney's glider had aborted at Boxtel when the towplane was shot down. He said, "We buried right up to the hitch in the sand. All personnel ended in a heap at the front of the glider.

"We had a communications trailer with equipment and personnel on this glider. We fired the glider. It was only a few minutes until the Dutch underground contacted us. The initial partisan contact was dressed as a priest and he walked with a limp."

S/Sgt. Grayson Davis had sprinted for the cover of a canal ditch, followed by his men. The men wondered where they had come to earth, as their aborted release was far short of the landing zone. Grayson wrote: "With nothing outstanding to orient our map with, I took Katkie and Reeser, a BAR team, with me to the nearest house hoping to find someone who spoke English and could tell me where we were. After knocking on the door, a young girl of 8 or 9 came to the door. She said the priest could orient my map and pointed up the road. The priest was riding a bicycle toward us. His coat was flying like Batman's cape as he came down the road. He did, indeed, orient us with the map— got two Dutch underground to guide us. The rest was easy. We walked to the LZ. It was dusk when we got to the company area. We had already been listed as MIA and everyone was glad to see us."

The glider carrying the heavy radio trailer was among the first to touch down. Sgt. Gerald Zimmerman said, "Our landing was perfect—better than on any problem or exercise we'd ever had. The jeep that was to pull our trailer parked just a few yards directly behind us on the landing zone. After driving all over the fields for a half hour trying to find the road to the Division CP, we met M/Sgt. Conrad Russell who directed us there."

After Cpl. Logan Koenig and his crew got the tail down and opened the nose section, it was easy. "We unloaded the four motorcycles. The glider load consisted of seven Signal Company men and the four bikes. Simple arithmetic said two men to a bike for transportation. The glider pilot elected to ride with me. I took off a-spinning and gave him a good ride to the end of the LZ, where he elected to wait for a jeep."

Medic T/4 Dale G. Weaver remembered, "Happy Dutch people were running across the field waving their arms. The glider with our trailer and medical supplies wrecked on landing. We lost four men in that one."

T/5 George A. Whitfield was with LTC David Gold, the division surgeon. After the glider had sailed over and through barbed-wire fences, it buried its nose in the soft dirt. Whitfield remembered some of the Dutch people didn't quite understand the English phrases they used in greeting the airborne. He remembered, "Some Dutch people ran out to shake our hands and said 'Good-bye!' "

Sgt. Alvin Kargas remembered, "After landing, a group of the glider pilots gathered and talked about forming a posse to attack the enemy. As far as I know, such action wasn't carried out."

Now that his job was over, glider pilot Hillyard pondered what he would do. "We were instructed before leaving on this mission that we get back to England by way of Brussels, Belgium, in order to be ready for other missions, if necessary. I headed for the control point as instructed and ran into a buddy walking down to the east toward Son. It was John Tyndall. I asked how he was and his reply, as always, was 'Just good to be alive!'

"As we proceeded down the road to the east toward Son, we could hear the flak that we had just come through. We now knew it was coming from Best and Tilburg.

"From about 600 feet off the deck came hordes of B-24s dropping parapacks of supplies and ammunition. Tyndall and I were still traveling east on this country road. Out of some of the parapacks came part of the supplies after having come loose from their bindings. They were falling all around us. I looked at him and said, 'Hey, a guy could get killed right here on the ground!' "

Sgt. Robert Bowen remembered, "Our mission was to secure the LZ for the resupply missions which were to follow. Germans fired at us from the opposite side of the LZ making the retrieval of supplies from gliders difficult. My squad went out in the LZ to bring back wounded from gliders."

Flight Officer Hillyard[35] closed his narrative for the day with this comment: "We finally approached the control point and began digging in for the night in a forest just north of Son. Believe it or not, with the exception of the incoming gliders and muffled flak sounds back to the west, and tow planes passing overhead, it was a very pleasant late afternoon. It reminded me of an air show."

---

35. Material is from copy of letter F/O Edward Hillyard sent to Ken Head, an Englishman, who has a museum at Membury Airport.

The radio trailer with jeep tow headed for the division command post at Son. Sergeant Zimmerman[36] wrote: "We were in an orchard behind a Son schoolhouse. We put the radio in operation as soon as we got there and I reported into the British XXX Corps net. The messages were going both ways, with speed, all night."

In describing how the 178 gliders that left England with his group had fared, Sgt. Ben Ottinger wrote: "Of the first 178 gliders leaving England, 14 failed to reach Holland."

Summarizing the 327th Glider Infantry Regiment experience for D plus 1 on September 18: "3rd Battalion and Regimental Headquarters Company took off from Aldermaston Airbase at 1130 and landed on the LZ near Son, Holland at 1515. 2nd Battalion took off from Newbury Airbase at 1145 and landed on the LZ near Son at 1530. A little .50 caliber and ack-ack was fired at planes and gliders while crossing the west coast of Holland. All units landed without opposition. Units assembled in woods south of the LZ outposted the area and had a quiet night."[37]

The second-day glider serials fared much better than those that arrived on D-Day. By avoiding the front lines and coming in from behind the German positions, the Allied planes and gliders avoided the intense anti-aircraft fire thrown up at them the previous day. It was only when they neared the Best-Oisterwijk-Boxtel area that intensive anti-aircraft fire was experienced, and that for only a short time.

D Plus 2 Glider Landings

Mobility had been the key factor in the planning of the 101st Airborne Division's part in the Market-Garden operation. MG Maxwell D. Taylor and his staff felt that rapid movement from hot spot to hot spot to stamp out threats to the corridor protected by the Screaming Eagles was the key ingredient to the success of their operation. Thus it was that in the planning of the operation, the artillery units received a lower priority in the flights to Holland.

With the delay in forward progress by the British XXX

---

36. Material is from the diary of Sgt. Gerald Zimmerman, which he kept throughout the Holland campaign in a small notebook.
37. *S-3 Periodical Report for 327th Glider Infantry Regiment.*

Corps, and the destruction of the key Wilhelmina Canal bridge at Son, which further delayed the advance of Allied armor, there had to be a shift in glider priorities.

The 82nd Airborne Division had been scheduled to receive most of the gliders to be flown on the nineteenth of September (D plus 2). Last-minute exchanges were made with the 101st being assigned 385 gliders to bring in the artillery and anti-tank units. Up to that time, the only *heavy* weapons on hand to fight armor and the German 88s were the 60mm and 81mm mortars, bazookas, machine guns, and the Gammon grenades.

Troop Carrier Command had two good days of flying weather on the seventeenth and eighteenth. The situation worsened on D plus 2 with heavy fog over the channel and the coastal areas. With the critical need for the support weapons of the artillery and anti-tank battalions for the outgunned infantrymen of the 101st, every effort was made to get the reinforcements to Holland.

In his book, 81st Troop Carrier Squadron crew member S/Sgt. Martin Wolfe[38] wrote:

> Our group briefing was short and scary. We learned about the fog and clouds over the Channel and about the build-up of German Flak capabilities. We would fly the "southern route" as on Sunday; but this time, instead of going over Belgium via the shortest route to the Eindhoven area, we would fly to the British held salient at the Albert Canal and then, turning straight north, fly right up "Hell's Highway" toward LZ "W." This would keep us as far away as possible from areas controlled by the Germans.
>
> Now (Colonel) Adriel Williams addressed the glider pilots. Most of them, again, would be without co-pilots. In view of the worsening weather, Williams said, he would not compel any man to pilot a glider who doubted his ability to make it to Holland under these conditions. But only a few of the Group's glider pilots took advantage of this disquieting offer.

A brief description of the weapons that the artillerymen of the 101st used to support the infantry units is given by PFC Luther E. Barrick, a member of the 907th Glider Field Artillery Battalion. He wrote: "When I came to the 907th, we had the 75mm 3-inch projectile that weighed 17 pounds with a five-mile range. The gun weighed approximately 1,700 pounds. A few months before D-Day, we were given the short range 105mm

38. Wolfe, Martin. *Green Light.* University of Pennsylvania Press, Philadelphia, 1989.

howitzer with a 4½ mile range. The 4½ inch projectile had a weight of 35 pounds. The 105mm packed much more power when it hit. Although heavier and harder to work, especially in mud up to the axle, we felt much more at home with it."

Cpl. Ray Hollenbeck had been trained as a paratrooper but was sent to a glider artillery battalion for the Holland mission. He felt some resentment from the men in the battery because of the extra fifty dollars' pay the parachutists received; a similar amount for hazardous duty hadn't been approved yet for glidermen. Recalling his introduction to this new method of air transportation, Hollenbeck wrote: "The first time I saw a glider was in the marshaling area. Being a paratrooper, I thought I was going to jump in Holland, but that was not to be. I was assigned to a glider like the rest of the men. We loaded a trailer which was laden with 105mm shells. The other men did all the lashing of the trailer to the glider to the rings that were in the floor. I didn't know a damned thing about lashing, whatsoever. After the men were through with their jobs, the pilot did his own inspection."

PFC Steve Koper had been to London on pass. When he came back to "B" Battery of the 377th Parachute Field Artillery Battalion, he found the battery gone. "They were at the marshaling area and had been assigned to their planes. There were a few of us left around camp with the cooks. They took us to the marshaling area and assigned us to gliders. The buddy of Pvt. Mike Michalek had been assigned to my glider and Michalek wanted me to switch with him. I told him we shouldn't because we were all assigned and the manifests were in triplicate form. If the glider went down, they wouldn't know who was who.

"Michalek was pacing the floor of the barrack—nervous—he had a feeling he was going to get it. In Normandy he had parachuted into a pasture and a cow stepped on his shoulder, dislocated it, and that is why he wasn't scheduled to jump on this mission. He really didn't have to go but one of the sergeants called him chicken so I guess his pride was hurt and so he went along."

Lashing a load down properly in a glider was extremely important. Knots in the ropes anchoring trailers, guns, and other equipment had to be firm and slip-proof. Shifting equipment could break through the floor, pop out through the thin canvas walls or slide forward or back, upsetting the delicate balance that was necessary for the pilot to maintain control of his craft. Robert Minick describes what happens when the knots aren't fastened properly:

> At Chilbolton, members of Sergeant Roy Brown's wire section were sitting around, admiring the sophisticated tie-down they had used on the load of 105mm ammunition. Soon the glider pilot arrived with a large box which he insisted must be tied down with the rest of the load. After having done such a dexterous job on the first tie-down, the men tried to talk the pilot out of the notion. Finally T/5 Stelzner, T/5 Bob Ernst and Pvt. Allen Anderson loosened the knots and threw the box on top of the ammo. Unfortunately, time was running out; they didn't bother to lash the load down quite as securely as they had done the first time.[39]

The gliders in which the artillerymen flew were usually overloaded. "There were three of us and a 105mm gun in my glider and some 105mm shells," recalled PFC Luther Barrick. "Our 105 made a full load, so the men and ammo put us a thousand pounds or so overweight. We always flew 800 pounds or more overweight."

F/O William Knickerbocker[40] wrote: "I checked out the glider on line and then to briefing. Ate lunch early and got equipment and back to the glider."

First Lieutenant Darlyle M. Watters of the 81st Troop Carrier Squadron was the leader of his serial of eighty tug ships and eighty gliders from Membury Air Base. Describing his load manifest, Watters wrote: "My fourteen consisted of glider infantry—one 1st lieutenant platoon leader, one staff sergeant and his squad."

PFC George Groh[41] wrote: "Just before noon on the 19th, our tow plane pilot called 'Good luck!' through the interphone and the *Roy White's Revenge* was on its way, part of a wave of reinforcements for the landings already made on Sunday, two days earlier. 2Lt. (Julian) Hoshal, our glider pilot, had named his ship for a friend of his who had been killed in Italy. We rendezvoused briefly over England and then struck out cross-channel for the

39. Minick, Robert. *Kilogram: The Story of the 907th Glider Field Artillery Battalion.* Private Printing, Hobart, IN, 1979, 132–33.
40. Combat diary kept by F/O William Knickerbocker for Holland mission.
41. From story PFC George Groh of "A" Company, 327th Glider Infantry Regiment, wrote for *Yank* magazine in World War II.

Continent. The fog closed in early and, at times, we could barely discern the outline of the tow ship just ahead."

Having been directed by the pilot to add an additional container to their well-lashed load of ammunition in the glider, Sgt. Roy Brown and his crew hadn't done as well on the second tie-down. Bob Minick[42] wrote:

> A short time after becoming airborne, the ammunition began shifting and finally broke a portion of the floor out of the glider. When the pilot saw the hole, with the shells dropping through it, he cut loose, circled around and headed back to England. He sat the glider down on the edge of the beach and the men waded ashore.

Recalling his mission, 1Lt. Darlyle Watters said, "Flight conditions were 'instrument' all the way over the English Channel. We were not supposed to fly in those conditions. Historically, our serial was given a radio recall. My C.O. didn't hear it or chose to ignore it. The back 40 gliders did hear, and did go back. My C.O. knew I had especially trained my squadron's glider pilots (I was the squadron glider officer) to fly in substandard weather thus may have ignored the recall knowing the need for the troops."

F/O William Knickerbocker[43] wrote: "The weather was really foul and we lost several gliders in the Channel and it didn't improve when we got over land so we kept losing gliders all the way. Two groups were ordered back to England but they couldn't contact us by radio. Most of the time we could only see four to five feet of the tow rope which was 100 yards long."

PFC Charles W. Hogan remembered that his pilot was F/O William Aussick. Cpl. Paul Smolinski was the co-pilot. Everything was fine until they neared the channel. Hogan wrote: "We began to run into fog—in and out. Our last encounter was too much. We couldn't even see where our tow rope tied to our glider. I don't really know what happened but I think we were below our tug ship and somehow our tow line seemed to catch—I always thought it became entangled in the glider wing. Anyway, Aussick seemed to be pretty excited and didn't want to cut loose. Finally, when we were about to fall apart in the air, he cast us loose and we headed for the water, which we couldn't see. I had

42. Minick, 133.
43. Knickerbocker diary.

my knife in my boot—took it out and cut the top of the glider open. Also, (Hardin) Workman and myself—we were in the jeep—kicked out the escape door. Aussick, for some reason, had on his flak jacket and Smolinski was trying to get him out of it. We had safety belts in the jeep. I stayed strapped in and I remember Workman squatted in the jeep seat ready to jump out of the escape door. We hit the water with a bang. I loosened my safety belt and went out the hole in the top. Kicking out the escape door was a mistake. Also, our life jackets were inflated and that was wrong. The rushing water came in through the door and swept Workman back into the tail section. I cut another hole and pulled him out and also helped Smolinski and Aussick. The tug ship dropped a life raft about a hundred yards from us and I started to go after it. My inflated 'Mae West' kept tipping me on my back and the water was so rough I gave up. Back on the wing again, I thought of my camera which was in my gas mask container. I got it out and the light materials you see in the foreground is what I had it wrapped in. I snapped several pictures.[44]

"F/O Aussick didn't have a life jacket. I reached down in the glider and cut a gas can loose, poured out the gas and tied a rope to him and the can. I don't know how long we were out there, probably two hours. We were picked up by a British PT boat and taken to Ramsgate, England."

One of the original members of the 101st, dating back to the activation at Camp Claiborne, Louisiana, PFC George A. Kempf has this recollection: "I happened to be one of the glidermen in our squad who were forced to ditch in the Channel on our way to Holland. Our pilot told us something was wrong. Our glider and tow rope were ahead of our tow craft. Somehow, due to clouds and fog, the flight had slowed down to 100 miles per hour and our glider was moving along at 120 mph. The pilot tried everything he could to get us back of the plane because he thought the towline would catch in the propellers and then there was silence until we were told to start heaving our equipment out and prepare for ditching. The pilot estimated we were out about 40 miles. As we circled, God must have been with us because the pilot and our squad sergeant saw an air-sea rescue ship coming toward us. The pilot brought us down tail first and

44. Picture of men on the glider wing in the channel in the insert.

the glider plopped down to the nose and wings when the English ship handed out a boat hook to us. We started counting heads and one was missing. It was the pilot. He was found in his seat and brought to the wing. A medic on the rescue boat said he was dead and thought the pilot died of a broken neck. He saved our lives by proper ditching procedures and yet lost his life in doing so. God bless his soul!"

That pilot may well have been F/O Edward M. Griffin of the 80th Troop Carrier Squadron whose towrope broke over the channel; he was killed on landing.[45]

"Over the English Channel, the fog was so thick that we could not see our tug plane," wrote Capt. Clifford G. Kjell, commander of 1st Battalion Headquarters Company of the 327th Glider Regiment. "When our pilot observed a tug rope cross ours he released the glider to avert a mid-air collision. When we hit the water, the cabin filled immediately, but there was about a two-foot space at the top of the fuselage. We took trench knives, cut the canvas, and clambered onto the wings. We spent 17 hours on the wings of that glider, being picked up on the morning of the 20th by a British motor torpedo boat."

Because so much fog was encountered, many tows and gliders became lost. Some landed on the continent short of the landing zone; others returned to England.

"It was a strange feeling coming out of the fog bank and being the only plane and glider in sight when there had been 90-plus when we entered the fog," wrote PFC John MacNider. "When we came out of the fog, over the Channel, and the tow pilot spotted a city, he called back and told the glider pilot it was Belgium. There was an old Luftwaffe strip there so we cut loose and landed. After the tow plane and glider pilots talked it over, they decided the strip was too short (for retow of the glider) so we loaded on the C-47 and returned to England."

As a replacement to the 101st Airborne Division, PFC Willard W. Phillips had arrived on the scene in June 1944. Recalling the glider ride to Holland, he wrote: "We crossed the Channel by ourselves. There were no other planes or gliders with us. When we got to Holland, the weather got bad and most of the

45. From excerpt of *80th Troop Carrier Squadron History* sent to Fr. Gerard Thuring by Roger Airgood.

planes turned back to England. Our tow plane took us to Belgium and we landed at the airport in Brussels. We had a jeep in our glider so we had transportation up to Holland."

When Jack Schott's glider[46] joined the mighty convoy, he was impressed with the magnificent sight being created by all the gliders in tow. After hitting the fog bank over the Channel, their glider emerged on the other side as the only one on the entire horizon. They were flying alone and almost at water level. When Schott looked at the compass, he told the glider pilot they had changed direction and were now heading west, on their way back to England. After the pilot told him he was crazy, they landed at the same airdrome from which they had departed.

In a letter he wrote to his fiancée on the first anniversary of the airborne operation in Holland, S/Sgt. William John related, "We flew in the fog for more than two hours and then we were over the coast of Holland. We could find no other planes or gliders and could not find the landing zone. The pilot of the plane was lost so he took the plane up above the clouds and the glider followed. The pilot of the glider told us he could not hold on much longer and would have to cut loose soon. We did not know where we were—over the channel, Holland, Belgium or Germany. However, the good Lord was with us and we flew for another two hours. The pilot saw a break in the clouds and cut loose, not knowing in which country we were going to land. Here was the catch—we landed about 35 miles south of London. At the time we landed, we jumped out of the glider with our weapons, ready to fight."

One of those gliders that returned safely to its home base carried Pvt. Harold Fransen. Bob Minick[47] wrote:

A few minutes after Pvt. Fransen exited from his glider, he looked up to his right just in time to witness a most tragic scene. Two of the "A" Battery gliders suddenly turned toward one another and rammed head on. For a split second the two entangled gliders seemed to hang in mid-air, and then broke apart. A jeep, its driver still sitting rigid at the steering wheel and his buddy slumped beside him, tore out through the front of one of the gliders and plummeted to the ground. The two gliders then crashed, one of them bursting into a brilliant

46. Minick, 134.
47. Ibid.

white flame from the phosphorus shells on board. Six artillerymen and the pilots lost their lives in the mishap.[48]

Having witnessed the collision of the two gliders from his battery over the airfield in England, Cpl. Ray Hollenbeck said, "No one could believe it. Just a short time before we were shaking hands and wishing each other luck and saying we'd see you in Holland. It was unbelievable—never got to Holland and already we had casualties."

More tragedy was to follow. This seemed to affect air force personnel only. Bob Minick[49] wrote:

> Corporal Lee Brake recalled that shortly after the glider crash occurred, the C-47s started coming in. One of the planes apparently had a mechanical problem which caused it to stop right on the runway. Just when a piece of ground equipment was attempting to tow it off to the side, another plane landed and blew a tire. It then swerved into the disabled plane, spawning another holocaust. This incident also decapitated the driver on the tractor.

T/4 Frank J. Looney had two glider rides for the Holland mission and never got there. The first time the glider ditched in the North Sea about forty miles out from Ramsgate, England, where the occupants were picked up by British air-sea rescue units. A few days later a second attempt was aborted due to torn fuselage on takeoff with the glider landing on English turf.

Platoon leader 1Lt. Kenneth L. Vyn's tow craft should have taken him back to England. He certainly wasn't happy with his situation. He explained: "We ran into dense fog and the tow pilot went too far left and we were 100 kilometers off course. (Found this out much later.) Upon landing, we were immediately engaged by a large enemy force from a tank outfit and were surrounded and captured."

F/O James A. Swanson of the 305th Squadron and members of his serial managed to regroup but passed over enemy territory bristling with guns. He wrote: "I had a load of 105mm ammunition—almost two tons, floor loaded, with four troopers and other miscellaneous equipment. I lost one man in the air. I took a number of hits, one knocked off the rudder, another

---

48. According to historian Martin Wolfe, the pilots were F/O Kenneth Hinkel and 2Lt. Adolph Riscky.
49. Minick, 134.

the left wing tip, another the right side of the cargo compartment with an almost continuous stream of small arms fire coming at us. The final hit was in the tow mechanism and with that we went down. We made contact with the underground almost on landing. Six weeks later we walked out."

Capt. Joseph K. Perkins served as the S-2 officer for the 321st Glider Field Artillery Battalion. He wrote: "Our glider carried a jeep with Lt. Col. Edward Carmichael, the battalion commander, his driver, six Jerry cans of gasoline and the floor covered with ten land mines (anti-tank) and myself.

"After clearing the heavy fog area, we had very heavy flak, but the first tug got through untouched. The second glider, less than 100 feet from us, was knocked down. It carried Captain Dunkelberg."

Flying with Captain Dunkelberg was PFC Victor Truesdale. He wrote: "Our tow plane was shot down before we arrived at the LZ in Holland and our pilot crash-landed the glider. We were immediately taken prisoner and spent six months in Stalag 30."

From his position behind the pilot, PFC George Groh[50] observed, "I was holding down the co-pilot's seat and, as Lt. Hoshal swung us north towards Holland, I saw him make motions for his flak suit. His judgment was confirmed a few minutes later when we crossed a patch of woods which blossomed suddenly with short, barking bursts of machine gun fire. It was our first of several such experiences. A glider at 500 feet is a clay pigeon. You just sit there feeling naked and helpless and big as a barn door, while the slugs pop through the canvas. Glancing back I could see some of the boys hunching instinctively toward the center of the glider, though it wasn't much use since one position was about as safe as another. Once I thought the pilot was hit, but when he saw I was worried about him he grinned and said, 'No, not yet!' That was all right with me. I had no desire to make like a glider pilot, at least not just now."

"The third day glider tow to Eindhoven was perhaps the mission which provided the heaviest losses for the 435th Troop Carrier Group.[51] There were many stirring examples of personal courage and devotion to duty on the part of troop carrier crew

50. Groh.
51. From the *History of the 435th Troop Carrier Group.*

members as they endeavored to bring their valuable glider loads over predesignated areas. Major Charles K. Boyd[52] and Captain Paul Joslyn stayed at the controls of their plane until the glider had cut loose, but it was too late for their personal safety. Flames initiated by ack-ack fire destroyed the plane before it left the LZ area."

"Cpl. Walter Holderer flew his first combat mission on D plus 2, glider tow. When his plane's fuel tank was pierced by small arms incendiaries, and flames began making headway, Cpl. Holderer grabbed a fire extinguisher, placed the nozzle in the small hole caused by the passage of the bullet, proceeded to put out the fire. His quick action undoubtedly saved the lives of all on board. In order to hold excitement to the minimum, Holderer refrained from telling his pilot of the incident until all were safely on the ground."[53]

For those who had safely run the gauntlet, it was now time to find a suitable landing spot.

PFC Steve Koper said, "With the glider being hit by small arms fire as it approached the landing zone, the pilot circled away from the area and made his approach from another direction."

Sgt. Ottie Brock said, "Our pilot had two previous combat landings elsewhere. He headed straight down when the tow was completed—no pattern approach. Later, in a ditch where we had taken cover, I saw several gliders get hit by ground fire while making pattern landings."

The combat experience of Cpl. John Nasea of the 321st in Holland was brief. He remembered a lot of flak and then it was quiet. "It was so quiet I didn't hear the one that hit me. I got hit coming down by an armor piercing .30 caliber bullet."

PFC George Groh[54] noted the enemy activity in the vicinity of the LZ. "There was a last burst of fire over the landing zone and then Hoshal swung us earthward in a hurry. Counting up on the ground, we found we'd been pretty lucky. A private sitting just back of the cockpit had been wounded in the face. I had caught a slug in the hip pocket which stopped half way through

52. Maj. Charles K. Boyd received the posthumous award of the Distinguished Service Cross.

53. *435th History.*

54. Groh.

a notebook. As for the rest, they were all right; there were holes all over but the slugs had been hitting where we weren't."

T/Sgt. Clifton Marshall had hoped to sit in the co-pilot's seat for the flight to Holland; however, he had been outranked by a major. Marshall remembered: "We crash-landed against a road bank and the major suffered one or both legs broken in the crash."

While watching from an irrigation ditch, which provided shelter from small-arms fire, Clifton Marshall noticed a flaming C-47 towing its glider to a safe release point. As he watched, the men jumped from the burning aircraft. Marshall noted, "The crew must have jumped out below 500 feet. The pilot and co-pilot made it but the crew chief didn't. We dragged them into a ditch but they jumped up and ran through the rifle fire to retrieve their parachute packing cards so they could thank the people who packed their parachutes."

For PFC Steve Koper, Michalek's premonition, described earlier, came to pass. Koper said, "The glider that Michalek was in crash-landed. The wheels stuck in soft earth and the glider flipped over, breaking Michalek's neck and he died instantly. Had I changed gliders I think it would have been my neck. What was meant to be. . . ."

After a slight nose-down/tail-up landing, Pvt. Tom Morrison needed help retrieving the equipment. "While holding up the front end of the glider to remove a small cargo of mortar rounds, the glider pilot was putting his Tommy gun down and, in the act of doing so, touched the trigger and many rounds went off before he realized it and, of course, he let go of the gun. Some of those rounds went right through the pilot's compartment which I was holding up."

Capt. Joseph Perkins was concerned that the division get its full consignment of artillery weapons. Such was not to be on this day. "We lost two cannoneers when the spade of a howitzer in another glider broke loose when the glider 'ground-looped.' Of twelve guns, we lost four in transit."

In summarizing the actions of two of the glider operations that involved the 79th Troop Carrier Squadron and the 305th Squadron one gets the feeling they were near-disasters.

Roger Airgood, historian for the 79th Squadron, related: "The mission was a flop as far as the 79th was concerned. Twenty-one planes with gliders took off with 155 airborne troops and

34,035 pounds of equipment to resupply troops already fighting in Holland. The formation ran into instrument weather when it reached the Channel and only four planes and gliders reached the LZ, the remaining 17 being scattered all over France, Belgium, southeast England, and their home base, Membury. No casualties."

F/O James A. Swanson of the 305th Squadron describes what happened to the twenty gliders flown by the squadron on the nineteenth of September: "The Germans had a field day with us. They threw up every thing they had. They had two days to stiffen their defenses and they did a real job. As a result of this, the score on the 305th Squadron was as follows: 5 glider pilots killed, 6 glider pilots missing in action, three glider pilots POW. Three gliders returned to England or friendly territory. These were the result of getting lost and hooking up with some other outfit during the various regroupings because of the weather. Three gliders landed near LZ 'W,' close enough to walk in. Due to the weather, fighters, light bombers and other troop carriers were recalled. The 305th missed the recall and we blundered on like we were going to win the war on our own."

Swanson added: "The tow ships didn't do much better than the gliders. Only a few made it back to England. Our commanding officer bellied his craft in on the coast. A couple were on fire and crews bailed out. Some crash-landed in farm fields. Nearly all were able to make it back to friendly territory."

In citing Troop Carrier Command losses, Martin Wolfe[55] provided the numbers for the September 19 missions as follows:

> No less than 17 gliders had to ditch in the English Channel on D + 2. A total of seventeen 53rd Wing C-47s were shot down. Thirty-six gliders were either confirmed as shot down or missing.

In summarizing all the glider missions for the 101st for September 19 (D plus 2), Rapport and Northwood[56] wrote:

> Men on that flight spoke of being able to see nothing except three feet of tow rope stretching out toward nowhere. Some glider pilots failing to bank when their planes did, turned over and had to cut loose. Eighty-two planes missed the LZ completely, and after flying

55. Wolfe.
56. Rapport, Leonard, and Arthur Northwood. *Rendezvous with Destiny* (3rd ed). 101st Airborne Division Association, Sweetwater, TN, 1948, 312–3.

circles over Holland, France, or Germany returned to England. Twenty-six gliders on that trip were never accounted for. Sixteen were known to have crash-landed in enemy territory, for some of the men in them got back. Thirty-one landed in friendly territory on the continent. Most of the occupants managed to rejoin their outfits within a few days.

An idea of the way this flight was cut to pieces by the fog can be gained from the figures. Of 136 jeeps that left England, only 79 safely reached the LZ. Of 68 guns only 40 came in. The 321st lost 3 and the 377th lost 1. Hardest hit was the flight of the 907th. All the planes towing its twelve 105mm howitzers turned back.

In all, 1,341 men arrived safely on the LZ, 554 of whom belonged to the 1st Battalion of the 327th and 159 to the 81st Anti-Aircraft Battalion. The rest were artillerymen, 337 from the 321st Glider Field Artillery Battalion, 190 from the 377th Parachute Field Artillery, 24 from the 907th Glider Field Artillery and the remaining 77 from Division Artillery.

Most of what didn't get in on D plus 2 stayed out for several days. Battery "B" of the 377th did come in on D plus 3 by parachute. The next glider flight was D plus 6 and it was small.

More than 500 men and essential equipment were flown to the Brussels airport. Men and equipment, in most cases, were with their outfits by D plus 10.

The twenty howitzers of the 321st and the 377th that did come in were the first guns to reach the division during the Holland operation.

The 907th Glider Field Artillery Battalion, with its short-barreled 105mm howitzers, were sorely missed for several days as not a single gun arrived on D plus 2, the nineteenth of September. The infantry had to resort to their 60mm and 81mm mortars, .30-caliber machine guns, bazookas, and rifle grenades as their "heavy" weapons.

EIGHT

The Son Bridge

Responding to the red smoke signal, men of the 1st Battalion of the 506th Parachute Infantry Regiment headed for the wooded area at the southern edge of the drop zone. Col. Robert F. Sink moved to the location immediately and began to send the men off in groups of fifteen to twenty with an officer. Three bridges were the objectives, with the main highway bridge as the key target. The two secondary spans, about fourteen hundred yards on either side of the highway bridge, were also to be seized. Company "A" was to go for the main bridge. The smaller bridge to the west was to be taken by "C" Company. "B" was in reserve. One of the 2nd Battalion units was to head for the third span, east of the main highway.

A few minutes after the first groups headed out on their missions, a Dutchman approached 1Lt. Norman Dike, the assistant S-2 for the regiment, and informed him that the two auxiliary bridges had been blown by the Germans several days earlier.

A log for Company "A" of the 506th Regiment was provided by 1Lt. William C. Kennedy, which provided a description of the rapid assembly by members of the company and the key assignment that had been given to them:

> Thirty-five minutes after the jump, the company commander, Captain Melvin O. Davis, and two officers, Lts. George Couch and George Retan, together with about 65 other men of the company moved from the assembly area toward the company objective. Company "A" had been given the principal mission of taking the main bridge across the Wilhelmina Canal, just south of Son. Sgts. (Burley) Sizemore, (Don) Barlowe and (Roy) Stringfellow were part of the group that moved to the bridge.

Almost half of 1st Platoon was late in arriving at the assembly area as they were dropped some distance from the rest of the 506th Regiment. A member of that group was Cpl. Charles Shoemaker, who related: "Most of the men were from 1st Platoon which was being led by 2Lt. James Diel. We didn't reach the unit before it left on its mission toward the Wilhelmina Canal bridge at Son."

Platoon leader 1Lt. David H. Galarneau had been tangled with an equipment bundle on his landing and sustained a multiple ankle fracture. As 2nd Platoon leader, he did manage to hobble off the drop zone and by late afternoon reached the hospital in Son. His assistant platoon leader, 2Lt. George Retan, had gone along with Captain Davis and the first elements of "A" Company. He was destined to become the first KIA for "A" Company.

"I was first scout," said Sgt. Don Brininstool. "Captain Davis was just a short distance away. About the first sixty men from 'A' Company headed for the bridge. I was on the left flank followed by Liddell, Borchers, Impink and Carter."

Brininstool added, "A new replacement ran up to me and said, 'If this is combat, it's not half bad!' I told him he hadn't seen anything yet. 'Just wait awhile!' About this time I heard the first shot and this young trooper must have been one of the first casualties after leaving the drop zone."

Sgt. Joseph P. Powers remembered the name of his plane as *Round Trip Ticket*, which he felt was a good omen. The return part of that trip would see him back in England in a few days. He wrote: "After the assembly, Captain Davis led us down a road toward Son with 2nd Platoon in the lead. We finally came to a halt in the backyard of what I was later told was a monastery or school for boys about to enter the priesthood."

The "A" Company log provides a rather complete picture of the action as the group neared Son and the bridge area:

About 400 yards southeast of the assembly point about half a squad of enemy riflemen fired on the force. However, this resistance was overcome in about five minutes and Captain Davis and his company pressed on about 800 yards from the first point of enemy contact and to the south. PFC Herbert Erickson, who was scouting to the front sighted two enemy riflemen who withdrew behind a barn when fired on. At this point the group was about 200 yards from the bridge and the objective. The 2nd Platoon was leading the attack. A

German 88 gun opened up, firing into the trees and above the heads of our troops. Sgt. Joe Powers of 2nd Platoon was hit by shrapnel at this time and was believed to be the first casualty.

Captain Davis urged the company forward. The enemy fire from the 88 gun increased in intensity and was joined by enemy mortars. In about fifteen minutes five men were killed and eight wounded. Among those killed was Lt. George Retan. The wounded included Lt. George Couch and 1st/Sgt. Burley Sizemore. Sgt. Don Barlowe ordered the company to withdraw about 25 yards to a rear position in a ditch that afforded comparative cover. This was about two hours from H-hour or jump time. Immediately thereafter, Major LaPrade appeared and took command of the situation.

PFC Nelson A. McFaul was in the midst of the action. He wrote: "Everyone assembled at the south end of the drop zone and were proceeding down a country lane toward Son. We entered a wooded area just north of a sanitarium and came under fire. It appeared to be artillery and mortar fire with explosions everywhere. The men ahead had stopped and were using the trees for protection. Sgt. Don Barlow and I tried to get them moving and to get behind the sanitarium for better protection against the artillery fire."

"We immediately came under some intense artillery and machine gun fire having been spotted entering our positions," said Sergeant Powers. "We had not been able to use the brick building of the monastery as cover so Captain Davis ordered us to move forward in the direction of the bridge which was our objective. Upon rising to move forward, I was flattened by an explosion and took a hunk of shrapnel in my right elbow, shattering it. I had lost my weapon so I crawled back in the direction we had come from meeting other members of the company who were moving up and they directed me to a medical officer who proceeded to treat me."

Nearby was PFC Nelson McFaul. He said, "I stopped to nudge someone when I was hit in the leg by a tree burst. I moved back out of the tree line and came upon Dick Harms, who had been wounded in the right shoulder. It didn't appear critical. I dressed it and sent a medic back to check him. At the time I was working on Harms, I heard 1/Sgt. Burley Sizemore yell at someone to get out here and put a tourniquet on his leg before he bled to death."

As the artillery, mortar, and machine-gun fire commenced

from the enemy positions, machine gunner Don Brininstool reacted. "We ran to get our machine gun in place. All hell broke loose. Liddell and Borchers placed our gun in position and I took over the gun with Liddell on my left and Borchers on my right with the remainder of the first wave still further right. A shell exploded near the gun. I thought half my face was blown off. I felt my face which was bleeding from the nose and both ears and covered with sand, but still in one piece. I checked with Liddell. He was hit around the elbow and Borchers was hit in the groin. After giving first aid and telling them to stay very still so we would not get another shell, I checked to see what other damage had been done.

"The Germans must have been watching us from the church tower. Capt. Davis was hit along with most of the first wave. The Germans had blown the bridges to the right and left of Son earlier. After finding a couple more troopers still walking, we headed for the main bridge."

As they caught up with the advance elements of Company "A," Cpl. Charles Shoemaker and the 1st Platoon contingent came upon the battered group. They moved past Sgt. Donald Barlow and the survivors of the air bursts and mortar barrages near the sanitarium. Captain Davis had been wounded, and 2Lt. George Retan had been killed. Shoemaker and his group moved on toward the bridge, which was number one priority. He wrote: "We got down to the canal and there was an 88 gun position that had been knocked out. A couple of our people were there. A very young German soldier was lying at the bottom of the gun pit. His belly had been opened from side to side. Another one was standing there wringing his hands. He told one of our people who spoke German that they had grown up together in the same village and were very close. Neither one of them was over sixteen years of age. He begged one of our men to put his friend out his misery. Of course, nobody would do that. Then he begged somebody to give him a gun so he could do it. Nobody offered him a gun. I don't know what happened from there on, as we kept moving."

With Company "A" as the point of the attack toward the Wilhelmina Canal bridge, Company "B" was following, ready to move in as support for the spearhead force. PFC John R. Garrigan wrote: "I do remember we were held up for a few minutes behind 'A' Company and we didn't know the reason at the time.

While waiting, a medic came by and noticed my hand was all bloody—how, I don't know—but he decided to fix it with a bandage. By the time he was done, we were told to move out and that is when I saw 'A' company as we went through them, all in bad shape. Captain Davis of 'A' Company was there, badly wounded.

"We hit the edge of the tree line and took off across the wide open field heading for the bridge, our objective. Duane Zentz and I headed for the center of the field where a German artillery piece was located. With the field buzzing with bullets, we finally made it to the gun emplacement and jumped in. The next move was for a little house on the edge of the canal. The soldiers crossing this field didn't have much of a chance. I saw so many of our boys going down. Zentz and I made the house which did have enemy, who were now running away from us as we turned the corner of a fence line. There was Joe Gendreau, a clean shot in the head. I felt a great loss at that moment but headed for the canal bridge just as it was blown up—another great disappointment."

Pvt. Robert W. Wiatt, a replacement for "C" Company for the Holland operation, remembered, "The mission of 'C' Company was to take a bridge west of the main bridge at Son. I joined a group of other 'Charley' Company men only to learn the bridge we were to take had already been destroyed. We then headed through some woods toward Son and the canal. We passed an 88mm gun that had been taken out by the Air Force. It was here that I saw the first dead person in my life."

As the action in the woods near the sanitarium wound down, Sgt. Joe Powers, the first "A" Company man to be wounded when the enemy fired tree bursts into the positions, describes what ensued shortly afterward as he was treated for his wound by a medical officer. "He ripped my sleeve open, checked the wound and gave me a shot of morphine. He bandaged my arm and offered a drink from his canteen. I had a canteen of water and told him so but he said, 'Drink this anyway!' I did and it was some of the best Scotch whiskey I had ever tasted. I thanked him and he tied my arm in a vertical position to a small bush and told me to lie there until I was picked up.

"From out of nowhere the Dutch civilians started appearing— men, women and children, oblivious of the danger to themselves. They piled cookies, cakes and other foods on my stomach as I lay there, coaxing me to eat and trying to make me comfortable. Between the morphine and the Scotch whiskey I wasn't feeling too badly about then."

After the 1st Battalion had been sent on its way in a flanking movement of the Wilhelmina bridge position, Col. Robert F. Sink learned from the Dutch resistance forces that the two smaller parallel bridges had been blown several days earlier. This added further impetus to the necessity to capture the main bridge before the same fate befell it.

As 2nd and 3rd Battalions and Regimental Headquarters personnel completed their assembly, some of the men had been confused by the smoke signals of the 502nd on DZ "B" and were late in reporting. The arrival of the glider echelons in the same fields a short time after the paratroopers had landed caused further delay.

PFC John Vlachos noted: "Men and women were running out on our drop zone picking up parachutes while we were still under fire. I crawled to the edge of the field where the woods began. There was a German ambulance well marked with Red Crosses that had been strafed by our fighter planes and set afire. I opened the door and saw two German medics and a nurse. They were burned and charred."[57]

On Colonel Sink's order, 2nd Battalion moved out, down the main road to Son. He followed it; after him came the platoon of "Charley" Company engineers, Regimental Headquarters Company, and the men of 3rd Battalion.

Marching down the road, Colonel Sink remembered several enemy tanks near Wolfswinkel that he had seen from his plane. He sent a patrol to investigate. Before the patrol could get there American fighters came overhead, saw the tanks, attacked, and knocked them out. Here was another demonstration of the air superiority that had made a daylight jump possible. The feelings of the men, already favorable toward the air force on account of the almost perfect jump, warmed even more.

T/5 Gordon E. King jumped with Capt. Charles Shettle as his radioman. He wrote: "We hadn't been on the ground long when Sink's jeep came in and I rode with him into Son because his operator had not shown up yet."

---

57. See story of Lisa van Overveld on page 29. The author also came upon the same scene as he moved through the wooded area.

King added: "We noted Mustangs strafing the highway even before we jumped and saw smoke where they had been operating as we headed for the highway and turned south toward the canal and Eindhoven. Sink couldn't wait to see if the bridge was still OK and headed south with 'yours truly' hanging on for dear life to the folded windshield while carrying my SCR-300 on my back and riding on the hood."

"Out in front of everybody was Sgt. Allen L. Westphal leading the entire regiment," recalled Sgt. Hugh E. Pritchard. "We were moving swiftly through the main street of Son. I was on the sidewalk on the left taking a little cover while Westphal was in the middle of the street at double-time and yelling, 'Come on you guys!' Suddenly a burst of German machine gun fire raked the street with one slug getting Westphal through the calf of the leg. He quickly crawled over to me and said, 'You know, that was stupid of me, wasn't it?' "

In the town of Son, a strategically placed 88mm gun covering the road opened fire. The advance elements went down. As a member of the leading platoon from Company "D," Sgt. Louis E. Truax wrote: "I was running down the street toward the Son bridge. I was on the right side and Sgt. Willis Phillips was on the left. We were going house to house. There was still food on the tables the Germans had left there. Phillips was killed by small arms fire from the Krauts still in the buildings or by a mortar shell."

As leader of the anti-tank section of 2nd Battalion, Sgt. Jack MacLean recalled when his group was called forward. "A pair of 88 guns were firing directly down the street and impeding our advance. We had the first of many such commands to follow with 'Bazookas up front!' Pvt. Glen Lindsey, highly skilled with his work with the weapon, moved forward into position, fired one round at the 88 nearest our group, disabling it and killing one of the Germans."

Six others fled the gun position heading toward the bridge. A "D" Company machine gunner finished off those men as they retreated.

The nearest 88 had held up "D" Company. About that time, Colonel Sink came upon the scene. Pvt. Paul Z. Martinez was there. He said, "Colonel Sink came up and asked, 'What's the hold up?' At the same time a couple guys were helping Allen

Westphal after he was wounded. Captain 'Mac' (Joe MacMillan) kept yelling at us to get across the canal."

Three troopers were within a hundred yards of the bridge when it was blown up by the enemy.

Sgt. Hugh Pritchard added to his account: "We were about 200 feet from the bridge when the Germans blew it. We jumped back under the cover of buildings while huge chunks of wood and other debris rained down all around us. I had no idea I was that close to the bridge, and I am sure that if Westphal had not been shot, creating a temporary delay, we (he, I, and others) would have been on that bridge when it went up."

Sgt. Jack MacLean continued his story: "I gave Lindsey some cover fire and headed for the bridge. Then it blew right in my face. I was dazed. I turned and headed for the embankment and saw Westphal facing south and placing fire across the canal. As I fired at enemy running out of a building I turned and saw troopers coming along the bank. They were not from 2nd Battalion so I headed back to my own people. I found Lindsey had been wounded and a medic had fixed his arm. Ray Taylor and Jeff Rice of 'D' Company were occupying the building just northwest of the canal."

One of the troopers moving toward the bridge along the canal bank from the west was Sgt. Philip Carney, who served as radio operator for 1st Battalion commander LTC James L. LaPrade and was close on the heels of his commander as they approached the bridge. Within fifty yards of the bridge, the Germans who had demolitions in place blew up the bridge. Sergeant Carney wrote: "We were so close that I got splinters in my face from the flying debris when we reached the bridge under fire from the other side."

Elements of 1st Battalion and the three rifle companies of 2nd Battalion had fought their way to within a hundred yards of the bridge. Colonel Sink was nearby, as was Major General Taylor, who had accompanied the troops of 1st Battalion. The first men from 1st Battalion had appeared just prior to the bridge being blown.

Moments after the explosion, LTC Jim LaPrade, along with Lt. Milford F. Weller and Sgt. Donald Dunning, came running up near the destroyed span, followed by Sgt. Philip Carney and his assistant, Cpl. Ogden Stutler. Carney added to his story: "Colonel LaPrade yelled at me, 'Sergeant, get those radios across to the other side.' LaPrade jumped into the canal and swam across to the other side. I looked around and found a piece of debris—a wooden plank. I placed the two radios on the plank, peeled off my combat jacket, my steel helmet and my M-1 rifle. I balanced them on the plank. I had Ogden Stutler with me and I told him to strip off some of his equipment so he could swim easier. Pushing off into the water with one hand holding on to the radios and the other hand holding on to the rest of my gear, kicking my feet for locomotion I started across the canal. Stutler had neglected to strip off some of his gear and as a result, halfway across the canal he yelled to me, 'I'm sinking, I'm sinking!'

"At that moment I had to decide what to save—him? the radios? or my equipment? I grabbed Cpl. Stutter by the back of his combat jacket with one hand and with the other held on to the two radios, and watched my steel helmet, combat jacket, and my M-1 rifle sink out of sight. Still kicking my feet, I was able to get them all across to the south side of the canal and Colonel LaPrade was able to use the radios."

Lt. Milford Weller and Sgt. Donald Dunning followed LTC Jim LaPrade in swimming across the canal. Other 1st Battalion men obtained a small rowboat and several squads were ferried to the south bank. Together with the group that swam across, they dispersed the enemy firing from the nearby houses.

To provide for "blown bridge" situations the 3rd Platoon of "C" Company of the 326th Engineer Battalion had jumped with the regiment. Though they didn't locate the bundles they had dropped from the planes, all three sticks had come down in a closely bunched group. With platoon leader 1Lt. Harold E. Young, they followed the 2nd Battalion toward Son and the bridge. Young wrote: "Within 20 minutes or so I heard an explosion up ahead. Instinctively, I knew that the bridge across the 80-foot-wide Wilhelmina Canal had been blown. Within three minutes word was passed back down the line 'Engineers up front!' From two years of training and the Normandy experience my platoon was well trained. We jogged along and went directly to the bridge which had been blown by the retreating German soldiers with a previously planted explosive.

"There was a circular concrete pier with about 20 feet of open water on each side. The infantry was jumping in and swimming from the north bank to the pier and from the pier to the south bank. We had no engineering equipment and we had to get a footbridge across to move the entire 506th Regiment across. We had trained for many kinds of improvisations but not this. The bridge was adjacent to the village of Son. I sent men to find hammers, nails, boards, planks, etc. Somebody located two boats which we placed midway from the shore to the pier. Then we made a rickety bridge that worked provided my men helped steady the infantry as they moved across. Before midnight the entire regiment had crossed. Some of my men located bigger and better planks and, in the middle of the night, replaced the rickety bridge with a fairly substantial one."

As the crossing of the makeshift bridge by over two thousand troops went on for several hours, men had to hunt down the remaining snipers in the area. PFC John Garrigan added to his story. "We set up positions on the bank of the canal until the bridge was passable and then we went on again. The enemy was still running. Finally it was time to hold up for the night."

Pvt. Robert Wiatt remembered: "We were under some fire at the time. We moved between some houses south of the canal with very little trouble and halted for the night in a ditch south of Son."

After the troops had crossed over the makeshift bridge, the men were posted toward Eindhoven on either side of the road. T/5 Charles McCallister had this recollection: "That night I drew the first shift at guard and when my turn was up, I believe a light rain was falling. I elected to sleep in a chicken coop, rather than the slit trench I had dug. By that time, nothing could have disturbed my sleep and the next morning I found myself covered with chicken mites, which gave me a lot of discomfort as I remember very well."

Earlier timetables had called for the 506th to take Eindhoven by 2000 hours on the seventeenth. A civilian report stated that a German regiment had just moved into town. Major General Taylor, in his conferences with British generals, had pointed out that it might not be possible to secure all the objectives on D-Day and suggested that Eindhoven might not be taken the first day. While talking with Colonel Sink at the bridge site, Taylor agreed that an overnight wait was advisable.

The "A" Company log provides the situation of the unit once the bridge objective was reached.

About 1900 hours, 1Lt. Bill Muir, who had assumed command, moved the company, less the 1st Platoon, to a bivouac area about a mile south of Son. Patrols were sent out from this point east and west of Son.

The 1st Platoon with 2Lt. James Diel commanding, was left on the south bank of the Wilhelmina Canal to defend the bridge from again falling into enemy hands and to prevent its further destruction. The night was uneventful.

According to PFC James H. Martin of "G" Company, his platoon was also detailed to remain on the north side of the canal. Their first night job was to guard Division Headquarters.

When the 506th Regiment launched its attack toward Eindhoven, the engineers had already begun work on an idea presented to platoon leader Harold E. Young. He wrote: "Early the next morning, a number of my men suggested that we build a raft to move jeeps back and forth. I was undecided. I went to see our battalion C.O. (LTC Hugh Moseley). When I got to General Taylor's headquarters, I heard him telling Moseley most emphatically that he wanted jeeps across that canal by noon. When Moseley came out I told him what the men had suggested. 'Go ahead and do it!' he said. I dog-trotted back to the canal. My enterprising men were already locating metal barrels to which they only had to make wooden bungs. How many barrels to hold a jeep? Somehow we decided on 16. These were assembled and held together in a wooden box with a flat top of boards to hold a jeep. We had some rope and tied it to each end to move the raft back and forth. The raft would hold one jeep and one man had to be on the raft to keep it from tilting too much. It worked and we took many men alone or jeeps across. The infantry had commandeered a panel body truck and they brought wounded to the south bank where they were put on the raft and taken to the north side. I sent my men looking for materials and in the afternoon they built a bigger and more substantial raft so we had two of them moving continuously.

"In a parachute outfit the men were always testing the officers. Sgt. Andrew Shlapak, the platoon sergeant, was on the south side. Just about the same time a truck load of wounded pulled up and General Taylor came up. Both wanted to move to the other side. Sgt. Shlapak yelled out, 'Shall I take the wounded or the General first?' Taylor was busy reading some reports. I yelled back, 'Take the wounded first!' and Taylor simply stepped back, not giving any thought to what was going on.

"It was a hot, sunny day and pulling the raft back and forth was tiring. We moved civilians across when the raft was free. Shortly before noon a gray-haired farmer came to the south side with two handsome work horses. He spoke Flemish and we couldn't understand him. We decided he wanted his horses on the north side so we took them over. But he didn't go away. He kept talking to us. Finally we took him and his horses back to the south side. In the middle of the night it occurred to me, finally, that he wanted us to use one horse on each side to pull the rope to relieve the tired men who were pulling.

"One of the glider engineer platoons came to relieve us the next morning. We demonstrated how to use both rafts with particular attention to the first one which was so rickety but had never failed us. As we left, we watched them put a jeep on the first raft and move it across to the south side. Just as it got to the south side, the jeep went overboard."

NINE

Eindhoven

Long before daylight, the Pulles family bakery was a beehive of activity on Monday morning, the eighteenth of September. The bakery was located on Kloosterdreef.

Bert Pulles, one of the sons of a family that had returned to Holland from Canada during the Depression in the early 1930s, had this description of the morning activities: "Dad, my brother John and I were up early, as bakers rise long before others to get the bread baked. That's all we were baking lately as there wasn't much in the line of ingredients available. I did the deliveries. We had a house to house route and sold bread to steady customers as was the custom in the old days. Shortly after daylight, my fiancée, Coby, came over. She often helped my mother in the store or with household chores.

"I went out on my 3-wheeled bread delivery bicycle and left our house to go on my first deliveries, turning the corner from Kloosterdreef onto Woenselschestraat. I noticed some Germans putting up a gun which I later heard was an 88mm weapon. I did not know much about guns or ammunition as I tried to have nothing to do with the Germans and ignored all these things. Going down Woenselschestraat, I noticed a bit further down the road another gun, same as the first, being put up and, remembering the planes and gliders passing over the day before, I thought I had better get back home and forget about the bread deliveries till I knew better what was happening."

From their overnight positions in the ditches and fields near Bokt, the men of the 506th Parachute Regiment began their moves toward Eindhoven at daybreak. Marshall[58] and Westover wrote:

58. From a historical narrative based on interviews of Col. Robert F. Sink, LTC Charles H. Chase, their officers and groups of enlisted men (Marshall and Westover).

The hour was 0730 when 3rd Battalion crossed the LD at Bokt with "H" and "I" astride the road and "G" and "HQ" going straight down the road. The country was flat and even and the two companies which were covering the regimental front were able to cover the fields and ditches at almost a marching pace. One platoon from "A" and the engineer detail were left to hold Son; it was sufficient for the task inasmuch as the 502nd had moved into a support position to strengthen 506's bid for Eindhoven. 1st and 2nd Battalions, with small flank patrols out, otherwise in regular march formation. Only 600 yards beyond the LD, 3rd Battalion encountered rifle and machine gun fire, and from that point all the way into Eindhoven, the column was opposed by little groups of infantry and occasional artillery fire, though the character of the resistance was so weak and irresolute that it had hardly more than a nuisance and delaying effect.

First Lieutenant Charles "Sandy" Santasiero was given the mission of leading the dawn attack toward Eindhoven. Colonel Sink had called for Santasiero the previous evening to be ready with his platoon. Sink's parting shot was, "Charlie—you punch the hole and I will pour in the men."

Santasiero described his mission: "At daybreak when the mist began to rise, I saw little ground cover and an open area about 500 yards before me. This ground had to be crossed on the double to reach the cover of buildings. With my men on the left and right of me, we went over the top. We began to receive rifle fire and I saw Krauts leave their fox holes and run for the buildings. We fought a running battle, not giving them time to organize or use their 88mm gun."

Sgt. Jack MacLean of the anti-tank platoon wrote: "Company 'I' started the assault down the left side of the road going toward Eindhoven and ran into some 88s that were mobile. We again heard 'Bazookas up front!' We met with Major Horton and an 'H' company officer whose platoon was to make a flanking movement. We ran into a couple machine gun emplacements and a couple riflemen. We fired a few rounds and were able to catch one 88 backing into an alley. We put three rounds into it, destroying it and killing the crew."

The combat career of 2Lt. David H. Forney was short-lived. As an assistant platoon leader in "H" Company, he arrived as a replacement for the Holland mission. He wrote: "My military career was cut short. Right outside of Son, I was hit with some kind of a shell and I never went back to duty again."[59]

As the spearhead of the 506th neared the outskirts of Eindhoven, enemy resistance stiffened.

First Lieutenant Santasiero continued his story: "At the edge of town, I wasted a Kraut out of a church steeple and waited for my men to dress up the line.

"Captain John Kiley came up to me, looking like an officer—bars, map case and binocs in full view. (Kiley was a close friend and I was concerned.) I said, 'God damn, Kiley! What in hell are you doing up here? You shine like a f—ing officer. You know the Krauts are waiting to kill officers. Please get your ass to the rear.' His reply, 'Sandy, not many of us (old timers) are left. I worry about you every time a mission bogs down—and you end up leading the attack for us.'

"Much to my sorrow, Kiley was killed by a sniper."

Pvt. William P. Galbraith was serving as runner for Captain Kiley in Holland. Recalling the actions of the eighteenth, Galbraith wrote: "I moved up to join Captain Kiley in the advance into Eindhoven. 'I' Company was on our right and 'H' Company was on our left. There was some small arms fire but not a lot. We got up to about fifty yards from a Catholic church. Kiley told me to go back and tell Major Horton to inform 'H' Company to get the hell up on line or we would be outflanked. I only went back a hundred yards where I saw James L. Brown from 'I' Company with an SCR-536 (walkie-talkie) radio. I told him 'Major Horton said for "H" Company to get the hell up on line,' that 'I' Company was receiving too much fire. The message went back. I hadn't even seen Major Horton. I got right back to Kiley. He asked me had I seen Horton. I said no, but that I got the job done. Kiley was standing behind a burned out German truck and next to a small cottage with a little courtyard in front. I was lying down on the left side of the road. I told Kiley he better get down. He said, 'If I get down, so will everyone else.' He no more than got the words out when a bullet hit him in the throat, killing him instantly. I shot at the openings in the church tower as I thought that was where the shot came from—also at some windows up the street on the right in front of the captain.

---

59. First Lieutenant Alex Andros said, "Dave Forney was so seriously hit that he spent four years in and out of military hospitals after the war."

I then ran across the street to see if there was anything I could do for the captain. There wasn't. I then asked 1st Sergeant Jerry Beam of 'I' Company if I could join them in their advance into Eindhoven. I then went back across the street and put three or four shots from my .45 automatic into the latch of the church door and then hit it with my shoulder in order to get inside the church. I landed on my fanny in the street. The door didn't give a damn bit."

PFCs George R. McMillan and Marion Hove served as scouts and pointed out enemy targets with tracer ammo. The two of them entered Eindhoven through backyards of the first group of houses. McMillan wrote: "We found two young women and a small child in a shed. We gave the ladies our American flag armbands and took off for the street in front of the houses. Hove and I made our way into the street and began a door to door run into town. No small arms fire encountered yet but we could feel the 88s over our heads. The houses were built close to the side walks and most had recessed front doors. Hove would cover and I moved, then I covered and Hove ran to the next doorway. We had penetrated Eindhoven some 300 feet and on the next dash made by Hove a German machine gun rattled a burst down the cobblestones. A bullet caught Hove in the foot. Other 3rd Platoon troopers were making their way up to us. The word was passed and help arrived for Hove. Bill Weber and Albert Cappelli were among the first to arrive."

PFC Joseph Harris of "H" Company recalled a buddy who was great in house-to-house fighting. Harris wrote: "We had a little fellow we called 'Tarky,' the best little house-to-house fighter you ever saw—a great little scout, too. He had a dummy grenade and he'd throw the grenade in the window and he'd follow it. He cleaned those places out in a hurry and Sergeant (Frank J.) Padisak would say, 'Wherever I go, Tarky, you follow me. You're the man I want with me in this house-to-house business."

Capt. Bernard J. Ryan, surgeon for 3rd Battalion of the 506th, wrote: "During the attack on Eindhoven, I was with 'H' Company and advanced with company headquarters, left wounded in farmhouses during the advance, giving plasma, etc. and leaving them in the care of the local people. We had no organized evacuation at first as the bridge behind us at Son had been blown. Major Louis R. Kent soon had a shuttle organized to move across the canal. I treated several of our casualties where they were hit, hanging plasma on their rifles with the enemy only a short way ahead of us. Almost all the casualties were from small arms fire. 1Lt. Fred Gibbs of 'G' Company warned me, 'You better keep down, Doc, they're in the next ditch!' as I passed him only to return a few minutes later to find that he had been shot and killed by the Krauts he was warning me about."[60]

First Lieutenant Alex Andros of "H" Company said his 3rd Platoon didn't have it bad going into Eindhoven but 1st Platoon caught a lot of hell from a German machine gun and its leader, 1Lt. Rudolph Bolte, was killed in the assault. The assistant platoon leader, 2Lt. David Forney, had been severely wounded shortly after the unit jumped off early that morning on its move toward Eindhoven. Andros was called over to assume command of the 1st Platoon. He said, "I went over there and most of the people were in a ditch on one side of the field, opposite a German machine gun. Sgt. Padisak had crawled up near the machine gun. I was getting ready to make another assault and told Sgt. Don Zahn to lay down some mortar fire, and we'd have a BAR provide covering fire. We were just getting ready to take off when one of the men came back and said, 'Forget it, Sgt. "Paddy" had already taken the machine gun out.'

"I do remember trying to flush out snipers by getting them to fire at us. Stupid as we were—we'd run across the road and have someone watch to see if we were fired on and pick out the spot where the shots came from and have one of our men pick them off. Fortunately, none of us got hit."

From his position at the front of the attacking force, First Lieutenant Santasiero continued his story: "We pressed the attack, came to a main street leading toward the center of town. I was in the lead with my men behind me on both sides of the street hugging doorways, fighting house to house. When we were close to a town square, rifle fire and a couple machine guns opened up on us. Firing was inaccurate. Sparks flew in all directions off the cobblestones of the road. I saw a foxhole in the road, jumped in and hollered for the man behind me to pass up

60. From an account Captain Ryan wrote in letter form to Maj. Louis R. Kent while recuperating in a hospital from wounds received during the Battle of the Bulge at Bastogne.

the light machine gun. I received the gun and started killing Krauts. Behind me the front of the building was blown out by an artillery round. I received a shower of bricks but continued to fire. When the second round hit the building with the same results, I began to work over the area up the road; then I saw sparks fly off the road in front of my gun, heard the whine of a large projectile go over my head and white phosphorus exploded against the building. All missed me."

The gun firing at Santasiero was one of the two guns described by Dutch underground members Hurks and Evers, and Bert Pulles, the bakery deliveryman.

Santasiero continued: "It was then that I knew they were firing an 88mm gun directly at me like a rifle (some feeling!). I saw the 88 up the road. I opened fire. The crew left the gun and started for the buildings. I had Sgt. Jim Shuler drop a few mortar rounds."

Pvt. Bill Galbraith, now without an assignment, continued his narrative: "I went up the street behind Jerry Beam and George McMillan. Some Kraut opened up on us with a machine gun. I stepped into a doorway that was inset about three feet and I thought to myself that he could wear that damned gun out as he couldn't possibly hit me where I was located. About that time an 88 shell hit the building across the street. It blew out the whole front of the building. The second one damn near tore my left leg off at the knee and put me on my butt in the street again. I crawled back into the doorway. Another round came in with shrapnel hitting me in the shoulder. After that I figured if I was going to live I'd have to get the hell out of there in spite of the machine gun. So, with my good leg, I started pushing myself back down the street toward the church. I got to the next house and a Dutchman by the name of Pete Klompmaker[61] opened the door and dragged me inside."

"As troopers moved in, small teams began checking each house," wrote PFC George McMillan. "It was discovered the Germans were using the basement windows to rake the street with heavy fire, while falling back toward the center of town. Word was passed that civilians were inside the buildings. The 3rd Platoon moved slowly forward until stopped by point blank 88mm fire. We were held back until 2nd battalion flanked the hot spot."

61. Verified by Peter Klompmaker in a September 21, 1988, interview.

Sgt. Donald G. Malarkey's recollection of the advance by the 2nd Battalion is as follows: "We came into the city from the northeast with scattered resistance but rounded up a lot of prisoners on tips from the Dutch people. In fact, at one time, we had so many men going after holed-up Germans that we had to stop following their leads."

T/5 Charlie McCallister had been relieved of the burden of carrying a heavy SCR-300 radio and was functioning as a rifleman. "A Dutch civilian came out of a house as I was going by and motioned me to follow him inside. I did so, and he led me to the kitchen in the back of the house, and as I entered I was facing five German soldiers, but they had stacked their weapons against the wall and raised their hands and surrendered when I walked in. I liberated one pistol and told the Dutchman to get the rest of the arms for the resistance people and then marched the Germans out into the street where they were quickly taken over by some of the other Dutch resistance folks. I hope my prisoners survived because the Dutch were really mad."

An enemy 88mm gun had been firing directly at First Lieutenant Santasiero in his foxhole position in the street, knocking down sections of the buildings behind him.

Santasiero added, "Major Horton came up and said, 'Charlie, the Dutch are on our side and I think you are destroying too many buildings!'

"I said, 'Major, what you are looking at was done by an 88 trying to kill me. We are about to finish this fight. Now tell it to the dead trooper in the street.'

"He departed as fast as he came. Those were the only words he spoke to me during the rest of the campaign. While this was going on, Colonel Sink sent the 2nd Battalion on a flanking attack which finished the battle."

Radioman Cpl. Joseph J. Hogenmiller wrote: "The battalions drove the small group of Germans back with gunfire, eliminating some of them where they stood. As the battalion began moving into the outskirts of Eindhoven, it was receiving direct fire down the street from two German 88mm gun positions and mortar fire. At this point, the 3rd Battalion came to a halt. Colonel Sink came forward looking over the situation and then ordered 2nd Battalion to swing around the 3rd Battalion on the left. LTC Robert Strayer, commander of 2nd Battalion quickly moved his force down an adjoining road toward the center of Eindhoven, peeling off Company 'F' (my company) to make a flank attack on the Germans."

Medic! Up Front!

"Easy" Company was also in on the 2nd Battalion maneuver as related by platoon leader 1Lt. Robert B. Brewer. "It all started when Colonel Robert Sink's lead element entering the northern outskirts of Eindhoven came head to head with a German strong point centered on a cursed Kraut 88mm gun astride our planned approach route. It was time for an alternate approach route and I was closest to that route.

"Capt. Clarence Hester (S-3 for 2nd Battalion) came up and told me to lead out around the left (east) of the main road and houses entering the city from the north. He gave me 15 minutes to get going. Quickly I quizzed the Dutch people there about the presence of Germans in that direction. I found that the school kids could understand my poor French. They would then interpret for their parents and pass the word back to me in French.

"I learned that the Germans had been in a fruit orchard astride my planned route just that morning. I therefore put two light machine guns on the upstairs porch of a house facing that orchard and had them reconnoiter the rear edge of the orchard by fire as we moved out. No response. But it alerted a German sniper (a sergeant-major with a Mauser carbine my guys later told me) on the top floor of the Philips electric factory. He then knew that we were coming around the back way.

"Because I'd had so little time previously to study our route, I had my map and binocs out as we made a standard approach march (two squads in column in front and two following and me in the middle) beyond the orchard across an open field, perhaps 600 meters across. The factory, about four stories high, was on our right front. I wanted to go to some cover, the gardens for starters, and planned to move on the double in that direction the moment any shooting began.

"At that moment I was hit. A round entered my right jaw and exited my left neck. Both holes, just below the third molar from the back, spouted blood immediately and blood flowed from my mouth like a fountain. I knew I was going into shock.

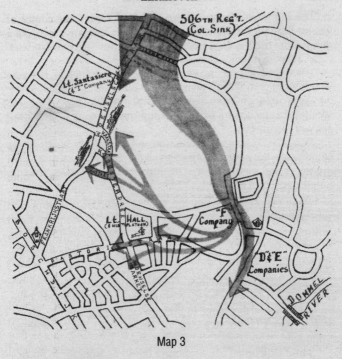

Map 3

"While the above was going on, I heard one of my men yell, 'Lieutenant Brewer's dead! Get going to those trees ahead!' and I remembered feeling good about that order. Someone was taking over."

S/Sgt. Albert L. Mampre was with the 2nd Battalion surgeon, 1Lt. Jackson R. Neavles, when a call came back from Company "E" for a "medic up front!" Mampre said, "There's a medic up there, why the call? (I was to go up and respond to the call.) The medical officer said, 'Goodbye Al, nice knowing you!' "

Mampre had been injured on the jump the day before and had considerable difficulty traveling down the road from Bokt during the day.

Mampre continued: "There wasn't much sense crawling out to him over the open field, so I hobbled out as I had been injured on the jump the day before and couldn't walk well.

"It was Lt. Bob Brewer down with a wound by a bullet that passed through his upper throat just before the jaw line. It was quiet at the time and, as I began patching him up, Pvt. Holland ('E' Company medic) came out to help.

"I was in the process of administering plasma to Brewer, which was very difficult because his veins had collapsed, when we were fired on from the houses across the field. Holland shouted that he was hit in the heel and scooted back to 'E' Company in the ditch.

"Dirt was kicking up around me and I heard the sharp crack and thought the plasma bottle was shattered. (I had such trouble mixing it and getting it started into Brewer.) I looked up and found it intact in my hand, so I lay down beside Brewer. He was yellow in color and not moving at all. In my best bedside manner, I said to Brewer, 'Are you dead? If so, I'm getting out of here!' He croaked back, barely audible and just understandable, 'No, but I don't know why not.' I said, 'Good, I'll stay with you.'

"Just after that I felt like a mule kicked my leg and when I checked I saw my right leg calf laid open to the bone.

"Three 'E' Company men came out to us when they saw us hit but they, too, were hit, one in the chest. I immediately gave myself a shot of morphine to prevent me from going into shock and so that I could take care of Brewer and the other three wounded.

"Some Dutchmen came running out to us from those houses and put Brewer on a ladder, using it as a litter. One tried to take my boot off but I wouldn't let him but he then helped me dress my wound. As he did this, the Dutchmen took Brewer and the others to the houses where the Germans were, rather than back to our lines.

"Fortunately, there was a deep set of wagon ruts that ran across the field to the house area and I could follow my patients with one leg (left and functional) in the rut and the right, which could not be straightened, on the ground and I made it to the house that the Dutchmen had taken my four patients. A woman next door was crying out to me (she saw my medic's insignia) that her husband was 'tote.' There was not much I could do for her or him.

"While I was patching up the wounded, others, including Sgt. Mike Ranney, came through. They had eliminated the German upstairs. I was beginning to throw up due to the morphine and asked the woman of the house for a basin. Her house was so clean.

"After patching everyone, including myself, the Dutch had a double decker cart and loaded all four on the cart, two on the first level and two on the top and we went to the crossroad at the end of the houses. I was trying to stay on my own two feet.

"As we were trying to decide which way to go to rejoin our troops, I wanting to go one way and one Dutchman wanting us to go the other (which was the wrong way), a platoon of Germans was going across a field on the other side of the houses and, upon spotting us, began running and firing at us.

"The Dutchmen ran with the double decker cart full of our wounded in the direction I wanted to go—toward Son and I, being quite helpless, dove head first into a round (German type) foxhole. Two Dutch men pulled me out and threw me on a wheelbarrow and with one on each handle ran hell bent for leather down the road after our other wounded men. None of us were hit during this firing and we were able to eventually get back to Son and medical help."

Flank Attack on the 88s

Cpl. Joe Hogenmiller, of 2nd Platoon of "F" Company, added to his narrative: "I received orders by radio from the company commander to have 1Lt. Russell Hall, platoon leader, along with Sgt. John Taylor, squad leader, to move our lead platoon onto Pastorestraat, when at the corner of Kloosterdreef they met the battalion executive, Capt. Charles Shettle, who told Lt. Hall that his platoon was to clear out the German 88mm battery. While conversing with a Dutchman, Shettle received information about the gun locations and the Dutchman promised to lead the men to them. The column continued to Kloosterdreef without knowing the situation or the nearness of the guns."

When he returned home without completing his bread delivery route, Bert Pulles related to his father, brother, Coby, and the rest of the family what he had seen. He then went back outside, running back and forth, peering down side streets and then dashing back to the shelter of home.

"Suddenly, I saw a group of armed soldiers coming down the street," he added. "I looked again to see if they were Germans, as they crossed the street and turned into the yard of a coal dealer who lived across the street. I asked, 'Are you English?' (Pulles was fluent in English, having lived in Canada and gone to school there.) Someone said, 'No, we are Americans!' My answer was, 'Better yet!' and proceeded to tell them about the German guns which I had seen earlier. I was so excited that I did not notice anything—just so happy to see American paratroopers that I could talk to. I am sure that I never noticed their ranks, if they had any. I just saw 12 or 15 young 'Gods' who came to liberate us. The only thing I noticed was the proudly-worn Screaming Eagle patch on their left shoulder—a badge I will never forget.

"I took them north on Kloosterdreef and left into the Runstraat, the street which was right across the street from our house and bakery shop. (We could see the whole street from our upstairs windows.) I led them north, going behind the houses which lined the Kloosterdreef till I thought they had gone forward as far as possible without being seen by the Germans. I then drew a small map on the ground with a little stick I picked up, telling them that three roads formed a triangle with Frankrystraat, Runstraat and Kloosterdreef and that the gun was placed on the northeast corner of this triangle and at a point where Woenselschestraat started.

"One of the men went forward to investigate. After possibly four or five minutes a call came 'Mortar and ammo!' and this was repeated all along the line of paratroopers. I remember a young Dutch fellow coming along just about then and he also—though he spoke no English—echoed the words, 'Mortar and ammo!' I then heard a loud explosion and bits of brick and mortar came raining down on us. The Germans had fired their gun and hit the building across the street housing a butcher shop. I found this out about ten minutes later as the Americans left me there and were going to the corner as the Germans surrendered at one gun. Before I went back, one American asked me if I wanted a cigarette. I think I was the first Dutchman in Eindhoven to go home with a carton of Camels.

"When I got back to our house, dad was limping because a piece of shrapnel had bounced off his leg, which stung but had barely broken the skin on his shin."

Radioman Joe Hogenmiller continued his story. "While the soldiers were moving forward, the civilians were on top of roofs and peering out of windows watching the paratroopers move in to take the gun position."

Meanwhile in the Pulles residence above the bakery shop, Coby, the fiancée of Bert Pulles, was distracted from her chores. Pulles added to his account: "Coby was all excited because while I was gone she had been cleaning upstairs, making up beds, etc. She had noticed two Germans, armed with rifles, coming down the street while we were behind the houses. She saw some paratroopers in the Runstraat and gestured to them that something was amiss. They hid in some doorways and when the Germans turned the corner they were captured and disarmed. They left the rifles leaning against the corner grocery store. Later, the grocer came out and I saw him sneaking the rifles into his store. (He probably has them still as souvenirs.)"

Sgt. John H. Taylor remembered that the 2nd Platoon moved to the left flank on the double, past the Philips factory and residential area. "Lt. Russell Hall took the 1st squad, moved between houses and through back yards. We came up behind a row of houses. Lt. Hall said, 'We'll get out across the street so we can get a better view.'

"Sherwood, me, Grodowski, Borden and Shrout went between houses with a wooden gate which was head high. I hesitated a moment. I looked up and saw a woman in a window on the second floor of a house waving her arms. Just then I saw the feet of two German soldiers entering a gate. We jumped out in the street and challenged them and grabbed them—two very surprised Krauts. They didn't seem to know we were in the vicinity. We pulled them inside. We noticed that the street curved— couldn't see around the corner. We crossed the street. It wasn't wide. It ran into a T-corner. As I got half way out into the street, I saw what we were looking for—the gun was about a hundred yards down the street—a big German 88, platform type."

This was probably the same gun that had been firing at 1Lt. Sandy Santasiero and his men of "I" Company earlier. The crew had earlier run for cover when Santasiero fired the .30-caliber machine gun at them from his position on the northern approach to the city.

Sgt. John Taylor continued: "The Germans saw me and Sherwood. They were cranking the gun to face our direction so they could fire down our street. I stopped and fired a whole clip from my rifle at them. I think I wounded two (verified two later).

Sherwood knelt down and fired a rifle grenade. It hit close to the gun. My empty clip did not eject from the rifle and I dived over behind a set of steps and Sherwood was behind me. The gun fired at us. It knocked the side of the house out just above our heads. When I looked down that street the muzzle looked ten feet in diameter. We couldn't see because of so much dust and debris from the explosion. Sherwood fired his grenade launcher from a high angle on a ground position like a mortar. In the meantime, Jacobs and Martin had gone down another street and our platoon and Griffin came in with mortar. They could fire that thing without a tripod, holding it between their knees. Sherwood got a grenade right in the house. Another gun opened up on the right. Sgt. George Martin could see it. The enemy machine gun fired, hitting the jacket of Martin's gun, sending a piece of shrapnel into his eye. (It was one of the few casualties we had in the operation.) We had them trapped. Gathered up a whole bunch of them pretty quick. A few of them tried to get away across a field. We ended up with 30 to 40 prisoners, quite a few wounded and killed."

Radioman Joe Hogenmiller provided his version of the battle to eradicate the two 88 gun positions. He said, "Lt. Hall called his rifle grenadiers and tommy-gunners to get forward to the head of the column. At a corner, a Dutchman stopped them and explained in English that the gun was just around the corner. Lt. Hall immediately sent his men to attack. The block between us and the gun was triangular in shape with Dutch homes on all three sides."

Hogenmiller continued: "The 2nd squad under Sgt. Charles Jacobs and 2Lt. Robert Perdue, assistant platoon leader, took the left side of the block on Woenselschestraat. The 3rd squad with Sgt. Frank Griffin, was kept in reserve position in the center of the block and the mortar was set up just a little forward. Lt. Hall, Sgt. John Taylor and I went with the 1st squad which was to move to the left and deploy between the houses of Kloosterdreef. Both assault squads took off through the backyard and then moved cautiously to the front of the houses. Not a shot was fired—the enemy seemed to have no idea of our presence.

"As the radio operator, I moved down the street keeping the company commander posted on movements of 2nd Platoon. As the 1st squad got in position, Sgt. George Martin saw a German soldier walking south on Kloosterdreef, shot at him but missed.

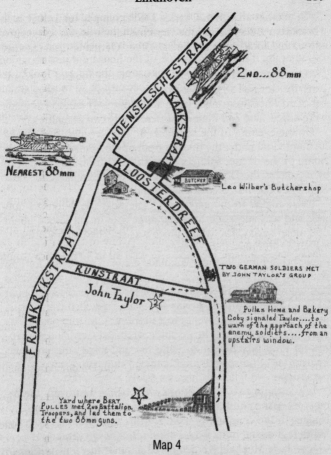

Map 4

"Lt. Hall, T/Sgt. Hugh Borden and Sgt. Taylor moved through a space between two of the buildings on Klooster, saw a Dutch woman waving at them out of a window, pointed down the street at several German soldiers walking toward the gun emplacement. Hall, Taylor and Borden jumped into the street ten feet behind them. Taylor yelled 'HALT!' and the others yelled 'Stop!' The Germans halted, offering no resistance, and were taken prisoners.

"In another area, Sgt. Charles Jacobs jumped up, rolled over a brick fence, surprised three Germans moving to an 88 gun position, and took them prisoners. Other Germans disabled that second gun.

"Due to the fast movements of the 2nd Platoon of 'F' Company, the German 88 gun positions were wiped out. A large number of prisoners were taken by 'F' Company—41 and 13 Germans were killed. The 2nd Platoon suffered only two casualties."

On the evening of the seventeenth, the Germans had placed an 88mm gun under the trees in front of the home of Mr. Evers. Some of the enemy soldiers were still wet from having had to swim across the Dommel River or the Wilhelmina Canal near Son. They had retreated south to Eindhoven.

Evers added to his narration: "The next day I looked outside and was surprised to see another gun in our street, about 150 meters away. The whole place was crowded with Germans. About 1130 hours the German commander asked whether we could bring him some tea. We made a cup of ersatz tea for him and, just when we brought it to the door, an explosion sounded and many Germans fled into our house. This was the beginning of the American attack. It was a grenade launched from a rifle and it exploded some twenty feet in front of the gun which was in front of our house. I heard some wounded Germans screaming for help. Machine guns, rifle fire and those rifle grenades made a lot of noise and, after some 15 minutes, I saw my first paratrooper—a fellow as big as a tree!"

While these two 88 positions were being destroyed, the remainder of the 2nd Battalion kept moving downtown toward the bridges in the central city area. By this time, before noon, the 506th regimental units were holding Eindhoven center.

Sgt. Jack MacLean remembered another incident farther in town. He wrote: "Our surgeon, Jackson Neavles, was trying to get the large double doors of a church open so we could set up an aid station as we had a lot of wounded men. He was pounding on the doors but getting no response from inside. I said, 'Let me open that damn door.' I put three .45 slugs in it but it didn't budge. I remembered they used a sturdy bar across those double doors. I said I'd get something that would knock them open. About that time another trooper approached me and told me how sacrilegious it was to fire on the church. I reminded him that the Germans were using them as OPs and snipers were also using the steeples to fire at us. I sent for a bazooka because I knew damn well we'd get in with that. By the time the bazooka arrived the little priest opened the door from the inside. He was complaining to the people around about the bullets that were zinging around his head as he neared the door."

In the meantime, Major General Taylor, using the facilities of the raft-ferry operated by the engineers, had driven down from Son to get a firsthand look at the progress of the 506th Regiment. While conversing with Colonel Sink, LTC Charles Chase relayed the information that 2nd Battalion troops had control of all four bridges over the Dommel River.

There were still small pockets of enemy soldiers who had been bypassed as the troops swept around the left flank of the 3rd Battalion troops. Several Dutch residents remember such incidents that occurred near their homes.

The family of underground member Jan Hurks had finished digging and covering a hasty air-raid shelter at 0600 hours on the eighteenth. The father sensed that there would be an attack toward Eindhoven from the Son drop zone before long. Jan Hurks wrote: "At 0900 hours, the Americans started to attack. They approached the Germans via a little ditch without them noticing it. The Germans were very surprised. After five or ten minutes the shooting stopped. Suddenly, two Germans walked toward our shelter and ordered us out. 'Raus!' Later, I saw them lying dead in the shelter. We ran quickly into the house. We all sought shelter under the kitchen table, since everything was trembling because of the gun the Germans had put 300 meters from our house last night. We were waiting in our house and at about 1000 hours it became very quiet. I crawled outside and, while crawling, I spotted two brown boots with laces, and a uniform all covered with dirt and branches. The soldier pointed a weapon at me and shouted, 'Hands up!' He then noticed my underground armband and asked me whether there were any Germans in our house. Actually I didn't know and said so. They searched the house but didn't find anyone. Then some 50 to 60 paratroopers showed up and paused in our yard. They had to wait for the British tankers."

Hurks continued: "When our neighbor saw the Americans in our yard he said there were still some Germans in his barn. In a split second all paratroopers jumped up and fixed their bayonets. All very quickly and disciplined—which impressed me a lot. One volunteered to see where they were. He fired his weapon to get some response but because there was dirt in the barrel, it blew up in his face. His comrades destroyed the gun out of anger. One of them, a dark complexioned soldier, stepped right over to our neighbor's barn and found the Germans. They were probably SS since they weren't wearing any uniform jackets so they couldn't be identified as such. Very harshly, the dark soldier led them away. About 1100 hours we heard the sound of Bren carriers. The paratroopers were very excited and started waving a bright colored flag. Those first British soldiers said the Americans had to join them in clearing the Woenselschestraat of Germans. They shot at everything that moved and a good friend of mine was killed by accident."

Two brothers, one thirteen and the other eleven, remembered the capture of a group of enemy soldiers in the early afternoon when most of the fighting had swept by.

Johan Vervoort, the elder, remembered, "A Dutchman informed an American that there were ten German soldiers in a shed nearby. The Americans were resting on the side of the Frankrystraat and with quick signs with his hands, the American in charge collected seven soldiers to get the Germans. We followed them since we knew something was going to happen. They started shooting at the shed and the Germans showed a white flag. They surrendered without a fight. They probably hid in the shed to be captured by Americans instead of by Dutch resistance fighters. Nevertheless, they were escorted away by the Dutch with their hands on their necks."

The younger brother, Jan, remembered, "When the American was informed of the presence of enemy soldiers in a building by the Dutchmen he said, 'Dammit.' They started to surround the Germans, one group attacking from the Hamsterstraat and one group attacking them from the back through the cemetery near Boschdijk Street. It took the Germans about 20 minutes to make up their minds."[62]

62. Material of Jan Hurks and the Vervoort brothers was translated by Peter Hendrikx.

244-Son

The fighting had not reached the heart of Eindhoven at 1130 hours when Joke van Hapert-Lathouwers received a call from her sister that set off a chain of events, as noted in her diary:

> Sept. 18—1130 hours—My sister, Gon, phoned me (illegal connection). She did Red Cross service work in the hospital. "Can't you go to the office" she said, "and have a look to see if you can put the troops in the north in touch with those in the south?" She was the leader. I always felt like that. "You saw what was going on in the air and here I can hear the guns in the south." Eindhoven was not yet completely liberated, but this was an order. I went to the telephone exchange in the middle of town.

"I remember the strange feeling on my way to the office," recalled Joke van Hapert-Lathouwers. "I felt a bit as if everyone was behind curtains, waiting for what? There was no one to be seen. The front door of the office was locked but on the left there was a grating which you could lift up and you could enter an air raid shelter. From the inside of the shelter, another door led to the exchange. I used this route to get into the office. This door was open. I kept listening for the ticking of a clock, thinking the exchange had been set to blow up. I heard nothing.

"I hardly knew where to start. I picked away all those lights going on and out. Then it was quiet. But not for long, because the St. Oedenrode line began ringing. I listened in and didn't expect to hear a real American saying, 'This is an Anglo-American line!' I nearly fell from my chair. After five years of war, I was used to the German language and now I wanted to tell that real American what my mission was but he did not understand me. I could not find the English words to express myself. I asked him to wait a minute. I took a little piece of paper and wrote on it in my simple English that I should try to put him through to the troops in the south of Eindhoven. When I had this all on paper, the real American was gone and the Oedenrode line did not respond to my ringing.

"At that moment the only thing I knew was there were Americans in St. Oedenrode so I could try to ring a number in a place nearby. Thinking of the direction of the gliders, I chose the village of Son, just above Eindhoven. I rang the number of the police, because on D-Day all policemen friendly to the Germans had fled. The telephone number was 244-Son. At once, I got an American officer and I told him what I had tried to tell the American in St. Oedenrode and asked him to wait near that 244 apparatus so I could ring him back.

"Between the north and south I did something else. It dawned on me that the exchange was intact and that it might be important to keep it like that. I phoned the illegal number of the underground and asked Peter Zuid (code name) to send some people to guard the entrances and exits of the building. Therefore, I had to open one of the exit doors so they could come in. Within a quarter hour they were there with arms under their capes.

"Then I concentrated my thoughts on that number in the south and asked myself who I could ring there. I decided to start just outside Eindhoven in the village of Aalst on the way to Valkenswaard. I thought of a family doctor, Doctor Wachters. He was well known and was reliable and was known for doing jobs for the underground movement.

"The doctor was surprised when he answered my ring. He tried for days but got no reply because there was only German military communications possible. The doctor wanted to speak to his mother, who was a bit ill. Would I try to contact her? I said I was sitting there with a mission and when I finished my task I would try to put him in touch with his mother. He asked me if there was anything he could do for me. I asked if he had seen any troop movement in Aalst. He said, 'No, but in front of my door are two peculiar little tanks. I see the helmets and they are English.' (They were really armored personnel carriers.) I asked the doctor if it would be dangerous for him to go outside and ask somebody from that little tank to come to the phone. 'No, I have a Red Cross band on my arm, will you wait a minute?!'

"After a few minutes, I had somebody from that little tank on the phone and put him through to the 244-Son number where my officer was still waiting. The call lasted four minutes. The carriers went back to Valkenswaard and told their headquarters that the telephone number of the 101st Airborne Division was 244-Son. Son was automatic traffic for Eindhoven, but in those hours it did not work. Only the telephone office could dial those numbers.

"That afternoon I got several calls from Son to Valkenswaard and from Valkenswaard to Son. At half past three the chief operator entered the phone room. She told me that the first liberators were in Eindhoven. I was relieved of my duties and on my way home I met the first American paratroopers dressed in overalls. I remember in nearly every pocket a little bottle (really hand grenades), I think for drinking fear away. They were very kind. We talked for a few minutes and on one of the last service orders of the Germans in our office, which I took away for my diary, I asked for autographs."

One of the paratroopers who wrote his signature for Joke van Hapert-Lathouwers was T/5 Lowell E. "Tim" Whitesel, who happened to be using a different mode of transportation and another route into Holland than most of the other men of his regiment.

Because the S-1 Section (personnel) had suffered grievous losses in Normandy, Col. Howard R. Johnson, commander of the 501st Parachute Infantry Regiment, had insisted that the revamped section travel to Holland via the seaborne route rather than by parachute or glider. One of those men was T/5 Lowell Whitesel. He wrote: "We went in seaborne and up to Brussels where we joined with General Dempsey's Armored Division of the British 2nd Army.

"We followed them into Eindhoven. I remember meeting a young girl on the outskirts of Eindhoven. She gave me a picture and taught me how to say 'I love you' in Dutch."

Several residents of Eindhoven remember their first impressions of the airborne troops as they arrived in the city.

Mrs. Maria Leyts was a fourteen-year-old in 1944. She wrote: "I lived in the Kerkstraat, next to the twin-towered Catarina church. We saw some big Americans coming from the Ten Hagestraat, wearing those strange uniforms with pockets all over, and with boots that had laces and buckles. We were cheering but they kept staring up at the towers of the church looking for Germans. We told them there weren't any in the church. We talked to them later and they gave me my first cigarette."

Willy F. J. van Ooyen was a five-year-old who has memories of the war that have been refreshed by his mother. He remembers: "One soldier handed his rifle to his mate and lifted me up. He was very kind to me. I remember he was unshaven and the strings of his helmet were loose."

A fourteen-year-old, Gerard van Boeckel, had an eye for small details and even with an occasion as monumental as the liberation of a city, he still remembers the appearances of the paratroopers, their equipment, and the little gifts they gave to the youngsters of Eindhoven. He hasn't forgotten. Van Boeckel wrote: "At 1130 on the 18th, our neighbor shouted to us, 'There are our friends to liberate us!' We all ran down the street near the church. We saw paras coming along both sides of the street, man after man. The first we realized was that we didn't hear them as they walked toward us with their rubber-soled boots. We were used to the German noises with the steel cleated boots. There was not much difference between a colonel and a sergeant. They all looked the same."

Celebration

Soldiers and civilians recalled the wild celebrations that went on in the afternoon when the last enemy soldiers surrendered.

"The reception by the Dutch people in Eindhoven was fantastic!" wrote Sgt. Hugh Pritchard. "They would have given us anything they had, and it was difficult to set up effective defenses with the friendly populace thronging all around. I will never forget Eindhoven."

The most vivid memory of the Market-Garden operation for Cpl. Richard F. Turner was witnessing the crowd in Holland on the day liberation came to them. "On D plus 1 when Eindhoven was liberated, its inhabitants were crowding around asking for autographs and offering weak beer and thin ham sandwiches to show their appreciation. The looks on their faces made the whole operation worthwhile."

Capt. Robert F. Harwick[63] wrote: "By early afternoon, the city was ours and we truly entered as conquerors and liberators. Those receptions are a thing to beggar description. If you can imagine all the spectators at an inaugural parade to suddenly swarm into, under and over the ranks—carrying fruit, pitchers of beer, sandwiches of dark bread or just waving Dutch flags or bits of orange cloth or just running, trying to touch you, every-

63. From a letter Capt. Robert F. Harwick wrote to Red Cross worker Helen Briggs from the Holland battlefields on October 4, 1944.

one happily yelling at the tops of their lungs, begging for a souvenir—the flag armband, the eagle insignia, a bar or badge or anything.

"Formations became impossible. Officers tried to keep the men in line. We still expected trouble. But men were literally pulled into homes to be fed or just talked to."

Gerard van Boeckel added to his story: "We gave the Americans tomatoes (the only produce available in the stores). They liked them. That day was like a dream. I got a K-ration with lemonade, biscuits, cigarettes (Camel, Philip Morris, Lucky Strikes), chewing gum, stew and corned beef. We got scarves made from green parachute nylon, which they were wearing around their necks. We got U.S.A. flags worn on their upper arms."

A few hours later the celebration developed a new vigor with the arrival of the British tanks, armored cars and the accompanying truck convoys. The streets were jammed with dancers. Festivities went on for hours.

Peter v.d. Heyden remembered, "The Americans were very friendly and gave us chocolate and chewing gum, also some biscuits we had never tasted before. They were delicious. They gave parachute silk to the girls, who used it for scarves. They gave so many things away that hardly anything was left for themselves."

Mrs. C. Boonman-Lammers was twenty-four years old at the time. She remembered: "I shook hands with them and rode on the tops of some of the tanks. We couldn't give them anything but love and kisses. My family had a fruit orchard and we picked all the fruits we could get and gave it to the boys, who were very tired."[64]

Willy van Ooyen remembered, "During the celebration a soldier was dancing with a girl from the Kip family when a shell exploded. The soldier, the girl and a man were wounded. Doctor Jansen treated the soldier first because he was the most important. The people fled to their houses."

First Lieutenant William C. Kennedy of "A" Company remembered entering the city at about 1630 as part of the 1st Battalion,

---

64. Mrs. C. Boonman-Lammers and her husband have tended the grave of 1Lt. Fred Gibbs all these years since the war.

which was in reserve at the time. He wrote: "We spent the night of the 18th with 2nd and 3rd Platoons quartered in a hotel."

Many of the citizens sent pictures of teenage boys and girls posed with American soldiers, some with their first cigarettes held delicately between fingers.

The war was still on. Officers tried valiantly to get their men out of the homes and back under military command. Capt. Robert F. Harwick, in his letter to Helen Briggs, explains what it took to get a semblance of order and then described that the liberation hadn't been without cost to his men and fellow officers. "It finally took a rumor of approaching tanks to thin the crowd enough to reach our objective in the town center. We took over the Cammandetur's old HQ and settled for a bit. Far from the end of our adventures! But the censor says 14 days before talking about combat.

"At this point, Kiley, Bolte and Gibbs have sent their best as do many men of Bolte's platoon. Kelly and Farnham are 'hurtin from workin' but want to be remembered."[65]

False Alarm

The troops were finally moved into strategic positions about the city. The civilian population was told to leave so the men could rest. Action wasn't long in coming.

T/5 Eugene E. Johnson of "H" Company wrote: "I remember after the celebrations we were sent to a schoolyard where we dug in for the night. The people were still coming down there and the officers and non-coms made them leave. We set up guards for the night. About 0300 hours in the morning, Sgt. Ralph Bennett came running around yelling, 'Get up, Get up!, We're gonna leave!' and the guys yelled, 'Oh, no!' but he finally got us going. We made a forced march through the city. They marched us out to an airfield to a runway and we stretched out when they told us to take a break. We were still carrying all of our heavy equipment from the drop zone. We set up a defensive line facing to the west."

"S-2 said there was an enemy counterattack coming from out

---

65. Harwick is trying to convey the information that the first men listed have been killed but censorship won't permit passage of the information at this time. Kelly and Farnham have been wounded.

of the west near the airport and that's why we were up there," said PFC James G. McCann.

The situation was the same for "G" Company. PFC James H. Martin wrote: "2nd Platoon under Lt. Ed Harrell marched out to an airfield to take care of a reported enemy group but that turned out to be a false alarm."

In a letter he wrote in diary form, chronicling the actions of several days, Peter v.d. Heyden described the actions of the day for the nineteenth:

> I woke up very early and went outside. British tanks were still passing through. I had never seen so many soldiers in town. The paras were still in position near the Dommel bridges on the Kanalstraat. We spent a few hours with them and learned our first English words. We also got some candy and some girls were smoking their first cigarettes. We also walked to other posts and all those paras were very friendly to us. In the late afternoon everything changed since the PAN told us to take the Dutch flags away. A German outfit threatened an attack on Eindhoven from the direction of Nuenen. The people went back to their houses.

First Battalion was sent in the direction of Nuenen in mid-morning to check out that report. First Lieutenant William C. Kennedy of "A" Company noted the action in the company log:

> About 1000 hours, the 2nd and 3rd Platoons mounted tanks (British) and went with these on reconnaissance east and west of the road connecting Eindhoven and Son.

During the afternoon of the nineteenth, 2nd Battalion was sent toward Helmond in response to a report that a large enemy tank force was getting ready for an attack on Eindhoven.

"One event that is still prominent in my memory was the movement to Helmond and back to Eindhoven during the afternoon and evening of the third day," wrote 1/Sgt. Carwood Lipton. "When we got there it was seen that we were over-extended and outgunned at Helmond so after a forced march of several hours, we were immediately marched back toward Eindhoven."

As a member of the anti-tank team for the 2nd Battalion, which amounted to no more than a few bazookas and rifle grenadiers, Sgt. Jack MacLean was near the front of the column as it marched toward Helmond. He wrote: "We were sent out to the east to a small town. We were right behind the lead unit and I remember one of the scouts came back exclaiming, 'My God, I've never seen so many tanks—the Germans have more tanks than we have people.' He described a field being full of enemy tanks. Our few bazookas weren't going to do a helluva lot of good. Word came back to us to pull back to Eindhoven and pull back real fast."

Sgt. Donald Malarkey was near the front of the column. "We joined British tanks to attack toward Helmond where major German forces were reported. The German panzers and infantry had set up a semi-circle defense, well concealed, on the west fringe of the city. The British tanks on the flanks and the 101st infantry were allowed to penetrate deep into the throat of the position before the Germans opened up. We were well in front when all hell broke loose. We had several people hit—our platoon leader, Lt. 'Buck' Compton, the worst. He took a machine gun blast through the butt as we were told to pull back to Eindhoven. Compton, who had been a guard on the UCLA football team, was too big for a couple of people to move. He wanted to be left for the Germans and told us to get the hell out of there. However, we tore a door off a Dutch farmhouse, rolled him on it, and four of us dragged him up the ditch along the road until we got him back to where we could get him on a British vehicle."

Sgt. John H. Taylor was also in on the move. He wrote: "We were drawing some machine gun fire and all of a sudden it was getting on toward dusk. We got orders to break off contact and did an about face. They brought trucks, some that looked like cattle trucks, and headed back toward Eindhoven as it was getting dark. All of a sudden, while we were moving back into the city, the Germans bombed it. They came over and dropped flares and just more or less flew at will over the city because there was little anti-aircraft fire from the British convoys. The Germans messed up the town pretty good. There were some fires."

The troops of 3rd Battalion, outposted along the runways at the airfield several miles west of Eindhoven, witnessed the bombing from a distance.

"We turned to watch as the sky lighted up over Eindhoven," wrote T/5 Eugene Johnson of "H" Company. "The bombers came over and gave the city a good going over. We turned right around and headed back all the way through town. There was much fire and the people were screaming and carrying on."

Gerard van Boeckel remembered the worst day for Eindhoven was the day after the liberation. "At 2030 hours, for an hour, 100 Junkers, 88s and Stukas bombed and strafed the whole town and the British 2nd Army convoys on their way to Arnhem. Over 200 civilians were killed. Many fires burned in town."

Ten-year-old Peter v.d. Heyden had run home when it was announced that an enemy tank force was approaching from the east. As night came, the enemy bombers appeared. He wrote in diary form the actions he witnessed:

> At 2000 hours all hell breaks loose. A bomb hits 25 meters from our house and it is a miracle we weren't hit. When the raid was over we went outside and saw the city burning. We ran to the Dommel bridge and saw dead soldiers, but we couldn't tell if they were British or Americans; it was too dark.

A girl of fourteen at the time of the liberation, Mrs. Maria Leyts lived close to the twin-towered Catarina church. On the night the city was bombed, many people were crowded into the basement of her family home. Mrs. Leyts wrote: "A bomb hit a few houses from our home but it damaged many of the surrounding ones. I was the first to be wounded. They brought me to an aid station nearby and I remember the Americans removed the mines from the road so we could cross. An American medic gave me first aid. He splinted the wounded leg and put some powder on it. He also gave me some 'powdered blood,' something we had never seen before. I had to be taken to a hospital, but I was refused admittance to the first one. I was young and had first aid already. There simply wasn't enough room. I was put on a cart and moved to another hospital where my leg was amputated the next day. I am still grateful to that American medic who gave me first aid."

Cpl. Steve Kovacs remembered the bombing. "Sgt. William R. Myers kept yelling for us to take cover when Stukas bombed us. He was out in the open with no cover."

Others killed in the attack included Sgt. Jim Davidson and PFC Robert J. Modracek.

A. J. van Hemme was twelve years old at the time a large number of paratroopers arrived near his home, which was close to the German military airport on the west side. Van Hemme wrote: "Paras were coming from the center of Eindhoven. They settled themselves in a garden in front of a farmer's house just opposite our home. I tried to visit with them but the contact was very short as they gave instructions to us to go into our homes. Perhaps they knew what was going to happen because a few minutes later German bombers started with the bombing of Eindhoven (not the part we lived in)."

One of the troopers who had been positioned near the airfield was PFC James G. McCann. After the bombing of the city, his group was sent quickly back to the bomb-ravaged areas. He wrote: "All of a sudden the Dutch people weren't so friendly anymore. They felt we had inside information that the bombing raid was coming and they thought we had moved out from the city to save our own necks without letting the civilians know so they could have moved out of danger. Members of the Dutch underground who were with us on our mission explained to them why we had been sent out there. The good feeling of friendship came back."

After returning to the city, PFC James H. Martin and his group got a dubious assignment. "We spent the next morning removing dud bombs from streets and buildings and dumping them in several canals. I shudder when I think how foolhardy that was."

The next few days the troops were sent off in many directions in anticipation of reported enemy moves. With support being provided by British armored units, the paratroopers had little difficulty in turning back potential threats.

A Possible Surrender

A few miles northwest of Eindhoven, the 502nd Parachute Infantry Regiment had been involved in a bitter and costly battle with an enemy force of approximately twenty-five hundred men. What had begun as a platoon mission to seize the highway bridge near Best, as a secondary objective in case the Son bridge was destroyed and unusable, had then become a fight involving 2nd and 3rd Battalions of the 502nd and two battalions of the 327th Glider Infantry Regiment before a decision was reached. Not until support armor arrived on the nineteenth had the 502nd been able to roll back the enemy from his positions on the north side of the canal. The highway span had been blown the day before as was the rail bridge a few hundred yards farther west.

On the twentieth, the 502nd moved from its defensive positions along the canal and moved north to St. Oedenrode where it set up a protective screen for the crucial Eindhoven-to-Nijmegen highway. Their positions were filled by 2nd and 3rd Battalions of the 327th, which maintained a defensive position near Best.

A report was received on the afternoon of September 20 by the S-2 Section of the 506th Parachute Infantry Regiment that with some persuasion it might be possible to get the defenders of Best to surrender. The information had been received from Dutch resistance members who had reports from enemy wounded that their comrades wished to surrender. During the afternoon of D plus 3, Capt. Richard Meason, Capt. Samuel "Shifty" Feiler, and a member of the Dutch underground were permitted to cross the damaged bridge over the Wilhelmina Canal south of Best. Blindfolded, the three men were led some five hundred yards toward the town to an enemy CP where they explained their mission to the German commander. Surrender was out of the question even though over a thousand prisoners had been taken in the area the day before. The three men were returned to the bridge with blindfolds once more in place. Their German escort guards had hoped a surrender could have been negotiated. They were downcast when their commander rejected the offer. The threesome recrossed the bridge, joined the rest of their party, and returned to Eindhoven in the late evening.

The 506th Unit After-Action Report for the twentieth provides a brief description of the action:

> During the day a report was received that 2,000 Germans wished to surrender in Best. Captain Meason and Captain Feiler went over and talked to the commandant but he would not surrender.[66]

Another attempt was made the following day because the Dutch still insisted that the Germans would surrender at Best, and possibly a show of force would convince them.

> September 21—During the day one platoon of "I" Company was sent to Best to try and get the German garrison to surrender, but again the Germans refused to capitulate.[67]

66. From 506th Unit After-Action Report dated December 10, 1944.
67. Ibid.

The assignment to make the second attempt to convince the Best defenders to surrender went to 1Lt. Charles Santasiero and his 2nd Platoon from "I" Company. He related: "The following day a runner came and said that the colonel (Sink) wanted to see me. When I arrived at the CP, the colonel introduced me to a Dutchman from the town of Best. The colonel said, 'Charlie, the town of Best is out of our sector. This man claims that the Krauts want to surrender. I have a truck and four 81mm mortars for you to use. The Dutchman will guide you to the blown-out bridge. The Dutchman will leave you at this point. He will not go with you. You will conceal your men, remove your sidearms, contact the "hostiles," give them two hours to surrender. If they do not respond, shoot the hell out of them.' (The Dutchman said around two thousand Krauts were in Best.) We arrived at the bridge. The Dutchman took off like a rabbit. My men made me a white flag. I started to cross the twisted steel with one eye on the canal, ready to dive in if fired on. While crossing, I saw a foxhole on the other side—no sign of life. I crawled up to the hole and hollered 'Achtung!' Two Krauts jumped up, smiled and dropped their rifles.

"I asked to see the officer in charge. Before they could act, an officer came up and proceeded to chew ass for not giving the alarm. I was blind-folded and, with a Kraut under each arm, was led away. We reached the CP. They did not remove my blindfold. I stated my case and the officer 'went on a fishing trip.' He wanted first to trade wounded paratroopers for Germans. He wanted written terms from our general and the clincher of them all was—he would surrender all of his command if he was allowed to join our forces and fight on our side to repel the Russians. I gave a negative answer, was escorted back to the bridge, blindfold removed. The officer asked for American cigarettes. We saluted and I returned to my men."

Assistant platoon leader 2Lt. Donald E. Replogle remembered the incident this way: "I remember going with the group with the white flag along the right side of the shoe factory. We walked up the railroad tracks. Then it was my job to go in the shoe factory with some of the platoon. We could see the Germans and the troops with the flag did not surprise them."

PFC Wilbur Fishel was part of the platoon. He remembered: "We walked up there along the railroad tracks in the morning to a footbridge with a white flag. Some Germans came over there to talk to them. In the meantime, we were lying beside the tracks and they were not gone long. They told us it was 'no go' and they went up into the shoe factory which was to our left—it was a two story building."

"They sent the 2nd Platoon of 'I' Company to see if a large German force would surrender," wrote Sgt. James Shuler, in charge of the mortar squad. "The Dutch underground believed a little show of force would do the trick. 1Lt. Santasiero went over the bridge with a white flag but the Germans would not surrender without some very lenient conditions, which the lieutenant had no authority to grant. We moved into position at a shoe factory across the canal from the Germans. As the enemy was making no effort to conceal themselves, the lieutenant decided to place mortar fire on them. We set up the mortar behind a brick wall. I wasn't in a position to observe, so Lt. Santasiero directed fire from the 2nd floor of the shoe factory."

Santasiero continued his story: "I placed the men in defensive positions in front of the factory, the mortars in the rear and Lt. Don Replogle and I went up to the 2nd floor to observe. We had a window facing Best. This was our observation post. I glassed the area—in front was flat land with cover in the Krauts' sector. Two hundred yards further was a building and off to the side were about a company of men gathered around a cooking fire. I said to Replogle to take a look, and said, 'I hope they remain that way until the truce is up.' I passed the information to Shuler, told him to zero in with the center gun only on my command. Time was up. We saw no sign of surrender, ordered Shuler to fire one round. The range was perfect, but far to the left. When the Krauts saw the explosion they turned, believing it was a dud, went back to cooking. I made a correction and said, 'Fire two rounds per gun, for effect.' I heard the 'wump' of the mortars going airborne, thinking they would never come down, when the first one hit the 'frying pan.' When the smoke cleared I saw only one German crawling."

PFC Wilbur Fishel added, "Santasiero was up on the 2nd floor with binoculars and told Shuler to set the mortars. The shot hit right in the midst of the men sitting around the fire. Santasiero said, 'OK, give 'em a couple more.' They did and soon after that all hell broke loose."

Santasiero added, "Then a direct fire shot from an 88mm hit

above the window. I said to Replogle, 'Get your ass out of here, the next one may come through the window.'

"We found the steel (exit) door jammed. The second round hit the casing on the side of the window. With our feet against the wall, we were able to open the door. We did not wait to see where the next round landed. We changed our position behind the railroad tracks and sent more 'letters of death' to Herman. From our rear we began to get artillery fire passing over our heads. It turned out to be a Limey artillery unit moving up the road. I talked to the officer in charge, gave him the picture and requested fire on targets out of range of our 81mm mortars. He was happy to do so. He started with the church steeple and began to work over the town of Best. Sergeant Ernie Mann and his men wiped out an enemy patrol. We reported back to Colonel Sink."

From that time on, Best became the target of the British army. In the following week they suffered heavy losses trying to move in on the enemy positions, which were centered in the stone factory.

TEN

The Fight for Best

Battle for the Best Bridge

The seizure of the highway bridge connecting Eindhoven with Best and Boxtel had not been considered with any interest on the part of the British, but MG Maxwell D. Taylor and his staff thought it might be a good idea to have an alternate route over the Wilhelmina Canal should it be found that the Son bridge was unusable. Therefore the division plan called for one company from 3rd Battalion of the 502nd Parachute Infantry Regiment to move quickly south from the drop zone to the bridge, a distance of approximately one mile, to seize the bridge.

The assignment was given to Capt. Robert E. Jones and the men of his "H" Company. The initial thrust was to be done by 1Lt. Ed Wierzbowski and the men of his 2nd Platoon. Accompanying them was a section of 3rd Battalion machine gunners and 3rd Platoon of "C" Company of the 326th Engineer Battalion under the command of 1Lt. Charles W. Moore.

Captain Jones reflected on delays in getting his company off the jump field and headed toward the objective and the frustration expressed by his battalion commander as he urged the troopers forward. Habits developed over long periods of training sometimes have a way of impeding progress. Captain Jones wrote: "To illustrate the point that men will do in combat what they did in training—as we left the DZ we ran into wire fences that surrounded the fields. True to their training on maneuvers 'not to destroy civilian property' the soldiers took the time to climb over, under or through the wire fences. This went on until Lt. Colonel Robert Cole, the battalion commander, in very forceful and clear rhetoric told them to 'cut the God-damned wire and quit wasting time! This was done quickly and the column moved out much more rapidly."

A large number of the men of 3rd Battalion had been lost to the division as the result of the heavy fighting for Carentan along its approach causeway in Normandy. As the result, there were many new faces in the ranks of each of the line companies. Captain Jones added: "As we left the DZ and headed toward the town of Best, I noticed as we progressed, more and more ammunition boxes appeared on the side of the road. The day was warm. Many of the soldiers were replacements and had not been in combat before and as they got tired they started dropping off the heavy boxes of machine gun ammunition. I don't believe any ammo bearer who had been in combat would ever do this."

Captain Jones continued his story: "The leading elements of our reinforced company lost the church steeple reference point while in the woods going toward Best. They came out at a point south of the town of Best. The company was fired on. I deployed the unit. We attacked a German convoy proceeding south toward the bridge over the Wilhelmina Canal."

Communications sergeant for "H" Company Joseph L. Ludwig wrote: "We set up the CP one hundred yards off the road. Two platoons moved across the road and into the outskirts of Best. They ran into many Germans who had escaped from Antwerp and coastal areas because of Montgomery stopping to tidy up his lines. They were headed for Eindhoven to return to Germany for refurnishing and reforming. Meanwhile, 2nd Platoon and attached engineers took off for the canal bridge. We did not see them again until the battle was over."

German defenders quickly responded to the threat that this force presented to Best. As the reinforced company tried to push the enemy back to seize the crossroads its members became widely scattered. The Germans were reinforced by a twelve-truck troop convoy that arrived on the scene. As Captain Jones was adjusting his lines to meet this new threat, LTC Robert G. Cole sent a radio message ordering Jones to get the engineers, the machine gunners, and the 2nd Platoon down to the bridge immediately. Without these support groups to rely on, Jones pulled the remainder of his company back into the wooded area.

From his new defensive position, Jones ordered Wierzbowski

and his 2nd Platoon, Lt. Charles Moore with his 3rd Platoon of attached engineers, and the machine gunners to move south, keeping to the cover of the wooded area, to get to the canal bridge as quickly as possible.

First Lieutenant Charles Moore recalled, "Lt. Ed Wierzbowski and I walked side by side when we left Best. Frankly, we lost control when we were ordered to move from Best to the bridge just before dark. Moving through the dense pine trees in single file in the dark started the problem. The Germans had fire lanes covered by machine guns which continually cut the line of march. I learned later that many of the men drifted back to battalion headquarters."

The enemy gunners fired on Wierzbowski's force as they passed the open firebreaks. Wierzbowski had his men swing wider to the left to be farther away from the machine-gun fire. With first scout PFC Joe E. Mann leading the way, the small group climbed up and over the bank discovering they had come out of the woods east of the bridge.

Moving through the darkness, they felt their way along the bank until they passed a loading zone. They realized they were still a quarter mile east of the bridge. Climbing back to the sheltered side of the canal bank, the group moved slowly for an hour until Wierzbowski felt he must be close to the bridge.

Leaving the others behind, Wierzbowski and Mann once more crossed to the canal side of the bank. This time they had crawled too far. A change of guard was taking place during their move and they were in the path of his walking beat. Any move to attack him would alert the sentry on the outpost on the far side of the bridge. The men couldn't move.

The remainder of the force waiting behind the bank wondered what was going on. Nothing was happening.

Suddenly, without warning, grenades were thrown toward them from the far side of the canal. Those men who were on the canal side of the bank began scrambling for the shelter of the leeward side. The sudden fire caused a stampede of a number of the men. They broke for the woods. Others began digging in on the sheltered side of the bank. A light rain began to fall.

First Lieutenant Moore added to his story: "We got to within fifty yards of the bridge. The bridge guards started firing. I withdrew over the top of the canal bank to find some cover.

"Nothing much happened during the night due to the darkness and rain. Sgt. Bob Likam, four of our men, and myself, started back toward Captain Jones and the rest of his company as we couldn't locate the rest of the platoon. 'H' Company had pulled back and we ended up in the middle of a two-pronged attack by the Germans who were attacking toward the bridge."

Capt. Robert Jones of "H" Company sent out three patrols to look for First Lieutenant Wierzbowski and his platoon. All three were stopped by enemy fire. In the meantime "H" Company took thirty-nine casualties the first night, most coming from artillery and mortar fire.

3rd Battalion Moves Up

When the first reports of the difficulties of "H" Company reached him, LTC John Michaelis, the regimental commander, realized Best would take more men than the original plan had called for in the planning stages. The fact that the highway and railroad bridges were still intact made the effort worthwhile now that the Son bridge had been blown.

After "H" Company had left hurriedly for Best, the remainder of 3rd Battalion had been busy securing the drop zone area and getting a feel for Holland.

T/5 John E. Fitzgerald served as runner for the battalion commander, LTC Robert G. Cole. His recollections included: "On the first day it looked like a picnic. Dutch civilians on bicycles and on foot were all around the landing zone. Many gave us gifts of flowers, apples and other fruits. Later in the evening, we ate a home-cooked meal prepared for the headquarters group by one of the Dutch families."

A replacement, Pvt. James W. Noreene, arrived on the 101st scene in August. He had never seen gliders land before his jump into Holland. The gliders arrived about a half hour after the last paratroopers were dropped. He wrote: "One aspect will stay with me forever and that is the terrible destruction of the gliders as they tried to land. I had never seen gliders land before and, after seeing so many crash landings, I was certainly glad to have come in by parachute. Gliders ran into bushes, trees, barns and haystacks and men and materials were strewn about and crumbled on the landing zone."

Noreene continued: "There was one event that I witnessed that turned out to be very interesting. That was the uncovering of an automobile which had been hidden under a large pile of hay inside of a farmer's barn. This farm was somewhere southwest of our drop zone. Someone in the group of battalion HQ men understood some Dutch—at least enough to find out that this farmer had driven the auto into the barn and piled hay over it at the time of the German invasion of his country. There the auto had remained through the years, right under the noses of the German occupation forces (the auto being put up on blocks) waiting for the day liberation would come to the Dutch."

When the order to move out had been given by Lieutenant Colonel Cole, 1Lt. Raymond I. Brock of the Mortar Platoon was still busy gathering his equipment off the drop fields. He wrote: "Some of the men commandeered a Dutchman with a cart and horse. They loaded the mortars and ammo on the cart and were paralleling the battalion on a road when battalion took off in a different direction. I had to high tail it to catch the equipment at dusk with Colonel Cole giving me hell for allowing this to happen. I located the cart at a farmhouse. I took those men and a few stragglers, a couple of wounded men on a short cut to the battalion destination and got there 45 minutes before they arrived. I was afraid battalion had changed its plans. It was dark as hell."

PFC Harry F. Johnson verified that story. "On our way to our positions, we came upon some Dutch farmers with horses and carts. We put our mortars on the cart. Before reaching our destination, we went one way and horse and cart went another. We were able to find them before the battle commenced."

T/5 John Fitzgerald described the battalion trip toward Best as follows: "We were marching in column formation when we came under fire from a group of Germans. A flare went off and everyone hit the ground. Fortunately for us, the Germans did not realize they had a whole battalion spread out on an exposed dike and the firing soon stopped. It was the first indication of things to come."

Fitzgerald added: "We arrived in a wooded area near Best at dawn and established our command post."

In the meantime, "H" Company was dug into the soft loam soil of the pine forest near Best. Sgt. Joe Ludwig closed the comments for the first day. "All that day and during the night we were getting the hell shot out of us."

Radio contact was the only link "H" Company had with its battalion until after first light the next morning.

2nd Battalion in Reserve

The 2nd Battalion was to be division reserve on D-Day and could be rushed to Son and Eindhoven if the need arose during the first day.

In a log he maintained for his company in Holland, Cpl. Pete Santini described the first-day events as he witnessed them:

> It took about an hour for the bulk of the battalion to assemble at their designated areas.
>
> We learned that four of our men had not left the planes. S/Sgt. George Boever had been wounded in the back and chest by flak. Sgt. Albert Bell and Pvt. Lawrence Brewer had also been wounded. Another man failed to jump because his main chute had broken open.
>
> The battalion moved to the vicinity of Son. The CP was set up in some woods. The machine gun platoon was split up. One section went with "Dog" Company and one with "Fox" Company. The mortar platoon was dispersed in the same area with the CP.

While 2nd Battalion was moving toward Son to be used as a backup force if needed by the 506th Parachute Infantry Regiment, one group of men was sent on a special assignment.

First Lieutenant James W. Tolar had jumped into Normandy with one of his squads to serve as security for a pathfinder team. He had another assignment in Holland. He wrote: "With my platoon of 42 men, overloaded with equipment, we hiked eight or ten miles to a bridge east of Son on the Wilhelmina Canal.[68] Our job was to observe, report on traffic and then disrupt it. It was very uneventful. Not a shot was fired by us. A heavy gun fired a few rounds. It was south of the canal. The most significant fact was that I knew we were being observed. The patrol spent the night in the area and returned to the battalion the next afternoon."

There was little or no combat action the first night for the men of 2nd Battalion. Guard duty was an annoyance but necessary for the security of units. PFC Emmert O. Parmley of "Fox" Company had this recollection of a distasteful assignment: "That night about midnight, 1Lt. Nick Schiltz awakened me. I said, 'What's up? Where are they?' He said, 'Time to check the outposts.' I could hardly believe what I heard. I did not relish the

68. The bridge was most likely the one at Gerven.

thought of wandering around in the middle of the night to see if anyone on guard was asleep. My first thought was that I don't know if I was going to like the new job as runner. I remembered the first night in France when I had shot at one of our own 'F' Company men, a medic by the name of Logeson. He did not respond to my challenge but kept coming toward me. I later asked him why. He said, 'I did not think you were calling to me as I was behind the lines.' To those on outposts there are no front lines. I have always been thankful I was such a lousy shot as it was Logeson who came to me and got me on my feet and to safety when I was hit in Normandy. I speak with pride and warm feeling toward Logeson, also of the other troopers I served with."

The men of "Fox" Company had moved into woods south of Wolfswinkel and set up a perimeter defense for the night. It had sent out a patrol to contact the 506th Regiment. This had been done and the patrol had returned before nightfall.

Contact with the 501st

The regiments always maintained contact with neighboring units by patrols. As mentioned in the previous paragraph, the "Fox" Company patrol had gone to Son to report in to the 506th Regiment and then returned to Wolfswinkel. Shortly after landing, the 502nd sent an S-2 patrol north to Veghel to establish contact with the 501st. This patrol was led by S-2 officer 1Lt. Sidney Clary and included PFC Robert Paczulla, PFC Richard M. Ladd, and two others.

PFC Richard Ladd wrote: "The S-2 section briefly assembled behind a small Dutch house which served as the temporary 502nd CP or collecting point near the main north–south road and the dirt road that went through the drop zone toward Best. 1Lt. Sidney Clary and four of us immediately left for Veghel. We passed through the 1st Battalion of the 502nd marching from the DZ to St. Oedenrode. We turned right just outside (south of) St. Oedenrode, skirted it and crossed the Dommel River and headed cross-country for about two hours. We came out on the main highway ¾ths of a mile south of Veghel. This trek or patrol was uneventful due to the 501st having things well in hand at Veghel. We reported to the 501st command post.

"We stayed in Veghel until dark and got a ride back down the highway on a farm truck with three or four Dutch underground members. We could only go half way due to several large trees felled across the highway. On the other side of the trees, we got a ride on a jeep in the rain almost to Son. Lt. Clary reported in to the 502nd CP but I am not sure just where as I don't recall seeing it in the dark near Wolfswinkel."

The Fight for Best on the Eighteenth

As dawn broke, Capt. Robert E. Jones of "H" Company still was out of communication with 1Lt. Ed Wierzbowski's 2nd Platoon. Third Battalion was still out of touch with "H" Company. Third Battalion had moved southwest during the night to reinforce the efforts of "H" Company, which was sensing more and more as each hour passed that it was outmanned and outgunned.

On the morning of the eighteenth, just as day was breaking, First Lieutenant Wierzbowski was in a position to observe the bridge over the Wilhelmina Canal. It was a single span over one hundred feet long. He noted barracks south of the canal and only twenty yards from the bridge with dug-in positions. Many soldiers could be seen in and around the positions. The Americans drew fire every time they raised their heads from enemy gunners on both sides of the span.

During the day, Wierzbowski's men shot up a bunch of stragglers who retreated past their positions. They had been pushed back by the troops of 2nd Battalion.

As he observed the proceedings, Wierzbowski noted a civilian and a soldier standing on the bridge. A short time later, the bridge went up in a tremendous explosion showering the countryside with bits of concrete and steel. He was in no position to notify division that the sought-for prize was no longer there for the taking.

PFC Joe Mann and Hoyle saw an 88mm ammunition and storage dump located about a hundred yards from their position. They sneaked up to a more advantageous position and destroyed it with two bazooka rounds. They shot six enemy soldiers who approached their advance position. In the firefight, Mann was hit twice by rifle bullets.

A little later the P-47s made a strafing pass that included the positions of Wierzbowski's platoon. They were not hurt by it.

Engineer Lt. James R. Watson sneaked forward to take a

closer look and was hit in the midsection. Medic PFC James Oravec crawled out to give him first aid. Wierzbowski then dragged Watson back 150 yards to the shelter of the large hole. Pvt. Onroe Luther and PFC Jacob Northrup were hit, both succumbing to their wounds. Mann was hit twice more, requiring both arms to be placed in slings. When Wierzbowski gave orders to have him evacuated to a safer foxhole, Mann pleaded to remain with the others.

First Lieutenant Otto Laier and Sgt. Thomas Betras of the engineers made a break to seek medical supplies for the group. As they moved back in the general direction of the 502nd troops, they were ambushed by enemy soldiers. Both were wounded but Betras eluded capture and returned to the 2nd Platoon positions near the bridge.

A British recon car arrived on the other side of the canal. It was fired on by the bridge defenders and moved to shelter behind a nearby building. From there its occupants fired automatic weapons at the Germans. The German garrison pulled out.

Cpl. Danny Corman of "H" Company found a small rowboat and crossed the canal to converse with the British. He came back with a medical kit. Wierzbowski then moved down to the edge of the canal and yelled across to them asking that they call division and request relief. The effort to reach division by radio failed. However, the British assured Wierzbowski that help would come soon—"Just stay put!"

About the same time Pvts. Lawrence Koller and Anthony Waldt and T/5 Vincent Laino prowled down to the derricks and came back with three German medics and a wounded enemy officer. The medics were put to work on the numerous wounded. The wounded were in desperate need of plasma and, due to its lack, several died.

Laino, a machine gunner from the engineers, manned a light .30-caliber machine gun near the bridge position and accounted for seven of the enemy and destroyed a German ammunition truck shortly after the bridge blew up. Later, as another enemy force approached the position, he accounted for twenty more of the enemy.

A fellow member of his platoon, Sgt. Adam Slusher, stated, "He was just great with that gun. We credited him with gunning down 75 of the enemy during the period."

The 502nd regimental after-action report described the gravity of the situation on the morning of the eighteenth:[69]

Action began at about 0520, on the 18th of September, when the enemy opened fire with automatic weapons on the battalions' positions on the front and left flank. It became heavier through the day, with artillery and mortar fire supporting and augmenting the fire of small arms and 20mm AA gun fire. This heavy fire kept up throughout the day, with the enemy seeming to fire in an area rather than at separate targets. In the morning, the enemy made two determined attacks supported by heavy artillery and mortar concentrations. These were repulsed with heavy losses to the enemy. However, during the morning, many casualties were caused by infiltrating enemy and the heavy concentration of fire poured into the pine growths in which the battalion had taken up its position. Support weapons of the battalion were limited to two 81mm mortars and five 60mm mortars. Supply lines to the battalion were long and hazardous and vehicles were not available.

The battalion actually established the road block near the town of Best and was preparing to take the bridges when it was overrun by numerically superior enemy and heavy artillery fire, causing it to withdraw southeast, at which time the leading element asked for assistance.

Communications sergeant Joe Ludwig of "H" Company remembered the seventeenth as bad but felt the eighteenth was worse, as he described the problems of 3rd Battalion and "H" Company in particular: "The second day was worse as we still had not made contact with 3rd Battalion. The Germans must have been getting reinforcements as the artillery fire and small arms seemed to be increasing in intensity. They also had two self-propelled 40mm guns which they kept moving around and shooting at us from different areas. The Germans were infiltrating the water ditches and hand grenades were being used and we were in bad shape."

One of those soldiers who came in closer contact with the 20mm or 40mm multipurpose guns being used with such devastating effectiveness during the Best operation was PFC James C. Sherriff of "G" Company. His unit had moved up during the night so the men were not aware of what was in their near sur-

69. From Narrative of Market-Garden for 502nd Parachute Infantry Regiment sent by S/Sgt. Fred Patheiger.

roundings. Sherriff said, "As daylight came, I spotted a gun off a couple hundred yards. There were two guys on a platform loading shells into it. It had a big shield on the front of it. When it turned to fire in another direction, I'd fire at the exposed gunners. I'd get off a burst or two and the machine gun would jam because I forgot to replace the recoil booster while cleaning it the day before. A little later something hit the end of the barrel while I was cocking it, so it would fire again. It peeled the perforated jacket of the gun like a can opener had done it. It went through the tripod and into my arm. I thought the gun had kicked me with its recoil. I called to 'Jug' (Don Jurgensen), 'You have just been promoted. You are now the gunner!' I added, 'We're trading holes when things quiet down. I'll count to three and we'll switch.' On the count of 'three!' I dived into his hole and he went into mine. His was about three feet deep—great. He yelled, 'You S.O.B., you didn't dig in!' My hole was rather shallow.

"Captain Abner Blatt, surgeon for 3rd Battalion, came over to look at my wound and got hit himself. Sgt. George Tobinas helped him to the aid station. I was ambulatory so I walked over and ended up guarding prisoners in a ditch."

The paratroops had no support from artillery units, which weren't scheduled to arrive until the following day. The British would reach Eindhoven during the late afternoon of the eighteenth and were not in communication so division couldn't call for supporting fire from that quarter.

Two men of the 3rd Battalion Mortar Platoon describe some of their action as the battle raged furiously in the Best area.

Mortar Platoon leader 1Lt. Ray I. Brock was caught in an open field. "I was returning from an OP near Best when Germans opened up with heavy small arms fire. I was caught out in an open clearing with no cover. I hugged the ground and was sure I would be hit with no one around to help. Fortunately, I escaped unscathed."

PFC Harry F. Johnson remembered: "On September 18th, after we ran out of AP shells for our mortars, we began shooting phosphorus mortar ammo. The Germans were strung out amongst the cabbages in a patch and, as they were hit by the phosphorus, they were jumping up and screaming like hell. One German was running toward us, wanting to surrender (with his hands up), when he was hit by an 88mm shell which completely disintegrated him."

In desperation, the 3rd Battalion commander would call for air support to overcome some of the superiority the enemy had in artillery and rapid-fire weaponry.

T/5 John E. Fitzgerald served as runner for 3rd Battalion commander LTC Robert G. Cole. He and radioman Robert Doran had a close relationship with Lieutenant Colonel Cole and were considered favorites. He said, "On the morning of the 18th, Colonel Cole shared a can of grapefruit with T/5 Robert Doran, his radio operator, and myself. He had carried it all the way from England. This and other acts of kindness were common to his character. We began to receive increasingly heavy fire as the morning wore on. The Germans were using anti-aircraft guns to defoliate the section of woods we were occupying. Casualties were mounting all around us. Cole soon realized his only option was to call for air support."

Regimental commander LTC John Michaelis became increasingly concerned with the lack of information of the CP of Lieutenant Colonel Cole's 3rd Battalion. PFC Richard M. Ladd was part of the group sent out to locate the CP. Ladd wrote: "Around noon on Monday, the 18th, Colonel John Michaelis dispatched a five-man patrol to try and locate LTC Robert Cole's CP. (Cole was not in radio contact with regiment.) We were to ascertain if the bridge had been taken. Our five-man S-2 patrol, led by Sergeant Graham Armstrong, included Tom Walsh, Paul Todd, Russell May and myself.

"Traveling in a west-southwest direction from the DZ, we were initially in open but rough ground. After about fifteen minutes, we received several rifle shots from a 15 to 18 man patrol crossing diagonally from our right and heading toward the southwest in the direction of the Wilhelmina Canal. For what purpose that patrol was traveling in an almost opposite direction has always been a mystery to me. I recognized its leader, 1Lt. Clarence Baker, a pleasant officer I had known at Chilton-Foliat. Days later I learned that subsequent to heated words with them about our being fired upon, Lt. Baker and his patrol were decimated near the canal.

"Within a quarter mile from that exchange, our patrol entered the Zonsche Forest (like a reforestation area with numerous fire lanes). At first we thought we were being directly fired upon by

Germans, but after pressing on across each fire lane we sensed the fire was mainly the residue of German shots being directed at our 3rd Battalion immediately ahead. After changing our line of advance frequently, due to the intensity of the enemy fire, we found 3rd Battalion companies dug in the woods. Sgt. Armstrong was directed to Colonel Cole's foxhole. He was successful in gaining Cole's attention and reported that Colonel Michaelis wanted to know if the canal bridge had been taken."

Lieutenant Colonel Cole at that time was agitated because the strafing by the fighter planes was hitting his positions as well as those of the Germans. He was also upset because he had just lost his radio operator.

T/5 John Fitzgerald describes the loss of his buddy. "T/5 Robert Doran, Cole's radio operator, was killed shortly before Colonel Cole. Doran was occupying a foxhole with me. As enemy fire was extremely heavy, both Colonel Cole and I repeatedly asked him to stay down. However, this interfered with his radio reception. He repeatedly got up from the hole, completely exposing himself to enemy fire, so he could send and receive critical messages. He died in the middle of sending a message."

Responding to regimental S-2 Sgt. Graham Armstrong's query as to the status of the highway bridge south of Best, Cole had matters of more importance at the moment. PFC Richard Ladd, who had been in the company of Sergeant Armstrong, described the scene: "Undoubtedly due to the exigency of his battalions' situation (enemy fire from almost three sides and the sudden impromptu strafing by U.S. Air Force P-47s) Cole exclaimed, 'To hell with the bridge!' or stronger words to that effect. Almost simultaneously, he leaped out of his foxhole and ran several yards out into an open area to more effectively display an orange parachute panel for recognition by the fighter bombers. He was struck down at that moment by a German bullet. This was possibly the most devastating rifle shot of the war for the 502nd."

Fitzgerald continued his story: "September 18th was one of the darkest days for the 3rd Battalion. The battalion had unknowingly come across a very large group of the enemy, who were trying to make their escape back to Germany by train. They were part of the armies retreating across Belgium and France. At the town of Best, they were ordered to stop and fight when their commanders became aware of the Allied airborne landings. The Germans had heavy concentrations of artillery and overwhelming small arms firepower. The enemy was also using 20mm anti-aircraft cannons to defoliate the section of the woods we were occupying. Fire was so intense that the trees began to burn. Casualties were mounting all around us. Colonel Cole decided that the only option left to him was to call for air support. When our P-47 fighters arrived, all hell broke loose as they started to strafe the area. He was becoming increasingly concerned for the safety of his men. He ordered and supervised the setting off of orange smoke bombs to our front. (The orange smoke indicated to pilots that friendly troops were near their target area.)

"As the planes continued their havoc, his concern increased. He decided to go into an open field to lay out a group of orange panels as an additional precaution. Just before he started toward the field he sent me to locate a jeep that was a short distance away. It was loaded with ammunition. We had been waiting for its arrival as our supply of ammo was almost out. I was only gone a few minutes. When I returned, I saw a group of men standing near the edge of the field. As I came closer, I saw the colonel's body on the ground. Kneeling down beside him, I looked up at the battalion surgeon and asked, 'Why don't you do something for him?' He replied, 'I'm sorry, John, there is nothing I can do for him now.' He had been shot by a sniper hidden in a house about a hundred yards from the field. We knew we had lost so much more than a battalion commander that day. I remember carrying the message to Major (John) Stopka, second in command, telling him that he was in charge of the battalion."

Some time during the morning, radio contact had been re-established between "H" Company and 3rd Battalion. Sgt. Joe Ludwig describes the strafing and a response to a radio message that left him wondering: "It was at this time that P-47s came over and strafed us and the Germans. They probably saved our rear ends because the Germans started pulling back from their attack. I remember looking at the trees. All the leaves were gone. After the P-47 attack, Captain Jones told me to get Battalion and tell them we were very low on ammunition. I called 'Blue Beaver' (code name) and Major John Stopka answered as Blue Beaver. It must have been shortly after Colonel Cole was killed by a sniper. I subconsciously wondered what had happened to Cole. During this time we never had any artillery support, unless you consider the P-47s as artillery."

The after-action report for the 502nd Regiment summarizes the activities for the afternoon of the eighteenth:

> During the afternoon of the 18th, the 3rd Battalion remained in position near the objective, denying the enemy the use of the bridges over the Wilhelmina Canal and the main highway to Eindhoven from Best. The battalion forced back two more limited scale attacks by the enemy. At 1330 hours, during a heavy attack by the enemy on the battalion position, five P-47s arrived just as the situation was becoming critical. Panels and orange smoke were displayed to identify the battalion lines. Following this action, aircraft strafed and bombed the enemy at very close quarters as the enemy had advanced to within one hundred yards of our battalion lines. This support, which was the first that the battalion had received, resulted in the enemy attack being repulsed with heavy losses in troops and equipment. At 1430 hours, during the strafing and bombing, the battalion commander was killed by rifle fire while observing the enemy from the battalion observation post, located near the front lines.[70]

During the late afternoon and evening of the eighteenth, troops of "I" Company managed to establish a roadblock on the highway south of Best and thereby gained control of approximately 250 yards of the highway, which provided access for relief and resupply of the enemy troops positioned along the canal.

Shortly after the death of LTC Robert G. Cole, the S-2 team, led by Sgt. Graham Armstrong, returned to the regimental CP with its report on the location of 3rd Battalion's command post. PFC Richard Ladd continued his story. "At dusk, the S-2 Section led Regimental HQ Company from the DZ down the dusty road toward the 3rd Battalion positions in the woods. We had passed several badly wounded men from 'I' Company on stretchers by the edge of the woods. Pvt. Bob Paczulla and I were acting as point for the company. Evidently there had been a lull in fighting for it was quiet and almost dark. As we reached the end of the woods on our left an open area presented itself. Paczulla and I started to continue into the open, but three 'I' Company men in a slit trench behind a .30 caliber machine gun said, 'Where ya goin?' We said, 'We're from Regimental Headquarters Company reinforcing 3rd Battalion.' One of them drawled, 'Ya better know somethin, this is the front raat cher.' Talk about a walk into oblivion, that could have been it!

"Our company got off the dusty track and hastily took up positions in the darkening woods, immediately behind 'I' Company. Foxholes were easily dug in the loamy soil beneath the pines."

2nd Battalion Joins the Fray

During the early-morning hours LTC John Michaelis, the regimental commander, had ordered LTC Steve Chappuis to move his 2nd Battalion out at first light to relieve the pressure on the hard-pressed 3rd Battalion troops.

From a diary kept by S/Sgt. Earl L. Cox in which he chronicled the activities of "F" Company for the entire Holland campaign. He provides a brief description of the moves of his unit for the eighteenth:

> At 0600 we moved southeast for an attack on Best. 0900 begin attack 300 to 400 yards behind "Easy" in Battalion reserve. Committed on right flank in line with "Easy" and "Dog." We managed to get into Best and captured 28 prisoners. Withdrew from Best due to enemy superiority. Formed on line in woods north of Wilhelmina Canal. Set up perimeter defense.

The fighting was extremely fierce for Companies "D" and "E" on the eighteenth. In a letter he had written to his buddy Pvt. William H. Stephens of "D" Company while both were in hospitals recuperating from their wounds, Pvt. Ruben LaMadrid[71] wrote about the casualties suffered by "Dog" Company in the battle for Best and the highway bridge: "I must have been ahead of the line when you got hit with the grenade. Cole told me about it the next morning. He also gave me your carbine. I carried it with me for three days until Lt. Bud Rainey made me throw it away. Warren Cole was killed the next morning and, also, John Kish. Remember Kish? He used to sleep in the bunk below me in England. Cpl. Jim Brodie got it about ten feet from where Lt. Baker died. Sgt. Lenwood Tuttle got it, too. Captain Bill Bolton was wounded the first day. Sgt. 'Cowboy' Harrison was KIA in Holland a week later. They gave him the DSC after he died."

71. From a letter Pvt. Ruben LaMadrid wrote to his buddy William H. Stephens on July 29, 1945. Stephens was recuperating from his wounds in a stateside hospital.

As a member of "E" Company, Cpl. Robert L. Gryder was in on the heavy fighting of the eighteenth. He wrote: "Company 'D' was on the left, 'E' was in the middle and 'F' Company was on the right. It was just like in training days after the firing started. You would get up and run ten paces and then hit the dirt, then up again as we moved across an open area. I could see troops to the right and left of me for 200 yards. People were being killed and wounded all around. We could not see the Germans so we were firing where we thought they were. Finally we crossed a road (Eindhoven–Boxtel highway) and there was no more firing.

"Several of us got together and someone said Captain Fred Drennon had been killed back in the field. We walked down the road a hundred yards or so and met some other guys not necessarily from our company. It seems we had overrun Best and were on our way back the way we had come.

"I felt something warm running down my left leg. A buddy cut my pants leg open and found blood. He ripped it to the thigh and found I had been hit with a .30 caliber bullet. By this time some of the others who had been wounded were gathering. Also, there were three or four German prisoners in the group. There were five of our wounded and the medic told us the first aid station and the German prisoner pen were just down the road a half mile. We were to take the prisoners and drop them off on the way to the aid station where we could get further treatment."

A trooper with excellent recall, PFC Emmert O. Parmley, preferred to write about others. "Our first action was the attack on Best. The first day of the attack, Lt. Nick Schiltz assigned me to Lt. Wolfe, his second in command. We were bringing up the rear of the platoon and were to see to it there were no stragglers.

"I like the Dutch people very much. I have often wondered about the Dutch men who were with us on the first day of the attack on Best. They were pulling two-wheeled carts for us, loaded with ammunition. I remember they wore colored bows on their jackets and am sure they had never been in combat before. We were still a long way from Best and there was only an occasional tracer bullet coming our way. They didn't seem to notice. As we approached the outskirts the tracers grew thicker. They kept pulling the carts but were looking around as if to ask, is there any danger, or for someone to say they did not have to go any further. No one was going to tell them not to go with us.

If I had to do it over I would, but at the time I know the thoughts of most of us were if they shoot at them, they are not shooting at us."

In the action the troops reached the outskirts of Best, under a heavy concentration of mortar and small-arms fire. First Lieutenant Nick Schiltz was out in front leading his platoon when he was brought down by enemy fire.

PFC Emmert Parmley was devastated. He wrote: "Lt. Schiltz was killed in this attack. As platoon runner, I should have been with him. I cannot but believe that being assigned to rear guard saved my life. I will never know if he did this on purpose. He was a fine, brave officer—carried a picture of his son in his helmet and looked at it often. His son appeared to be about one year old. When later, in the courtyard by a house in the outskirts of Best, I looked in his helmet which was on a gun that marked where he fell, the picture was still there. There were also flowers put there by the Dutch people."

"At the Battle of Best, when the 2nd Battalion started across the wheat field in battalion formation, I was a corporal—when I reached the other side, I was a sergeant," wrote Howard J. Matthews of "Fox" Company. "On reaching the far side of the field, I jumped into another ditch beside the road. Then I dashed across the road and jumped into another ditch, looked left and right and found I was in a ditch with many German soldiers. I shot two of them next to me, then noticed they were unarmed. Sgt. Tom Terrell was at the end of the line yelling at me that these were his prisoners.

"Meanwhile, Frank Tiedeman came sprinting across the road, jumped into the same ditch and saw all the Germans and jumped out and ran back across the road. He started shooting and threw a hand grenade. He finally noticed Terrell and me waving frantically at him. He and two other 'F' Company men came over and we started down the ditch and were able to put fire on the quad-twenty anti-aircraft guns that were firing on the battalion in the wheat field. We were able to drive them off.

"I lost a good boyhood friend, 2Lt. Robert Sickles, when we were in the wheat field near Best. We grew up on the same block in Detroit. He was in 'E' Company."

The entry in the 2nd Battalion journal by Cpl. Pete Santini gives readers a vivid eyewitness picture of the day's events as they unfolded on the eighteenth in an area extending from the drop zones to the Best area.

We moved out at about 0800 toward the town of Best. The field we jumped on had to be crossed again. About midway across the field, the leading companies contacted the enemy.

The CP was set up in a farmhouse which was located approximately in the center of the field.

Enemy mortar, artillery and small arms fire was very heavy. The casualties began to roll in. Captains George Lage and Ernest Shacklett, our battalion surgeons, and the men in the aid station went to work. The medics, as usual, were right on the job.

The fighting was fierce and the casualty toll began to rise by leaps and bounds. The fighting went on for hours. We were badly outnumbered and had no artillery support. Our 81mm and 60mm mortars were doing a good job.

About 1450 hours, gliders began to come in. We were right smack in the field where they were going to land. Wave after wave, they came in and landed. It was an awe-inspiring sight. The men in the front lines were unable to enjoy this beautiful show of air supremacy but I'm sure the enemy must have felt some fear.

The bombers followed the towed gliders in and dropped our resupply. Most of the supplies landed on the field but some landed in territory held by the Jerries.

Captain Lage and some of the medics went out to pick up some wounded. A sniper got Captain Lage through the right shoulder. The wound was low and quite possibly punctured his lung. He was bleeding badly and had already lost a lot of blood. Captain Shacklett had to give him two units of blood plasma before we were able to evacuate him. No jeeps or ambulances were available and the aid station and the CP were under artillery fire. A Jerry car, which had been captured, was used to evacuate Captain Lage or "Doc" as he was more commonly known.

The casualties were still pouring in. Captain Shacklett and S/Sgt. Ernest Labadie, with the few remaining aid men, had more work than it seemed possible to do. However, they worked tirelessly and did a wonderful job.

Sgt. Louis Zotti, Cpl. Dave Jackendoff and a few more men from company HQ, helped the medics carry wounded in from the field. An incident which struck me as peculiar happened while the CP was under heavy mortar fire. Pvt. Floyd Ankeny, a man who has been in the company almost since its beginning, gave his foxhole to one of the new men who had never been under fire before and calmly began to dig himself another hole. I questioned him later and asked him why he did it. His answer was, "I thought the new man was a little frightened." Who wasn't!

The enemy was pushed back and the CP advanced. The company paid quite a price to get off that field. Fourteen men wounded and five killed.

It was already midday when 1Lt. James W. Tolar and his forty-two-man platoon returned from their reconnaissance trip east of Son where they had been sent to check out a highway bridge. They had moved out directly, striking out cross-country from the jump field. Now, as they returned to 2nd Battalion, Tolar reported to the battalion commander. "We rejoined the battalion at midday. The first person I saw was 2nd Battalion commander, Lt. Colonel Steve Chappuis. He asked the number of men I had. I said 42. He said I had as many as he did. He said we were attacking immediately. He had plans of his own and they did not include going to Best. We lost three officers wounded and some enlisted men KIA and otherwise.

"We had just moved out, not knowing where the enemy was. PFC Paul Dely, a scout, had gotten only 20 or 30 steps in front when the action started like a match in a powder keg. The enemy was in a road with banks about four feet. They were only about fifty to sixty yards to our front. Dely was half way between us. No protection was offered us but Dely dove behind a haystack which screened him from enemy view and it apparently never occurred to the enemy to fire through the haystack.

"Dely stepped from behind his cover and threw a grenade into the road and announced it was for Hitler. Immediately the men nearest tossed their grenades over to Dely. He repeated his toss over and over, designating each time a different member of Hitler's staff as the intended recipient."

Cpl. Robert L. Gryder was one of five walking wounded sent back by a medic who had no transportation to offer them. They had four prisoners in tow. These were to be left at the POW cage near the aid station. Gryder wrote: "As the five of us were marching down the road, a 20mm gun opened up on us and we all dived into the ditch. After about five minutes, the gun stopped firing. In another 10 to 15 minutes we decided to get up and see what was going on. We punched the Germans with our rifles but they never moved. The five of us Americans started

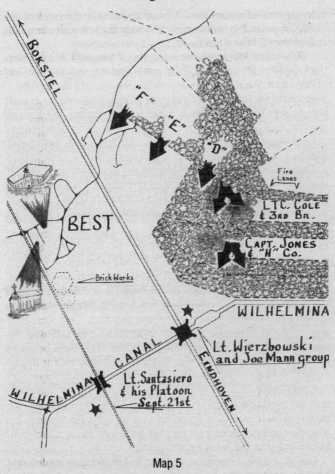

Map 5

walking down the road again. However, we were fired on. Again we dove into the ditch alongside the road. After a while, maybe 30 minutes, we decided we had to do something. Since I was the only one who could walk well, I began a series of moves, leaving the ditch and darting in three or four directions. In each case I was fired on and scrambled back to the ditch. After about another hour we looked down the road and saw two columns of

German soldiers, possible 200, marching down the road toward us. As soon as they got within 50 yards of us, we stood up and one of the Germans ran up and took our weapons.

"This crazy looking German kid was assigned to take us to the rear area. He carried a P-38 pistol and was waving it wildly all the time. We marched back. When we were in the middle of an orchard the German kid got even wilder, gesturing to us to do something. We did not know what he was saying. We thought the end was near. However, he finally climbed up in a tree and started throwing apples down to us. We felt a little better after that.

"Since all of us were wounded, he got us in a truck he flagged down on the road and they took us to a Dutch hospital in either Schijndel or s'Hertogenbosch. I do remember them putting me in the operating room with a big skylight overhead. I could see P-47s very low overhead."

Cpl. Pete Santini noted the difficulty of locating the forward command post of 2nd Battalion as they moved forward to keep pace with the line company troops.

> Pushing forward we met Lt. Hughes with about 60 prisoners, going toward the rear. Sgt. Leonard Langford and Cpl. Reggie Davies were acting as prisoner guards.
>
> When we arrived at the place the forward CP was supposed to be, we found it had moved forward. The companies had the enemy on the run and were hot on their heels. Instructions were left for us to wait for Lt. Milford Bliss, who would guide us to our new positions. Lt. Bliss arrived and we started out. Again, when we arrived at the designated position, the CP and forward CPs had moved.
>
> Captain James Martin and Cpl. Otto Fick had some of his S-2 men on patrol in an effort to locate the forward echelons. We were lost babes in the woods, but in enemy territory that isn't funny.
>
> It was beginning to get dark. Luckily, we contacted the rest of the battalion. About 2100 hours we moved out and joined them in their new position. We set up in the woods for the night. We knew the enemy was close, but just how close, we never realized until the next morning. The night was almost silent.

Daybreak at the Bridge

During the late afternoon 1Lt. Nick Mottola and his platoon of men from "D" Company had become separated from their unit.

They ended up at the Wierzbowski position near the highway bridge and were quickly moved into positions on the flank of Wierzbowski's decimated force.

In the night the enemy attacked Mottola's flank positions and the men fell back, overcome by superior numbers that had turned their flank. The men fell back to the canal, swimming or taking advantage of the few small rowboats on the bank. They moved east along the south bank of the canal and recrossed it well to the east. Wierzbowski's men were scarcely aware of what was happening to Mottola's force.

As the misty dawn broke on the nineteenth, Wierzbowski's men hadn't repositioned themselves to take over the gap left by the departed "D" Company platoon. With the coming of day enemy troops had moved up into grenade-throwing positions. They were within twenty feet of the large holes occupied by several Americans.

An enemy hand grenade exploded on the machine gun of T/5 Vincent Laino of the engineers, taking out one eye and temporarily blinding the other. By using his sense of touch, Laino was able to locate and hurl back another grenade that landed near his feet, thus saving his own life and those of three of his comrades.

Having been wounded in both arms the day before while attacking a nearby ammunition dump with a bazooka, PFC Joe E. Mann was leaning against the side of the hole he shared with several others. An enemy potato masher dropped into the hole. With both arms held firmly in place by slings, Mann spotted the missile and yelled "Grenade" and fell back on the grenade, taking the full force of the explosion in his back. The action saved the lives of others though several took fragments in their bodies.[72]

The survivors of Wierzbowski's small force surrendered to the enemy but were freed later that afternoon when 2nd Battalion troops came through the position.

Ongoing Fight for Best

The 2nd Battalion had moved into position on a line during the night, scheduled to attack toward the German positions along

---

72. PFC Joe E. Mann received the Congressional Medal of Honor while T/5 Vincent Laino was awarded the Silver Star.

the highway, in the woods, and along the canal. Cpl. Pete Santini chronicled the actions:

> We were scheduled to attack at 0600 hours. At about 0550, the first shots for the day went off. It was quiet for a moment and then it seemed like all "Hell broke loose."
>
> Mortars, 88mm, 20mm, machine pistols, rifles, and our own mortars, machine guns, tommy guns, rifles, carbines, shots from all directions, a bedlam of noise which was impossible to describe. This went on all morning. Again the Jerries had us outnumbered. Their artillery was giving us "Hell" and we still weren't able to give them any in return.

With the dawn attack about to take place on the nineteenth, PFC Emmert Parmley provided a picture of the landscape before his group as it prepared to take off in a rush toward the enemy positions near Best. "On the second day of attack, 'F' Company's line was about 150 yards west and parallel to the highway running north along the canal to Best. We were not too far north of the canal. The Germans were dug in on the east side of the highway. It was still dark and we were waiting for daylight to begin our attack. We were in position, 2nd Platoon was on the left of the 'F' Company front which was the west edge of a small tree plantation—none of them over ten to twelve feet tall. To our right was an open field down to the highway. It was through these trees that our captain, LeGrand 'Legs' Johnson, led the attack at daylight. I recall waiting in the dark for the order to attack. A weapons company .30 caliber light machine gun was next to me on the right. It was getting lighter. I could make out the buildings along the highway. I had moved to this position in the dark so did not know what was in front of us.

"To my right about 20 feet, I heard a lot of radio squawk and static. It was Captain Johnson and radioman Sgt. Albert Mazzeo with the radio strapped to his back. They were going into the trees leading down to the highway.

"At the same time I saw Germans coming out of the buildings along the highway on the west side. The machine gunner next to me opened up. I heard no order to fire. We all opened fire about the same time up and down the line. We were on top of the ground. There had been no holes dug for we knew we were going to attack in the morning. I had an M-1 Garand and had fired three or four clips when I heard the order to attack. I ran for the projection of trees on our left."

Sgt. Franklin "Ray" Blasingame wrote about one of his friends in action the second day as 2nd Battalion moved out. "As the battle for Best got under way, E. O. Parmley was first scout out. It was just daylight and as he moved out of the woods toward the enemy and onto the road separating the woods we had stayed in all night, and the woods across the road where the Germans were, a Kraut stepped up on the road just opposite Parmley. The German fired but missed but by that time ole Parmley woke up and saw the German injecting another round and, with his Garand at the hip, 'Blam, Blam, Blam' and the Kraut was done for.

"About that time S/Sgt. Wilson L. Lee, an old timer with the 502nd, took a shot in the groin and gut from a German gun. It must have been painful because he screamed a lot before he died. The gun was a 20mm piece."

The enemy fire was hot and heavy as the troopers approached the enemy positions. Parmley was looking for protection. He added to his story: "When I got to trees, there was little protection—no holes where I was located. I saw a little indentation about two inches deep where a mortar shell had probably hit. It looked like the Grand Canyon to me so I dived in."

Parmley continued: "In desperate situations, some person usually takes over. On this day it was former 1st sergeant, bull-horn voiced Rolland Fair. I don't know if he had any rank at the time, as he was a private most of the time. His only weapon that day was a British Welby army pistol—and his deep voice. He constantly exposed himself, waving that big revolver with the ring in the butt like he was going to throw it at someone. I am certain the Germans in Best heard him roar out orders.

"I heard him bellow, 'E. O.!' (He always called me E. O.) 'Damn it E. O., go back to Battalion, tell Lt. Atkins to send us up a machine gun. We need help!'

"I hated to leave my 'big hole' but off I went. I found Lt. Atkins but he had no gun to send. I found that all of 'F' company was in bad shape. I saw no one on the line we had departed from that morning. There was no one in the woods that led down to the highway—the same trees through which Captain Johnson had attacked earlier in the morning. If Germans had attacked at this time—we were wide open."

Parmley continued: "Rolland Fair took charge of the situation. With his bull-horn voice, he directed our withdrawal back to our original line from which we departed that morning. We expected a counterattack. Fair had us dig in. A trooper named Bloomfield dug a hole with me on the original line about the center of the tree line that led down to the highway. We dug one together as that was much faster—and we dug a deep one. In front of our line was a fire break about 12 to 15 feet wide before the trees led down to the highway. About ten feet to the left of Bloomfield and me was a .30 caliber machine gun whose chatter sounded good. Next to us on the right, about five feet away, was a replacement named John Hovey. He kept looking for Germans. I told him to dig in—'you are not going to see them!' He dug a little more but would not keep his head down. Bullets were making that cracking sound like breaking sticks, which meant they were close. There was also a German 20mm gun firing. John Hovey continued to look for Germans. He was enthusiastic about fighting. I do not believe he was scared at all. If it was possible, he was too good a soldier. It had to happen. I heard him call 'Medic!' I yelled back, 'No medic here. You will have to crawl back to the rear.' He went crawling back with blood all over his face."

The early-morning attack took a heavy toll on the 2nd Battalion troopers. Cpl. Pete Santini describes the action from a different perspective:

Our casualty rate was on the upswing again. Men were coming in the aid station from all directions. Captain Shacklett and S/Sgt. Ernest Labadie and the aid men had their hands full again. The way these medics worked was a marvelous thing to observe.

Shells were landing all around them, but they never seemed to notice. The wounded were their responsibility and they were taking care of them.

Captain Martin came down and directed all available men to go back and dig some slit trenches for the wounded. Again "CO HQ" went to work and dug for everything they were worth. I was scared but I kept right on digging, too.

Tanks Come to the Rescue

The British had reached the site of the demolished Son bridge the evening before and their engineers had toiled through the night installing a Bailey bridge over the Wilhelmina Canal. Shortly after 0600 on the morning of the nineteenth, armor began moving northward. A squadron of tanks was assigned to the 101st Division. Major General Taylor sent some of them to the hard-pressed troops of the 502nd.

The British armor approached from the rear of the regimental positions. They appeared first in the regimental command post area. PFC Richard Ladd described the scene in his area: "Around noon we became conscious of a sound of armor approaching from the DZ. Enemy fire abruptly slackened. A lone British major with a scarlet cloth cap on his head and a white lanyard running to his sidearm, strode into the woods and inquired loudly as to the location of the regimental C.O. Someone responded quickly, 'He's over there in that hole.' The strange officer appeared to be seven feet tall from my humble vantage point. A brief conference with Colonel John Michaelis was followed by a throaty roar as six Churchills and one Challenger tank advanced along the road parallel to the wood line. At the first crack of 76mm fire from the Churchills and the flame thrower on the Challenger, the men of the 2nd and 3rd Battalions began to move forward. A host of German infantry was streaming to our positions within a half hour. A miscellaneous group of S-2 and Regimental HQ Company men escorted over 1,100 prisoners back to the DZ that afternoon."

The men on the firing line were elated at the arrival of the tanks. Now they had some support. Now the odds were evening out.

"When the English Churchill reached our lines, it seemed everyone leaped out of their holes as if ejected by some force at the same time," added Private First Class Parmley. "We were all yelling and were going to charge but the tank commander was a very calm person and said, 'Let's not be hasty, lads, perhaps we can give Jerry something to think about.' At this time the tank was on our line at the left edge of the trees that led to the highway. He fired the big gun. It looked like an air burst just in front of the buildings on the highway.

"There were a few white flags but not many. He fired again. This brought results. The Germans on the left started surrendering as the tank moved across our front to the right of the trees that ran down to the highway and fired again on the right side of the trees. They started surrendering all up and down the line—

so many we just motioned them to the rear. They looked like good troops. Many had camouflage capes on, like the German paratroopers wore, but I did not see any paratrooper helmets on them. We then moved out to occupy the buildings and land in front of us. I was surprised to see the number of Germans we had killed. We had gotten a large number of the ones that spent the night in the buildings and were coming out to occupy the trenches that morning. Had they left ten minutes sooner, we would have missed them.

"I was first scout when we moved out. This was my first experience in going through houses, checking to see if any Germans were in them. We were still enthused and spirits were high from all the prisoners we had taken. We had won the battle. We should have been tired but I do not remember being tired. It had been a long day and was getting dark. I remember, on outpost that night, fires burning around Best. They could be seen for miles."

The entry for the log of "Fox" Company as recorded for September 19 by S/Sgt. Earl L. Cox sums up the company actions for the day:

> 0600 attack towards canal on right flank of White (2nd Bn.). We advanced ahead of other units but had to pull back on line as enemy resistance was too stiff. 0830 set up defensive position on edge of woods. At 1430 British tanks arrived. Tide of battle changes in our favor and we start pushing the enemy back. Enemy starts surrendering in bunches running across open field to our position. Some were machine-gunned by own troops. Move to defensive position. We were on the right.

Cpl. Pete Santini continues describing the events as they unfolded after the arrival of the British armor in their sector of the line:

> Some English tanks came up to assist us. They laid down a terrific artillery barrage. Now the odds were even. We finally could give those Jerries some of their own medicine.
>
> The first barrage must have made "Christians" of the master race because they started surrendering. They came in groups of 50 to 60, from all directions.
>
> We held our fire and allowed as many to surrender as wanted. These were lined up and thoroughly searched for concealed weapons.

I estimate there were between 500 and 600 of them. About twice as many of them as there were of us, but they still surrendered.

After they were searched, they were taken to the division PW camp by Captain Martin and some guards.

Not all of the enemy troops were ready to surrender as the troops moved through the woods and fields with their newly arrived tank support. The 502nd after-action report[73] describes an enemy move that created problems for command post personnel:

> . . . As the enemy positions were reached, small groups began to surrender. These groups became larger and larger until they numbered fifty or more. A collecting point was established in an open field which was soon covered with prisoners. As the advance continued toward the canal, the enemy withdrew toward the woods on the left flank of the 2nd Battalion. They entered these and were in a position to attack the left flank and rear of the regiment. Fortunately, this fact was discovered and every available man in the battalion command post group rushed to man positions to surround the woods. The fire of this group combined with fire from the left flank company, and one tank forced the surrender of about 400 of the enemy who were in the woods.
>
> During the height of the battle, a group of about fifty enemy penetrated the right flank and were advancing from the rear toward the regimental command post before they were discovered. They were engaged by the command post personnel and routed with considerable losses. By 1730 hours, all enemy resistance had ceased and the bridge area was under firm control. The regiment immediately established a defensive position to protect it. . . .

Regimental Headquarters Company had its forward CP just behind the front lines. S-2 member Richard Ladd had a vivid description of the fighting that swept up to and almost over command personnel. "All hell broke loose with the Germans attacking from two, almost three, sides. I was unable to shoot because I was several feet into the woods from the road, even though the Germans kept pressing closer. A few yards from me, a slit trench containing the regimental message center received a direct mortar round, killing Pvt. Alex DeLulio and T/5 Edwin Wood.

"The voice and admonishments of our company commander,

73. Patheiger, op. cit.

Captain Cecil Simmons, remained audible over the tumult and intensity of the attack. Simmons, an officer not generally idolized by his men, shouted commands like, 'Look out on the left! There's three Krauts in the ditch! *Get em!*' Like him or not, this choir director sure gave a young soldier confidence. You knew 'Big Cece' wasn't missing much. . . . The situation seemed most uncertain for three hours that afternoon because of the strength of the German fire into 2nd and 3rd Battalions.''

Medical Evacuation

Evacuation of the wounded by ambulance or jeep on the eighteenth and nineteenth had been an impossibility. No vehicles were available. With the arrival of the British tanks the tide of battle began to change. Members of the division medical company moved in to fill the gaps caused by the wounding of Capt. George Lage and other members of the medical detachment.

First Lieutenant Henry Barnes, medical evacuation officer for the 326th Medical Company, was assigned to look after those needs with the 502nd Regiment. He describes the difficulty getting to the Best area to evacuate wounded: "On D plus 2 I tried to find one of the battalion aid stations. I stooped over to ask one of the colonels sitting under a tree scanning a map for the location of one of the aid stations. Just as I bent over, a bullet buried itself in the tree over my head. The colonel muttered, 'Someone get that sniper!' and casually showed me the location of the aid station.

"In trying to get there, my driver and I ran into another sniper and we had to lie in a slit trench for five minutes before someone got him.

"I was lying on top of my driver who chortled the whole time because it was the first time he had beaten me to a hole during the war. As I peered out of the hole I could see down one of the lanes through the woods but I couldn't rise up any higher or the sniper would fire at me.

"Finally we got out and got to the aid station only to find it had been a German aid post and had just been captured. A medical sergeant was digging a grave for his newly dead comrades and there were no wounded there. German bodies floated in the canal and grim troopers were bayoneting every bush and firing short bursts into the undergrowth. One soldier pointed out some

British tanks a short distance away and said, 'Those tanks saved us and they ran over the German wounded, flattening them like pancakes.'

"I tried to get up to the station through another lane and got to where two lieutenants were directing an attack. One wanted to use my jeep for hauling ammunition but I asked him how we could then save him if he was wounded.

"Then my last trip for the afternoon was along the extreme left flank and my driver and I got up to a group dug in behind a brick wall. As soon as I arrived, an English lieutenant crawled over to me with his face white with fear. I stared in amazement at a bullet that had pierced the front of his helmet with only the point of the slug touching his forehead. There was only a tiny trickle of blood running down his nose. While lying behind the wall staring at him, I got up on my knees to wipe off the blood when a shot rang out behind me and a bullet passed over my right shoulder and buried itself in the brick wall spattering dust and grime into my eyes. Two men silently detached themselves from the group, and crawled back to get the sniper.

"I thought we were surrounded but a moment later a gangly youth crawled up and said in a southern drawl, 'I almost gotcha, didn't I?' He added, 'I saw someone move and took a shot.'

"I was so glad that we weren't surrounded that I didn't even reprimand him. I then returned to my jeep, taking the British officer with me.

"After contacting Major Doug Davidson, the regimental surgeon of the 502nd, I then knew the location of the aid stations and decided to evacuate that night."

During the three days of heavy fighting, the enemy had tied up over twenty-five hundred troops in battling to keep the 502nd Regiment from seizing the Best highway bridge. The enemy had been unable to send reinforcements to the beleaguered force in Eindhoven. The road had been effectively closed by the roadblocks set up by "I" Company.

The after-action report for the Market-Garden campaign describes the casualties inflicted on the enemy during this period and the weapons captured or destroyed. It also shows the heavy price the regiment paid to achieve its victory.

. . . Subsequent investigation showed that the area covered by the regiment on the 17th, 18th and 19th of September, had contained some 2,500 enemy troops. Of these, 1,042 were captured, and an estimated 800 were killed. This last figure was reported by a British unit which later occupied the area and buried the dead. Reinforcing his normal complement of machine guns and mortars, the enemy had eight 88mm guns, two 75mm anti-tank guns and five 20mm anti-aircraft guns.

Casualties in the regiment were particularly heavy. The 2nd Battalion lost all three rifle company commanders, the executive officer, the S-2, and the S-4, while the 3rd Battalion lost its commander. Total casualties were 29 officers and 420 enlisted men.

Civilian Suffering

During the heavy fighting of the nineteenth, a Dutch family had been caught in the cross fire of the Americans and the Germans. Christ van Rooy, a twenty-year-old living in the Best area during the fighting, recalled, "The children of a Dutch family were in a shelter which the eldest son had dug earlier that morning. The mother was in the basement of the home. In the hole with the older boy were five young children. A German soldier hiding in the ditch near the shelter saw the Americans approaching, got up and attempted to run away. He was shot. Thinking he had come from the hole and assuming there were more enemy soldiers hiding in it, an American tossed a grenade into the shelter. The eldest son grabbed it and rose to throw it out of the hole. He was shot dead. The children began to cry and the Americans realized there were only little ones in the shelter. It was a terrible tragedy."

Van Rooy related the plight of another family in the same area on the same day. "A family which lived near the canal bridge had to seek shelter with neighbors and friends each night for several days because their home was being used by the enemy. The second night they had been forced to stay in a hay barn as many people were forced to leave their homes in the expanding battle area. On the morning of the 19th they had gone back to their home but had left their blankets to be used again that night. As the fighting swirled around the hay barn, German soldiers discovered the blankets and sensed that American soldiers had slept there. The Wijrooven family, occupants of the farm and owners of the barn, were in a bomb shelter away from the farm buildings. Enemy soldiers approached the shelter and accused the family of sheltering the hated Americans. Despite the protestations of the family, the youngest son of ten was taken from the shelter as a hostage. He was crying as he was led away. An older brother brother jumped from the hole and asked to be exchanged for the little brother. One of the Germans took his pistol and shot the older boy. Wounded, he attempted to crawl to the shelter of the barn. The Germans shot him with a machine gun, killing him. The father saw this, ran out toward his son and was shot in the legs by the German soldier. He was badly wounded."

For being Good Samaritans, the Wijrooven family had lost a son and the father was crippled for life.

The 327th Joins the Fray

With an estimated enemy force of twenty-five hundred battling the troops of the 502nd on the nineteenth, and before the arrival of British armor and artillery support, division felt that the 2nd and 3rd Battalions of the 327th Glider Infantry Regiment in the vicinity of Oud Meer (old lake) in the reforestation area northwest of Son should be sent to support the embattled 502nd.

Shortly after daylight, BG A. C. McAuliffe, artillery commander for the 101st, had gone to the 327th command post where he ordered 2nd and 3rd Battalions attached to the 502nd. LTC Ray C. Allen, commander of the 3rd, moved his men northwestward as soon as he received the assignment. He hurried on ahead in his jeep toward the 502nd CP.

Along the way he came upon a group of two hundred enemy soldiers marching southwest to reinforce the large contingent already in the Best area. Allen had been greeted by fire from the enemy force but managed to escape with only a bullet hole in a ration box in his pocket. He hurried back to his troops and urged them on to trap the group before they reached their destination. The Germans had quickened their pace and the glidermen were only able to get at the stragglers, of which seventy-five were killed or captured.

By this time a squadron of British tanks and some British artillery units had been assigned to the 101st and moved out with 2nd Battalion from its bivouac area near Wolfswinkel. BG Gerald J. Higgins had taken charge of the combined forces and outlined the roles for each. His purpose was to clear all the Germans out of the area west of the Son canal bridge to the road bridge at Best.

The 502nd, using the Eindhoven–Best highway as its right flank, would push south to the canal. The many scattered enemy troops in the Zonsche Forest (pine plantation) would be handled by the 327th with 2nd Battalion moving west and south from the vicinity of Oud Meer located in the middle of the forest. The 3rd Battalion (formerly known as 1st Battalion of the 401st Glider Infantry Regiment) was to go north to isolate the enemy near the canal and to provide cover for the glider landings scheduled for later that day.

T/5 Jack Millman[74] wrote: "Our first encounter was the next day. Our company had split into two fighting teams and were mopping up through a wooded area which the paratroopers had by-passed on their way to Eindhoven.

"It was at the junction of two fire breaks that we met two Jerry machine guns, supported by a squad of riflemen. I was with the company commander, the 2nd Platoon and part of the weapons platoon. The 2nd Platoon sergeant shot one, wounding him, and killed another. The advance squad leader used a tommy gun on another. They never did find his face. The rest were taken prisoners and sent to the rear.

"From there we went about a hundred yards to the canal, where we turned right to make contact with the 1st Platoon and the rest of the company which had been advancing parallel with us. We met them about three hundred yards down the canal near a large factory. We consolidated there along the edge of the woods, where they had taken a few prisoners. We took prisoners there until it began to get dark. Then we went back to a battalion area and dug in for the night."

With 2nd Platoon under 1Lt. Frank H. Hibbard and T/Sgt. Manuel Hidalgo, it followed a sandy road down through the woods with half of the platoon on the left and the other on the right until enemy rifle and machine-gun fire greeted them. Automatic weapons were brought forward. These served to distract the enemy while the half platoons moved left and right around the obstacle. One of the men who could understand German felt the enemy wanted to surrender. Hibbard sent back a message to bring up Sgt. Lloyd Gross, who was fluent in German.

74. From a copy of a letter T/5 Jack Millman wrote to his parents on June 27, 1945.

The platoon didn't wait for him and continued on with their enveloping move.

A few of the enemy were shot, some seeming not to be aware a fight was going on. Both elements of the platoon had gotten around the strong point and the enemy began to surrender individually and in small groups.

Technical Sergeant Hidalgo and Sgt. Carl J. Hanlon moved down the road shouting for the enemy to surrender. Backed by the numbers of Americans and their position to the rear of the enemy forces, they began to surrender in ever-increasing numbers. A total of 159 prisoners were taken. Many more had been killed but not a single casualty had been suffered in the move by the 327th to clear the woods.

Evacuating Wounded at Night

First Lieutenant Henry Barnes had decided he would carry on evacuation of the wounded from the 502nd regimental and battalion aid stations during the night of September 19. He and his driver had been under fire on many of the evacuation trips during the day, and he felt traveling over the flat, open spaces that marked the drop zones made them a target for enemy gunners on the northern and western fringes of the division landing areas. It was safer to travel at night. He wrote:

"Northeast of Son, on the extreme tip of landing zone 'W,' during the bombing of Eindhoven (Sept. 19), I went up to evacuate some wounded from one of the 502nd aid stations. I waited until it was dark and drove with my driver and two medical replacements who wished to go for the ride. The plowed fields were covered with parachutes and gliders and near a farm house with a woods northeast of us. This was just a few hundred yards north of where my glider crash-landed.

"My driver and I, both veterans of Normandy, too tired to dig in, rolled up and slept in a parachute, our first real sleep since landing. We were waiting until it was dark so we could go forward, unobserved in the flat country. The two new men each dug a large slit trench because we were receiving light scattered artillery fire and we were uneasy with the parachute flares over Eindhoven lighting the sky for the bombers.

"A German plane, on fire, seared the dusk as it tried to get back north making an ominous start for the evening.

"Voices could be heard during our sleep and when my driver and I awoke about midnight, we found no trace of the two new men, so we went on past the house 50 yards west of us along the road up to the battalion aid station and when we were about a hundred yards or so past the house, loud explosions, gun fire and shouting could be heard.

"We worried about passing the house on our return trip with our wounded. We took the wounded back, delaying our return trip for about three or four hours until it was just getting light and, as we neared the house, we picked up a chaplain who explained that a German patrol had captured sixteen Americans and he had been the only one to escape into the darkness by crawling out the front door. We took him and the wounded to the hospital in Son."

ELEVEN

St. Oedenrode

As division commander MG Maxwell D. Taylor stood looking over his shoulder. LTC Patrick Cassidy, commander of 1st Battalion of the 502nd Parachute Regiment, watched as one plane carrying men from "A" Company burst into flames as they passed over the enemy lines near the Belgian–Dutch border. A short time later the plane on his immediate left, flown by Maj. Dan Elam of the 435th Troop Carrier Group, was hit and the left engine and wing were burning fiercely. Pilot Elam continued to maintain his position in the formation.

To the front and over the drop zone the last serial of the 506th Regiment was just finishing its drop, having been slightly off course and four minutes late. Col. Frank J. MacNees, pilot of Cassidy's plane, rose to a higher elevation, followed by the remaining planes of his serial so as not to endanger any of the stragglers floating down to his front.

As they passed over the wooded area at the southern edge of drop zone "C," the green light was flashed on in the lead plane. Cassidy, still intently watching the progress of the Elam craft, had to be nudged by his division commander that the green light was on. With that he had led the members of the stick out over the freshly plowed fields near Son. The planes carrying the remainder of his 1st Battalion had flashed the "go" signal to the troopers as they moved over the same fields.

Upon landing, Cassidy had spotted the red assembly smoke for 1st Battalion and had headed in that direction. Unfortunately it was the assembly marker for 1st Battalion of the 506th Regiment. Cassidy should have received the green light a mile or so farther north in the drop area to be closer to his D-Day objective in St. Oedenrode. For General Taylor and his Division Headquarters echelon, it was only a short distance into the wooded area where he and his men quickly joined elements of the 506th in its movement toward Son.

After locating the proper assembly marker, set up at an intersection of two country lanes, Cassidy arrived to find much of his battalion already assembled. Also gathered with the group was 2nd Platoon of "C" Company of the 326th Engineers along with company commander Capt. Joseph Crilley and company headquarters.

The task of 1st Battalion was to take St. Oedenrode, one of the key points on the Screaming Eagle section of the highway leading north to Arnhem. Company "C" was to lead out, followed by 1st Battalion Headquarters. "A" Company followed as the reserve unit. "B" Company was sent on a flanking movement to the right. Two key highway bridges over the Dommel River were located in St. Oedenrode.

As a Holland replacement for "C" Company, Pvt. Gerald B. Johnston hunted desperately for a bundle with a blue parachute. He hoped to find the bazooka he was assigned to use against marauding tanks. He found his assistant, Pvt. Kenneth Parker, but with shells landing nearby, he lost sight of him. Johnston wrote: "I lost Parker in the crowd and then saw the assembly smoke at the edge of the field. I was really torn up at this point—join up without a bazooka or keep looking and maybe miss the assembly. I ran into Lt. Robert Lake. He told me to join up and so I headed for the smoke—no bazooka."

"It seemed like everybody made good landings," wrote S/Sgt. Roy W. Nickrent. "As the crossroad was easy to spot, I had no trouble finding the battalion CO, Lt. Col. Cassidy, at that spot ready to move out. It was but a few minutes before the battalion was on the march to St. Oedenrode. There was a feeling of elation as the troops moved away from the assembly area. We had very few jump casualties and spirits were high. The men were eager to tie into the Germans."

As the 1st Battalion moved off the drop zone and headed for St. Oedenrode, the men could see fighter support in the form of P-51s strafing enemy positions behind the tree line near the southern end of the village. The fighters had been circling high overhead while the parachute drops were being made. Having spotted fire from enemy positions in the orchard, the pilots had noticed enemy tanks and dropped down in sweeping power dives to remove these as threats to the advancing paratroopers.

Platoon sergeant Richard F. Johnson remembered the American P-51s and British Spitfires gave the men very good support on the drop. "The Germans tried to get tanks to our DZ but these planes took care of everyone of them. We could see the tanks in the near distance."

For Pvt. James W. Flanagan, there was little enemy action the first day. He wrote: "We formed up and started our attack on St. Oedenrode. We had little action going into town. My platoon was to set up a road block at the intersection of the Schijndel to St. Oedenrode and Eindhoven to Nijmegen (Hell's Highway)."

Pvt. Gerald Johnston added: "After the company formed up and headed toward St. Oedenrode, we could hear distant small arms fire, whether in front of us or near the drop zone we had left, I could not tell. 'Charley' Company was in the lead toward St. Oedenrode. We were not the lead platoon. At one point, the call came from up front for 'bazooka forward!' All I could do was relay the call back. Someone eventually trotted forward."

Up with the forward elements of "C" Company were members of the 2nd Platoon of "Charley" engineers. T/5 Carl F. Kelley accompanied them as the platoon medic. He recalled, "We took a little dirt road headed for St. Oedenrode. We got to the main highway and started up the road. There were some trees between us and the town. We could see two fighter planes and watched them coming in. As they were diving down we could see the rockets let go but we couldn't see what they were firing at. As we got out onto the road there was a little bend. Just as we came to that bend, there were two German tanks, one had been following the other. Both were knocked out. The lead tank's engine was still running. I was with 'Stub' Clark and a kid named Wendell Stackhouse, the company barber. There was a dead German up in the hatch. Clark said if we could get the German out of there he could drive the tank off the road. Stackhouse was up on the tank with someone trying to help him pull the German out. Whatever the foot of the dead German touched or hit, it caused an explosion. Pvt. Stackhouse was blown off the tank by the blast, which drove his barber tools through the pocket of his jacket and they protruded through his body. He was dead."

Some time later Pvt. Gerald Johnston came by. "As we moved forward we came to a light tank sitting in the road that had burned. There was a burned German soldier just part way out of the top hatch who looked like he had been caught there by an internal explosion. My first war casualty vision—on the ground alongside, was one of our men, badly cut up, dead from an explosive injury. I've wondered ever since, did the bazooka man who trotted forward get the tank? Was that him on the ground?"

Johnston continued: "There had been some casualties up ahead and the 2nd Platoon was sent through the people on the ground. I was lead scout at this point. We went around a bend in the road toward a bridge. To my left was a German soldier, wounded, leaning against a house. On my right were several people in a ditch, with one or more wounded—one of them was Lt. Mort Smit of the 3rd Platoon. Just as I was appreciating my surroundings and noting I couldn't see any Germans across the bridge, I was hit. I fell to my knees, blood running out of my sleeve and I couldn't grab onto my rifle. Someone in the ditch pulled me in by my foot and my part of the invasion of Holland was over.

"Captain Fred Hancock went by shortly thereafter, after Hollingsworth and others in the platoon rushed the bridge and got into the ditch on the far side. Howard Crotts was hit over there."

PFC Robert Marohn wrote: "As we came up to the village, the shooting started and things got hot. I was told to check out a large house. I went through it thoroughly from bottom to top. No one was there. When I came out, the platoon had continued to move into the village and I was alone. I headed in the same direction and was going up the main street when Sgt. Ken Kochenour, of our platoon, came out of an alley. He asked if I was thirsty. Naturally, I said yes. He led me back into the alley and to the side door of a building. We went into a barroom. It was a small Dutch pub. Ken went behind the bar and drew us each a large glass of beer. It really hit the spot. We could hear the machine guns down the street. The war was still on. We finished the beer, checked out the building and then continued to the street. A little further on we saw some German boots in the window of a small shop. We went in and several Dutch people who were in there led us to the kitchen and pointed to a door. It led to the cellar. Three German NCOs had taken refuge there. They came up at our invitation. We relieved them of their pistols. They were with a finance unit. The next day was to be pay day for the troops in that area. They opened the trunk of a car parked out front. In it was an attaché case filled with new money. Kochenour took one bill as a souvenir, the rest were turned over to Captain Jim Hatch, Battalion S-2 officer, along with the prisoners. We continued on and caught up with the rest of the company."

Capt. James J. Hatch remembered what he had done while the actual fighting was going on in the approach to St. Oedenrode. "While the line companies were securing positions around St. Oedenrode, my runner and I sneaked into the town. We found one German trying to slink away. I slowed him down with a bullet but he was able to keep going. We went to the town hall which had been the German CP. The phone was ringing. I picked it up and heard a string of German, too fast for me to understand, even with a year of German in college. Finally I said, 'Heil Hitler!' and hung up. Next, the burgomeister of St. Oedenrode came over. He lived next to the town hall. I told him we were U.S. paratroopers holding the road for British tanks which were coming the next day. He had his people out in the street shortly, dancing and celebrating freedom."

Fr. Arnold deGroot had watched in fascination from the third-floor window of a factory as the paratroopers and gliders descended on the fields of the Zonsche Heath three kilometers southwest of his vantage point. When the fighter planes approached in the direction of the factory, firing at the enemy tanks and trucks, the witnesses hastily left the factory and headed for a safer haven. Father deGroot wrote: "We passed through yards and cellars until we reached the Martinus home. There, we rested to calm our emotions. On the market field, Germans hid behind walls and trees. Soon I heard another kind of gun firing, not knowing it was American. I went down into the cellar with the other inhabitants. It was a little after 1700 hours. On the cellar grating we heard footsteps and a voice speaking over a radio. I said, 'I just heard English being spoken!' Nobody believed me. Then somebody tried to open the door. 'Those are Germans,' others said. 'Go open the door quickly before they shoot!' It was a partisan yelling 'Americans!'

"We saw them all over the market square, but there were no civilians. We all stormed outside toward those straight-forward guys and stammered our English welcome. Then we walked past the closed houses and soon the market square was filled with townspeople. The Americans gave away packages of cigarettes, sometimes four or five at a time. It was incredible to us.

"The burgomeister got back his chain of office, after being suspended for two and a half years. He was congratulated and we danced around him.

"Then the resistance members told us to go back home again and to pass the word to others. German prisoners were being brought to the town hall. The leader of the guards was a civilian. He told us, 'It isn't over yet!' Shortly afterward, the shooting started again."

Father deGroot continued: "The underground men took cover behind trees and against houses, moving toward the sound of the shooting. Some 60 Germans retreated from the village toward the farms and woods near the Dommel River behind the Oda monastery. From there they fired into the village with the underground firing back. Soon the underground occupied the garden of the Oda monastery adjoining the Dommel River. From there they fired their captured German rifles from behind the stone wall.

"I was with the civilians on the deserted market square while the Americans marched toward the bridge and the Dommel River. Then someone yelled, 'Fire at St. Oda!' I hurried there to see whether Our Lord should be taken out of the church. Luckily, just the barn was burning, caused by a tracer bullet into the hay. The inhabitants of the Oda monastery were all in the corridor, frightened as they were due to the bullets. I was able to clear the corridor for the firemen who were expected to arrive. We pushed everyone into the ward with two frightened nuns guarding them. Many of them had to be carried inside until the corridor was cleared. To extinguish the fire was more dangerous than the fire itself because of the bullets. The firemen lay flat on the floor, trying to direct the spray of water but it didn't work so they stopped. I directed them to a building next door to the blazing barn from which they continued to direct the water from their hose."

The Americans sent riflemen and machine gunners to the monastery where they took over the positions on the stone wall facing the enemy soldiers beyond the river.

Father deGroot added to his story: "In the meantime the Americans continued fighting. Two wounded were carried into the monastery. While I was in the adjoining building, an American came asking for a doctor and a priest. He pointed to two wounded soldiers in the garden. Both were Catholics. I absolved them and ran back to get some Holy Oil. When I returned, one of them had died. I went to the other, who had a bullet in his arm. He was talking and I knew he was out of danger. I went back to the first one. A few other Americans were praying around us. Then the officer of the Americans who were defending the position approached me, being furious about the Germans shooting at two nurses who were taking care of the wounded on the other side of the garden wall. This was the first English I could completely understand. It was almost 2000 hours."

Meanwhile, back at the hospital for the infirm and handicapped that had been partly taken over by the German air force surgeon and his three men, Nurse Koos van Schaik had her hands full. Paratroopers of 1st Battalion had appeared in the hospital, removed all weapons from the enemy wounded and placed guards at the doors. Nurse van Schaik describes the experiences with her first encounter with the American surgeon:

At half past five, I ran into a Chinese soldier in the front hall—A Chinese-American with a Red Cross band around his arm and the Red Cross on his helmet.

He said, "I am Captain Choy, commanding officer of the medical staff. Do you speak English?"

"A little sir," I replied.

"You have the German medical staff here, have you not?"

"Yes sir."

I showed him the operating room and the rooms with the wounded. He said, "All right, tell the German doctor that he can continue to work here. I will send him all the German wounded and next door I will open a station for our soldiers. Will you go with me to pick up some Americans? Do you have a stretcher?"

I followed him. Riet Hoonhout was helping me carry the stretcher. Dr. Choy walked in front, moving fast and light in his rubber-soled combat boots—catlike—so different from the heavy German iron-cleated boots.

Where was he taking us? We had not been out of the building this far. We went through the back yard, past the Odagesticht, the convent next door. It was also a home for senior citizens.

Behind the convent the Oda Farm is on fire, a direct hit. Firemen are trying to put the fire out, pigs are running loose all over the place. Suddenly the water of the firehose clatters on our shoulders when we pass the burning barn. The captain keeps on going. Where is he taking us?

Finally, we come to the last garden of the convent, which is separated from the fields behind it by a high stone wall. A wooden gate opens up to the meadows along the Dommel River.

Two Americans are lying on the ground. Five others are manning the machine guns on the wall. They are firing without stopping.

I look over the wall to the woods at the other side of the small river. "Is that the front line?" I asked Captain Choy.

"No," he replied, pointing with his finger to the ground. "It is right here!"

He bends over the first soldier. "Not this one. He is dead; take the second one, but hurry, we are standing under fire here!"

I just wondered how these two casualties came here. Now I realize, they have been right here on this spot!

Their machine guns are positioned on the wall. Two paratroopers who have followed us are now taking their places. It is almost impossible to make ourselves understood because of the rattling of the guns. From the field, the fire is being returned and the Americans dive behind the wall. Crouching low, we have been able to get the soldier on the stretcher and start back to the convent. Under a rain of sparks we passed the burning barn, stepping over firehoses, wading through ankle-deep puddle of water. The stretcher is heavy and our strength seems to have ebbed from all the terrible things that happened around us. We have to bring him in and maybe we have to go back for others.

Thank heaven we make it safely to the convent and take the soldier inside to the operating room of Oda. Captain Choy introduced us to Captain Best, another airborne medical officer. We cut the uniform—what a pity to ruin such nice material—but we must hurry. While the doctors try to stop the heavy bleeding in his arm, Riet and I take off the rest of the trooper's clothes. Under his blouse he has a belt of grenades. I freeze. I do not know how to handle these things. Carefully, I unfasten the buckle.

"Just drop it on the floor in the corner," Captain Best says. "I will take care of them."

Riet finds two more grenades in his pocket. The pins are still in them, but we are frightened. "Don't drop them Riet!" I say. Again Riet puts her hand in his pockets, before we remove the pants but now she removes an apple. We cannot help laughing in spite of the tension.

When the doctors are finished with him we carry him to one of the rooms in the sick bay. In the hall we have to step over the big firehose that had been laid from the street through the building to the backyard. Water is running in all directions and the nuns are trying to scoop it up and get it over the threshold.

Alongside the corridor are two stretchers with dead Americans. Carefully we maneuver to pass with our stretcher. My heart cries at this tragedy. They have come from so far to help us and, after a few hours, they are lying here dead and mutilated at our feet.

We put the young American in bed. "What is your name," I ask him. "Dennis." "Thank you Dennis for all you have done for us!" He says "It is nothing, thank you for your treatment. You Dutch people are very good to us. The war will soon be over now."

In the meantime, other elements of 1st Battalion had made their approaches into St. Oedenrode from different directions.

Sgt. Thomas E. Earhart remembered that several key personnel were disabled in the early hours of fighting. "On the first day, Captain Fred Hancock was wounded. So was Lt. Smit. Sgt. Kochenour was hit. It all happened while 'C' Company was gaining control of the first bridge."

As "B" Company had assembled on the drop zone, 1Lt. Allen C. Barham sent his 2nd Platoon scouts toward Nijnsel. When company commander Capt. Cleveland R. Fitzgerald gave the word, Barham sent his platoon on its way. "The 2nd Platoon attacked Nijnsel where Dutch intelligence reports stated that Germans were located."

A member of 2nd Platoon, PFC Forrest J. Nichols, remembered, "Our platoon assembled quickly. We attached ourselves to Joop Oosterwijk of the Dutch underground. He led us on the patrol to Nijnsel."

While looking for the footbridge to enter St. Oedenrode from the southeast, the remainder of "B" Company came upon a second highway bridge that hadn't been considered in the planning stages. On their approach, a small German unit was closing in on the same bridge with the aim of destroying it. A bazooka round took care of that squad's explosives as well as the squad. A larger group of enemy soldiers had taken up positions in the cemetery beside the church.

Sgt. Arthur Parker followed 1st Battalion into St. Oedenrode. His job would be with the 377th Parachute Field Artillery Battalion when they arrived on the scene on D plus 2. He was also to provide bazooka protection and an anti-tank defense for the infantry if the artillery pieces were not recovered. Parker describes his first day: "We headed into St. Oedenrode, heard firing all around us from the cemetery by the church. We fired back and the Germans faded away to the northeast. We saw our first dead paratrooper lying right in front of the church. We entered the town without any trouble and the Dutch people were coming out with their pieces of orange cloth. Everybody had something orange. They were offering us pitchers of milk. We drank a few glasses and tried to tell the people that the war wasn't over yet and that the Germans would try to take the town back. They were so happy to see the Americans that they did not care."

As the first-day activities wound down, Fr. Arnold deGroot was beginning to feel hungry, after a day without eating. He wrote: "I was getting hungry and went back to the factory. On the way, I met another brother who informed me the factory was now being used as a first aid station with 12 wounded, one of whom was a German. Those cigarettes made us thirsty. We weren't used to them anymore. We went to our neighbors of the parish who invited us to drink German champagne with them. The enemy left lots of champagne. We celebrated the liberation with a peace cigar and sang Wilhelmus (National Anthem) for the first time. We told the others of our experiences and it was 0130 when we went to bed."

Fr. Hermen Peeters, now seventy-five years old, remembered liberation this way: "On Sunday evening there was a German jeep which had been captured. It contained many bottles of brandy and boxes of cigars. I hadn't eaten. The Americans gave the priests two bottles of brandy so they could celebrate. I became very sick because I drank brandy on an empty stomach. I was one of many who were very sick that night."

It was almost 2000 hours when the Americans ceased firing for the day. They were still being fired upon from two places across the Dommel River but those Germans were far away toward Rijzinger, a small hamlet toward Schijndel.

The Seven Jeeps

The 502nd after-action report makes mention of a patrol encountering twelve men and five jeeps on the road to Schijndel. No mention is made of the other two that were part of the same convoy.

On the 18th of September, the town was attacked from the south by a strong enemy force. One company of the battalion met this determined attack and repulsed it, overrunning enemy mortar positions and capturing a number of prisoners. A patrol which had been sent to reconnoiter the road to Schijndel saw twelve men and five jeeps of the 1st Airborne Army, who, after taking the wrong road, found themselves a mile in enemy territory, pinned down by enemy small arms and mortar fire. Two squads were sent forward to relieve the situation. They drove the enemy back and rescued the men and jeeps.

On the morning of the eighteenth, Colonel Cartwright of the 1st Allied Airborne Army headquarters wanted to move up Hell's Highway toward Veghel and other towns to the north. Division Headquarters had provided him with two jeeploads of men from Division Recon Platoon to cover them in their move. Other jeeps were destined for the 501st Parachute Infantry Regiment, which was in the Veghel area. The jeeps had arrived on landing zone "W" just north of Son. All had arrived safely except the one driven by PFC Tony Wysocki. Having narrowly escaped with his life, or from serious injury, when the glider carrying Wysocki and his jeep had collided with another over the landing zone, the glider had been badly damaged on impact in the crash. (See story on page 89.)

After spending the night at Division Headquarters in the church school near Son, Wysocki was headed for Veghel as a passenger. He wrote: "Early at dawn, Thompson and a lieutenant came from Veghel to escort us back to Veghel. We had seven jeeps. I was in the second jeep with Thompson, Brown and two other men. As we left Son, we made a turn to the left at an intersection. It was the wrong way. We headed for Best.[75] As we approached a road and made our turn, there was a German machine gunner at a road block. He fired a burst at us and we opened up on him. There was another gunner on the other side of the road. We couldn't stop so we proceeded on ahead to get out of the range of the machine guns. As we did this, we came into this little town. To our surprise, it was filled with Germans. The road led to a circular roundabout so we went to the right and hoped to circle around and come right back. We thought we

75. Wysocki was wrong. They ended up headed for Schijndel or Olland.

were part of a Western the way we were going through and shooting up the town—loaded as it was with Germans.

"We lost the first jeep and I don't know what happened to the five behind us because we couldn't stop. We thought by opening fire on the machine gunners we'd warn the others behind us. We proceeded out of town on a country road which was only a two-laner with ditches on both sides. Lo and behold, here comes a convoy of Germans. We were shooting at them as we went by—close enough to reach out and shake hands. Near the end of the convoy, somebody got out with a machine gun and was going to spray us with it. At the same time somebody threw a grenade into the jeep. It went off. We hit the German and went to the right and hit a tree head on. I was thrown into a ditch. In the meantime the Germans had halted their convoy. They were on the other side of the road in the ditch. I crawled behind a house. I was just going to reload the .45 when I heard 'Achtung!' That soldier had a 'cannon' in his hand. I could see the rifling in the barrel. That was my experience in Holland. They lined us up in front of the house . . . the five of us. I can recall an elderly couple who came out of the house with water and rags to wipe our wounds and, in the meantime, the Germans questioned us a bit and then loaded us on a truck and took us to a hospital."

Though he didn't realize it at the time, Sgt. Elmer Weber of the Division Recon Platoon was a participant in the "Seven Jeeps" incident. He wrote: "Driving the jeep was Paul Goswick. Riding in front was a major (probably from the 1st Allied Airborne Army) from headquarters. In the back seat were Cpl. Robert Boyle and myself. We had only gone a mile or two when we came to the top of a small hill where we met a German tank and a platoon of German soldiers coming up the other side. They immediately opened fire and, as we dove in the ditch, Boyle was hit. We managed to get him over into the ditch and found out he had been hit in the back and was paralyzed from the waist down. Realizing our only hope was to withdraw, we made Cpl. Boyle as comfortable as possible. After crawling about 500 yards we suddenly came under heavy mortar fire. Assessing the situation, we decided the shelling was coming from behind a haystack several hundred yards away. We fired tracers into it and set it afire. Sure enough, out ran two German soldiers. We got rid of them in short order. As soon as we got back to our own unit, I asked Captain Thomas Wilder for a squad of men to accompany me in getting Cpl. Boyle out. By the time we got back there the Germans had withdrawn. The jeep was ruined but we brought Boyle out OK. Unfortunately, he died that night in the hospital."

Another soldier who played a part in the incident was Pvt. James W. Flanagan from "C" Company of the 502nd Parachute Regiment. He had this recollection: "My platoon set up a road block at the intersection of the Schijndel–St. Oedenrode and the Son to Veghel roads. At this point we bedded down for the night.

"On the morning of the 18th, a convoy of jeeps came through our road block. The private on the block told the Army Air Corps major that the Germans were up the road toward Schijndel. The major said he could read a map and proceeded to go up the road. The convoy was ambushed and sent back a request for help. The second platoon sent a patrol up the road (two squads) under Sgt. Willis O. Bird. I was acting as platoon scout. I went out on the point with Junior Leafty, taking turns, covering and moving up the road side ditch.

"We continued this movement up the road for about a mile, until we came to a sturdy looking house with a couple of windows facing our line of approach. The windows were open with the curtains pulled back, a pretty good warning. It was Leafty's turn to dash ahead. He had to cross a culvert (too small to crawl through) so while I covered him, he took a mad dash and scrambled over. An MG-42 cut loose from the window close to the road. I let them have a full clip of M-1 ball—and I ducked down into the ditch just in time as another MG-42 mowed the bushes that I had been behind. Leafty was OK. I was OK. Sgt. W. O. Bird was working up the ditch about 25 yards behind me. About this time, I heard the 'pum—pum—pum—pump' of someone stuffing a mortar in an expert manner. I had previously learned to pay attention to little things like that. I was wondering who was going to be on the receiving end. The first hit about 100 yards to my left. Number two about 75 yards. Three about 50 yards and about then I was getting a little perturbed. Number four hit about 25 yards away and I knew that the next one was going to be close so I coiled up in a ball on the side of the ditch. I heard the flutter of the tail fins as it came in. I didn't hear it explode. I was booted up the slope and into the air several feet.

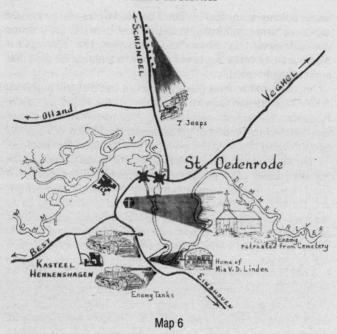

Map 6

Everything in slow motion until I started down and I really bounced when I hit the asphalt road—flat on my stomach. I was out of things for a while. Don't know how long. I came back to reality. Realized I was lying in a much-exposed position and bullets were buzzing around. I wasn't feeling anything and nothing seemed to work. I finally got my right arm in action. I could see that I had taken a steel fragment through my left wrist and I wasn't ready to check my legs. I couldn't feel them. I crawled over to the ditch and someone pulled me in. I was given a shot of morphine and a couple of bandages were applied to the worst wounds. By this time I was bloody from the hips down, looking like hell. I noticed my old M-1 rifle lying in the ditch with a splintered stock.

"Right about now I wanted to get out of where I was, but the aid man said it would be a while before they could get a stretcher in. So I lay back and cooled it since I was lying in the same ditch that I was hit in and I didn't want any more mortar shells landing in my hip pocket. I decided to crawl out. I could move my arms and legs by this time. I crawled for perhaps 200–300 yards. My elbows and knees were raw. I decided it would be a lot easier if I could walk down that asphalt road. So, I picked up a scrap piece of lumber to assist me and climbed out of the ditch and walked down the road. I hobbled along in plain sight of everyone. No problem. I guess they could see I was out of this war.

"Probably three-quarters of a mile down the road a jeep raced up to meet me—did a fast 180 degree turn and I flopped in the front seat for a fast trip to the hospital in St. Oedenrode—right to the door. I got out and walked into the receiving room. I was immediately grabbed by the Catholic nuns and aid men and in no time at all I was stripped bare—washed and inspected, powdered with sulfa and whatever and bandaged, issued a hospital gown and put to bed and all this happened before breakfast. Sure a hell of a thing to go to war before you have your morning coffee."

Private Flanagan failed in his part of the rescue effort of the seven jeeps and their occupants. The only jeep that got away was the one containing the colonel, and he was the one who had requested help for the rescue of his party.

Sgt. Willis O. Bird and other members of 2nd Platoon of "C" Company continued the rescue efforts, using the cover of the roadside ditches the men had set out. They had been spotted by the enemy a thousand yards from the jeeps when the enemy began to fire upon them.

With covering fire from the two squads, Privates Culverhouse and Duval made their way up to the jeeps, managed to climb on board the first two, got them started, turned them around, and dashed off toward the American lines. Both jeeps were hit several times but the men got them back safely. With covering fire continuing from the two accompanying squads, 2Lt. Joshua Mewborn and Pvt. Junior Leafty, along with two medics, were able to get hold of most of the wounded. With that, the entire group withdrew to St. Oedenrode.

Evacuating Enemy Wounded

Small-unit actions had been taking place along several other side roads that didn't involve rescuing men from the seven jeeps. Enemy units had suffered heavy losses. On the afternoon of the eighteenth, the firing died down and the battlefield was silent. Capt. Frank Choy, the American surgeon, told the nurses that the German doctor could go out to pick up his wounded. Nurse Koos van Schaik continues her story in diary form:

The German doctor cannot go alone in the car. Three Americans and I go along. One drives and the other two sit on the fenders with hands on triggers. The doctor and I sit in the back. We turned towards the road to Schijndel and were stopped by paratroopers in a ditch. "You are entering No Man's Land!" one of them calls. One of the troopers explained our mission. We continued for about 500 meters and had to get out of the car as there was a tree across the road. I realized I was completely dressed in white and could be spotted a mile away. One of the paratroopers stayed by our side. The others remained with the car. The doctor walked straight out and called several times in German: "Don't shoot, hold your fire, this is the Red Cross!"

We passed a burning house and came to a ditch along some woods. We climbed over some debris. Suddenly we saw a lot of abandoned German equipment in the ditch with Germans lying about. Again the surgeon called out loudly: "Rotes Kreuz hier, nicht schiessen!" A projectile whistled over our heads. "What was that?" I asked the American.

"Not so good," he whispered. "German artillery!"

Suddenly four or five German soldiers came out of the woods, machine guns in hand, for a confrontation. The surgeon was a very tall and broad fellow and he stood high on the ridge of the embankment. The Germans were young and hesitated a moment, recognizing a German officer, before they spoke. They told the doctor that they cannot hold their position and they cannot take care of their wounded and are going to retreat. The doctor tried to talk them into surrendering, but one replied, pointing at the American, "Wir konnen ihn doch einfach umlegen und Sie konnen mitkomen!" (We can finish him off and you can come with us!)

The surgeon raised his voice, "Are you crazy? You see I am a doctor," and pointing to the school far away beyond the field, "I have over 75 wounded comrades there, you want me to abandon them? And what about these men here? You are outnumbered and you do not have a chance!"

The American and I were standing motionless. My heart beat pounded in my ear. My throat was dry and I couldn't swallow.

The surgeon told the soldiers that if they did not want to surrender they should at least move away now and hold their fire till we were back in the village as we will now collect and take their worst wounded with us. They agreed and moved away quickly. The doctor checked the dead ones to make sure they were really dead. One soldier was lying in a deep ditch. He called out to us. He could barely speak. He had a chest wound and was bleeding badly. The doctor picked him up under the arms and I grabbed him by the feet. He was so heavy and I had great difficulty lifting him over the embankment and carrying him to the car. The doctor told me to get into the car first. We put the soldier crossways over my knees. The American was covering us from behind, walking, facing the woods behind us, with his gun at the ready. It remained quiet. The German medics were waiting for us and helped to remove the soldier from my lap. My uniform was stained with blood and some of the nurses asked if I was wounded. I couldn't speak, shook my head and ran into the kitchen for water. I put my head on my arm and sobbed. I could not surrender to my emotions and went upstairs to change my uniform apron before I went back to the car.

Wolff and Hahn, the two German medics, pushed me aside and said "You aren't going out there again. We will go." The Americans jumped on the car and they left for the same location again.

A short time later civilians brought in a little three year old girl who was bleeding profusely from the neck. The Unterarzt told them to put her on the table. Captain Choy came in and gave directions to one of the guards to get blood plasma from next door. The girl lost consciousness. The doctor applied pressure. Captain Choy wanted to put a needle in the little arm, but the veins were too small.

We all watched, praying for a miracle. The surgeon explained that he will try to do it with his instruments. He made a quick incision in the elbow. The guards were back and had opened the blood plasma can. Captain Choy got it ready and the flow started. We all held our breath. Then the little girl opened her eyes and said, "Een beetje water." (A little water, please.) There wasn't a dry eye in the room.

Fr. Arnold deGroot described how little of the country had been liberated beyond the width of the corridor near St. Oedenrode. "The Germans were in Boxtel and Olland. Many were hidden in the Eerde area. Some people in a five kilometer radius still weren't liberated—Best, Liemde, and Eerde. The situation in Schijndel was unknown since nobody could travel to those villages. Two kilometers past the Damianus Foundation on the boundary between St. Oedenrode and Schijndel many shots were heard. The Americans fired mortars from the Damianus

Foundation so we were sent to the shelter of the farm. Since I preferred to be in the village, I left using the main road. This way everybody could see me and they didn't fire at me. I met Americans near the Doelen who asked me how far it was to the railroad. That is where the Germans were and they headed for them. Those men had incredible courage."

St. Oedenrode on the Nineteenth

The day had started as one of elation as the first tanks came up the corridor having passed over the newly installed Bailey bridge at Son. The excitement was recorded in the diary of Nurse Koos van Schaik of the Dutch Red Cross, who was on duty at an aid station jointly operated by a small German air force medical team, the civilian nurses and members of the 1st Battalion surgical team. Koos van Schaik wrote:

Sept. 19—Willy (Ogg) and I go with Miss Kosterman to the marketplace. I don't recognize the village. Is this St. Oedenrode? Flags, flags everywhere. Even the smallest house has the tricolor bunting, red, white and blue, reaching out to the middle of the street.

British tanks thunder over the market, slide around the corner at the church. We cannot make ourselves understood due to the rattle of the treads. The people cheer and cheer. The entire village is here. It is overwhelming. The British laugh when they see the enthusiasm of the population. They hold up their thumbs as a greeting and victory sign. The children are throwing paper streamers called serpentines. The long colored paper ribbons get stuck on the aerials of the tanks and fly along in big wavy curls. The tank commanders are sitting in the turrets with their earphones on. They duck to avoid the flags. In Belgium the population had written with chalk on the vehicles, "Greetings from Scheldewindeke, Flandres. In Edingen everything is O.K."

Also the French have left their visiting cards. "Bon souvenir d' arras." The Dutch are not far behind: "Welcome in Valkenswaard, Greetings to Nelly T. in Nynsel. Here everything O.K." Family news for relatives and friends down the road. People become ingenious.

A big armored car with the words "Korps Mariniers Rotterdam" gets a tremendous ovation—the first Dutch soldiers, Corps Royal Marines Rotterdam, who have been in England after the fall of Holland in 1940.

This is the liberation army. The American paratroopers have taken the road from Eindhoven on north. Now the tanks have to hurry to Nijmegen to save the bridges. On and on the tanks roll by. In between are Red Cross ambulances, also smaller staff cars. Motorcycles and dispatchers are shooting in and out of the convoy. The Red Cross soldiers wave at us when they see our nurses' uniforms with the Red Cross armband. We laugh and wave back at them. The Americans around us look a lot better than yesterday, much more cheerful. They thank God that the army has arrived. Apparently it has been very risky.

And we still cannot understand that we are standing in the same St. Oedenrode of yesterday and of last week. All the colors and all that orange!

It is so overwhelming that we cannot comprehend that this is real. A few days ago we were standing on this very spot watching the Germans retreat.

The people now laugh and cry at the same time. Our ambulant old folks have permission to come and look for themselves. "Nurse, is it peace now? Are we now going back to Scheweniger?"

"Not quite, we need a little more patience!" Willy replies.

A few hours later, on the outposts where the troops of "C" Company of the 502nd mount their guard, the scene changes to one of watchfulness, wonder at what will happen. The tension returns.

After helping unload the second-day serial of gliders on the eighteenth, underground member Johan Scheutjens had been sent out on a scouting mission. He wrote: "On the evening of the 18th, a colleague and I went back on reconnaissance looking for more Germans. We learned from the citizens of Olland that a large group of Germans was on its way to Olland and that there were also many Germans in Schijndel to the northeast. We returned to our base and informed our commander who in turn notified the paratroopers."

The report passed on by Johan Scheutjens was sent to the forward company of 1st Battalion. When Capt. Fred Hancock of "C" Company received the warning, he immediately sent out a patrol under Lt. Harry Larson to intercept the enemy force. Very shortly Larson's men came under fire but did force the enemy outposts to retreat. As the enemy force moved to outflank his men, Larson fell back until his patrol was on line with Lt. Joshua Mewborn's platoon. Soon all of "C" Company was in on the fight.

Paddy McCrory's Tank

Watching from a height in his command post, LTC Pat Cassidy sensed that "C" Company was hard-pressed and fighting a reinforced company-sized enemy force. Cassidy remembered a partly disabled British tank that had limped into town earlier and was now parked in town. He asked its commander, Sgt. Paddy McCrory, if he could give "C" Company some support.

McCrory was quick to respond in the affirmative but said he was short on crew. S/Sgt. Roy Nickrent, operations sergeant for Cassidy, and Pvt. John J. O'Brien were detailed to fill out the makeshift crew. The tank could travel no faster than a slow double time in leading out with the company attack. With O'Brien inside helping McCrory with chores, Nickrent rode up in the turret calling out targets of opportunity. McCrory spotted a three-gun 20mm anti-aircraft battery that had been providing support for the enemy move toward St. Oedenrode. Before the battery could get off an answering round, McCrory had wiped out all three gun positions. A German truck in a field tried to make a getaway toward Schijndel. McCrory got it with one shot from the tank's cannon. The truck, loaded with ammunition, exploded all over the countryside.

Small-arms fire ricocheted off the tank's armor as firing increased. It was prudent for Staff Sergeant Nickrent to get down from his exposed position, where he followed along behind the tank firing bursts from his tommy gun. Enemy soldiers in the ditches began to surrender in small groups.

When firing abated to the front, Private O'Brien climbed up into the turret where he had a better view. He continued to fire a Sten gun into the ditches and bushes along the road, routing more Germans into the open. While in the exposed position, an enemy sniper picked off O'Brien with a bullet to the head.

S/Sgt. Roy W. Nickrent remembered that Lieutenant Colonel Cassidy sent him and Pvt. John J. O'Brien along as a makeshift crew in Paddy McCrory's crippled tank. He wrote: "As the tank could only go about five miles an hour, it gave us time to survey the terrain ahead and McCrory could get a fix on it and blast it. Everything that was in that Irishman's way was blasted out. He was a great soldier!

"As for heroics, the action of Pvt. John O'Brien from the

hatch of McCrory's crippled tank displayed total disregard for his own safety. He stood up and fired his automatic weapon at the enemy troops—however, one enemy round caught him in the head."

Sgt. Arthur Parker of the 377th Parachute Field Artillery Battalion was one of seventeen men who had parachuted into Holland on D-Day as part of the forward echelon for Division Artillery. They were led by three officers from Headquarters Battery. This group provided the fire direction, forward observers, survey section, radio, and wiremen. The rest of the battalion came in over the next three days, one battery by parachute and the rest by glider.

First Lieutenant Herbert Perry was one of the three officers who jumped with the forward echelon of Division Artillery. After finding the equipment bundle, several of the team headed for St. Oedenrode carrying the contents of the bundle. They set up a station in an orchard. In the morning they went back to the DZ to pick up the rest of their equipment only to find the parachute infantrymen battling the Germans for possession of the drop zone on which they had landed.

From an entry he had made in the diary of 1/Sgt. F. G. Fitzgerald[76] of "C" Battery during the campaign, Perry described his actions for September 19 as follows:

> The British tanks started coming through at 1000 hours. Boy, did they look good. The Jerries had pushed in from the north and west during the night to within 1,500 yards of the St. Oedenrode bridge.
>
> About noon, Lt. Col. Cassidy asked me if we had an artillery OP and I told him only the church steeple. He asked me how I thought we could do from the mortar OP and I said I would go look at it. It was a thousand yards north of the bridge.
>
> On the way out there we ran into some Jerries. They had infiltrated through the lines and were in considerable strength. We went back and got some 12 or 15 troopers and were driving the rats back slowly, when one of the tanks came up and speeded our push. We pushed them back about 600 yards and then they came pouring out of the woods with their hands in the air. One of them got Sgt. Earl Johnson just before he decided to surrender. A great guy, a big loss to the FO section. The mortar OP was no good for artillery. You couldn't see 1,000 yards.

76. From the diary of 1/Sgt. F. G. Fitzgerald for September 19, 1944.

A member of the forward observer team, Pvt. Gordon E. Hannigan, recalled being with Sgt. Earl Johnson during the action. He wrote: "Taking the part of an infantryman was how Sergeant Johnson was wounded. He was about 32 years old and had a 12 year old daughter. I thought at the time, 'Boy, is he ever old!' I was 19 and his daughter was only 7 years younger than I. I found out very soon that he was a much better man than I.

"I was with Sgt. Johnson when he was wounded. We were trying to take a section of road and the Germans were holed up in a farmhouse. Sgt. Johnson was hit in the neck. He was carried back and I tried to administer first aid. He was conscious all the time. I was trying to give him a shot of morphine from my first aid kit to relieve the pain. In the stress of the moment, I forgot to puncture the end of the syringe and Sgt. Johnson said, 'Hannigan, are you doing it right?' I finally got it open. The medics took him to an aid station and I found out later that he had died. I had lost a friend."

Reinforcements

Second and 3rd Battalions of the 502nd spent the evening of the nineteenth in position along the Wilhelmina Canal near the blown highway bridge and outposted along the Eindhoven–Best highway. Cpl. Pete Santini describes the evening and the trip the following day to join 1st Battalion up in St. Oedenrode.

September 20—The night was rather peaceful. A few 88s and some mortar fire but they were very scattered.

We left the position about 1530 hours and started toward St. Oedenrode. We had to cross the jump field again. It was a fast march. While we were crossing the fields a number of C-47s came over. They dropped some equipment bundles first. To our amazement, some men began bailing out. It was a battery of the 377th Parachute Field Artillery Battalion bringing in some much needed artillery. The men must have been quite scared. I can well imagine how they must have felt at seeing the field they were jumping on completely surrounded. However, we shouted a few reassuring words to them and told them to take it easy while struggling to get out of their chutes. We moved into Division reserve and hadn't been there but about an hour when the line companies were ordered to move out to support an attack. The CP was left back as a rear echelon.

As a member of "B" Battery of the 377th Parachute Field Artillery Battalion, PFC Walter M. Tibbetts was one of those paratroopers who appeared suddenly overhead as 2nd and 3rd Battalions of the 502nd were crossing the landing fields. Tibbetts wrote: "We in the gun crews had a 'door load' to push out ahead of us, part of our gun, and the rest of it was under the plane in racks that were dropped as we jumped. We could see a lot that was going on, both around us outside and also down below. Our flight of planes hit the coast five miles south of the flight path and we went directly over a large German anti-aircraft battery. We were flying in 'low down' and I could see very well the Germans running in all directions, jumping on their guns and opening up on us. The planes broke formation and scattered in all directions, circled back over the Channel, regrouped and got on the correct course. I don't think we lost a plane in the incident. It surprised the Germans as much as it surprised us. We were so low and just in and out. We got the most flak and anti-aircraft fire just before the drop zone. That is where our plane was hit."

The 377th Field Artillery Battalion minus "B" Battery went into Holland by glider on D plus 2 while "B" Battery went by parachute the following day.

Sgt. Robert J. Kane of "B" Battery remembered, "As far as 'B' Battery and its jump, we really took a kidding for arriving a day late. In a discussion we had in the marshaling area, it was explained why the men of our battery parachuted instead of going in by glider with the rest of the battalion. One of the officers said it was his understanding that because of the general mix-up in Normandy, the army wanted to give parachute artillery another crack at a combat jump.

"The jump itself was like a parade field jump in the states. The field was firmly secured. We did, however, run into a great deal of ground fire on the flight in. Our flight dispersed over the Channel and regrouped. The second route in gave us much less ground fire."

Regimental Staff Hit Hard

The narrative of the 502nd Parachute Infantry Regiment for the Market-Garden operation provides a description of action that took place on the twenty-first and twenty-second in the regimental area:

During the night of the 21st and the 22nd of September, orders were issued for an attack of the Regiment less one Battalion, supported by a squadron of tanks. The objective was a road which crossed the St. Oedenrode–Eindhoven highway at a point approximately 2,500 yards north of St. Oedenrode. The attack was launched at 0630 hours across open ground against heavy machine gun, AT gun, artillery, and 20mm and 40mm gun fire, but inch by inch the enemy was pushed back 1,500 yards. At about 1000 hours, the regimental commander, the S-3, the S-2, the assistant S-3, and several enlisted men of the regimental staff became casualties; however, the attack continued without slackening. Five 88mm guns and two 40mm guns were knocked out by the regiment, and 140 prisoners taken. Because of the fact that positions could not be consolidated, the regiment drew back and once again took up defensive positions about 1,500 yards north and east of St. Oedenrode.

LTC John Michaelis had moved his regimental CP forward so he could be near the action. He was with members of his regimental staff along with LTC Paul Danahy, division G-2, and Maj. Harold W. Hannah of G-3, Maj. Harry Elkins and 1Lt. Thomas Swirczynski of the 377th demanding changes in his supporting artillery when a tree burst exploded above the group splattering the whole group with shell fragments. A total of fourteen men became casualties, including the two division staff officers.

Capt. George Buker, the regimental S-2 officer, remembered that September 22 was his last day in action with the 101st. "An enemy shell landed near a gathering of the regimental staff killing the regimental commander's orderly, PFC Garland Mills, and wounding several staff officers."

Maj. Harold W. Hannah of the division G-3 staff happened to be present with LTC Paul Danahy as observers at the meeting when the shell hit. He wrote: "Early in the morning of the 22nd, I was hit along with others outside of St. Oedenrode when I was contacting them in reference to regimental plans. I walked back to my jeep which was behind a tank. Two of our lads saw the bleeding from my shoulder and insisted on injecting their morphine syrettes."

Both officers, as well as the others, were evacuated and flown back to a hospital in England and missed out on further actions of the 101st.

Move Toward Schijndel

On the twenty-second, there was fierce fighting in the Schijndel–Eerde area by 1st and 3rd Battalions of the 501st battling to keep the enemy from moving south to cut the northbound highway. Part of the 502nd was sent up the St. Oedenrode–Schijndel highway to relieve some of the pressure being felt by the 501st troops.

In his diary entry for the twenty-second, S/Sgt. Earl L. Cox of "Fox" Company of the 502nd wrote:

> Attacked to the north in the direction of Schijndel at 0630, assisted by tanks. Met stiff resistance, advanced approximately 700 yards driving enemy out. Dug in and held what we gained. At 1600, we pulled back to where we started at 0630 to consolidate positions. 3rd Platoon still protecting Division CP.

PFC E. O. Parmley must have been in on that maneuver. He wrote: "We were around St. Oedenrode a lot during the next week or so. Our next move was an attack near St. Oedenrode. We had a Sherman tank with our platoon along with a British crew. It was a dawn attack. I was next to the tank on its right side. We just formed a line with the tank and walked at a normal pace with the tank waiting for the Germans to open up. In front of us was a line of trees and a farm house on the right about 100 yards away. The trees ended directly in front of our tank. From the left end of the line of large trees a 20mm gun opened up on the tank. I do not believe we were over 75 yards from their lines. All of their fire seemed to be directed to our tank. I thought to myself, being next to a tank is not the place to be. What worried me most as I hit the ground was the realization that I had a gasoline stove strapped to my back. It was full of gasoline. I promised myself I would never go into another attack with a gas stove even close to me.

"The 20mm gun was no match for the tank. The tank did not even waste a 76mm shell on it. The three Germans manning the gun were cut down by the tank's machine gun. They were brave but foolish soldiers and their gun was not dug in. There were a few branches off a tree for camouflage. That is all they had for protection. With the 20mm gone, we took their positions with a few prisoners."

Parmley continued: "Later in the day our bazooka man, Ray

(Calfboy) Blasingame had no other weapon than his bazooka. He carried it like a rifle. For some reason, he became detached from the rest of us and in a fence row he came upon a German who saw the bazooka pointed at him. 'Calfboy' said the guy's eyes almost popped out of his head. 'Calfboy' came proudly marching his trophy back to the company and the German had his hands as high as they would go."

War Correspondent Walter Cronkite

Walter Cronkite was one of several war correspondents on hand to report from the battle scene in Holland. He had arrived on board the same glider that carried BG Anthony C. McAuliffe, the artillery commander of the 101st Division. In one of his dispatches sent from the battlefront, he describes his visit to the prisoner-of-war cage of the 101st Division, which was set up near the town of St. Oedenrode. A censored copy of his eye-witness report was transmitted by radioman T/4 Iving M. Schmidt of the 101st Signal Company to the rear base in England on September 22. The message[77] reads as follows:

22101 Cronkite add Vidor requote funny thing is we don't find any Nazis among them. Their morale pretty low and they're all decided now they never were much in favor of Hitler anyway. I visited prisoner area which large field surrounded dunes providing perfect guard posts.

Germans were sorry looking lot. They are pilots who never flew planes, paratroops who never jumped. They are sixteen year olds jerked from Nazi military schools and rushed toward front lines. There were men of sixty from labor and home guard detachments. In this enclosure is bottom of Hitler's manpower barrel. Major Robert L. Gregory, Birmingham, Alabama provost marshall of this airborne unit "I don't believe there is a Four F left in Germany. We seem to have captured all of them in last couple of days."

We only have two real problems here. One is when trucks come to evacuate prisoners to the rear. These boys had enough of war and we are still catching few shells around here. They really fight to get on those trucks going back. Other problem is when we try to feed them captured German rations instead of American rations—see that big

77. Copy of Walter Cronkite dispatch message provided by Sgt. Patrick Macri of message center of the 101st Airborne Signal Company.

hole they are digging over there. That is to throw German rations in. They also are getting finicky about our own rations. They learned what is in each ration box and scrap among themselves over favorite breakfast, lunch and dinner units. Enditem.

Signed Cronkite

Recon Trip of Johan Scheutjens

Much action took place between St. Oedenrode and Schijndel and Eerde on September 25. The road had been cut northeast of Koevering on the evening of the twenty-fourth. The Germans were also pressing hard on the 501st positions in and around Eerde. On the twenty-fifth, underground member Johan Scheutjens went on a reconnaissance mission toward Schijndel. He wrote: "I was ordered by our commander to go on recon between St. Oedenrode and Schijndel because I was thoroughly acquainted with the terrain. If possible, I was to return by way of Olland. I was dressed in a pair of worn-out coveralls and carried a pail given to me by a farmer. During the trip I walked right smack into some Germans. They asked me what I was looking for. I told them some cows had broken out of the field and I was looking for them. Fortunately, there were some cows in the field. The Germans let me go and I went toward the cows. I came to a farm where there were many Germans. By coincidence, I knew the farmer who lived there. I greeted him and inquired about his family. I asked for the loan of a raincoat, which he gave me.

"About an hour later, I went on my way. After having reconnoitered St. Oedenrode and Schijndel, I went toward Olland. I had an uncle there and he put me up for the night.

"The next morning I started for St. Oedenrode by way of Olland. As I reached Olland, I was picked up by the Germans. They placed me behind a house near a woodshed where I was guarded by two Germans with rifles at the ready. All of a sudden, like a bolt of lightning, the sky lit up with a shell burst from the direction of St. Oedenrode. The Germans ran for cover and I fled to safety on the other side of the building. As I was very familiar with the terrain, I ran zigzag as fast as I could. The Germans fired at me. All I could think of was to get away. I found a farmhouse and luckily saw no more Germans. I continued on to St. Oedenrode and came back to safe territory.

"I immediately went to my commander and informed him of my experience. He shook hands and said, 'A job well done.' "[78]

Arnhem Survivors

The survivors of the battle for Arnhem and its bridge had been rescued by the British and were on their way south and back to England. They passed the positions of the American soldiers along Hell's Highway in the vicinity of Uden, Veghel, and St. Oedenrode.

Communications sergeant Joe Ludwig of "H" Company witnessed an event that was to have a lasting impression on him: "On D plus 10 (September 27) we were moving up the corridor in the vicinity of Uden in two columns along both sides of the road. It was late in the afternoon when we saw troops and trucks in the distance. Automatically, without a word or signal, we pulled off to both sides of the road. Those who were able and the walking wounded slowly passed by us followed by truck loads of wounded and sick. We looked at them and they looked at us but no one said a word. It was the British paras returning from Arnhem (what was left of them). They were beat up, sick, tired, wounded, dirty and covered with blood and mud but there was something about their bearing that filled us with respect and admiration. They had been defeated, through no fault of their own, but not conquered. After they passed, we continued on our march. No one said a word. We were all lost in our own thoughts. *There but for the Grace of God go we!*"

Several miles farther down the road, the marching men and the slow-moving trucks passed through Veghel. Sgt. Gerald Zimmerman of Signal Company witnessed their passing and remembered the incident in his diary notations:

It was at Veghel that I saw the British Airbornes coming back from the Arnhem front. These boys were very quiet when coming back, but you could see they still had good spirit. All our hats are off to those boys who fought so furiously and for so long with overwhelming odds against them. I know that they will always be remembered—the two thousand living who got out, and the six

78. Translated by Cpl. Arie Van Dort, a former member of the 326th Engineers who had been born in St. Oedenrode.

thousand dead, wounded and prisoners who didn't return. A battalion that tried to reach them was wiped out.

The action in the St. Oedenrode area continued to wind down as fresh British armored columns and infantry moved slowly up the corridor, pushing the enemy out of their positions on either side of Hell's Highway.

TWELVE

Veghel

The 501st Seizes Veghel

The assignment of the 501st Parachute Infantry Regiment was to quickly seize the four bridges in and near the town of Veghel. Two of the spans were along the highway that would carry the British XXX Corps on its move up the corridor to Arnhem to provide relief for its airborne forces. One of those bridges was a narrow lift span crossing the Zuid-Willems-Vaart Canal at the southwest edge of Veghel. The other bridge crossed the Aa River in the town itself. Two railroad bridges, one over the same canal on the west side of town and a shorter span over the Aa River on the north side of town, were also to be seized.

When the regimental staff made its plans it was decided to add a separate drop zone for 1st Battalion so that if the enemy had a strong force along the canal, 1st Battalion would have been in position to attack it from behind. First Battalion was to seize the two bridges farthest to the east.

Two of the 1st Battalion troopers related the change of drop zone for their unit, and one provided the reasoning for the move.

As communications officer for 1st Battalion, 1Lt. Frank L. Fitter remembered: "1st Battalion had a separate drop zone of its own. It was called 'A-1' and was about four kilometers northwest of Veghel."

"A day or so before the mission, Colonel Johnson had our drop zone changed to the east side of the canal," wrote Sgt. Chester L. Brooks, who was operations sergeant for the battalion. "Otherwise, all the troopers would have jumped on the west side. This would have made it easier for the Germans to resist us."

In its briefings, the 1st Battalion commanders had directed that any man who landed where he saw a bridge was to go directly to it for the purpose of securing it. Specific assignments had been made for one platoon of "A" Company to go at once to the lower railroad bridge and one platoon from "C" Company was to seize the upper bridge over the Aa River. A platoon from "B" was to head for the road bridge in Veghel.

The loss of 1Lt. Charles Faith's pathfinder plane meant there were no directional signals in place when LTC Harry W. O. Kinnard's 1st Battalion arrived shortly after 1300 hours as the lead echelon for the 101st. The lead plane had to depend on the skill of its pilot and navigator to determine the locations of the fields in which to drop the six-hundred-man battalion. They missed!

Kinnard landed near a road and at once saw a large building that was identified on a map as the "Kasteel." Holland is full of castles; there were several of them in the area. He didn't know where he was. He sent Pvt. Alphonse Batts, of the S-2 Section, to make inquiries. Batts found a Hollander who informed him that they had landed at Kameran, a distance of six miles from Veghel, which was their objective.

Capt. David Kingston, one of the medical officers of the 501st, had landed in a tree just in front of the castle and hurt his ankle sliding out of the tree. Fr. Francis Sampson, Catholic chaplain for the regiment, had made his second water landing. In Normandy, he came down in the Douve River. In Holland, he landed in the moat that surrounds the castle.

Having gained knowledge of his whereabouts, Kinnard assembled his battalion at the crossroad near the Kasteel. Orange smoke was put out and red flags were waved. The battalion had been dropped in a compact group and this made assembly that much easier. Within fifteen minutes, all company commanders had reported.

As far as has been determined, only one man was killed on the DZ. PFC Ernest A. Lambert of "B" Company reported: "Pvt. Robert Peninger was killed on the jump at the drop zone from ground fire. He was dead when he hit the ground."

Platoon sergeant Maurice C. White had a bad ankle injury on the jump. Maj. Sammie N. Homan, executive officer for the battalion, had sprained his ankle due to his combat boot buckle being caught in his risers, giving him a poor landing position.

It was decided to use the Kasteel as a temporary battalion aid station. Capt. William Burd of Regimental Headquarters Company was told to clear the locals away except for a detail that he would use for collecting the equipment bundles. Capt. David Kingston would tend the jump injured who numbered some eight cripples. He also had about forty-six men of his own plus the locals, whom he was using to collect supplies from the surrounding fields.

The Dutch people from the neighborhood crowded around them quickly, offering fruit and other gifts and asking if they could be of help. Some of the numerous bicycles were quickly put to use. Several were requisitioned by key jump-injured personnel.

S/Sgt. Maurice White said, "I hurt my ankle very bad on the jump but I hobbled around fairly well. On the march from the DZ to Veghel, a Dutch family gave me a bicycle to ride. There was very little resistance going into Veghel."

Sgt. Chester Brooks said, "After landing, Major Homan, Wilcox and I acquired bikes from the caretaker of the castle and two other men who were standing on the road leading to the castle from the main road to Veghel. Homan had sprained his knee on the jump and eventually had to give up riding the bike."

Expressing concern for his injured, Lieutenant Colonel Kinnard told Captain Kingston that the battalion would have to move out on its mission and that he was being left with the jump injured and with Captain Burd and his group. After Burd located transport, the remaining group would then move on down to Veghel.

Captain Kingston recalled the occasion. "We had a dozen or more people with injuries—several leg fractures. There were no bullet wounds that I recall. The C.O. of the drop (Col. Kinnard) came by and said, 'We've got to get going, Doc; I can leave you a squad.' I replied, 'If that's the best you can do, Colonel, don't leave the squad, that would just get us killed!'

"So the troops departed. We were busy rounding up casualties and putting on splints, etc. and had our aid station in an outbuilding of the castle, but inside the wall. I sent one of my men out with a rifle to get us some transportation. We had a hay wagon and thought that if we could get something to pull the wagon, we could move everybody to Veghel."

The rest of 1st Battalion headed for Veghel. The approach march was led by "B" Company as advance guard; "A" Company covered the flanks and "C" served as rear guard with

Headquarters Company coming down the road in the center of the formation.

Having lost his helmet for the first time on a jump, Sgt. Chester Brooks described his quick trip to Veghel. "We had five miles (8 kilometers) to Veghel. Wilcox of S-2 and I, after Homan dropped out, headed for the first bridge on the top of the dike. First time I ever rode into combat on a bike. We arrived at the bridge and almost simultaneously a squad from 3rd Battalion arrived. Wilcox headed for town and I biked to the next bridge—a squad had just arrived. I then headed into Veghel from the opposite direction than that of 1st Battalion. I biked past a maintenance garage which the Dutch told me had German soldiers inside. I met the point of the battalion led by Captain Harry Howard. I told him where the Germans were located. He set up a machine gun to cover the front of the building and I took a couple men to cover the rear of the garage. It was Sunday and there were all kinds of kids following us. I tried to wave them away but they followed. Howard or someone shouted for the Germans to surrender and were answered by rifle fire. The machine gun opened up and mothers came from all directions grabbing kids. That action was over quickly without any casualties on either side.

"I noticed a hand waving to me from a doorway of what looked like a large house so, in proper military manner, I slipped along the side of the building to the doorway, jumped in with my gun ready and discovered it was a bar. The 'waver' drew me a beer. After pedaling five miles into town and all over town and running around, that beer disappeared fast. He drew one or two more and then I decided to rejoin the war effort and slipped over to the door. The point of what may have been 2nd Battalion was coming down the street. The two men on point were each watching upstairs windows and doors opposite them but didn't see me and I made some appropriate remark like 'Looking for someone?' I almost got shot for my efforts as they swung their guns on me."

As part of the advance guard that was advancing on foot, PFC Gerald J. Beckerman of "B" Company remembered that he and Pina had been ordered by Lt. John Sallin to take the right flank. "I remember what a rough time we had trying to keep up with the platoon as they went double-timing down the road into

Veghel. It was very quiet. I don't think I used my rifle till the second or third day."

Supply sergeant Clive Barney landed close to the assembly area at the crossroad. He described the first action to improve his supply operation: "A German truck came along and Cpl. (Albert) Hutton and I promptly liberated it for a supply truck."

A trooper from another company, Cpl. Chester E. Ostby, wrote, "We ran into some German trucks and shot them up. The trucks that were still usable were emptied of their contents. A box broke open and was full of money. No time to salvage any of it."

As his group marched into Veghel, T/4 Earl H. Tyndall Jr. had a real surprise. "A young Dutch girl came up to me and offered me an ice cream sandwich. My first thought was, 'Good Lord, here I am sent 50 miles behind German lines on Sunday afternoon without any opposition and munching on an ice cream sandwich!'"

The radio he carried had broken loose from the ripcord-rope attachment on his harness as he had attempted to lower it just before his landing. However, T/5 Frank J. Carpenter retrieved the broken piece of equipment and was carrying it strapped to his back. "We were marching south from the castle along a road beside the canal. We did not see a German nor did we hear a shot fired. The doors were opening in the houses as we approached Veghel. I felt a tug on my leg and there was a little boy with a red wagon. He was trying to tell me to put my radio in the wagon and he'd pull it along side. I was trying to tell him as best I could that I had to carry the radio. All of a sudden it dawned on me that since the radio was broken, what the heck, it wasn't doing any good on my back so I obliged him by putting it in his little wagon and we marched along. He was about the happiest little Dutch boy in the entire country. You could see the pride in his face. That was our welcome to Veghel."

With "B" Company entering Veghel at double time from the drop zone, there was bound to be some opposition along the way. Cpl. Donald W. Wilson remembered, "We went into Veghel on the run. Ed Smythe and I were together. We went down an alley. There was a trooper there who had been shot in the hand. We sent him across the street to a church to get some help for his hand. Then we went through a gate in a high board fence and started up to the back door of a house. We were close to the house when the Germans inside shot at us. We got powder burns from their shots. We were not hurt. Smythe took a bullet right through the top of his helmet; the one that hit me hit the edge of my helmet with the shoulder of the bullet—this deflected it so that it went up and just put a sizeable dent in my helmet. We got out to the alley and regrouped. We put a bazooka round in the house and the six or eight Germans gave up."

While the frontal attack was in progress, Lieutenant Colonel Kinnard had sent his demo officer, Lt. Lee J. Bowers, one mile up the railroad to blow a section of the track. He learned that all the bridges were in good hands. Capt. Harry Howard's men had moved into the center of town. They had engaged in several small firefights, killed a few, captured some, and looked to be in good shape. Having heard from regiment that an enemy tank had broken through at the highway bridge over the canal, Kinnard put out bazooka teams to cover the northern, eastern, and southern approaches to the village. Sgt. Chester Brooks had contacted men of 2nd Battalion so the town was relatively secure.

T/5 Frank Carpenter describes his company move after the fighting had died down. "We moved into the center of town and into the northeastern section. We pulled up alongside the railroad tracks and that was the perimeter defense "C" Company was to form and scout out just beyond the railroad and the road back was really a parallel road back towards the castle. That is where we stopped and spent our first night in Holland. It was completely uneventful as far as enemy action was concerned."

"B" Company was sent to cover Veghel on the southeast and Company "A" was to cover Veghel bridge.

Lt. Howard Holt, of the regimental group, arrived with word that a firefight had developed at the Kasteel and that Burd and his men were being roughly handled. He had just left the area and had heard the firing. Discounting the story, but as a precaution, Kinnard sent his battalion supply officer, 1Lt. Clark Howell, and a few men west to the Kasteel to look things over.

Capt. David Kingston, at the Kasteel with the jump-injured, had expected to be on the road heading for Veghel in short order. Having located a hay wagon, he needed a vehicle to pull it. He had sent out one of his men with a rifle to get some transportation. He wrote: "After a while my man returned with a German ambulance he had captured along with two German casualties, a medical officer and a driver. He backed the ambulance up to the entrance to the castle yard. We unloaded the German casualties. Then we loaded two of our casualties into the ambulance and were starting to bring out the hay wagon when I looked up the tree-lined avenue and saw a column of twos approaching. They were wearing gray uniforms, so we retreated inside the wall to await developments. Although we had a Red Cross flag flying, and no one shooting at them, they dropped two mortar rounds into the center of the compound. My crew and the injured were inside an outbuilding so there were no injuries from the mortar rounds. When the first shell exploded, Captain (William) Burd appeared. I don't know where he had been but he came up to me inside the compound and asked me what was going on. I told him about the Germans out front. He then said he was going to climb over the back wall to escape. I tried to dissuade him, pointing out that the Germans probably had point men on that side of the castle, but he went anyway. At any rate, about ten minutes after the mortar shells, the Germans stormed in and took us prisoner. To give him credit, the German medical officer chewed out the platoon commander for the mortar shells."

A radio message from Lt. Clark Howell informed Lieutenant Colonel Kinnard that the men at Kasteel were in a hot firefight with a force of approximately fifty Germans who had a number of mortars. Kinnard asked permission of Colonel Johnson to send "C" Company to the rescue. Johnson sent his response—send one platoon. Your job is to defend Veghel.

Military historian for the European Theater of Operations BG S.L.A. Marshall[79] wrote: "It was almost dark when 1Lt. Louis Rafferty and 3rd Platoon started. Meanwhile a few men who had been around Kasteel but had gotten away before the Germans closed in, straggled into the CP. They said the situation was hot and that the defense did not appear to be organized. Rafferty and his men got as far as Heeswijk, ran into a small group of enemy in the dark, were aggressively opposed, and proceeded to dig in for the night—800 yards short of the objective. Kinnard alerted the rest of 'C' to move if needed. There was no contact with the enemy around Veghel that night for 1st Battalion except that then, and through the next morning,

79. From an unpublished after-action report by historian BG S.L.A. Marshall.

German vehicles continued to blunder into the roadblocks and were promptly captured or destroyed.

"Rafferty reported soon after first light that the Germans were in Kasteel and that he was being opposed by two platoons which were closing around both of his flanks. Kinnard said to Johnson, 'I'll have to pull him back or support him,' and Johnson replied, 'Then pull him back.' Rafferty disengaged and fell back on Veghel. There was no other action on D plus one."

Drop Zone "A"

The 1st Battalion got its green light at 1301 hours over the misdrop area near Kameran. The remainder of the 501st Parachute Infantry Regiment came down in compact groups south and west of the small hamlet of Eerde, two miles from its nearest targets, the railroad and highway bridges over the Zuid-Willems-Vaart Canal.

Accompanying the "Geronimos" of the 501st Regiment were two platoons of engineers from "A" and "B" Companies of the 326th Engineer Battalion. Their assignment was to build an auxiliary bridge next to the highway bridge over the canal at the southwest end of town.

Cpl. Bruce M. Beyer kept a log for his 2nd Battalion (501st) until he was wounded on September 24, a week after he entered Holland. In his first entry he provides the timing as the unit makes its flight to the drop zone; he describes the drop area, missions of the men, and the establishment of the battalion command post in Veghel.

Took off from Aldermaston, England at 1030A. Crossed land about 1150. Over our lines much waving from civilian populace. Yellow smoke indicating our front lines about 1240. Light flak received about 1255 (no damage). Jumped at 1306. Landing was unopposed. Terrain flat, sandy, frequent patches of pine trees. Civilians much in evidence, cordial. Dropped about one mile west of designated DZ. Light injuries sustained on jump.

'D' Company secured bridge. Captured three Germans, one bus, one car, killed one German.

Battalion entered Veghel about 1430, marching along main road running NE–SW. Battalion occupied sawmill, Battalion CP, staff, S-2 and message-center.

Some aerial photographs the men had studied during the briefings a day or two before the mission provided some worry for S/Sgt. John Bacon of "H" Company. He wrote: "The photos taken of the drop zone several days before the jump did not show two white objects in the right side of the Eerde drop zone. I saw them when I left the plane. This bothered me. Between the photo-taking and the jump, some Dutchmen had cut down two large trees. Those stumps looked bad from the air."

The stumps may have resembled anti-aircraft guns pointing to the sky. Other 3rd Battalion troopers made use of the fallen trees—perhaps too late.

"Our battalion commander, Lt. Col. Robert Ballard had dispersed his staff among the rifle companies for the jump," related 1Lt. Bill Sefton. "As battalion S-2, I was assigned to a plane from 'Dog' Company. Since the platoon leader was on board I clambered aboard as #4 man in the stick. For whatever reason, we jumped a few hundred yards short of the DZ. Even so, Dutch underground members were on hand with carts to gather the equipment bundles. Since my S-2 section was dispersed throughout the air train, I ignored the tumult of troop leaders trying to assemble their units and struck out for the battalion objectives, the highway and railway bridges over the Willems-Vaart Canal at Veghel."

Having arrived in England while the 101st was in action in the Normandy campaign, Pvt. John G. Cavaluzzo experienced his first combat in Holland. "The landing was fairly quiet. Dick Leighton and I had to climb the sand dunes in Eerde to see what was ahead. We felt a sense of elation in the first encounters."

Pvt. Clyde O. Bruders remembered that a windmill stood at one edge of the drop zone. "A group of our men captured about 18 Germans who had a machine gun in that mill. They apparently were afraid to open fire because there were so many of us."

Action didn't last long for PFC Norman A. Nelson. He was wounded early in the fighting. He did take part in the capture of the first Germans in the Eerde area. "I did help in capturing German soldiers who came out of an old Dutch windmill. We loaded some badly wounded Germans onto a three-wheeled Dutch truck."

"Colonel Howard Johnson talked to the three regimental intelligence teams just before we took off for the Holland invasion," wrote PFC Carl H. Cartledge.[80] "Each team had a bridge to take as quickly as possible after landing. Ours was the rail bridge at Veghel, and if we got it, then down the road on the other side to the road bridge over the Willems-Vaart Canal. He told us how important the bridges were and how quickly we must move out and seize them before they could be blown. He wanted the bridges by 1300 and he, I suppose to inspire us, said that the first man over any of the bridges would be awarded a Silver Star, but not to stop at the bridges—the battalions were right behind us, and to keep moving forward, even through the town of Veghel if all went well."

In describing the move toward the objectives, PFC Carl H. Cartledge wrote: "We took off for the bridges but Frank 'Chief' Sayers was nowhere to be seen. We left without him—Becker, Teichman, Thorne, Brown and myself. We followed the railroad tracks at a trot and waved the Dutch people back into their homes as they ran out to greet us. They were all in their Sunday church clothes. For those minutes it just didn't seem like war to them, and perhaps even to us. We took the bridge in 29 minutes. As we were crossing the bridge there was 'Chief' Sayers bandaging a German he had shot through the shoulder. Thorne shot a German motorcycle rider as he crossed the bridge. (The fool had stopped and jumped off his cycle with his machine pistol and was going to win the battle of the bridge by himself.) I suppose Thorne was the first across but 'Chief' had the bridge already before we got there. Brown got three more Germans as we crossed the bridge onto the road. 'Chief' got the first bridge on the Holland mission and the first German, but no one got a Silver Star."

After the pathfinders had marked drop zone "A," they joined the leading elements of the 501st on their move into Veghel. T/5 Glenn Braddock wrote: "We had barely cleared the town square where the canal came to a dead end—other troops had gone on—when someone yelled, 'There's Krauts running into that building to the left!' Sgt. John O'Shaughnessey took after them on a run with me close behind and several others followed. Some went around to the other side of the building. O'Shaughnessey

80. Material taken from two letters PFC Carl H. Cartledge wrote to relatives of Pvt. Frank Sayers after he learned his Indian buddy had died in the Minnesota north woods where he returned after the war. Letters were dated October 18, 1980, and November 20, 1980.

kicked open the door and threw in a grenade. I was about to pull the pin on one but he ran inside with his Tommy gun blazing. I didn't see any movements so I did not fire but ran with him, others following towards and out a door on the opposite side of the room. Just prior to reaching the door we heard heavy firing and upon reaching the outside discovered that the troopers who had run around to the back of the warehouse had disposed of the enemy. I did not go over to count the bodies but I recall there were four in one group and a couple more farther away."

"We seized Veghel quite quickly with minimum opposition," said 2Lt. Robert P. O'Connell in describing his first combat experience. "In working along a street fight in Veghel, we killed three Krauts and, as we moved up the street, I jumped over their bodies and thought—30 seconds ago they were alive! The reality of the war came to me then."

Cpl. Charles J. Ritzler had landed very near the bridge and went on into town. He wrote: "Everyone seemed glad to see us. I was stopped at the second bridge by snipers. Got on top of a house and started firing."

First Lieutenant Bill Sefton continued: "I passed through the village of Eerde where I encountered Lt. Hugo Sims, the S-2 officer for the regiment. He told me that a few members of the regimental staff were attempting to establish a CP there until the situation clarified and if I saw Colonel Johnson, would I please inform him of this development. I kept on going toward Veghel and eventually arrived there and found the 2nd Battalion assembling on the far side of the canal. There was the usual amount of confusion and, while we were standing around, Colonel Ballard was sending off troops and officers in this direction and that. A bus came roaring along the road down the north side of the canal right through our assembly area. As it went by, you could see several German soldiers looking out the windows at all the Geronimos. They were pulling their soft overseas caps over their ears and heading for the floor. Ballard yelled, 'Stop that bus!' and everyone opened fire on it. The bus went another hundred yards and careened into a ditch. As we got to it and had it thoroughly surrounded, we found that the only wounded person was the driver, who had part of one ear shot off."

Capt. Eber H. Thomas, one of the supply officers for the 501st, remembered the same incident this way: "As soon as we crossed the road bridge into Veghel, a German bus approached.

The bus ran into a ditch after some shots were fired. The bus had a Red Cross on it but it was loaded with ammo. Colonel Johnson and his men were at the bridge. I was assigned an area along the branch canal into Veghel."

Cpl. Eugene Flanagan on the bus action: "We caught a vehicle with supplies heading for the front with four Germans. They were taken prisoners. A car came down the road. Colonel Johnson hollered, 'Shoot him in the head—I want his car!' "

Having just arrived in time to help shoot up a bus that was fleeing from the Veghel scene, 1Lt. Bill Sefton reported that it was the only action near the 2nd Battalion command post in the first half hour. He added, "Somewhere in that time I acquired a bicycle—some civilian simply handed it to me. Colonel Ballard, seeing I was the only mounted officer he had, said, 'Sefton, go down, cross the bridge, go up the other side and see how 'Dog' Company is doing at the railroad bridge.' As I got to the middle of the highway bridge over the canal, there was Colonel Johnson in full glory directing troops in all directions. I remembered seeing Lt. Sims so I reported and said, 'Colonel Johnson, see that church spire over there, part of your regimental staff is in that little village.' The colonel pointed to a small car driven by one of the regimental S-2 staff. It was full of bullet holes and blood. It turned out that part of the advance element had wiped out a small group of rear guard Krauts. Thus, a vehicle was on hand. Johnson said, 'Fine Sefton, get in that car and go tell them to get up here.' I said, 'Yes sir, Colonel, but Colonel Ballard has sent me down to 'Dog' Company and—' Johnson interrupted, 'Sefton, get in that car and go tell my staff to get here!'

"I felt the least I could do was go tell Ballard what had happened and so when Johnson turned his back I retraced my pedaling, advised Colonel Ballard that Colonel Johnson wanted me to go to Eerde and tell his staff to come up.

"Ballard said, 'Sefton, I told you to go to "Dog" Company, now go to "Dog" Company!'

"I was trying to sneak back across the bridge pushing the bicycle. Johnson had his back turned. He wheeled around and saw me and said, 'Sefton, haven't you gone yet? Get in that car and go now!'

"A full colonel outranks a lieutenant colonel and I felt that I could get to the village in the little car and back before Ballard knew that I had taken a detour. The car had a rumble seat, a flat tire and the driver was from the S-2 section. I hopped in the rumble seat and said to the driver to get on down the highway and get me to Eerde. The road ran straight out for about 400 yards and then took a slight turn to the right toward Eindhoven.

"Just as we got to the turn, there were two GIs in a foxhole beside the road with a bazooka and they yelled, 'Get off the road—there's a tank coming!' The S-2 driver simply cut the wheel and nosed the vehicle into the ditch. About that time the GIs said, 'It's OK, it's a Limey tank!'

"Now, of course, we were wearing American uniforms and had an American flag sewn on our left shoulder and I walked out on the highway and sure enough this tank came barreling down the highway toward me—a medium tank. The tank commander was standing up in the turret and waving his hand. I immediately started to think, what word should I greet him with, certainly there would be a *Stars and Stripes* reporter right behind him in a jeep and while I'm pondering this important question, I am listening to a little voice in my mind—that's a funny color for a Limey tank. They paint theirs O.D., like ours—that one is black and yellow but it must be a Limey tank—he's wearing a black cap. No, Limeys wear black berets. What army wears a black cap?—and about that time I realized I was looking at the black German cross painted on the front of the tank and the guy who waved at me had a Luger in his hand and he was now about thirty-five yards away and his jaw had dropped open and he was bringing the Luger to bear. I had my M-1 rifle under my right arm and I crouched in the middle of the road and brought it up like a Kentucky squirrel hunter trying to snap off a shot before he did. He shot first and I heard the snap of his round past my left ear. I shot from the hip and he threw up his hands and went down the turret. To this day I don't know if I shot him through the navel or missed him by ten yards. I jumped aside as the tank thundered by and yelled to the bazooka men to get him. They were tracking him at ten yards' range and the gunner was pulling the trigger but nothing was happening. I could see that he had not activated the round; not attached the wire to the little coil in the back that allowed him to fire it. So I was yelling at him like crazy until the number 2 man realized what I was saying, tapped the gunner on the shoulder and reached back to arm the shell by putting the wire through the coil. By this time the tank was fifty yards down the road and going like a bat out of hell. The bazooka man had a good aim and since I was almost behind the bazooka I could see the round come out like a fast ball by a good pitcher. It hit the turret and bounced straight into the air. He had not armed the warhead by pulling the pin before he put it in the tube. I stood there firing bursts of three with my M-1 which was supposed to be the signal for armored attack and trying to hit the crack between the chassis and turret on the grounds that somewhere in our basic training if you put a round right in there you could partially disable the tank. It didn't work worth a darn."

Members of "G" Company of the 3rd Battalion had been sent south from the drop zone to establish roadblocks on the highway between Veghel and St. Oedenrode.

PFC Eugene Cavanagh remembered, "We made it out to the highway just as a German tank[81] and an officer's car came along. Someone hit the car, wounding the driver and the officer (major). With the help of Dutch farmers, we pulled trees across the road to block it off. We were ordered to place a machine gun in a farmer's rose bed alongside of the road. He helped us dig the hole only to have us move off after we dug up his plants."

Communications corporal James S. White wrote: "After landing at Eerde, I was sent to run a telephone line to 'G' Company which had cut the road between Veghel and St. Oedenrode. As we neared the highway there was some small arms fire just ahead of me on the road. As we soon found out, the forward men of 'G' Company had fired at a German jeep when it wouldn't stop. A German major was wounded in the arm. He was very upset when he didn't get away."

Mortar sergeant John Urbank of "G" Company remembered the incident as follows: "We sent a point to the road. A light German tank came down the road. Buford Perry fired a rocket at it—missed. Bill Nemeth, first scout, thought the British had broken through and waved a greeting. The tank commander took his binoculars down and waved back and drove on by. We captured a Volkswagen following. A private, sergeant and a Czech major were in it. Were they mad because we let the tank

81. The German tank was most likely the one that escaped destruction when a trio of tanks was strafed by fighters at St. Oedenrode earlier in the day, as described by Pierre Drenters.

go by and captured them instead! The major called us gangsters."

First Lieutenant Sefton continued: "The tank roared on down toward the bridge and Colonel Johnson reportedly thought it was the first Limey tank to come into Veghel because we'd been told earlier that Montgomery had indeed broken through. The tank opened up with a machine gun but not a soul was hit but Johnson and all the Geronimos on the bridge ended up dangling from the supports while the tank roared across town. It went clear down the twisting street, came out in the main section of town where priests were passing out beer and pretzels and people were dancing in the street, made a right turn and went right down the main street being pursued by a pathfinder sergeant who was shooting a .45 pistol into the motor section in an attempt to disable it and by Cpl. Robert Goble of my S-2 section vainly trying to stick his M-1 rifle in between the tread and the bogie wheels. The tank kept firing the machine gun but not a soul was hit. The crowd parted like the Red Sea for Moses and when last seen the tank was merrily on its way out of town."

Cpl. Charles Ritzler was in the top of a Dutch home firing at snipers near the second bridge when he heard a loud commotion behind him. He added to his story: "A German tank came from behind and I emptied a clip from my Tommy gun at it—no effect."

"As we approached the bridge at the Willems-Vaart Canal, a Kraut tank tore by us on Hell's Highway," recalled 2Lt. Robert O'Connell. "Our company missed this tank and Colonel Johnson was angry."

In the initial assault on Veghel, T/5 Glenn Braddock of the pathfinders had been in the first group. He wrote: "At the end of the canal the Germans had dug and built a well camouflaged gun emplacement. It was empty except for some trash and we were given the task of maintaining a cross-road blockade.

"Civilians had started to gather around and when someone said, 'Hear that clanking?—our tanks are pretty well on time to support us.' Support us hell! That's a light Kraut tank—someone get a bazooka team. All we were armed with were our rifles and Tommies.

"Earlier I had passed a bazooka team and started back when I heard the burp gun on the tank and then the heavier boom of an artillery piece. Then shots from rifles and submachine guns. Our men made the turret gunner duck inside—evidently he saw me just before he ducked down inside. The tank turned my way and I ran like hell for the street in back of the building on the corner—turned out there was a helluva high rock fence and I couldn't get through. Just as the tank rounded the corner and swung toward me, I kicked open the house door and barreled inside. There was a loud boom as I crossed into another room with two women and a small boy huddled tight to the opposite wall. I waved at them and then heard the tank going back past the other end of the building past the gun emplacement and on out of town with the troopers still firing at it."

Cpl. Eugene Flanagan added to his story: "A tank was spotted and I was told to get up front (as a bazooka man) where Colonel Johnson was located. I was too late. Someone else must have got the tank."

No one did, but lots of men had a shot, or maybe more, at it.

Because he had some training in handling of racing pigeons as a youth, Pvt. Arthur M. Crook was given the assignment of looking after the carrier pigeons for the 501st. He recalled, "I thought my dad would really get a charge out of knowing that his son was handling birds in an invasion and I planned to transmit some epic message via homing pigeon after we landed near Veghel. In my mind I composed dozens of memorable messages—'Relax—situation in hand—The Screaming Eagle and Geronimo have landed!' etc., etc.

"As it turned out, some officer wrote the messages and put them in the capsules. I don't even know what they said. I never found out if the pigeons made it back to their home cote in England."

Construction of Temporary Bridge

One platoon in each of "A" and "B" Companies of the 326th Airborne Engineer Battalion was parachute trained. They were assigned to jump on drop zone "A" at Eerde in support of the 501st Parachute Infantry Regiment. The first-day assignment of both engineer groups was to move to Veghel where they assisted in securing the highway bridge across the Zuid-Willems-Vaart Canal, one-half mile southeast of Veghel. A defense line was to be set up on the west bank of the canal.

Because of the narrowness of the existing lift bridge over the canal, the span was too narrow for the passage of the heavy Allied tanks that would be moving north toward Arnhem along what was to become known as Hell's Highway.

The 3rd Platoon of Company "B," 326th Engineers, had been assigned to jump with the 2nd Battalion of the 501st Regiment. Their mission was to help secure the highway bridge in Veghel over the canal, to reinforce it, and also to build a second bridge close at hand that would hold seventy-ton tanks and other heavy traffic. The second bridge was to pass over the lock of the canal a few feet from the existing span. The engineers were assisted by members of the underground and teachers from the Veghel Technical School.

Work was begun almost immediately after the defense line near the bridge had been established. Engineers and underground workers set about collecting materials such as heavy timbers and iron beams for the project.

PFC Harry G. Yaworski was a member of 3rd Platoon. He wrote: "Our objective was the canal bridge. Three of us were assigned to an outpost at a crossroad and I missed the actual entry into Veghel.

"We came out on a road and there was a German truck—doors open and motor running."

Engineer Pvt. Edward P. Carowick was impressed with the "wonderful cooperation of the Dutch in helping get materials for, and transporting materials to the bridge site, such as I-beams and heavy timber. They provided welding equipment and the support in helping to construct the second bridge."

PFC Harry G. Yaworski continued his story: "At the Veghel bridge, three Dutch underground men appeared (with orange arm bands) and began working on a bridge next to the existing one."

In later action that night, Yaworski recalled, "I drove a German truck with what appeared to be railroad ties on it for under support for the bridge. No one seemed too keen on driving a German truck at night. I recall 'searching the gears'—they were different from anything I had previously driven. I recall arc-welding under the bridge. Those three underground guys accomplished a lot in a short time."

Liaison Between Regiments

Having returned to his unit a short time before the Holland operation from a long stint of recuperation from wounds received in Normandy, S/Sgt. Robert J. Houston[82] no longer had a platoon to command. He was given the task of making contact with the 502nd Parachute Infantry Regiment, which was to take St. Oedenrode, a few miles south of Drop Zone "A."

Houston wrote:

> The captain told me to take four men, go to St. Oedenrode, contact a 502nd officer, and report back before dark. The rest of the company would be either in Eerde or Veghel when we got back. It was a sort of "Message to Garcia" assignment.
>
> I picked Henry Boda, Frank Samolek, Lenny Lloyd and Joe Cerra. We started across the fields straight south toward St. Oedenrode, which was about three miles away. The country was very flat, and most of the fields seemed to be pastures for the dairy cows. We weren't on a main road, so didn't see many people or any German soldiers. The country roads and lanes were usually bordered by tall poplar trees which gave some concealment as we walked beside them. We looked for Dutch windmills, but the only one in the vicinity was at the edge of the village of Eerde.
>
> As we approached St. Oedenrode, at about three o'clock, we heard rifle fire; but it had stopped by the time we reached the outskirts of the village. As we came into the center of the village, people began to come out of their houses with orange flags and flowers. There was a crowd in the square, and everyone shaking hands with Americans and giving them apples and other food. This was really "liberation," and we were glad to be in on it, even though the 1st Battalion of the 502nd had done all the work. There had evidently been a small German garrison in the town. Twenty of them had been killed and fifty-eight captured by the time our patrol arrived. They had started to blow up a bridge but were stopped in time, so that part of the corridor was open.
>
> Civilians continued to crowd around, and it seemed that we had shaken hands with a hundred people. We found the battalion headquarters in a big red brick school building on one side of the square. I reported about the 501st in Eerde and Veghel and about our patrol. An

82. Houston, Robert J. *D-Day to Bastogne.* Exposition Press, Smithtown, NY, 1980, 52–4.

officer warned us that some of the German soldiers from St. Oedenrode had escaped from the village and might be between us and
Eerde now. The officer was trying to convince the Dutch people that
the war wasn't over and that the streets should be cleared. Suddenly,
there was firing not far away and the street cleared in a hurry.

We started back, keeping beside trees and bushes as much as possible for concealment. We had gone about halfway when we saw a
small group of German soldiers coming across a field toward us.
They hadn't seen us, so we crouched down in the roadside ditch
until they were just a few feet away. They were bunched together, so
our first shots killed all but one. My tommy gun worked well, in
spite of having been dropped earlier in the afternoon. The one German not hit shouted, "Kamerad!" so we had a prisoner. One of the
men suggested that we should leave him with "the other Nazi bastards," but we brought him along to be questioned by regimental intelligence men.

We continued on toward Eerde and didn't have any more excitement. We found battalion headquarters, left our guest with people
there and reported about St. Oedenrode and the area between the
501st and 502nd. A sergeant in battalion headquarters told us that
the 1st and 2nd battalions of our regiment had captured the bridges
at Veghel, so our part of the corridor was under control. He said that
"H" Company was digging in just beyond the windmill on the edge
of the village, so we went out there and rejoined our company.

First Counterattack at Veghel

It wasn't long in coming. The Germans moved quickly to stamp
out the threat to their flanks at Veghel.

When the defense of Veghel was reorganized a few hours before dark on the seventeenth, "E" Company of the 501st was
given the northwest sector of the town to defend and they didn't
have the exact area in their directive. The Mortar Platoon didn't
have an opportunity to register their weapons.

A member of the platoon that faced the brunt of the German
attack on the sector, PFC Samuel L. Raborn described the involvement of his company in the fighting near the railroad
bridge over the canal: "At the time we dug in on a road beside a
canal, I had anti-tank grenades on a hole on the canal bank.
Johnny Altick, Frank McClure and Ernest Lightfoot had their
machine guns just across the road and a telephone line leading
back to company commander, 1Lt. Frank Gregg. The Jerries

(paratroopers from a town just north of s'Hertogenbosch) threw an attack at our platoon. They thought we were a small group (and we were). I don't know where the other companies were. It was rough. We lost half of my platoon and we were pushed back to the railroad and bridge and there made another stand."[83]

"Easy" Company was not well prepared when an enemy force of approximately three hundred came down the east bank of the canal in the midst of the night fog, infiltrating through the positions in a surprise attack. Fighting centered on a huge warehouse three hundred yards northwest of the railroad bridge on the east bank of the canal. At 0200 hours, burp-gun fire was heard to the front, and a few minutes later the outposts were overrun or pushed back to the MLR. There were three attacks, with the heaviest occurring about 0400. At one critical stage, 1Lt. Joseph C. MacGregor, the platoon leader, though badly wounded, managed to hold off the Germans with his tommy gun until his men were able to draw back to a defensive line. He was later dragged to safety. Seven men were killed by German grenades, tree bursts, and machine pistols. At least twenty-six more were wounded. Among the latter was the company commander, 1Lt. Frank Gregg.

"Dog" Company extended to the left along the railroad track westward from the positions of "Easy" Company. PFC George E. Willey, who was with "D" Company on this date, remembered: "We were ordered to dig positions along the railroad."

The action in Holland was the first for Pvt. John G. Cavaluzzo of "D" Company. This was his first night of combat. "I was on outpost with Dick Leighton and a third replacement. 'E' Company was engaged in close-in fighting to our right. This had us sweating because we feared getting cut off from our MLR. It actually sounded as though the Krauts had gotten behind us."

From a citation for the posthumous award of the Silver Star for bravery in the fight around the railroad bridge, the following description is provided on the actions for platoon leader 1Lt. Joseph C. MacGregor:

> . . . the overwhelming superiority of the enemy greatly taxed the strength of his platoon and Lt. MacGregor was ordered to withdraw his men. Realizing that a critical situation had developed and that rapid withdrawal was imperative, Lt. MacGregor remained at the

83. From a letter PFC Samuel L. Raborn wrote to the family of T/5 John Altick, who was killed near the end of the war. Letter dated 1945.

center of the road junction fully exposed to enemy fire, and directed the movement of his confused forces. Desperately shouting orders to his men, he held back the onrushing enemy by firing his submachine gun from his exposed position, killing several of the enemy. This afforded his men sufficient time to effect an orderly and safe withdrawal. Although seriously wounded, he remained to direct his troops until the position was overrun and he became, temporarily, a prisoner. He was rescued the following day by counterattacking, friendly forces. . . .[84]

Third Platoon of "B" Company of the 326th Engineers played a supporting role with 2nd Battalion of the 501st being responsible for the construction of a second bridge over the Willems-Vaart Canal, a mile southeast of the railroad span. They were called upon to reinforce "E" Company when it was being pushed back near the railroad bridge. The 2nd Squad of 3rd Platoon moved along a mile of the west bank of the canal and were part of an ambush of an undetermined number of the enemy.

As part of the squad involved in the ambush, Pvt. Edward Carowick remembered the incident: "I think the ambush was the turning point of that action. Rip Reardon could really throw. He was responsible for most of the casualties when the Germans were ambushed. Most of the men passed their hand grenades to Reardon. He threw them right on target. I heard most of the persons involved state that they could not have been thrown that far but Reardon did it."

PFC Harry G. Yaworski of the engineers remembered the ambush. "One of our men came upon a German soldier rising out of a ditch and coming toward him. He shot him in the midsection. Our man was never the same guy after that. He didn't know whether the German made a movement to surrender or was coming up to shoot him."

Though wounded, 1Lt. Frank Gregg had been able to remain in command of his company. With the arrival of daybreak, he was able to commit his reserve platoon effectively and the Germans were forced back.

PFC Samuel Raborn added to his letter: "Later in the day we got battalion support, attacked and killed or captured the Jerries."

84. General Order 33, Headquarters, 101st Airborne Division, U.S. Army, March 30, 1945.

Radioman John Marohn wrote in praise of his mortar sergeant of "E" Company: "I remember Sgt. Lester Miller who was a ridgerunner from West Virginia and in charge of our mortar section. He never took the bipod or base plate with him— only the tube. While on the canal, he had the uncanny accuracy to place the tube between his legs; after a good view of what he wanted to hit, told the crew to put so many increments on a round, sight the angle of the tube and fire a round and hit the target. He was uncanny in judging distance."

In the entry in the 2nd Battalion log for the eighteenth, Cpl. Bruce M. Beyer noted:

> Heavy fighting, much contact, enemy driven off by 81mm mortar fire.

"The first night we were hit by a battalion of German parachutists and some SS Troops," wrote Sgt. Eddie Turner.[85] "They were brave fighters and also intelligent. Our company caught the impact of all their fighting ability and, at daybreak the next morning, we had lost more men in that one night's fighting than we had during all of our fighting in Normandy."

PFC George Willey was a member of "D" Company on the seventeenth but was transferred to "E" Company to help fill in the lost numbers after this action. He wrote: "The first night 'Easy' Company lost 28 men in 30 minutes as German AA guns fired in the trees over their heads. I was transferred to 'Easy' Company the next morning to help bring up the strength of the company."

First and 2nd Battalions had an opportunity to take a breather for a day or so. Units of 3rd Battalion and, particularly, "I" Company had their problems on the eighteenth.

---

85. From a letter Sgt. Eddie Turner wrote to the family of his close buddy T/5 John Altick in May 1945.

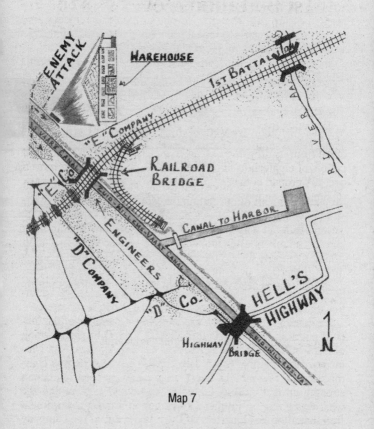

Map 7

THIRTEEN

1st Battalion Moves North

1st Battalion Heads North

The Dutch underground had brought in word that there were seven hundred enemy soldiers in Dinter. This little community had been on the route of march as 1st Battalion had moved down from its drop area at Kameran on the seventeenth. Several patrols of eighteen to thirty men had drawn fire as they moved over the ground between the roads and the river. The little town of Beug was supposed to mark the limit of 1st Battalion's patrolling but LTC Harry Kinnard asked permission to send a patrol all the way to Kasteel to see what had happened to the men who had been left behind as jump casualties with medical captain David Kingston and Regimental Headquarters Company C.O. William Burd. "C" Company was given the mission and S/Sgt. William DeHuff took charge of the patrol. He took along an SCR-300 radio and from the time he and his men left the battalion area in Veghel, every stage of his progress was reported.

Radioman T/5 Frank J. Carpenter was a member of the De-Huff patrol to Heeswijk-Dinter and the Kasteel on the morning of September 19. Carpenter related his experiences: "As I remember the briefing, S/Sgt. Bill DeHuff gave us (he was commissioned a few months later), we were to proceed in platoon strength up that road as far as the castle and explore and see what was going on up there. I had gotten a radio replacement from battalion headquarters so I was taken out of the company HQ and attached to DeHuff for the patrol. We started off the railroad tracks moving northwest on the road, scouts out in platoon formation and the Dutch riding along beside us on their bicycles. They would ride on down the road and come back and tell us what was up ahead. After one of the young Dutchmen came back down the road, DeHuff told us there was a machine gun near and pulled us up out of MG range. He went forward with somebody. I can't say they had a flag of truce but they had in mind the setting up of a meeting. A German sergeant came out and talked to DeHuff. I was back in the platoon so I don't know what was said. I do remember that DeHuff said something like we were the lead element of a massive striking force supported by artillery and we were moving down on them. The sergeant was discouraged enough and figured this was exactly what was going to happen and surrendered his whole machine gun section. We walked on down the road. Prior to reaching Dinter, which was another 1,000 yards away, we ran into a sizable force. We deployed again. We were informed by the Dutch underground of the presence of this force. They'd ride forward and spot these strong points and come back and tell us about them. There were three or four of these Dutchmen. The information was excellent—exactly where every German was in position and how they were deployed. I don't know how they got away with it—certainly at the risk to their own lives.

"We must have been close to the Dinter intersection or just beyond the Heeswijk intersection. DeHuff went forward again and brought us up as close as he could without getting in range of their small arms fire. He went forward again and was met by a German sergeant-major. The fellow was not much older than DeHuff. They discussed things and on this occasion I was with them. What it amounted to, he was quite discouraged as the officers had all taken off and left things in his hands. He felt this wasn't the thing to do and, inasmuch as there was a massive American column coming right up the road behind us, it would be better to save lives. He surrendered the whole group—platoon in strength. DeHuff lined them up with the people we had picked up earlier—not a shot had been fired and this was several hours into the morning. A couple of guys were dispatched to guard them and they were sent back to Veghel. That was the end of their war.

"Unbeknown to us, deployed between this road that we were on and the canal on our left was probably an enemy force of battalion size and this was the group that the next day would be facing 'A' and 'B' Companies when they made their push up the road. We proceeded on and went as far as the castle."

Radioman Carpenter continued: "We pulled into the castle

and DeHuff deployed everyone around it. We even went into the gatehouse and raised the drawbridge. We figured if they tried to hit us they'd have a hard time getting in. The old caretaker kept trying to discourage us from raising it and he seemed to be telling us it didn't work well. DeHuff made up his mind and up went the drawbridge. DeHuff took one man and headed off in the direction of s'Hertogenbosch. There had been a rumor that there was a major German force in there and he was going to scout it out. He left. I was really outside the range of my radio set now but I climbed up on the tower of the castle and all over the darned place trying to call 1st Battalion but wasn't able to reach them. For some reason or other, I went out in the yard and, standing there, gave them a call and *Bingo*—battalion came in clear as a bell. I dug my foxhole right in the middle of the rose garden where I made contact.

"Things were very relaxed. We saw no Germans whatsoever. We had let the drawbridge down so DeHuff could leave on his scouting mission. We toured the castle. (Dave) Klinger came up and said, 'My God, this place has a torture chamber in it!' We had never seen one, so we toured it.

"One of the fellows had run across a German ambulance.[86] They had abandoned it when they ran out and couldn't get it started. The guys worked on it for most of the day and got it running. There had been a lot of supplies accumulated that had been dragged off the jump field so we loaded everything we could into this ambulance and then we were concerned that we were hauling weapons in it and if we did get captured, we would be accused of using the ambulance for purposes for which it wasn't intended so we rigged a parachute to cover the crosses. Then we sat down and rested and waited for DeHuff to return.

"The battalion was quite concerned as to the whereabouts of DeHuff. He finally came back. He called Battalion on the radio and gave them a report of what he had seen, which was a major German armored force in the town of s'Hertogenbosch. Battalion relayed the information to Colonel Kinnard.

"Upon his return DeHuff told Kinnard, 'I'm now at Kasteel. The wounded are gone. There are no signs of our men here but bloody bandages. The DZ is almost clear of bundles. I have found one 81mm and one 60mm mortar and have them with me.

86. See comments of Capt. David Kingston on page 227.

The mission is complete. Our (Burd) force has been lost. What are your instructions?' "

Carpenter added to his narrative. "We were told to wait for a while and pretty soon the order came to move DeHuff's platoon back to Heeswijk—right away! That was all that was said. We packed everything, took the ambulance, went back towards Heeswijk."

Lieutenant Colonel Kinnard had asked permission to send "C" to Heeswijk and Dinter, with one platoon at the former place, so as to outpost the entire force. He figured the main threat to regiment was from that flank. Colonel Johnson approved and "C" was sent on its way. The move of "C" Company initiated a whole series of events that came to engage first 1st Battalion, and then the entire regiment. It was obvious the Germans had infiltrated in considerable strength along the north side of the canal as any attempt at movement along the highway during the third day drew fire. They made one attempt to get at the third bridge but were driven back. They also hit hard at the planes flying resupply missions into the DZ. Lieutenant Colonel Kinnard felt that a passive, close-in defense of the Veghel area might, in the long run, be the costlier way and that taking offensive measures against the enemy was more likely to preserve the corridor.

T/5 Frank Carpenter was not aware that the rest of his company was on the move in their direction. "What we didn't know, in the meantime, was that Captain Phillips had been moving up the same road we had traveled earlier, with the rest of 'C' Company. When we got into Heeswijk or Dinter by that road that branched off to the Canal, we met Captain Phillips.

"By now it was damned close to dark. We settled down for the night. We deployed in a circle around the village. We got filled in on what was going on. At dawn the next day, or shortly thereafter, 'A' and 'B' Companies were to attack from Veghel northwest toward the canal and the road we had come up. We were to set up a blocking position on the road that went from Heeswijk-Dinter over to the canal. At dawn the next morning, that is exactly what we did. We started down the road toward the canal and 'A' and 'B' Companies started their attack from the vicinity of Veghel. I, of course, was listening to all of this on the radio.

"Shortly after we swung left from the Dinter-Heeswijk intersection, we ran into enemy fire and had to fight our way to the canal. Capt. Phillips was leading us. The platoons were well deployed. We pushed our way through whatever Germans were in front of us to a drawbridge at the canal and anchored ourselves in position."

Having served as radioman for Lieutenant Colonel Kinnard for the first few days of the invasion, T/5 Joe Haller Jr. was then sent to Capt. Robert H. Phillips of "C" Company for the northward adventure. In actions near the canal bridge, Haller described the part he played: "I remember down by the canal, the Germans raised a white flag. They wanted to give up. They had me, because I could speak German, and one other fellow, who was to cover me, go down there to talk to the Germans. They opened fire on us. We jumped into the canal. I yelled to Captain Phillips—'Let em have it!' Our men opened fire again for about half an hour and the Germans gave up. We got about fifty prisoners. A lot were real young and some were very old fellows. They weren't good soldiers and the young ones didn't even shave yet."

Carpenter added to his story: "I don't remember any (German) officers in these actions. One had come flying around the corner in the sidecar of a motorcycle at the drawbridge intersection. They were shot and killed right there at the drawbridge. We had our first casualty. He was hit and killed there in the middle of the road right by the drawbridge."

The most vivid memory of Holland action for Pvt. John R. Thomas occurred in this action. "When Sgt. (Arnold) Krombholtz and I were crossing the bridge near Schijndel (he was lead or point and I was flank guard and had pulled in to cross the canal bridge) we were about ten feet apart when a sniper got him in the head. He made no sound whatever."

Lieutenant Colonel Kinnard decided to have "C" Company deploy to the south of Heeswijk and to include the bridge over the canal within its ground. He then used "C" as the dustpan, and the other two companies of 1st Battalion as the broom sweeping toward it. The distance of the sweep was about five miles and it covered the ground between the highway and the canal. The sector was bisected almost evenly by the Aa River. The attack jumped off at 0930 and "C" started its move from Heeswijk to the canal at about the same time. "B" was on the left with its left shoulder to the canal. "A" was on the right, echeloned to the right rear and guiding on "B."

T/5 Frank Carpenter had mentioned earlier about the assistance of Dutch underground members riding forward and spotting German positions and reporting back with the information to the advancing paratroopers. First Lieutenant Sumpter Blackmon of "A" Company describes the work of one of these men. "Hans Kropman was a Dutchman. We were getting ready to move out that morning. 'C' Company had already gone the day before. Hans Kropman came up to me and said, 'I want to help.' He spoke fluent English. I said we need it. I gave him a rifle and a helmet off a soldier who didn't need it anymore. The first thing he did after setting aside his weapon and helmet was to get on a bicycle and roll five miles up the road. We met him a mile north of Veghel and he came back and told us exactly where the Germans were located. He told us we were going to run into them right here—and pinpointed their position on the map. That made it possible for Lt. (Henry) Puhalski and his 3rd Platoon to cross the canal on the east flank, moving north to capture over two hundred men with a group of 45 men.

"The Dutch were a kind of funny folk," said Blackmon, choking up. "They were the finest folks I ever saw. I couldn't ask for any more cooperation than they gave us during the entire time we were in Holland.

"Going up there I had a German motorcycle and rode the thing up one side of the canal and down the other side to move along the canal. There was one Dutch house in that area. I was called to the home on the canal and the occupants noted I was an American and they brought out an American Air Force man who had been shot down two days before. He joined us in our fight. He added one more to our force. He carried two boxes of ammunition for us."

As Lt. Henry Puhalski's 3rd Platoon moved forward, hoping to sweep the German forces before it into the dustpan, tragedy struck.

Sgt. Wesley Bates of 3rd Platoon recalled, "I knew hatred for the first time when Lt. Henry Puhalski was killed. The Germans put up a white flag and then shot him when he stood up."

Executive officer for "A" Company 1Lt. Sumpter Blackmon, recalled the action that led to his friend Puhalski losing his life. "He was fighting on the right side going up toward Dinter and his 3rd Platoon was moving up nicely and they saw white flags being waved up in front of them. Puhalski started moving up and was shot. This taught us a lot. We didn't worry about white flags anymore. If a man stood up, we would honor him. We didn't pay any attention to flags."

Reflecting a bit on his part in the "Dustpan Operation," Capt. Ian Hamilton, commander of "B" Company said, "My recollection is that following our delay and hesitation when we recognized white flags adorning bushes and some of the trees, we did make a rather rapid move, especially along the left front of our designated zone—principally us in a ditch which took us to the flank and even rear of the German opposition. These people we dispatched in short order. I allowed myself the privilege of picking up a German Schmizzer pistol and appropriate ammunition, which I utilized in a later engagement."

When the two "brooming" companies completed their sweep and the German force was gathered in the dustpan, a decision had to be made as to the disposition of the 1st Battalion forces, five miles north of Veghel.

With the air force man participating in the actions of his unit, 1Lt. Sumpter Blackmon related how they used the Dutch personnel. "We had German trucks and the Dutch were driving them. They took some people back to Veghel. We thought we were going to spend the night in Dinter. Some of the men were up in Heeswijk."

Night Attack on Schijndel

Reports had come in to 501st headquarters that trucks carrying an enemy force of two thousand men were moving through Schijndel in the direction of St. Oedenrode. Lieutenant Colonel Kinnard had received the news at 1700 hours and was directed to move his battalion immediately from the Heeswijk-Dinter area, travel south along the main highway, under cover of darkness. Third Battalion was to move from Eerde through Weibosch and approach Schijndel from the south. Third Battalion was to start its move at 2200 hours.

First Lieutenant Sumpter Blackmon added, "We thought we were going to stay in Dinter but we moved out of there and the Germans moved back in. We traveled from Dinter to Schijndel that night, starting about ten o'clock. That was the darkest night I have ever seen in my life. We couldn't see our hands in front of us. We had to kind of feel our way along. We weren't about to fire because we wanted to get over there without firing anything.

They would fire and we'd just hit the side of the road but kept moving."

T/5 Frank Carpenter continued his story: "The direction of the attack changed. We started heading south to Schijndel. 'C' Company took the lead and it was 1st Platoon in the forefront. We started marching down the road, scouts out, guards on the right and left. It was complete darkness. The company was strung out on the road behind them. The first thing we ran into was some minor rifle fire up ahead of us. Everything stopped. Everybody laid down on the side of the road. Captain Phillips wondered what was going on. He was quite agitated and wanted to get the attack on the move. He was hollering up the road, 'Git your ass in gear!' I was standing right behind him, perhaps three feet away, when he turned to face the rear to get the next platoon going and to deploy them along the side and to go around this minor problem. He was swinging them out on the left when all of a sudden an ack-ack gun started firing. A couple of tracers went right by the two of us and we dove into the ditch. He said, 'I guess there's more up there than I figured on.' The enemy ack-ack wagon took off in the dark."

As a member of "B" Company, PFC Gerald J. Beckerman remembered the same incident. "We were crossing many open fields under German fire, hearing the small arms fire whizzing by and making a thud sound as they hit the ground near you. Luckily none of them had my name on them. I remember chasing a group down a road. They had a 20mm anti-aircraft gun. They would stop around a bend and wait for us to come near, fire a clip point blank at us and then take off."

In Veghel, Dutch underground member Mike Nooijen was asked on the evening of the twenty-first if he knew the way to Schijndel. Working with service company of the 501st Regiment, he was asked to direct them to Schijndel where anticipated fighting was to take place the next day. Nooijen was in on the move by way of Dinter during the very dark night experienced by the other members of 1st Battalion.

Nooijen wrote: "I knew the way. I was lugging for 200 yards—then waiting again, then heavy machine gun fire, then quiet again—walk some more, then stop again. I thought, how will I ever see the Germans in the dark.

"One kilometer further down the road we found a delivery

truck of Paul Kaiser, with the name 'Paulientje' painted on the side. It was ours. We put all of our gear and ammunition in it and set out again for Schijndel but the going was slow. Shots were fired and we had to jump from the truck more than once for cover. We passed an American checkpoint where a stranded Citroën was sitting with two wounded, high ranking, German officers. I learned a new phrase—'stupid Krauts.' We reached Schijndel and were told to park the auto, loaded with ammunition, behind the church."

Recalling the night attack on Schijndel, Capt. Ian Hamilton of "B" Company remembered, "I recall Colonel Kinnard convening a meeting of company commanders before we entered the town and he opened it up to suggestions. It was my thought and one which I expressed that we would simply slip into town, take the Grange, take city hall, take all the watering holes (saloons and bars) and dare the Germans to take them back from us in the morning. Colonel Kinnard accepted the proposal and issued orders that fundamentally provided for us to do just that."

T/5 Frank Carpenter was shaken by the next order of his commander. "We got down to Schijndel and got word from Captain Phillips to fix bayonets. Nobody had ever said to fix bayonets before, even though we were veterans of Normandy. There were many emotional thoughts going through our minds as we drew our bayonets and fixed them to our rifles and moved into town. The only enemy soldiers we got were Germans who had been fast asleep. They woke up and came out to see what was going on. They were billeted in the houses. I remember we moved into the houses and set up the CP. I found a nice, thick rug and curled up and promptly went to sleep. It was pretty late that night when we got there."

PFC Paul E. Sanders was another who remembered the bayonet incident. "We were ordered to fix bayonets for hand to hand combat. We knew that all the enemy soldiers hadn't left. I did not have to fight hand to hand. Some of our men did."

Cpl. Chester Ostby of "B" Company remembered "the night attack on Schijndel down a very narrow street. It was pitch dark. A German opened up with a machine gun. We were jammed up due to the darkness. Not a man was hit but the sparks flew. Then a horse came galloping down the street. No one got hurt."

S/Sgt. Maurice C. White remembered: "We were part of a night attack on Schijndel. I had obtained a German motorcycle with a side-car that I rode in when possible because of my bad ankle. Had a .30 cal. machine gun mounted on the side-car. In Schijndel, we were searching the town and I opened a door to a bar and there were two German soldiers. I closed the door, took a cap off a Gammon grenade, tossed it in the room; result—two German soldiers pasted to the bar. The same night a German soldier came riding into town on a motorcycle. The command was to stop him, but don't hit the gas tank. Several opened fire and three grenades were tossed. Needless to say, we got the soldier but also destroyed the motorcycle."

The leading elements of 1st Battalion arrived in Schijndel about midnight. In a short time, the leader of the local underground unit arrived to confer with Lieutenant Colonel Kinnard. He asked in what ways could his men be of most assistance. Kinnard asked that he first send his best English-speaking member. This was done quickly. The member was told to inform the Dutch people to stay off the streets, display no bunting or flags, and for the people not to show their friendliness to the American troops. Kinnard felt certain his troops would remain only a few days and the German troops would return. He didn't want the civilian populace to suffer at the hands of the returning enemy forces. The underground was also asked to pinpoint the enemy strong points in and around town. The Dutch found a good-sized force near the railroad station, which was in position to block the approach of 3rd Battalion moving up from Eerde.

With "A" Company bringing up the rear of the 1st Battalion force, 1Lt. Sumpter Blackmon arrived later than the first elements. He had this comment: "We went into Schijndel about 0300 hours in the morning. It was another good move because we captured a German headquarters with the battalion under Colonel Kinnard."

The troops of 1st Battalion had their hands full with the coming of daylight. T/5 Frank Carpenter recalled: "In the morning, we set up some road blocks on the different roads leading into Schijndel from the north, east and west. These started paying dividends right away as word hadn't gotten back to the German lines that we were there and they drove in and our guys captured vehicle after vehicle as they arrived in that little town."

"We took the town filled with enemy soldiers," wrote Sgt. Robert R. Chapman. "In the morning, Krauts came out of bedrooms to walk into our guys in the kitchen. The U.S. Army Field Service Regulations warn never to do what we did."

Though he had access to the church steeple, Lieutenant Colonel Kinnard found that the ground mist concealed the movements of approaching enemy soldiers as they neared the town center.

Cpl. Donald W. Wilson remembered the action the next morning. "The following day, we drove the Germans out of the town and an ammunition dump seemed to be burning close by. The shrapnel kept falling all around us. In the early morning, I was walking down a street when a German machine gun opened up at one end of the block. I jumped right through the front window of the nearest house."

PFC Ernest A. Lambert remembered that one of his friends died in Schijndel. "Pvt. James F. Stallings was killed in Schijndel the day after the night attack when the Germans attacked across a big field, killed by rifle fire in the convent garden. After the attack was repulsed, he was buried there. I often wondered if his body had ever been reinterred in a military cemetery." (Later reinterred at Molenhoek and then moved to Maryland.)

Cpl. Chester Ostby remembered the daylight fighting and running into enemy tanks. "The attack out of Schijndel is where we ran into enemy tanks. We withdrew into town. We all stopped in a tavern and drank beer until an officer told us there was a war going on and to get the hell out there and fight it."

Company "A" was positioned on the east side of Schijndel. First Lieutenant Sumpter Blackmon describes the actions in which his men were involved. "The Germans were right smart and tried to lure us outside the town to fight them. Colonel Kinnard took a group to open the highway. I had a group to protect his right flank. The Germans were pretty strong outside. On his right flank were two tanks and I don't know how many men, but I had a group of 'A' Company men and we were under heavy fire from those tanks—and I don't know how many foot soldiers were with them. The infantry stayed about 800 yards away and we couldn't do a thing about them. We didn't have anything but rifle fire to put out at them and they'd fire into our area and they were afraid to come closer with the tanks because they thought we had bazookas or something. They had been told we could knock out their tanks at 300 yards. After they would fire and shell us the ground troops would advance toward our lines and we'd let them get to within a hundred yards of us and open up with everything we had and the tanks would hesitate, afraid to fire because their men were between us. We felt safe from the tank fire when they were between us. We felt safe from the tank fire when they were that close. We thought it was easy but that is where I got hit. It wasn't enough to put me out of action. I guess it went on for about three hours. We had good cover. Those tanks were firing right over us and we were down low in the ditches. We'd stick our heads up to see if any Germans were coming."

Another soldier had trouble getting close enough to the German tanks to fire at them. PFC Paul E. Sanders wrote: "Captain Bob Phillips and I were ordered to try knocking out a German tank which was giving us trouble. We took my bazooka and gave chase, fired a few rounds of ammo but we never did get close enough to knock it out."

Radioman Frank Carpenter wrote: "Later in the day we pulled an attack toward s'Hertogenbosch. We had two battalions on line. Whatever happened above at higher headquarters caused us to be ordered back to Veghel. There had been a breach in the main highway and we were to go back and help close it."

Underground member Mike Nooijen had accompanied 1st Battalion on its mission to Dinter, Heeswijk, and Schijndel as a guide and helper with the supply people. He described the morning moves and the sudden decision to depart. "With the arrival of daylight, American soldiers were coming in dumping German weapons and ammunition into our auto. A lot of gun fire was going out from the church steeple where snipers were shooting at the Germans. The faces of the soldiers became somber. The 'walkie-talkies' were very busy. The men were looking over a map. They were going to retreat. Did I know the road to Heeswijk? Of course. It had to be quick."

Medic Pvt. Jack L. Gehrs had been working in the regimental aid station in Veghel but was sent along on the Schijndel mission. He remembered when the 501st decided to pull back to Eerde. "As we were pulling out of town, the townsfolk were lined up along the street watching us leave. Their faces were so sad looking."

Frank Carpenter described the move back toward Eerde.

"The Germans were pressing us. The 1st Battalion went through us and led the way back to Eerde. Our company ended up as the rear guard for the battalion. We ended up in the little town of Weibosch between Schijndel and Eerde and just outside the little village. We settled down for the night in nearby fields."

T/4 Earl H. Tyndall Jr. was part of 1st Battalion Headquarters Company and remembered the adventure of the morning of the twenty-second: "We were able to capture a butchered calf which was still on the table ready to be cut. Since I had some experience in a slaughterhouse during the summer with my father, I volunteered to cut and cook the meal that evening. That night we were in an open field and Colonel Kinnard stated that we were going to do like the cowboys and Indians. We set up in a circle and defended in all directions. That night, in a farmhouse, I cut the veal, cooked it in rendered fat from the carcass, and we all enjoyed veal steaks that evening."

Mike Nooijen and Sgt. Chester Brooks were part of a segment that moved back, retracing their steps from the night before. They headed for Dinter where a platoon of "C" Company had set up a roadblock to protect the rear of 1st Battalion when it moved south to Schijndel. Included with that platoon were members of the headquarters section of the 1st Battalion. They had been under attack by a small German force during the day.

Sgt. Chester Brooks had this recollection from the battalion point of view: "We cleared out the area and then were ordered to attack Dinter, which we did that night. We left a squad of cooks, the mail orderly, Amos (the Bear) Hathaway and others to protect our rear and took a number of prisoners at Dinter. We were ordered to Veghel. I was to go back and pick up the group protecting our rear in Heeswijk."

Mike Nooijen was put in the front seat with the driver for the truck they had confiscated the night before. He wrote: "I was beside the driver of the truck to guide him through the turns. Just before crossing the Heeswijk canal bridge, we came under fire but did not get hit. At Heeswijk we got some rest—but nobody could rest. By the old town hall, at Heeswijk-Dinter, there arrived every hour a little guy on his bicycle reporting the locations of the Germans. They said it was the town secretary. It was getting dark. By the bridge there were still some crates with German ammunition we had to pick up. An officer ran over to pick up the last crate. We fired covering shots over his head. He threw the crate in the delivery truck. More enemy tanks were reported. Shells began to fall. The underground men threw away their German rifles and we loaded the men in the delivery auto. Suddenly, a big swear word from an officer. Again, we had to retreat. I felt it as a humiliation. The driver stepped on the gas and away we went. We were under fire. It was scary. The driver kept going at full speed. Other vehicles came on—jeeps, ambulances . . . everything. We reached Veghel."

Sgt. Chester Brooks was sent back to pick up the group serving as rear guard. He wrote: "An officer was in charge. We found they had picked up a German (Polish) prisoner during an attack on their position by an armored half-track. I learned Hathaway had been hit. The lieutenant had a camouflaged German car. I appropriated it and we drove to get 'the Bear.' A cook named Davis drove with me on the running board. We did not see the half-track but were told it was out there. When we got to Hathaway, we discovered he had an unexploded 20mm shell in him and was in what we perceived to be poor condition. We had no medic but saw that we needed a stretcher. Davis drove back and got one and we loaded Amos on top of the car and drove to the hospital in Veghel."

1st Battalion Moves into Eerde

The men of "C" Company had served as rear guard for 1st Battalion in the move south from Schijndel. They had stopped for the night in the outskirts of Weibosch, in the nearby fields. In the morning, 1st Battalion had gone on toward Eerde.

T/5 Frank Carpenter describes an adventure in getting nourishment for his friends on the morning of the twenty-third. "Woke up in the morning and we were hungry—hadn't had much to eat since we left Veghel earlier. We remembered passing a bakery[87] in the little town so the supply sergeant, or his assistant, and I took the motorcycle with its side-car (captured earlier) and went back to the bakery. No one there spoke English but they got the idea a large number of men were hungry so

---

87. Carpenter found out in recent years that the Germans did not harm the Dutch baker and his family. The family, in turn, wondered if the Americans ever got out alive from their predicament.

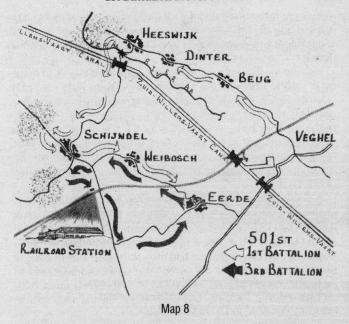

Map 8

the whole family set up a production line making sandwiches. They split the little loaves of bread, slapped butter and jelly between. The girls stacked them in cardboard boxes for us. About that time, a Dutchman entered and announced that Germans were coming in from the north side of the town from the direction of Schijndel, along the same road we had followed the day before. We peeked around the corner of the building, up the road, and sure as hell there were German scouts coming down the road. We grabbed every box in a hurry. I jumped in the sidecar. The boxes were stacked on and around me. We fired up the danged thing and roared out from behind the building. By this time the German scout was so close he was dumbfounded when we came roaring out. Of course, it was a German motorcycle with side-car so it gave us just enough time to surprise him and he didn't fire until it was too late. We went south down the road towards Eerde, took some corners real fast—heard some shots fired, but they weren't close."

Carpenter continued: "When we got back to the company,

they were just pulling out. We sat alongside the road in the side-car passing out the jelly and butter sandwiches to the men and everybody was munching as they marched down the road to Eerde.

"As we walked into Eerde, to our right were two sand dunes with a little valley or dip between them. They were off to the west of Eerde. We were ordered to surround the town and face the west with the possibility of the Germans coming down the same road we had just traveled. The CP was in the end house leading into town. From the upstairs window, which faced west, we had an unobstructed view over the windmill which was between us and the sand dunes. The dunes were about five hundred yards away."

On the twenty-third, the 1st Battalion had moved from Weibosch into the Eerde area. "C" Company placed a roadblock on the railroad crossing along the Eerde–Weibosch road with company headquarters in the first house at the bend near the windmill. Most of the troops faced west into the sand dunes. "B" Company was a quarter mile east of the roadblock set up by "C" at the rail crossing. They had blocks on two country lanes entering Eerde. "A" Company was at the south end of Eerde near the end of the ten- to thirty-foot-high dunes.

Communications officer 1Lt. Frank Fitter of 1st Battalion remembered the approach to Eerde. "We had quite a bit of resistance. Colonel Kinnard led a group out to the west toward Eerde. We went there. The rifle companies had gone up earlier. 'B' Company was outside the town. Colonel Kinnard asked Captain Harry Howard to get somebody into town—it was late in the evening, to contact the underground. They were to meet us at one of the churches. Captain Howard turned to me and said, 'Come on, let's go!' So we went up to 'B' Company, which was spread out along the road. We told the commanding officer that we were going into the town. By then it was dark. Howard said, 'Don't fire down the street as we will be coming out the same way.' As we entered the town under the cover of darkness, we knew there were Germans inside the town. We hadn't gone more than a block when a German, riding a cart pulled by a horse, came out of a side street. Howard and I jumped in a doorway. The whole of 'B' Company opened up. I remember to this day that bullets ricocheted off the walls and the street sending sparks flying."

Cpl. Donald W. Wilson of "B" Company was involved in the action. He wrote: "The night we went into Eerde, James Rehmert and another soldier were on opposite sides of the street when a German came down the street driving a horse hitched to an ammunition cart. Rehmert and the other guy both had Thompson subs and seemed to be shooting right at each other with that German between them. They killed the German and the horse, but I couldn't understand how they kept from shooting each other."

Fitter continued his story: "They finally stopped firing and we went on to the church. We couldn't contact anybody. Captain Howard said, 'We are probably at the wrong church.'[88] We said there was only one thing to do—go to the other church which was some distance on the other side of town. We worked our way over to the next church and I stayed outside, kind of as a sentry, while Howard knocked on the door and was let in. I stayed outside for what seemed like 15 to 30 minutes and became concerned. There wasn't anybody around so I went up and knocked on the door and was admitted. The Catholic priest, Rev. Joseph Willenborg, turned out to be head of the underground. He and Howard were in a little room that was blacked out with only a single candle burning. They were drinking good church wine. I immediately joined them for a glass or two. The priest was a very interesting person and talked to us for 30 minutes or so and told us he thought a good many of the Germans had left town but there were still some around. Howard and I said our farewells and came on back and 'B' Company did not fire on us as we came through."

First Lieutenant Fitter added: "The next morning, 1st Battalion moved in and caught the Germans by surprise. The Germans fled and left a field kitchen. We passed the food out to some of the U.S. troops for, as I recall, the field kitchen was intact with all the hot food on the stoves. We did not eat it. Colonel Kinnard called the priest and told him to give it to the civilians and to do it quickly. I'm sure the underground took over the food that was cooked and it was dispersed to the Dutch civilians. They were really fine people and helped us out."

---

88. First Lieutenant Frank Fitter was mistaken in thinking there were two churches. John van Geffen related that Fitter mistook the monastery, with its small steeple, for a second church.

Daybreak on the twenty-fourth brought several surprises to the men of the 1st Battalion. S/Sgt. Maurice C. White of "C" Company had his platoon on outpost duty, which included a roadblock at the railroad crossing entering Eerde from the northwest. He wrote: "The next morning an enemy force was observed approaching our position from the west, along the railroad tracks. It was estimated to be a company of infantry and three tanks. I kept my platoon in position until they were across the road from us. Then we rejoined the company in Eerde. The Germans advanced to the sand dunes and we were pinned down for a while."

When Lieutenant Colonel Kinnard got the message, the enemy force was already looking down at his positions from the tops of the dunes.

With the coming of daylight, 1Lt. Sumpter Blackmon was better able to see the company positions. He pointed out: "We were a little bit careless to be real honest about it. We had moved into Eerde and had not outposted it properly. Those sand dunes were piles of dirt about 20 feet high and had 8-inch trees growing out of them. The Germans had been there for some time and had good observation. They were harassing us. I was in a house with Captain Stanfield Stach. We were placing our men out and checking on a map when the whole side of the house blew in on us. The shell was a direct hit over our heads and threw all the stuff on our maps on the table. They had occupied the area for at least a day or so before we got there. Colonel Kinnard decided we should move them out because they were harassing us too much."

Sgt. Guy M. Sessions of "C" Company remembered the developing action in the dunes. "The gunfight in the sand dunes— as I recall moving into the sand dunes area, everything was quiet and peaceful. We were assigned positions right smack dab in the middle of the rather large sand area, probably four or five acres in size. We couldn't understand why we were ordered to dig fox holes in such exposed positions and still can't to this day. There was also a hump of dirt, like a berm, with pine trees growing from it about fifty yards to our front. It was obvious this could give cover to the enemy if they could get that close to us. There was also a Dutch windmill about 100 yards to our rear and, of course, the Germans thought we were using it for an observation post—and we probably were."

The town of Eerde had taken a pounding from enemy mortars and artillery shelling since the eighteenth when 3rd Battalion had been subjected to the bombardment. Company "I" in particular had been hit hard around the railroad station at the north end of town. Sgt. Jacob H. Wingard had been picked off by a sniper's bullet while observing in the windmill.

The house occupied by T/5 Frank Carpenter was serving as the CP for "C" Company. It was the home of John van Geffen and his parents. The family was no longer staying at home. John van Geffen wrote: "During the time of the heavy fighting, and after, our home was very heavily damaged. My family and many others stayed in the priest house of Father Joseph Willenborg. There were 40 or more refugees staying in his house. Father Willenborg slept on the floor."

The paratroopers didn't have long to wait before the enemy attacks began on their positions around Eerde.

Sgt. Guy Sessions wrote: "When the attack came it was more or less a frontal attack and we could see German troops advancing steadily forward until they were in very close range. Close enough for me to yell, 'Hande Hoch! Surrender!' Well, they yelled the same thing back to me. I answered by getting my bazooka man to put a round into an area where a small group of Germans seemed to be concentrated. In the meantime, a German 88 zeroed in on the windmill and was methodically taking it apart brick by brick. By this time there was a good sized concentration of the enemy using the berm for cover—estimate a company directly attacking my front (platoon area). My machine gunner had left his position, for what reason I'm not sure, so I ran and jumped into his foxhole to try to get the gun in operation again. I found the machine gun jammed, maybe he had gone to look for another weapon. I got the gun working. Evidently it had gotten so hot and needed to cool. I began firing short bursts toward the enemy—close range—30 to 50 yards. A bullet landed very close to my head and I thought I had been hit. I reached up to my right temple, expecting to feel blood, but the bullet had hit into the sand on the side of the foxhole and it was the sand hitting my head that I had felt. After what seemed like hours, the Germans began to withdraw and we reassembled for a counterattack."

PFC John Hopke remembered the fighting in the sand dunes.

His recollection was a vivid one. "I was a machine gunner with Stan Leck. We decided to give the gun a good cleaning as it was fired a lot and, with all the sand around, it needed cleaning. We then covered the gun with a shelter half. I told Leck I would go down the line and gab with a few of the guys for a couple minutes and then I would come back and he could go. Agreed, good deal. I got out of the hole and took five or six steps when I heard the pop of a mortar. I hit the ground and, after the explosion, I looked around. Good God! Leck got hit right on the head. What a mess!"

Lieutenant Colonel Kinnard called for the tank support that had appeared the day before. When they were in position to move out with the infantry, the troops would move into the dunes.

T/5 Frank Carpenter related: "We got into a fire fight with the Krauts. They weren't pressing us from the north but they did occupy the high ground which we should have done. The battalion finally decided we'd have to take the damned thing and we were to have a platoon of British tanks which were being sent forward to us. The tanks were a little late getting there but when they did, some time in the early afternoon, down the road out of Eerde comes this tank column. The tank commander sent two tanks out on the right, two on the left and he stayed on the road and pulled up alongside the building we were using as a CP. We were just waiting for him to start the attack. The English lieutenant was up in the turret and yelling down to Captain Phillips that he wouldn't go into an attack with us or take orders from Captain Phillips until his battalion commander told him to do so.

"You didn't talk to Captain Phillips that way! Phillips was madder than a wet hen. I saw an argument ensuing so I turned around and rested my radio against the back of the tank and kept looking up at the tank commander and back to Captain Phillips and that lieutenant wasn't going to budge until he had orders from his commander.

"Coincidentally about this time in that little gap in the sand dunes, wide enough for a tank to come through, a German tank had rolled up in there. We didn't see it at first and the tank cut loose. He fired one round and hit the British tank we were standing beside, just below the gun tube and out the other side. It was an AP shell. Had it been another type, we'd all have been killed. When I tilted my head, that lieutenant flew through the air, falling down beside me and rolled into a little ditch, screaming bloody murder. He'd been ripped open in the groin and one leg was almost off at the hip. He was yelling, 'Save my men, save my men!'

"While this was going on the German gunner had turned his gun and had taken a shot at another tank that had pulled up by the windmill, knocked it out, traversed the gun tube to his right, fired a third round and hit the third tank, traversed it all the way left, beyond the windmill where the other two tanks were located, fired two more rounds and knocked them all out. He fired five shots and knocked out five tanks, all just as fast as it took to load those shells and move that gun. So here is this lieutenant who had just gotten into an argument with the captain when he should have been moving with him, certainly would not have lost all five of his tanks. Some of the tankers got out. The bow gunner and driver got out of the tank beside us. I don't know what got out of the others. We never went back to find out. What a tragic waste and the platoon didn't get off a single shot! We could see the German tank after he took his first shot."

S/Sgt. Clive Barney verified Carpenter's story. "The same tank chased us off a field where we had been picking up supplies. We knew the British tanks were at our CP so we sent a couple men ahead to warn them and we hoped the Tiger would chase the rest of us right to the CP. Afterward, the Tiger was chased off with a bazooka."

Radioman Joe Haller was near the church when the tank incident occurred. He said, "Some British tanks went out there near Eerde and got shot up by 88s. The guys were burned to a crisp. The hands were up in the air as if reaching for the hatch cover. That was right behind and to the right of the windmill."

The tank support the paratroopers had hoped for in the assault on the German positions in the sand dunes was gone—gone before it had commenced.

The British commander withdrew the remaining tanks claiming there were too many anti-tank weapons in the dunes, making the use of tanks in that situation too great a risk. The anti-tank work had been done by an extremely accurate gunner on a German tank nestled in the dunes.

When the tank support failed to materialize, the 501st still had the artillery to support them. The tall church steeple in Eerde was the site of several observation posts. First Battalion officers and men took turns calling directions for mortar fire. Officers from the 907th Glider Field Artillery Battalion had been sent forward to direct the fire of their guns positioned south of the St. Oedenrode–Veghel highway and four hundred yards west of the highway bridge over the canal.

In his book *Kilogram,* Bob Minick describes the work of the forward observers of the 907th Glider Field Artillery Battalion in support of the 501st in the dunes fighting at Eerde on the twenty-fourth:

> Lt. Bates Stinson's team was directed into the Eerde area and assigned to work with the 1st Battalion. Upon driving into the town, Sgt. Edward Paprocki, Cpl. Francis Withers and Cpl. Carl Edstrom came under artillery fire and took cover in the basement window wells of a Catholic convent. As the shelling continued, the three troopers could hear the nuns praying in the basement. A phosphorus shell burned a hole in one of their jeeps' tires. After they put the spare tire on, Lt. Stinson directed them to meet him at a forward observation post about a half mile up the railroad track. They were to drive up one side of the embankment while Stinson reconnoitered the opposite side. When they finally arrived at the rendezvous point, they learned Stinson had been hit by mortar fire and was evacuated.
>
> While Stinson's team was working in the forward position, Lt. Frank Toth, PFC George Pinkham, PFC LeRoy Stewart and Pvt. Ken Course were operating from the church steeple in Eerde. When the German artillery singled out the steeple as their prime target, the team left the church and set up shop behind a schoolhouse located in a small orchard. While in this position, Pinkham, Stewart and Course were all wounded when the Germans shifted their attention from the steeple to the schoolhouse. The troopers were evacuated to a field hospital set up in Veghel, about two miles away.
>
> Later in the same day, Lt. Gerald C. Taylor and Privates Tom Logue and Douglas Solomon did excellent work from the same steeple. By this time the fighting had extended to the north and east of the town but the 501st officers still felt the sand dunes were the critical terrain feature. Plans to clear the dunes were immediately put into action.
>
> With the parachute infantry carrying out a bold attack and with Lt. Taylor from his vantage point, keeping the artillery moving three to four hundred yards ahead of the attacking paratroopers, the Germans were finally driven back.[89]

89. Minick, 151–2.

The attack went ahead without tank support. Capt. Stanfield Stach's "A" Company had support of a section of light machine guns and a mortar observer, and with "C" Company providing a base of fire to force the enemy soldiers to keep their heads down, the attack began at 1215. Second Lieutenant Cecil O. Fuquay, with his 2nd Platoon, charged forward leading the way.

Sweeping in from the south, "A" Company moved quickly up through the nearest dunes. One squad did a flanking movement to the left, behind them. With the men yelling as they charged across the open area, it was not long before enemy soldiers began to throw down their arms and fled from the onrushing troopers. Moving in groups of two and three, the men rushed into the positions, sometimes clubbing the enemies with rifle butts rather than resorting to bullets.

When it was over, fifteen of the enemy were dead, seven were taken prisoner, and the rest fled back through the dunes.

The assault was carried out entirely by Company "A" followed closely by 1Lt. George Murn's light machine gunners. The mortar fire was being directed by Capt. Harry Howard and others from his group in the shattered steeple of the church.

Second Platoon continued to move forward and came under fire from the next group of dunes. With the enemy attacking them with machine-gun, mortar, grenade, and small-arms fire, 2nd Platoon continued in short spurts, taking advantage of thick scrub brush that screened them from view. The men put out more fire, concentrating on any movement they might spot ahead. Gradually, the southern dunes were cleared. The 60mm mortars were doing an outstanding job keeping ahead of the men, thanks to those observers in the steeple. The fire from the 105s was too far out in front of the men to be of much use.

As the men reached a stretch of flat and barren ground, they came into the view of a German tank positioned a thousand yards to the west. Its first burst killed Second Lieutenant Fuquay and Cpl. Bronislaw Kraska. Platoon sergeant John Kushner was badly wounded. Only one squad leader was left.

Company commander Stach sent 1Lt. James C. Murphy to take command of 2nd Platoon. He reorganized what was left of the platoon and found it was no longer in condition to spearhead an attack. He was going to put it in reserve position but before he could act on it, he was called to 1st Platoon when Lt. Harry Mosier received critical wounds and his platoon sergeant,

George H. Adams, was killed. Private Jack Bleffer acted as platoon leader until First Lieutenant Murphy got back.

Without a leader, 2nd Platoon was left to slug it out before they could be moved back to a reserve position. Exec officer Sumpter Blackmon described their individual actions:[90] "I saw one man throwing rocks, hitting the scrub to one side of him. The rocks hitting the scrub produced action. The enemy fired at it. He got a line on the enemy fire position and knocked it out. I saw three men consult among themselves, then get their heads down and charge straight into an enemy machine gun nest twenty-five yards away, and take it without loss. This was the way it went the rest of the day."

Lt. Monk Mier's 3rd Platoon was committed on the right with the mission of driving the enemy to the west into the open fields where the machine gunners and what was left of 2nd Platoon would have a field day. When its forward files reached the northernmost edge of the dunes it turned west, covering ground on the run. They overran the remaining enemy positions. The ones who weren't killed or did not surrender fled into the steady hail of the machine gunners on 2nd Platoon's front.

And so ended the struggle for the sand dunes. The enemy artillery continued to vent its anger at the men directing fire from the tall church spire, much of it having been blown away earlier.

The Eerde Church Steeple

First Battalion company clerk T/4 Earl H. Tyndall remembered the dunes fighting and part played by the forward observers in the Eerde church tower. He wrote: "One outstanding memory is that the church steeple made an excellent observation post and artillery and mortar observers were up in this steeple together with Capt. Harry Howard and me. After getting two direct hits on the steeple, Captain Howard ordered all the enlisted men to leave. I started down the stairs and, after going part way down, remembered that my raincoat was still in the steeple and that was my only means of keeping warm at night. Naturally, I went back to retrieve the raincoat. While there, a field phone rang and I answered it and was asked to observe a mortar round, which I

90. Rapport, Leonard, and Arthur Northwood. *Rendezvous with Destiny* (3rd ed). 101st Airborne Division Association, Sweetwater, TN, 1948, 367.

did. After that time, Captain Howard gave me a direct order to leave the steeple. I tried to tell him I was just recovering my raincoat and he kept telling me to leave."

First Lieutenant Frank Fitter also remembered the church spire being used for observation purposes. "Two of our mortar platoon people were in the steeple as observers for our mortar gunners who were firing on the Germans just outside of town and the Germans got wise and put a few rounds through the steeple. The Germans had some tanks hidden in haystacks, very well camouflaged but we knew they were there. So, Harry Howard—he was quite a guy, he says 'I'm going up there myself to direct some of that fire!' Ole Harry climbed up there where he was in position to call it to the gunners. The Germans leveled on the steeple again. They knocked ole Harry out of there. He fell down the stairs with a bunch of bricks falling on him. I thought he was hurt bad. We ran over there and pulled him out. He was bruised but wasn't hurt much. He said, 'I'll fix those guys!' So that night he got the only American flag we had and took it up and hung it in the opening of what remained of the steeple. The next morning those Germans just leveled that doggone steeple. We went up and dug out the flag. Ole Harry said, 'That's the only souvenir I want out of this war!' and he took the flag."

During the heavy fighting in and around Eerde, Bernadette van Geffen, wife of John, had lived with her parents in the Eerde railroad station. Along with her parents and other family members and friends, much time was spent in the family air-raid shelter nearby. She said, "One of the enemy tanks, which was responsible for the destruction of the steeple on the church, was in position near the air raid shelter and one of my brothers could hear an observer giving the tank gunner directions on firing at the church steeple. He would give the meters right or left and then on target."

John van Geffen and his family felt the display of the flag in the shattered steeple was a clear message to the Germans. "It was clearly visible to the Germans in the sand dunes and in the direction of Schijndel as a sign 'We stay where we are.' "

Ammo Truck Explodes

While the observations were going on, there was a terrific explosion off to the northeast in the direction of "B" Company. It was noticed by men battling in the sand dunes. One of those was Sgt. Guy Sessions. "We heard the explosion and could see the smoke about 200 yards away to our rear. We didn't know what had happened at the time but suspected it resulted in casualties. We learned that a supply truck had blown up killing eight or nine of our men."

Capt. Ian Hamilton of "B" Company remembered he lost his close friend 1Lt. Robert Schorsch in Eerde. "I had spent nearly an hour in the church steeple using excellent binoculars taken from a German major we had killed a few days before. I descended the winding staircase of the church, passed right by the just arrived truck and walked away to inspect positions. The explosion caused me to run back to see what happened. Men were lying about, some were crawling, others obviously dead. I ran to Bob Schorsch who was lying on the ground and jerking. I grabbed him and pulled him to a sitting position but he was bleeding from his nose and mouth and was trying to speak. In a few minutes he was gone."

As a twenty-year-old, Mike Nooijen had volunteered his services as soon as he could hurry to the Eerde area from Schijndel where he had witnessed them descending on the seventeenth. He had been assigned to help move supplies to and from a central storage area. On this date, they were hauling ammunition. The small delivery auto his group had requisitioned in Schijndel finally broke down approaching Eerde. Nooijen wrote: "We unloaded the ammunition and set her on fire. I felt sad. I don't know where but along came a captured German army truck which was full of German ammunition. We put ours with it. We were given food and rest in a civilian shelter.

"The next morning we left with the ammunition truck. In front of the farm of Harie van de Pol, we came to a stop. Tjallie wanted to introduce the Dutchmen to his friends. We were drinking coffee between two piles of bundled sticks (used for firewood).

"A tremendous bang—shell fragments flying everywhere—two in my arm (found that out later). The farmhouse was on fire with shells exploding all around. Everything and everybody was in a panic. It was an inferno. I fled with a stream of men and jumped over everything in the way. I ran faster than a hare. A couple hundred meters further stood an officer with a drawn .45 pistol. I understood him to say that he who tried to run further would be stopped by him. Who was this hero? We were standing with about twenty men around him. He gave stern commands and he got respect. Tjallie and I stayed behind. We were to lay dead comrades in one row. I counted 8 or 10. They were my friends from the first hours. I was not able to keep the tears from my eyes even though I tried to hide them."

The destroyed ammunition was critical to the 1st Battalion troops whose supply had been diminishing by the day's actions.

FOURTEEN

Eerde

Action in Eerde

Fourteen-year-old John H. van Geffen had watched the paratroopers float to earth from the entrance to the family air-raid shelter in Eerde.

The 3rd Battalion of the 501st Parachute Regiment was to secure the small town and also establish a roadblock south of Eerde to prevent the movement of enemy troops toward Veghel while 1st and 2nd Battalion troops secured the four bridges.

Capt. Jack E. Thornton, commanding officer of Headquarters Company, wrote: "Before we were even organized after the jump, Henk Zijlman approached the drop zone in full Dutch military uniform and offered to join the battalion and act as interpreter. His English was very good and he served with us until we were relieved."

The move for the 3rd Battalion men was the shortest distance to reach an objective. PFC Laurence R. Burgoon came off the drop zone carrying two boxes of machine-gun ammunition. He wrote: "We took up an outpost at the rail station. That evening, a German patrol knocked it out."

Shortly after daybreak, heavy rifle and machine-gun fire was heard from the direction of the German positions, which had suddenly filled during the night. They were in the sand dunes approximately five hundred yards west of the van Geffen home. The paratroopers had formed a defensive line around Eerde and its windmill, which was being used as an observation post.

The Germans were advancing along the railroad track, moving from west to east in the direction of the Eerde railroad station.

John H. van Geffen recalled, "Many Germans were attacking

the Americans who had lines about the windmill and the Eerde railroad station."

The first action against the enemy in the Eerde area took place in front of the men of "I" Company. Sgt. James D. Edgar wrote: "We (2nd Platoon under Lt. John Ell) set up a road block. The next morning all hell broke loose. It was a foul-up on both sides. We had the Germans in an ambush but Lt. Ell thought the enemy wanted to surrender. By the time we pointed out they were carrying weapons, it was too late. It turned into a 'Cowboys and Indians' deal—in gardens, around barns, through hedgerows, fences, ditches, houses—all of it was there. We fought all day, begging for help. We found out Lt. Ell had told headquarters we were fighting a patrol. By this time, he was dead. Finally when we were down to one clip per man, S/Sgt. Frank Sciaccotti got on the radio and called for help. He was told to 'Hold at all costs!' His answer was, 'I have four rounds per man. You tell me how to do it and I'll try!' We were ordered to fall back. As we fell back, we met help coming on the run. The Germans started falling back, too."

Cpl. Richard L. Klein made sergeant in a most unwanted way on the eighteenth. With small-arms and machine-gun fire beginning to hit the area around the railroad station and the windmill, 1Lt. Lydle Hilton began to utilize the vantage point of the tall windmill near the sand dunes as an observation post. Corporal Klein wrote: "Lt. Hilton, Sgt. Jake Wingard and I were in the only windmill in Eerde directing fire on the sand dunes immediately in front of us. Jake, who was my best buddy, took a rifle round into his chest and matter of factly said, 'I'm dead—I'm dead!' He was."

Having returned to the family home from the shelter at early dawn, the van Geffen family wasn't there long before the heavy firing broke out. The children were ordered to lie on the floor. The father had smelled smoke. He went out to the barn to investigate to see if the pungent smoke odor was rising from that building. It was not. The shutters in the home were closed on all the windows so visibility to the outside was blocked off.

In midmorning the van Geffen home began to take numerous hits, both small arms and artillery. The elder van Geffen rushed outside as the barn was burning. He wanted to save the family pig. When the anxious mother looked for the father, part of the house collapsed when it was hit by several mortar shells.

As American paratroopers moved toward the German positions by way of the van Geffen backyard, one soldier stopped at the door to urge the family to seek shelter in the church. They didn't understand his directions, as no one in the family spoke English, so the paratrooper made a quick sketch of the church, pointed to it, then pointed to the family and then back to the church. The family realized the message he was conveying to them. The van Geffens followed the ditch toward the church and were directed to the relative safety of the priest house, which had a fine cellar.

Pvt. Henry G. Taylor was a member of Sgt. Jim Edgar's squad. He recalled the early actions near the railroad grade and the depot. "On the second day, I let a truck load of Germans pass the railroad crossing and then hell broke loose. Bob Kester was killed. John Quinlan was shot through the stomach, which broke his spine. It was four hours before we got him to an aid station. Lt. Ell was killed on the road while walking among trees. We were being attacked by two German tanks with 88s and infantry. They killed all but four of us in Edgar's squad."

Another member of the squad was Pvt. Marvin C. Wolfe. He recalled: "We had no opposition the first day. We moved into place. Early the next morning, we had a battle in the sand dunes along a railroad track beside a railroad station. Lt. Ell was killed there—also Quinlan."

Wolfe added, "I was a machine gunner and Henry Taylor was my assistant. We were along a railroad track, protecting the right side of our company and we looked up and there stood the biggest darned German you ever saw holding a burp gun. He looked at us, dropped his gun and took off. He was on the other side of the track.

"We were being pushed back and our machine gun wouldn't fire another round. Lt. Ell was there and told us he would stay and cover for us. He did and that is when he was killed."

Sergeant Edgar added to his story: "We had a man named Poole who had been 'shell-shocked' before. He was as good a man as any in a small arms situation but let a mortar or artillery shell fall close and that was all for him. Poole and I were fighting rear guard for the platoon in its withdrawal. He was on one side of the track and I was on the other. We were doing pretty well with M-1s when they began using a small mortar. They 'walked it' down the track. One round landed close to Poole. I thought it hit him. I peeked over and there he sat, staring at nothing. I crossed over, grabbed him and ran down the track, him with no rifle and no helmet. We came to a culvert under the track. I crawled under and Poole got half way in and froze on me. I dragged him out and caught up with the platoon."

With only the weapons they carried with them when they dropped on the fields the day before, the 3rd Battalion troopers were outmanned and forced to fall back toward Veghel.

They would have to return to Eerde and the sand dunes in a few days. The area continued to be a threat to the 101st positions.

On the nineteenth of September, the 501st was centered in Veghel. The 1st Battalion was on the north and northwest side. Second Battalion was in the south and on the east flank. Third Battalion was near the canal facing west. Col. Howard R. Johnson decided to outpost his forces away from Veghel with the exception of 2nd Battalion, which had the responsibility of protecting the regimental command post and the four bridges. Third Battalion was sent back to Eerde. "C" Company was sent north toward Heeswijk-Dinter.

PFC James P. Monaghan of "G" Company was in on the move back to Eerde on the nineteenth. He wrote: "We were moving up through Eerde and there was considerable small arms fire coming from the other side of the railroad track. This in itself was expected, but what amazed me was I saw an elderly woman down on her knees scrubbing the steps in front of her house."

For several days the 3rd Battalion was in defensive positions on the outskirts of Eerde. Pvt. Jesse C. Garcia of "G" Company was serving as runner for his commander, Capt. Vernon Kraeger. He said, "I was there as a runner in case the radio failed. We were dug in around a perimeter and I was a short distance from the captain. Evidently I was dug in too deep. I didn't hear him calling me. He crawled out of his foxhole and looked down in my position. I remember looking up and seeing the captain. He said, 'Garcia, if you dig that foxhole any deeper, I'll consider you AWOL!'"

A fond memory of Captain Kraeger was provided by Monaghan: "We were on outpost duty and I recall Captain Kraeger standing near a GI's foxhole and telling him that if he was going to hit the Germans, who were running across an opening 300 yards away, he would have to lead them with his shots."

On another occasion Private Garcia accompanied Captain Kraeger to battalion headquarters where his commander conversed with Col. Julian Ewell and Col. George Griswold. They came under fire. Garcia wrote: "I don't know if we were spotted by a few Krauts or not but they opened fire with small arms fire. I hit the ground immediately. Neither Captain Kraeger or the two colonels ever flinched or jumped. I remember Colonel Ewell saying in his southern twang, 'Well, I guess we better take cover.' They were real men in combat."

A day or so later, some British tanks were attached to 3rd Battalion. T/5 William Schwerin was a 3rd Battalion radioman. He recalled: "We were sitting behind a building by an English tank. I was awake and a shell hit about 200 yards away. Colonel Ewell looked up and said, 'Schwerin, where was that explosion?' After telling him, he got us on our feet and we just moved around the building when a shell hit the tank, killing the crew members and wounding one of the CP group in the thigh."

Private Garcia added another memory of his commander. "We had a skirmish with Krauts in a woods. The captain was naturally at the front line (if not ahead of it) and I was about 20 feet away. He received his first wound, a bullet in the arm. The medic told him to go back to the rear medical unit. I heard him say, 'I'm all right' and when he was asked again, he refused. I remember he stayed at his position firing steadily with his carbine since we could see the Krauts not very far away."

Private First Class Monaghan added another story: "One day we were moving up a road and came under some very accurate artillery or tank fire. I had noticed earlier a burned out Sherman tank that had received a hit in the turret. This convinced me it was tank fire. Warren Reudy and I were down in a very small ditch when a shell exploded so close that it covered us with dirt. After seeing that neither of us were hurt, I looked up and there on the road, just as calm as could be with not a care in the world, was Captain Kraeger. I said, 'Hey Captain, when are we going to get out of this mess?' He replied very calmly, 'Don't worry Monaghan, I got you in and I will get you out.' Well, that was all I needed, and he did get us out. He was one of the greatest leaders I ever met."

For three days, 3rd Battalion was in a perimeter defense around Eerde. Patrols went out each day and night. Both forces were feeling out the other.

The 3rd Moves Up to Schijndel

While 1st Battalion had jumped off in its attack as night fell, 3rd Battalion was ordered to move out at 2200 hours.

S/Sgt. Robert J. Houston of "H" Company describes his actions in the nighttime movement toward Schijndel as follows:

During the day on September 21, men from the Dutch underground had brought word to Colonel Johnson that German forces were building up in Schijndel. Colonel Johnson, not one to wait for somebody to hit him, ordered an attack by 1st and 3rd Battalions. The 1st Battalion would come in from Heeswijk while we moved up from Eerde. There was some question about the wisdom of making such an attack at night, but that was the word; our company commanders had orders to move out at ten o'clock. Company "H" organized along a lane and was to move out from the line of departure with platoons and squads in line rather than in marching column. We heard a machine gun fire in the distance and now and then the b-r-r-r-p of a Schmizzer, as we leaned against the bank of a ditch beside our lane. It was a cloudy, dark night; so much the better, nobody could see us coming. We had orders to keep the line straight so if there was firing we wouldn't hit each other.

When ten o'clock came on our wrist watches, Sgt. Euel Langlinais and I got up out of the ditch and started to move ahead. We moved ahead in line and put some rifle fire into the spot from which the machine gun was firing. It hadn't been firing directly at us, so no one in "H" Company was hit as we moved slowly across the first long field. We went along carefully to keep from getting scattered in the darkness. There was no more firing as we continued toward Schijndel, about three miles from our line of departure.

We had been walking for an hour when directly in front of us, we saw the shape of a house with vehicles parked around it. We were moving quietly, so they didn't expect any company. A squad went up to the house and reported back that there were six German army vehicles with no one on guard. The captain thought this was a good job for the first sergeant and sent Joe Henderson to the door with a private who could speak German. The 3rd Platoon went along as the reception committee.

Sergeant Henderson knocked loudly on the door, and the private called, "Come out, I have a message for you!"

The door opened and the sergeant shined his flashlight on a sleepy looking lieutenant. He didn't realize that his guests were

Americans and asked what the message was. The private told him that the message was twenty rifles aimed at him and he should tell his men to come out without their weapons. I snapped on my flashlight and let him see a few of the rifles to emphasize the message. He called out and German soldiers began to appear. We soon had twenty in a bunch behind the house, where they could be watched until it was light enough to take them back.[91]

Sgt. Jim Edgar was in on the same attack toward Schijndel as a member of "I" Company. He wrote: "We shoved off before midnight. 'I' and 'H' Company with Captain Stanley led the attack, one company on one side of the road and the other across the road. 'G' and 'HQ' were following. My squad was on the 'H' Company flank. I had a clip of tracers to show 'H' Company how we were progressing. 'H' Company had a man doing the same at their point. It turned wild—everybody hollering and screaming and we were moving along. We were running over more Germans than we were killing. We were in a ditch along the road. I put my tracers in and fired up in the air to alert 'H' Company of our progress. I lowered my rifle. Just then a German let go with a machine pistol. A full clip went between my body and arm (tracers). One caught me in the elbow. Then my helmet was blown away. With the Germans up in the road, Walter Franklin stepped on me and stopped. The rest of the squad moved by telling me Sears, Kellar and another man were down on the road, wounded.

"I got up and went to get my wounded. We put them in a house along the road. One house was on fire. Along came 'G' Company. I asked them for a medic. They refused. I got hot and told them they were always so far behind they didn't need a medic. We gave each other first aid as best we could. Then a German came in and gave up. He went out and gathered several more. When daylight came I had five or six Germans. These were not the type of Germans we fought on D-Day. The Germans got a garden gate and carried Sears to a crossroad where we ran into Captain Stanley of 'H' Company. He talked to me and picked me up and set me on the hood of a jeep and drove me into town to either a monastery or church."

Col. Julian Ewell's forces, with Companies "H" and "I" in the lead, entered Schijndel from the southeast at daybreak. His forces had been fired on by the same truck that mounted a 20mm cannon and a machine gun that had harassed 1st Battalion on its approach march during the previous night.

Ewell had held his forces back so that the two battalions would not be firing at each other after 1st Battalion reached the center of the town from the north. His troops moved northwest quickly using the railroad as its left flank.

S/Sgt. Robert Houston's group had come upon a house with six small German trucks parked around it during the night. They had captured twenty enemy soldiers without a shot being fired. When daylight arrived, they moved forward, with paratroopers driving each of the six vehicles. Houston continued his account:

Sergeant Henderson checked the six small trucks and found that they were all in working order. The captain told him to bring them along when we moved into Schijndel. As soon as we could see the town a few hundred yards ahead, the order came to move across the fields directly toward it. Sgt. Henderson and I, with one squad, would bring the trucks by the road, which swung a little to the left.

The company moved out and, after waiting fifteen minutes, we started slowly up the road. We had gone just a little way when we saw a company of German soldiers marching in close order in a field to our left front. They were heading for the road we were on. Joe continued to drive along slowly while I jumped off on the right to tell the two men in each truck to follow closely and not to fire until Sergeant Henderson threw a grenade. The column was almost to the road now and we could see the Krauts looking at "their trucks."

Joe timed it so he would come up to them just before the head of the column reached the road. He stopped the truck, threw his grenade, and the rest of us jumped down behind the trucks firing as fast as we could. The Germans were so surprised that we all had taken cover before any fire came back at us. The rest of "H" Company heard all the noise and swung back to come in on the flank of the company that was now shooting at us. In a few minutes white flags began to appear from the ditch that crossed the field, and what was left of their company surrendered. "H" Company hadn't reached Schijndel yet, but we knew of one outfit that wouldn't slow traffic in the corridor.

The six trucks were casualties of this encounter, so we left them and went on into the village. Officers had told the people to stay off the streets and not to welcome Americans because we weren't sure how long we would stay. Even with this warning, there was a lot of cookies and other food passed out of doors and windows to soldiers resting by the houses. We didn't get involved in any more fighting around Schijndel, but the 1st Battalion had a great deal of action all morning.[92]

The monastery at the eastern edge of Schijndel was being utilized as an aid station by 3rd Battalion. The battle raged on the outside. Sgt. Jim Edgar had been taken to a large monastery or church that served as an aid station. He wrote: "This building had huge double doors and the windows came almost to the floor. A captain was ministering to the needs of the wounded. When the shells began getting close he put all of us on the floor. Small arms fire began to come closer. The captain was looking for somebody. He jerked open a closet and found a man hiding. He yanked him out and the man bolted to one of the big doors. That was as far as he got. As he opened the door he got hit in the belly. By this time the walking wounded like myself were looking for some kind of weapons but for some reason the firing stopped."

As 3rd Battalion came up the road from Weibosch to Schijndel they were followed by enemy troops who were harassing from the rear. An example of such action is described by T/5 William Schwerin: "It seemed that while we attacked Schijndel the Germans were back in the Eerde area. As we walked into Schijndel we were fired on from behind and Sgt. Gerald Suter was shot in the back. He was lying on the ground and convulsing almost like a man having an attack of epilepsy. It reminded me of a wounded rabbit that flexes and straightens its body in rapid motion."

While 3rd Battalion was busy in the fighting on the southern and western fringes of Schijndel, its communications section was busy bringing wire forward so battalion could maintain telephone contact with regiment and other units of the division.

S/Sgt. Chester J. Wetsig, communications chief for 3rd Battalion, wrote: "The morning after the night attack on Schijndel, I was ordered from our Eerde position to bring our battalion CP forward and complete line communications. When I arrived in

92. Houston, 58.

Schijndel, I asked the S-3 for future plans and he said we were to stay there in defense."

Meanwhile, the wiremen were slowly moving up along the Schijndel–Eerde highway putting the communications wire in place. Wire communications corporal James S. White said, "The battle for Schijndel was a very confusing time and later developed into a very fierce battle in Eerde and other points close by as our regiment tried to keep the highway open.

"As a lineman, I was with some other wiremen laying a telephone line to the attacking companies as they moved toward Schijndel. Somewhere in the area of Weibosch we realized our supply of wire was short so Sgt. Chester Wetsig sent William Murphy and myself back to Eerde to take up some of the wire we had laid the night before that wasn't being used any longer. It was already daylight when we got back to Eerde and started rolling our wire along the road to Schijndel. As we approached a crossing of the railroad, and I was in front, I saw a German soldier coming toward me from the railroad crossing. I was so startled at seeing an enemy soldier in this area as I knew according to our battle plan no enemy was supposed to be here. As I stood wondering what the enemy soldier was going to do, he turned off the road to a field to our left and, as I looked to where he was going, I discovered more to my surprise that at least a company of Germans was just to my left in a field passing me in battle formation on their way to Eerde. I have always thanked the Lord for a few small buildings along the side of that road that kept me from their view. At this time, for some reason, I looked up at the railroad crossing and the area was also filled with enemy soldiers. By this time we realized this was no place for two linesmen with carbines as their only defense, so again we were seemingly blessed by our guardian angel who was with Murphy and me. As we were about to see things were hopeless, a Red Cross jeep came up the road headed for Schijndel. As the jeep driver saw the enemy all over the place, he turned the jeep around as quickly as possible and headed back for Eerde and, as you can guess, Murphy and I somehow found riding room on that jeep. There was some small arms fire coming after us but we all escaped without harm.

"Some minutes later, Sgt. Wetsig and T/4 Tom Murphy drove through the railroad crossing which we had just left and almost ran over some German soldiers still there. They too made their

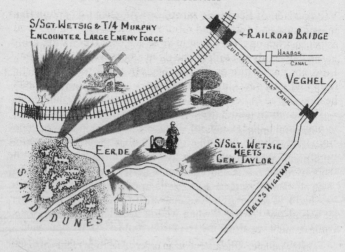

Map 9 illustrates action involving S/Sgt. Chester J. Wetsig's encounter with enemy force. 1—Rail crossing where he met a large enemy force. 2—Where the speeding vehicle failed to negotiate a sharp curve. 3—Where Wetsig met General Taylor and his group.

escape in a hail of small arms fire but overturned their German jeep (which was taken from the Germans the first day) just below the crossing, but made it on foot and without harm to Eerde."

On his way back from Schijndel where he had been told the 3rd Battalion would be in a defensive position for some time, S/Sgt. Chester J. Wetsig was headed back for supplies. He wrote: "I decided I had better get to the regimental area in Veghel to get my spare radio batteries, etc. Enroute, at a railroad crossing outside of Eerde, we had to drive through 450 Germans, all armed, plus a Tiger tank. T/4 Thomas P. Murphy was with me on the ride. Lt. Mathwin was captured at the same location a short time later. After we rolled over (with a commandeered German car) we followed the ditch to Eerde where we found Jim White and Bill Murphy who had run into the Germans while trying to lay wire to Schijndel. A messenger appeared and I borrowed his motor bike and headed for Veghel to report to Regiment this enemy information when I ran into General Taylor and a lot of

VIPs outside of Eerde. He turned around after I gave him this information and I went and reported to the British on the road as per instructions. They sent in three armored recon cars. I followed and nearly got killed. The three recons were knocked out. I did not find White or the two Murphys so I returned to the right and later saw Colonel Ewell who told me we were again headquartered in Eerde. I rejoined the following morning."

The wiremen hadn't been aware that there had been a change in plans and both 1st and 3rd Battalions were on their way back from the Schijndel area. In all likelihood, some of those enemy troops were on their way to the railroad and highway bridges in the Veghel area.

At that time, 1st and 3rd Battalions were still engaged with the enemy up in Schijndel. S/Sgt. Robert J. Houston of "H" Company remembered that the 501st Parachute Regiment lost all interest in holding Schijndel in the middle of the day.

> In the middle of the afternoon an order came from regiment to the 3rd Battalion to disengage and go back to Eerde. Another German force was attacking Veghel from the northwest and the 2nd Battalion holding the corridor there would need reinforcements. We weren't actually in a fire fight now, so we simply turned our backs and marched down the road toward St. Oedenrode and then turned off and came into Eerde from the south. While we had been away a German patrol had come into the village. There weren't many of them but they were shooting at us as we approached the village. "H" Company spread out in a skirmish line to clean them out. We worked our way up to the houses and were moving from building to building when a sniper killed Sgt. Langlinais. Our men spotted the house that the shot came from and it was soon riddled. All the patrol were either killed or captured and we let our friends in the shelters know that we were back.
>
> We moved through the village and dug in for the night in our old area beyond the windmill. This was beginning to seem like home; we kept time again by the clock in the church tower.[93]

Who's Surrendering?

On the afternoon of the twenty-second, when 3rd Battalion had returned from the Schijndel area, the line companies had gone

---

93. Houston, 59.

into their MLR positions north and west of Eerde. S/Sgt. John McPherson had taken out a patrol to see how much enemy buildup could be discerned to his platoon front. Sgt. James E. Breier was on that patrol. He describes what happened in a confusing event. "We had walked out about a mile when the point of the patrol, Pvt. John Posluszney, halted us with an upraised arm. He had noted what he thought was a white flag of surrender being waved out in front of him. S/Sgt. John McPherson moved forward and called me to accompany him as I was fluent in German.

"The two of us went up beyond Posluszney about a quarter of a mile to where the Germans were in the ditches. As we marched up, they ordered us to surrender. McPherson, who is a fiery Southerner, was vehement and started cussing. 'We're not surrendering, you are!'

"It so happened the supposedly white flag Posluszney had seen was an orange flag. With the afternoon sun hitting it at a certain angle, it did appear white to Posluszney. It was really a marker used for communicating with their artillery people.

"We were forced into the hedgerow with a group of machine gunners from the 5th Herman Goering Panzer Division. They had captured us.

"I spoke directly to the German officer in command. He turned to his sergeant and said that if I didn't shut my mouth and speak to the sergeant he'd have me shot. I was being reminded that I was subordinate to his rank. I spoke to the German sergeant who then relayed the message to the nearby lieutenant. My message was that they were surrendering to us. He said, 'No way, you are my prisoners!'

"McPherson and I were separated. While they questioned me, I kept insisting they were our prisoners as they had raised a white flag. He insisted that it was their artillery marker.

"Another officer and a sergeant took me beyond their company. We were taken back to battalion. There I talked to the S-2. I related the same surrender story. They moved me up to regiment. One of the officers had a patch over his eye. I spoke to one officer in English. He told me they were going to lose the war. They didn't have a chance. All the officers kept asking me, 'Why are you fighting us? You are German, like us.' They couldn't understand why I was fighting them as I was of German stock.

"Regiment sent me to division where I told the story again.

On the way I observed things. The division CP was in a monastery. I didn't know what town it was. At division I was taken to a large room that had sand tables of our positions and where they were situated facing us. I saw all of this. I found it fascinating. I was intrigued with the passing of high ranking officers who greeted each other with 'Heil Hitler!'

"I was moved to a small room where they continued their questioning. The two interrogators left the room. The sergeant came in to serve as my guard. I was sitting near the window looking out. There was a railroad station to the right of the monastery which seemed to be run by nuns. I observed all of this. The officer in charge of interrogation returned and noticed me facing the window. He 'reamed' that poor sergeant for permitting me to sit and observe the outside.

"The Germans came to the conclusion that because I had come voluntarily I wasn't really a prisoner of war. Under the circumstances, they would send me back. I was quartered for the night with the sergeants. I had an opportunity to become friendly with one of them. He asked me, 'If I volunteer to take you back, will I get all the chocolate and cigarettes?' I said I'd get him all he wanted. So he volunteered along with one of the men from his squad. The next day they carried a big white bed sheet with me between them. They took me through an outpost of the 327th Glider Infantry Regiment. That is where a major took the pistol from the sergeant and I had to insist that he give it back as they brought me voluntarily and they must be permitted to return. They sent the buck private back to the German lines to get the story verified about my being taken up there and it took three or four days to get Sergeant McPherson released as the enemy continued to hold him until their two men were returned."

FIFTEEN

The Division CP at Son

The division parachute echelon, including MG Maxwell D. Taylor and BG Gerald J. Higgins, jumped with 1st Battalion of the 502nd Parachute Infantry Regiment. BG A. C. McAuliffe was scheduled to arrive by glider on D plus 1. Col. Thomas L. Sherburne arrived in the lead glider on the seventeenth, a short time after the parachutists had landed. The first glider serial brought in the Division Recon Platoon, radio jeeps, motorcycles, and equipment trailers of Division Signal Company, units of the 326th Medical Company with its surgical team and a portable field hospital, and division command personnel.

As the headquarters group reached the wooded area south of the DZ, T/4 George E. Koskimaki announced to the staff that he was already in contact with the parachute units that had landed on drop zones "B" and "C." The 501st Parachute Regiment was out of range of the SCR-300 radio that he and others carried on these missions.

After exiting from a burning plane, Maj. H. W. "Hank" Hannah of the G-3 staff headed for the CP. He wrote: "I went with General Taylor toward Son; heard the bridge blow up. The CP was in a school building near an orchard. A little Dutch girl gave me some milk for coffee from a cow she had milked. The Dutch were wild about the GIs—many mugs of beer were proffered."

M/Sgt. Conrad Russell of Signal Company and others were joined by Col. Thomas Sherburne in providing guide service to the troops coming off the glider landing fields. They directed them to the assembly areas so they could continue on to their first-day command post locations.

Cpl. James L. Evans served as a wireman for the Division Artillery forward echelon. He had taken over steering the glider

During a 1987 research trip to the battle sites in Holland, the author was taken to the Eerde cemetery by former underground member Albert Marinus, who showed him where the local underground had hidden its weapons during the occupation.

The members of the pathfinder team of Capt. Frank Brown, which dropped on DZ "A" to mark the fields for the 501st Parachute Infantry Regiment less 1st Battalion. The drop occurred near Eerde. The plane carrying 1Lt. Charles Faith and his stick, which was scheduled to mark DZ "A-1" northwest of Veghel, was shot down just after crossing the front lines of Eindhoven.

Paratroopers march out through the morning fog toward their waiting planes. Some are carrying cumbersome loads, which are to be dropped with them.

A jumpmaster checks his men as they climb aboard the waiting C-47. The man facing the camera is making final adjustments in attaching his rifle (in a Griswold container) to his parachute harness.

Troopers waiting for takeoff. Censor has rubbed out identification marks on the helmets.

Gen. Maxwell D. Taylor and jumpmaster LTC Patrick Cassidy look out from the doorway of Col. Frank J. MacNees' "Brass Hat."

Paratroopers landing on the DZ at Son. They suffered only light casualties due to jump injuries. Most considered it a "Parade Ground" jump. The troop carrier planes were not so fortunate as seventeen of them were shot from the sky.

Men of the 506th Regiment extricating the occupants of F/O Thornton C. Schofield's glider, which collided with another over the LZ near Son. Miraculously, the four occupants came out alive. The pilot of the other glider died as the result of his injuries.

As PFC Tony Wysocki crawled from the wreckage, the action was recorded on 8mm film by a glider pilot who had arrived safely with the same serial of gliders. Wysocki received a copy of the film.

Members of the 327th Regimental Headquarters Company just before takeoff.

Medical personnel of the 327th Glider Regiment back a jeep into the cargo section of the glider. The pilot and co-pilot will occupy the hinged section in flight. Note the Griswold nose on the glider.

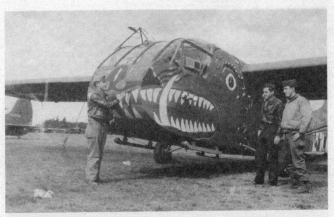

F/O W. V. Zajac and 101st platoon leader 1Lt. Martin H. Stutman watch as Sgt. S. R. Romero puts the finishing touches on a fierce airborne monster prior to the third-day glider flights.

PFC Charles W. Hogan snaps a picture of his glider mates as they anxiously scan the horizon for a rescue ship that will pick them up from their ditched craft in the English Channel. Their CG-4A was one of seventeen carrying 101st troops that ended in the Channel on D plus 2.

Soldier maintains communication with a "walkie-talkie" radio between his platoon and company headquarters.

Dutch citizens point out locations of enemy soldiers on a map to Eindhoven liberators.

Prisoners captured in Eindhoven on September 18th are on their way to a PW enclosure.

The 3rd Battalion line company commanders in Holland were Champ Baker (I), Robert E. Jones (H), and George Barrett (G).

LTC Robert G. Cole, commander of 3rd Battalion of the 502nd, killed by a sniper near Best.

Nurse Koos van Schaik of the Dutch Red Cross was busy ministering to the needs of the old and handicapped during the crucial days just before the liberation of St. Oedenrode. Excerpts from her diary are used in several chapters of the text as she relates her experiences and her work, including cooperation with the German surgeon and his medics when the facility was taken over by the enemy. She later worked with American surgeons Frank Choy and William Best.

On the 40th anniversary of Market-Garden in September 1984, Koos van Schaik (Jacoba Milovich) joined former German surgeon Dr. Ewald Pieper and fellow nurse Willy Ogg for a reunion at the site of the hospital and aid station.

The picturesque castle (Henkenshagen) at the west edge of St. Oedenrode served as the CP for the 101st Airborne Division for a time during the Market-Garden battles. An MP stands guard at the drawbridge over the moat while radio operator T/4 George Koskimaki is busy at his post beside the air-raid shelter. Division ordnance commander LTC Roger Parkinson, T/5 Ancel D. Mullen of the 326th Engineers, and an eight-year-old Dutch boy were killed by enemy shelling in the wooded area behind the castle.

Heeswijk-Dinter castle where 1st Battalion of the 501st was dropped. Father Francis Sampson and others landed in the moat. Others had tree landings.

Auxiliary bridge built beside the main canal bridge southwest of Veghel by 326th Engineers and instructors from the Veghel vocational school.

As T/5 Oscar Mendoza descended to the DZ near Eerde, he suffered a shrapnel wound to the jaw. After receiving treatment, he refused to be evacuated and was given an assignment to gather equipment bundles from the DZ. The three-wheeled "tri-cycle" provided a suitable vehicle for his purpose. He then transported the bundles to the proper supply storage points.

The church steeple in Eerde suffered extensive damage from the shelling over a period of several days. The spire provided an excellent observation post for members of 1st Battalion and forward observers of the 907th Glider Field Artillery Battalion. Capt. Harry Howard very defiantly raised the American flag in the opening at the top on the evening of the twenty-fourth. Enemy artillery knocked it down early the next morning.

The windmill at the edge of the sand dunes in Eerde also provided good observation. Sgt. Jake Wingard died in the windmill on the morning of September 18th when picked off by an enemy sniper. After that incident, the windmill became the target for enemy artillery.

North Brabant Sanitarium or Zonhove was taken over on the afternoon of September 17th as the hospital of the 101st Airborne Division. Zonhove was only a few hundred yards northeast of the blown Wilhelmina Canal bridge.

A British tank crosses the Bailey bridge over the Wilhelmina Canal at Son. The span was constructed during the night of September 18th.

A group of twenty-two soldiers of the 101st Airborne Division whose gliders made forced landings near s'Hertogenbosch pose with their Dutch friends who provided safe haven for them until British forces reached the area five weeks later.

A picture of the railroad trestle which crosses the Neder Rijn west of Arnhem and east of Driel. Radio operator T/5 Frank Carpenter of "C" Company of the 501st Parachute Infantry Regiment destroyed an enemy tank with a British anti-tank gun just as it approached the "C" Company positions from under the railroad by way of the viaduct on October 5th.

Members of a machine gun team of the 501st Parachute Infantry Regiment maintain a watchful vigil on the top of the dike near Heteren. At times the enemy was positioned on the opposite side of the slope of the dike. The adversaries often resorted to tossing hand grenades at each other. Most of the time the grenades rolled harmlessly to the foot of the slope before exploding. That problem was solved by Sgt. Laurence Lamb, who attached cord from parachute risers to the grenades.

Maj. Oliver Horton, commander of 3rd Battalion of the 506th Regiment, was killed by shrapnel as he approached the railroad station near Opheusden in the midst of the heavy fighting in the morning of October 5th.

Company "G" schoolhouse CP was destroyed by enemy shelling at dawn on October 5th.

Windmill used as aid station by 1st Battalion on October 6th. The wounded were evacuated at night.

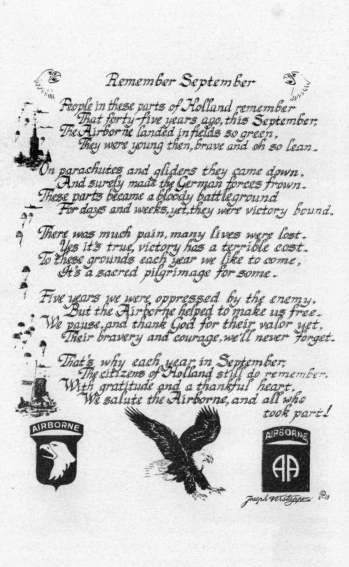

Remember September

People in these parts of Holland remember
 That forty-five years ago, this September,
The Airborne landed in fields so green,
 They were young then, brave and oh so lean.

On parachutes and gliders they came down,
 And surely made the German forces frown.
These parts became a bloody battleground
 For days and weeks, yet, they were victory bound.

There was much pain, many lives were lost.
 Yes it's true, victory has a terrible cost.
To these grounds each year we like to come,
 It's a sacred pilgrimage for some.

Five years we were oppressed by the enemy,
 But the Airborne helped to make us free.
We pause, and thank God for their valor yet,
 Their bravery and courage, we'll never forget.

That's why each year in September,
 The citizens of Holland still do remember.
With gratitude and a thankful heart,
 We salute the Airborne, and all who
 took part!

Joseph Verstappen ©-89

when both the pilot and co-pilot had been hit. The pilot was able to land the craft after Evans managed to bring him back to consciousness. Evans and members of his team moved into Son shortly after dark on D-Day. They moved into a grammar school and he slept under a two-horse cart in an attached shed.

According to PFC James H. Martin, his platoon from "G" Company of the 506th Regiment was assigned to guard the division command post the first night. First Platoon of "A" Company had the responsibility of protecting the bridge area while the 1st Platoon of "C" Company of the 326th Engineer Battalion went about the task of building floats to transport jeeps and other small vehicles across the canal until a new bridge could be brought up and put into position.

One of the long-range, powerful SCR-499 radios failed to make it. Its towplane was shot down in the same vicinity in which the *Clay Pigeon,* carrying men of "C" Company of the 506th, lay in a smoking pile of debris. The stories of the survivors of the troop carrier crash and the radiomen with the radio trailer will be related in a later chapter.

A fifty-two-man contingent of the 326th Airborne Medical Company, which included a surgical team, arrived by glider on Sunday afternoon on the landing zone just north of the boundary of the Zonsche Forest a short time after the last paratroopers had dropped in the area. They immediately started setting up a Red Cross–marked tent to serve as a temporary field hospital. Within an hour, the medical group was ready to receive casualties.

After a good landing, one of the first spectacles T/5 W. Paul Nabours witnessed was a collision almost overhead. He wrote: "I saw two gliders colliding in the air only 30 to 40 feet above the ground. We did some assisting of the seriously injured and then started to set up our hospital tent. We had it all stretched out, ready to erect, when we received word to go into Son where we set up on the ground floor of what was (at that time) a TB sanitarium."

First Lieutenant Henry Barnes had served as co-pilot in his glider. After the jeep it contained was removed, Barnes and his small contingent went about the job they were assigned for the mission. "We toured the landing zone in our jeep and began to take the injured to the south end of the field where we put up a squad tent. All fifty-two of our personnel arrived safely, including the attached surgical team.

"Two of the gliders (which landed on the LZ) hit head-on during the landing and it was hours before all the injured were removed from the entangled wreckage. One pilot, piteously crying and moaning through his gravely smashed face, lasted until noon of the second day before he died.

"The tent served as a temporary hospital until later in the day when most of the group and the equipment were moved into a small hospital in Son. I was using the tent as a collecting point. I found myself alone with three men by night fall. We felt a little silly in this big tent full of wounded in the middle of a field that had been a landing zone for a great invasion. None of us were armed and our tent stood out like a sore thumb but we were unharmed and safe about sixteen miles behind the enemy lines."

The North Brabant Sanitarium, a short distance northwest of the bridge over the Wilhelmina Canal in Son, became the hospital administered by the 326th Airborne Medical Company and the 3rd Auxiliary Surgical Team in the late afternoon of September 17. At the time of the arrival of the airborne, it housed about a hundred patients who suffered from infectious diseases, many of them being victims of tuberculosis. It had survived the war free from German interference, as the enemy had no desire to be quartered in TB-infected premises. The sanitarium was run by the Alexian Brothers, a Belgian-based order. On hand was a staff of twenty-five brothers who handled the duties of nursing the patients.

As the forward elements of the 506th Parachute Infantry Regiment had approached the Son canal bridge, some of the scouts contacted the sanitarium and saw the possibilities of it being used as a hospital.

T/5 Paul Nabours had been one of those who had been busy setting up the Red Cross tent on the landing zone when he was directed to head for Son to the North Brabant Sanitarium. He wrote: "The TB patients had been moved to the cellar. We used the whole ground floor for several days."

Kees Wittebrood, a historian in Son, wrote of the arrival of the 326th medics to the sanitarium: "The company had brought the entire equipment for an operating theater with them in the gliders. Within an hour, the sanitarium had been fitted out as efficiently as possible by the men of the medical company. They started by partitioning off five operating theaters in the west wing of the main building, adjoining the laboratory and the doctors' rooms. The Americans provided their own electrical power supplies. Blood plasma, blankets, sheets, bandages, plaster and cotton wool were brought in in incredible quantities.

"The lighter casualties were given beds in the basement and corridors of the main building. The badly wounded lay in the west wing, near the operating theaters. After they had been operated on, they were moved to the verandas.

"The evacuation of the TB patients started immediately after the landing. Where there were no medical objections, walking patients were allowed to go home."[94]

A key role was played by Brother Gabriel Janssen,[95] one of the staff members at the North Brabant Sanitarium. He described the work going on during those crucial days: "Our sanitarium was obviously more convenient for these severe casualties than the field hospital. When the American medical staff started converting our sanitarium into a hospital that afternoon about six o'clock, everything went like clockwork. First of all, five operating theaters were laid out and twenty surgeons went straight to work, mainly removing shrapnel and bullets, but with occasional amputations. The surgeons did a wonderful job, relieving one another when they were too fatigued to continue."

Sgt. Joe Powers had been near the point of the attack formation as "A" Company of the 506th Parachute Infantry Regiment had moved to capture the Son canal bridge. His path had led behind the sanitarium where the platoon was hit by tree bursts from 88mm shells, mortar shrapnel, and small-arms fire. He is believed to have been the first man hit as the platoon moved from behind the cover of the boys' school. He had been treated by one of the battalion surgeons and had a shot of morphine. The surgeon had insisted he take a drink from a canteen he offered, which contained excellent bourbon whiskey. His arm had been splinted and while he lay quietly waiting for pickup by other medical personnel, he was showered with gifts of cake,

94. Wittebrood, Kees. *History of Zonhove.* Son, Holland, 1979.
95. Ibid.

cookies, and other food from Dutch people who appeared miraculously from hiding places.

Powers continued his story: "Sometime before dark I was picked up by medics in some kind of a German vehicle and taken to the same brick building in the yard of which I had been hit. They had turned it into an aid station. The basement was full of wounded lying on the floor and on some makeshift cots. As I was ambulatory, I started walking around to check for some of my own men. Almost the first one I saw was my cousin, John, who had a nasty looking chest wound but he was being well taken care of by the doctors who naturally were treating the most seriously wounded first. I think most of my platoon was there. Those who weren't were already dead, I found out later. Captain Davis was there, too, seriously wounded."

PFC Charles Randall of "B" Company was another who had been hit by shrapnel from one of the ack-ack guns firing at the men and planes over the drop zone. When he awakened after his operation, he discovered the war was over for him and that he'd be handicapped for life. The surgeon had removed a jagged piece of steel from his arm. His Dutch friend Kees Witte-brood[96] described the incident: "The major who carried out the operation—one of the first at Zonhove—had removed a sharp piece of steel measuring three inches by half an inch thick from Chuck's left arm. Carefully the surgeon explained everything he had done and why he'd been obliged to amputate the arm. As the surgeon spoke, Chuck's thoughts went back to a one-armed kid he had known years ago in the Boy Scouts. He recalled that this boy could do everything despite his handicap and the thought immediately gave him courage, so that the news that his own arm had been amputated did not shatter him."

PFC Nelson McFaul had been hit by shrapnel from a tree burst in the same attack that injured Sgt. Joe Powers. He had this recollection: "I was wounded the first day and was placed in a bed in a makeshift hospital—a TB sanitarium which was on the outskirts of Son. The patient next to me was our captain, Melvin Davis. They took him into the operating room which was beyond the wall behind my bed. Two doctors were examining him and one said, 'I think we're going to have to amputate.' The other doctor wasn't sure and said he

96. Ibid.

wanted to check with Major Crandall. The major came and examined Captain Davis and determined that the legs could be saved. After an operation of approximately two hours, they brought Captain Davis back—with both legs."

Kees Wittebrood describes the assistance provided by the staff at the sanitarium: "The staff and patients of the sanitarium who had remained in the safety of the cellars of the main building during the first days' fighting, emerged from their shelter the following day. The Brothers offered to assist in caring for the wounded. They were magnificent. They prepared hot chocolate at regular intervals (using the free, fresh milk delivered daily by farms from Son and Breugel), made beds, kept the operating theaters clean, and even held cigarettes to the lips of the incapacitated soldiers or helped them to eat at mealtime."[97]

Bert Sanders was a seventeen-year-old boy living in the small town of Gerven, which was located three miles southeast of the Son bridge as the crow flies. It was also a mile south of the Wilhelmina Canal. On the morning of the seventeenth he had been in church with his family and had heard the bombing and strafing in the distance. Later, the people had rushed out of their homes when others had spotted paratroopers and gliders landing in the distance near Son. The few German soldiers in Gerven remained concealed under the trees and because the action was in the distance, they did not fire their guns. In a diary he kept of those momentous days, Sanders noted these operations for September 17:

> Everyone is anxious and the police warned us about what might happen.
> In the evening, we heard the rattle of machine gun fire coming from Son. You can even hear the guns in Valkenswaard.

While another radio team member provided a breathing spell, T/4 George E. Koskimaki had time to jot observations into a substitute diary in which he recorded the daily events of the Holland campaign. The original diary was back in England with the rest of his personal belongings. The daily notations were recorded on the onionskin sheets found at the back of signal corps message books, which were later transcribed to the formal diary. Koskimaki reasoned that if in danger of capture, he

97. Ibid.

could dispose of his notes by eating them. For the eighteenth, he had a brief entry along with a letter he wrote several weeks later to his fiancée in Detroit. The diary entry kept memories fresh in his mind.

We set up our first CP (Command Post) in an apple orchard in Son last night. Reflecting a bit on yesterday, I was in radio communication with almost every major unit of the division that arrived by parachute within fifteen minutes. Our infantry boys captured Eindhoven today.

I went into town for the first time and bought a pair of wooden shoes. Also traded some of my invasion money for genuine Dutch currency. People here want cigarettes more than anything else. We use our cigarettes for bartering.

A group of B-24 bombers swept over us very low today and dropped supplies. The equipment chutes barely opened on time before the equipment hit the ground. Some of the bundles landed within fifty yards of the division CP.

On the morning of the eighteenth, Cpl. James L. Evans was still without equipment of his own. He collected the telephones and wire from the German 88mm anti-aircraft gun emplacements in and around Son and set up a local net for the headquarters until their own wire equipment arrived on D plus 2.

Being a normal curious teenager, Bert Sanders was joined by a few of his friends. They were anxious to see what had happened to the north and west of Gerven. Sanders[98] chronicled his actions:

Monday, September 18—Everything is very uncertain but Harry v. d. Maut, Frans de Laat and I wanted to see what happened. We walked toward the Wilhelmina Canal and we saw the Dutch flag hanging from the collapsed bridge. We were surprised since Gerven (where I lived) was still in German hands. We were told that four Americans in a jeep just passed on the other side of the canal. We were put across the canal since the bridge was demolished. We heard that those Americans stopped at a haystack to look around and asked "Germans here?" Then we knew they were Americans. When the patrol returned from their mission everyone started waving and shouting for joy. One of them gave me a pack of cigarettes. Here we met our first liberators and I guess I showed my pack of cigarettes at least ten times to prove I was right. Then we crossed the canal again

98. The diary of Bert Sanders was translated into English by Peter Hendrikx.

and went back to Gerven. The three of us are as far as I know, the first from Gerven to have met the liberators.

After lunch, I saw gliders landing in the distance but no paratroopers were dropped like yesterday. Four of us decided to go to Son to see what happened. We crossed the canal again and since there were no Americans or Germans we thought it was quite safe to go further. It seems that the north side of the canal is liberated since we saw a resistance fighter on a motor bike.

Suddenly planes fly over very slowly, dropping food and ammunition. They drop everywhere around us and we are in the middle of it all. Then we reached Son, which was busier than at fair time. It was crowded with Americans coming from the woods and with Germans with their hands on their heads. Everywhere are little flat cars (jeeps). We tried to talk to one of the drivers but our English is not good. Nevertheless, he gave us some cigarettes and chocolate. We also met a Dutchman who had been in England for four years. Now they have dropped him here. We went to my aunt who lived near the drop zone. It was late but it was worth it. The whole area was scattered with gliders. In the woods the soldiers were getting ready for the night. One was sleeping, another looked on in silence and another was making a fire. All are very quiet.

When we returned to Son, volunteers are needed for tomorrow. Jack v. d. Maas and I decided to come back tomorrow. When we reached the Son bridge we were not allowed to cross. We walked over the dike and through the fields to the other bridge and we reached Gerven very late. Still, here in Gerven, there were no Americans or Germans to be seen.

After accompanying the 1st Battalion of the 502nd Parachute Regiment on its D-Day mission to St. Oedenrode, 2nd Platoon of "Charley" Company of the 326th Engineers marched down to Son where they joined 1st Platoon in the vicinity of the demolished bridge. 1st Platoon continued to operate the ferries it had constructed for hauling vehicles back and forth across the canal. 2nd Platoon removed the wreckage of the bridge in preparation for the Bailey bridge site. At 2100 hours, both platoons reverted to 326th Engineer control and a platoon from "B" Company, which had arrived by glider earlier, took over the job of ferry service. The two "C" Company platoons moved to the engineer battalion bivouac area a half mile north of Son where they joined the battalion glider elements that arrived by glider that afternoon.

One of the engineer officers who arrived on the eighteenth by glider was 1Lt. Ralph D. Pickens. He was given directions by the Dutch as to how to reach Son after he had been directed to move to the bridge area. Pickens described his early action. "My 1st Platoon laid a hasty mine field south of the Son bridge. My men also operated the ferries."

By now, the Dutchman Bert Sanders was fascinated with the actions taking place and felt there was a need for him to help. However, he got caught up in the actions and was exposed to the same enemy rifle and machine-gun fire that was directed at the American soldiers. This is his account of the following day:

Tuesday, September 19—In the early morning Jack Maas and I went to Son again—by bike this time. When we reached the Son bridge, we saw the Bailey bridge which wasn't there yesterday. Many tanks and scout cars were crossing the bridge coming from Eindhoven. Finally, they have contacted the paratroopers.

We had to be at our checkpoint at 0800 but this is 0900 in Dutch time. Lots of volunteers are waiting but there was much to be seen. At 0900 a few officers and Dutchmen came over and sent us towards Best. There are soldiers everywhere. We pass a crashed aircraft and we saw the bodies of dead soldiers. I think they were German but you can hardly recognize them. You can hear the shooting now and suddenly we had to hide in a ditch. The bullets whistled around our heads. I heard one volunteer say, "What did we start?" and "I didn't expect this!" Then a horse cart shows up and helpers are needed. Some of us joined the horse cart and we rode towards Best. The shooting stopped and after a while we saw an American patrol. They said we should get off the cart. We were on the edge of an open field and that patrol was watching the other side of the field. Suddenly the firing started and we were in the middle of it. We all jumped at the same time on the horse cart and sped back. When we were away from the shooting, we loaded the parachutes and bundles on the cart. Lots of soldiers passed, all going toward Best.

We joined some Americans for a meal which was a K-ration. We talked a bit with them and we asked one man what he did and where he came from. He seemed to be a farmer and he told us he had only four horses. We were very disappointed to learn that he uses a tractor instead of cowboys. A command sounded and there he went again—a farmer from America fighting the Germans.

We also had to do some more work. We had to collect mines and we were told not to pile more than four high. This didn't take long and then we went to a farmer who gave us sandwiches and milk. It was very busy here and lots of tanks are passing by and many gliders are scattered everywhere. One glider had landed behind the farm and we climbed into it and examined it inside out. A British tanker approached us and asked us whether the farmer wanted to sell a chicken. We asked him. He didn't mind so we were all after the chicken. Then we walked back and got a ride in a jeep. The shooting started again. By now there were not many volunteers left. It had become dangerous. My friend Jack also left and I saw him walking back toward Son. After a while the shooting lessened and we had a chance to talk with the soldiers. They said at 1500 a new lift of gliders would land. Since it was almost three o'clock, we saw the gliders landing nearby. We ran to the open field where they landed. There were still gliders standing from the first lift. A few soldiers were waving flags for the gliders and we joined them. They gave us cigarettes. The shooting started again and we saw the dust and dirt coming from explosions. We saw a plane which was hit by flak. One parachute opened, another did not and one caught fire. The Americans jumped up and said we should go to the other side of the road. There we saw uniforms, helmets and cigarettes. I put on a helmet. We are covered with dirt from an explosion so we ran away from this scene. We saw a glider landing nearby and walked over to see how they unloaded. The nose of the glider was lifted so a jeep could roll out. In the meantime, all the gliders had landed.[99]

Reports had come in to 101st Airborne Division headquarters of German armor massing to the southeast. The British were also in the process of widening the salient at its base on either side of Eindhoven. No one was sure whose tanks were on the move in the Son area.

The 1st Platoon of "A" Company of the 506th had been left behind to provide bridge security for the engineers while they carried on their chores of ferrying light vehicles across the canal at Son. A second platoon of engineers was busy clearing the debris away from the bridge footings in preparation for the arrival of a Bailey bridge with British engineers. First Platoon was led by 2Lt. James Diel who had received a battlefield commission after Normandy. Cpl. Charles Shoemaker was one of his soldiers.

Shoemaker and his group had become aware of the fact that their "soft" assignment was about to change. He related: "On the 19th, Lt. Diel mentioned the fact that they had a report from

99. Sanders diary.

Dutch partisans that there was a German force a couple miles down the canal. The Dutch didn't know if it was moving in our direction. It made everyone edgy. It was possible other units were sent out to look for them."

First Lieutenant Fred Starrett from Division Artillery and Dutch army officer Lieutenant Dubois had come up from a reconnaissance trip in the Eindhoven area a short time earlier. They were sent to check out the report of tank movements to the east. Leaving their jeep south of the Wilhelmina Canal, the men had proceeded on foot accompanied by LTC Ned B. Moore, Cpl. Jerry Janes and Pvt. John J. McCarthy, the latter two a bazooka team from 1st Platoon of "A" Company of the 506th. The remainder of the platoon stayed at their posts to guard the approaches to the bridge.

Cpl. Charles Shoemaker continued his account: "Along about 1700 hours I remember distinctly two Dutchmen riding up hell-bent-for-leather on their bicycles from down the canal bank to the east. They hopped off and started talking excitedly in broken English. The news they had was that there were five or six German tanks coming up along the canal bank and they were very close in. They did have foot troops with them. We were pretty well spread out on that side of the road. All we could do was sit there and wait for them."

Moving along the canal, First Lieutenant Starrett's group had seen movement in the trees about three hundred yards to their front. A well-camouflaged enemy tank burst from the cover of the tree line and was headed in their direction and toward the bridge. The tank had a clear shot at the bridge, as the canal ran straight and true in that direction. The first shot hit a truck, exploding it on the bridge, thereby stopping traffic.

The Dutch lieutenant was sent back to make telephone contact with the division command post to inform them that at least six armored vehicles and accompanying infantry were in the woods a half mile east of the bridge. The first tank began moving toward the bridge along the raised bank of the canal followed by four supporting infantrymen, firing its machine gun and cannon. The bridge defenders responded with their lighter weapons. LTC Ned Moore's group was caught in the cross fire. First Lieutenant Rodney Adams and a few others jumped into the canal to swim to the northern bank. Adams drowned during his effort.

Meanwhile, T/4 George E. Koskimaki was monitoring his radio in a foxhole in the orchard adjacent to Division Headquarters when he received a message alerting division to the approaching danger. His diary entry expresses the concern for the hectic actions involving the division CP on September 19:

> Had a bad scare when enemy tanks got within a couple hundred yards of the CP and shelled headquarters and the bridge over the canal. They apparently saw me run into the building with the message that enemy tanks were nearby. As soon as I got into the building, a shell crashed through the tile roof as I handed the message to an aide. They also fired on the observer who was in the tower beside the headquarters building. He came down in a hurry.

Cpl. Jim Evans also recalled an observation post in a steeple next to Division Headquarters. It was equipped with a phone, and two observers used it until a tank shell hit the steeple.

T/4 Robert A. Schmitz of Division Headquarters Company had come in with the second wave of gliders on the eighteenth. His recollection of the incident was that "on the second day, the Germans attacked Son. I was eating in the school yard when a shell from a tank hit the steeple with an observer in it. The fight started and we scattered. I spent the night at the 326th Engineer area."

In closer proximity to the tank, Moore, McCarthy, and Janes found shelter in a small hole. The bazooka team fired two rounds, missing the tank. The third round hit but failed to stop the tank.

Cpl. Charles Shoemaker, one of the bridge defenders, continued his story: "Here came one—he looked about the size of a house! That is the one that mauled a truck on the bridge. It got kind of confusing. We didn't know if it was a big force coming up our way. At that time, there was a platoon of engineers and a platoon of infantry on the south side of the canal. We couldn't do a helluva lot about it if there were a dozen or more tanks coming our way. During that attack, Jim Hoenscheidt was in a very precarious position near the edge of the canal with the Germans firing directly at him from the other side of the canal. He threw a partly eaten apple toward the Germans. They thought it was a grenade and ducked. This gave him the opportunity to get out of his predicament and he raced to the sheltered side of the levee. Lt. Jim Diel was killed in that area about 20 to 25 yards out from the last house.

"The lead tank was knocked out. The rest of the tanks backed off but didn't go far. We kept getting some fire from them during the night. We had some British help. A couple of Bren gun carriers came up. The people on them off-loaded to the outside edges of the houses. We had pulled back to the houses and were in backyards."

A Trooper Named Hovi

T/5 Paul J. Quaiver of "A" Company of the engineers remembered a replacement named Pvt. Lauri W. Hovi who had arrived in the 326th Engineer Battalion a short time before the division departed for the marshaling area. Describing the action of the nineteenth, Quaiver wrote: "At the company area just about 1900 hours, as the sun was going down, hell seemed to break loose in a farmyard which was just across the road. A German tank set a hay stack on fire and was moving around the area firing its weapons. Most of us were in foxholes that the Germans had vacated and Hovi was hit as he stood outside his fox hole. He was taken to a convent nearby which was used by the medics and he was dead on arrival. For Hovi, the war was brief and fatal; others have lived through their war to tell about it, even brag about it. We can't speak for the Hovis but we should not neglect them, for they paid the price some of us were never 'tagged for.' "

81st to the Rescue

Adverse weather conditions on the nineteenth affected the arrival of the artillery and anti-tank support groups at a time when they would be called upon to move right into the heat of battle after arriving in the assembly areas just off the landing zones.

Only forty-seven of the eighty-one gliders carrying the 81st Anti-Tank Battalion arrived at LZ "W" on the nineteenth. Only fourteen of the twenty-four six-pounder (57mm) guns arrived that day.

That part of the airborne echelon of the 81st Anti-Tank Battalion that reached the landing zone safely, came in under heavy enemy flak and small arms fire. Immediately on landing, this echelon, suffering from loss of key personnel and vital equipment, was rushed to the defense of the Son bridge and the town of Son, facing attacking enemy forces of armor and infantry, which was penetrating from the southeast cutting the road between Son and Eindhoven. Under heavy enemy artillery and small arms fire, one enemy Mark V (Panther) tank was destroyed at approximately 1900 hours which was four hours after landing.[100]

One of the more fortunate units to arrive on the Son landing zone on September 19, after battling fog most of the way, was "B" Battery of the 81st Anti-Tank Battalion commanded by Capt. Alphonse G. Gueymard. With very little pause, the battery was rushed to Son to help stem the attack that was taking place just about the time they were assembling off the fields. Gueymard wrote: "My battery 'B' landed in a very satisfactory way and assembled rapidly. Shortly after landing, we were informed that tanks were in the vicinity of Son. I proceeded forward with the 2nd Platoon and ran into General Higgins who directed us to the Son bridge area. The Germans had cut the highway immediately south of the bridge, stopping all movement of the British 2nd Army. Upon reaching the bridge, enemy small arms fire was evident and we returned the same. We observed a large tank on the south side of the canal due east of the bridge. We were able to get an anti-tank gun behind a house and fired at the tank which was moving along the levee. Our first round disabled the tank and the crew jumped out and disappeared. Several other rounds were fired for good measure. The Germans on the south side of the canal were retreating to the east and my platoon conducted a fire fight for several minutes. Some of the Germans escaped to the east. That night we crossed a platoon of guns over the bridge and put them into position south and east as a protective force to the bridge which was again opened for traffic. Some members of the 327th were also in the area."

A member of 2nd Platoon assigned to a gun that was positioned in another part of Son, Cpl. Rogie Roberts, recalled: "There was only small arms fire—nothing to be worried about and we moved into position around the town. My gun position was on the northeast side. There were quite a few German bodies and several dead Americans in the area which indicated a rather severe fight before we arrived. Other than that, we fired a few rounds from our 57mm anti-tank gun at a tree line that someone reported seeing movement and whoever was there had moved on."

100. From *History of the 81st Airborne Anti-aircraft and Anti-tank Battalion.*

The 327th Arrives on the Scene

The 1st Battalion of the 327th Glider Infantry Regiment didn't fare much better in its arrival in Holland. It, too, was rushed to Son to squelch the enemy threat on Son and the canal bridge.

PFC George Groh[101] of "A" Company remembered: "1Lt. Ernest Walker assembled about a hundred men and we set up a temporary defense. The rest of the company was scattered all the way from London to Brussels. The Division HQ sent a call for help shortly after we arrived, and about a dozen of us piled into a pair of jeeps and hurried down to Son, a nearby village. They'd beaten off the attack by the time we got there."

Another member of "A" Company who came in that afternoon and who was sent with his group scurrying in the direction of the bridge was S/Sgt. Jack L. Williamson. He wrote: "We got over to the highway and were sent south. Someone from Division Headquarters was there. He said the CP was under attack and for me to take my squad and the three men he gave me to attack the Germans. We moved but a damned 90mm mortar was shooting at us and scaring the hell out of us—especially me. We got out a ways and there on the ground was a young paratrooper, blond hair and blue eyes—a good looking kid—and from the top of his back down below his buttocks he was nothing but raw meat—clothes all gone. His helmet was tipped forward and his head was to one side. He said, 'Hi, trooper! You want this machine gun?' (a .30 caliber air-cooled weapon) 'I won't need it. Take it and give 'em hell!' I slung my .45 submachine gun and took the .30 cal. We advanced and crossed a small canal. I gave the machine gun to Pvt. Ernest J. Miller. The three paratroopers who were with us took the armored vehicle, which evidently had been captured earlier, and drove it back to our lines. One of them was standing up in it and waving an orange identification flag to let the others know there were Americans in an enemy vehicle. I unhooked the mortar, dragged it over to the canal and threw it in. I guess it is still there today. There were two dead Germans on the bank. I was so hepped up that I kicked both of them into the canal. On the way back, I stopped where the little paratrooper lay. He was dead. It still hurts me to think about it.

101. Groh, op. cit.

We moved to the north around the Wilhelmina Canal. We spent the night dug in on the dike. That night a German self-propelled gun came up to the wood bridge and shot up some British vehicles," concluded Staff Sergeant Williamson.

Another 1st Battalion company of the 327th, "C" Company, with Capt. Walter L. Miller Jr. in command, had been rushed to the bridge site on the evening of the nineteenth. On hand were its 1st Platoon, Company Headquarters and the light machine-gun and mortar sections. The rest of the company was somewhere between England and Holland. Captain Miller had selected a good site on which to establish his four-hundred-yard defense line. The terrain offered little cover to attackers with very few shallow ditches that would conceal enemy movement. The six-pounder, anti-tank guns of the 81st kept the supporting tanks at a respectable distance.

One of the soldiers who was part of Capt. Walter L. Miller's "C" Company was PFC George K. Mullins. He remembered setting up that first night near a windmill. He wrote: "Moving under cover of darkness, we approached the windmill to get grazing fire. During the night you could hear tanks moving some five hundred yards away to the east. No sweat, it must be our own tanks. The Germans couldn't be that close."

After the first attack had been repulsed, additional enemy armor and troops joined the fray. The glidermen were joined by a platoon and a half of the engineers who were positioned around the bridge. Part of 1st Battalion of the 506th Regiment had been moving by, and these men were rushed in to bolster the line.

That evening, the city of Eindhoven was bombed. "C" Company of the 506th had been ordered to move to Son to bolster its defenses. They were moving up the road when the bombing raid commenced. Pvt. Robert W. Wiatt wrote: "As we passed outside of Eindhoven, the Germans began to drop flares and their bombs. We were ordered off the road and dug in. When it was realized that we were in no danger from the bombing, we continued on our way to Son."

Capt. William Pyne, commander of "C" Company, remembered that his unit was positioned outside of Eindhoven on the nineteenth in a defensive position. "When the bombing started, we were ordered to move. We had an underground guy with us. He wore a white armband. He said he would lead us fast. He scared the hell out of me. I fretted and worried that he might be leading us into a trap. I remember 1/Sgt. Joe Reed kept him covered all the while as we were marching north. I'm sure he was a brave Dutchman but he was under a whole lot of suspicion. However, he got us up where we were supposed to be."

Pvt. Robert W. Wiatt continued his story: "We got there in the middle of the night, dead tired and bedded down north of the canal on the west side of the road in some nearby houses."

Second Attack on Son

The troops of the 107th Panzer Brigade attacked Son again on the twentieth. Some were part of the force that came down along the bank of the Wilhelmina Canal and then moved back into the shelter of the woods on the south bank a half mile or so from the Son bridge. Others moved into the area alongside roads from the southeast.

Division Headquarters was anxious to learn how and where the enemy tanks were crossing the river to get within range of Son. The assignment went to Capt. Thomas P. Wilder and members of his Division Recon Platoon.

Before daybreak on the twentieth, Wilder and two jeeps loaded with his men traveled south of Son, took a heading southeast of town. Along the route they encountered a British officer and his driver on a similar mission—only he was looking for an alternate route along which his tanks might get into the area to drive off the enemy armor. After the combined group had traveled another mile, they came upon a large group of soldiers moving across the road in front of the British vehicle, which was in the lead.

As one soldier passed the British armored car in the dim light, he nodded a greeting to the colonel and continued on to join his group.

Wilder was startled at seeing the uniform of the soldier who had passed and asked the British officer why he had stopped. The colonel replied, "Those are your lads, aren't they?"

"No way, those are Krauts!" responded Wilder.

The country lane was too narrow to turn the vehicles. This was followed by the slow process of backing for some distance to a wider area where turns could be completed.

It was then that the Germans realized the vehicles were not

carrying their own troops. They began firing but in the dim light of early morning no damage was done. Along the return route two machine-gun posts were set up and these were relieved later by larger infantry forces.

At Division Headquarters, Sgt. Elmer Weber of the Division Recon Platoon was on duty, He wrote: "As communications sergeant of the Recon Platoon, my jeep was usually parked near G-2 where I kept radio contact with the different patrols and relayed information to General Taylor. One morning, just a few days after we landed in Holland, Capt. Tom Wilder called in that they had just spotted four German tanks; he gave me their location and said they were headed toward the Division CP. I rushed the message up to General Taylor. He looked at the map spread out on his desk and said, 'Show me on the map where they are.' I pointed out the location to him and he said, 'Have Wilder verify the location as we have a platoon of men in that area.' I went back to the radio and before I could contact Capt. Wilder an 88mm shell came through the CP. We didn't need any verification."

"The morning of the 20th was just a little confusing," added Cpl. Charles Shoemaker. "I remember the Germans attacked again. They didn't come right straight up the canal bank. They were a bit off and away from the canal. They hit us again but it didn't last too long. By that time we had some help. I remember a bunch of British tanks just beyond the houses and they were breaking out across the fields and attacking the Germans."

PFC George Mullins continued his story: "Morning broke. Anti-tank mines were being laid east of the windmill. As the early morning passed, things began to happen. The truck convoys and war machinery were rolling by. Small arms fire began to come across the fields. 88s fired point blank at the trucks. A smoke screen went up on the east side of the highway.

"I got relieved from my machine gun and moved in behind the windmill. I took over someone's foxhole—mighty shallow for me. I dug a few feet more. I then moved back near a cross by the windmill to take a look at the ditch that runs along the east side of the road. I came face to face with one of our generals by himself. 'This is a hot spot isn't it soldier?' he said to me. We chatted a bit. Then he headed up the road. Back in my foxhole, I noted the anti-tank gun crew that had moved in earlier was getting ready for action.

"Then all hell broke loose. Bullets began to pop in. A Sherman tank rolled up. It stopped thirty to fifty feet from me, then another one pulled up. I saw Captain Miller climb on one of the tanks to warn them about the mine fields. Then I saw the first tank that rolled in take two rounds high on his turret from a Tiger.

"Meanwhile, I heard 'Mullins! Get your machine gun!' I headed for the gun at the same time the anti-tank gunner fired his first round at the tank. The shell passed a couple feet over our heads and the muzzle blast was ten feet or more. At this instant, the second tank took a round from the Tiger. The tanker put it in reverse, spun her around and headed straight for my hole and stopped right over me.

"During this time Pvt. Herschel C. Parker immediately jumped out of his foxhole and ran around the north side of the windmill into the foxhole behind the machine gun and began firing, thus repulsing the German infantry that was moving up with the tank. It caused the tank to button up. A fuel truck near us took a round and was burning on the highway. How was I going to get out of this one? Lots of steel was sitting directly over my head. Looking out between the tracks, I could see Captain Miller. 'Captain Miller!' I yelled. He peered under the tank. 'Should I crawl out?' 'No, no, stay put. Stay there,' he shouted a second time. He then climbed on the turret. I'm sure the tank guys didn't have it all together after taking the round from the Tiger. 'Move this thing, you are on top of one of my men,' the captain yelled.

"The engine roared to life and, instead of this chunk of steel moving forward, it spun to the left. I lay flat at the bottom of the hole with my forehead on my arm to save a space to breathe.

"The soil was very loose and the tracks of the tank mashed this loose soil down on me. I felt the tank leave. I put all the pressure that I could possibly exert upward. The first thing I heard Captain Miller yelling was 'Get out of there, get out of there!' I don't know if he or someone there gave me a hand in getting out. I'd say Captain Miller had his hands full keeping everything in order. By this time another tank had showed up. During the turmoil the anti-tank gunners had knocked out the Tiger and now hooked up the gun to their jeep and high-tailed it out of there to another position. What a great gun and crew that was!

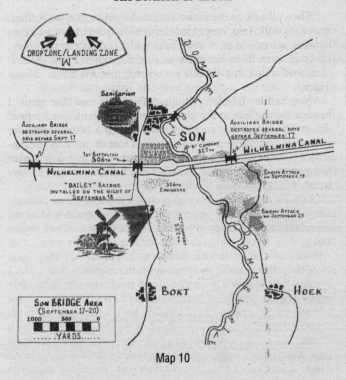

Map 10

"Things quieted down for a bit. The Tiger in front was turning. Word came, 'Get ready, we are going to counter-attack!' "

One of the engineer platoons involved in the continued fighting around the Son bridge on the twentieth was led by 1Lt. Harold E. Young. He wrote: "We were engineers but we spent a lot of time fighting as infantry out of necessity. We were back at battalion headquarters after being relieved of our bridge and rafting duties. The glider pilots were told to stay with the engineers until means were available to take them out. They were there. Suddenly, I was told to take my platoon and to report to a glider infantry company commander. I did and he put us on his left flank. My men were in ditches alongside the trees. I had a runner at the company HQ. He came back and told me to report to the captain, which I did. He told us to synchronize watches and that at a certain time there would be a five minute rolling barrage and then we were to move out with fixed bayonets. I ran back and told my men. It was in the middle of the day. The barrage started and I wondered how I would move myself out. A whistle blew and that did it. I got up and ran forward and all of my men came out with their bayonets shining in the sun. The Germans just came out of holes and surrendered. We moved forward about 500 yards with my main function cutting barbed wire on the fences as I had a pair of linesman's pliers. Now we were really nervous. I saw about six German soldiers in the grass to my left. I yelled to Fritz Balboni and another guy and they swiveled around and blasted those German helmets. Yes sir, we really riddled a big bunch of green cabbages. Back at battalion HQ the big joke was that the British army was moving east along the highway and Lieutenant Young and his platoon and an infantry company were charging south with fixed bayonets."

Some of the airborne troopers wondered what glider pilots did after landing their aircraft behind enemy lines. This is what F/O William Knickerbocker wrote in his diary for D plus 3:

Son, Holland—Cheese and tea then Morian and I headed for Son to get in the fight. Heard small arms fire from hill back of town where Jerries were trying to make a push on our bridge. We joined a paratroop engineer outfit and lined up in a hedgerow. To get into our ditch, we had to step into a puddle of blood between the legs of a dead German machine gunner who was staring up at us. "Over the top" and we went so fast we over-ran the German first line before they could fire a shot. Had to fight from then on. Got ahead of our own mortar fire and pinned down in a turnip patch. Missed command to go forward and sniper left behind kept me pinned down for an hour. Every time I moved I got a slug next to me. More Americans came up and I caught up with my bunch. Narrow escapes with machine guns and snipers. Left at 2 P.M. with everything quiet. Found two friends and headed north for Nijmegen.[102]

Pvt. Robert W. Wiatt and the men of "C" Company of the 506th had arrived at midnight after a forced march from Eindhoven. His company commander may well have picked off that

102. Diary entry of F/O William Knickerbocker for Wednesday, September 20, 1944 (D plus 3) at Son.

troublesome sniper who kept glider pilot Bill Knickerbocker pinned down. Wiatt added to his story: "Soon after first light we found the German army on the other side of the road. Needless to say, the fight was on. I was an ammo bearer with a machine gun crew and those boxes of ammo that I had carried all over the place came into use that morning. After we drove some Germans out of a small wooded area, we took up a position on the back side of the canal bank. Every time we tried to fire the machine gun we got sniper fire from the other side of the canal. I am very glad that the sniper was a poor shot because while the other two members of our machine gun crew went to the left and right—I fired the machine gun to draw the sniper's fire. This did work and one of the fellows spotted the sniper and that was the end of that."

Capt. Bill Pyne remembered that his company was ordered to take positions near the canal at Son on the twentieth. "We had no tank support in our area. Tiger tanks were reported moving in from our left toward the bridge. Elements of "C" Company moved off the road and down to the left. We got to the canal. At that time heavy tank fire hit us and killed Lt. Harold Cramer. A sniper in a second story window of a house down on the canal shot Sgt. Albert C. Smith. He fired with considerable effect. Somebody came up to me and said there was a sniper and he pointed to the window from which he had been firing. He was giving us a problem. I remember going forward with that man and getting into a firing position. I carried an M-1 on the mission. I saw the sniper's weapon pushed out of the window and I fired into the lower corner of the window. That was the last action from that sniper."

In describing his involvement at the Son bridge area on the twentieth, Cpl. Richard F. Turner of 1st Battalion (506th) wrote: "When 'B' Company was assisting in the defense of the Son bridge, most of 1st Battalion was stretched out along the canal. The battalion commander (LTC James L. LaPrade, later KIA at Bastogne), 1Lt. Herbert Viertel and I were lying on the sloping canal bank on the opposite side of a house at which the enemy (3 tanks in an open field about 500 yards away) was firing. The battalion commander thought he heard some movement inside the house. Lying on his stomach on the side of the down slope of the canal bank, he threw a hand grenade at a window of the house. The grenade hit the window sill and came rolling down the hill toward Lt. Viertel and me. The battalion commander yelled, 'Duck' to us. We already had. The grenade exploded harmlessly about ten feet from us, as the blast from the grenade was a level higher than our heads. The commander blamed his poor aim on the map case he was carrying, saying his arm caught the case as he threw the grenade. He then motioned for me to follow him. We crouched and ran up to the window he'd missed. Standing on either side of the window, beside it, we each threw two grenades inside. Neither of us missed that time. About an hour later, after things quieted down, an elderly Dutch man and woman came out of the basement. They were carrying a pitcher of warm beer which they gave to us, their 'liberators.' Apparently some noise or movement from this elderly couple is what caught the attention of LTC LaPrade, causing him and me to completely wreck the living room of their home with grenades."

"Jerry put up a stiff fight at first," wrote PFC George Groh[103] as he described some of the fighting involving his group on the twentieth. "We drove him out into an open field interspersed with drainage ditches and he started giving up. PFC Ernest Miller pulled off the big coup of the attack. Miller was charging from ditch to ditch, firing his BAR, when it blew up in his face. His momentum carried him into the next ditch where he brandished his trench knife. The occupants—three Jerries armed with machine guns and a mortar—threw their weapons away, shouted 'American!' and surrendered."

Describing his part in the counterattack south and east of the Son bridge, PFC George Mullins wrote: "We headed out toward the southeast with all the guns blazing. The smoking Tiger was to my right. I was told that the two Germans in it bit the dust.

"We came to the road where I heard the tank noise the night before. It had farmhouses on the west side of it. I ran around one of the houses to the west side, looking for Krauts. I saw a dugout. I pulled a hand grenade from my belt. Clear the way before entering—it was a lesson I learned in Normandy when a lieutenant trooper stepped in front of a dugout and got blown away by a machine gun. Instead, this time I entered the dugout against my better judgment. In the dim light a Dutch family was huddled together. My eyes focused on a little girl decked out in

103. Groh, op. cit.

her farm clothes. We stared at each other. The family was so scared. None of us spoke a word."

Mullins continued: "Out back and around the farmhouse, to the northeast, I heard a battle with small arms (our guns) raging, then across the field I saw Germans running like hell to save their necks. I understand we took some casualties in our rifle platoon. We pulled back to the windmill. A British truck with soldiers in the back had taken a round from a tank and a shell had hit the rear side killing most of them. The truck came and stopped behind the buildings."

Mullins added, "It was decided to send the supporting tanks down that side road with us riding on them. We were to pursue the enemy tanks that had been shooting at the bridge and at the town of Son. The engineers checked out a high, narrow bridge over a stream (probably the Dommel River bridge northeast of Eindhoven). I couldn't believe that bridge would support a tank but it did. We went through open fields with so much dust it was difficult to see anything. When the tanks stopped to size up the situation, we slid off and took cover. A man ran across the street to our front. Our tank put a round in a house. Moving up, we contacted the Dutch people and found the Germans had moved out. As we pulled out, the Dutch people gave us apples and eggs as we marched back."

The highlight of the twentieth for S/Sgt. Jack Williamson was a patrol he led. "We came upon two civilians and I asked for identification. One was an old fellow and he looked scared. He was shaking. The other fellow was built like a tank and mean as hell looking. I did not know what their identification cards said but the one the big fellow had was full of swastikas. I decided the old man was a farmer and let him go. Guess I should have brought him along, too. I told the big fellow to come along with us. He said, 'Nein, Icht mus arbeiten!' I said, 'You better move—and now!' Here we were, ten men armed to the teeth and he says 'No!' I pushed my gun in his stomach and said, 'Move!' He still refused. He was standing there, straddle-legged and giving me the dirtiest look. I fired three rounds into the ground between his feet. He didn't even flinch. My men thought I had killed him. Very slowly he turned around and we started back, very grudgingly, step by step. After we got back to the canal, I told a couple of the men to take him to Colonel Salee, our battalion commander. Later on I was told he turned out to be one helluva German—SS officer and paratrooper and during the questioning, something didn't suit him and he spit right in the colonel's face. I don't know for sure, but I guess they killed him."

Major General Ridgway Stalled

During the morning of the twentieth, Major General Taylor had conferred with 1st Allied Airborne Army commander LTG Lewis Brereton, in the headquarters of 506th Parachute Regiment commander Col. Robert F. Sink. Brereton had then headed north in the direction of Nijmegen and Arnhem for an inspection trying to move in and out of the long convoys headed north.

MG Matthew P. Ridgway had flown from England to Eindhoven and was anxious to move up the corridor to the Nijmegen area. With his aide and a jeep and driver he had picked up in a motor pool at the airport, he was in the midst of the British convoy moving up the corridor between Eindhoven and Son when it came to a mysterious halt. After waiting for some time, he noted nothing was happening. There was no firing heard to the front. He went forward to check and found that the road was supposedly under fire from an enemy attack. He waited some more. No one in the column seemed to be doing anything about clearing the blockage. He had no command authority in the situation. Proceeding on foot, the general, his aide, and the jeep driver walked the few kilometers to Son.

Angered by the delay, Ridgway sent the driver back to pick up the jeep. He headed for the 101st command post where he conferred with headquarters personnel. Major General Taylor was still in Eindhoven.

Ridgway learned that Lieutenant General Brereton was somewhere up ahead in the convoy column. Ridgway was anxious to confer with him. He was directed into an orchard where Signal Company had a number of radios in operation. Perhaps he could make contact with his superior.

The notation for September 20, 1944, in the diary of T/4 George E. Koskimaki is as follows:

Had Generals Ridgway and Brereton on my radio. General Ridgway wanted to contact his commander. I had been in touch with the unit earlier. Now I couldn't raise them with my SCR-300 so I climbed to the roof of a chicken coop where contact was made immediately. Ridgway climbed on the roof to talk to Brereton. I had to caution him about using clear text over the air.

Koskimaki added, "I was embarrassed when General Ridgway walked into the orchard and asked me if I was in contact with the 18th Corps. (General Brereton was traveling with that group.) I answered in the affirmative as I had exchanged information with their operator a short time before. When I tried again at his request, there was no response to my calls. I reasoned that because their radio was moving forward, they had most likely moved out of the range of my radio. I looked about and spotted a chicken coop with a slanting roof. General Ridgway gave me a boost and then handed me the radio. The corps operator came in loud and clear. I gave the general a hand as he clambered up onto the roof. He seemed annoyed when I cautioned him about security in using clear text. He was happy, however, to make contact with General Brereton."

Brothers Meet Again

On the afternoon of the twentieth, the remainder of "A" Company of the 506th Regiment had joined 1st Platoon and was now positioned on the west side of the road between Son and St. Oedenrode providing security for division as well as its service area. Cpl. Charles Shoemaker continued his story: "We were outposting the division on the 20th. That is when I ran into my half-brother Bob Hamilton again. Lou Braasch, Dave Diener, Jerry Janes and myself were in a machine gun position. We heard noises and knew nobody that would do us any good should be out there. Everybody was ready. One of the guys pulled the pin on a grenade. We were a little jumpy with all the Krauts in the vicinity. I heard a nice Yankee voice say 'Quiet!' and another said, 'I can't—I stepped in a f—ing hole!' and unless he was born and raised in the States—Germans didn't generally come across like that. I hollered and, of course, it turned out to be my brother, Bob. There were two or three glider pilots there. They had been outposted around the landing zone since late afternoon and were now beginning to make their way back to Eindhoven and eventually on to England. Glider pilots were free spirits to begin with. They were rather hard to control on the ground. Dave Clark wasn't too far away and he came over and asked about his buddy, Bob Gilman. (See page 93.) Bob Hamilton told him about Gilman being killed on take-off the day before."

With the fighting having almost reached the doorstep of Division Headquarters in the past two days, it was decided to move the command CP to the small castle Henkenshage on the western edge of St. Oedenrode, where it would be more centrally located with the division's fighting forces. The 502nd would move its 2nd and 3rd Battalions to St. Oedenrode on the evening of the twentieth. First Battalion of the 506th was now positioned in a perimeter defense of the Son bridge area. The 501st was four miles north of St. Oedenrode in Eerde and Veghel. The remainder of the 506th would move north from Eindhoven as soon as the two British flank corps came abreast in their movements parallel to the northbound highway.

SIXTEEN

Black Friday

The information about enemy movements along the corridor continued to filter in to Division Headquarters. The signs were ominous. The enemy was about to launch massive attacks in the Veghel area. The underground couriers brought more and more news to their leaders who, in turn, funneled it to the division commanders. Reports came in from east and west.

The 107th Panzer Brigade, after failing in its mission to cut the highway and destroy the Bailey bridge at Son on September 21, moved under cover of darkness toward Erp. The target was the bridge over the Aa River, which they hoped to seize.

Two days earlier, division had anticipated such a move and had ordered the bridge at Erp destroyed along with another one over the Willems-Vaart Canal near Keldonk, two and a half miles southwest of Veghel.

The unit log kept by Cpl. Bruce M. Beyer for 2nd Battalion Headquarters Company of the 501st Parachute Regiment tells of a successful mission on a bridge that didn't take place. The job wasn't completed:

> Wednesday, Sept. 20—S-2 patrol and Demo to Erp. Blew bridge to prevent German armor from crossing.

The 2nd Battalion S-2 leader, 1Lt. Bill Sefton, was sent out on numerous patrols. One of them had been ordered by division in anticipation of an enemy move toward Veghel from the east. Sefton said, "Colonel Ballard sent me out with a mine-laying party to set up a bridge for demolition to a town northeast of Veghel. It was a hike of several miles. The mine-laying party got out and set up their explosives across the top of the bridge surface. I left an outpost there and went back and reported to Colonel Ballard that they were indeed mining the bridge and that area must certainly be secure. It turned out that an enemy column came along—an armored infantry outfit. I heard later it was an SS unit. The patrol detonated their charge which put a *half-inch crack* across the bridge surface. They fired their rounds and wisely withdrew. It developed into the first real threat to Veghel."

The other bridge at Keldonk was handled by members of the 326th Airborne Engineer Battalion. The unit history cited the action of one of its platoons for September 22 in blocking the movements of enemy forces:

> The 3rd Platoon of "A" Company sent one squad on orders to destroy the bridge across the Zuid-Willems-Vaart Canal two and a half miles southeast of Veghel (near Keldonk). Two enlisted men were slightly wounded in this action.

The mission of destroying the bridge near Keldonk was successful. The mission of mining and then destroying the bridge at Erp, when danger was imminent, was not done satisfactorily. The 107th Panzer Brigade had found an opening.

When word had come through via the Dutch underground that the enemy was massing near Erp for an armored attack against Veghel, LTC Robert Ballard had sent a battalion S-2 patrol under the leadership of 1Lt. Bill Sefton. The combined S-2 and demo patrol he had headed earlier had not been successful in blowing the bridge, or the enemy had repaired the damage and a strong attack was in the making on the morning of the twenty-second. Sefton related: "I took a patrol and went up the left flank to determine how deep they were and how serious were their intentions. We had gone up two or three miles and decided to cut across and toward the highway but I had premonitions that I used to get in combat that told me not to go across that flat field, which was probably 300–400 yards wide, to the tree line along the road where there were some farm houses that I could see which again were about a quarter mile this side of the highway that the Germans were attacking along. I took my field glasses and studied the trees and houses and I guess what was really bothering me was that there was no movement whatsoever—not a chicken, not a dog—nothing.

"We had a couple of aggressive Geronimos in the S-2 section saying 'Lieutenant, there has got to be a barrel of Lugers over there. Let's go!' I had this terrible feeling that it would be a mistake. While I'm sitting there, torn by indecision, a tank well off to the northeast fired a round toward the town, over our heads. We had one carbine with a rifle grenade in the group, but I seized on that as the reason not to cross the open field and said, 'Let's go knock out that tank first.'

"About that time I could see 'Dog' Company coming up from the same route we had taken and Colonel Ballard had committed it to making a flanking attack. So I changed my mind and said, 'Let's hook on to this company's flank.' The company didn't get more than 10 to 15 yards out in the field when all hell broke loose from the other direction where the flank protection of the German column was well ensconced in the trees and bushes I had been studying to no avail. They probably would have let my little patrol walk right up to their gun muzzles but they couldn't afford to take that chance with a full rifle company. 'Dog' Company returned fire very aggressively and moved across the field with me on their flank. They pushed up to the road by the farm houses where the German outpost units had been as flank security and I found myself in the ditch on the right flank of the company and the ditch went another 200 yards to the next little crossroad.

"I asked the platoon leader if there was anybody on his flank and he said no. I said I'd take my section down there and turn his flank for him. There was a lot of ground fire, MG fire in particular, from the Germans who were only 50 to 80 yards away and it was skimming right across the road so we stayed crawling down the ditch on our side of the road with the twigs coming down on our backs from the machine gun fire going through the brush above us.

"I was leading the patrol and as I got to a slit trench at the bottom of the ditch, looking in, there were four little kids, the oldest couldn't have been more than four or five years old. They were all blond, curly headed, scrubbed clean, wearing little blue coveralls and I stuck my hairy, unshaven visage over the edge and they all said, 'Allo, Allo!' I crawled around and on in the next ditch were the parents, holding a baby, and they were scared to death, hugging the bottom of the ditch.

"We went on, moved toward the end of the ditch and found ourselves right across this little road from the house on the far side. It was the house of this family. I left the rest of the patrol there and said, 'Goble, let's run across and see who the hell we are up against from inside the house.' Like so many Dutch houses, there was a barn, a stable that was actually part of the same building. We got in and it had a little Gothic window on the far side in the direction in which the Germans were located. I pulled up a milk can and was sitting on it, looking out the window, with Goble standing beside me, when a German soldier suddenly materialized out of the ground about 35 yards away and started running slightly diagonally away from me and all I could think of saying was 'Look at him go!'

"Goble said, 'Aren't you going to shoot him?' and I said, 'Oh yah'—I forgot I had loaded my M-1 with tracers to point out potential targets to the patrol. When I fired, it looked like a long red finger reached out and I don't know if I just singed his buttocks or got him in the hips but he went into a flat dive and disappeared. We never did push clear to the highway. 'D' Company eventually withdrew. We retraced our steps back to Battalion. Ballard had moved the battalion CP over to the edge of town, in the direction of the attack."

The Dutch underground continued to warn the Americans of impending attack from both east and west. In the early morning of the twenty-second, they sent reports of enemy movements northward from Helmond and Erp. Another column was moving east from the Boxtel area. With the 1st and 3rd Battalions occupied in the fighting around Schijndel, only the 2nd Battalion of the 501st was set up in perimeter defense around Veghel.

Anticipating that the Germans would head for Uden as a potential cutoff point, division had ordered the 506th Regiment, less 1st Battalion, to move north as quickly as possible—to get to Uden before the Germans arrived.

In a report he prepared in the early weeks of the Market-Garden operation, assistant division commander BG Gerald Higgins[104] wrote:

> September 22: At 0300 the 3rd Battalion of the 506th Parachute Infantry closed in the St. Oedenrode area, moving up from Eindhoven. At 0500, orders were received that this battalion, as well as all other elements of the regiment, would move to Uden without delay. Movement was to be made by motor and marching. The 3rd Battalion began its move to Uden by marching at 0900. The 2nd Battalion

104. Higgins, op. cit.

initiated its movements piecemeal as transportation became available during the day.

The advance detachment of the 506th, consisting of approximately 150 officers and men from Regimental Headquarters and other units of the regiment, passed through Veghel at 1000. Immediately after passing through, the enemy cut the main highway between Veghel and Uden.

What must have been one of the first instances of a unit being adversely affected by the enemy penetration of the north–south road toward Arnhem involved this British support unit. It must have occurred about the time the road was cut, stopping the flow of 506th troops up to Uden.

One of the functions of a regimental or battalion S-2 section was to send out small patrols in areas where suspected build-ups of enemy forces were taking place and to alert the friendly forces to the possibility of impending attack. PFC Carl Cartledge[105] of the 501st Regimental S-2 Section describes one such patrol incident: "We were walking down the road from our outpost to four trucks with 40mm anti-aircraft guns behind and the men had stopped for tea. I explained that we five men were the only Americans within a half mile or so, and the enemy could see them from the distance. The British captain told this American private how presumptuous I was to tell him what to do. Frank 'Chief' Sayers laughed when I came back and he said, 'Well, you told him once!' It was an expression he used and he meant, 'Damned fool, once is enough!' He was right. In about ten minutes, all hell broke loose and we helped evacuate the bodies and the wounded much later. The trucks and guns burned all that afternoon."

In describing the actions in the Veghel area, 2Lt. Robert O'Connell wrote: "On September 22, Companies 'D' and 'E' of the 501st were generally southeast of Veghel. Both companies came under direct 88 fire to our left front."

Pvt. William J. Houston of "D" Company had been on outpost at the highway bridge over the canal southeast of Veghel. He wrote: "We moved through Veghel and north of the town, flanking the highway. Pvt. George Kos and I were sent out on outpost for the night. About daylight Kos said to me, 'Houston,

105. Cartledge, op. cit.

if we get attacked today we are going to get it.' I played that remark down.

"We were going to advance when the Germans beat us to it. The first sign of it was a sniper got me in the left shoulder—no bone hit. Kos and I were standing behind two separate trees, firing at the Germans coming across the field. We were on the left flank so we saw a bazooka shell bounce off the tank when it was swinging its gun around us. The British had several tanks three or four hundred yards back of us. They got the tank. We also saw the 88 that got us. I shot at the 88—it was a trailer gun. About that time it hit Kos. Nothing was left but from the waist down. I was blown in the air. When I came down I thought my leg was blown off, but I found I was lying on it and only a piece of shrapnel had hit me in the right leg. After the enemy tank was knocked out, the attack stopped. I went back with some other men to the aid station which was back of us, through the English tank area. One of them had been knocked out."

After Houston was treated, he was sent off with others in the direction of the railroad bridge where a small group from his unit was holding that strategic bridge.

Machine gunner Cpl. Glen A. Derber didn't see any real action in the first few days. That changed suddenly. "My first heavy action occurred on the 22nd when a report came in that 40 tanks supported by infantry were approaching. We pulled out of our positions and force marched across town to meet them. Some distance from town, as we started to cross a large turnip field, a German machine gun opened up on us and I saw the tracers coming at us and hitting the dirt not 15 feet away. I hit the dirt too and tried to locate the enemy so I could take him out with my .03 rifle with a grenade launcher and 5 rifle grenades. We proceeded towards the enemy and they sent me down a ditch to set up my gun on the left flank. (This seemed to be the standard way of utilizing Headquarters Company weapons.) Directly across the field from me was a farm house with a lane to its left and a field to its right. A few riflemen came to join us and formed an MLR and a German tank appeared in the far corner of the field. My assistant gunner manned the LMG (light machine gun) while I prepared to use my grenade launcher on the tank. A burst from a BAR to my right caused the tank commander to button up and a nearby rifleman was lobbing rifle grenades at the tank so I saved mine.

"About this time two Germans carrying a white flag appeared from behind a brick house on the far side of the field and approached our positions. Someone on the right yelled to 'cease fire' but we could see the enemy deploying to our left in a maneuver to outflank us. The two Germans dropped the white flag and ran back towards the brick house. I had unloaded the grenade and inserted two tracers into my .03 while this was taking place. (The tracers were to tell me if I was zeroed in because I'd never had a chance to fire this weapon on the rifle range.) I stood up and carefully aimed at one of the fleeing enemy. Locked in my mind is the image of that tracer as it reached out and tapped that Kraut on the back just to the right of his backbone. He rounded the corner of the house and pitched forward out of sight. Someone on the right later confirmed that he was dead. It was my first kill and I was so elated that I began to whoop and holler and forgot, for a few seconds, that bullets were flying around."

In his report, Brigadier General Higgins provided an hour-by-hour report of events as they unfolded in the Veghel area.

By 1200, the 2nd Battalion of the 501st, astride the Veghel–Erp road, was being hard pressed. Additional troops were started toward Veghel and General McAuliffe was placed in command of troops in that area and charged with defense of the town and bridges. At about 1400, enemy tanks cut the highway northeast of Veghel and destroyed transport parked on the highway. Battery "B", 81st Anti-Tank Battalion arrived at the same time, went into action on the highway and immediately destroyed a Mark V tank leading the attack. The 2nd Battalion 506th took position on the left of the 2nd Battalion 501st, with the 1st Battalion 401st Glider Infantry on its left. With the assistance of the British artillery gathered from the highway, the attack from Erp was repulsed by dark. At about 1400, enemy infantry, with tank support, attacked astride the Canal from the northwest toward the highway bridge southwest of Veghel. Company "D" 506th, which was in Veghel on its way to Uden, was turned around, deployed near the bridge and repulsed the attack, with the assistance of elements of the 44th Tank Regiment.

During the afternoon, the enemy launched an attack against the town from the north and were finally halted just short of the railroad bridge by elements of the 2nd Battalion, 501st, and one platoon of "H" Company, 506th, which had taken up a defensive position there a short time before.[106]

106. Higgins, op. cit.

The entry in the 501st 2nd Battalion log by Cpl. Bruce M. Beyer provides the reader with the scope of the battle taking place in the Veghel area:

> Friday, Sept. 22—At 1100 German armor and artillery in the vicinity of Erp, SE of Veghel. Commenced shelling. Lt. Wolf wounded in hand by shrapnel. Sgt. Mero captured 12 Germans near grain elevator in town. Had binoculars shot away. Germans attacking Veghel at 1215. Forward CP established SE edge of Veghel. Heavy fighting. Three German tanks knocked out by AT guns. Support given by rocket-firing Typhoons, British tanks and artillery. CP established in new position 2000 hours. Casualties medium.

The enemy was now on the outskirts and other units got into the fray. Second Battalion of the 506th Parachute Infantry Regiment was just passing the sector on its way to Uden when they were diverted.

As radioman for his "F" Company platoon, Cpl. Joe Hogenmiller had good knowledge of the movements of his regiment, battalion and company. He wrote: "On the 22nd, the Dutch underground warned the 101st Division commander of enemy movements east of the corridor near Helmond and west of it near Boxtel.

"In response, the 101st commander moved to rush the 506th Regiment to Uden with Colonel Charles Chase, executive officer of the 506th, as leader of the advance party. They reached Uden at 1100. Shortly after 1100, the Germans cut the road north of Veghel and the regiment was isolated until 1700 the next day. Colonel Chase's small group of Regimental Headquarters Company and a platoon from the 2nd Battalion, held off the Germans all night.

"The 2nd Battalion of the 506th moved into Veghel. General A. C. McAuliffe, assistant division commander, rushed us out to the Uden road in time to meet the advancing German armored division on the outskirts of Veghel."

Part of the 2nd Battalion had already been trucked up to the Veghel-Uden area. Now it was the turn of "F" Company. "We were driven up in big trailer trucks," wrote Sgt. John H. Taylor. "From Eindhoven we went back up through Son, right over the bridge which had been repaired, and moved on up to Veghel. We did a right turn. It was in the middle of the afternoon. We unloaded very hurriedly and lined up alongside the trucks. We started to move out of Veghel and the 2nd Platoon was the rear element of the column. We moved out and got just clear of the town on a road and drew some small arms fire taking place up ahead.

"Someone from Battalion came down the road and told us to do an about face. We were on the wrong road. We turned around and went right back to Veghel. We did a right turn. We cleared up the last part of the village."

Taylor continued: "As we moved out on the road with another group of houses on each side of the road, there was a British convoy parked alongside the road. (See story of PFC Carl Cartledge on page 317.) Just as we swung out to get around these trucks, we heard a noise and looked up. A couple of German tanks were coming across an open spot on the left hand side of the road. We hit the ditch about the time the tank fired and hit a truck. It blew up. I was down in the ditch and a British soldier came slipping and sliding in the mud and fell right beside me. For a moment our equipment belts were tangled. After a few seconds I heard a loud report behind me and the tank burst into flames. One of the 81st Anti-Tank Battalion 57mm guns had been wheeled up behind a jeep and turned around and they fired and hit the tank with the first shot."

PFC William E. True of the same company, but different platoon, recalled the incident plus another involving Dutch civilians. True wrote: "As we pulled into town, we detrucked in a little park-like area, German artillery and probably tank fire was heavy all around us. An American gun crew in the middle of the street was exchanging head-on fire with a German Tiger tank. I was terribly impressed with the guts of those gunners, because it seemed like their gun was a mere pea-shooter (57mm), facing up to the much heavier fire power of the tank. I don't recall how that gun crew made out with the tank since my platoon's assignment was to make a northward sweep of the town for a block or two west of the street where the tank battle was going on."

Having gone into action almost from the moment they came off the landing zone on the nineteenth, the men of the 81st Anti-Tank Battalion and particularly "B" Battery were in the thick of the battle. Cpl. Rogie Roberts describes the actions of their move to Veghel on the twenty-second: "We were still in the Son area when our Captain Gueymard came to us and told us to move to the town of Veghel where an attack by enemy tanks had been reported. We hooked up the gun to the jeep and left. It took us about 15 to 20 minutes to get there. I was quite surprised when we got there—the attack was in full swing. We went through the town and stopped on the north side where someone was screaming 'Tanks! Tanks!' We swung the gun around in the middle of the street and set up on the cobblestone roadway. This was not a good idea as the gun had a rather strong recoil and would slide or jump back when not anchored. We waited. In the meantime, from a corn field to our right, we began receiving rather heavy small arms fire which was hitting on the building about four feet over our heads. A British truck was blazing on our right. As it burned, ammunition began exploding. It was getting rather hairy. Smoke began to drift across the street. A tank suddenly appeared. It was a Mark V German medium Panther tank, moving across our direct front at about 100 yards— the length of a football field—possibly closer. I could see it quite clearly even though the smoke was down to ground level. I went down on one knee to get at the sights for aiming the gun. As I looked through the scope I could see nothing but smoke from the burning truck. This obscured my sighting. I stood up, took another look. I could see the tank clearly from a standing position. Someone on the sidelines was screaming 'Fire! Fire!' I yelled, 'I'll fire when I can see it!' I can remember it quite vividly as I was in the middle of the street. I went back to the gun, put my eyes again to view finder and waited. A little gust of wind lifted the smoke which gave me a brief view of the tank. I quickly depressed the gun and fired. I hit the tank between the tracks where fire began to belch out. Smoke was rising from the turret. The two German soldiers jumped out and started running. American soldiers in the ditch beside the road immediately fired and brought them down.

"The edge of the gun shield hit my knee and I went down in the street. The recoil of the gun had knocked me down. I thought my knee cap was broken. At first I didn't know what happened. My own gun had kicked me. Captain Gueymard said to put another round in the tank. I said, 'Captain, I can't move!' Gueymard then loaded the gun and fired it himself. The tank was already burning and I didn't see any reason for firing again. Captain Gueymard called for another round. By this time I was up and hobbling. I moved back to the gun and fired the third round. It was unnecessary but, in the heat of battle, it was one of those things."

Capt. "Fonse" Gueymard remembered the affair this way: "The attack on September 22nd by the Germans on the north edge of Veghel was an exciting affair for me. My battery was down the road south of Veghel when I received word from General McAuliffe that the Germans were attacking Veghel with tanks and to get up there in a hurry. I gathered a couple of guns and we took off for Veghel as fast as possible. On reaching the northern edge of the village, it was obvious that a fire fight was occurring and, in the middle of the highway, we saw a Mark V tank moving toward the infantry defense and firing intensely. One gun was available and we detached it from the jeep and set it up in the middle of the highway. The gunner was Cpl. Rogie Roberts and I acted as loader. The driver of the jeep was Howard Wortham. We fired immediately and the first shot knocked out the tank. A few additional rounds were fired and the attack stopped. On setting up the gun, we were a bit excited and forgot to set the brakes. As a result, the gun recoiled, knocked me down and fractured Roberts' kneecap. Colonel X. B. Cox and several others were there by the time the firing took place. Later the remainder of my battery arrived and we took positions with the infantry on the east side of Veghel."

"One of the amazing things that happened before the firing began," added Cpl. Rogie Roberts. "We needed some ammunition from the jeep when we were setting up the gun. There was a flight officer[107] (glider pilot) who came up and started unloading ammunition from the jeep and bringing it forward to the gun in the midst of all the small arms fire. He had gone in with the 82nd and this amazed me. This man was helping us—his job was done. He could take off and run but here he was unloading the jeep as if nothing was happening.

"Only a few minutes before we shot the tank, General McAuliffe told me that a tank was to the north of Veghel and to see what I could find out about it," wrote LTC X. B. Cox Jr., commander of the 81st Anti-Tank Battalion. "I located one of my anti-tank guns just outside of the command post and we

107. Author's note: Tom Berry responded to a reunion notice I had placed in the St. Louis newspaper. He described to me on the phone the above incident from his vantage point. I put him in touch with members of the 81st Anti-Tank Battalion. He got in touch with Rogie Roberts in 1985. He was that glider pilot.

went to the edge of town. We saw the tank, set up the gun, knocked out the tank and within some 30 to 45 minutes I reported back to General McAuliffe what had happened. (Long years after the war was over, General McAuliffe was still talking about how fast the mission had been completed.)"

Having passed by the anti-tank gun in the street, PFC William True of "F" Company of the 506th continued on his way. He wrote: "Fortunately, we encountered no Germans, neither tanks nor infantry as we moved through our assignment area. One thing did occur that impressed me with the effect of battles on the civilian population. I observed what appeared to be an underground storage dugout (called a root cellar by some) with angled double trap doors which closed. Suspecting there might be Germans hiding in the cellars just waiting for an opportune time to come out, I opened the trap door and very cautiously proceeded down the stairs with the safety off my rifle which I was holding in front of me. There turned out to be two or three old men, several women and a few children huddled together and obviously terrified. As I turned back up the steps, I gave heartfelt thanks to someone above for having given me the intelligence and courage not to follow my first cautious inclination which had been to toss a grenade into the dugout and take no chances."

Memories of a similar action in the corridor still create nighttime problems for T/5 Loy Rasmussen, who also served in "F" Company. He recalled: "I still have nightmares over what might have happened in Holland if I had reacted as trained. I was sent by my platoon leader, 1Lt. Frank McFadden, with two other men to check out a farm house and to flush out any enemy snipers who might be hiding there. I burst through the door while the other two went left and right around the building. As I charged in, I saw a box-like lid raise slightly and go down very quickly. I should have sprayed the box with my tommy gun but I held back for some reason. I called out in the few German words I knew—'Come out with your hands up!'

"An old bald-headed man and his wife, and I presume their daughter with a small baby on her arm, emerged from the box which must have been an entrance to the house from the cellar.

"Had I fired, as was my first impulse, the deaths of those four innocent people would have been on my mind to this day. It is enough that I've had nightmares about it from time to time since the war."

Meanwhile, in the 2nd Platoon sector, Sgt. John Taylor began to notice that many of his men were missing. "Things got hot and heavy, Jerry Farley got a tank with a bazooka up the road after a bit of a fire fight. Meanwhile, 3rd Platoon was having quite a fight on the other side of the road. One of the German tanks had pulled up on the right hand side of the road and I guess the British called in the Typhoons and they came in—they were diving right at 'em and knocked it out and set it on fire. The action was hot and heavy. In the middle of it I heard Lt. Hall holler, 'Get to the left flank!' We didn't have any flank and we had to keep the enemy from getting around us. I hollered for the 1st squad to follow me and we went down that ditch— got out where we could see what was going on and got into position to keep them from coming around our flank. I had a bunch of men missing and couldn't figure out where they were. We got settled down and I started looking for my men. One trooper up the road mentioned that some of them got hit when the truck blew up. I went up the street where I found them all. Grodowski had been hit in the leg. Ochoa had been bunged up some. Robbins had been hit in the heel. Watkins had been hit real bad; in fact, he died a few minutes later with his head in my lap. We had things pretty well settled down that afternoon. I don't know what the situation was as far as the British were concerned. They left trucks and everything.

"I think it was Haney—we could smell something cooking. It smelled pretty good. We crawled up the side of the road and sure enough they had a steel pot on a little stove; we retrieved the pot and ate the contents."

In an action that took place in the near vicinity of Taylor's platoon, T/5 Loy Rasmussen remembered: "I was out as part of a patrol that had become separated and I came upon an abandoned vehicle which mounted a 20mm cannon. A soldier from another unit was there also. He had some knowledge of the weapon. Down the road came two German tanks with their 88mm cannons looming as large as telephone poles as they approached our area. I had only an M-1 which doesn't do anything for stopping a tank. I kept hoping the other trooper would fire but he kept holding back. When the lead tank was within easy range he fired the weapon, aiming for the tracks. He hit the tank and we took off running before they could zero in on us. We never knew how effective the firing had been."

As "D" Company of the 506th was detrucking near the highway bridge over the Willems-Vaart Canal, they were called on to repulse the main force of enemy troops moving toward them from the north.

Sgt. Hugh Pritchard of "D" Company provided a copy of a citation from his regimental commander, Col. Robert F. Sink, to his unit that read:

> On the 22nd September 1944, at 1400 hours, "D" Company, commanded by 1Lt. Joe F. McMillan, detrucked at Veghel, Holland and immediately was committed to repulse an attack which was a serious threat to the main highway bridge over the Zuid-Willems-Vaart Canal on the outskirts of Veghel. "D" Company promptly attacked to the northwest along the canal against superior enemy forces estimated at 200 men with supporting mortars and a self-propelled gun. As a result of this prompt and aggressive action by "D" Company, 35 of the enemy were captured and approximately 75 enemy were killed, and the canal bridge which was vital to the success of the Holland operation was prevented from falling into enemy hands.

Sgt. Jack MacLean's anti-tank team had spent the night in the Nunen area, northeast of Eindhoven, in support of "D" Company. It had been a quiet occasion. During the morning, a bunch of American six-by-six trucks appeared on the scene. The men were quickly on-loaded. They headed for Veghel where rumor had it that the Germans had broken through. MacLean wrote: "We had to get there in a hurry. The attack was broken up and we took a lot of prisoners in the woods west of the highway. Sgt. Jeff Rice was pumping mortars into the wooded area and we fired several bazooka rounds and rifle grenades. We got some 40 Germans to surrender along with a disabled tank. When the prisoners came up on the road, other troopers fired at them, causing the enemy to dive back in the ditches for cover. We had a time getting them out of there. We recaptured a Piper Cub pilot. He had been shot down earlier. He was furious because we almost killed him. He was caught in our barrage."

PFC Donald G. Harms[108] of 2nd Battalion of the 506th was moving up by truck with his company toward a new position in

---

108. From General Order 47, 101st Airborne Division, December 4, 1944, citing PFC Donald G. Harms for the posthumous award of the Silver Star.

Uden when it was subjected to an attack by enemy artillery fire. The men were forced to leave the trucks and set out on foot. Enemy infantry and armor suddenly launched an attack on the company. Realizing the seriousness of the situation, Harms jumped into an abandoned jeep and towed an anti-tank gun to a position within range of the enemy. Despite heavy fire from an enemy tank, he moved the gun into position and helped man it. This gun disabled the tank. He then went forward, still under fire, and evacuated two wounded men. His aggressive actions were of great assistance in breaking up the enemy attack and enabled the company to set up a defense, thereby saving many lives and several trucks in the supply column.

The British armor had arrived in Veghel and some of it was located near the aid station set up by the 50th Field Hospital. This brought much enemy counter-battery fire into the area. The hospital commandant had requested permission to move into the Catholic convent, which was larger and cleaner. The move had been completed on the twenty-first.

First Lieutenant William Dimmerling arrived in Holland six days before the guns of the 907th Glider Field Artillery Battalion reached the battle area. He had parachuted as a forward observer with the 501st Parachute Regiment. He was able to use his expertise as an artillery spotter with the supporting British artillery.

On the morning of the twenty-second, Dimmerling attended Mass at the convent church in Veghel. One of the nuns presented him with a rosary she had brought back from her last visit to Lourdes in France. Accompanied by PFC William Wakeland and Pvt. William Copeland, Dimmerling had gone up into the steeple of the church to spot for the artillery.

As he was establishing a base point registration, Dimmerling noted a large concentration of enemy troops to the northwest and called for immediate fire. In three rounds, Dimmerling was on target and the artillery was raising havoc as it dropped shell after shell on the disoriented and confused enemy troops.

It didn't take the Germans long to realize an artillery spotter was at work. A look to the surrounding landscape showed the steeple of the convent church with possible movement by our soldiers. Enemy artillery was directed toward the church with five direct hits being made on the tower while other rounds landed in the courtyard below. The nun who had given the rosary to Dimmerling was one of several nuns killed while others were wounded.

The fire mission was completed. Only then did Dimmerling and his men come down from their observation post. A short time later the steeple was demolished by the continuing enemy barrage.

First Lieutenant Robert Radmann describes the actions affecting the aid station on the twenty-second: "The next morning we again became the target of the Germans. All that day and night we were under constant mortar attack. Just after sundown we were hit twice and three of our wounded were killed, one being a German soldier. Eight of the sisters were hit and five died the next day. A German officer we had as a patient, was quite upset about the attack as he knew we had our Red Cross placed on the roof of the convent facing the direction of the German attackers. He was most upset that the Red Cross was being overlooked and suggested that we take him under a white flag to the German attackers and he would advise them of their violation. He was certain that we were being fired on regardless of the Red Cross because the Germans had used the convent tower for observation and felt our troops were doing the same. Before a decision could be made on this matter, we were hit again and this time the German officer was hit and in no condition to be moved. Although we were never hit again, we were constantly being restricted in our operation of the aid station."

On the twenty-first of September, PFC Elroy Huwe was hit by shrapnel in the lower right abdomen. He talked the medics into letting him stay with his company. They consented if he would come back to the regimental aid station each day to have the wound redressed. He wrote: "The next day I went to the aid station to have the wound rebandaged and just after the job was finished and I was leaving the aid station, which was located near a church in Veghel, German artillery started coming in. The aid station was receiving quite a few hits. I saw a door ajar and noted several men lying on the floor. I dove between a couple of them. (Safer in crowds you know!) After the shelling was over, I got up but noted none of the men were moving. I took a long hard look and realized they were all dead. I had sought shelter among the KIAs. I left with a strange feeling."

To the people of Veghel, Friday, September 22, 1944, is known as Black Friday. Mrs. Josephine van Herpen-Hout, a twenty-year-old at the time, recalled the day when two of the paratroopers rushed in to warn them to get to a shelter. She wrote: "Suddenly on Friday, they ran into the house and told us to get into the cellar. They had to get back quickly to their unit. They'd just left and the shooting began. Artillery explosions, bullets and tanks—the Germans had come back. We went to the neighbor's cellar as that one was much better than ours. It was good we did, too—as two shells landed in our kitchen, right on the cook stove where the food was sitting. Nothing was left. The other landed in the cellar. We had to flee to the part of Veghel which was across the River Aa. There was no shooting there. They must have known that the soldiers were all in the center of the town. We heard there was a German observation post in the church tower of Erp (next village to the east) which signaled to the German tanks and artillery where they had to shoot.

"We had to run to our sister's house at the other end. I'll never forget the heavy shooting—dead soldiers, wounded. A leg with a boot still on it, hanging in a tree. We never thought we could come out alive, but luckily we did.

"We were also glad the temporary hospital that was in the town center had moved on Thursday. There were hundreds of soldiers, even Germans. We were allowed to talk to them. I will never forget all that screaming and crying for help. One was filled (his back) with straw. We all felt so much pity for them, so far away from home. They were all brought in from the fight around Schijndel, Veghel and Eerde."

The twenty-second started as a "laid-back" kind of day for Cpl. Charles Ritzler and the other two members of his small detachment positioned at the railroad bridge over the Willems-Vaart Canal. It would gradually change and he would eventually meet his former platoon leader from Camp McCall days. In his notebook diary, he chronicled the day's activities:

On outpost all day. Dynamited for fish but no luck. Roasted corn and ate tomatoes. Were ordered in during the afternoon and went back to the bridge. I was given Clyde Schneider and Bob Miller with their machine gun to hold the railway bridge. Don't know what they could be thinking of when they kept only us three. Were fired upon about two hours before darkness and we were in for it. It was the flank of the force attacking the main bridge a mile further down. Just as it got hot we made contact with Lt. (Clark) Heggeness who had 17 men. Fired till dark and had to stand by while 3 tanks looked us over at about 300 yards. Had good shooting. I used about 400 rounds from my tommy gun. Took 18 prisoners. Lost one man from a hand grenade. Pushed out a few men just over the bridge and prepared for a hot night.

It is possible that 1Lt. Clark Heggeness of "H" Company of the 506th Parachute Infantry Regiment was not aware that he was bringing reinforcements to men of his former "D" Company, 501st Regiment, when he was ordered to move in the direction of the railroad bridge over the canal. In describing his move, Heggeness wrote: "We had proceeded a quarter to a half mile west of the highway along the south side of a canal. All of a sudden we could hear a loud roaring sound. What that obviously meant was there were some German tanks in the area and, from the sound, we could tell they were approaching from the southwest. It wasn't long before we could make out two Tiger tanks coming through the trees from the south along with a few disorganized infantrymen—maybe 30 or 40.

"Since they were coming from a wooded area where tanks could not navigate freely, I think the enemy intended to cross a small bridge over the canal (it might have been a railroad bridge) and then proceed east, where the area was open, to cut the highway or have an open shot at vehicles on the highway.

"I thank God that I remembered what I had learned in infantry school, i.e., the only way to protect a structure is to get away from it. We fanned out from where we were near the bridge, half of us crawling to the north and the other half to the south, so we could have an open field of fire toward the bridge. The two Tiger tanks came up almost side by side through the trees and, as they came close to the bridge, we started shooting bazookas at the tanks and rifle fire at the infantrymen. It so happened that I was in the group to the north of the bridge. We were very lucky because as the tanks approached, their turrets were open but nobody was looking out. I don't think they saw us at first but, as you know, when a big black tank comes up with its 88 moving around and pointing in your direction in a menacing manner, it makes you wonder why in the world you were there and not some place else. We were extremely fortunate to have a bazooka on each side of the bridge and, while they were unable to do any damage to the tanks, they did scare the drivers. The tanks started shooting their 88s but they didn't seem to know where we were because they were firing all over blindly. Also, our rifle fire caused the infantrymen to drop down in their tracks and eventually start crawling backwards. It was sort of wooded so it was pretty easy for them to get away. We did not have a machine gun but we had a couple of BARs. Although the tanks certainly had the edge on us, they started to back up as their infantry began to disappear. They backed up facing us and shooting rather wildly as they retreated. I really don't think any of our men got hit, but we did have to do our laundry afterwards. I have to give credit to the bazooka men because, without them, I am sure the tanks would have been more aggressive and probably would just have run over us."

First Lieutenant Heggeness continued his story: "After a short wait, we proceeded to patrol in the direction taken by the retreating tanks. We could not re-contact them. It was not long, however, before we saw an English tank and we were filled with elation (for a few seconds). However, we soon learned it was a British tank captured by the Germans. We waved our flags to identify ourselves. All we got in return were some very unfriendly shots from the tank and rifle fire from the infantry. We then threw smoke grenades and got out of there. I believe one or two of our men were killed and several more wounded because we had believed that English tank was friendly."

Recalling the action near Veghel after the Germans cut the highway, PFC Thomas P. Fitzmaurice said, "The firing was pretty heavy when we were knocking out that roadblock and we looked up and saw an American tank—we were supposed to have British support and everybody was remarking about the British being up front. Then we looked again and they were Germans. They started firing point blank at us. Those shells sounded like dropping a piece of meat on a hot skillet when they went over your head."

PFC Joseph Harris was with Heggeness. "The 3rd Platoon was sent off on a side road as the Germans had captured an American tank and were using it against us. That's where Hahn, Purdie and one other guy were killed. They were Sergeant Padisak's buddies and were killed by concussion from one of the shells."

Action was hot and heavy on the east side of Veghel as the

enemy artillery and mortars pounded the positions of the para-troopers.

"The worst action I can remember was Veghel," wrote PFC James H. Martin of "G" Company. "We were in and out of town quite a few times over several days. The first evening we were deployed along a road with a small hedge in front of an apple orchard. I and my second gunner had just completed a couple of pretty good foxholes when Sgt. Oscar Saxvik said we would have to move on back in the orchard as he wanted to put Sgt. Harold Brucker and 'Jiggs' Rogers in our positions because they had a phone and a radio and he wanted them close by. I re-member protesting bitterly to no avail so we moved and were still digging in when a concentrated shelling occurred. It lasted 15 or 20 minutes. When it was over, Saxvik came back and said, 'I hope you sons-of-a-bitches are satisfied now!' Brucker and Rogers had taken a direct hit and were killed."

PFC Jim Martin also remembered, "There was a dead GI lying at the main intersection in town and when we came back in after being pushed out, some civilian had covered everything but his feet and legs with a raincoat and there was a small bunch of flowers which had been placed on his body. I was very touched by this act of concern."

When the Germans cut the highway between Veghel and Uden, part of "E" Company of the 506th was in Uden with LTC Charles Chase and Regimental Headquarters Company. Capt. Richard Winters and 1/Sgt. Carwood Lipton were part of the advance element. Sgt. Don Malarkey, a member of S/Sgt. William J. Guarnere's platoon, was caught in Veghel during the heavy shelling. He said, "The 'E' Company members wondered about Captain Winters and the rest of the company. The size and depth of the attack was so heavy we thought the rest of the company on the Uden side of the block would be wiped out as we assumed the enemy force had also sent a column to the north.

"Captain Winters, in Uden, thought a similar fate had be-fallen us. He had positioned the rest of the company near a street intersection in shop buildings on the south side of the town waiting for the German tanks to turn to the north. They had been able to view the assault on Veghel from a towering church steeple located near their position. Winters thought Veghel might be overrun so he discussed the possibility with the remaining elements of the company. Winters then decided they would make their stand, even if it was their last. Although the next 24 hours were tense, the German forces were routed and a last ditch defense of Uden did not have to be made."

As a member of the advance group in Uden, 1/Sgt. Carwood Lipton had these recollections: "We set up a defensive plan and set booby traps and kept up fire from different positions so the Krauts would think we were a large force. Some British were there, too. Captain Richard Winters told me to organize as many men as I could find into one defensive position. I tried to man-handle one Britisher into the defense when he seemed to be reluctant and he stopped me short by pointing out that he was a major and not accustomed to being ordered about by a first sergeant—even American."

With the battle swirling about them, the medics and surgeons of the 506th were extremely busy picking up the numerous casualties resulting from the heavy fighting. Capt. Bernard J. Ryan, one of the two surgeons with 3rd Battalion, described activities: "At the second battle of Veghel, Captain (Stanley) Morgan and I were with 3rd Battalion Headquarters, or 'G' Company, alternating at crawling up ditches to evacuate casualties. We would sometimes crawl two or three hundred yards. Some Krauts in an English recon drove right up beside our jeep, dropped a grenade in the jeep, wounding the driver, while we were picking up casualties in the twilight."

When he couldn't comply with the wishes of a trooper, Cpl. Henry R. Ritter felt very guilty as he departed. "I remember standing near a badly wounded man being cared for by medics. The guy's lower jaw had been blown off. He was in shock and he didn't know it. I was smoking a cigarette and this trooper motioned to me that he wanted a drag on my cigarette.

"Oh, that was bad. How do you tell a guy that he hasn't got a mouth in which to put a cigarette. I didn't know what to do so I just walked away."

The heavy fighting continued all along the highway between Veghel and the enemy roadblock on the highway between the two towns.

Radioman Cpl. Joe Hogenmiller added to his story: "The 2nd Battalion commander was given orders to set up a line of defense

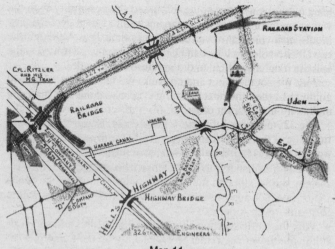

Map 11

with company machine gunners positioned up front of our lines and to hold there. The Battalion was equipped with mortars, machine guns and rifles. We were facing a German armored division."

With "F" Company in the midst of heavy fighting, Sgt. John Taylor was busy moving his men around. He said, "We moved up to the next crossroad and set up a line of defense and our left flank was still open. This was the time Bob James and Jayko went out to the left on patrol and went all up and down that road for quite a ways and did not make contact with anyone who was supposed to be there. We knew our flank was open. The 3rd Platoon was over on the right side of the road. I don't know about 1st Platoon—either over there too or in reserve.

"During the night we could hear tanks and vehicles of some sort moving around in front of us and we told our people on crew-shared weapons not to open up unless they absolutely had to. The enemy was probably trying to bait us to commit our automatic weapons so they could pinpoint our positions and put mortars in on them. We decided to move a machine gun out there in the middle of the night. We crawled up a ditch—I was in the lead and, as I crawled up through some bushes, I put my hand on someone's leg and sort of froze momentarily. I knew he was alive, whoever it was, and in a second I heard someone say in a British voice, 'Are you American or German?' There were two British soldiers who had been hiding in that ditch since that episode that afternoon and they were pretty shook up and scared. We got them out and on back. We knew something was going to happen the next morning. There was too much movement out there in front of us."

The 327th Glider Infantry Regiment got its marching orders from the Son area before noon on the twenty-second. Trucks were available for 3rd Battalion but Regimental HQ and 1st and 2nd Battalions had to march the total distance.

PFC Robert Jessup got the dubious assignment of "road guide" to direct the battalions northward along the safe roads. He wrote: "My most memorable experience was when I came up missing in action. We were moving our CP to Veghel. I was placed at an intersection as road guide. The medical jeep was to be the last vehicle in route of march. They were to pick me up. Shelling started somewhere (near St. Oedenrode) up the line so a radio message was sent changing the route of march. Suddenly no troops were coming by, no jeep, nothing! Darkness came and there I stood. When you're in combat, you are lost. I finally saw a gas stove light up. I eased toward it and heard some British GIs talking. I hailed them and went cautiously toward them. They had a big laugh at my predicament, fed me and gave me a bed roll. (Next day dawned bright and clear. Traffic wasn't moving north. The Germans cut 'Hell's Highway' between me and Veghel and I stayed with the British for three days until a convoy went north.)"

In a letter he wrote to his parents, T/5 Jack E. Millman described the action of the move to Veghel and the resultant shelling. "We marched 10 to 12 miles to Veghel, arriving in the afternoon. We started digging in at the edge of town and the Germans started some heavy shelling. They threw everything at us but the kitchen sink. I dug a foxhole in thirty minutes. We lost quite a few men in that barrage."

PFC Denis M. Parson, also of "G" Company, felt "the Germans observed our movement to the courtyard."

The most vivid memory of the Holland campaign for 1Lt. Thomas J. Niland, S-2 leader for 2nd Battalion of the 327th, was the shelling they experienced in the churchyard in Veghel.

"We had just moved in and were the division reserve. The men were digging in when we received a tremendous shelling which took a great toll. I was then ordered to get the battalion out of there and we moved through Veghel to a location just south of town. I and several men went back to the churchyard area to see if we could account for any wounded left behind. It seemed like the Germans knew exactly where we were and there was nothing you could do but lay and wait in the ditch until the barrage was over."

T/5 Glenn E. Braddock may have had a related experience. He had been a member of the pathfinder team that marked drop zone "A" at Eerde. After that mission was over he had joined other team members in the assault on Veghel.

Miles from his home unit, which was the 502nd Parachute Infantry Regiment in the St. Oedenrode area, Braddock had no specific assignment after the DZ mission. He was assigned to guard prisoners. He describes the surroundings in which he was operating. "There was a courtyard and some kind of a brick convent with high stone walls around part of it and this was used as team headquarters and also as a prisoner compound.

"It was here that I received another education, when guarding prisoners, don't expose yourself unnecessarily to any outside elements. The other team members were out on a combined scouting and mop-up operation with the Limey tanks and I had missed out, having been away escorting a prisoner for interrogation and so I was on guard duty by myself. The Krauts were all moved inside to one big room with only one door leading out to a hallway. The outside door was set in just far enough so it could not be seen, unless one was standing in the doorway. We had a machine gun positioned there in case of a prisoner break.

"The Germans started shelling the area and I looked inside the room—most of the prisoners were crowded down low against the wall. I had heard one or two conversing in broken English with some of the guards earlier so I knew that at least one of them could convey the message I was about to give— 'Your comrades are shelling us. I'm the only guard here but I have a gun set up outside, out of sight. I'm going to cover this doorway and anyone trying to escape will be shot. Stay where you are.'

"I got to feeling so cocky that after the shelling stopped I ventured outside the hallway door to view the damage wreaked by the artillery. I damn near got hit. A hunk of stonewall on the building whizzed past me and the snap of a bullet going by. I jumped back and, as nothing happened, I jerked my head out and right back—another chunk of stone off the wall. Whoever it was, wasn't fooling. I got inside and stayed there.

"A few hours later the tanks came back into town and our men were way behind. They came around the back door where the sniper had been trying to get me and I told them to get the hell away from that side of the building unless they wanted to help the poppies grow.

"Earlier there was a group of underground personnel who attached themselves to our organization. I don't believe we had given them an invite—they just joined us. So, when I told the fellows I thought the shots came from the church steeple almost two blocks away, the Dutch patriots had a talk among themselves and headed for the church. No shots were fired in their direction so we stayed in a safe position to watch the action.

"Upon arriving at the church, some went inside while the others took up positions outside. Shortly, the inside group came back out with a prisoner with hands behind his head. He was escorted to the side of the church with Dutch about four feet on either side of him. Meanwhile, the group that stayed on the outside of the church had more or less lined up to one side of the church steps. It was to this side the prisoner was marched. As soon as he cleared the steps everyone stopped and I presumed he was told to turn facing away from the church for no sooner did he turn than a volley of shots was fired from the group that stood away from the steps. I heard scuttle butt later that the prisoner was a female."

One wonders if there was a connection between the extremely accurate artillery fire and the sniper in the steeple. The location of the glidermen of the 327th was in the same vicinity.

As the day came to a close, the 101st Airborne Division was being hit from the northeast where the road had been cut. It was having a difficult time holding back the strong push from the direction of Erp. Two attacks had come from the north and northwest with enemy soldiers with armor moving toward both the railroad and highway bridges over the Willems-Vaart Canal. Armor support and artillery were much needed.

Sgt. Gerald Zimmerman was operating a powerful SCR-499 radio set at the forward command post of the 101st Airborne Division in Veghel on the night of September 22–23. He was called on to send a crucial message to the British 30th Corps, which was in the Nijmegen area. The enemy had cut the road between Veghel and Uden. There was a desperate need for armored support. Zimmerman wrote:

> One night I had to send an "O" (urgent) message to XXX Corps to get help from the "Desert Rat." The reception was bad and I had a helluva time getting through. Two people came to check to see if the message got through. I had so much trouble I told the second one to be quiet until I had finished. It turned out to be General Tony (McAuliffe). If I hadn't gotten the message through, I guess my tail would have been mud. The general understood and thanked me.[109]

109. From a diary Sgt. Gerald Zimmerman kept during the Holland campaign.

SEVENTEEN

Send Us Some Tanks!

In response to the urgent radio message sent by Sgt. Gerald Zimmerman, with Brigadier General McAuliffe looking over his shoulder, the British commanders up in Nijmegen responded by sending a brigade of tanks to help the paratroopers open the road link between Veghel and Uden. It would be some time before the armored vehicles arrived. In the meantime, the war went on.

The 2nd Battalion of the 506th was pushing north from Veghel hoping to link up with the tank force coming south. The 2nd Battalion of the 501st continued its battle in the southeast section of the town with the bulk of its force facing the enemy as it continued to exploit its Erp bridgehead. The 326th Engineers were in position facing the enemy moving along the Willems-Vaart Canal from the direction of Keldonk. To the north, a small band of "D" Company men were separated from the 2nd Battalion of the 501st facing the prospective onslaught of a company-sized force supported by two tanks. Troopers of the 327th were spread out around the railroad station covering the approaches from the north. Others were in position along the railroad tracks extending from the railroad bridge over the canal to the railroad bridge over the Aa River. Other 327th troops faced the enemy to the northwest of the canal highway bridge on the southwest side of the village.

The entry for the 506th Unit After-Action Report for the twenty-third has this brief account of the day's fighting for its troops:

D + 6—Soon after dawn the enemy launched small scale attacks against the defensive positions southeast of Veghel. These were held off without difficulty. During the night plans were drawn up which called for a British armored brigade, recalled from the Nijmegen area, to advance on Veghel from Uden, join forces with the 2nd Battalion of the 506th, which was to advance from Veghel toward Uden, and clear the road in order that the flow of traffic might be resumed. Following that, the armored brigade was to swing sharply south and cut off the enemy escape route through Erp.

Plans drawn up during the night called for "F" Company to lead in the attack to open the road to the north at daybreak. Sgt. Russell Schwenk was the squad leader in 3rd Platoon of "Fox" Company. He remembered that platoon leader 1Lt. Raymond Schmitz came back all shook up from the battalion officers' meeting in which attack plans for the twenty-third were issued to the companies. Schwenk wrote: "Our platoon leader was very visibly shaken and practically shell-shocked. What we learned from him we got by questioning. 3rd Platoon was to lead the attack—right smack into the Germans and their tanks. These orders, as everyone knew (someone was about to go), were Lt. Schmitz' warrant. The road on which we were to move was strewn with wreckage from a British convoy which the Jerries had smashed the day before. The trucks were still burning."

To the rear and left of 3rd Platoon was Sgt. John H. Taylor with his 2nd Platoon. They had listened to the German vehicular movement to their front all night long. His men knew they were in for heavy fighting in the morning.

"Sure enough, about two hours before daylight, they shelled us pretty good. They came in with those half-tracks and we didn't have a very good position and we couldn't see as daylight hadn't broken. We had an open spot. Lt. Hall, Haney and myself were behind a little rise and had tried to move the machine gun there when the half-tracks initially came out. I noticed Lt. Hall was sort of up on his knees and all of a sudden that half-track opened up and it caught Hall on the left side of the body and spun him around like a top. I hollered at him, 'Is it bad?' He was hurting but thought he could make it back to a ditch back where he could have some cover to get to an aid station. He started crawling across an open spot and was moving real good the last time I turned and looked at him. About the same time Frank Griffin was wounded in the arm—Joe Hogenmiller was wounded. They had to cross an open spot to get some cover and things got pretty bad for a while. I think most of the attack that morning was concentrated on our side of the road."

The Germans were making their move before daylight in the

area to 2nd Platoon's front. In the meantime, 3rd Platoon was to begin its drive north. Sgt. Russell Schwenk described the move. "We started the attack, 3rd Platoon on the road to Uden or until we were stopped. 1st squad on the right, 2nd squad on the left, scouts on the flanks, 3rd and mortar squads following in reserve. After moving only a hundred yards, a big BANG!, totally unexpected. One of the burning trucks had exploded. It was loaded with ammo—HD stuff—Wow! Everyone who was able, back-pedaled as the stuff continued to explode. After the explosions had ceased, the truck was still smoking. We proceeded to the area of the explosion and found Lt. Schmitz and radioman Pvt. Carl Pein, both dead, victims of concussion as they had been closest to the truck when it blew up.

"I was leading on the right, crawling along side of the road in a ditch. Sgt. Charles H. Reese was doing the same on the left side. The Jerries, noting the explosion and the confusion, thought this would be a good time to attack. I couldn't believe my eyes. Three Tiger tanks came rolling down the road toward us—all guns blazing. 88 shells exploded off the road. Smaller turret guns swinging and firing continuously. This was not a good place to be. We had some cover as the roadside ditches were about two feet deep. We sat tight and watched. I pulled a grenade from my belt and was preparing to lay it in the treads of the first tank as it passed. There was a .57mm anti-tank gun back aways. Why hadn't he fired? Just then the gun did fire and nailed the tank pretty good, spun him to the left, away from me and toward Sgt. Reese. At the time the tank was almost between us. I could count the bolts on the tread. A quick look to the rear and I noticed the other two tanks had turned back—they had no infantry with them. The disabled tank turned into a field for 30 yards and began to burn. The men who tried to crawl out of the turret were easy targets for our guys. Scratch one Tiger and crew. Shortly after that I found Sgt. Reese, seriously injured, shot through the lung. End of the war for him."

"B" Battery of the 81st Anti-Tank Battalion had come upon the scene of a tank attack the day before like a fire brigade. They had quickly put out the fire of one tank. It is most likely that they were there to take care of the tank right in front of Sgt. Russell Schwenk as "B" Battery was attached to the 506th Regiment at the time. Capt. "Fonse" Gueymard, its commander, wrote: "The following morning the Germans attacked with tanks and infantry and we knocked out another Mark V and two armored vehicles."

Sgt. Russell Schwenk continued his account: "Again, there was a lull in battle and 3rd Platoon withdrew. 2nd Platoon then advanced as far as they could on the left of the road. 1st Platoon was doing the same on the right. Shortly thereafter, my squad was sent further to the left to the flank of 2nd Platoon. After the squad was positioned, I returned to the rear area for more info and machine gun ammo. I used a covered drainage ditch for the ammo trip. However, on return I decided to be brave, also was curious. I took a short cut across an open field directly behind the 2nd Platoon position. Field was about 100 yards across. Secured ammo and other equipment and made the trip at double time. I had barely reached the safety of the ditch when three mortar rounds bracketed the field I had just crossed. I warned my squad of the danger but didn't get the information to 2nd Platoon. Bad failure on my part."

Sgt. John Taylor continued his story: "Orel Lev went into the upstairs of a house where he had a better view of the half-tracks. He was able to stop them and was later awarded the DSC, posthumously, for his actions."

The citation for PFC Orel Lev's heroism revealed that his platoon was protecting the left flank of the defense when the enemy attacked that flank with three half-tracks, one Mark IV tank and infantry troops. The platoon was forced to withdraw after suffering heavy casualties, but Lev elected to remain and cover the withdrawal of the platoon. Although exposed to heavy enemy fire, he fired his rocket launcher at the leading half-track and killed four of the enemy. At this time, the fire from the tank became a very serious threat to the withdrawing platoon since its fire was being directed by the commander from an open turret. Realizing this, Lev killed the tank commander and halted the advance of the tank.[110]

"We had quite a time there," continued Sergeant Taylor. "The situation went on for quite a while and we finally stabilized again and found that Lt. Hall had been hit by a mortar shell and was dead and we had lost quite a few people."

110. General Orders 11, Headquarters, 18th Airborne Corps, December 9, 1944. Posthumous award of DSC to PFC Orel H. Lev.

"All the company commanders of the 2nd Battalion notified their radiomen with orders for their platoon leaders to set up their line of defense in their assigned areas, facing the north toward Uden," wrote Cpl. Joe Hogenmiller. "I relayed the message to Lt. (Russell) Hall, platoon leader, and Lt. Hall sent his machine gunners across an open field several hundred yards beyond an old barn to set up positions. Leaving his platoon on built-up lines, keeping machine gunners covered with fire, Lt. Hall, with me as radioman and along with Sgt. (Frank) Griffin, mortar squad leader, all moved to the old barn, setting up a command post to observe the front attack by the Germans and their movement toward our lines.

"A short time after we reached the old barn, I received orders from the company commander for Lt. Hall to pull his advance machine gunners back to the main line and to move the CP to the main line.

"I passed this information to Lt. Hall; then, in turn, Lt. Hall called in his machine gunners and sent Sgt. Griffin to the rear, crossing an open field, then sending me next.

"The machine gunners were overrun by the Germans. Sgt. Griffin was seriously wounded in the arm but continued to the rear without stopping. I was hit in the calf of the left leg by a .30 caliber bullet when I was half way across the field. I continued to run the stretch to the main line without stopping. Lt. Hall was killed at the old barn in Veghel."

After the fighting subsided, it was time to count the losses. Sergeant Taylor continued his narrative. "After we got organized we settled down. That morning 2nd Platoon had suffered 16 men killed and wounded. You could see in one 24-hour period that we had as many casualties as we had in all of Normandy.

"We got some British tanks that were back in town to back us up and we got things pretty well covered. I was the only sergeant left in the platoon. We didn't have a platoon leader. There was only a little enemy fire occasionally. I decided I'd better get over to the company CP and find out what the situation was going to be since I had the platoon at the time.

"You can hear a mortar shell when there isn't any noise. Just before it hits, you hear a little flutter—so I heard a little flutter and went head first prone into the mud in the bottom of the ditch and I heard something chug. I looked over my shoulder after lying there a few seconds and could see the fin of a heavy mortar shell sticking up in the mud behind me. Well I know that miracles do happen—why that shell never went off I'll never know. It was within five feet of my feet. I didn't linger around and got out and over to where Lt. McFadden was and he could determine what could be worked out.

"We had a new officer come in just before the Holland trip, 1Lt. Edward G. Thomas. It wasn't long before Lt. Thomas came over and said he was going to take over the platoon. He proved to be a very good combat leader.

"It was now about 3 o'clock that afternoon. We got word to move out. We went straight up the highway. We didn't meet anything. We went up a few miles and took a road to the right and I was moving along a ditch—wasn't very deep, waist high bushes and we were moving through an orchard area. We spotted a German half-track out there several hundred yards. We were going around in the hope of cutting that dude off and about this time I was looking up to locate the half-track from my new position when all of a sudden I stepped over a bush and an enemy officer raised up right in front of me. He touched my rifle and it went to the side and I was eyeball to eyeball with this dude. He was hollering 'Kamerad, Kamerad, Kamerad!'

"I just grabbed him, hollered, and shoved him up on the road. I didn't even get a chance to search him. I could have gotten a good Luger and a watch from him. I had to swing out and get to where I had a good view of the half-track and that son-of-a-gun took off like a scared ape. It was gone cause they spotted us. We checked out that area and didn't run into any small arms fire."

The Germans to the front of "F" Company had just melted away.

"D" Company was in on the action, too. Sgt. Louis Truax remembers losing a close buddy during the corridor fighting of the twenty-third. "Cpl. Jack Mattz was a native American Indian from Crescent City, California. Moving house to house up toward Uden we were fired on by a Kraut tank just south of Veghel. Mattz and I and several others spotted the tank, and with a bazooka we welded the turret to the tank. He backed off with only his machine gun going. We then started through Veghel. The Krauts started walking 88 shells down the street behind us. They came closer and closer until one hit immediately behind me. The shell threw me up against a British M-8 armored car. I got a pencil-sized piece of shrapnel in one leg. I believe the same shell blew Jack Mattz to the great beyond. I never saw him again."

Sgt. Jack MacLean must have been hit by the same shell. He wrote: "We got up into Veghel and the Germans started bombarding the town with real heavy stuff. Something big came in and blew up the building I was standing next to. When I became aware of my surroundings, I was lying in the middle of the street. I crawled under a knocked out half-track where I was bleeding from my wounds. Sgt. Jack Sandridge of "D" company came along and patched me up. I asked about my buddy, Jack Mattz. Jack said, 'Sorry, Mattz has had it!' "

The hero of the tank/anti-tank gun encounter of the day before, Cpl. Rogie Roberts of "B" Battery, wasn't in a position to work the gun when there were plenty of targets on the twenty-third. Nursing a badly swollen knee (broken kneecap) suffered when the 57mm anti-tank gun had recoiled when he had fired at the German tank, Roberts found that he couldn't dig a foxhole for the night because of the painful knee injury. His buddy, Pvt. Dan Freda, offered to share his hole. Roberts had taken him up on the offer. The platoon CP was in a small house near the southern end of Veghel. Roberts recalled: "I slept well that night. I was so tired. Still couldn't walk well in the morning. I called back to Captain Gueymard and he said I should be evacuated back to battalion to have someone look at my leg. I left the backyard and went down the driveway and got to the front of the house. I heard an explosion in the back yard. I couldn't imagine what it was. It was too painful for me to go back. I had taken perhaps ten steps when Sgt. Ray Rathbun caught up with me. He was bleeding from the face. 'What happened to you? I just left!' He said there was a direct hit on Freda's foxhole. I had again escaped by the skin of my teeth. Pvt. Freda had been killed."

501st Continues to Hold

Most of Company "D" was on line facing toward Erp as day broke on the twenty-third. During the past several days they had moved about meeting enemy penetrations as they developed on the east side of Veghel from the direction of Erp.

Cpl. Jack Hampton was in his foxhole wondering how he was going to respond to the tank approaching his position. "I remember the tank was about 100 yards from my position and moving in. We had been issued a British type (Gammon) grenade, a soft pliable substance wrapped in a black cloth with a drawstring. As the tank moved closer I thought to myself what am I supposed to do with the plastic stuff. I didn't know how to use it."

During the night, Pvt. Bobby G. Hunter and two buddies had been sent out on outpost in front of the lines, which were situated at the northeast corner of the Veghel–Erp road. Hunter describes the experience: "We dug a hole big enough for the three of us which was about 18 inches deep. It was deep enough to get below the surface but absolutely no protection against tanks. Each would guard an hour while the other two slept. I was asleep when early in the morning (you could see but it wasn't full daylight), Finch wakened me and said, 'God damn man, there's a tank coming straight at us.' We protested, but I took a peek. Finch said, in a warning tone, 'Don't let him see you!' I remember easing back down in the hole and looking at both of them for a few seconds and then I asked, 'Now, what in hell are we going to do?' No answers. The tank was firing its cannon and machine gun and coming on slowly, seemed not to be in a hurry.

"I don't remember being particularly scared nor did Finch and Schmidt. My mind was working as well as ever and we talked in normal tones. The only solution any of us could come up with was to wait until it was close enough to use our Gammon grenades and try to damage its tracks. I figured our chance of doing this was slim at best. If you kept your head down you knew you couldn't run as we were about a hundred yards in front of the MLR and about an equal distance from the drainage ditch. The field was flat with absolutely no cover. The machine gun on the tank would have cut us down before we had run thirty yards. We stayed.

"When the tank was about 40 to 50 yards from our hole it was knocked out by Jack Rider, a cook. After the loss of their tank the Germans soon withdrew and we made it back to the MLR."

Cpl. Jack Hampton also heaved a sigh of relief. He added, "Someone fired a bazooka that blasted the tank right through the turret. That stopped the German attack. Rumor spread that it was one of the company cooks who fired the shot. Needless to say, our opinion and respect for this particular group immediately elevated to the highest degree."

Other members of "D" Company as well as the other companies of 2nd Battalion were heavily embroiled in the same vicinity.

The journal kept by Cpl. Bruce M. Beyer showed the heavy casualties being inflicted on the paratroopers on the twenty-third:

> Quiet during the night. Lt. Ed Brash wounded. Lts. Volango and Frase (E Co.) KIA along with Sgt. Joyner and Sgt. Chorzempa. Captain Norwood (A/326 Eng) KIA. Medics Boss and Furtak KIA. Casualties medium to heavy.
>
> Heavy firing from Germans to southeast all day, resulting in a number of casualties. Church and hospital have been hit frequently by artillery fire. Garrity and Foster KIA. Several German concentrations landed near CP. Owner of house KIA by shrapnel. Battery of British artillery has been returning German fire. They are located near CP. T/5 Jack R. Rider got a German tank with a bazooka this A.M.

Several days had gone by during which S/Sgt. Edward Jurecko and his platoon were involved in bitter fighting. He didn't have time to jot down his notes. Though the action was still hot and furious, he did find time to transcribe his observations of the actions as they unfolded on the twenty-third:

> It's been four days now since I last had a chance to write. We have been battling furiously. The Germans have been doing their utmost to cut off the British supply lines. Our mission is to keep it open. My men are getting little sleep and very little food. Last night, myself and the 1st squad of my platoon were caught in the middle of an open field. Lt. Brash and Pvt. Jerrytone were wounded and Pvt. George Smith was killed. It is raining now (1300 hours). We have just been attacked by the enemy. Two of our tanks have been knocked out. The enemy lost one. The enemy's artillery and mortar barrage has been terrific. Casualties in the company have been high. I just lost Sgt. Choate, KIA by artillery fire. Pvt. Bryan wounded. . . .

While the heavy mortar and artillery barrages were wreaking havoc on 2nd Battalion and "D" Company in particular, Cpl. Sam R. Pope was busy maintaining communications between the two units. He wrote: "When the enemy attacked 'D' Company and our telephone line went out, I took off to repair it and found that it had been cut by shell fire about 100 yards from the

'D' Company CP. Instead of trying to patch it, I tied on to a reel of wire and ran a new line over to the CP. As I was tying on to the company phone, a mortar round came in. I ducked down in the foxhole I was in. These holes must have been dug by the Germans as I never saw such well-dug holes by our folks. As I raised up I said something to the trooper next to me—one of my replacements—and when he failed to respond I looked his way and saw that the mortar round had killed him.

"I went back to our company area and as I approached it I found Ted Steets sitting on a stump with his chin cupped in both hands. He was obviously depressed and as I tried to cheer him up he said that he felt his time had come."

Pvt. William J. Houston was one of the "D" Company men who was shunted around from one trouble spot to another. After he had been wounded on the twenty-second, at the same time Pvt. George Kos was killed, he had gone to the aid station to be patched up. From there he was directed to the railroad bridge over the canal. He wrote: "I was put on outpost with someone else. It was raining that night and I did something that night I didn't normally do. I went to sleep standing up. I awoke in time to catch my rifle. Then it seemed every bush across the little road was moving. I awakened the other trooper who was with me and told him I was going to throw a grenade. Afterward, I told him to cover me and I went across the road to see what had fallen. (Nothing!) Boy, did I start something that night. Grenades—grenades. They were going off to my right and left. We had seen some Germans in the vicinity the evening before. When in doubt, throw a grenade."

In his diary entry for September 23, Cpl. Charles Ritzler refers to the grenade tossing that occurred in the early morning of the big attack on the railroad bridge position over the Willems-Vaart Canal:

Awake nearly all night. Men continually throwing grenades at any little sound. We loaded machine gun belts with the stray bullets we could find. Estimated 300 Germans at our front. We had 15. Could get no relief as every man was needed at the main bridge. They attacked at dawn and we had duck shooting and mowed them down. Machine gun got down to half a box of ammo and Miller and Schneider were shooting at men with carbines instead of using the

MG. Fired my Tommy gun occasionally so as to give the effects of a machine gun. Glad I carried a lot of ammo. One more attack was beaten off and more than 20 prisoners came in—mostly wounded. Glider boys finally swept across our front and cleared our area. 40 dead were counted. It was good work. Gliders then took over the bridge. I could get no info on our company or even the regiment, last reported trying to stave off another attack from NE of town. So we just hung around the bridge the rest of the day and cleaned our weapons. Found an empty house and all three of us went to sleep on the floor. Gliders had plenty of men at the bridge.[111]

Farther to the southwest, along the Willems-Vaart Canal, a road parallels the canal. Men of "A" Company of the 326th Engineers had earlier helped construct a second bridge over the canal adjacent to the original highway bridge. They had blown the bridge over the canal near Keldonk on the twenty-second, thus preventing enemy armor from using that route for its attack on the key bridges at Veghel.

A call had come to the engineers from 2nd Battalion of the 501st for mines. First Lieutenant Ralph D. Pickens wrote: "I was assigned to one of the combat teams and had delivered our hasty mine field to the combat team commander. The battle situation was very fluid and he decided not to employ the mines—ordering me to find a safe place in the southern end of town to store them until he determined whether or not to use them. Captain Tom Norwood, on foot, hailed me down in my jeep and ordered me to return to engineer headquarters and deliver his request for anti-tank mines. I left to do so and could hear enemy tanks approaching. Later, I was informed that Captain Norwood had been killed by one of these very tanks."

The utilization of anti-tank mines was important to the 326th Engineer Battalion inasmuch as strong artillery support had not yet materialized from the divisions' artillery battalions. It may be that T/5 Robert G. Salley was carrying out Captain Norwood's request for mines, which had been forwarded to engineer headquarters. Salley wrote: "Captain Nancarrow and I took a load of mines to Captain Norwood at Veghel but he was killed moments before we arrived."

111. Pvt. Robert W. Miller and PFC Clyde Schneider were decorated with the Silver Star, and Cpl. Charles Ritzler was presented with the British Military Medal by Field Marshal Sir Bernard Montgomery for his efforts.

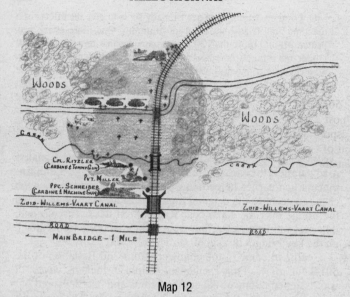

Map 12

"Schneider had a good hole right by the railroad. Miller and I covered the creek to his front. Machine gun covered all the railroad to the house at the bend. Crosses are where we found dead Germans."

The *Statistical History of the 326th Engineer Battalion* indicates its men were heavily involved in the actions of the twenty-third:

> A squad of 3rd Platoon of "A" Company placed and covered a road block on the road by the canal, one and a half miles southeast of the bridge. This bridge was attacked by two enemy tanks and supporting infantry about 1430 hours. During this action Captain Thomas Norwood was seriously wounded and later died as the result.

Two members of the Dutch underground were involved in actions in the same area with the engineers on the twenty-third. Tonny Kuyper and Nellie Wijnen were asked to retrieve an abandoned enemy motorcycle between the lines as they reconnoitered enemy positions in the Keldonk area near the canal. On the twenty-second Kuyper had pedaled his bike to the area of the canal bridge at Keldonk to determine the presence of enemy soldiers in the area. He had observed them in positions on the north side of the blown bridge. The following day Kuyper and Wijnen repeated the trek of approximately two and a half miles. They noted the enemy had advanced a considerable distance to the northwest along the canal bank. The job assigned to them was to pinpoint the enemy positions. They had also noted the abandoned motorcycle on its side. Kuyper wrote: "Since the Americans needed transportation badly, they asked if we could bring the motorcycle back to their position. We were more than happy to help any way we could. When we reached the motorcycle, I put it on its wheels and tried to start it. All of a sudden the machine guns began to chatter. I dropped the cycle and took cover in a roadside ditch. Nellie did the same diving for the ditch on the other side of the road."

The two Dutch fighters were across the road from each other and, after a short time, Wijnen began calling out. She had been hit by one of the machine-gun bullets, which had pierced her ankle. When the firing eased up, Kuyper rushed to the other side of the road where he applied a tourniquet. After that they began to crawl along the ditch toward Veghel. It was a difficult and painful time for Wijnen. After they had moved a hundred yards toward the American positions, the paratroopers began to provide covering mortar fire, which forced the enemy to hold their fire and retreat. An American medic worked his way down the ditch and provided more adequate treatment. Then several of the soldiers rushed forward and carried her to the highway bridge at Veghel. The motorcycle was not retrieved for the Americans.

"Black Friday" (the twenty-second) had been a terrible day for the medical personnel, nuns, and wounded at the hospital converted from the convent in Veghel. First Lieutenant Robert Radmann looked over their means of transport. "The next morning the shelling stopped. We discovered our only means of company transportation, our jeep, had been hit and was a smoldering wreck. At the entrance of the convent a dud mortar shell was lying and, if it had exploded, would surely have killed many of our patients and members of our company. By noon that day, Veghel had been secured and the road to Nijmegen was open."

Not quite that early. The log written by Cpl. Bruce Beyer has a later time sequence.

Heavy German attack beaten off about 1600. German withdrawal? Advance elements of CP moved out about 1800 to SE. We took the initiative in attack along with about ten English Sherman tanks and elements of the 506th. Occupied positions Germans had withdrawn from. Evidence of German Tiger tanks. Several prisoners taken. 1830 hours—this battalion in reserve. Place taken in line by 2nd Battalion of 506th. Returned to CP.

Wire section (Sgt. Page) has been doing good work under adverse conditions of keeping lines open. 2030—situation quiet.

During the afternoon elements of the British armored brigade, which had proceeded south from the Uden area, joined forces with the troops of the 2nd Battalion of the 506th. The enemy forces caught in between had made a hasty withdrawal toward Erp. The linkup had occurred at 1700 hours; shortly thereafter, contact with the German forces was lost.

As the battle swirled about them, two members of 2nd Battalion of the 501st still had time to note in diaries or logs the passage of another huge armada of planes and gliders on the twenty-third.

In the log he kept for 2nd Battalion Headquarters Company, Cpl. Bruce Beyer noted:

A skytrain of at least a thousand C-47s towing gliders came over SW to NE of town about 1700. Also Sterling bombers bring supplies. Overhead cover by Thunderbolts. C-47s passed over flak areas. Several C-47s shot down. Supplies being dropped in No-Man's Land.

In his diary entry, S/Sgt. Edward Jurecko expressed admiration for the courage of the C-47 pilots:

(1615 hours)—Thousands of transports and gliders are now passing overhead. As I watched from my foxhole, I saw transports being shot down out of the sky. They didn't stand a chance. Flak is heavy in this area. Those boys have a lot of guts to fly those big, slow-moving planes over here. We are thankful for the supplies they are bringing.

A notation in the *Tactical Operations of the 101st Airborne Division* describes the arrival of the remainder of the gliderborne elements of the 101st Division:[112]

112. Higgins, BG Gerald J. *Tactical Operations of the 101st Airborne Division, Annex No. 4,* September 23, 1944.

During the day a 4th glider serial arrived bringing remaining elements of the 327th Glider Infantry and the 907th Glider Field Artillery Battalion. These troops were immediately moved to the Veghel area, and the 907th Field Artillery Battalion was placed in direct support of the 501st Parachute Infantry. The 321st Glider Field Artillery Battalion was attached to the 506th Parachute Infantry and fired several missions during the day.

The last glider serial arrived on the afternoon of the twenty-third. It brought in the remaining elements of the 327th, which had failed to arrive in Holland on the nineteenth. The 907th Glider Field Artillery Battalion had been the most handicapped of all the divisional units, as only 24 men of the battalion of more than 550 had arrived on the landing zone on the nineteenth. The 501st Regiment was the infantry group they normally supported. These troops were moved immediately to the Veghel area upon arrival. The battalion staff and the battery commanders and the advance parties moved forward on reconnaissance of the area. At 2100 the entire battalion moved into an advance bivouac area from which they would move in support of the 501st the following morning.

The glider in which PFC Luther Barrick arrived on the afternoon of the twenty-third also carried a trooper who was extremely upset during the entire ride. He had been on the earlier aborted mission, and the second experience seemed worse than the first. Barrick wrote: "There was a young trooper on board who kept repeating the same words over and over again, 'It's hell—boys—I'm telling you it's hell' all the way and sweat ran off his brow like rain. He was really scared. When we landed we got our 105mm howitzer out of the glider with the help of the Dutch. We moved to our assembly area and then on to our location. Shortly, we had the gun dug in. PFC Mike Coladonato and I were sent to 'B' Battery to help out. They only had 67 men accounted for out of 135. We were sent to the number 3 gun with Sgt. Jack Bumgardner's crew."

Cpl. Ray Hollenbeck remembered that the civilians were a big help on the ground: "They assisted us in unloading and provided directions as to where we should go. We had problems getting enough vehicles for the 105s and trailers."

Much of "B" Battery had landed far behind enemy lines. Some were in the Boxtel area. Others were at Den Dungen and s'Hertogenbosch. Very few would reach the battalion positions in time to offer assistance in the battles to be fought around Eerde and Veghel.

With the guns in position south of the highway and not far west of the highway bridge over the canal, the 907th would be ready to support the 501st in its battle around Eerde on the twenty-fourth.

EIGHTEEN

Third Road Cut

Reconnaissance in the direction of Erp shortly after dawn on September 24 indicated the enemy had made good his escape to the southeast. The area along the highway between Veghel and Uden was clear of enemy troops. The 506th Parachute Infantry Regiment along with its support units, the 321st Glider Field Artillery Battalion and "B" Battery of the 81st Anti-Tank Battalion, was ordered to Uden to take over the defense of that area.

The 327th Glider Infantry Regiment was assigned the task of defending Veghel. To 2nd Battalion went the assignment of providing cover eastward to Erp.

With no enemy activity noted between the two towns, 1Lt. Thomas J. Niland, S-2 leader for 2nd Battalion of the 327th, had looked forward to a breather at Erp. He wrote: "On September 24th I remember going to the village of Erp and thought that I was going to be in a very secure, lovely position of running a small Dutch village. It seemed like a pleasant place. The people were glad to be rid of the German forces. The remaining enemies did not put up much resistance and withdrew upon our arrival. I had already started to set up the town for the battalion commander and was going to start interrogating some of the people to see if there had been any collaborators in the area. We would be living in houses and having a few of the comforts of life; however, the British arrived within the hour and we returned to the battle."

The 907th Glider Field Artillery Battalion, with its heavier snub-nosed 105mm howitzers, had arrived on the afternoon of the twenty-third. In combat situations they usually supported the 501st. The commander of the 907th, LTC Clarence Nelson, was in Veghel conferring with Col. Howard Johnson to coordinate attack plans. The forward observers arrived in Eerde to be in position to spot for the howitzers situated some four hundred yards west and south of the highway bridge over the Willems-Vaart Canal.

With the 327th taking over their former battle areas, 2nd Battalion of the 501st Parachute Infantry Regiment was released from its defensive assignments in Veghel and moved to join the 501st Regiment in its continuing battle in and around Eerde.

Shelling at the Railroad Bridge

The log kept by Cpl. Bruce M. Beyer describes the roundabout move by 2nd Battalion to cross the railroad bridge in its move toward Eerde, where it was to go into regimental reserve.

> September 24, Sunday—One week since drop. Fairly quiet during the night. Some artillery fire received. Report that German guns have moved into position in the east.
>
> Evacuated KIAs (Lts. Frase and Volango, Kos, Smith, Sgt. Choate of "D" Company, T/5 Foster), Schnoor, Goshorn, Henigman, Noyes wounded yesterday. Battalion alerted for move 1100. Moved out through town to NE about 1230. Moved along road other side of town leading to railroad bridge across the canal. Received artillery fire from east. Advance elements of CP halted, took cover in ditch. 1320 several concentrations received in tree bursts above us wounding Aguilar in the wrist and leg, Sgt. Holden in legs and back, myself in right calf and thigh, Sgt. Mero severely wounded in right shoulder, arm and stomach. Medical aid rendered by medics Shurg and Tuel—helped by Baynes and Ghiardi. Lay in ditch as four more concentrations received. No further injuries sustained by group. Capt. Rhett approached group 1400 through ditch perpendicular to ours. Informed us CP set up 100 yards to the rear. Holden and I crawled back through ditch. Sgt. Lewis evacuated us to medical company in Veghel at 1500. Tetanus shot received. Sulfanilimide sprinkled in wound and dressed.

The Holland campaign ended for Cpl. Bruce Beyer; no further notations appeared in the battalion log for this period.

Another 2nd Battalion soldier weathered the same shelling. Communications corporal Sam Pope was in on the move at about the same time. He wrote: "I remember the day 2nd Battalion went along the railroad toward Eerde. We came under fire from somewhere by 88mm artillery. As we marched along the railroad, Ted Steets was next in line behind me. We turned left onto a road (or lane) between rows of cottonwood trees. About a hundred yards up the road several shells exploded. A tree burst directly over me sent shrapnel that chewed up the tail of my jacket and one piece punctured my canteen and cut a gash in my right buttock—just a flesh wound but the water running down my leg from the canteen made me think I was bleeding badly. The fact it was cold water as opposed to hot blood did not register.

"From there I proceeded another hundred yards or so and more shell fire came in so I piled into the roadside ditch with several other guys but the 88s came in landing on the road just a few feet from us and I don't know how many guys got hit. I received two minute pieces of shrapnel that jarred as if someone was hitting me with a pick handle.

"I know that T/4 Joe E. Mero was hit there. He was trying to locate the enemy through a pair of binoculars when those shells began coming in. I don't know if he was killed outright or died later. (Mero succumbed to his wounds on October 6.)

"I learned later that Ted Steets never moved from the place where my canteen was punctured. Someone said he got a direct hit. Earlier, while we were on the railroad bridge, Cpl. Buster E. Williams was killed.

"About the time the 88 barrage ended, I looked up and saw Captain Edmund Rhett going by so I got on the road and followed him to our CP where I was told we would not need wire put in that night. I really don't know who was responsible for that but it very likely saved me from becoming a victim of what some folks call battle fatigue. I was really shook up—about as close as I suppose a man can be without cracking up. The respite from duty saved me. The next day I was able to carry on."

Second Battalion sergeant major S/Sgt. John L. Ghiardi remembered the terrible shelling the battalion underwent as it moved toward Eerde by way of the railroad bridge. "We were being led by Major Raymond Bottomly along the road hedged by trees on both sides in the direction of Eerde. I ended the day slightly shell-shocked. Steets was killed instantly and Mero, seriously wounded, died some days later. I just got away with a few shrapnel scratches, largely because I crawled about 30 to 40 yards into the open field, away from the direction from which the shells were coming."

Company "D" was caught in the same barrage. Pvt. Bobby G. Hunter described the move toward Eerde: "As we started this maneuver, some of the guys were caught on the road and under trees. John Marnye and Francis McKeown were killed instantly. Wayne McClung died on the way to the aid station. Schmitt and Louis Kill were also wounded."

Two soldiers from Division Artillery units witnessed the enemy 88 and small-arms fire being directed at the 501st units that were on the move to Eerde.

Cpl. James L. Evans had moved up to Veghel along with the advance elements of Division Headquarters. With his wire communications group, he was to help coordinate the liaison between the artillery units and the infantry. PFC John P. Oyach was serving as radioman for the 907th commander, LTC Clarence Nelson. Oyach was in Veghel with Nelson, who was conferring with Colonel Johnson.

In a heavy action at the western end of Veghel, Cpl. James Evans recalled, "I was a wire corporal as the attack developed. I was in the building at the 'Kingfish' switchboard alongside the spur canal leading into town. At first we barricaded the windows and prepared to defend. The switchboard operator told me my 907th line was cut so I took my test phone and walked the line down the right side of the spur canal to its intersection with the main canal. A concrete bridge over the spur was being hit many times with rifle and machine gun fire and ricochets from where the Germans were firing at the troops and trying to stop some Americans from crossing the canal on the railroad bridge with the high overhead steel support structures.

"I was crouched by a concrete post on the bridge corner waiting for an opportunity to cross when suddenly all shooting stopped. To my amazement, two or three Americans marched onto the railroad bridge with a large Red Cross flag. They got all the wounded off the bridge and took them back. As soon as they were off, more Americans charged across the bridge and all hell broke loose again. Then I realized I should have crossed my bridge but I knew I had witnessed one of the best scenes of my war experience."

LTC Clarence Nelson, with his driver PFC Walter Litwak and radioman PFC John Oyach, were in Eerde during the barrage. Oyach recalled: "The Germans threw some heavy artillery on us. I was positioned on a roof top by an infantry officer to spot for Heinies coming up the canal. I considered myself very lucky. I had been standing beside a chimney and then moved to get a better view of the canal. A German artillery shell blew the chimney to bits. I could have been a goner in my original position."

Highway Cut Third Time

During the morning of the twenty-fourth, the enemy hammered at the positions of the 1st and 3rd Battalions of the 501st in the Eerde area. Unable to break through in that area, a force of approximately two hundred Germans, supported by a self-propelled gun and two tanks, slipped past the west part of the sand dunes area down a secondary road, heading for Koevering.

The men of the 502nd had been kept apprised of the situation by members of the Dutch underground. Companies "D" and "H" were sent north to intercept the enemy. The German force moved quickly and was almost in Koevering when the 502nd men arrived.

In the meantime, Lt. John Sherry and Lt. Jack Williamson were up in their Piper Cub L-4 observation plane, spotting for the artillery supporting the 501st in Eerde. Not realizing the enemy was so close to the main highway, the pilot was making low sweeping passes over and along the highway when the plane was brought down by small-arms fire. Both artillery officers were killed in the crash.

In late afternoon, the enemy force found an open lane between the 501st and the 502nd just north of Koevering and cut the highway. Word got back quickly from both ends of the break.

The artillerymen of the 907th, positioned just south of the highway near the canal bridge, noticed that traffic had stopped. Convoys had ceased passing their positions. To the south, they noticed ominous black clouds of smoke.

At Division Headquarters at the Henkenshage castle, on the west side of St. Oedenrode, T/4 George E. Koskimaki was on duty at his SCR-300 radio beside the moat. He was operating in the G-2 Net for the division when an urgent call came through to stop all traffic, as the highway had been cut for the third time. The event was recorded in his diary for September 24:

Germans cut the St. Oedenrode–Veghel highway. Our SCR-300 radio is the only communication the cutoff troops have with the outside world tonight.

Koskimaki added, "I had a call earlier on the radio to cut off all northbound traffic in town because the German armor was blowing up the equipment of the British, who were stopped beside the road. I ran into the castle to inform headquarters. They called the MP post in town. The MPs stopped the traffic."

The firing batteries of the 907th Field Artillery Battalion were among the first to sense something was wrong. Hearing the gunfire and seeing the smoke clouds rising south of their positions, a quick call went to 501st headquarters where Lieutenant Colonel Nelson was conferring with the 501st regimental commander. Nelson ordered "B" Battery to defend the battalion positions while "A" Battery was to continue firing its mission.

Capt. Gerald McGlone, commander of "B" Battery, pulled his guns from their pits and placed them in position to fire directly down the road at any approaching enemy. A light machine gun and two of the heavier .50-caliber guns were taken down from their mounts on the trucks and placed in dug-in positions. The battalion's bazookas were brought forward and placed in strategic locations.

Remembering his experience from that night, PFC Luther Barrick wrote: "The night the Germans cut the road south of Veghel, our artillery was receiving rifle and machine gun fire. Because me and Mike Coladonato were always together, Sarge said, 'Mike, you and Barrick take grenades and a bazooka and your rifles and go along with the lieutenant.' We were placed out on the flank in front of our artillery pieces a few hundred yards to help protect the other men. Also, a few men were sent out on patrol to find how close the Germans were to our positions."

Cpl. Ray Hollenbeck and Pvt. Walter Lyszczarz were a bazooka team that day. Hollenbeck recalled: "We were about a hundred yards out in front of 'A' Battery. We chose a shallow ditch for our set up, then quietly waited for the enemy to appear. During our two hour posting, we heard the movement of tanks but never knew whether they were German or British."

It was already dark when Maj. William Pasley and Capt. Gerald McGlone had gone down the road for a personal reconnaissance. Along the way, they met the British brigadier general who commanded the tank unit that had been caught in the German breakthrough. The British officer explained where he had deployed his remaining tanks and troops to counter further moves by the enemy. The artillery officers were aware that a large number of vehicles had been caught in the melee with burning vehicles at both ends of the convoy. This prevented the trucks and support vehicles in the middle of the column from escaping, and the Germans could blow them up at their leisure without fear of them getting away. A total of forty vehicles were destroyed in a two-day period in that section of the highway.

Resupply Mission

The 501st Parachute Infantry Regiment had its hands full holding back the German troops that were moving toward the highway from the Schijndel area. To make matters worse, the truck bringing in the resupply of ammunition from Veghel had blown up near the "B" Company CP, killing eight or nine of the men present to unload the vehicle. (See page 269.)

Operations sergeant Chester Brooks had caught quite a bit of small shrapnel in his legs, near the church in Eerde, while eating during the day. It hadn't been very serious but it hampered his walking. He felt he would be able to perform a mission for which they asked for volunteers. Brooks wrote: "A request came in for someone to volunteer to drive a jeep and trailer to Veghel to get supplies as we were somewhat cut off by German tanks on the Veghel–Eindhoven road. I volunteered. Kenneth Merchant, my assistant for operations, volunteered to go with me. We kept off the main road as much as possible but finally had to go along it. There was a British tank burning right by our road junction and a German tank was not far off toward Eindhoven. It was dark or damp dusky night as we so often had in Holland. We drove toward Veghel and passed another British tank which wasn't firing and then on to the bridge entrance to Veghel. Troopers jumped up at us from all sides asking how we got there. I said we just came down the road and they said, 'That's impossible. There was a German tank here a few minutes ago!' I said, 'I know, we just drove past it.' That didn't convince them until someone recognized Merchant. We got our supplies and retraced our route. We weren't feeling very brave with clover-leafs of mortar ammo on the hood, boxes of machine gun ammo in the back seat and an assortment of ammo in the trailer. Merchant asked me how we were going to find our road, as it was really dark by then. I said we'd drive to that burning tank and turn right. The only trouble was the tank we came to that was burning was the one we'd passed that was not firing. You can imagine our anxiety when we continued on, thinking that German tank was waiting for us. Fortunately, he wasn't. We came to the other burning tank and found our way back to Battalion without further incident."

Fourteen-year-old Joseph Verstappen had been awakened from a sound sleep by rapping heard on a basement window of a house where four Dutch families had taken refuge for the night. He recalled the incident: "The night we had to get out of the house we found out later, from my cousins Jack and Pete Verstappen, that it was Germans who had knocked on the door and windows. They had taken Jack and Pete with them on a big truck. They wanted to go to Schijndel and they were drunk celebrating the victory over the 'Englanders'—that is what they called the British, when they broke through the corridor between St. Oedenrode and Veghel at Koevering. The Germans were so drunk they ran into a fallen tree and ordered the two boys to help them but they ran away. When the boys returned to the farmhouse, they found it was empty. The others had gone south."

The after-action report for Market-Garden provided by S/Sgt. Fred Patheiger provides a detailed description of the fighting on the twenty-fifth by units of the 502nd as they attacked northward with units of the British 50th Division from the St. Oedenrode area:

During the night, the enemy, who had gotten into position on the exposed right flank of the regiment, had dug in on either side of the road and had emplaced 88mm guns in concealed positions, with fields of fire down the highway. To open this, the only route of communication with the British army north of St. Oedenrode, one battalion, plus one company and ten tanks attached, attacked at dawn of the 25th. Almost immediately, four of the supporting tanks were knocked out by 88mm fire and the company accompanying the tanks were pinned down by small arms and fire from automatic weapons and artillery. Four more tanks were brought up to assist the advance, but were put out of action by enemy 88mm fire almost immediately upon getting into position. When the 88mm guns were

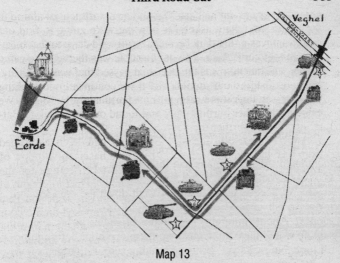

Map 13

Sergeant Brooks identifies the numbers on his map as follows: "I have marked the map along the only route that seems logical. The numbers 1, 2, 3, and 4 locate the following: (1) German tank. The British tank (2) was burning. I don't recall which side of the road the German tank was on but the British tank was on our side of the road. I hoped that the flames from the British tank, rather than light us up, would make it more difficult for the Germans to see us. I kept the British tank between us and the Germans. We were in the dark most of the time. The 2nd British tank (3) was down the road—we drove past it. It didn't fire while we were there. It had been knocked out by the time we came back. (4) is where we encountered the road block by the Veghel highway bridge and were challenged."

spotted, friendly troops were so close to them that it was unsafe to bring artillery fire upon them. One 57mm AT gun was brought up and laid on the 88mm gun which was in a position behind a hedgerow near the road. Several hits were made on the 88mm gun and it was put out of action. However, two other 88mm guns were bringing fire on both the troops who were advancing along the ditches on either side of the road and those through the fields. By doggedly pushing up the ditches which ran through the fields and on either side of the road, automatic and small arms fire was brought on these two guns and forced them to withdraw. In a fire fight that lasted until 1800 hours the evening of the 25th, the enemy was pushed back bit by bit and finally forced to withdraw to the north thereby clearing the road in the battalion sector. The enemy suffered severe casualties in this action and the many prisoners captured stated that it was their mission to cut the road and hold their positions at all costs.[113]

Recalling the action when the road was cut to the north of the 502nd positions around St. Oedenrode, Capt. Jim Hatch remembered: "The Germans had infantry and one or two 88mm guns at the outset. The 502nd was to attack the position at daybreak. We needed tank support. I went down the road looking for a British general officer who might provide us with tank support. About midnight, I located a brigadier in his van. He said he would have three tanks up there one hour before jump-off time. No tanks yet. I was up making sure we jumped off on time. Next thing the 88s started firing. I looked back and three British tanks drove out on the road and the 88s put them out of action before they fired a shot. The infantry finally moved the Germans out. I finally got the word on the tanks. They were replacements for the fighting up north. The drivers were ferrying them north and had no combat experience. I hope I never meet up with that brigadier general!"

Back to Veghel

There wasn't going to be much of a rest for the men of the 506th Regiment after they had been instrumental in reopening the Veghel-to-Uden segment of the highway. They had spent much of the afternoon of the twenty-fourth hiking up the highway to Uden to provide a defensive screen for that community. The 506th Unit After-Action Report for the twenty-fifth indicates a sudden change in the division planning:

At 0030 a Division liaison officer brought orders to Uden for the 506th PIR to move to Veghel to open the road south of Veghel where it had been cut again. The unit commanders received the order at 0130. The regiment was to pass the IP at 0345. Order of march:

113. Narrative of Market-Garden for 502nd Parachute Infantry Regiment.

3rd Bn., 1st Bn., Regt'l HQ and HQ Co., and 2nd Bn. The column arrived at Veghel at 0530 and waited for orders on the NE side of town.

Orders were received for an attack astride the Veghel–St. Oedenrode highway to the south. The attack jumped off at 0830 with 3rd Bn. leading, with one-half squadron of tanks attached and 1st Bn. following to the right rear. 2nd Bn. in reserve. At 1130 the 3rd Bn. was held up so the 1st Bn. was needed to protect the right flank of the regiment and was to make contact with the 501st PIR on the right. The 2nd Bn. with one-half squadron tanks attached were committed to make a wide flanking movement to the left. This attack progressed slowly because of many rumors of friendly forces in the 2nd Bn. area. Darkness came with 3rd Bn. and 1st Bn. on line facing south and 2nd Bn. facing west with contact between 2nd and 3rd Bns. Plans were made during the night for the 2nd and 3rd Bns. to make a coordinated attack in the morning.

Sgt. John Taylor and his 2nd Platoon had returned from their venture up a side road between Veghel and Erp in late afternoon on the twenty-fourth. They were looking forward to a well-earned rest. Taylor wrote: "We thought we'd move into an orchard there. We had drawn some rations and they'd got our bedrolls up to us. We pitched some pup tents in the orchard and thought we were going to get a few days' rest. We straightened out everything and boy, about two o'clock the next morning, word came—'Roll it up, we're moving out! Drop your bedrolls at the gate.'

"Golly, we hadn't even had a hot meal so we took off before daylight. The Germans had cut the road again, south of Veghel."

As a member of 3rd Battalion, the advance element in the march back to Veghel, 1Lt. Alex Andros recalled: "One of the big problems of the Holland campaign was keeping the road open. Seems like we were constantly busy marching up and down trying to keep it open. We had just arrived from Veghel and were ordered to march back to Veghel. The Germans had broken through and blockaded the road again. We marched all the way back—got there around 0500 in the morning. Dawn was just breaking and we were given an order to launch an attack along the road. We were on the right side going south. The Germans were set up in positions along the road.

"The landscape was very flat and the enemy had some good grazing fire set up and you couldn't move over the ground. That grazing fire was really low. The musette bag on my back had the top ripped off by machine gun fire. As I passed the mortar men, a round dinged off the barrel of the 60mm mortar tube and it was sticking out only a foot above the ground level. It was only up and down the ditches and it took us all day until we got to the point where we could do any good.

"One of our 3rd Battalion companies made a flanking move pretty late in the afternoon and I recall Sgt. Charles E. Richards' squad from the 3rd Platoon was right up front about fifty yards from the enemy positions along with Lt. Willie Miller. I crawled up to them and asked how they were doing. Richards said, 'The hell with this—we can't take this anymore. Let's get up and go!'

"He got up—that whole squad got up and they charged into the Germans. The enemy gave up. At that time, there were very few of them left. Apparently, during the day, most of them had pulled out and left a handful of guys. These few guys kept us at bay all that time. The troops we overran were German paratroopers. They were quite young."

Second Battalion was ordered to make a wide, flanking movement to the left and almost directly south along a secondary road that roughly paralleled the main highway. They were then to swing right and head west hoping to outflank the enemy roadblocks.

Sgt. John H. Taylor added to his story: "We went down the main road, swung left below Veghel and this took an all-day deal and we really hit the spot just before dark, and with the British coming up from the south to meet us we had to be careful not to shoot at our Allies. We cleared out our section of the road, moved across it and held there for the night."

When the 3rd Battalion was stopped by heavy mortar and artillery fire, 1st Battalion was ordered to swing right to protect the right flank and to make contact with the 501st on its right.

As a member of 1st Battalion Headquarters Company, PFC Giles N. Thurman was in on the attack south from Uden to Veghel. He wrote: "I remember the British convoy of trucks and tanks, bumper to bumper, getting knocked out and burning. I remember the attack we were in when a British tank, captured by the Germans, came through our lines and a German threw a potato masher grenade from it which killed 1Lt. Warren Frye. I was with him when he died."

"We were back on the road heading south through Veghel," wrote Pvt. Robert W. Wiatt, a "C" Company replacement for

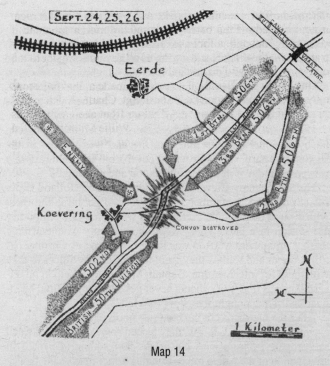

Map 14

the Holland mission. "The Germans had cut our one highway link. There had been heavy fighting. We got to an area where we were pinned down by German fire on the right side of the road. The fire was very heavy from machine guns and 20mm guns. By afternoon things slacked off a bit and we were able to attack and drive the Germans from the field. We ran into a Sherman tank that was in use by the Germans. We took some casualties but someone put the tank out of action with a British grenade. We spent the night in ditches that divided the fields. We got a bit of rain that night and some visitors in the form of an enemy patrol. Someone in the next ditch from the one I was in heard the patrol and fired at them. It was very dark and the Germans headed for our ditch, not knowing we were there. Five of them, one wounded, jumped in the ditch on top of me and a foxhole mate. We did not know who they were or what was going on.

One of the patrol members spoke and we knew they were Germans. We jumped out of the ditch and ordered those Jerries to surrender. They did with the exception of the wounded one who was still in the ditch. Not knowing what he was doing there—he was shot. Later, as we searched the four remaining members of the patrol, one of them began to slink away into the darkness—he, too, was shot. We tied the other three together with a piece of parachute cord and took them back to the company CP."

During the day, several of the men of 3rd Battalion had been hit by shrapnel and machine-gun fire and were placed in the shelter of a barn, which provided cover from the light rain that was coming down in the late afternoon and evening.

For Sgt. Stanley Clever of "G" Company, the Holland experience ended on September 25. He wrote: "I got hit in the chest with a burst of machine gun fire and was taken to a temporary aid station in a barn. There were about twenty wounded men there. Captain Jim Morton was lying beside me. A German patrol came in and told us they were looking for an officer to take with them for interrogation. Captain Morton told them in no uncertain terms that 'our officers never get out of regimental headquarters.' They bought that story and left."

After the Germans cut the road just north of Koevering on the evening of the twenty-fourth, they placed some of their tanks and self-propelled 88mm guns out on the flanks alongside roads in anticipation of the Allied forces bringing armor in from the flanks.

As the tanks were moving to strategic positions east of Koevering, they would meet a bazooka/machine-gun team from the 377th Parachute Field Artillery Battalion before the arrival of the 506th Regiment.

Lieutenant Shaw's Bazooka Team

At the 502nd end of the enemy road cut, action was also heavy. As noted by Sgt. Arthur Parker of the 377th Parachute Field Artillery Battalion positioned near St. Oedenrode, "The Germans cut the road again and took one of our gun batteries under fire and Colonel Harry Elkins heard there were enemy tanks coming to support the infantry that had our guns under fire. He sent Lt. Kenneth Shaw and myself as a bazooka team and George Vogel and Cpl. Barlett with a light machine gun to cover us. We

went about a mile north of St. Oedenrode where a paved road
went east of the main highway. There were woods on one side
and open fields on the other side and the ditches were filled with
German dead. We headed east through the woods. We heard
tanks coming down the road. Didn't know if they were friend or
foe. Our machine gunners set up their gun and Lt. Shaw and I
moved east into a little depression overlooking the road and
loaded the bazooka. Soon, the tanks came into view and we saw
the muzzle brake on the gun so we knew they were German.
From our position, we could see only two tanks but later found
out there were six more behind them. The tanks could not get
off the road due to the deep ditches on both sides. As the lead
tank came into range, I let fly with the first rocket. It did not explode. This alerted the infantry riding on the tank and they
started firing our way. Lt. Shaw loaded another rocket into the
bazooka and slapped me on the butt and I fired again. This time
the rocket exploded right under the top track and the tank
stopped. A lot of smoke but no fire or explosion inside the
tank. The infantry bailed off the tank and ran up the road where
our machine gunners opened fire on them as they took to
the ditches. The second tank fired a few rounds in our direction
and their machine guns sprayed the woods around us. We
loaded the bazooka again and waited. The second tank moved
up behind the dead tank and tried to nudge it off the road. All
this time the cannon was moving from side to side in a menacing manner, looking for us while their machine gunner was cutting branches off the trees with his bursts. As the tank tried to
push the other tank it was almost stopped and Lt. Shaw gave me
another pat on the butt and we put this rocket dead center in the
second tank and it went up in smoke and flames. Our machine
gunners kept a steady stream of fire on the infantry that supported the tanks. The other tanks down the road laid some heavy
fire on us in the woods. The tree bursts drove us into the ditches.
We fired one more rocket at the tanks like a mortar round but
they were now out of range. By this time, someone's artillery
was firing at the tanks and they retreated. We had only two rockets left so we got the hell out of there real fast."[114]

---

114. Sgt. Art Parker was awarded the Silver Star for his actions but was disappointed the others received no recognition.

"E" Company Comes in from the East

As a member of the 2nd Battalion, which was involved in the flanking movement to the left of 1st and 3rd Battalions, 1/Sgt. Carwood Lipton of "E" Company wrote: "When the Krauts cut the road again, 'E' Company was sent to find their main body. Captain Dick Winters put us in an extreme spread formation and we proceeded in approach march, expecting to draw their fire, to find them. When we were in the middle of a very large open area, they opened up on us with small arms, mortar and direct fire from tanks in woods adjacent to the open area.

"We hit the ground, which was slightly rolling, and gave some cover to the men. I heard Bill Guarnere yelling and setting up the 2nd Platoon machine guns and mortar in the middle of the area to fire on the woods. The tank fire was skipping right over me so I crawled for the woods we had just left when suddenly I saw someone standing right by me. I looked up and it was Captain Winters, trying to pinpoint where the Kraut fire was coming from. Feeling somewhat foolish, I stood up and together we tried to evaluate the situation.

"It was obvious that the 'E' Company men were pinned down in the middle of the field. They were firing at the enemy positions in the far tree line. Our men needed more ammunition so I ran back to some Sherman tanks (manned by Britishers) back on the road and got some ammo boxes with .30 caliber machine gun belts from them. I saw Sgt. Floyd Talbert, who had made it off the field, so I gave him two boxes and I took two and we ran out to where our machine gunners were set up in the middle of the field. When we arrived, the Krauts laid in heavy mortar fire on the positions so we all pulled back to our tree line.

"The Sherman tanks were behind us on the road and, as we could see the German positions and three of their tanks on the far side of the field, we yelled to our tanks to come up to fire on them. The British lead tank left the road and came forward through the trees. We were yelling to the commander that the German tanks were right across the field (about 400 yards) and the British tank officer had the hatch open and was standing up with field glasses looking in that direction. For some inexplicable reason, the British tank continued to move forward until its front pushed out of the woods into the open field.

"Within 15 seconds, a 76mm shell from one of the German Panther tanks slammed into the British tank, hitting the shield around its 75mm gun and deflected up without penetrating it. When it hit, I was standing right by the tank and I must have jumped six feet and dove for cover in a ditch. I knew there would be more shells right away. They weren't long in coming.

"The second shell from the Panther came about 15 to 20 seconds later. The Sherman was open throttle in reverse to back into the woods again but it was too late. That second shell hit below the 75mm gun shield and penetrated the armor. The tank commander's hands were blown off and he was trying to get out of the hatch using his arms when the third shell hit the tank, blowing him out and killing him and setting the tank on fire. It burned all night with its ammo exploding at intervals."

From a different position in the "E" Company attack formation, Sgt. Donald Malarkey was in on the same action but had another view of what unfolded. He wrote: "We were working with British tanks and had reached a pine thicket that was several hundred yards east of the Eindhoven–Nijmegen highway. We spotted a German tank west of our position with just its turret and 88mm gun showing. We had five tanks attached to us. We got the tank commander and took him to a sandy knoll where the Tiger could be seen clearly through a small opening in the trees. He brought a tank up, spun the tracks into the knoll so they could lower the 75mm cannon enough to get on the turret of the Tiger. When that was accomplished he suddenly decided he didn't want to fire from that position because he would only get one shot and, if he missed, the Tiger would take him. About a hundred yards to the south there was a finger-sized strip of 25-foot-tall pine trees. The strip was about 40 yards wide and ran for a distance of 200 yards. The tank commander decided to line his five tanks behind the trees and move through them together with all the Shermans opening fire from the edge of the pine trees prior to breaking out into the sandy field. The 2nd Platoon spaced themselves between the tanks moving through them assaulting across the field to the Veghel road.

"We had not moved more than halfway through the pine strip when it became obvious a mistake had been made. The Tiger, in rapid succession, poured 88mm shells into the woods, knocking all five tanks out in a minute or so. We were able to pull some of the crew members out of the tanks. Several were on fire and we threw sand and blankets on them to douse the flames. Once this was done, we moved across the open ground. When the first machine gun fire rattled, our new platoon leader stuck his head in the sand and so ended his career with the 101st. Platoon sergeant Bill Guarnere and squad leader Joe Toye controlled the men and completed the crossing. I had the mortar squad and was busy getting fire on a German machine gun position. Once the Shermans were knocked out, the Tiger jauntily pulled out. Its machine guns were of no use as they were below the crown of the road, which was fortunate for 2nd Platoon," Malarkey concluded.

First Sergeant Lipton finished his account: "We set up a defensive position for the night and Captain Winters told us that he would personally see that anyone who knocked out one of the German tanks that night would get a Silver Star. We couldn't find them, however, and the next morning when we attacked the German positions, we found that they had all withdrawn."

As the 506th fought to snuff out the enemy roadblocks from the north and east during the day on the twenty-fifth, the British 50th Division with strong armored forces advanced from the south. Companies "D" and "H" of the 502nd provided bases of fire for the British troops.

A Medevac Team

The 502nd Parachute Infantry Regiment was involved at the south end of the German breakthrough point. First Lieutenant Henry Barnes and his driver T/5 George Whitfield had gone forward to evacuate wounded from the action. Barnes wrote: "We came upon a heavy mortar crew of the British army. We asked for directions. They were located north of St. Oedenrode, on the main highway going to Veghel, near Koevering. As we were talking, one of them suddenly cursed and pointed out to me a heavy smoke that loomed up about a mile ahead of us. It rose near a thinner smoke. He said, 'There goes another one,' and went on to explain that a German 88mm gun had knocked out a second tank on the road ahead.

"We went on up to see if we could get the wounded out and by the time we went a mile a sad sight greeted us. Along the highway were four tanks in line, two Churchills and two Shermans. Each had been knocked out and were on fire. There was a large, dry dike on each side of the road and these tanks provided an almost complete blockade of the road.

"We parked our jeep behind the tanks in back of a small house the size of an American garage. I loaded two German wounded into the back seat and, getting into the jeep, I leaned over to talk to an English soldier in a foxhole who was pointing out where a Bren gun carrier had been blown up, when a thunderous crash showered plaster and brick on us and blew the two prisoners out of the back seat, stunning all of us.

"Apparently the crew of the self-propelled 88 (that had knocked out the four tanks through the frontal armor) had seen us drive up and fired at us. The gun was so close that we had not even heard the muzzle blast before the shell exploded. We scrambled on to the jeep and, as we drove back with the wounded, the building was hit again.

"After leaving the wounded at Son, we drove back more cautiously and searched the still burning tanks for wounded and found four British tankers seriously wounded, but already bandaged by the aidmen of the 502nd and we took them back to a British hospital in a convent in Son. The rest, approximately eight, were either shot or burned to death.

"As I crawled toward the tanks, along the dry ditch beside the dike, I came upon three dead soldiers, a dead Englishman and a dead American facing a dead German; three different nationalities in a thirty-foot space. Under the German was a machine pistol or 'burp' gun partially loaded. I crawled on past the burning tanks and jumped down into a culvert under the road. It was empty except for a wounded German who had a belly wound and a hand blown off. He was near death so I gave him some morphine to lessen the pain. I peered out of the ditch on the other side of the road to see if I could spot a Bren gun carrier and a sad sight greeted my eyes. A house was on fire just above me and in front of the house, which was on a sharp curve, was a convoy of trucks, both English and American, bumper to bumper, some were still ablaze. It was a desolate and tragic scene with no one in sight.

"I crawled back to get help for the German and found that my driver had taken back some more wounded. The tanks, still afire, blocked the road to such an extent that he couldn't back up with the litter wounded on the jeep. He had to turn around on the main highway in sight of the self-propelled gun and he took a chance and drew no fire."

T/5 George Whitfield, the jeep driver for the medevac team, described how he concealed the jeep-ambulance behind a small building across from the burning tanks and proceeded to crawl along a ditch parallel to the road until he reached some men hiding in a culvert, close to the forward burning tank.

> With assistance from a rifleman, he managed to crawl forward to reach two wounded soldiers; they were placed on the side of the road.
>
> Noting their serious injuries, Whitfield gave what medical aid he could and then crawled back about 100 yards to reach his concealed jeep. Without hesitating and giving no thought to his own safety, he drove past the rear burning tank toward the forward burning tank from which artillery ammunition had begun exploding.
>
> After loading the two soldiers onto his vehicle, and in direct line of enemy fire, Whitfield turned the jeep around as gently as possible to avoid causing additional pain to the wounded.
>
> He then returned to the aid station and from there continued on to the nearest hospital where he left the two injured soldiers.
>
> Then, retracing his route past the rear burning tank, he concealed his jeep once more and crawled to the forward burning tank where he conducted a search for wounded in the exposed front area.
>
> Upon ascertaining there were no casualties, he returned to his jeep, only to find it covered with debris—the result of a direct hit on the building by enemy fire. While cleaning the debris from his jeep, Whitfield noticed two walking wounded lying nearby in a slit trench.
>
> Despite another direct hit on the building, acting once again without hesitation or regard to his own personal safety, he drove forward onto the road. Stopping in full view of the enemy, he got the two wounded men into the back seat, drove forward approximately thirty yards, then stopped again. This time, he loaded a litter patient and another walking wounded—all the while remaining in full view of the enemy. He then made the return trip to the aid station and back to the hospital, safely delivering all wounded in his care.

For his bravery that day, T/5 George Whitfield was awarded the Distinguished Service Cross.[115]

115. From the article "Daring Rescue Mission Remembered" by Rebecca Bunch in the *Chowan Herald* of Edenton, NC, sent by T/5 Herbert Zickuhr of the 326th Airborne Medical Company. Verified by T/5 George Whitfield.

First Lieutenant Henry Barnes had been working on wounded farther to the rear when Whitfield had made his two jeep-ambulance runs to the hospital in Son. Barnes wrote: "I went back to the culvert to help the German and jumped down into the culvert and almost landed on another enemy soldier standing right in front of me. I found myself holding the German's machine pistol in my hand.

"After a few minutes, I began to rage internally. The one thing wrong with being a medic is that he seldom gets a chance to explode or to shoot at the enemy. He is always on the receiving end, without much chance of getting even. I was determined to bring back the wounded German and to look for the Bren gun carrier so I picked up an English medic who was allowed to carry a rifle and I had my machine pistol and we circled another way around. We came across an American machine gun crew who were unconscious but had already been bandaged. Apparently they had been hit by mortar fire. We evacuated them. We then went further to the left and moved past an outpost line by crawling along a small drainage ditch. A German fired a 'burp' gun at us. We crawled back as mortar fire came in and the two outposts cursed us for stirring up the front.

"I was getting madder and madder. I sent back the English medic and as I left, one of the English soldiers, still firing the heavy mortars sweeping the woods ahead of us in an effort to knock out the self-propelled gun, stopped me and asked me if I found Trooper Jones, the driver of the Bren gun, and if he was dead, would I please bring back his raincoat. He said he had lost his and would have to pay for another unless he could find one.

"I went along the side of the road, parallel to the one on which the tanks were stuck, and came upon a sergeant of some 502nd men lounging under a tree. Asking for an armed guard so I could get some wounded, I was refused. I then went on until I found a lieutenant and he gave me a squad and out we went in the dusk. We found the carrier and dead beside it were three men, including Trooper Jones. I remembered to take the raincoat and we returned. I gave it to the English soldier and went back to our parked jeep.

"I then went back to the tanks and saw, near the spot where the machine gun crew had been hit, a GI crawling slowly along. He had a groin wound and was dragging his M-1 rifle. Crawling ahead of him, about fifty feet, was a wounded German and the GI was following him. We pulled the jeep onto the road, put the GI on and then started to load the German. I was so fatigued by then that I could barely lift my end of the litter (as you had to raise it almost head high to put it on the brackets). A shell whistled by from that self-propelled 88 gun—I got the loaded stretcher on it in no time and we retired."

Highway Reopens

The twenty-sixth dawned as a soggy, rainy day. The diary of First Sergeant F. G. Fitzgerald provides a view from the southern end of the enemy salient where the 377th Parachute Field Artillery Battalion was in support of the 502nd Regiment.

26 Sept.—Weather is very bad with a lot of rain falling. "Hell's Highway" still cut but an attack is scheduled for 1800 hours. Battery has fired quite heavy since early morning in conjunction with the coming attack. "H" Company 502nd PIR supported by tanks and artillery successfully reopened "Hell's Highway" at 0930 hours. No traffic is yet allowed to use the road because of 88s zeroed on the road.[116]

The enemy had removed much of its forces during the night but a few self-propelled guns, tanks, and some 20mm guns were still in support of the infantry keeping the road closed.

Back along the main highway, PFC George R. McMillan of "I" Company of the 506th 3rd Battalion remembered having to battle the elements as well as the Germans. He wrote: "In 2nd squad of the 3rd Platoon, we were soaking wet. It was raining. We flanked the Germans by using a drainage ditch. Enemy soldiers were visible through a culvert. My M-1 jammed. Bill Weber handed me another rifle while calmly catching a potato masher grenade and flipping it away. Weber tossed a frag grenade and knocked out and captured a 20mm anti-tank gun and crew."

PFC Wilbur Fishel was in the same platoon. He remembered when George McMillan fired through a big culvert and hit a German on the other side. "I yelled, 'Did you get him George?' He said, 'Yeah, I got em right in the ass!' There was one guy

116. Diary of "C" Battery of the 377th Parachute Field Artillery Battalion as kept by 1/Sgt. F. G. Fitzgerald.

catching grenades and throwing them back at the Germans. We weren't getting any British tank support at the time."

Pvt. Ralph E. King of "H" Company remembered they were fighting some German paratroopers. "I don't know if they were qualified chutists as they were young kids. They were firing in the hedgerows. I also remember the deaths of three troopers. The Germans were firing tree bursts. They'd zero in on you and fire into the trees. That was how I got hit on the 26th."

Second Battalion of the 506th Regiment had made a wide swing to the left south of Veghel in the hope of outflanking the enemy force that had cut the road near Koevering. First and 3rd Battalions were on the left and right of the main highway facing south as day broke on the twenty-sixth. Second Battalion faced west. F Company had delivered a "left hook" to the German force. Sgt. John Taylor wrote: "2nd Battalion was heading in the general direction of Uden. We were moving along a road parallel to the main highway. A big fire fight broke out on our left front. I drew my patrol assignment again—seems like I always drew those assignments. Orders were to take three men and see what was going on over there.

"We had some real open terrain so we scooted across and we drew some small arms fire. Finally, we got over to a big, deep ditch and started moving up and ran into an almost complete company of British soldiers. They were lined up and down this big drainage ditch and there was a big culvert that went under the road and apparently they had stormed through the culvert. The ditch went up several hundred yards and made a curve. A German machine gunner was up there. He had blasted them and wounded four or five of the men. I talked to the British commander. He wanted to know if we would go up and take that machine gun out.

" 'Hell no, I'm not going to go up there! One of your tanks is sitting beside that big ole tree over there 300 to 400 yards away. All he'd have to do is move over with that big gun and fire into the ditch and he'd get that guy out of there.'

"The officer said, 'Would you mind going over there and pointing that gun out to them?'

"I went over and talked to the tank commander and he got a couple rounds into the ditch. I don't know if they got out of the situation or not but they were just lined up along the sides of the ditch and every time they'd try to get up there the German would open up on them.

"We went back to the company and caught up to the column. Got a ride on a truck and ended up in the same apple orchard we had left earlier in Uden."

NINETEEN

Behind Enemy Lines

Aborted Landings Behind Enemy Lines

In the earlier chapters we read about the personal experiences of the soldiers as they went about accomplishing the assigned missions of the units. They have worked for months and even years with the men they served with. But now, here are experiences of men who come to rely in life-and-death situations on people they have never seen before and learn to what extent people will go to gain their long-lost freedoms. The airborne troopers will now meet the Dutch people.

A few troop carrier planes had to be aborted over heavily defended enemy positions. Gliders had to cut loose from tow craft that were going down in flames. There were no reserve platoons and battalions that could rush forward to provide relief in critical situations. Now they relied on the resistance fighters, the members of the underground who had been busy for over four years preparing for the aerial invasion that was coming down upon them.

Mary van Hoof and her half brother Adrian Goossens were schoolteachers in a community near the Belgian–Dutch border, and both were involved in the work of the underground. On the seventeenth of September, she had been cycling when suddenly an armada of bombers flew over their village. She felt their liberation was at hand. Later in the day she saw more planes, which made her very excited. She wrote: "That same Sunday around 1330 hours, after dinner, we heard and saw another group of planes, some were towing gliders. We and our neighbors were dancing and waving with white sheets, jumping for joy, but then suddenly—oh, it was awful to see—burning planes came down, losing wings and burning chutes with unlucky soldiers in the air. What to do now? I hastened by cycle to the right side, hoping to give some help.

"Just beside a little stream, I saw a glider on a potato field. Nobody was around. I called in never spoken school English, 'Be not afraid—I come to help you! I am your friend.' An American soldier named Lt. Hartz came crawling out of a ditch. One by one more of them appeared. Farmers from the neighborhood came and looked in surprise when they heard me speaking in English, which none of them understood."

T/Sgt. Harry Tinkcom had landed safely, coming down into some trees whose branches held him up, momentarily, just above ground level. He released his harness and dropped to the ground. He got rid of his Mae West and found a place of concealment between two trees. He looked about, listening for the sounds of war, and noted the passing of a serial of gliders that was taking a pounding from the same anti-aircraft guns that had brought down the *Clay Pigeon*.

Tinkcom heard voices and a crackling in the bushes. "Hello, hello. We are friends, where are you?"

Raising himself cautiously, Tinkcom saw a priest and another man running about, looking for the parachutists.

The priest was concerned that Tinkcom was badly wounded as blood trickled down his nose and forehead. He had a cut over the left eye and another on the bridge of his nose.

He asked if they had seen other parachutes. "Yes, there were three of them that came down." So S/Sgt. Joe Curreri and the paratrooper had made it safely.

The priest came over and put one hand on Tinkcom's shoulder and with great sincerity said, "We have much gladness that you are here, for we have been waiting for you a long time, a long, long time."

The priest wanted to know if there would be many paratroopers coming. Suspicious now, but with little knowledge of the scope of the operation, Tinkcom said only, "I hope there are many of them, for our sake."

As the men walked out of the woods, they came upon a parachute backpack and Tinkcom noted, with satisfaction, that it belonged to Curreri.

His concern now was for the fate of the two pilots. Had they survived the crash? He asked the two men if they had seen a crashed airplane. They had.

At that moment, three more civilians ran up. "The Germans are coming!" one said breathlessly.

"Quick," shouted the priest. "Run that way into the woods. Go a little way and lie down. I come soon with bread and milk."

The plane towing the glider in which T/4 Artie Kitterman, T/4 Mike Lewis, and PFC Jack Kessel were riding was shot down just after it passed over the Belgian–Dutch border. The same gunners who shot down the *Clay Pigeon* were probably the ones who brought down this tow craft as well as several others forced to come down in the same vicinity. Kitterman's glider had come down in a potato field and came to rest with its nose buried in a haystack. Besides the three signalmen and pilot, the glider carried a powerful SCR-499 radio set installed in a quarter-ton trailer. The men had decided beforehand that Kitterman would take the ax (to be used for emergency purposes) to break out the windshield in front of the pilot's compartment so he could escape. The radio trailer filled its storage area so tightly that only four inches of space was left on either side and over the top. As Kitterman went out of the side door to break the windshield, the men found the pilot had crawled through a tight space under the trailer.

Kitterman related his story: "We left the glider with the trailer in it as fast as we could because we figured the Germans had seen us land and would come after us. About one-quarter mile away was a woods and from this potato patch to the woods was a ditch about shoulder deep. We went down that ditch to the woods. We had not been in the woods long when we heard a small explosion back at the glider and then saw smoke rising from it. We thought the Germans had burned it and at that time let it go at that. It was getting late afternoon by then and we had no idea which way to start out so we decided to stay in the woods that night. After dark, someone came into the woods and called 'Comrade.' We weren't about to answer him, thinking he was a German. It turned out to be a member of the Dutch Underground but we didn't respond."

Mary van Hoof may have been on hand when the radio trailer was removed from the glider. She wrote: "One of the liberators opened the front of the glider and a carrier came out. They asked me to go with them but I said I would follow on my bicycle. About ten minutes later, in a small woods, they were looking at a map while on each edge of the field I saw a para with a gun. One man named Brabec seemed to be in charge. He asked me where exactly they were located as he was very anxious to get to Son. It was dangerous in this area and I asked them to wait a little while for my brother. 'Help will come soon. He is helping on the left side of the field.' The Americans were so anxious and I know Germans were in all the nearby villages.

"Luckily, after ten minutes, my brother Adrian Goossens arrived with his comrades Frans Widenburg, Jan Gooskens and Piet Watershoof. He and Brabec and F/O Hartz decided to go to the other side of our village. In the meantime, the group had grown to ten persons and three jeeps."

T/Sgt. Harry Tinkcom had dashed into the brush and concealed himself in a patch of weeds. He had been there about fifteen minutes when Father Gysbers returned with a young boy who was carrying a round loaf of brown bread, a bucket of milk, and a jar of butter. The priest left again and as Tinkcom munched his food he watched as two P-47s circled the spot where the troublesome guns had been firing. The first one went into a power dive firing its machine guns and dropped a bomb and rose back to an altitude of about two thousand feet. The gun persisted in firing at more troop carrier planes, which were returning from their glider-towing mission. The second plane dived and dropped a bomb. No more firing came from that gun position.

The priest appeared again, this time with another young man who had seen a burned plane with a big O on its tail. He handed Tinkcom a piece of blackened aluminum as a souvenir of the plane. He hadn't seen any bodies around the plane's shattered fuselage.

While discussing ways to get out of the predicament and moving to a location that contained friendly troops, Tinkcom had produced his evasion kit with good cloth maps, forty dollars in Belgian, French, and Dutch money, a compass, and a hacksaw blade. The priest had exclaimed, *"Très fantastique!"* in admiration of the completeness of the American equipment.

As they talked, two partisans came up with PFC George D. Doxzen, who had exited the plane just behind Tinkcom. His face had been badly cut by his shovel handle when he landed on top of a barbed-wire fence. Tinkcom dusted some sulfanilimide powder into the wound.

PFC George D. Doxzen's recollection of the events following

the landing are somewhat sketchy whereas Tinkcom had chronicled his experiences shortly after returning to England. Doxzen recalled: "I met some Dutch civilians who took me to a field where there were three jeeps and 17 GIs whose gliders had landed in the vicinity due to their towplanes being shot down.

"We set up a perimeter defense around the field. We were set up in teams, one automatic weapon and one rifle to a team. My teammate was a staff sergeant from Boston named Quinn."

T/Sgt. Tinkcom was taken to another area, where he found the two pilots of *Clay Pigeon*. The three had marveled that all of them were still alive. Some time later, crew chief S/Sgt. Joe Curreri showed up in the company of three partisans.

Beex, one of the partisans, was admiring Doxzen's M-1 rifle and insisted on carrying it. He said, "For many years no have one. Once soldier, now soldier again for partisans rise soon." A bit apprehensive about this, for he was taking no one at face value, Tinkcom asked Doxzen if "the thunderstick was hep to jive?"

"No," said Doxzen, "no BBs in it. This double talk has its uses after all, doesn't it?"

Tinkcom was ashamed of his suspicions but care was necessary. The enemy was everywhere and his cleverness was undoubted.

As the group proceeded along the edge of the woods they stopped and one of the partisans whistled twice. Another partisan appeared and led them up a lane past three glider infantrymen who were standing guard with a BAR. Soon they came to three jeeps and several soldiers, possibly twenty of them. Their tug ships had been shot down and the glider pilots had landed their craft safely.

Shortly after dusk it began to rain. The two badly injured pilots were made as comfortable as possible. The glider troopers were well armed and equipped. Without regard for their own comfort, they gave several blankets to the two lieutenants and though the blankets soon became heavy with water, they never complained.

In another section of the woods, possibly facing a different field, T/4 Artie Kitterman and his group had ignored the calls from someone coaxing them to respond. Taking no chances, they had remained silent as night came on. Kitterman wrote: "There was a road on the far side of the woods and we heard voices of people walking on the road that night. The next morning I went to the road edge of the woods and watched people walking or riding by on bicycles. I thought I would take a chance with an older man and went out on the road and stopped him. He could speak a few words of poor English but I finally figured he wanted us to stay there and he would get the Dutch underground to come to the woods. An hour or so later, two men came and told us they had some injured Americans in another woods and wanted to take us over there to be with them. They led us about two miles across fields to the other woods. They had other men across the fields from us watching for any Germans who might see us.

"In these woods were about twelve Americans and one German the Dutch were holding. They wanted us to keep him because they didn't want to be caught with him in their custody. That evening, they brought us some sandwiches and cigarettes and did this each day we were with them. They told us they would get the British to come and get us out so we decided to go along with that."

The morning of the eighteenth brought disturbing news to Tinkcom and his group. Seven partisans came to the encampment to inform the men that three German armored cars were in the nearby village searching for downed airmen. They knew the men had to be somewhere in the vicinity. The glidermen began to make immediate preparations to stop the armored cars and to drive off the Germans should they enter the woods. Though it was a small group, they could produce a respectable amount of firepower. In their arsenal they had a bazooka, a BAR, a .50-caliber machine gun, some Thompson submachine guns, M-1 Garands, carbines, and about a bushel of grenades and several packets of explosives.

While the alert was on, a doctor and a nurse came from the village to care for the wounded men. The doctor pronounced their treated condition as "ver goot."

Before noon the men were informed that the Germans had gone, overlooking a wounded American lieutenant who was hiding in one of the village houses. Everyone laughed heartily over this.

In the afternoon several partisans approached with extensive maps and plans where the little unit would be able to leave the woods in jeeps to join a larger force that was holding a bridge.

Little-used roads could be negotiated for the greater part of the trip but, at one point, a main road employed by the enemy for troop movements had to be crossed. The partisans predicted that this would be a short but dangerous time, but they were sure the crossing could be effected. The leader of the partisans in that sector, Adrian Goossens, a quiet young student, had an amazing amount of military information at his fingertips, and he knew the territory as well as he knew his own backyard.

After all parts of the projected plan had been considered, the soldiers packed their equipment and moved quietly out on their way to the bridge, guided by two enthusiastic partisans.

PFC George Doxzen was part of this three-jeep force making the attempt to get through to Allied forces in the Eindhoven area. He wrote: "We spent the night in the field and the next morning we departed for Eindhoven. The jeeps were manned with a driver, a machine gunner in the center and a rifleman on the right in the front seat and one man facing right and one facing left and one facing to the rear in the back seat.

"As we approached each road intersection, a member of the Dutch Underground would be waiting at the corner. If it was safe to proceed, he would wave us on. If there were Krauts in the area, he would wave us back and we would go into the woods and deploy. By this method we reached Eindhoven and I rejoined my unit."

The air force men stayed behind to look after the injured pilots. This included S/Sgt. Bela Benko, who had narrowly escaped with his life from a burning plane by shoving his arms through the parachute harness with no time to buckle it on but had managed to land safely in the same area.

Many partisans had been filtering in and out of the woods all day long. All were friendly and agreeable. Language was a barrier, but it was apparent to anyone that they were a determinedly courageous group, willing to go to almost any lengths to defeat the Germans. For many years they had labored and many had died to free their beloved Holland. For the past four years, said one of them, their organization had lost an average of over three hundred men a month. When caught by the Germans, their fate was certain death. Had any of them been found giving aid to fallen airmen they would have been executed immediately and without ceremony. Well aware of this, they nevertheless took great chances and performed their jobs with a lightheartededness toward death that was amazing.

The quiet young student, Adrian Goossens, related that he had been challenged that morning by a German. He said, "I was riding along on my bicycle when a German halted me. 'I mus hab dot bike,' he said. So I stuck in the tire this." He produced a pin. "Den German ride and ssss go tire. German swear and I laugh. He throw bicycle away. I 'air' tire with this when German go." He pulled a bicycle pump from his coat pocket. That was one of his favorite tricks and he used it often. He knew hundreds of ways to annoy and delay the "Master Race."

After the glidermen had left, Goossens took Tinkcom and the air force men to a new place of concealment located in a woodlot of a friendly farmer named Karl Smulders. He had carted over a plentiful supply of straw and a large tarpaulin.

Just as the five men were preparing for badly needed rest that night, two partisans appeared with seven more Americans who had also been shot down. These consisted of three glidermen, Sgt. Mike Lewis, T/4 Artie Kitterman, and PFC John Kessel; a glider pilot, F/O P. Hartz; a crew chief, T/Sgt. Gerard H. Pitt, and a crew radioman, S/Sgt. D. R. Dunham; and another paratrooper from the *Clay Pigeon,* Pvt. Lucian Hopkins. Hopkins told the men that they had come down right on top of a nest of Germans. He said nine had been captured, six killed, and he and another man, Pvt. Moses Lopez, had managed to escape, but Lopez had been shot in the back with the bullet entering from the side. He was being cared for in a farmer's home.[117]

All of the above men had been brought in by the partisans to the hiding place to permit easier contact. That night the men slept soundly while big guns roared in the distance. Occasionally, machine guns and rifles would sputter. Then it would be quiet.

Farmer Karl Smulders kept the men supplied with food. The priest, Father Gysbers, visited them on the nineteenth. More C-47s passed overhead towing gliders. While the Thunderbolts and Mustangs were overhead, the anti-aircraft guns remained si-

117. In his brief report, Pvt. Moses Lopez said that he was wounded and was eventually captured. The farmer was executed but others were released. It is hoped the Dutch family wasn't punished.

lent. When the fighter planes were off in the distance, the guns blasted away at the big, defenseless troop carrier planes.

Before nightfall, Goossens came up with the news that over a hundred Germans were dug in in the woods between the hiding airmen and the village. They were probably retreating or fighting a rear-guard action for others.

On the twentieth, the number of Germans around the village of Hoogeloon had increased to three hundred. Goossens felt it was their responsibility to fight a rear-guard action. The men had to remain extremely quiet now so as not to stir up suspicion of their presence.

While sitting there staring at the sky or the ground, they were startled to hear a noise in a nearby field. To their amazement, they saw three civilians approaching with a heavily loaded wheelbarrow. On it were piled headsets, tuning coils, blankets, and a case of K-rations. The glidermen had had a huge SCR-499 radio, much larger than a mine car, in one of the gliders. It had been hidden by the partisans shortly after the glider landed. On the preceding day, after the glidermen had made anxious inquiry about it, the partisans thought they wanted it. This was a mistaken impression for actually the radio in that time and place would be a hindrance and a danger. Tinkcom asked one of the glidermen to make it clear that they did not need the mobile unit, that it would be best for all concerned to leave it where it was concealed.

There the matter rested. But in the afternoon, much to their consternation, they saw the farmer and two others coming across the field with the huge SCR-499 hitched behind a two-wheeled cart. The situation was alarming and yet amusing. They admired the daring of those men who had skirted the German lines with that radio in full view of everyone, but their very desire to help constituted a danger. Just to be seen near it would have meant their death.

T/4 Artie Kitterman was just as amazed when he saw them coming across the field. He added this to the story: "The Dutch had taken the radio trailer from the glider and then burned the glider but not before removing the wheels and tires from it. These were also brought to us. The radio had all the tubes and coils out of it—even the wiring diagrams had been removed from the transmitter. Earlier, other underground men brought the parts to us and we now had a usable radio set (500 watt transmitter and two receivers). They brought us everything except the cigarettes I had left in the trailer."

But since the set was out there in the field, there was nothing to do but thank the partisans, drag it into the woods, and bury it under a camouflage cover. It was an anxious twenty minutes. About two hours before, paratrooper Hopkins, while on guard duty, had seen three Germans moving across a field not a hundred yards away with a roll of telephone wire. Once the set had been concealed, everyone breathed easier.

The men dug foxholes, concentrating first on good-sized holes for the wounded pilots. If they had to make a stand against an enemy assault, they had better have good cover. They worried that the Germans would select their position as a likely defensive position of their own.

That night a German prisoner had been brought in by the partisans. He had been captured some time before, but sensing the Americans were to be relieved by the British shortly, he was moved up to the woods area where they were concealed. He cooperated with the men but to make sure, his hands were bound. The men learned he wanted only for the war to end so he could get back to his wife, who was an opera singer.

The next morning, farmer Karl Smulders came with tea and sandwiches. The men were eating when a lad came running through the trees and, pointing toward the village, shouting breathlessly, "Germans, Germans come!" Then he disappeared.

The injured pilots were quickly placed into their foxholes and tucked in with straw, blankets, and raincoats. Those who hadn't dug foxholes took cover at various vantage points previously decided upon.

Shortly thereafter, heavy firing broke out in the village. From the direction of fire it was clear that the Germans were around the airmen to the south, in a semicircle. After about an hour the firing abated. Later, only spasmodic firing occurred.

At 1330 a terrific din began in the village and the woods below the Americans. Apparently the main struggle was on. Heavy artillery shells went overhead, sounding like distant freight trains. These shells were coming from a northeasterly direction, indicating that either the British or German guns had moved into new locations. Mortar shells exploded nearby and an occasional bullet whipped through the trees or ricocheted off with an angry whine. The sounds were mixed with the chatter of machine guns and mortar explosions.

A German officer came by on the nearby road with his bicycle. He stopped to survey the battle scene. The men argued that he should be shot before he brought more men into the area. After looking around, the officer pedaled back in the direction of the village. Would he return with more men?

The question was soon answered. In less than a half hour, wagons were heard on the road and several came into view along with about thirty German soldiers. They drove up and stopped opposite the hiding men. The Germans were setting up a machine gun at the corner of the woods just across from them.

For over an hour the Germans moved about at the corner of the road and in the woods, at times close enough to knock leaves down on some of the Americans.

There was some sort of an altercation among the enemy soldiers at the machine gun. Soon it was taken down and the wagons were turned around and driven back in the direction from which they had come.

The Americans decided the position was too dangerous. They moved up a nearby hedgerow, carrying their injured with them. They reasoned the Germans would not cross a large field nearby and the Americans could go into a cornfield to hide among the tall cornstalks. They hadn't reached the rows of cornstalks when there was a wild scrambling below them and voices could be heard in the woods they had just left. Everyone was sure the Germans were in on them and that the game was up. Swearing softly, Tinkcom took a grenade from his pocket.

It wasn't the Germans at all. It was the partisans, who had expressed dismay when they found the empty foxholes and thought the men had been taken by the Germans.

Adrian Goossens was bringing good news. "The British are coming!" he shouted. From then on he was often referred to as "Paul Revere." He had promised the day before that he would be in the first tank that came to relieve his charges.

"But where are the British?" Tinkcom asked. "Hey, fellows, this is premature."

He had just finished speaking when bullets began to whine through the bushes. Everyone hit the ground in a hurry.

"What the hell is this?" Tinkcom muttered to Joe Curreri. "Something is wrong here!"

His doubts were soon dissipated. There was a clanking farther down along the hedgerow and there appeared several British Bren carriers carrying nonchalant but watchful Tommies. The British had come and what a welcome sight they were!

T/4 Artie Kitterman wrote: "We began to hear shooting and it kept coming closer to us. It was the British in five small armored cars and they had been shooting as they came although they had seen no enemy soldiers along the road. Within three minutes three Dutch underground appeared from the main road side of the woods. Some of us were out in the open beside the woods talking and shaking hands when a German rear guard from the earlier group opened fire on us with a machine gun from across the open field. The British sent two of the armored cars up the road. There was some firing. When they came back, they announced that the gunner wouldn't bother us any more. They hooked our radio-trailer to the back of one of the vehicles, loaded all of us into their armored cars and went back the way they had come. They continued shooting into the trees on both sides of the road as we went along. We headed for a nearby village."

Tinkcom related that the village of Hoogeloon had been liberated a short time before. The inhabitants lined the streets, shouting and waving at the bedraggled and dirty Americans who had not washed or shaved in five days. When the carriers stopped, a civilian came up with a bottle of champagne that had been hidden from the Germans. There was backslapping and handshaking as the Americans walked over to the British CP. Evidence of the recent fight was to be seen everywhere, smashed windows, bullet-pocked facades, and bloody pavements.

At the field kitchen, set up in a brick building, several British soldiers who had not yet eaten insisted that the Americans use their mess kits. After eating, they washed in a house where a German had been killed by a grenade. The lady of the house chuckled over the incident and pointed to the blood with great satisfaction.

The Oirschot Landings

The small village of Oirschot, situated seven miles west of the Son landing zone, witnessed at least two aborted glider landings in its vicinity on the eighteenth. In one instance, the glider carrying 1Lt. Ray J. Hiltunen and two of his 326th Engineers crashed when the left wing was shot off. All occupants were killed.

In another instance, H.L.A. DeBeer was a thirteen-year-old living in Oirschot. He remembered a Waco glider crash-landing in the Oirschot-Best area on September 18. "One American was captured by the Germans who led him through the village. He was a tall man which surprised me since I was always told that paras were very small men. He was allowed to rest and, since I was only 13 years old, I was allowed to approach him. The German paratroopers led him away very roughly. He spent a while at a farm of the van de Kerkhof family and then he was led back to the market square. It seemed the Germans didn't know what to do with him. They were very nervous."

A third glider came down in a field near Oirschot on the nineteenth, the day the glider landings were so badly scrambled with numerous craft landing far and wide, missing the landing zones by many miles.

The story of a Dutch doctor, who treated men of the 101st Airborne Division when they became ill some time after their glider had made a premature landing short of the Son fields, was related by his daughter, Maryke Muller.

"During the war my father, Dr. Harry Scholman, practiced medicine in the village of Oirschot, near Eindhoven, in southern Holland. On the 19th of September, a glider carrying U.S. soldiers overshot its target and landed in a field just outside Oirschot. After several days of hiding, without rations, the soldiers ate some root crops that had been sprayed with chemicals to prevent insect damage and, as a result, they became violently ill.

"They eventually made contact with a farmer who informed my father of the situation. He immediately met the soldiers in their hiding place and, as they would not give up their arms and enter his Red Cross hospital, he installed them in an abandoned farm cellar and provided the necessary medical treatment as well as bringing them a daily hot meal."

Maryke Muller[118] concluded: "Eventually they recovered and he believes they attempted to cross the lines and return to their units. My father has no record of their names because they did not enter the hospital. However, they did leave him a mess tin (canteen cup) in their hiding place on which were scratched the names: Bob Ernst, Our Bill, Snowden, Pinhead and Kirk, Ltd. Some of them were from New York and Ohio."

Shelter in Den Dungen

A British Horsa glider had come down east of s'Hertogenbosch on the afternoon of the eighteenth when its towrope had been severed by the explosion of an ack-ack shell. The following day, an American CG-4A glider carrying men of "B" Battery of the 907th Field Artillery had come down several miles farther east and near the Willems-Vaart Canal.

T/5 Sam Brandenburg was the leader of the glider carrying the men from "B" Battery. The area over which they flew had witnessed the passing of Allied troop carrier planes and gliders for three days. On this date the Germans were waiting for them. They had brought in more anti-aircraft guns. Considerably more flak was thrown up at the planes and gliders on the nineteenth and as a result at least three gliders had to make aborted landings.

The plane towing Brandenburg's glider had taken considerable evasive action as it passed over the flak area, and glider pilot F/O Weldon McBride found he could not keep up with the moves of the tow craft. He had to cut loose.

PFC Lester Chaskins was also on board the glider. He wrote:

118. Author's note: The above letter was forwarded to me in 1980. The name Bob Ernst rang a bell from somewhere. With little more than a pause, I went to my personnel files and thumbed through the 907th Glider Field Artillery Battalion rosters and found a Cpl. Robert A. Ernst. I further noticed I had an address for him in Aurora, Nebraska. With help from the telephone operator, I was shortly in touch with Bob. It was his canteen cup that was described in the letter I read to him over the phone. He liked to scratch the nicknames of his buddies onto his mess equipment. I quickly got the names of the others: Sgt. Roy "Snowden" Brown, T/5 Bill R. "Our Bill" Stelzner, John Kirk from Queens, New York, and Pvt. Allen "Pinhead" Anderson from West Virginia. I had the address for Brown and got further verification from him. The information was quickly passed to Miss Muller. She and her father then knew the men had survived the war.

"I smashed my head on something very hard. I don't even remember how I got out of the glider. We were all crouched beside it when two civilians appeared, as if by magic. One of them spoke good English and immediately told us that he was from the Dutch underground. He said the Germans were very near and that we must leave at once. Leo Tousignant didn't trust them and remained behind."

Brandenburg described his experience: "After we hit the ground, I crawled out of the front end of the glider. The Germans were firing at us. One of the men, Pvt. Leo Tousignant, grabbed the pilot's grease gun and began spraying the woods from which the Germans were approaching. About then the underground boys came from the opposite direction yelling 'Comrade' and motioning us to come that way."

Private Tousignant held the Germans at bay long enough for the men to get clear of the area. A short time later he was killed when enemy soldiers got in position to fire at him from the flanks. Pvt. Lee Watkins held back to fire several more bursts as the men hurried away.

Peter and Tom van Breevoort had been on the run ever since they escaped from a prison bus in s'Hertogenbosch that was taking them to the train to be transported to a concentration camp in Germany. At the time of the airborne invasion, they were working for farmer Voets in Den Dugen. He provided them with food and shelter. The two brothers had been working for the underground since 1942.

On the nineteenth, while working in the fields, the brothers witnessed the emergency landing of a glider. Peter van Breevoort wrote: "Tom and I ran towards the glider but, because of heavy firing, could not go near. We remained close by. While waiting, Harry van de Broek joined us. Suddenly, we saw five Americans walking in our direction. Harry had a better knowledge of roads and together we led the Americans to safety. We hid in a bean field where the foliage was quite high."

Brandenburg added, "They hid us in a bean field till after dark. Someone brought a Dutch doctor, Prinsen. He had a Red Cross band on his arm. Before he began treating us, he asked for a cigarette. I remember he said, 'The first good smoke in five years!' After he was through treating the wounded and injured, they took us to a cellar where we stayed most of the time."

Lester Chaskins remembered that the doctor was there for

some time. It was already dark. He said, "I remember a German plane flying over us at tree-top level obviously looking for us. How he missed us, I'll never know. Had my first drink of milk from a helmet. It tasted strong. You could tell I was a city boy."

Peter van Breevoort continued his account: "When it was dark, we and the men were hidden in the field; we could hear the Germans on the roads searching for the crew of the downed glider. We waited until they passed and we led the men to a more permanent hiding place. Along the way we picked some peaches for them. The men were delighted. The men were brought to a small cabin which stood in an apple orchard and it was originally used as a storage place for empty crates. The inside was separated into two rooms by a wall that had a very small window. The front had two big doors, the back only one. During the day, the men stayed in the smaller back-room and at night they slept in a manure pit near the cabin. It had been cleaned and filled with hay and blankets. Every night the men were lowered down into the pit and it was covered with a lid until early the next morning when they were taken out.

"A few days later we picked up three English pilots at another farm who had roamed around in the open and brought them to the same place where the Americans were hiding.

"A week later we were awakened from sleep to go and bring another pilot to safety. He was in great danger because his hiding place inside a haystack was surrounded by German artillery. With great difficulty, we were able to bring him safely to where the others were hidden. This was a great joy to the three English pilots for he was their fourth crew member."

One of the British glider pilots who had spent some time in the underground shelter provided a description of it and what living conditions in it were like:

It consisted of a concrete and cement sewer pipe roughly four and a half feet in diameter and about sixteen feet in length. At one end—the entrance—was a hole two and a half feet square, down which we had to squeeze to enter. The other end was sealed. The entrance hole was covered with a wooden lid and this in turn covered with muddy straw and refuse, thus effectively camouflaging it from even close inspection. The one disadvantage we had to suffer from it was that at the same time it obstructed most of the daylight and fresh air, too.

Some indication of the state of the air may be gained by the fact that when we lit matches, it was almost impossible to keep them lit, so impure was the air.

The top point of the shelter was roughly six or eight inches below ground level and covered with earth; the shelter had been made habitable by the provision of straw, blankets and one bucket for sanitary use.[119]

Peter van Breevoort continued his story: "One morning when I dropped by, I saw all pale faces! A German patrol had opened the two big doors in the front to see what was inside the cabin. Through the tiny window, the men had watched in horror. Luckily, the Germans did not look at the back of the cabin and disappeared without discovering the hiding place."

T/5 Sam Brandenburg remembered the incident. "They brought four British soldiers to the cellar but they didn't stay but a few days because it was too crowded. One day they put us in a small room in the back of a farm building. While there, the British glider pilot found a dog collar. He put it around his head like a crown and got on a stool with a stick in his hand. He said he was the King of England. We were all laughing. Someone said, 'Shh—be quiet!' Two German soldiers came into the big room of the building. They looked around and left. If they had come to the little room—that would have been a different story."

Brandenburg added: "Someone would come before daylight and after dark and say, 'Good buddy.' We knew that was our food. We also got plenty of fruit.

"When the coast was clear, they would let us get out and get some exercise. There was a woman present. I don't remember her name but they trusted her. They brought her to the cellar. She memorized our names. Henk said the Germans would let her go through the lines. She brought back word for us to lay low and not to try to make it back to our outfit because it was too far."

It became unsafe for the van Breevoort brothers to continue operating in the area. Peter wrote: "It was unwise for Tom and myself to remain at the farm because people around were mistaking us for the airbornes and we did not want to bring any hiding men into jeopardy. The only thing left for us to do was to try

119. Anonymous. *Royal Army Ordnance Corps Gazette,* January 1945, 8.

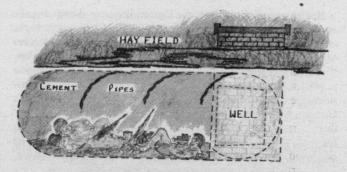

Sewage holding tank where airbornes hid.

to make contact with the British army. Crossing the front line, we reached the British. They took both of us to Veghel, but they were unable to assist us and did not allow us to go back in case the Germans might catch us."

PFC Lester Chaskins closed his account with this: "The Underground hid us for forty days, in Den Dungen, at the risk of their lives and all of the people in town. Peter and Tom van Breevoort and Henk Schakenraad—even the police chief gave up food rations to make our stay comfortable."

The van Breevoort brothers persisted. Though they had been told by the British not to return to Den Dungen, they went back. Peter wrote: "In spite of their suggestion, we did manage to get back to Den Düngen, which had been liberated and we never did see the pilots or the airbornes again."[120]

Shelter in the Boxtel Area

Some of these narrations give the reader some insight into the problems facing the 907th Glider Field Artillery Battalion on the nineteenth (D plus 2) when only 24 men of a 550-man battalion made it safely to the landing zone at Son. As mentioned earlier, they were scattered all over Holland, Belgium, and France, and whole flights of them had returned to England. Fog had been the major problem.

120. Peter van Breevort has visited with Sam Brandenburg, Lester Chaskins, Peter Sirak, and one of the British glider pilots since the war and the men had happy reunions.

Having encountered the same fog conditions as the other gliders carrying 907th personnel, F/O William Richmond's flight manifest listed the following troopers on board: Sgt. John Minick, Cpl. Tyrus Brunton, and PFC Harry Salleroli and a jeep. Richmond recalled that he gave Sergeant Minick a cram course in piloting the glider. Near the landing zone they received considerable small-arms fire. After flying past it and out over the German border, the towplane circled around and came in higher than normal for cutoff. Richmond pushed the control column forward, putting the craft into a steep dive, picked up the run to one hundred mph, and made the best landing he had ever made.

Robert Minick[121] describes the adventures of this glider crew and their contacts with the underground:

Richmond looked out and saw a large group of Dutch civilians rushing up to the glider. They helped unload PFC Salleroli's jeep, then hid it in a barn.

Shortly after the underground concealed Salleroli's jeep, they furnished the men with civilian clothing, and then led them to a tobacco farm. There they spent the next three days dodging German search parties. The first thing the underground did was collect all the American cigarettes. Then they furnished those who smoked with a domestic brand. They knew the Germans would detect the aroma of the American tobacco immediately. Next they were fed and treated like kings.

On the second day, two different patrols searched the farmhouse. The first patrol had fifteen Jerries and the second one about forty. While the patrols searched the buildings and grounds, the four Americans would hide in the tobacco fields. At one point during the search, the Germans were within forty yards of them and the men could hear the Krauts talking. The men had to lie quietly under the tobacco leaves for two hours on two different occasions. But then things got better. After the second patrol left, the men were not disturbed by any more searches.

Shortly after dawn of the fourth day, all four decided to make a break for it. The underground had helped map out a safe route and then lined the route with small strips of white bed sheeting which would show up in the darkness. The 907th men linked up with some troopers of the 82nd and, with one man lying across the hood manning a tommy gun, they began their mad dash. They headed toward their objective down winding, narrow back roads, ignoring challenges from enemy sentries and outpost guards. Wild shots were fired at them but, luckily, no one was hit. After a long and grueling trip, they successfully rejoined their unit.

A 907th glider, piloted by F/O James Swanson, landed in a field east of Boxtel. Arriving with Swanson were Sgt. William Lange, PFCs Eugene Langston and Nick Marucas. Robert Minick[122] describes their adventure:

They noticed a group of Germans converging on them from across the field. As the 907th troopers began running toward a wooded area, they spotted a Dutch civilian who was trying desperately to get their attention. When they reached the fence surrounding the field, the Dutchman parted the wire for them and introduced himself as a member of the underground. Together, they ran for a short distance before stopping at a farmhouse. While the Dutch guide was out in front checking the road, the troopers refreshed themselves with a glass of cold milk. Having made certain that the road was clear of enemy troop movements, the guide again ran them for quite some distance until they reached a wooded area. He motioned for them to sit down and keep quiet, then left. The long conditioning hikes and runs at Bragg and Newbury had served them well. Later that evening, the Dutch guide returned with an English-speaking doctor, who asked if they needed medical attention. He then assured them that they were in good hands. He advised them to do what they were told and then quietly disappeared into the darkness.

After several days went by, the underground moved them to a farm where they hid in a small wood shed. They covered themselves with bundles of twigs, emerging only long enough to eat and occasionally listen to the BBC broadcast over a radio hidden in the attic of the farmhouse. Three days later, the Germans moved into the farmyard and set up an anti-aircraft gun right at the back door of the house. Obviously, the situation was rapidly deteriorating. Since Swanson, Lange, Marucas and Langston had made up their minds that they would never be captured without a fight, they remained hidden in the shed and the game of cat and mouse continued.

The crowning blow came when the Germans began using the corner of the shed to urinate against. Since the shed had several wide openings in between the laths, the men were always guaranteed of a fine misty spray every time one of the Germans visited the makeshift latrine. It was time to vacate the premises.

122. Minick, 144–5.

On a dark, rainy night, when flights were non-existent and when there was no need for the German gunners to be out of doors, an underground member opened the door and led the men out and away from the shed. For the next thirteen miles they followed one another by holding onto a rope knotted at intervals. This would keep them from becoming lost in the darkness. They were finally led to a campsite in the woods occupied by seven men from the Headquarters Battery. Here they remained with Sgt. Harold Wohlford, Sgt. Alvin Ettingoff, Sgt. Bill Doss, T/5 Robert Weaks, T/5 Rex Willoughby, Cpl. Perry Acord and Pvt. Herman Hohman. After successfully eluding the Germans for twenty-three days, the entire group of men was led in pairs to the maternity hospital in Schijndel. Before their trip through the German army, men were ordered to don civilian clothing provided by the underground and to shave their beards.

Flight officer Swanson's cover was a small child furnished by a most patriotic underground member. Swanson began his stroll holding the little girl with his right hand and tightly clenching his cocked .45 in a coat pocket with his left hand. Sgt. Wohlford recalls walking right down the side of a well-traveled road. Almost immediately they were passed by German tanks and half-tracks.

When they arrived at the hospital, they were placed in a room behind a large door that had a TB sign hanging on it. The German patrols always avoided this door when passing through the wards and hallways.

Throughout the hectic period spent at the hospital, the underground carried on its extensive and highly dangerous operations. It included the nuns, the local priest, Protestant ministers, doctors, police and bargemen, and nothing was too risky for them to try. On one occasion, when the German division headquarters was set up in the hospital basement, all civilian passes had to be re-stamped or revalidated. A young lay teacher in the local Catholic school, pretty and very shapely, went into the office containing the new stamp and, by sitting on the desk of the officer in charge and flashing her pretty limbs about, she was able to get his mind off the stamp. She then stamped the hem of her slip and the underground had a reproduction working within an hour.

Prior to the invasion, the hospital had also been a way station for getting downed RAF and 8th Air Force crews out of continental Europe and back to the United Kingdom.

The 907th Artillery Battalion wasn't the only unit to find landing sites in the Boxtel-Esch area. Parts of Headquarters Company of 1st Battalion of the 401st Glider Infantry were mis-dropped in that region on the eighteenth. Several gliders carrying men of Headquarters Company of 1st Battalion of the 327th also ended up in the area and eventually joined with 82nd Airborne, British 1st Airborne, and men of the Polish Airborne Brigade.

The glider in which Sgt. Willie R. Hiney arrived in Holland near Boxtel was hit by numerous rounds of small arms, which made it sound "like someone typing on loose paper." The tow-plane was hit in the rudder and immediately cut the glider loose.

Hiney wrote: "We had a communications trailer loaded with equipment and personnel. We fired the glider. It was only a few minutes until the Dutch underground contacted us. The initial contact was dressed as a priest and walked with a limp. They hid us out in the countryside for a few days. We were some distance from Boxtel. The group was getting larger, creating more difficulty. They decided to move us into an insane asylum. Here we stayed until an SS headquarters moved in downstairs. It became too difficult to get food in so we moved one night. There were about twenty of us by this time, including some British soldiers. There was also an escaped German officer who was in the group which had attempted to assassinate Hitler earlier. He was with the Dutch Underground and joined our group the night we left the asylum. He and some underground people took care of the sentry so we could get out.

"Sgt. Russell Vaught was in charge of the group. He and I were in agreement with the Dutch that we take the officer with us in the group which was a good decision. He spoke several languages and was very helpful in stealing rations out of German kitchens for the group. Vaught could speak broken French as he was from Louisiana. He and the German would go in and get the food and bring it to a cart and horse which I and an underground person had waiting.

"This went on for some time with the delays that required that we must get through to the British lines. One night they said they would advance to where we were hiding but they did not make it for a few days.

"One of the most frightening experiences was that we had rounded up the Nazi sympathizers and around a hundred and fifty troops and had them as a group. Then the British did not come until the next day. We had very little ammunition to hold them from breaking out on us. There were about 45 people in our group at the time. The next morning we were relieved by the British."

The men in S/Sgt. Michael A. Bokesch's glider were members of the Mortar Platoon. His group flew into Holland on the nineteenth, the day the glider landings were so badly scattered because of bad weather. His contact with the underground was almost immediate. He wrote: "I was the only one who spoke German (similar to Dutch). I had to challenge the oncoming Dutch underground member, Marinus Verhagen. He was wearing light blue coveralls and had blond hair and looked very German. He and I remained constant companions, along with Klaus and Frances Dekker (the latter two were sweethearts). Their guidance, directions and judgment were most heroic and certainly contributed to our success and final escape.

"When darkness fell the first evening, it was a chilling experience. We were led to safety in a wooded area by a 'monk.' At dawn the following day, some unarmed enemy soldiers approached my guard area. They wanted to surrender. I told them to get lost.

"Within a few days, the underground linked our group with men of the 401st Battalion, then men of the British 1st Airborne Division, then the Polish Parachute Brigade members. After six weeks we had members of the 8th and 9th Air Force—pilots, fighter and bomber crew members, some who had been shot down two years before and hid out with the aid of the underground."

Citing one of his buddies, Bokesch wrote: "S/Sgt. John Burke had the qualities of leadership that inspired others, including officers of the Air Force and British Airborne that his judgment was always in the best interest of all. (Burke was killed at Bastogne.)"

Bokesch added, "We were assisted by the Dutch—radio communications, food. They provided us with black bread, jelly and milk. When they learned the enemy was nearing our hideout area, they would move us to an alternative hideout. They always planned ahead."

Unknown to the Allied troops was the fact the food they were eating was being carted to a farm by a thirteen-year-old boy.

When the British fired on the church steeple in Oirschot on the second of October, the church was burned. The townspeople were evacuated by the Germans. The DeBeer family was sent to

Boxtel, where the parents stayed in one home and the thirteen-year-old boy was placed with a neighbor. H.L.A. DeBeer wrote: "My parents stayed with the van Hooff family and I stayed with the van Kuyks, next door. The van Hooffs also hid a Jewish man named Katam. Although he was in hiding, he was a member of the resistance using the name of Franssen. When we arrived in Boxtel we learned there was a refuge at the Campina Heath. Mr. Katam brought 11 American survivors from a glider crash-landing to the refuge.

"After a few days, I was told to carry something to the Campina Heath. Being 13 years of age, the Germans wouldn't pay much attention to my travels. I was told not to speak about my travels to anyone. What started with small packages ended up with transporting push carts, which I had to bring to a farm just outside Boxtel. I brought bread, baked by baker van de Laar, and jam. If I was stopped by the Germans, I had to say it was for the evacuated civilians."

Sgt. Joseph Nyeste of Headquarters Company, 1st Battalion of the 327th, landed in an area near Boxtel heavily patrolled by German troops. His group was found and immediately hidden by Gabriel Sauer from the Hague, who was a member of a group searching for lost soldiers and men of the airborne. Soon they were met by seventeen-year-old Marinus Verhagen from Esch, who was also seeking Allied soldiers.

Trying to keep the airbornes out of the hands of the Germans, the two underground men decided to get help. Contact was made with Klaus Dekker, a Boxtel resistance worker. With the help of his brother, Roel, he organized an immediate rescue party with a number of trusted men. They managed to gather and help 106 men—airbornes and pilots. They assisted them until the liberation of Boxtel.

For six weeks Sgt. Joe Nyeste and his comrades remained in the woods of Campina. They found the ideal hiding place in the hills, digging foxholes and shelters against the cold and rain, and to sleep.

S/Sgt. Michael Bokesch ended his narration. "My most vivid memory of the Holland operation was at dusk when we made our trek from the forest to take over the town of Boxtel where friendly troops (Scots) were on the other side of the canal, subsequently leading to our escape."

Involved in the same festive occasion, Sgt. Joe Nyeste added,

"They greeted us as liberators, made us policemen and that evening, with three other comrades, we arrested the first collaborators."

Nyeste remembered that a man came to him saying, "My wife is sick at home and she would love to see a 'Liberator.' I went with the man to see his wife."

The Scots were really the liberators in this case. Without them in position across the canal, the liberation would have been delayed for some time.

This chapter provides only a sampling of the wonderful assistance provided by the Dutch underground resistance groups who did so much to shield, feed, and eventually steer the airborne soldiers to their own units. Many of the friendships developed in those days over forty years ago still continue. The airborne soldier salutes his Dutch compatriots!

TWENTY

Watch on the Rhine

The regimental intelligence teams of the 501st Parachute Infantry Regiment were probably the first units of the 101st to be deployed on the island. PFC Carl H. Cartledge wrote: "Towards the beginning of October, the three S-2 teams headed north to the island south of Arnhem, Holland, bounded on the north by the Neder Rijn and on the south by the Waal. The #2 team was in a windmill at Driel, the #3 team was in a windmill at Opheusden, and we were in an old bell tower at Heteren. All three teams were on the dike of the Rhine. The British airborne operation on the north bank was winding down, not much going on our side of the river for the moment. We took over from a British division, and they pulled back. Our own troops had not yet arrived from Veghel. In the next day and a half, one of the most amazing events happened and I still wonder at the outcome.

"There were less than twenty men for several miles of the Rhine bank on our side. The British had moved several miles back and the 101st Airborne couldn't get up the jammed highway to us. The Germans had crossed the river in force at several points, ours being one of them. Our radios were hooked to each other, but our base station was many miles away at Veghel and out of touch. I estimated that about an enemy company had pulled into the brick factory below us. It later turned out to be a battalion. The enemy soldiers were fat and slow on their feet—and very cautious. We knew they were green as grass. A couple of shots their way and they all went flat. All that day we kept shooting at them at distances in excess of 500 yards, far beyond their own capabilities.

"We ranged up and down the dike sounding like any army, yelling orders to no one and then moving. They fired back with machine guns and mortars, riddling the trees and houses and scaring hell out of the cows. Our own artillery was Frank 'Chief' Sayers. His carbine grenade launcher was our mortar and big gun. Of course he couldn't reach them; they were too far away and were digging furiously. (We later saw their trenches and they were things of beauty—every shovel of dirt was hauled away somewhere, so our aircraft wouldn't be able to photograph them.) They got ready for a major battle. Chiefs grenades blasted the fields in front of them. They waited for us to attack.

"By the time evening rolled around that first day, we were just about out of ammo. We had one box of hand grenades to throw down the dike that night, and Waldo Brown had a .45 pistol loaded with one clip, and that was it. They could have walked through us but we decided to stick it out. We built fires all along the dike and continued to yell back and forth. We had never known the Germans to attack at night, and they had looked so green, we figured if they did attack we'd take them with our knives and rearm ourselves with their guns. Anyhow, our battalions must surely be getting close even though we could get no one on our radios yet.

"The following morning the Germans were well dug in among the bushes in front of the brick factory. They must have dug all night and were waiting for our attack. They were firing at the trees behind us again. There were a lot of dead cows in the fields between us. They must have killed them during the night thinking they were being attacked. About mid-morning Waldo Brown put on a British airborne beret, took out his pistol with our last ammo in it, walked to the top of the dike, cursed them at the top of his voice and then calmly emptied his .45 at them, turned his back and walked back down. We heard them talking excitedly about that for fifteen minutes or more. But they hadn't fired at him at all. About noon the 2nd Battalion of the 501st spread out along the dike."[123]

The 1st Battalion of the 501st Parachute Regiment had been ordered to move into the area of the dike between Driel and the railroad viaduct where it crossed the Neder Rijn south and west of Arnhem.

First Lieutenant Frank Fitter, communications officer of the 1st Battalion, was part of the advance party. He said, "I remember when we moved up to relieve the British near Driel. As com-

123. PFC Carl Cartledge, letters to family of Pvt. Frank Sayers.

munications officer, I was in the advance party. We went up to make contact for the relief and just as we got there, they were under a pretty heavy artillery barrage. We jumped out of our jeep and ran into their headquarters which was in a house that was all sand-bagged. They had a bunch of noisy radios—had fire control on one side and the CP group on the other. The commander welcomed us in the ole British tradition with: 'We're in a bit of a battle now but would you chaps care for a toddy of rum?' We told him, 'No, go on with your business.' But he insisted, so we drank. And then when this was over, we made the plans for the relief. There were only three of us—the battalion CO, myself and the adjutant."

First Lieutenant Sumpter Blackmon remembered the move to the island. He said, "The drivers came to pick us up to relieve the British. They did not want to drive into the fields to turn around because there were so many dead bodies and we were subject to a lot of enemy firing. I got into the lead truck and the driver permitted me to take the wheel. I turned around in the field and got back on the road. I noticed when we got up on the Island between Nijmegen and Arnhem and were ready to disembark from the trucks, paratroopers were driving all the trucks behind me. The regular drivers didn't wish to drive the way our paratroopers wanted them to drive. When we got out of our trucks we got one of the best pep talks ever given to us. We were kind of teed off with the British for not coming through on time and not supporting us with barrages as requested at Eerde and for not getting up there to relieve the British in Arnhem.

"As we dismounted, a British major came by when we were unloading and said, 'Go get 'em, troopers—you're the best soldiers in the world!' I noticed he went on by the other trucks repeating the same message. That just fired us up."

Because the enemy had excellent observation from the high ground across the river from Driel, the men were dropped off many miles short of their destination. The officers didn't want their men to become casualties to the highly accurate German artillery before reaching their assigned positions.

Replacement Pvt. John Cavaluzzo of "D" Company in 2nd Battalion was headed for the area previously described by PFC Carl Cartledge. He wrote: "We had to arrive at our position in the dark, necessitating a quick march from where the trucks had dropped us. The Krauts had full observation."

Sgt. Guy Sessions wrote: "We had been transported in trucks most of the way but now we were to replace the British who were dug in along the Lower Rhine. We had already met our British guide and he was leading us to the 'C' Company area."

"After we got off the trucks we had a long walk and trudged well into the night up into Driel and then turned east to the dike area," said T/5 Frank Carpenter. "We were awfully tired as we had been walking literally parallel to that dike from west to east. The 1st platoon made a left flank and went north toward the dike on a little road that was an entrance to a farm and house that was tucked up next to the dike. Company HQ and the next platoon made a swing around and then, for some reason, we stopped. There was something going on at the front. Captain Phillips went up and put all of us in the ditch beside the little road that led north. We laid down in it."

Sgt. Harold L. Paulson said, "Company 'C' called all squad leaders forward to show them their areas. When I went back to get my squad, someone had moved them about 50 feet where they all promptly laid down for needed shut-eye. While I was stumbling around in the dark, trying to find them, the Krauts laid down a mortar barrage. Before I found my squad, I was knocked down three times from concussions of close hits and never received a scratch."

T/5 Carpenter added: "Pretty soon there was some firing, machine gun, German, and our stuff, and combat action from that house, shooting back toward us. About that time six or eight mortar rounds came in on us. The first rounds hit right where that road went from going east into the yard. It hit right at the junction of the roads just like it was zeroed in. Then they started dropping the shells toward the north, one after another, each one closer than the others right up the road. The darned things were literally hitting on the road and our guys were lying off the side of the road on each side of it. We were pinned down. One exploded on the road right above my head. I got a little shook up. It was the one time I was ready to break in the entire war. The supply sergeant was lying next to me. I started getting up and he put his arm and hand on my back and pushed me down and about that time another round went off and had I gotten up on the road, I'd sure have gotten some shrapnel. After that shot there was no more firing.

"Captain Phillips got up and came back down the road, realizing part of the company HQ and parts of two other platoons were still on the road and hadn't turned in. He ordered us to go toward the dike and cross over a fence and go on over into an orchard on the other side of the barbed wire fence. We were told the British were in the orchard. It was the exact corner of the dike and the railroad viaduct.

"The guy in front of me started over the barbed wire fence and a flare went off. The Germans in the farmhouse had fired the flare. Everybody who was moving up in that field, froze—even the guy on the other side—we grabbed the fellow that was up on the top strand of wire and steadied him so he didn't move. It was like an eternity before that flare went out. We took off running across the field and into the orchard, then infiltrated our way into the British area. Captain Phillips relieved the British and they were ordered to infiltrate back and to reassemble at Nijmegen.

"What we didn't realize is that the Germans had come over the dike and filtered into our area. As we had moved in, they had evidently moved in behind us and we were now basically surrounded. The British left about this same time but they had to leave a Bren gun carrier and an anti-tank gun of some sort—maybe a six pounder, plus a sergeant and about three or four men who were the gun crew. They were to move out the next day when the lines opened up. They stayed with us when the rest left."

"It was every man for himself to get out of the orchard and into our area," wrote S/Sgt. Maurice C. White. "I lost two good men from my platoon in that orchard. PFC Joe Alberico was killed and PFC Frank Beck was wounded. Beck had his jaw blown off by shrapnel. (He spent 2½ years in army hospitals getting his jaw rebuilt.) We were able to get in position at the junction of the river and railroad."

As darkness brightened into day, the action really picked up. T/5 Frank Carpenter stated: "The Germans started coming in on us from the west. They were shooting at us and throwing hand grenades over the dike and we were throwing grenades the other way. There wasn't much up on the railroad but the Germans were trying to stick their heads through that viaduct and taking some shots and this went on all day. We lost three guys, that I can recall, to snipers in that area. We dug foxholes into the side of the dike and one guy, the operations sergeant, Milton Nelson, got it. One guy was walking when he should have been running through an open place and he got it and a third guy was down in the orchard when he got it. We think the same sniper was in the farmhouse we had run into the night before. Since we were surrounded, the battalion commander ordered 'A' Company to begin an attack from Driel towards us with platoons on line and they did. They had a helluva fight."

First Lieutenant Sumpter Blackmon said, "We were relieving and replacing the British up there and Captain Phillips of 'C' Company was down right at the railroad track where it goes across the river from Nijmegen to Arnhem. His right flank was on the railroad. We stretched out down the dike toward Driel, which is two miles down to the west.

"The 506th was at Driel and we were next to them and at night sent 'C' and 'B' Companies to relieve the British and the major of the unit we were relieving told us there was a small patrol down between the two companies we were relieving. I asked him, 'How big a patrol?' and he said 'It is a small patrol—rather small patrol, not many,' and I asked him, 'How many, as many as ten?' and he said 'Seven or eight,' and the next day we went down to get that patrol out of there. Company 'A' had gone into Holland with 8 officers and about 144 enlisted men. After some of the bitterest fighting 'A' Company had experienced in the Eerde and Weibosch areas, 'A' Company had 56 strong for the Island operation."

Blackmon added: "We were ordered to get the patrol out and to connect with 'C' Company. As for support for our men, we couldn't get any artillery fire down there. It was just between the companies and it was just too dangerous to bring in any artillery fire."

S/Sgt. Clive Barney remembered an incident with some British tanks. "They shot at us up on the island. Captain Phillips told me the tank commander had been given the 'C' Company command post coordinates and thought they were their targets. They were supposed to work over the hill, across the river. I'll never forget Phillips' coolness under fire on many occasions, but the one I remember most (because at the time I thought it was funny) was his walking into the British barrage waving a white flag."

First Lieutenant Frank Fitter had something to add concerning the artillery support. "On one occasion I recall the British backing us up. We had a lot of British artillery. I don't know how many of those 6-pounder guns were behind us but it was quite a few. They would run tanks up behind us and fire and then withdraw. We put up with that for quite a while and then Captain Harry Howard said, 'I'm going to put a stop to that!' He went to the battalion commander and said, 'We don't need any more of that—those guys come up and fire like hell and leave and we get all the counter-battery fire and besides, they are not doing any good anyway.' They kind of backed off after that."

First Lieutenant Blackmon continued his story: "We were ordered to get the patrol out and connect with 'C' Company. I felt we had plenty of ammunition for the .30 caliber machine guns and we had four or five of the weapons. We took three machine guns and put them near the dike. All three of them opened up on the left flank of the enemy who were over on the left side. The gunners were firing all the way across the sector through apple trees and orchards. We had instructed Lt. Harry Mier that those machine guns march their fire and stay just ahead of us as we advanced through the apple orchards over into the enemy territory. As we moved along, we were able to set one of the barns on fire. We used a mortar to do that. We put about fifty rounds of mortar fire in there right ahead of our troops—wasn't over two hundred yards across there. We were lucky to get the Germans excited and they started to give ground and run away. They'd left one of their machine guns and we were about to run out of ammunition by the time we got to their positions. I grabbed the enemy machine gun. The Germans were going down a ditch away from us. I leveled that gun and fired right down the ditch—I thought I was gonna be firing that way, but I guess about ten rounds went down the ditch but I ended up on my back, firing straight up in the air. That was when some men in the company said, 'They're not up there, sir!' That German machine gun pushed me right back on my fanny."

When asked why the company was down to only fifty-six men for this sweep through the orchard, Blackmon said, "We never got replacements while we were in the line. One thing about the paratroops—they never sent any new men on the front lines. That is why some of the companies were down to platoon size (50 men) due to no replacements being brought in—battalion reserve was myself and 12 enlisted men."

T/5 Frank Carpenter continued his description of the battle

from the "C" Company viewpoint. "The more they ('A' Company) squeezed the Germans, the more the Germans realized they were caught between us. They were getting shot from both sides. The only way they had out was to go over the dike and it was just a matter of time before they broke en masse and we were gonna have a field day and that's what happened.

"Sometime in the middle of the afternoon they tried to go up over the bank, to run up to the top and across the dike where the rest of their units were. We cut loose and had them pinned right between us and boy they just kept falling off that bank one after another. They finally gave up and sent in a German officer with a white flag and asked *us* to surrender. Captain Phillips laughed—if anyone was going to surrender, it was the Germans—'You get out of here!' All they were doing was sizing up our positions and trying to note our strength. They went back and the fighting resumed for a while longer. Then what few Germans were left were either captured, killed or wounded by our fire or by 'A' Company."

Blackmon finished his story: "After some of our bitterest fighting, 'A' Company killed 25 to 30 and captured 65. As we moved these prisoners to the rear, a heavy German barrage caught us as we left the cover of the dike. This barrage took two of my three guards and 15 to 20 of the prisoners. Hans Kropman was injured bringing those prisoners in."

Hans Kropman had volunteered his services during the very first days of Market-Garden and had stayed with "A" Company. Describing his part in the attack near Driel, Kropman related: "The screaming 'Screaming Eagles' surprised the enemy and, after a fierce but short battle, we took about 75 prisoners.

"It was nearing daybreak and there were still plenty of other Germans around us. Captain Stach ordered a few men to take the prisoners to the rear so he did not have to worry about them.

"I asked Stach if I should go along with these men but he said, 'I might need you here.' However, a short time later he changed his mind and said, 'Hans, maybe you better go along with them in case they need an interpreter.' I tried to catch up with them and when I got there, all of a sudden, the Germans started shooting at us (as well as at our prisoners). I was hit by shrapnel from a mortar shell and later moved to a field dressing station."

T/5 Frank Carpenter summarized the action after the prisoners were marched to the rear. "After 'A' Company was done, they just swung north and laid up against the bank of the dike just like we were, so we had one continuous line and the 'good ole guys' from 'A' Company had saved the 'good ole guys' from 'C' Company.'"

To Capt. Ian Hamilton and the men of "B" Company went an assignment to clean out the farm complex that had given so much trouble to Capt. Bob Phillips and his men during the previous night and daylight hours of October 5.

Captain Hamilton said, "Lt. Ronald I. Murray, commanding the 3rd Platoon, led a wasteful attack to 'straighten the line' as a farm building complex was on our side of the dike and we were ordered to take it. I first directed British artillery on the position, augmented it with some company mortar fire, but the enemy held as Murray's men advanced into small arms fire. He was killed along with a couple of others. Several men were wounded. Immediately after the attack I busted one of my sergeants to a buck-ass private for failure to supply supporting machine gun fire from the left flank. He said the gun jammed but when I pulled the trigger of the gun, still in place, it fired perfectly. This occurred in an apple orchard."

PFC Lawrence C. Lutz was with Lieutenant Murray in the action. He wrote: "The 3rd Platoon under Lt. Murray's command, moved into an apple orchard near Driel on the Island. As we moved on, a shot rang out and Lt. Murray fell with a sniper's bullet to the head. PFC Joe Braml got up to go to Lt. Murray's aid and before I could get the words out for him to be careful, he was shot and killed. Even today I still regard this as the most traumatic moment of my life."

As an aside, Lutz wrote:

In my opinion, 1Lt. Ronald L. Murray was one of the most complete men I have ever known. A man of wit and charm with a compassion for the men under his command that made all of us respect and admire him. I had emotional problems as a young trooper and he gave me the ear when I needed it. My love for him was like father and son.

As for PFC Joe J. Braml, we met at Camp McCall and, being in the same rifle squad, we became good friends. We ate and drank together, cried and bitched to one another, went on pass together. After the Normandy operation we returned to England and took a seven-day furlough together—obviously pretty good buddies.

As Captain Hamilton and his men moved farther into the orchards and the farm complex, he noted what appeared to be carnage. He said, "We moved up into that area and took up assigned positions and while so doing we came upon mounds of bodies. My presumption was that the British had butchered a number of Germans and the Germans had done the same to a number of British. There were too many dead bodies piled that close together, to otherwise have been killed in the normal course of infantry warfare."

The scene he witnessed was most likely the result of the pile-up of German dead, killed while trying to retreat to the dike when caught between Companies "A" and "C" earlier.

With the shelling of the area and the resulting slaughter of the captured prisoners and guards, a lull fell over the area.

Sgt. Harold L. Paulson noted, "When the British pulled out they left a machine gun. They said it wouldn't work. I told my gunner to play around with it in his spare time and see if he could fix it. A couple hours later Tom Gatewood said he thought he had fixed it and could he test it. I told him to fire a sweeping burst out front. Later we found a dead German who had been hiding in the weeds."

Action picked up again before darkness fell. S/Sgt. Maurice White said, "The British left some equipment. A German tank came down the dike and under the railroad and stopped. T/5 Frank Carpenter (1st Platoon) bore-sighted a British five-pounder (anti-tank gun) and fired one round and knocked out the tank."

For T/5 Frank Carpenter it was a more personal matter. He said, "Evening fell and there were a heckuva lot of Germans over there. We heard at least two tanks fire up. They were on the other side of the railroad viaduct on the dike road so we could hear them but couldn't see them. All of a sudden, Germans appeared on the bank of the railroad, which was to our east, firing down into us. Germans came over the dike side and were firing over the top of it and the two tanks started moving.

"Inside a little building were the British gun crew and the gun tube was pointed smack at that viaduct and I was standing there with a radio on my back. The British sergeant was urging his men to get to the gun. They said something to the effect that a mortar round had blown the front sight off and they wouldn't move out of that building, which was pretty substantial. He was yelling at them and the tanks were coming—one tank had

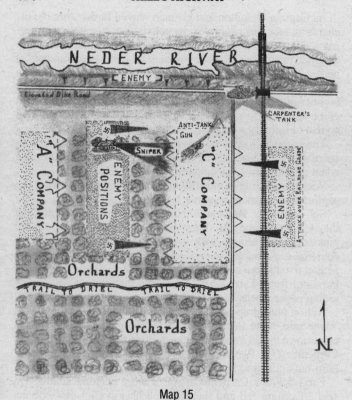

Map 15

breached the viaduct opening and started shooting at us—all the guns in 'C' Company were firing. I was standing outside that little building and looked down and saw the gun. I had never fired one of them, never had seen one before, nor been close to one. I grabbed another guy and said, 'Come on, let's see if we can make that gun work!' I darted about five yards and jumped in the hole they had dug for the gun. I didn't know if it was loaded. I fooled around, pulling all kinds of levers and finally got the breach open. Out popped a shell. It was loaded. I tried to push it back in. That was not how you did it. You slammed it in and the pawls released and the breach closed. I didn't know how to fire the gun. The tank gunner was spraying the building with machine gun fire. The sturdy walls prevented penetration. There was a lot of hollering and screaming going on. While working all the levers, I hit something that caused the gun to go off. The gun jumped in the air. There was a helluva lot of smoke and flame. I told the guy I was with to jump into the hole. I didn't know if the gun was going to explode. The shell had hit the tank. It exploded. I was still standing there. The gun was smoking.

"The guys in the tank tried to get out. Hell, they were mowed down by our guys. They never had a chance. The other tank—the gun crew—knew what they were doing. They weren't going to come through that (viaduct) opening. They put it in reverse and backed out of the way. The attack which the Germans had started was smashed and stalled in place. They all went back over the bank on both sides of the dike and railroad bridge and that was about it for the night.

"Needless to say, when the tank was hit, everybody was swatting me on the back and yelling. I was cheering and crying and glad I was alive but I was the first anti-tank gunner in 'C' Company." (T/5 Frank Carpenter was awarded the Silver Star for his actions.)

2nd Battalion at Heteren

As the truck convoys bearing the 501st Parachute Infantry Regiment had moved along the roads from Nijmegen to the island, they had tried to hug the dike area along the Waal River and then turned to the north before swinging east. Second Battalion had dropped out of the convoy, dropping the men short of their assigned areas.

The diary of Cpl. Charles J. Ritzler of "D" Company provides some background for the scene to be played out over the next two months along the dike of the southern bank of the Neder Rijn.

Oct. 4—Woke up at 0400 this morning, rolled our bedrolls and walked out to trucks. From there we went north about 8 miles from Arnhem where the British had been driven back this side of the Rhine. We walked five miles to the line and relieved the remaining British about dark. Subject to shelling all of the time—men won't be able to stand this too long. They hammer us all the time.

Pvt. William J. Houston remembers his stay up on the island this way: "I guess it was the next day we went up to the dike. They told us that two companies of English soldiers nearly got wiped out just before we got there. They had gone across the dike to take this brick factory between the Dutch Rhine and the dike. This was our position along the dike until we were pulled back."

"I remember marching into the area of the lower Rhine River," said Pvt. Henry A. DeSimone. "We were relieving the English. They didn't care about smoke coming from chimneys in the houses they were in. We were on one side of the dike and the Germans on the other side."

Because of heavy fighting, S/Sgt. Ed Jurecko had been unable to jot down notes in his diary for extended periods. His first comments on the island episodes appeared in October 12 notes while he was recovering from wounds suffered during a mortar attack on October 7:

> Many days have passed. We moved north to reinforce the British. Her airborne units had been hit hard and were disorganized. Our mission was to hold the counterattacks of the enemy and to prevent Jerry from establishing any more than the one beachhead they had on our side of the river. We occupied the British positions and were amazed at the number of enemy that were on our side of the river. We had wonderful concealment about 400 yards from the enemy on the sloping 20–30 foot high dike in which we dug our foxholes and prepared for come what may. It came!

Second Battalion moved into position along the dike between Heteren and Driel. The Germans shelled the positions constantly but the men had excellent shelter in their foxholes dug in to the leeward side of the dikes along the road that led from Opheusden to the railroad viaduct that crossed over to the Arnhem area. The men were sent out on listening posts, sniped at the Germans, and lobbed grenades to the far side of the road bank.

The diary entry for October 5 by Cpl. Charles Ritzler covers several actions:

> Germans shelled all night. They have plenty of stuff across the river. Took Manzi and Beck on a listening post at dark but a machine gun opened up on us and we were forced in. We sniped at Germans all day. They weren't very cautious. The British have been letting

them run around—things are now changed. Jerries attacked 3rd Platoon and got close enough to throw hand grenades—wounded six and killed two (Cooter and Pennington). Cooter was an old Toccoa man. Arviso, Johnson and Worth were among the injured.

Intelligence officer for 2nd Battalion 1Lt. Bill Sefton remembers the action along the dike. "When we got up to the Neder Rhine we took over positions from the British unit that was there and the position was the main dike on our side of the river. The interesting thing was that the British were holding one shoulder of the road and the Germans the other. Neither side dared stick a head above the dike. You could hear the enemy coughing, sneezing and talking. The dike was 20 to 25 feet high with sloping sides and if you threw a grenade across, it either missed the foxhole you were throwing at and rolled harmlessly to the bottom of the dike or if it rolled in the foxhole, they had time to throw it back."

Cpl. Glen A. Derber had this memory of the dike: "My most vivid memory of the Holland campaign is the 'Grenade Court' section of the dike where the Germans were dug in on one side of the dike and our men on the other side, separated only by a blacktop road with a fence on each side."

Up along the dike, facing the Neder Rijn, activity had slowed down to exchanges of hand grenades and sniping in the 2nd Battalion area.

Cpl. Jack Hampton describes a somewhat humorous incident: "The rumor was that we were relieving a British unit and that their attitude in defense of that area was somewhat loose. It must have been so because one morning, soon after we got there, I looked over the dike to the field beyond and saw dirt being shoveled out of a hole some 50 to 75 yards in front of me. The German was making headway on the hole because I couldn't see his head. I assumed he was stooped over so as not to expose himself. Well, he must have gotten warm because the digging stopped and soon he laid a jacket up by the hole. Then on top of the jacket he laid a bottle of probably wine or cognac. Then he went vigorously back to work on the hole. I thought—such arrogance! I'm going to teach that so and so a lesson. I told the other guys to 'watch this' and took a bead on the bottle with my trusty M-1 and squeezed off a round, shattering the bottle into a million pieces. Now I don't understand the German language but I'm sure they could hear the cursing all the way back to Veghel. After that there was very little activity in that area."

Pvt. David M. Smith was a member of the 501st Regimental S-2 Section at one of the three OPs along the dike. The S-2 teams had been on the scene for a day and a half as the sole 101st protectors until the regiment had arrived during the predawn hours of the fifth. He was surprised with the visit of the regimental commander to his post in the bell tower at Heteren, not far from where Col. Howard Johnson had set up his command post. Smith wrote: "I was in an OP in a very thin defensive line. Three other S-2 men and myself were on duty observing there. One of our guys was running around in his long johns because his pants burned. He had been close to a white phosphorus burst. The long johns were filthy (as were all of us). Suddenly the colonel (Johnson) and several of his staff came to the tower for a look at the German lines across the river. As soon as the old man saw our long-john clad man he hit the ceiling. He said, 'Major, I want this man in a pair of pants in less than an hour!' The major took off and was back in about a half an hour with pants (the right size, too!)."

Throughout the division, Col. Howard R. Johnson, commander of the 501st Parachute Infantry Regiment, was known as "quite a character" by other troopers. Pvt. Clyde O. Bruders of service company describes an incident that illustrates why the "Geronimos" of the 501st loved their unpredictable leader. "I spent most of my time in this area on guard at the regimental command post and the only thing that stands out in my mind was the evening before Colonel Johnson was killed. An English artillery group was in position around the CP. At dusk that evening, the English started lighting fires and turned on search lights. Colonel Johnson told me to contact them and tell them to turn off the lights and douse the fires as they were drawing enemy fire. The English sergeant I spoke to refused, saying his 'ole man' did not say so. I informed the colonel of his answer. Colonel Johnson told me to go back and tell him that '*my* Colonel' wanted the lights out and if they were not put out I was to shoot them out. He still refused. The colonel said, 'Put them out!' I fired one shot and the lights went out."

After a day and a night of exchanging grenades, little damage was being done to either side. It didn't take ingenious paratroopers long to devise better ways of conveying the grenades to the enemy positions.

"The situation lasted one or two nights until some GI had a brain storm," said 1Lt. Bill Sefton. "He tied a bunch of boot laces together and attached a white phosphorus grenade on one end while hanging on to the other end. The cord was just long enough to reach across the road and dangled a few feet on the other side. They burned the Germans out in one or two nights."

"While on this raised highway near Driel we were tossing grenades back and forth, not doing much damage to either side," wrote Sgt. Lawrence C. Lamb. "I, myself, unraveled silk threads from parachute suspension lines. We tied one end to the road fence cable, the other end to our grenade. These grenades stayed where they hit the ground. A couple hours of exchange and the Krauts gave up on that part of 'Hell's Highway' as we called it."

Cpl. Glen Derber wrote: "The riflemen dug in our side were tying suspension lines to the grenades so they would not roll harmlessly down the opposite side of the dike when they threw them across. They were hauling grenades by the jeep load."

Col. Howard Johnson had been inspecting the positions of the 2nd Battalion along the dike on the afternoon of the sixth. The men of "F" Company had just repulsed an attack along their segment of the dike front.

Communications corporal Sam R. Pope of 2nd Battalion HQ was working in the area. He wrote: "I remember the day on the Island when Colonel Johnson was killed. I walked past him and several other officers—around the corner of the house they were standing by, as the shell came in. Later I was told that he was killed and I presume that was the shell that killed him. One or two seconds later and I could have been in on that one."

"I was in the 2nd Platoon CP when I heard a round coming in," wrote 2Lt. Robert O'Connell. "It was one of the few rounds that day. It came in at an angle—not from directly across the Rhine. I heard Colonel Johnson had been hit and ran over there about 50 to 75 yards to my left. I saw a crowd around Johnson on the ground and sensed disaster and went back to my platoon."

Attending the mortally wounded colonel on the ground was Capt. Louis Axelroad, one of the 2nd Battalion surgeons. Men gathered around the flamboyant commander heard him say weakly, "Take care of my boys."

Sgt. Chester Brooks, operations sergeant for 1st Battalion, had been jolted by a fragment of a shell in the Driel region on the sixth and had been sent to an aid station, perhaps the same one Colonel Johnson was taken to. Brooks wrote: "We could not get off the island until dark as the Germans evidently had the exits covered with artillery fire. We were evacuated after dark by 'Ducks' and picked up by ambulance on the other side. I was not aware of the Colonel until one of the medics offered him a cigarette and he was exasperated and said, 'Don't you know I don't smoke!' I didn't realize his situation was serious until quite some time later when he asked a medic in a rather weak voice, 'How much farther, Doc?' We got to a field hospital and I learned a little later that he died during the night."

The numbers of enemy soldiers in front of the 501st Regiment positions were steadily increasing. The movement across the river was occurring during hours of darkness. Flares were sent up to spot the movements so they could be dealt with by the artillery.

From an entry in the diary of S/Sgt. Ed Jurecko, describing action that took place on the night of October 6:

> The next night we sent parachute flares up over the river and spotted at least ten rubber boats coming our way, loaded with Krauts. It was a massacre.

In the bell tower at Heteren, Pvt. David Smith and his team were at their posts. Smith wrote: "I was observing the Kraut lines when all of a sudden I saw at least a reinforced company begin crossing the river in rubber assault boats. I called it in and they put every piece of artillery available in the area (American and British) on a sector in front of the tower to the river. Very few Germans got back to the other side. Soon the Krauts wised up and started shelling the tower. They got a direct hit on the roof with me looking out of a hole in the wall. I went tumbling down to the floor below. I went back up to the roof with one of the other guys and continued to observe while the other two men stood guard."

In his diary entry for October 6, Cpl. Charles Ritzler mentioned the flares and also the movement of heavy-caliber machine guns to the line.

Sniped all day. Got one. Shot bazooka at the old factory where Jerries are hiding out. Planes dive-bombed it about 1400, really is a racket when they let them go. Lewis got it in the stomach by mortar. Moved two .50 caliber machine guns in our line. They will help a lot. Shot flares up all night (every 2½ hours) then opened up with all our weapons so they got little sleep last night. Went to my hole about 0300 this morning.

Heavier weaponry was requested by the 501st to reach out farther to the enemy positions six hundred yards to the front and to the locations across the river. In a diary notation for October 6, 1/Sgt. G. F. Fitzgerald of "C" Battery of the 377th Parachute Field Artillery Battalion wrote:

The 501st asked for a .50 caliber machine gun. We sent Cpl. Bernie Jankowski, T/5 Baker, Joe Chadwick and Dave Older with a .50 caliber up to protect the right flank of "D" Company.

A member of that gun crew, T/5 Albert S. Baker, related: "I was with Cpl. Bernard Jankowski and others on an outpost with the .50 cal. machine gun. A lieutenant came up and 'asked us to volunteer' to go with the infantry with our MG up on the levee. We went and then dug in up on the bank. An infantry lieutenant came by and told us to open fire towards the Rhine River. Cpl. Jankowski said, not unless there are targets we can see. The next day the lieutenant came back with a sergeant and asked if he could use our gun. Jankowski consented. The lieutenant got into my foxhole with a walkie-talkie radio and gave orders to a nearby mortar crew. The infantry sergeant lay beside my foxhole observing through field glasses. The mortar fire was two hundred yards short. Then the Germans came back with a barrage of their own. The sergeant was hit. When it was over, the lieutenant left. Cpl. Jankowski turned to me and said, 'See, Baker, if we had opened up with that .50 caliber the Germans wouldn't have quit firing until we were wiped out.' He added, 'Now if the Germans were coming across that field in an attack we would mow them down.' We never did get to fire that .50 caliber on the levee."

Pvt. Gordon E. Hannigan had jumped as a forward observer on the seventeenth and did a lot of that work up on the dike. The officers of the 501st may have liked having the firepower of the .50-caliber MGs on the dike but the infantry soldiers in the positions didn't care for them. Hannigan noted: "Every now and then our 'C' Battery would send a .50 caliber machine gun to fire across the river. The infantry didn't care for that because anything larger than a .30 caliber promptly brought incoming mortar fire."

The diary notation for "C" Battery mentions the shelling that the .50-caliber gunners underwent along with mention of the grenade throwing carried on by both sides:

> 1st Sergeant Fitzgerald and others went forward to the 501st area to check on the .50 caliber MG crew and Lt. Bernie Carr's party. The .50 cal. was truly in a hot spot with a few near misses by mortar fire. A bit below them, Americans and Germans were throwing grenades across the dike at each other.

Second Battalion intelligence section leader Bill Sefton described the positioning of the troops along the dike and the main positions of the enemy soldiers. "I remember how dark the nights were and our positions on that dike were merely 2 and 3 man strong points 50 to 100 yards apart. There was a lot of patrol activity across the river. The Germans still had a bridgehead on our side. Since our foxholes were on the nearside of the dike and there was a two-lane road across the top of the dike, you had literally 200–300 yards of dead space on the other side of the dike. Once the Germans got that close there was little you could do to fire at them."

Every so often a trooper hazarded a peek over to the other side in daylight. Some got bullets through the head. Others were more fortunate, being saved by a glancing blow that didn't penetrate the helmet. Two men remembered the incident, though they have not been in contact since the end of World War II.

Pvt. William J. Houston wrote: "One of our men, Henry T. Harbison, got a bullet through his helmet while peeking over the dike. I'm sure he still has a crease in his skull. I looked over the dike but tried to blend in with something."

"I remember another humorous incident," recalled Cpl. Jack Hampton of "D" Company. "It could have been a tragic event. We were along the top of the dike trying to observe any German activity. It had been very quiet and we had become complacent. Henry Harbison was one of the guys looking boldly across the dike when suddenly we heard a loud 'boink' and saw Henry tumbling head over heels backward to the bottom of the dike.

Our first reaction was—a sniper got Harbison! He lay there a few seconds and then jumped up and said, 'Did he get me?' We laughed out of relief that Henry was O.K. I can't say the same for his helmet as there was a neat crease right in the middle from front to back probably an inch or more deep that made it look like humps on a camel's back. We became more cautious after that."

As noted in his diary, October 7 was a bad day for 1st Platoon of "D" Company. Corporal Ritzler wrote:

Saturday was a bad day. Jurecko, our platoon sergeant, got it while shooting a mortar. We brought Koss from the 2nd Platoon to act as platoon sergeant. Jurecko was a good man. Our colonel also got it. He died early this morning. Mortars hit a yard from Schneider's hole. He was okay but it knocked the side of the machine gun in. Finally brought Cooter's and Pennington's bodies down. Medics didn't come to get them though so if they're here tomorrow noon we'll bury them ourselves. We used the same tactics and shot up flares all night and kept up a steady stream of fire.

"Not long after we got up on the dike, some of our 'D' Company men got it as the result of a tree burst," wrote Pvt. William Houston. "This was the time I heard my first 'Screaming meemies.' Corporal Stevens caught some hogs eating on the troopers killed by the tree burst and shot them. I guess he caught them just in time."

"In this area, I encountered the bodies of PFC Walter Cooter and Pvt. Jesse Pennington," wrote 2Lt. Bob O'Connell. "They had been there for some days and the pigs were getting to them. I was irate as were the men in my platoon as they had not been attended to or cared for. I contacted the chaplain's office and the bodies were removed."

In a continuing entry into his diary written while recuperating in a hospital, S/Sgt. Ed Jurecko described a tense mortar situation that took place on the seventh of October:

1st Platoon sergeant Stanley Koss' section was being attacked the other side of the dike at night. I remember listening to his plea for help on the field phone to the company commander, safe in his bunker. His men were dying in the attack. Next day he threatened to kill the company commander with a .45 revolver. On that day he recommended me as an ex–mortar sergeant to pull back his platoon and for me to direct the mortar fire at the dug-in enemy opposite his vacated position at the top of the dike. With radio, I was effective in dropping rounds into their foxholes until I was detected and fired on and wounded.

Pvt. William J. Houston remembered the same incident. "We tried to drop the 60mm mortar shells close to the road that runs along the top of the dike but the guys on the mortar were afraid to shoot them almost straight up in case the wind caught them just right and they would come right back on us."

"Our 60mm mortar men had backed off a ways and were attempting to lob their shells just fifty feet in front of their own line," wrote Cpl. Glen Derber. "Those guys were good! I still can't believe that happened. We could see the German cigarette smoke from our positions on top of the dike."

A rifle grenadier and a sniper specialist, Cpl. Glen Derber seemed to enjoy stalking the enemy. He wrote: "I got involved when someone came down the line looking for a rifle grenade launcher to try and knock out a German machine gun set up in a foxhole about 75 yards out from the far side of the dike. I volunteered and asked someone to cover me with a tommy gun while I set up and lobbed grenades at the position. I had the foxhole pretty well bracketed but ran out of grenades so destroyed the gun with bullets and then went off to get more grenades. When I got back the two Krauts had retreated (I wondered why no one shot them) into a nearby woods. The Krauts pulled out under cover of darkness but the next day they put a sniper on that section of the dike and shot two troopers through the head as they were observing. I, of course, had to go over there and try to locate that sniper and neutralize him. Having previously knocked off a Kraut at 700 yards, I thought it would be easy. I tried the old trick of putting my helmet in view at one location and observing with field glasses from another but it didn't work and I gave up when a bullet hit the opposite side of the road, just six inches higher and there would have been three casualties shot through the head. And I never heard or saw where the shot came from. I was brave but I wasn't foolish. Anyhow, my sergeant reprimanded me for leaving my gun position to go hunting Nazis on my own."

The machine guns, snipers, and mortars kept the enemy at bay during daylight hours but there was much movement at night and the firing of flares tended to keep both sides honest. First Lieutenant Bill Sefton wrote: "They didn't attempt to approach us in daylight but there was a lot of night activity. I remember one night we had run out of flares. There seemed to be a lot of bustle on the German side. We had some concern about the possibility of a night attack. We did manage to find one of those little British 50mm mortars and a whole case of their little smoke bombs so at dusk we had the mortar set up and dropped smoke all over the German positions. They assumed that we were going to attack so they fired their flares up all night long."

"I remember one day I borrowed a pair of field glasses and searched the other side of the Rhine," said Pvt. William J. Houston. "I spotted a German welding on a tank by the flashing of the welder. I don't remember just who got the British artillery on that target but they really laid the shells on that tank."

Sticking one's head up to observe enemy activity was hazardous to one's health. There were ways of taking advantage of a good position using concealment. Second Lieutenant Bob O'Connell wrote: "I had a position in the attic of a demolished house where, from a small window, I had good visibility across the Rhine. I had binoculars and laid back from the window as this was too dangerous as the Krauts could see our every move. After searching, I spotted a camouflaged tank well across the river, too far for rifle fire. I called for a forward observer and Lt. Dimmerling of the 907th came up as a spotter. It took only two rounds to zero in and the tank was hit with a barrage. The tank took off down the road covered with smoke and fire. We counted it as a hit."

"We occupied houses during the day and dug into the dike at night," wrote PFC George E. Willey. "Only the attic could be used to look over the dike for German activity.

"Sergeant Bill Forman had me fire many rounds of mortar on a railroad car we suspected of being used by Germans for observation and his direction of fire was outstanding."

Once the enemy moved away from the far side of the dike and moved into the brick factory, the men were sent out on listening posts.

Corporal Ritzler describes what those experiences were like as noted in his diary for October 11:

Wednesday: We were sent out clear to the river on an outpost and really spent a sleepless night but no Heinies showed up. Came in around 0500 in the morning—cold and wet. We had three mortar hits on the house while we were gone.

One of those involved in these patrol actions was Pvt. William J. Houston. He wrote: "After so long the Germans got tired of dodging grenades and moved out from the other side of the dike. I remember Henry Harbison and I going out on an outpost on the Dutch Rhine. While I was on watch, Harbison took a nap and what a nap that was! He snored so loud that I eased away from him. It was no sleeping for me that night."

First Lieutenant Sefton remembered: "The enemy retreated to a brick factory on our side of the river and stayed there for another week or so before the sniping and artillery fire made it untenable for them and they finally withdrew across the river."

The brick factory continued to be a sore spot for the 101st and the British. Bombing with many hits had failed to dislodge the enemy from its position. A frontal assault had to be made.

Cpl. Charles Ritzler's diary entry for October 12 gave a terse report of the actions.

> We made contact with the British on our right and took the brick factory that had the machine gun in it so we have this side of the river pretty well cleaned out. Came in just before dark.

Sgt. Lawrence Lamb of "D" Company was involved in the attack on the brick factory. He wrote: "We took very heavy losses there. We lost several on October 12, including myself."

PFC Carl Cartledge, of the regimental S-2 Section, was still at his observation post when the battalions were involved in the fighting along the dikes. He wrote: "I remember the line company guys on our right in the brick factory who got wiped out with mortars and how we carried one back over the dike and wondered if he lived."

During this time period the 501st Regiment was on line between Driel and Heteren. Extending westward from Heteren to the Randwyck area, men of 2nd Battalion of the 506th Parachute Regiment held the line along the dike.

What the American troops didn't realize was that the enemy had zeroed in on the dike positions long before they arrived. The enemy had fought the British and the Polish brigade along the dike during the two weeks before the arrival of the 101st.

Consequently, when automatic weapons were fired from certain locations, the Germans knew the exact range and responded immediately.

The 506th on the Dike

The men of the 101st had been told by the British they were relieving that the dike area was quiet with only limited patrol action to be expected. The grenade tossing seems to have been in the 2nd Battalion area of the 501st. The response to the use of the heavy .50-caliber machine guns was the same for 2nd Battalion of the 506th. "Fox" Company, which had taken heavy casualties in the corridor fighting near Veghel, was hit hard again.

PFC Bill True remembers his group was hit pretty hard the first day they moved up on line. He wrote: "My most harrowing experience on the Island occurred the first day we were sent to take up defensive positions on the dike. There was a windmill right at the dike in our platoon sector. The lieutenant told us to dig in behind it in an apple orchard. The Germans had obviously observed our movements and probably suspected we had lookouts up in the windmill. They started an intensive artillery barrage at us. Some of the shells were hitting the windmill and the top of the dike. Most were falling in the orchard where we were trying to dig in. On at least four or five occasions, I was nearly buried by the earth thrown up by the artillery fire. Our lieutenant finally got the right idea and we ended up digging our foxholes on our side of the dike, just below the top."

True added to his narrative: "The next day, while talking to a 2nd Platoon man who had been assigned to help pick up the pieces of his buddies, I became aware that he was barely rational and not fully in control of himself. I learned later that he was sent to the rear someplace to rest and I'm not sure if he ever returned. There, but for the grace of God, go I."

Sgt. John Taylor's 2nd Platoon was to replace 3rd Platoon up on the dike where that group had taken a beating the night before. He wrote: "We had the job of setting this place up so we could defend it. Maning Haney and Clarence Shrout went back in the orchard and found a .50 caliber machine gun. It apparently belonged to the 81st as it was an anti-aircraft type weapon. They took it up on the dike and put it on our left flank. Then we got two more machine guns and put them down on our sector.

Meanwhile, we got hold of 1st sergeant Charley Malley to scrounge up a bunch of grenades for us. Every position had quite a few hand grenades and we made contact with the artillery and we got two concentrations zeroed in. They were called *FISH ONE* and *FISH TWO*. One was just over the dike in front of our positions and the other was over by the river bank.

"Right here (at Randwyck) the Rhine River makes a bend away from us. It was the only place where the Germans were on our side of the river and there was a string of trees that came up toward our place and that is where the Germans came in the night before. We'd expected them there so Haney's gun was down on the left flank and Bernard Tom and Kenneth Hull had another machine gun there along the right flank and somebody in the outfit had another gun down there also.

"2nd Platoon was down to 30–35 men. We had lost 17 men earlier. We started the operation with 48 enlisted men and two officers—both of whom had been lost.

"Shortly after dark all hell broke loose. We called for artillery. We know it was close, right over our heads, on the other side of the dike. Got a report that a shell got Orel Lev, Tom and Hull. Our telephone lines were all out. We had no communication. 1st Platoon on our left had a radio. Lt. Thomas thought it was our own artillery but we learned later it was mortar fire. The Germans had pinpointed these two machine gun positions and got mortars on them."

Sergeant Taylor added, "Lt. Thomas told me to get word to the radio to call off the artillery. On the way down to the position, Kiosnowski shot at me. He missed. I gave him the password—guess he didn't hear me. Just about the time I got to Haney's position—30 yards away—all of a sudden it exploded. It killed Haney and Shrout and wounded Carlino. The Germans had spotted our automatic weapons firing and had called in mortar fire."

Almost immediately upon arriving at its positions along the dike on the south bank of the Rhine River, the company commander of "E" Company was requested to establish an observation post near the riverbank and, from the place of concealment, report back to the artillery units any appropriate targets they might find. The British had been hearing a lot of vehicular movement across the river and wanted to find out about it and possibly disrupt or destroy movement of enemy forces.

Sgt. Donald Malarkey described his part of the operation: "At the meeting, we looked at maps and aerial photographs while the British officers explained how we could assist them. They said I could build a camouflaged 'duck-blind' type of observation post with good visibility of the tree-lined east–west road. I was to report all vehicle movement and identify it in relation to predesignated landmarks. Information was to be reported by SCR-300 radio to the British officer who was located at our CP south of the dike."

"A call went out for Sgt. Malarkey, myself and Pvt. Eugene Jackson to report to company headquarters," wrote T/5 Roderick Bain. "Captain Winters informed us that we were to form a three-man patrol and under cover of darkness the following morning, proceed to the bank of the lower Rhine River, set up a concealed observation post and, with my SCR-300 radio, point out targets of opportunity on the Arnhem side of the river, radio back to the British artillery unit to our rear, give the correct coordinates and generally raise havoc with the German forces."

Sergeant Malarkey finished making a blind for himself and set about preparing for observation of the enemy movements. He wrote: "When I finished, I lay down in the ditch facing to the east so I could detect the first glimmer of light. Almost simultaneously with the first sign of light, I detected a movement against the skyline 65 to 70 yards up the ditch. I kicked Jackson, who was behind me, and whispered to him that something was moving in the ditch. He, in turn, alerted Bain while I switched the safety off on my tommy gun and got behind an orchard tree on the edge of the ditch. I saw the outline of a head bob up and down so I challenged them. No response. However, I did not open fire as I somehow thought it might be a friendly patrol—I knew differently almost immediately when I noted a German police dog sniffing the barrel of my tommy gun. At that moment the training instruction vacated me that specifically said, 'When a German patrol is led by a dog, shoot the dog first.'

"My second challenge evoked a 'Me friend!' and in the quickening light I could see something white being waved. I told Jackson to move up the ditch ready to fire and I would blast them with my tommy gun if there was any trouble. He yelled back that there were seven Krauts. I ran up the ditch and kept them covered while Jackson searched them for weapons. I told Bain to get Captain Winters on the radio so we could find out what he wanted us to do. By now it was daylight and bringing them back across open country would be dangerous. I thought we would have to hold them till dark but Winters said to get them to hell back so they could be interrogated."

T/5 Rod Bain added, "I radioed back to our CP in order to alert our outposts what had transpired. Sgt. Malarkey and Jackson lined up the Krauts and away we went running full bore for the dike. The terrain was flatter than a pancake and we had visions of being gunned down with bullets in the back from the Germans situated on the other side of the river. It didn't take long to hot foot it to the dike and safety. By the time we got there, the SCR-300 felt like a piano on my back."

Sergeant Malarkey added to his account: "I expected we would come under German machine gun fire but we did not hear any weapons fired until we got to the dike, well out of effective range. I ran up ahead of the prisoners when we got to the blacktop roadway that crossed the dike. I wanted to be in front so our outposts would spot me. The hobnailed boots of the Germans sounded as if the German army was coming to Private Don Moone who was on outpost duty on the backside of the dike.

"We didn't hear much in the way of details about the patrol once we had turned them over to be taken to division."

As a footnote to the above action, the following item appeared in the 506th After-Action Report for October 5:

> Company "E" reported seven enemy captured in their sector. The prisoners are enroute to the Combat Team PWE at 0920.

A Purple Heart for Major General Taylor

The commanding general of the 101st Airborne Division learned the hard way that firing mortars, like .50-caliber machine guns, brought an immediate response from the enemy on the north side of the river.

Capt. Steve Karabinos[124] wrote: "General Maxwell Taylor was 99 percent right on whatever decisions he made. The one time he was wrong was when he didn't listen to a private and thereby got himself a Purple Heart. On that particular day he

---

124. From a letter Capt. Steve Karabinos wrote to John Taylor, eldest son of MG Maxwell D. Taylor, on April 4, 1987.

wanted to go to a mortar observation post where we could look across the Neder Rijn River to the other side. The OP was located in a solid stone building right on the dike. Since the ground across the river had higher elevation, it meant our movements to the OP were under German observation. We (General Taylor, Charles Kartus, the driver, and myself) parked our jeep behind another building which was about 200 yards from the OP. We got into the OP and climbed to the top floor and through peep holes we looked across the river and saw nothing but desolation. The General turned to one of the boys and said, 'Private, how about directing one of our mortar sections to drop a few rounds across the river.' The private replied, 'If I were you, sir, I wouldn't do that.' General, 'Why not?' Private: 'Well sir, we have no target of opportunity to fire at, and if we shoot over there, the Jerries will only fire back at us.' General: 'Fire away soldier, we want to see what goes on over there.' So with that, the private picked up his telephone and called his mortar section, gave them coordinates of their target and told them to fire about six rounds. We watched the shells land across the river, hitting their target, but we could see no other activity or damage to any extent. After watching six rounds, the General told the private that was enough and with that we proceeded to climb down out of the OP. We got out of the building and stopped to talk to the battalion commander who hurried over when he heard the General was in the area. He and the General talked at some length. It wasn't long after we heard a gun go off from across the river and the whistling of a shell as it came down and hit the other side of the dike knocking mud across the top and splattering us. Of course, we had good cover so no harm was done. I looked at the General, for I felt more would be coming in, but since he didn't say anything, I started back to the jeep with him following me and Kartus bringing up the rear."

Captain Karabinos continued: "As we walked away from the dike, we also walked away from cover and came under German observation. Again we heard the same gun go off and again the whistling of the shell as it bore down, but this one landed 25 yards to our left. I turned to the General and said to him we are under observation and we better start double-timing for cover, which we did. I hardly said the above when we heard the gun go off again and this time the whistling seemed to be right on top of us. By this time we were along side of a building and I was near turning the corner when suddenly I found myself being hurled some five feet through the air, but fortunately behind the building. I then proceeded to pick myself up and came back to the side of the building to see how the General and Kartus had fared. The General was just picking himself off the ground and I asked, 'How are you, General?' He replied, 'The sonsabitches got me in the ass!' I helped him to his feet and then picked Kartus up. He was hit in the left arm, both of them being hit by shrapnel. I was OK except my wristwatch got busted. I hurriedly got both of them under cover as several more rounds came in."

The commanding general of the 101st Airborne Division was out of circulation for ten days.

TWENTY-ONE

Opheusden

The logical way to use airborne troops is to have them strike swiftly, seize key points, hold these until armor and regular ground troops pass through them, and remove them quickly to prepare for still more such operations.

Such was not to be in Holland. Instead of going back to England or a new base camp yet to be established on the mainland in France, the Screaming Eagles of the 101st Division were directed to move up to the island, a landmass between the lower Rhine (Neder Rijn), which flowed past Arnhem, and the Waal River with Nijmegen on its south bank. The British VIII and XII Corps were moving up on the flanks of the corridor, or Hell's Highway as the troops chose to call it. Progress was slow but steady. Thus the American 82nd and 101st Airborne Divisions were called upon to continue their actions under a British command.

The area assigned to the 101st extended from Elst (along the main Nijmegen–Arnhem highway) westward to Opheusden, a distance of ten miles. The land was flat with numerous orchards throughout its area. The troops would be handicapped in that travel in daylight would be hazardous as the Germans occupied high ground on the north side of the Neder Rijn and had little difficulty observing the movements of the Allied forces. Several small bridgeheads were in existence in the Heteren-Driel area. During flood stage, the landmass of the island was often below the level of the Rhine and Waal Rivers. The land was protected by sturdy dikes twenty to thirty feet above the landmass. The dike had a narrow two-lane highway running along most of its length on both sides of the so-called island.

The 506th Unit After-Action Report describes the move north with its attached units:

Oct. 3—The Combat Team (consisting of 506th Parachute Infantry, 321st GFA Battalion, Batteries A-B-D-E-F of the 81st Abn. AA & AT Battalion and Co. "B" 326th Engineer Battalion) moved by motor from Uden to Nijmegen on the 2nd. Combat team commenced move to vicinity of Andelst-Zetten at 1300 hours. Transportation shortage caused four hour delay and move was completed at 1830. Relief of 214th British Brigade completed at 2100 hours and the British unit moved out.

Describing his move to the Dodewaard-Opheusden area, "D" Battery (81st) commander Capt. William G. Joe wrote: "As 'D' and 'B' Batteries were normally in direct support of the 506th, we accompanied them across the Waal at Nijmegen. The regimental HQ was established in a town to the east of Opheusden. 2nd Battalion was on the north up against the levee. 3rd Battalion was ordered to relieve the British regiment on the west. Naturally, our two batteries went in support of 3rd Battalion. The British assured us that all was quiet—nothing happening and they seemed to believe that—their casual attitude reflected it."

A Holland replacement, Pvt. Billy J. Waites of "G" Company, recalled arriving in the Opheusden area. "We relieved some Limeys. They told us there would be a German patrol that came through town at night. The British said to leave them alone and we would have no trouble with them."

PFC Leonard T. Schmidt remembered that his group had just relieved the British and they remarked, "There's nothing out there in front of you but a small patrol. It turned out to be considerably more."

Capt. William Joe continued his story: "The 3rd Battalion moved in generally where the British had vacated. I set up the Battery CP where the weapons commander had a set up near Dodewaard but nearer the small brick kiln and jam plant.

"Work had just begun for 'B' and 'D'. Our weapons were different and positions had to be selected with back up positions and routes for resupply. Fields of fire had to be compatible with the infantry squads and platoons. We didn't depend upon the infantry companies for any support other than maintaining contact. On the 1/4 ton Jeep, we carried our own rations, gas, ammo, and maybe a blanket roll. Of course, with peaceful assurances of the British, we brought up the kitchen and supply truck with the bed rolls. Since we were so busy setting up defensive positions, we temporarily stashed the bedrolls in the windmill located near the railroad depot in Opheusden.

"There was a lot of flat ground between the dikes and, in some cases, outside the dikes to the water's edge. But around the villages and, particularly in the rear of houses, there were small trees, orchards of fruit trees and heavy vegetation along the drainage ditches. There were lines of trees along the roads. We needed a little high ground to reach out 1,000 to 1,500 yards with those .50 caliber machine guns; short of that we had to get right on the MLR to get maximum effective use of the guns. And, of course, no infantry man wanted to be near the damn things if they started firing. All of our men appreciated that fact."

First Lieutenant Walter Kron, leader of the 2nd Platoon of "D" Battery, was very proud of his gun crews. "In the .50-caliber machine gun, we had a devastating weapon. Why, when they cut loose, it was like an earthquake. The paratroops tumbled out of their places and made themselves scarce. They didn't want any part of those blasting demons, even though they were damn glad that we were there."

Capt. William Joe continued: "After the British moved out, we were still digging in all the next day. You ever try to dig in a pedestal mount down low enough so that you could provide effective fire? The following day we had a few intermittent rounds of artillery to fall along the roads, then a couple of rounds around the road intersections, a couple near the railroad depot, etc. We used to be a heavy weapons company. Our sergeants felt they (Germans) were either harassing us or zeroing in and our non-coms knew we were under observation. Out in the flats, the infantry had listening posts at night and would withdraw at daybreak or when the fog and mist lifted. Near the railroad tracks, the 506th was using the drainage ditches to travel back and forth. My men told me that it was a thing of beauty to watch the German gunner walk his rounds down those ditches, turn the corner, walk down the horizontal ditch; they were clearing out any positions we might be thinking of putting in there."

Captain Joe goes on to describe the locations of his heavy .50-caliber machine guns. "In Opheusden, we considered the right flank and the left edge of town to be critical areas. On the right flank the road left the middle of the town going west with houses, vegetation and trees quite a ways out. We had a gun there and I believe there was a .57mm there, too. Coming back nearer the town center we had another gun. There was another gun between the railroad station and the center of town. It was difficult to get a good field of fire because of the underbrush. The left gun in Opheusden, under Cpl. Jim Lindsey, was at the railroad crossing. We had to cover the right side of the railroad embankment and the flats to the left of the tracks, all flat farm land cut into large square plots by irrigation ditches."

Though the 506th Unit After-Action Report mentions only light enemy artillery shelling of the 1st Battalion area on the fourth, it felt like a full-scale barrage to PFC Richard E. Turner. "Enroute to Opheusden, 'B' Company and the 1st Battalion were in slit trenches. Much artillery and mortar fire was coming in. My head was about one foot lower than loose dirt piled at the end of the trench. My walkie-talkie was sitting on top of the dirt. A mortar shell hit the loose dirt about a foot from my head, blowing my helmet off and rifle from my arms. The blast put shrapnel holes through the radio and blew it and my helmet and rifle about twenty feet away. It ruined the radio but missed me."

It was considered an obscure little town by many, but Opheusden will be remembered by the men who fought so savagely to hold the area around it. First Lieutenant Alex Andros of "H" Company said, "On the overall ETO scheme of things it was no big deal but as far as 3rd Platoon and probably the whole company was concerned, it was one of the most ferocious single battles in which 'H' Company ever engaged, at least the point of view of casualties.

"I had 3rd Platoon. We were to tie in with 'G' Company on our right. The line was about 400 yards from the main road through town and I was asked by Captain Jim Walker to connect that line from 'G' Company to 1st Platoon, who were back about 400 yards where the main railroad track crossed the main road. The position he suggested was in a completely open area with some cover to our front. It would have been very easy for the enemy to get up there and we would have been dead ducks. We had no way of getting in or out of there. So I told him I either go up or I go back and we decided to go up. We tied in with 'G' Company up to the railroad track and that was our position. Lt. Bob Stroud's 1st Platoon was back 400 yards on the main road by the railroad tracks, but on the other side of the tracks. As I recall, the night before a German patrol came up and we were told not to do any firing to reveal our positions. They fired some Schmizzers and a couple of Very pistol flares and no one responded so apparently they were trying to feel us out."

Andros added: "I had sent two guys out on outpost in a house about 150 yards in front of our line on the far side of the railroad embankment and just before dawn they came back to report to Sergeant Samuel Hefner that Germans were moving down the railroad tracks. Hefner and a couple of guys went up along the track about fifty yards ahead of our lines. Here comes this group of Germans moving in a very close formation. Of course, they didn't see Hefner and they weren't expecting anything and when they got within twenty yards, Hefner opened up with his tommy gun and the other guys started firing—probably killed or wounded fifteen to twenty of them, then immediately took off for our lines and got us ready for the main attack."

The opening paragraph of the 506th Unit After-Action Report for the fifth of October chronicles the first hours of the enemy attack on the 3rd Battalion positions:

> Enemy attacking in 3rd Battalion sector (Opheusden) at 0300 hours. At 0600 hours enemy attacking in strength along entire 3rd Battalion front. 3rd Battalion reports enemy using civilians as a screen for their advance. Medium artillery shelling of combat team command post at 0700. Combat team commander and S-3 depart for 3rd Battalion at 0730. The enemy continues to press its attack and the 3rd Battalion commits its reserve at 0845 hours.

In an account written from his hospital bed after being wounded in the Ardennes campaign, Capt. Bernard J. Ryan,[125] surgeon for 3rd Battalion, described the first morning at Opheusden: "Early in the morning of October 5, Captain Stanley Morgan and I were suddenly awakened before daylight when a heavy shell landed within a few feet of the aid station shattering the windows and scattering glass on our bed. This signaled the beginning of a three-day attack by the 363rd Volksgrenadier Division. Both of our company CPs in the sector were hit before daybreak and both company commanders were wounded. There were incessant artillery and mortar bar-

---

125. From a letter Capt. Bernard J. Ryan wrote to Maj. Louis R. Kent, surgeon for the 506th Parachute Infantry Regiment, from his hospital bed after being wounded in the Battle of the Bulge at Bastogne.

rages followed by a heavy infantry attack. The 'G' Company CP was forced to move slightly to the rear leaving the battalion aid station forward. Casualties began pouring in so rapidly and in such large numbers that any movement of the aid station was impossible."

T/5 Edward R. Vetch, serving as runner for "G" Company, had vivid memories of his combat actions in Opheusden and has since visited the battle area. He wrote: "The German attack on our front in Opheusden in the early morning of October 5th found me at the company CP, a schoolhouse near the center of town as the artillery hit with a roar as thick as a hailstorm at the crack of dawn. I had taken off my boots for the first time since coming to Holland as the English told us it was a quiet place as we moved in the evening before. At least six rounds hit us directly at once.

"The whole roof and part of one wall were blown in at one time as the initial barrage landed. I was in my sleeping bag along a wall and was pretty well buried under debris. It was no easy job to get out with two or three hundred pounds on top of you and smoke and dust so thick you couldn't see your hand in front of your face. Then to find my boot, which I was using as a pillow. There were yells for MEDIC! everywhere, as 3rd Platoon of Sergeant Ross Minor was in a thatched-roof barn just behind the school. It, too, had taken a direct hit and was on fire. We found Captain Joe Doughty near the center of the school where he had bunked in a small room. He was buried so deep we had to dig him out and he was hurt pretty bad. He told me to get to Lt. Eugene Rowe and 2nd Platoon to see if they needed help as they were on the MLR on the northwest edge of town which was a roar of small arms fire by then."

In a letter he wrote to the wife of one of his fellow officers who had been seriously wounded, Capt. James C. Morton[126] gave her a "Censor passed" version of the fighting at Opheusden and the wounding of her husband, Capt. Joseph Doughty of "G" Company. "Joe was hit at daybreak in the opening phase of the attack. A German shell crashed into his CP and a piece of shrapnel got Joe dangerously near the eye. He had to be evacuated."

126. From a copy of a letter Capt. James C. Morton wrote to Mrs. Joe Doughty from a hospital bed on March 8, 1945.

T/5 Edward Vetch continued his story: "The MLR was in a drainage ditch along an apple orchard on the edge of town. As I got there, Lt. Rowe was in his CP, a small cement building right on the edge of the ditch. The Germans were in the orchard directly in front and so close I could see the black boots through the branches. Everyone was firing continuously. Charles Lewis, with his machine gun was by a little bridge going over the ditch to the aid station and an old people's home on the left front. Another machine gun was to the right. The door of the CP building was on the back side from the orchard and a window was on the left side. As I talked to Lt. Rowe, he suddenly pulled his .45 and reached out of the window and shot straight down. I glanced back out the door and a German soldier lurched out beside the building with blood gushing from his mouth. Lt. Rowe had shot him through the back of the neck.

"About this time a German got a line of fire down the ditch from the right with a machine gun and 2nd Platoon started taking casualties and had to drop back to the buildings at the edge of town. The machine gunner to our right was instantly killed. Lt. Rowe told me to try to get the gun. It was 50 to 75 yards away. I ran around the corner of the building and jumped in the ditch to get some protection from the fire which was coming in from the front of the orchard. I sort of expected the German gunner to open up at any moment, but I found out later Charley Maggio had picked him off with an M-1. I pulled the gun out of the tripod and as I did so I badly burned my left hand on the barrel jacket. It was so hot! Most of the ditch was empty by then except for the dead the gunner got when he shot straight down the ditch before Maggio got him. I ran back about 100 yards in record time as the small arms fire coming from the orchard was very heavy.

"I got to the church, a large brick one with the roof blown off by the barrage. There was a small hole in the end facing the orchard—it was an ideal position. I ran up on the altar, feeling a little bit guilty, but not for very long as they were coming out of the orchard for the ditch we had just left. I was on my knees with the gun lying at the bottom of the hole and plenty of targets 100 yards ahead and less than half a belt of ammo. Before I got through it, Ray Duran came running in with two boxes and orders for me to report back to Lt. Rowe to help place Sergeant Miner's 3rd Platoon that was in the barn behind the school as reserve platoon so I would know where everyone was when I had to find them in a hurry. I couldn't leave before just one more belt which didn't take long as they kept coming out of that orchard."

Describing the actions involving his support troops from Battery "D" of the 81st AA & AT Battalion, Capt. William Joe relates: "On Thursday morning (Oct. 5) early, first light, and real foggy, it 'hit the fan.' Most of it was coming down in Opheusden and it continued until the fog lifted a little so we could see smaller stuff, mortars and light artillery hitting the road intersections and around the houses. Our single telephone (it was quite a ways from my CP to the railroad station) didn't last long. We depended on our radio contact with the platoon headquarters. I presumed everything came to a standstill because of all the artillery fire in a small area. I heard a report that the Germans attacked down the road on the right flank of Opheusden with civilians in front of them. Perhaps these were civilians coming toward our lines to get out of the way of advancing Germans."

Captain Joe continued: "Things got confused from the reports received at the CP on the left infantry company ('I') in Dodewaard. Everybody had their hands full. In Opheusden, Cpl. Art Lynn's squad was cut off and pinned down in the vicinity of some houses on the right flank along with some of the infantry. The enemy pushed through the center of town. Here is where a gun was overrun. Lt. Bob Hollingsworth was hit in the groin by shell fire and had to be evacuated. The gun at the railroad station held its own and stopped the Germans on the north side of the tracks heading toward the south edge of the village. The men later reported that in the far distance the enemy was crossing over the railroad tracks to the south side of the tracks. I'm told Jim Lindsey's gun didn't stop them but it certainly slowed them down. We had .50 cal. ammo loaded for anti-aircraft fire—two ball, armor piercing, explosive (blue-tipped magnesium) and tracer. I can imagine when the rounds hit the rails, cross ties and rock ballast there was a helluva ear blasting sound, and red tracers skittering in every direction and the bright flash of exploding magnesium rounds. One of my men told me—'First you see the enemy soldier, then you see a white flash when a .50 caliber magnesium round hit, then you see this object (man) fly backwards'—he sounded quite awed."

Describing the dawn attack on his "H" Company platoon position, 1Lt. Alex Andros related: "At dawn they finally attacked. At this time our platoon was reinforced by a machine gun squad from Company 'B' of the 326th Engineers. We had a total of 44 guys with us. Sgt. Charles Richard's squad was on the right tying in with 'G.' George Montillo was on the left side—he was supporting squad but also protecting the left flank along the railroad embankment in case the Germans came over the embankment—to protect our rear. Sgt. Frank Kleckner was right up front.

"When the attack started it got pretty heavy with quite a bit of mortar and artillery fire coming in and that's where Sgt. Harry Clawson was seriously wounded (and subsequently died). Things got pretty bad around there. It must have been around 0830–0900 in the morning. We were suffering a lot of casualties so I sent this kid, Elmer Swanson (we couldn't get our radio going) to bring up some litter bearers. Capt. Stanley Morgan was the medic. He came up and went into the house where Clawson and Thomas were located. About 0930 or so, Colonel Bob Sink arrived and he asked me what the hell was going on. I told him we were getting our butts kicked. So he said, 'Can you hold on for another half hour? The 1st Battalion is coming up and they'll counterattack through you.' All I said was 'Yeah, we can hang on for a half hour.' But I think we stayed on about an hour and a half. When the Germans started getting behind the railroad tracks—we were keeping them away—you could see them behind the railroad embankment so Sgt. Samuel Hefner, who was the mortar squad sergeant, took his 60mm mortar tube without base plate and put it on the ground and there was a little haystack behind the station house and I said I'd spot for him. He stripped all the increments off the charges on the mortar shells and dropped the first one and the damned thing went straight up and I saw it coming down and I thought it was dropping right back down into the barrel. The shell landed about ten yards away from us and not too far from this guy who was under the hay wagon. But after that, it was all Hefner needed. He just dropped those rounds right along the back of that embankment. You could hear those Germans yelling. It must have been pretty effective. Ten minutes later we didn't have any shells left."

The *Unit History of the 326th Airborne Engineers* describes the actions in the Opheusden area that involved its men:

In the early morning, the Germans made a big drive from the west and were pushing on a line from the west direction in the vicinity of the town of Opheusden. By order of the regimental commander of the 506th, and with permission from division, the company was converted to infantrymen, due to the shortage of men at the time of the drive. The mission of the company was carried out—that being the 1st Platoon moved on a line on the north side of the railroad track facing the west toward Opheusden. The 3rd Platoon to move on a line on the south side of the railroad track. Company headquarters and 2nd Platoon were alerted and remained in bivouac area as a reserve platoon. The 1st and 3rd Platoons were to move forward through the defensive position of the 506th Parachute Infantry, who were dug in, until contact was made with the enemy, the objective being to determine how far the enemy lines were. Captain Froemke was killed while moving across an open field. Lt. William Deas assumed command. The battle became more furious on the north side of the tracks, with infantry and engineers fighting in the same line pushing forward toward town. Terrific fighting continued on both sides of the tracks through the remainder of the day and night.

PFC Thomas P. Fitzmaurice of "H" Company said, "The engineers were coming in as reinforcements and they were coming in at a bad time. Their captain (Donald Froemke) stopped them. They pulled over in a ditch and wanted to know where the CP was and just as we gave them the directions, an 88 shell came in and evidently landed at his feet. I didn't know where he went or what happened. My helmet flew about 20 yards out into a field and I wasn't about to go after it and I really felt naked without it. It was about two hours later before I could find another one. The captain was blown about a hundred yards and was completely dismembered."

PFC Frank Halloran was one of the engineers of "B" Company who was sent forward to assist the 3rd Battalion of the 506th in repulsing an attack on Opheusden. He wrote: "On the morning of October 5, at about 0800, Colonel Sink came up to where 'B' Company was dug in. He wanted us to assist Major Horton's 3rd Battalion west of Opheusden. Colonel Sink led the company up a dirt road. I was on the lead right flank behind Sink. As we approached the small town we could hear heavy machine gun fire and German artillery as we came upon five houses on the right. Colonel Sink told one squad to drop off behind the houses and assist 'H' Company. The lieutenant in

'H' Company (2Lt. Willie Miller) was wounded in the neck and he told us to proceed behind the houses, cross a small bridge and spread out in a drainage ditch about 100 yards behind the houses and a dirt street. Colonel Sink proceeded with the rest of the company to assist 'H' Company at the railroad station. The German 88s were landing in the drainage ditch so we moved back to the houses. The mud was up to our hips in the ditches. One of my friends was hit by machine gun fire crossing the small 15-yard-long bridge over the ditches. I was the last one out. As we came back to the houses, the 'H' Company lieutenant asked me and another engineer to jump the wire fences between the houses and work our way down to the bridge at the end of the street. We did this by protecting each other as we jumped the five-foot fences. We defended the last two houses we were behind.

"The German infantry was attempting to come up to the houses through the tall purple cabbage fields behind the houses. I got hit on the right knee cap and a few minutes later an 88 shell blew me and the shed I was behind about five feet in the air. I didn't have my helmet and my Thompson submachine gun was gone. I was hit pretty bad in the right arm. Two engineers rolled me down a ditch alongside the dirt street bridge. I really felt pretty helpless with no helmet and no weapon."

First Lieutenant Robert Stroud describes the action near Opheusden. "The 1st Platoon was told to go to the junction of the main road and the railroad track and we extended to our left. Louis Vecchi's squad was on the right. Hank DiCarlo's squad on the left, and Bob Martin's squad in reserve along with the mortar squad. Things were relatively quiet for a while and then they started throwing stuff at us. We were pretty well protected—most of the guys—except those fellows on the left who had to be in the fields. I had the CP right there in the little concrete signal station. We, at one time, had a few Germans who were trying to come up to surrender—about six of them, waving a flag. We were trying to get them in. Vecchi was holding fire on them and they were coming right up. A British Bren gun carrier came up and saw them coming in and just deliberately fired into 'em, killing most of them—the rest went back. A little later Major Oliver Horton, our battalion commander, came up to look over the situation and saw where our platoon was placed. We went out about a hundred yards in front of our lines between a couple houses to try to spot the Germans. At that time, as we were looking around, we were mortared. As the rounds came in, we immediately hit the ground. After they stopped, I got up but Major Horton didn't. I turned him over and saw he was white and bubbling at the mouth. I pulled him back as far as I could and then some of the fellows in the platoon moved him back farther and we saw he was pretty well gone. A little later, after the firing stabilized, we were told the 1st Battalion was supposed to come through and make an attack through our position. We waited then."

PFC Frank Halloran was now incapacitated, having been hit when an enemy shell hit the small building he was using as cover. In the shelter of a ditch beside the dirt street, he waited for medical assistance. "Not long afterward, a jeep came up the dirt road. They took a stretcher and picked me up and put me in the rear of their jeep. (The medics were John Gring and Stanley Matycich of the 321st Glider Field Artillery.) The engineers and 'H' Company opened up with machine guns on the cabbage field so we could cross the 30-foot bridge. After the bridge we made a left turn and there was a trooper lying in the middle of the dirt road. John Gring knew it was Major Horton and he was dead. Gring put him across the hood of the jeep. The fighting at the railroad station behind us was getting real heavy. We went about 100 yards in the jeep when an 88 came over and 'Matty,' the driver, thought it was going to land right in the jeep so he slammed on the brakes and Gring had a helluva time trying to keep Major Horton's body from falling in the mud. I almost landed in the front seat. The shell landed in the woods, off to the side of the road. We found the 1st aid station of the 907th Artillery. There were a lot of cows and women and children in the barn."

With the enemy soldiers coming around his flanks, First Lieutenant Andros said: "I sent Johnson to contact Richards and get ready to pull out. He came right back and said they were being overrun. You could see the Germans coming around the rear and we knew they were getting around our left so it was time to pull out so I went to Captain Stanley Morgan and said, 'We've got to get those guys out of here' and he said, 'You can't move these guys!' So he stayed with the severely wounded. There was no way we could get them out."

Capt. Bernard Ryan[127] wrote: "During the early morning of October 5th, Captain Stanley H. Morgan, with surgical technician T/5 Walter Pelcher, immediately responded to a call that several wounded of 'H' Company were in a nearby barn and needed medical attention. They were at a platoon CP. While caring for these casualties the Germans forced the platoon to withdraw. Captain Morgan told Pelcher to leave and he himself stayed with the wounded and was taken prisoner, and remained so for the rest of the war."

Andros added: "During the intense shelling I was with my radio corporal, Franklin Stroble. He was trying to get his walkie-talkie to work and I was chatting with him. A round came in. We both hit the deck. It killed him. All I got was a little flesh wound and a dent in my helmet. I was very fortunate. It was one of those things—luck was on my side that day."

Assigned to one of the machine-gun teams in support of 3rd Battalion troops, PFC Leonard T. Schmidt remembers losing his close buddy Carl Pease in the first-day action. "He and I were in this gun position. I relieved someone on the machine gun outpost and the Germans zeroed in on the gun with about 12 rounds of mortar and it is fantastic how small one can get down in a foxhole. I think I could have been in my steel helmet. They knocked the gun over. We decided that since they had the gun zeroed in, we would move to a position on the other side of the ditch. We were under an apple tree. It was early morning. You could hear the Germans talking but it sounded like English and I said to Pease, 'Hey, if they're English they've got no business being out in front of us without our knowing it.' I told Pease, 'Either you start firing or I will!' and that was his demise. He was shot through the skull. It was like sitting and talking to somebody and, all of a sudden, you are by yourself.

"I couldn't get the gun to fire. I went back to have someone look at Pease and ran into some riflemen and asked if they could get a medic and one said there were no medics up in this area. One of them went and looked at Pease and came back and said, 'He's dead!'

"It was my first experience at seeing a buddy dead from that close and having to push his body off the gun so I could try to operate it."

127. Ryan, ibid.

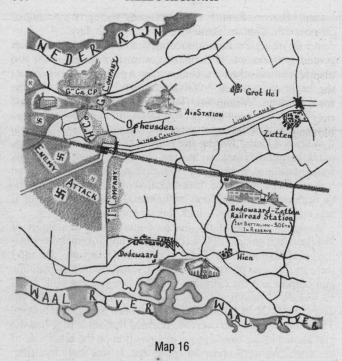

Map 16

"By the afternoon of October 5th, the Germans had taken
most of the town of Opheusden and had the aid station surrounded," wrote Capt. Bernard Ryan. "German soldiers in the
attack could be seen all around the aid station. Unescorted
German wounded came in for treatment. At about 1900 hours,
while I was administering plasma to a soldier, a heavy shell
struck directly in the next room, throwing me violently to the
floor in plaster and debris. The shell had blown out the front of
the building and entered a room where four German litter
wounded, including an officer, were none the worse for the experience after we dug them out. Pandemonium reigned in
Opheusden that day and evening, the town was burning and
shells were landing everywhere. One was as likely to encounter
a German as an American. All the wounded were finally evacuated by midnight and our 3rd Battalion had retired to Dode-

waard, having been relieved by the 1st Battalion. We evacuated 79 seriously wounded from the aid station that day."

As the company runner, T/5 Ed Vetch had kept the officers posted as to the whereabouts of the various platoons. He had also served a stint on a machine gun. And now he was part of the battalion pullback. "We were slowly pushed back as the town came down around us. By dark there were fires burning all over and Opheusden was in shambles with tanks right in town blowing down anything that stood or moved as we pulled out with what was left of 'G' Company. I never did know how many casualties we took that day, but it was high, I am sure. I know we lost five gunners that day so I lucked out again."

"There was a very heavy artillery barrage with an all-out attack by the Germans," wrote S/Sgt. Merville Grimes of "G" Company. "We had a large number of German prisoners in the basement of a house but had to leave them when we retreated."

First Lieutenant Robert Stroud of "H" Company added to his narrative: "Under cover of darkness, we moved back under orders to assemble at the battalion command post which was about a mile back. When we started moving back we were getting mortar fire and artillery at us on the road at the same time. We got back to the battalion CP and were told this was a mistake—we weren't supposed to pull back but to return to our former position. We went back and told our platoon that we were to turn around. We started back, ran into 'G' Company coming back with a bunch of prisoners—it looked like 50 to 60 of them. We then had gotten orders for the next day to move out to our left to take up positions where the other companies had vacated and it was toward Dodewaard. We moved into that position."

T/5 Ed Vetch added: "We were in groups dropping back to some English that were supposed to have an MLR along the road from Dodewaard. It started misting and raining and was so dark one might as well have kept his eyes closed. I think you could have seen just as much. After about a half hour of stumbling along in the dark we ran head on into a bunch of Krauts sleeping around a haystack by a blown down farmhouse and barn. Their guard or someone hollered and we hit the dirt as they opened up on us from less than 100 yards. Charles Lewis and I became separated and worked our way into the orchard as it quieted down and continued down a ditch in the orchard. We passed another group of Krauts in the orchard on our left so close we could hear them talking and they were lost also. A while later, we came to a road on a low dike and lay there for some time, listening and wondering where to go. We decided to crawl up on the road and see what was on the other side. Just as we got up on the road, a gun was cocked in the ditch on the other side. I yelled, 'Don't shoot, we're Americans!' He gave a password but I told him we had none and were from the 101st coming from Opheusden. He said to come in slow as they had us covered. They were Scottish and were on the British MLR.

"We found most of 'G' Company already back in the orchard, some were digging slit trenches to sleep in, as we had a long, hard day and everyone was dead tired as it was nearly midnight. Neither Chuck Lewis or I felt like digging and it was comparatively quiet—only a harassing shell now and then. We curled up by an apple tree near a drainage ditch and dropped off to sleep."

1st Battalion Moves Up

As pressure from the enemy continued to mount along the 3rd Battalion front on the morning of the fifth, Colonel Sink called for his 1st Battalion, which was in reserve near the Andelst-Zetten railroad station, to move forward and pass through the troops of "H" and "G" Company. They were to take over the sector extending from the railroad station to the eastern edge of Opheusden up to the bank of the Neder Rijn.

As the relief was being completed, the 3rd Battalion troops were ordered to move to the south side of the tracks to take up positions on the right flank of "I" Company. Thus "I" Company was responsible for the line extending from the bank of the Waal through the village of Dodewaard. "G" and "H" would hold the area between Dodewaard and the railroad station, which was the area through which the enemy was filtering most of its troops to the Opheusden sector.

As part of the 1st Battalion forces that moved through the 3rd Battalion positions on the fifth to take up that part of the MLR that extended north from the railroad station and highway intersection to the eastern edge of Opheusden, Sgt. Don Brininstool must have wondered if the boast of one of three enemy soldiers captured the previous day would come to pass. He wrote: "My squad was sent out in an open field. All night we could hear the German tanks and other vehicles moving into position for the morning attack. At daybreak, we could see their tanks about 300 yards away. I sent my men back into the woods about 200 yards in back of us. Sylber Speer was first. He was like a jack-in-the-box. First you saw him run, then machine gun fire from a tank. I remember thinking they must have got him. Then Speer would come up running again. Then (Don) Burgett had his turn, followed by Justo Correa. I was the last one to make my run for the woods. I was carrying a .30 caliber bi-pod type machine gun. At the edge of the woods was a wire fence. After clearing the fence, I was knocked to the ground. At first I thought an 88 shell had put me down. I had been hit at the base of my neck by one of the bi-pod legs. I picked up the machine gun and my squad and headed back into the houses for more protection from the tanks. After reaching the houses, I looked at my machine gun. An MG bullet from one of the tanks had torn through the jacket (outer barrel) of my gun and this is what had knocked me down, probably saving my life as I must have been down when the 88 shell went boom."

Cpl. Donald Patton had served as a scout as "B" Company moved up on line the day before. He didn't remember much action occurring on the fifth but at sunset his group had turned northwest at the railroad station and set up a bivouac for the night, headquartered in the house and in the orchard west of the house. The men had dug in for night protection. He had led a two-man patrol to the west along the tracks and then north and circling back to company headquarters. He had reported that he hadn't seen enemy or friends, nothing during the two-and-a-half-hour patrol that ended at midnight.

In a letter Patton[128] wrote to a friend in Holland, he described his experience on the morning of the sixth: "At daybreak, it was extremely foggy and I got out of my foxhole and looked around, greeting Sgt. Ernest King and suddenly, in a break in the fog, we saw a complete semi-circle of German tanks lined up to the west at about one hundred meters approaching our orchard positions at a slow, deliberate speed. Soon I saw more tanks along the road and on the railroad tracks to the direct south of our po-

128. From a letter Cpl. Donald Patton wrote to J. M. van Alphen in Holland in 1982.

sition. Sgt. King and I hollered at our first line of men to retreat and get out of there for we had only a couple of grenade launchers, three bazookas, light machine guns and rifles immediately available with sleepy-eyed soldiers. By the time we rushed back, the Germans had already pulled in front of the house (headquarters) and had started into the open field east of the north–south road to Opheusden and the dike road.

"There appeared to be hundreds of tanks—though I would venture 50 or more were in action that early morning coming at us from three different directions. As I was wounded in the next hour, I was literally out of action and had little more than ear sounds and rumors to substantiate my thoughts."

"Daybreak came and so did the Krauts," wrote S/Sgt. Charles A. Mitchell. "Out of the morning mist the tanks came with supporting infantry directly into the left flank of 3rd Platoon's squad led by Sergeant John Boitano. He had positioned himself on the second floor of a house along the road to try to delay the tanks with a large self-made grenade, the size of a pillow, which I felt was an exercise in futility, as well as the loss of a fine squad leader I could not afford to lose. I used a lot of profanity to get him out of there."

"Everything was fine—quiet on the morning of the 6th when all hell broke loose," wrote Sgt. John N. Boitano.[129] "I had a big sack of explosives which I was going to drop on a tank from the house. A tree was in the way. I was the last to leave the house. That day, we attacked three times and beat back the Krauts. We all ran toward the windmill. I saw a really good friend with his leg almost torn off. I stopped running to get him back to the windmill. He was 190 pounds and I was 135. I thought any minute we were going to heaven."

In a letter he wrote to his former platoon sergeant, Sgt. Charles R. Weise reminisced about the action of October 6. "The tanks moved up on the railroad and fired directly at us. The 3rd Platoon squads, 1st and 2nd, were dug in at the apple orchard on the outskirts of Opheusden. In firing directly at us, one 88mm shell landed adjacent to my hole and the front of the shell broke through the wall of my fox hole. Thank God it was a dud! I left my hole immediately. We received word to withdraw. After the

129. According to his friends, Sgt. John Boitano was awarded the Silver Star for his efforts.

2nd squad left I positioned myself near an out-building and had every 1st squad man tactically withdrawing one at a time. As soon as the last man left, I started to withdraw but heard one incoming shell—close—I slid half my body sidewise into a drainage ditch and the shell hit very close. Shrapnel entered my back causing paralysis to my lower body and bleeding from a stomach wound. I started pulling myself back to where the others went."

S/Sgt. Charles A. Mitchell picked up the story: "In fairly good order, we withdrew across the yards and fields we had moved across the day before, taking numerous casualties, as we went toward the aid station. Machine gunner Don Patton was hit and I think John Boitano assisted him to the windmill. Another squad leader, Sergeant Charles R. Weise, went down directly in front of me. He yelled, 'Mitch, I'm hit!' With his better than six-foot frame on my back, we all moved back as those tanks hesitated but kept firing. As I came to a drainage ditch, I hesitated for a moment, but with a pat on the back by my old friend, Charlie Weise, I lowered him into the ditch on my back and crossed the muck to the other bank. At the windmill, we placed him on a stretcher inside. I changed pants with a dead soldier."

As has been mentioned earlier in the chapter, the men of "D" Battery of the 81st AA and AT Battalion were up front with the infantry men of the 506th. The paratroopers steered clear of the big .50-caliber machine guns. And sadly, the 81st men weren't kept alerted as to the moves of the infantry.

"That morning (2nd day) the right squad in the open closest to Opheusden came in without their gun," wrote Capt. William G. Joe of "D" Battery. "When the enemy attack came down the center after we pulled out of Opheusden, the Germans were putting down small arms fire and artillery. When daylight came, that .50 caliber MG squad looked around and there was no infantry around anywhere. They had pulled back the right flank without notifying our squad. They pulled the breech block, disabling the gun and ran."

This may have been the same .50-caliber machine gun found by Cpl. Charles Shoemaker and the remainder of his team. "On the second day our machine gun team had been pushed out. We were across a water-filled ditch or small canal. Just to our left was a bridge going across it. When we moved over there we found a .50 caliber machine gun in a position—ammo and all.

Daylight or a little after, a British tank came up beside us. The tank commander stuck his head out of the hatch and said, 'We've got word the Germans are going to attack through this area. They've got quite a few armored vehicles and a helluva lot of infantry.'

"Just about that time a streak of fire came zipping across his bow. He was right. There was a bunch of tanks out there in the little woods off to our right and one of them was trying to get him. He just stopped in midword and away that tank went as he backed out of the line of fire.

"We looked out to our left and we could see down a drainage ditch, probably 150 yards straight ahead. The field on both sides had low grass and it looked for all the world like the German army was doing close order drill out there. They were coming from two different directions into that drainage ditch. This was a machine gunner's dream. So we laid the .50 caliber on them. I hit the butterflies and nothing happened. Jack Braasch came out and looked at it and I guess it was pure instinct. Something was broke. Would you believe the coincidence—we got 25 rounds out of our .30 caliber and it quit. It had a broken firing pin and we didn't have a spare one. The decision was made—took about five seconds. There were three of us and there were probably three thousand of them—it looked like to us. We decided to use that bridge and get back over to the other side."

The most memorable time on the island for PFC Fred T. Smith was in the little town of Opheusden. He wrote: "We took the town in late afternoon and the next day the Germans threw tanks at us. S/Sgt. C. A. Mitchell ordered, 'Let's get into the buildings and make a stand there because we can't fight tanks in the open.'

"As we were leaving, I looked back and saw foot troops with the tanks. I thought they might catch our company in the open, so I went back to my little fox hole and started to lay down some covering fire. There was somebody else doing the same because I could hear an M-1 firing. I think it was Sgt. Edgar P. Dodd. When the M-1 stopped firing, I decided to get out of there.

"As I was trying to get to the company, I passed an old barn. I could see a medical jeep inside, through an open window. As I passed the barn I saw Sgt. Dodd and one other in front of me. At that time, a shell came screaming in and both men were hit very bad. I did what I could for them. Dodd looked at me and asked if I was leaving them there. I said I would be back for them.

"I found S/Sgt. Mitchell and told him that Sgt. Dodd was hit and would he go back with me to get him. He said, 'OK—how far is it?' I didn't want him to know so I started back and he followed.

"As we got to them, he looked at me and said, 'Well, we can't carry both men!' I told him not to worry. I knew where a jeep was located."

S/Sgt. Charles Mitchell wrote: "Fred Smith's reference to the wild jeep ride took place on the morning of the 6th, as the enemy had probed our positions all night before with strong patrols. None were successful, but any astute commander would get the message. Captain Heber Minton was well aware of what to expect at daybreak. He and I both concurred our penetration to the 3rd phase line left little cover for the expected assault the following morning. Several attempts to discuss this with the Battalion HQ failed to gain permission to withdraw to better covered and prepared positions. The thought of protection of the aid station in the windmill, so full of wounded and dying, dominated all thinking at battalion for the moment, as the day had produced many dead and wounded.

"At some pause here, young Freddie Smith ran up to me with tears in his eyes and his eyes big with excitement. 'Sarge, Dodd's hit and we have left him to die.' Realizing he had to be calmed down, I asked him to draw a sketch on the ground where we might find him. He did so and I assigned the position to the gun crew and Smitty and I made out way to where Dodd lay along a rock wall, face down and groaning at our touch. Directly over the 8-foot wall, the Kraut squad of about ten men were taking a break, rifles stacked with a tank, big gun lowered, having their ersatz coffee and brown crackers.

"To say the least, we were faced with an impossible task, when Fred whispered, 'I know where a jeep is.' We moved around a corner and less than 20 yards away sat the prettiest jeep that ever came out of Detroit—medical outfit complete with stretcher. We didn't hesitate a bit—rolled it back beside Dodd and I held my hand over his mouth to stifle his groans and rolled him on the stretcher. As we lifted him (over 200 pounds) on to the jeep we noticed off to the side a 'B' Company man, (Pvt. William J.) Yorko, who we thought dead but his breathing told us we had to load him up, too. A huge fellow, he made not a sound as we put him into the right seat. With Smitty under the wheel, I in the back leaning over Dodd to hold him in and holding Yorko's jacket collar, I nodded to Smitty and that jeep sounded like a P-47. Out of there we roared as the Krauts scrambled for stacked weapons. I gave no concern for the tank, its gun was down and parked beside the wall, had no way to hit us.

"Smitty to this day swears I chewed him out as he nearly turned the damn jeep over as we made a curve back to the aid station, where we unloaded Dodd hastily and, before we could unload Yorko, a shell exploded, a near direct hit, destroying the jeep, killing Yorko and seriously wounded the medic officer attending him."

Fred Smith gave his version: "Just as we got back to the field hospital at the old windmill and had carried Dodd inside, a tank fired right at the jeep and killed the other wounded man and shrapnel hit a medical officer who came out to help him."

Sgt. Charles Weise had been brought to the windmill aid station earlier by platoon sergeant Charles A. Mitchell. Though in terrible pain, he was aware of the heavy enemy fire beating against the sturdy building. He was lying between Don Patton and Sgt. Edgar Dodd, who were both in his platoon. Patton had a large piece of metal protruding through both sides of one leg and was in extreme pain. Weise said, "The windmill was continuously being shelled. Much shrapnel was flying through the windows and double doors. There were more men being carried out who had died than those being brought in. I was doped and bleeding from the mouth, nose, ears, etc. because I also was suffering from concussion. I stirred one time because they had a hold on me and were going to take me to the 'dead pile.' Don Patton and I were close buddies, he says, 'Charlie, give me your hand'—this dreamer. He clasped my hand and started praying aloud. It seemed like immediately the war stopped. We were not getting shelled. The medics stopped to listen. It was a very stirring moment in my life. As soon as he stopped praying, shrapnel came in again and struck one of the doctors in the abdomen. He fell backwards, grasping his innards, and the medics got very busy trying to care for him. But the religious concept was so fantastic. . . ."

Witnessing the episode was medic PFC Robert "Buck" Barger, who was attached to 1st Battalion from the 326th Medical Company for evacuation purposes. He wrote: "Lt. Colonel James L. LaPrade was given orders to evacuate and leave the wounded and the medics. He refused to do that. On the last day our assistant battalion surgeon walked out the door of the windmill. We heard an explosion and he came flying through the doorway. He had a small hole in his abdomen and his intestines were oozing out. Captain Joseph Warren told us to wet some gauze compresses and put them on his abdomen. They eventually brought some German prisoners and they carried him out and back to our lines. To my knowledge he survived."

Third Battalion surgeon Capt. Bernard J. Ryan, whose aid station had been farther west and closer to the railroad–highway intersection, remembered the incident. He wrote: "1Lt. Cyrus L. Worrell, medical officer for the 1st Battalion was seriously wounded as the battle continued. He was hit outside the aid station when a piece of shrapnel eviscerated him, causing the loss of several feet of intestines and other internal injuries. He had formerly been a flight surgeon and had volunteered for parachute duty."

In other actions in the same area, "B" Company communications corporal Henry Gogola remembers a scary experience during the Opheusden fighting. "We were in a ditch about fifty yards or so from the road when, suddenly, we saw what I believe was a Tiger tank looking right down our throats. His machine gun was chattering to pin us down. It fired an artillery round in our direction. The ground shook like Jell-O. I know that I bounced up and was slammed back down. I heard a scream close by and saw PFC Bill Arledge not more than eight feet to my side. He had a good part of his torso blown away but was still alive—barely. I shot him up with morphine. There was not much more I could do for him. He was gone within a very short time. Another friend lost."

With the enemy pushing forward with tanks and infantry and heavy barrages of artillery and mortar rounds, 1st Battalion was forced to shorten its lines to keep from being outflanked. S/Sgt. Charles Mitchell wrote: "Hastily, Captain Minton prepared a modest perimeter defense of the windmill at a curve and crossroad nearby. Our big gun was a .57mm, which someone quipped, 'At least it might knock the paint off one of those tanks.'"

However, those .57mm guns (six-pounders), manned by men

of the 81st AA and AT Battalion, destroyed many of the German tanks during the Holland campaign.

In the actions south of the railroad station and the north–south highway position toward Dodewaard, the 3rd Battalion was holding its own. The 1st Battalion was having real problems as they were pitted against so much enemy armor and very heavy concentrations of artillery fire. The 506th Unit After-Action Report for October 6 reads:

> The 1st Battalion had to pull back to the eastern edge of Opheusden. The 1st Battalion was ordered to hold their present position until noon, which they did, and the 5th Battalion DCLI (Duke of Cromwell Light Infantry) would move up on their left flank at this time. The Combat Team commander ordered a counter-attack to commence at 1230. Because of numerous delays, the attack did not begin until 1345, following a 15 minute artillery preparation. The plan was as follows: 1st Bn. on the right, 5th Bn. DCLI on the left, with the main east–west street of Opheusden as the boundary. The attack was to proceed through the town of Opheusden to the western edge and deny the enemy the use of the town. The attack moved forward about 300 yards where extremely heavy enemy artillery and mortar fire stopped it. During this attack, the enemy was infiltrating around the 1st Battalion's right flank and the British left flank. Both battalions had to withdraw their flanks to meet this threat. Under existing circumstances, it was impossible to evacuate the wounded.

Sgt. Don Brininstool was in on the counterattack to drive the Germans out of Opheusden. He relates: "The Germans had about half of the town and we had the other half. Word came that we were to hold the town and the British would send troops in. The English arrived with about 300 men. They said, 'You take the houses and we will take the flank open ground to our left.' We were doing a good job of clearing out the houses but the battle didn't last too long as the Germans mowed the English down except for about thirty of them. We heard their major had said, 'A bloody good show while it lasted.' "

Cpl. Charles Shoemaker was another trooper who remembered the incident. He said: "I remember watching a British unit attack across some fields. They just lined up and away they went. About 25 yards later, only three or four of them were still running. There were five or six of us outposted nearby. Another

British platoon came in, lined up, started running—same thing happened."

Capt. William Joe had been told about the same incident by someone from the 506th. He wrote: "When the British were ordered to retake the railroad crossing, their unit marched up the road like they were on parade. They lost a lot of people but they reached the crossing and later had to give it up."

Another 506th trooper who was in on the afternoon counterattack through the east side of the village was PFC Giles M. Thurman. His vivid memory is not so much of the battle but of the civilian wounded he came upon in one of the homes. Thurman wrote: "Some first aid training I had received in the CCC (Civilian Conservation Corps) earlier came in handy. In the attack on the village of Opheusden, I was a lead scout for the platoon. I came through a barnyard, heard voices and kicked open a door—don't know to this day why I didn't blast away but what I found will live in my memory as long as I live. An older woman was dead, a boy of 15 or 16 had a gaping hole between his shoulder and elbow on his right arm and a beautiful girl of about the same age with a large piece of shrapnel in her leg, almost to her crotch. I threw my weapon down and took the morphine and bandages from three of our people and dressed the boy's wound, bandaged him and then took the girl, removed the shrapnel, gave her a morphine shot, tagged them and sent for the medics. I was congratulated for this later. (The Dutch were the Roelofse family.)

"The house was about 100 yards in front of the windmill we were using as an aid station. All the wounds were from artillery fire air bursts."

PFC John R. Garrigan was in on the two-pronged attack to retake the areas of Opheusden that had been lost earlier. He wrote: "I was now a squad leader on the afternoon of the 2:30 attack. Bill Oatman and I took off with a machine gun, jumped a couple of ditches, ran through a tobacco field with the rest of 1st Platoon with us. We finally came to a five-foot[130] fence which was the German defense on the other side—a lot of them nothing but young boys. All this time Oatman was firing his weapon and we finally came to a decision. We could go no fur-

---

130. Probably the same fence encountered by PFC Frank Halloran the day before in the engineer attack with "H" Company.

ther. Some of the boys were in a house up on the road and some of them jumped the fence. The English soldiers were fighting to our left. Sgt. Robert Kane was one who jumped the fence and we never saw him again. We went back after dark to find him but it was not to be. That night, in some backyard, we started digging in for the night when along came a mortar barrage—one shell landed in the hole next to one occupied by Jose Alvarez and myself. Both boys in the hole never knew what hit them."

Medic Robert Barger remembers the hectic time they had at the windmill aid station as the enemy closed in around it. "Lt. Colonel LaPrade ordered the riflemen to come by the aid station and pick up the wounded. We moved out under cover of darkness. We walked by a good-sized farmyard and down to an orchard. I would guess the distance (from barnyard to orchard) was a couple hundred yards or so. A group of five or six of us medics went back up to the farmyard to sleep in the barn."

Covering the final evacuation of the wounded from the windmill in Opheusden was an assignment of the line companies of 1st Battalion. Sgt. Don Brininstool of "A" Company remembered: "About 0200 hours we were ordered out. It seemed like we marched all night long. I don't think anybody had had much rest in the past 48 hours which made the march seem longer. We settled into an apple orchard."

The Apple Orchard Battle

The average line company foot soldier knew little or nothing of the big picture. The men of the 1st Battalion of the 506th knew they were being relieved during the night of the sixth but didn't know who the relief unit was or where they were at a particular moment. Thus it was that LTC Ray Allen's 3rd Battalion of the 327th Glider Infantry men ended up only a few hundred yards to the west and north of LTC James LaPrade's 506th men. The 506th men had moved right through the open area left by Lieutenant Colonel Allen when he assigned his troops their positions along their north–south line.

A brief explanation is necessary here to explain how this move had taken place.

After a relatively quiet period of a week or so in the Veghel area, the 327th Regiment was sent north on the morning of the sixth to replace a British unit in the Elst region. However, with the 506th having taken such huge losses during the fifth and the sixth in the Opheusden area, the 327th Glider Infantry Regiment was moved quickly west to a new line of responsibility. The 2nd and 3rd Battalions were temporarily attached to the 506th. The 3rd Battalion, which was formerly the 1st Battalion of the 401st, was commanded by LTC Ray Allen. His battalion was to be responsible for the northern half of a new defense line that extended from a point twelve hundred yards east of Opheusden, south to and including the railroad tracks. Allen's forces would cover a distance of two thousand yards from the lower Rhine south.

As 1st Battalion of the 506th was making its orderly withdrawal from Opheusden, Allen's forces went on line with Company "A" taking over the northern sector nearest the river. "B" Company established its position from the railroad north. An open space of five hundred yards was left between the two units. This would be covered only by fire. Company "C" was the reserve unit. The men were in position by midnight.

Sgt. Ben "Doc" Ottinger remembered the action in the Opheusden area. "We were ordered to relieve the 506th. However, Colonel Allen and Colonel Sink got into a heated argument about this small town of about 100 buildings. Colonel Allen didn't want to enter the town but would rather set up south and east along the railroad tracks where we would have better observation. The Division G-2 sided with Colonel Allen. Colonel Ray Allen put my 'B' Company and 'A' Company on line and held 'C' in reserve. He also left a gap of 500 yards between 'A' and 'B' in which to lure the Germans into a trap."

The enemy started moving across in front of "B" Company at 0400.

Sergeant Ottinger continued his story: "This proved to be a death trap for the Germans. The next morning about 300 Germans started moving on 'B' Company's flank. Lt. John O'Halloran waited until the Germans were about 75 yards away before he gave the order to fire. I had a BAR. Boy, did we have a field day! What was left retreated.

"Later in the morning, we weren't so lucky. The enemy approached, this time with tanks. We couldn't stop all of it. Some got through. Their artillery set in. Tree bursts were taking a heavy toll on us. We were in an apple orchard. On October 7th, our company suffered 47 casualties, 17 of them being killed."

The enemy force that attacked through the "B" Company line at daybreak was a fresh battalion. It attacked eastward along the railroad, then swung slightly northward in front of "B" Company, which was taking a heavy plastering from enemy artillery and mortars. A large segment of the enemy battalion swept past the glider outposts, passing between "A" and "B" Companies and right into the orchard where 1st Battalion of the 506th was bivouacked for the night.

Medic Robert Barger had gone to sleep in the hayloft of a barn a few hundred yards northwest of the orchard where the bulk of 1st Battalion was resting. He wrote: "The next morning I was awakened by one of our guys. He said the place was crawling with Germans. There must have been 250–300 of them. They never entered the barn and I'll never know why. They finally regrouped and started down the road in the direction of the orchard. They did not know or see our battalion dug into the orchard."

Sgt. Don Brininstool added: "At daybreak, all hell broke loose again. We were supposedly in back of our own lines but not 200 yards away must have been 400 Germans. I heard a grenade explode. I jumped up, grabbed a machine gun and ran into a ditch and put the gun in action along with a couple other machine guns. Within minutes all you could see was white flags. The Germans said they had fought the men of the 101st before and didn't want any more of us. They also said they had heard us come in just before daybreak and thought we were their prisoners."

A vivid memory of PFC Richard E. Turner of "B" Company occurred just west of Hemmen (near Opheusden). He wrote: "A fresh battalion of enemy troops marched into an area where 1st Battalion was resting early in the morning, and got caught in cross fire of two machine guns (one on each corner) of 1st Battalion's perimeter (rectangular) defense. Over 200 prisoners were taken and more than 50 bodies were on the field. One of the machine gunners was from 'B' Company. The whole scene was like out of a movie, where the 'bad guys' are easily seen. Some of us with rifles didn't bother to fire them. The machine guns were doing too good a job and the rifles weren't needed."

During the height of the enemy attack, what was left of "C" Company of the 506th was led by its remaining officer, 1Lt. Albert Hassenzahl, on a move around the left flank. When this twenty-seven-man force was stopped in its encircling maneuver, it called for mortar fire—which it got. Thus it was able to complete its trapping move.

Still at the haybarn northwest of the orchard, medic Barger finished his narrative. "Our guys waited until the last minute and then opened fire. They probably killed approximately fifty and captured the rest. About that time, one of the Krauts broke and came running up the ditch that ran beside the barn. We had a little medic who wore two pistols. The guns almost weighed him down. Anyway, he threw the back door of the barn open and yelled, 'Halt!' The Kraut kept running and this guy pulled both pistols and fired. It killed the Kraut and damned near knocked the medic on his rear from the recoil."

The October 7 entry in the log of "A" Company provided by 1Lt. William C. Kennedy summarizes the results of the orchard battle:

> About 0600, enemy infantry appeared from the west of the company and battalion position. Both sides opened fire. Within one hour the battalion had taken 231 prisoners, counted between 50 and 60 dead and between 25 and 30 wounded. Our battalion casualties were small; 2 dead and 5 wounded. Company "A" suffered no casualties in this encounter.

During the two days of fighting for Opheusden, the 506th Regiment lost 14 officers and 186 enlisted men. None of the 1st Battalion line companies was larger than a platoon in strength. The fight to hold the defensive line in the Opheusden area was turned over to the 327th Glider Regiment. Hard fighting would continue for another eight days.

October 8 Battles

The fighting along the defensive line of 3rd Battalion of the 327th continued with the enemy pounding the positions continuously with artillery and mortar fire.

Sgt. Ben Ottinger of "B" Company (401st designation) was hit by shrapnel from one of the large shells. He wrote: "On the 8th, I was wounded as the Krauts continued the heavy artillery fire. I was on the right flank with my buddy, Clyde Futch. We were dug in deep. We were the last two on the end where the 500-yard gap was located. The British brought up six artillery observers with a radio and set up fifty feet from me and Futch. Needless to say, they got a direct hit on the radio. Five of them were killed. Futch and I were wounded. I crawled out of our foxhole and went looking for a medic for Futch. He had a bad wound just above his ear. I got down to the next foxhole, which was occupied by S/Sgt. Roger Seamon, and fell. He pulled me in head first and gave me a shot of morphine. I was evacuated on the hood of a jeep and sent to an aid station which was in a barn."

(Later Ottinger was visited in the hospital by buddies who survived the battle and told him the company had only thirty-three men left when the battle was over.)

Company "A" was on the northern end of the 3rd Battalion line. The men there were no better off when it came to shelling than the men of "B" Company.

S/Sgt. Philip Fry of "A" Company remembered the argument that developed between Lieutenant Colonel Allen and Colonel Sink over the positioning of the 3rd Battalion troops. He describes the terrible shelling of the positions: "Man, did we take a shellacking there! The Krauts shelled us for 45 minutes; blew us out of our holes. The Germans came down between 1st Battalion of the 506th and the 401st. They hit us about four times that night. I'd never heard it before or since but they used whistles for commands. I know ole Sgt. Brown shot that machine gun until it wouldn't fire no more. The M-1s got so hot with all the casmoline (if you didn't get it all out) it would burn your hands.

"One of my buddies got blown out of the hole and he took off—couldn't take it anymore. Never saw him again until we got back to Mourmelon. I still have ringing in my ears from all that shelling."

One of the forward observers assigned to the 401st Glider Infantry was 1Lt. James A. Robinson of the 377th. He realized the enemy was using the signalman's station house as a command post. A few days earlier it had served the same purpose for 1Lt. Robert Stroud of "H" Company of the 506th. Now the 101st wanted the building destroyed. Robinson wrote: "There was a railroad station near the road intersection and, as I found out by shooting at it, it was well fortified and made of concrete. I called for a lot of rounds and couldn't destroy it. Then I put 'WP' (White Phosphorus) on it and I couldn't burn it out. We were getting a great amount of machine gun and mortar fire on us. We were in very open country except for the apple trees. The intense fire fight lasted two to three hours.

"There was a young German soldier approaching our position and we motioned for him to come on in. He was hesitant but he kept coming. He did come in and, in my excitement, I grabbed him by the throat and he was glad to be pulled down. His own troops were trying to machine gun him. I discovered I didn't have a firearm and he did. I disarmed him and he was very docile as he lay there while I continued to direct artillery fire."

The enemy also directed attacks on "A" and "B" Companies of 1st Battalion of the 327th in their defensive positions south of the railroad tracks. British observers on hand with the 327th related that the barrage dropped on "C" Company was the worst they had experienced since El Alamein in Africa. It was estimated that two thousand rounds fell in the 327th area in a fifteen-minute period. It was thought that "C" Company was wiped out, and a platoon from "A" Company was ready to rush in to replace them as soon as the barrage lifted.

Company "C" had moved up on line during the night of the eighth. PFC George K. Mullins describes his part in the action: "Each man in 'Charley' Company moved in to take up his position near the ditch that ran along the west side of the road. My machine gun squad moved to the west side of a house. We heard a noise in the basement. Our platoon leader yelled out, 'Who's down there?' A German burp gun spoke out not far away. After that little episode we kept the noise down a bit. We dug our foxholes. Daylight was approaching.

"We noted the terrain was level—good grazing fire for machine guns. A corn patch was to my right with a BAR in position out in front on the opposite side from me. The enemy artillery began to zero in on us all up and down the line. Some time around noon, an 88 shell made a direct hit into a foxhole killing both riflemen. Darkness approached and the shelling got heavier. South of me our company CP was taking a beating from the German artillery. That building got too hot and the HQ people wasted no time getting out of the back door. Just a few feet away my close friend, Joe Henn, was smoking up a storm. The heavier the barrage, the more smoke came out of his hole. Now it was dark. All hell broke loose. Just how many 88s do those Krauts have? I've been under artillery fire from Normandy to this place and never experienced anything like this. The whole front was getting it at the same time."

As the heavy enemy shelling lifted when the troops neared the American lines, eight enemy tanks supported the 1409th Fortress Battalion and two decimated battalions of the 959th Infantry Regiment focused their attack on the areas defended by "A" and "C" Companies of the 327th. British and American artillery opened up on their advancing troops. Air bursts were called for that exploded less than a hundred yards from the glider infantry positions. The infantrymen fired so fast and so long that machine guns and rifles refused to function properly.

PFC George Mullins continued his account: "Over the sounds of the intense shelling, I heard the enemy coming closer and closer with all the fire power that he could produce. Their machine guns, burp guns and rifles were sending an endless stream of lead in our direction. Not a single shot was being fired by our men in the line.

" 'No damn Kraut is going to take me in the bottom of my foxhole!' I said to Herschel Parker. He said, 'Stay down, too much artillery, you'll get your head shot off!' Staying low, I opened up with machine gun fire. After a few bursts I believe every man on that line began firing. Out in front the enemy began screaming, yelling and charging. Then a whistle blew for them to regroup and to charge again. There would definitely be no sleep tonight.

"Between bursts from my machine gun, I sensed a shell coming in too close for comfort. I ducked. The shell exploded in front of the gun—so close it should have blown the weapon in on top of us. I took a piece of hot shrapnel in the back side of the shoulder. 'I'm hit!' I yelled. 'Where?' asked Parker. 'Clean through!' Parker took over the gun. I couldn't find any blood on the other side so I assured Parker that I was OK. The situation wasn't helped any by the bellowing of the dying cattle close by. It was too dark to see them.

"An automatic weapon opened up very close to the BAR. The tracers from his gun were spraying through the corn field and then rising until they were going straight up.

"The machine gun began to get sluggish. Finally, I was pulling the bolt back and firing it single fire. Parker decided to clean it. He took it into the foxhole. It was pitch dark. I stood over him with my carbine at the ready looking for the enemy. Parker disassembled the gun and cleaned it without hesitation or any mistakes; he then reassembled it and placed it back on its tripod. It fired like a new gun.

"During the height of the attack, one of our 60mm mortar men sat in back of his mortar tube with ammo bearers passing shells to him from both sides. As soon as one shell left the barrel another went down the tube.

"Daylight finally arrived.

"Curiosity got the best of me. I crawled out of my foxhole and went through the corn patch to see why enemy tracers were being fired straight up. There, within a few feet of the BAR man, lay the biggest German, all decked out in battle gear with his finger frozen to the trigger of his automatic weapon which was still pointed skyward.

"Little did we know that 'C' company had been scratched as an existing unit. It had been reported that the enemy had taken over our company foxholes. Not true! The company commander showed up to find our biggest concern was a shortage of ammunition. Parker and I had less than a box left for our machine gun. There were enemy dead only a few feet in front of our foxholes."

S/Sgt. Jack Williamson of "Able" Company

S/Sgt. Jack Williamson had to take over a platoon in a critical situation when its leader became reluctant to act. "One day the Germans started a big attack and they came through the fields. We had a sergeant who should have been in charge of the platoon. He wouldn't get out of his foxhole. He was scared. I was scared but he was more scared than I was. I couldn't run off so I started giving orders. I said, 'Move that reserve squad down there to the left!' The squad leader said, 'Are you in charge?' I said, 'Hell yes!' The mortar sergeant came up and asked, 'Where shall I fire the mortars?' I pointed out toward the advancing Germans and said, 'There, damn it, get to firing!' It looked like we were sure gonna be overrun. I called back to our company commander, Capt. J. B. Johnson, and asked him if we should pull back. He said, 'No, hold your ground! Don't move your positions one bit.' I told him to send us up a resupply of ammo. 'Are you in charge?' I said yes. We had British artillery support. I went upstairs in this house and the British forward observer, a captain, with two enlisted men were there. I said, 'Get your artillery firing!' Man was he cool. He looked out of the window and said, 'Oh yes, by jove.' He turned to his sergeant, 'Would you crank up your radio.' They all seemed cool and calm. I wasn't, as it was the first time I was in charge of such a situation. The Germans were getting real close. We captured one. He had been impressed into the army from the Alsace-Lorraine area.

"The resupply hadn't arrived. I told the men to fix bayonets and then called back to the captain and said, 'Where the hell is my resupply of ammo?' He said, 'Jack, you should have had it.' I didn't. The two men who were supposed to have delivered it in a jeep came half way, dumped it and went back. When Captain Johnson found that out he got after these men and they told him what they had done. PFC Ken Rippel took out his .45 pistol and told the two men, 'We're going to get that ammo and we're going to take it right up to those men on the line or I'll kill you!' He would have, too. So there they came right up to the front.

"By this time the British artillery was firing. I mean it stopped the attack—boom—boom—boom, right up and down the line. I was upstairs with that British observer and I couldn't believe what I saw. He said, 'I say, Sergeant, now we'll give them a little air burst,' and he did, very effectively. Now for a little white phosphorus to top it off. I had never seen white phosphorus before. Those shells came in—white stuff went spewing up into the air and I mean those Germans were screaming, hollering. It was pitiful. They put up a white flag. Three Germans came forward. They wanted two hours to pick up their dead and wounded. Our commanders gave it to them. After that day, I was platoon sergeant."

Staff Sergeant Williamson describes the actions of one soldier in his platoon. "We had one man who wasn't firing his gun during the attack. I said as I was running back and forth along the line, 'What the hell is the matter with you? Get to firing that gun!' He said it was against his religion to kill. I said, 'What the hell are you doing in an airborne outfit? Git firing that damned gun.' I looked back and I'll be damned—he was firing that gun straight up in the air. Well, hell, I had to keep moving down the line. When I came back by him, he was dead. I looked down at him and said, 'I hope the hell you're satisfied!' "

There was seldom a six-hour period between October 5 and 15 that the enemy didn't launch an attack against the lines of the 101st. By the fifteenth, the 363rd German Infantry Division was almost completely wiped out. The enemy then fell back about a mile and a half and the two sides resorted to patrolling the no-man's-land in between.

TWENTY-TWO

Dodewaard and Hien

Dodewaard

William van Wely, along with his parents and three sisters, had witnessed the landings of the British 1st Airborne Division several miles north of their Dodewaard home. They wondered when the Allied liberating forces would reach them.

"On the 23rd of September we heard that some English had been sighted in towns east of us so we expected them on Sunday, the 24th. As members of the underground, several of us were waiting for them by the church close to the Geurts jam factory. Our waiting was not in vain. Along came a scout car on wheels and we met our first liberators of the British 2nd Army. The commander had been born in Arnhem and had fled to England in 1940. We gave them all the information they were looking for—layout of minefields, German strength and their positions, etc. In the first week there were no fixed front lines— just some exploring and feeling things out. There weren't many Germans in the nearest towns. Shortly thereafter they started moving in to retake the Nijmegen bridge."

The Americans started arriving on the scene on the third of October. Van Wely described the first encounter. "We saw a strange sight—helmets bobbing in a dry ditch coming toward us. Upon reaching our farm they came out toward the barn. They were wearing uniforms we had never seen before; hand grenades hanging from their breasts, bayonets stuck in their boots, pockets loaded with ammunition, rifles and shovels on their backs. Luckily, my youngest sister, Jean, a teacher, spoke English and she asked them what army they belonged to and what country. Then we heard they were paratroopers of the

101st Airborne Division coming from Nijmegen to set up a defensive line to protect the Nijmegen bridge.

"Within five minutes they were digging holes to stand in and placed machine guns at the edge of the holes facing the west from which the Germans started advancing shortly. Our farm was right in the front line which started on the Waal River and ran toward Opheusden. It didn't take long to find out what that meant.

"I helped as much as I could with the digging, directing their fire, because I knew the area as well as my own pockets. Much fire came from our neighbor's place. Hoogakker was a carpenter and wagon builder. The Germans used his work bench to place a machine gun on so it could fire in our direction. Later on we heard that our fire knocked out that gun position.

"Mortar fire started increasing by the hour with hits on our house and barns. My mother and sisters, who were still at home at the time, made sandwiches and coffee for the men. My sisters jumped from foxhole to foxhole to give it to the soldiers. It was a miracle they were not hit and killed.

"Our father had been killed a few days before while on the road with his horse and wagon. A direct hit from German artillery fired from across the Rhine River opposite Opheusden killed him and the horse. This was also the day we buried dad."

While van Wely was at home with his mother and sisters for a few days so he could be present to console them, Jan Tornga and underground members Panke Derksen, Nic Augustines, and others picked up eight German frogmen who had been heading up the Waal River intent on blowing up the Nijmegen bridge.

The American paratroopers who had arrived at the van Wely farm and other positions in Dodewaard were from "I" Company of the 506th Regiment. Their assignment was to cover the area from the railroad track near Opheusden, all the way south to the Waal River at Dodewaard, far too great a distance for a single parachute infantry company to cover. However, they were supported by part of "D" Battery of the 81st Anti-Tank Battalion and British artillery.

Capt. William Joe of "Dog" Battery had some of his .50-caliber machine guns positioned in Opheusden but he also had some in the Dodewaard area. He describes the positioning of his heavy weapons: "The right gun in Dodewaard was down the road leading west with very little protective cover. They could cover the open space to the right and reach out to the single farm house in the distance between the village and the railroad tracks. To their left they could reach a clump of trees just to the west of the village and a large growth of trees in the distance beyond the town. That patch of woods was too close for comfort and a natural jumping-off spot for an attack. Cpl. Guy Stone's gun was placed in the church to go over the vegetation in the immediate front and to reach that large growth of woods in the distance, and from that tower he could cover a lot of ground."

Captain Joe continued: "With 'I' Company of the 3rd Battalion covering the line from the Waal River dike to the Dodewaard-Opheusden railroad station, 1Lt. Walter Kron was supporting them with several .50 caliber machine gun crews."

PFC George R. McMillan of "I" Company describes what it was like on the thinly held line to his front. "Company 'I' was holding an area between Dodewaard and Opheusden consisting of a few farm houses, barns and outdoor toilets. Acres of apple trees were ripe with fruit. On October 4, we spotted the Germans crossing the fields in front of us, heading east to Opheusden. A call to Lt. Replogle got the response that we should stay out of sight and watch. The rest of the day at 3rd Platoon, John Jacobs dug up and cooked vegetables. A trooper named Emery hung frag grenades in the trees throughout the apple orchard with trip wires running to a central control point located in an outhouse. Word came down that starting at dusk, Division and English artillery units would ring our positions with steel. Enemy artillery fire had been coming overhead all day long—close but no direct hits. The friendly barrage began and lasted all night non-stop. At times shrapnel from our own shells rained down on us. Daylight arrived. The shelling stopped. Sgt. Jim Siesennop gave us the word, 'Send out a patrol!' Jerry O'Christie, Bill Weber and I skirted Emery's orchard, moved west until we could see the railroad tracks at the point where they turned north and crossed the upper river. Stalled equipment sat on the dike road. From our position, we viewed the fields which were covered with dead Germans. For as far as we could see, there were dead. Among all the fallen bodies, small groups of German soldiers staggered about drunklike, fifty or so in number. Artillery fire commenced so we moved quickly out of range."

At another outpost, with the same 3rd Platoon, PFC Wilbur Fishel remembered when cows inadvertently gave his position away to an enemy sniper. He said, "I was in a ditch with another guy. He had just stood up and was hit in the chest by the sniper. Every time I put my head up to look around, the sniper shot at me. I tried to crawl through a culvert to get aid for the wounded trooper but there wasn't enough room to go through. Near us in the field were some cows that followed my every move, turning their heads to watch me. This kept the sniper informed of my location and he kept the gun pointed in the direction in which the cows were watching. Another soldier came up, sent from the company to find out what the firing was all about and he was hit as he dropped into the ditch beside me. Finally, a British tank came up after bazooka shells failed to explode when they hit the thatched roof of the farmhouse in which the sniper was hiding. One round from the tank's big gun was all that was needed. There was no more firing at us from the house."

The reason why there were so many cows in the fields during the periods of heavy shelling may have been due to gates being left open by Americans or because of a decision by the Dutch underground members.

Underground member William van Wely remembered: "We lost all of our cattle in the first week. The gate to the pasture was left open by an anti-tank gun crew. The milk cows went in the direction of the Germans so that was the end of milking and in a way, it was a relief.

"Now I could give all my time to helping our group after mother and sisters were removed from the front line area. Home and barns got so many direct hits from German mortar fire that window glass was all shattered and buildings could burst into flame anytime. Luckily that never happened. Our commander, Jan Tornga, told my family to get out before it was too late. The whole town was evacuated and our task as a group, with the help of others, was to go through town as far as possible to open barns, cattle and hog pens, to let the animals out. At that time, we realized it was not a question of a few days when the populations could move back into their homes. As often as possible, I went back to the farm because mother asked me to feed the canaries and pigeons."

Underground leader Jan Tornga remembered how his men utilized an abandoned enemy truck. He said, "Panke Derksen and Nic Augustines located a German truck while on patrol. They weren't sure if Germans were in the vicinity so they asked for support and under cover of the fire, crept up to the truck. They couldn't start it. The Germans didn't bother them so they went back and got a horse and pulled the truck back to the American lines. The truck had no gasoline. Once the tank was filled, the truck was operable. The Americans used it for a while and then torched it."

The German rifles being used by the underground members created a problem with the Americans. Tornga added: "We were equipped with German rifles. We weren't permitted to fire them because the sounds confused the paratroopers. They took away our German weapons, gave us American helmets and rifles and also provided me with a pair of binoculars so I could better observe the Germans. This way I knew where to direct their fire."

One day William van Wely got a shock at what he saw upon arrival at home and was extremely angry with his American friends. He wrote: "One day when I reached home and entered the kitchen—what was left of it, I had a shock. Mother had raised approximately 50 pullets from day one with warm water bottles. By September–October, they had just started laying. When I looked on the table, covered with mother's best table linen—chicken drumsticks—ready for eating—I became raging mad. The soldiers had killed all the hens. That was the end of my mother's care and work!

"Luckily, at that moment, the Germans started an attack using all their weaponry—artillery, mortars and machine guns. Instead of eating the chickens, the Americans sprinted out to their positions. My friends took me along to seek cover. It was a terrible attack. The Germans covered the whole front line with fire. A mortar round fell ten feet from where I lay all covered with mud. I didn't get a scratch! We had to run along a dry ditch toward the 101st mortar line while the Germans kept following us with their mortar fire. What happened to the chicken dinners, I never did know."

In describing the work of patrolling by his underground group, William van Wely related: "We spent much time in seeing that the civilians were moved to safer places behind the lines. We had a red, white and blue armband which identified us and allowed us to pass through the Allied lines. One time we were stopped by an Army patrol on the road. They asked us who we were and what we intended to do. With a few words of English we had picked up and using our arm and hand movements, we tried to express ourselves. Then one of them started speaking in Dutch to us. You should have seen our faces! The soldier must have been of Dutch ancestry. They let us through.

"Our biggest handicap was not being able to speak English. When you were on guard duty with them, there was not much talk and those hours were long, especially at night. Our task with them was to stop all civilians from entering the front line areas and, if found in a forbidden area, those civilians were to be arrested and turned over to the MPs."

The 502nd Regiment moved to the western end of the Allied line to take up positions in the area of Dodewaard and Hien. Cpl. Pete Santini describes the change of scenery and a new experience, guard duty with members of the Dutch underground:

Oct. 13—We are going to move up to relieve the 327th Glider Infantry. It is only about one and a half miles to their positions. The trucks will not be able to bring up supplies except at night. The Jerries have good observation and fire artillery at all vehicles they see on the road. We reached our objective at 1740 hours. The town is very small. The name is Dodewaard. The Battalion staff and message center are set up in a schoolhouse. The company is set up in a small but comfortable house. "G" Company is supplying one platoon for CP guard. Two platoons of "G" are in battalion reserve. There are six men from the Underground working with the battalion. They will pull guard on Number 1 post. Each man will be on two hours and off ten.

Oct. 14—Five new men from the Underground have come to relieve the six men who pulled guard last night. One is quite a young man—his name is John. He speaks English fairly well and seems to be fairly well educated. His father is mayor of the town.

At about 1900 hours the guard on Number 3 post brought in an elderly couple. The woman seemed to be hysterical. The man appears to be quite capable of taking care of himself despite his age. The old man has been taken to Bn. HQ. for questioning. We are trying to make the old lady comfortable. I've made some tea for her. We are going to let her and her husband sleep here in the house because if they try to travel at night they might accidentally get shot. From what I can gather, it seems that the Germans have taken possession of their home. They were told to go to the rear of the German lines because of the artillery which our guns kept throwing their way. This old couple chose to come over to the American lines instead. They hid under a dike for four hours until it was getting dark and then started toward our lines. The men in the first outpost spotted them but allowed them to pass. At the next outpost, which is a double sentry post, one of the sentries halted them and escorted them to the company CP. The old man gave us a lot of valuable information. He is 66 years old and she's 62. We will see to it that they arrive at their destination in the morning.

Oct. 15—It's raining again, as usual. The old couple is still with us. They had breakfast with us. The old gent still has quite an appetite. We were impressed by an incident which happened while they were eating. The old woman suddenly stopped eating, reached across the table to straighten out the old gent's tie—women are still the same, no matter what country they are from.[131]

Van Wely continued his story: "Some of the Dutch tried to steal in desperation, others tried to reach their homes for the purpose of saving some clothes. Personally, I picked up clothes for people from their homes or dug their money up from the gardens where they had buried it. In a crazy time, you do crazy things, risking your life for other people's possessions."

The effectiveness of the British artillery has been mentioned on several occasions previously. First Lieutenant Allen C. Barham of "B" Company and 1Lt. Ray Brock of HQ Company of 3rd Battalion describe such actions that affected them.

First Lieutenant Allen Barham remembered one night when the unit had moved back up on the MLR near Dodewaard. "We put a guard on the winery close by. We were assisted by the Dutch underground. The Germans were moving at night and with the assistance of a British artillery officer we pinpointed the line of wagons and trucks. He asked for and got a 'Yoke 4' on 120 guns—that meant 480 rounds. We observed the slaughter from the second floor window of a house. We could hear the screams of men and the neighing of horses. They moved around all night like wild people."

Members of the mortar platoon were alert twenty-four hours a day in the steeples of various churches, looking for enemy movement and for artillery flashes at night. Mortar platoon leader

131. Author's note: While I was interviewing William van Wely at his home in Grimsby, Ontario, in December 1987, Wely began to describe the incident and I stopped him and gave the punch line. He thought I had been one of the 502nd guards with whom he had pulled guard duty.

1Lt. Raymond I. Brock of 3rd Battalion recalled: "S/Sgt. Karol Southard, Cpl. Floyd Wilson and I were manning an OP in the church tower of Dodewaard. We always manned our OPs at night, too, and during the early hours of the morning. Battalion HQ received some artillery fire. Knowing that we were alert, Battalion called and asked if we had picked up any artillery flashes. Fortunately Cpl. Wilson had plotted them so Battalion asked if we could locate the German artillery positions as we were being supported by twelve 18-pounders of British artillery. I said I'd try to locate their position so I drew a line from our CP back along the azimuth Wilson had taken across the Rhine off the map. I then started looking for the logical artillery positions and settled on a saddle between two hills, just across the Rhine. I called the grid co-ordinates to Battalion and they relayed the information that the British fire three rounds. When the rounds were fired I could not see any bursts so I reported, 'Lost bursts!' 'Down 300 yards.' Battalion said the British were going to fire all twelve guns for effect. I said, 'Don't do that. I don't know where the original three rounds landed.' Battalion said the British wanted to use all guns as our area had been quiet and they needed the exercise. I said, 'OK, it's not my money!' They did the whole bit and did we get results! When the shells landed, all hell broke loose. We could see the explosions and smoke and heard the noise in the church tower. Wilson, Southard and I were jumping around in the tower with our arms around each other. Battalion thought from the noise that the tower had been hit."

First Lieutenant Brock was extremely proud of the work of his 81mm Mortar Platoon of 3rd Battalion of the 502nd Regiment.

"Volunteered" for Patrol

Line company soldiers were not anxious to be called upon to take part in day or night patrol activity, though each unit had men who were skilled in the art of this type of work. A few relished the experience and volunteered themselves and buddies to go along on these missions. Such was the case for Holland replacement Pvt. Patrick G. Fergus of "F" Company who seemed to enjoy going on patrols. He wrote: "Patrolling was my thing and I went on many of them. One person I wanted out there was someone I could count on in a bind. 'E. O.' Parmley was one of them. His favorite comment was, 'You son-of-a-bitch—you're gonna get me killed yet!' "

PFC Emmert O. Parmley remembered the "gung-ho" Fergus. He wrote: "Our platoon was to furnish two men for a patrol. It was to be a four man move. S-2 from 2nd Battalion was to send two men. Our platoon sergeant, Gerald Scheier assembled part of the platoon and called for two volunteers. I heard a voice call out, 'E.O. and I will go!' and before I could say anything, Sgt. Scheier said, 'Done! Come to company headquarters and get some sleep. You go at midnight.' Who volunteered me? It was that fellow from Brooklyn—Fergus. I think he liked me but this seemed a funny way to show it. I liked him but not that much.

"Our mission was to cross the enemy lines, observe their strength, the type of troops, and to find out all we could about them. The plan was that at midnight our people would lay a barrage on their front lines. We would then cross no-man's land under this barrage, get as close as possible to their lines, then wait for the second barrage which would lift 100 yards which the Germans didn't know. When the second barrage came, we were to run across their lines into small trees which were on their front line. There we were to get good positions to observe, for after the second barrage we'd send up flares which would light up everything like daylight.

"All went as planned—the first barrage on time and target. We got almost to their lines. We waited for the second barrage. We heard it coming. We got up and moved toward their lines but the first shell landed in the same place. We thought it was a short round as it always seemed like there was a short round in most shelling—but they were all short. The barrage did not raise 100 yards as it was supposed to. We could not make it across their lines and were lying in a field in front of their positions, no more than 15 to 20 yards—then up went the flares. I knew we were close to their lines as I saw the glow of a cigarette just moments before the first flare. I heard a cough, also the clearing of a throat. I could imagine a German drawing a bead on me. I will never know why the four of us were not spotted as the flares lit up the field like daylight. None of us moved. Our only chance was to lie still with the hope the flares would soon burn out, which they did. Our officers and men awaiting our return were relieved to find all four of us made it back okay."

S-2 Patrols

The S-2 sections of regiments and battalions were constantly involved in patrol activity, day or night. The work of the 502nd Regiment in the Dodewaard-Hien area was to hold back any offensive by enemy forces. One purpose of the patrol was to make judgments as to where future moves by the enemy might be anticipated and in what strength they would come.

Recalling his most harrowing experience on the island, PFC Richard Ladd wrote: "As a five man patrol, led by Sergeant Paul Todd one night east of Dodewaard—we were hugging the base of the dike as we tried to advance quietly in the rain past the front doors and yards of abandoned Dutch houses facing the dike. After a quarter mile, we reached some wooden stairs leading to the roadway on the top. At this instant, Pvt. Louis Migliarese whispered that he thought he saw a helmet in the gloom on top of the dike. I reported this to Todd and he and Pvt. Jack Ott went upside of the dike to investigate. Two shots followed by a tommy gun burst. Two Krauts were killed, dug in at the top of the stairs. As shots ended, we were flared by the Germans. Like day light we saw that not 30 yards in front of us was the enemy MLR. Their line opened up with much firing. Machine gun bullets plopped into the dike next to us. However, we made our way back, the houses helped serve as a buffer and each time a flare went off we would freeze, looking away from the enemy. We five returned unscathed and called British artillery fire down on the position of the German MLR. Next day, in the course of patrolling, we discovered the German line had moved back a good mile to the east."

Citing creature comforts on the island, PFC Richard Ladd has this to add: "From mid-October to November 20, the S-2 Section of the 502nd operated out of the town hall in Dodewaard. This was a heavily constructed building which we used as a 'Cossack Post' at night and a base for patrols during the day. I named it 'Fortress Dodewaard' and it stuck with some of the men."

PFC Thomas E. Walsh was a member of the same S-2 Section. He remembered: "Night patrols were a daily occurrence. Manning an OP in the courthouse (town hall) of Dodewaard was an interesting experience. It was the first time in my life I'd spent time in jail. The courthouse basement offered the best protection from artillery fire, and the cots in the jail cells weren't that uncomfortable.

"Upstairs in a window of the courthouse, a .50 caliber machine gun was set up during daylight. At night windows were sealed to conceal our occupation. Patrols from both sides passed our position. German patrols with hushed voices in guttural accents passed through town. American combat patrols led by Capt. Paul Dovholuk alternated passing our position."

A Loudspeaker Calls for Surrender

PFC Emmert (E.O.) Parmley remembers one particular day on outpost duty up near Dodewaard. "We were at this particular outpost at least two weeks. One day, orders came from HQ that we were going to try coaxing the Germans to surrender. We usually referred to the enemy as 'Hans' and 'Fritz.' In fact, many times we challenged each other with 'Is dot you, Fritz?' and the answer was, 'Yaah, Hans!'

"The plan called for us to open fire with all our guns on command and to fire until the 'cease fire' command was given. Loud speakers were brought up to tell the enemy the advantages of surrendering. We promised no harm if they surrendered. On the command, 'Cease fire!' not another shot was to be fired.

"On this particular day, all went as planned. The loud speakers bellowed out, 'Commence firing!' and we did. We fired everything we had. We were in a ditch and the bazooka man was lying up on the shoulder of the road that ran in front of our position and had the bazooka lying on his back. He blew his shoe off. Our machine gunner clamped down on the trigger and did not release until the loud speakers bellowed 'Cease fire! Everyone cease fire!—No more shots are to be fired!'

"The loudspeakers then started telling the Germans how nice we would be to them if they surrendered—which some of them were believing—until our machine gun fired. No one was on the gun when it fired. We looked at one another and it fired again. The person on the loud speaker bellowed, 'Get the name of the man that fired those shots!' We all started laughing—in fact we got hysterical. The gun had gotten so hot, when a shell went into the chamber it fired after the cartridge was there for a couple of seconds. All we did was laugh and listen to the voice on the loud speaker say all it was going to do to the man who was firing those shots. Needless to say, we took no prisoners that day."

In his diary notation for the sixteenth of October, Cpl. Pete Santini missed out on the humor of the occasion:

> There is a big show scheduled to take place at 1430 hours this afternoon. The leading roles will be played by the Jerries and our artillery. They will be supported by our mortars and machine guns. The whole plot is to give Jerry a good pounding in a coordinated, concentrated shelling. The machine guns will be used to pick off those who leave their holes in an attempt to get away from the artillery. Maybe they will realize how futile it is to hold out and they may surrender before they are completely annihilated. The show went over with a big bang, and a few crashes. However, it didn't seem to have the proper effect on the Jerries. Their answer was to return some of the fire.

During the same afternoon, a team of photographers and writers from *Life* magazine appeared on the scene. They wanted to photograph the capturing of prisoners.

The diary of S/Sgt. Earl Cox of "F" Company had this notation for October 16:

> At 1435, a combat patrol sent out to houses at our immediate front supported by tanks and artillery. Captured two prisoners. Mission successful. Artillery from enemy had direct hit on CP. No casualties. Moved CP to house next door. Patrol action was photographed.

"I remember an incident that took place up on the Island," wrote Cpl. Howard Matthews. "Lt. Col. Allen Ginder came up to the front lines of 'F' Company with three reporters from *Life* magazine. They wanted pictures of Germans being taken prisoner. A squad from 3rd Platoon went out with them across a field and into a woods in the German lines.

"When they left, we took a machine gun and moved to the left of a field and down a drainage ditch of the field the 3rd Platoon squad crossed. We spotted a German squad moving down the ditch trying to cut off the 3rd Platoon squad. We opened fire on them killing several and two of them raised their hands and surrendered and came down the ditch to us. Meanwhile, the German troops in the woods opened fire on Ginder and the squad. Ginder was wounded in the hip and leg. He was carried back with other men from the squad. The *Life* magazine people were unhappy because they were not used to being shot at. LTC Ginder was unhappy because he got shot. But then the *Life* magazine people were happy when I gave them two Germans to take back with them."

Cpl. Pete Santini's entry in the company log for the sixteenth showed the following:

> While the shelling was going on, "Fox" Company sent out a patrol assisted by a tank, and pulled a surprise raid on the Jerries. Their mission was to get at least one prisoner. The patrol returned in a short time with two prisoners. The mission was accomplished without any casualties.
>
> About 1600 hours the Jerries zeroed in on "Fox" Company's CP. There was no one in the building at the time. A British tank pulled in behind the building and parked there. As the tank commander was about to get out of the tank, a mortar shell hit him on the head and blew it completely off. Lt. Col. Ginder was hit by a shot in the lower abdomen. It made a nasty looking wound and shattered his pelvic bone. PFC George Chicoine was also wounded at the same time. Both men were evacuated.

It was most fortunate that the heavy fighting was over before the 502nd Regiment moved into the lines near Dodewaard on October 13, as the battle for Best had taken an exceedingly heavy toll of its fighting men.

Capt. J. Roy Martin of 2nd Battalion remembered: "2nd Battalion wasn't very effective after the heavy fighting in the Best area where only the battalion commander and myself were left. The rest of the battalion staff and all the company commanders had been killed or wounded. We were so badly shot up in that action that we really were not very effective thereafter."

TWENTY-THREE

Other Memorable Experiences

The 3rd Battalion of the 506th Parachute Regiment had lost its commander on October 5, the first day of heavy fighting in the Opheusden area. Maj. Oliver Horton died when hit by shrapnel from a mortar round near the railroad crossing. He was replaced by Capt. Robert Harwick, who in turn almost became another casualty.

Captain Harwick wrote:[132] "I was commanding 3rd and got ambushed while in a jeep. The driver was killed and the jeep went off the dike into the canal. Clark Heggeness and I walked a mile or so in a water-filled ditch but did get away. After it was over, I found I could wear a Purple Heart. A soft touch."

Describing an incident that was hair raising, 1Lt. Clark Heggeness of "H" Company wrote: "One day, Captain (Robert) Harwick asked me to accompany him in a jeep along the dike to reconnoiter the area and to make certain that there were no enemy. We were sitting side-by-side up high behind the driver, sort of like VIPs riding in a parade. A river was to our left. The road was on the dike and there were trees and brush to the right. We had gone maybe a half mile and, as we came around a curve, lo and behold, there was a German machine gun nest next to a tree not more than 25 or 30 yards ahead. When they saw the jeep coming, the machine gunner opened up and started shooting and all I could see was a host of tracers and what seemed to be red streamers coming right at us, with loud cracking noises indicating the bullets were going by very close. The jeep driver (who we learned later was killed) lost control of the jeep and it hit a stump just to the left of the road. Captain Harwick and I

132. From a letter Capt. Robert Harwick wrote to Red Cross worker Helen Briggs from Holland on November 21, 1944.

then catapulted into the air, landing in about three or four feet of water and about ten feet from the bank in the midst of reeds and bulrushes. Luckily, we were not injured by our 'flight,' and we were lucky to land in the water instead of on the ground and, also, that the water was not over our heads.

"Pretty soon we heard several Germans on the bank of the river. They were laughing and we could see them pushing the reeds back and forth with the ends of their rifles, apparently looking for us. I don't know if they were trying to help us or were going to shoot us, but the water sure was cold! After a minute or two they left and, after we couldn't hear them for a long time (and I mean long!!), we waded back through the reeds to where the jeep was. It was a mess, up against a tree stump with the front end bashed in, and we could see that the Germans had apparently taken some papers (maps?) and carbines from the jeep, or else they had been thrown out by the impact. We saw the driver who was slumped over the steering wheel. He had a bullet hole just above his eyes right in the middle of the forehead. I'll never know, for the life of me, why the good Lord picked him and not the captain or me. We then waded and walked (very carefully) back to our units."

Haircuts

Second Platoon of "F" Company of the 506th hadn't had sleep for three nights when they got orders to pull guard duty at the division command post at Slijk-Ewijk. Sgt. John Taylor related: "Here I was with 30 men who hadn't slept in three days and had hardly anything to eat. We got briefed by a division officer. Lt. Ed Thomas got us something to eat. Everybody was fed by midnight. Lt. Thomas and I were on the go all night long checking the posts.

"We got back about 1500 hours from that assignment. They trucked us back to our bivouac area. As we drove up in the trucks to unload, 'F' Company was falling out for inspection. We had a new C.O., Lt. Wyland (not his real name). I hadn't met him before. As we got off the truck, he told Lt. Thomas to fall out the 2nd Platoon to stand inspection also. Keep in mind, these men had been without sleep for approximately four days and four nights so we fell in and had the inspection. We were not prepared for it and the C.O. reamed us out pretty good and I was told that two of my men needed haircuts and he wanted me to have these men get haircuts before I went to sleep that night and to report to him when I got the task done.

"We got the men back in the orchard. Getting haircuts was no problem as George Lovell had his clippers along and, in a little while, we had the men's hair clipped.

"This didn't set well with me. It didn't set well with Lt. Thomas and it didn't go over well with the men—the initial confrontation with the new company commander. Here was a new man who didn't realize what the men had been through for many days. He should have informed himself and not forced them to stand inspection—and to chew them out about anything and then to have me report to him to let him know the haircuts had been completed. I guess the mean streak showed in me. We had the men's hair cut by 1900 hours that evening. I knew where the C.O. was bedded down, in a house, I waited until about 0100 hours and made my way up to the house. I awakened the good company commander and informed him that I had managed to get haircuts for the men. This didn't set too well with him, having been awakened from a sound sleep. I did exactly what he told me to do, except I did it on my time schedule."

Counter-Battery Fire

The firing batteries of the various artillery battalions were not the only ones subject to counter-battery fire. The fire control centers were sometimes hit.

As for his most harrowing experience on the island, Sgt. Arthur Parker wrote: "S/Sgt. Frank Van Duzer and I decided to spend the night in the big red schoolhouse in Zetten as our big covered foxhole was taking on water. We moved into a small room on the first floor near the door and spread our bed rolls. Just as we got settled, our first sergeant and his telephone operator decided they wanted the room. The first sergeant made us move out. We found a clean place on the 3rd floor and bedded down. That night, the Germans shelled us with some heavy artillery and the first round came in right through the window of the small room which was now occupied by the first sergeant. He was badly wounded and his switchboard operator was killed. The Germans tried to bring the school house down around our heads. We barely got out of there and back to our wet, but safe, dugout. Several men were killed and wounded that night."

T/Sgt. Cliff Marshall wrote: "The school on the edge of Zetten was close behind a big barn and we thought it offered protection from the German rockets. There was a small stage with a trap door and Major Julian Rosemond and myself and a few others went below when the rocket hit. I was temporarily pinned by the foundation walls—not even hurt. 1/Sgt. Noah Lauten was seriously injured. I then became first sergeant."

Capt. Joseph K. Perkins wrote: "I was acting as duty officer in the fire direction center in a house in Zetten when a 200mm delayed action shell fell only thirty feet away. It landed in a 'dry' canal by the road and buried itself so deep all energy went straight up. The poor guard was sent home in shock."

The diary of 1/Sgt. F. G. Fitzgerald of "C" Battery of the 377th Parachute Field Artillery Battalion describes an incident that took the lives of several of the battery men:

Oct. 9—Jerry continued to throw a lot of artillery around and launched a counterattack in our immediate front after a 15 minute artillery preparation. They suddenly swung the concentration into our area positions while we were in the midst of a fire mission. Heavy (152mm) shells landed in the area killing Exec. Lt. John Sluzewich and S/Sgt. Peter Lutz and seriously wounded Cpl. Myron Burge, PFC Larry Davis and Pvt. Six, slightly wounding Pvt. Fred Conrad, Olinger, Kline and Sgt. Fitzgerald. Despite the hardship of losing the nerve center of the firing battery, the mission was completed. (Davis and Burge died of their wounds a day or two later.)

Shelling of a Rest Area

Communications sergeant Chester Wetsig wrote: "After we had been in contact with the enemy over some 30 days, continuously, we were taken back to a large house for a two-day rest and showers. The new battalion exec officer, a captain, called all the battalion HQ non-coms together. I was sitting in front of a window with fellows standing to the right and left of me. The two on either side of me were killed and quite a few others were wounded when a shell hit and exploded near the window. T/5 W. J. Radel and W. J. Dellapenta were killed that day."

T/5 William Schwerin was in the same room. He remembered: "While we were in reserve up on the Neder Rhine, all the non-coms in Headquarters Company were in a corner room of a building. A shell hit outside the window killing Pvt. William Dellapenta and T/5 Walter Radel but missed Sgt. Wetsig, who was sitting between them."

T/5 Raymond Lappegaard was a member of the communications section and was also in the room that day. He wrote: "On one occasion we were about five miles back in a so-called rest area. We were in a school building and were attending a non-coms meeting on the wrong side of the building one night. I was standing in the corner of the room. An 88mm shell landed very close to the window sill. There were about twenty men in the room. Radel and Dellapenta were killed. The explosion knocked me unconscious. When I woke up I was still shaking for about half an hour."

Division CP Hit at Slijk-Ewijk

The division command post was shelled in Son on September 19 and 20 with no loss of life. It was shelled again at the Henkenshage castle in St. Oedenrode on September 26, resulting in the death of LTC Roger Parkinson, the division ordnance officer. The following day T/5 Ancel D. Mullen and a young Dutch boy were killed by another shell in the same area. The third shelling occurred shortly before the division was to move south to its next station in Mourmelon in France.

M/Sgt. Charles R. Norton of the division G-2 Section remembered: "The Division CP was bombed in Normandy and shelled in Holland. I was leaving the CP when the shells started coming in. One struck the building where the message center was located. One landed in the orchard and exploded near the CP tent damaging the trailer, tent and some equipment inside. No one was injured in the tent. I spent some time in a ditch before continuing to my quarters. On my way, I was passed by a cyclist who was reported to be directing the firing."

PFC William K. Crews of the division MP Platoon remembered the incident. "While on guard duty at a brick barn, which was being used as a division headquarters, it was hit by shell fire. Bricks were blown everywhere by the explosion. I ran under the shelter of a tree. I was hit on the foot by a brick but no injury resulted."

Cpl. E. Logan Koenig of Signal Company remembered: "The Division had moved up to a location where the CP was in an orchard. Signal Supply was set up in a barn, attached Holland style, to a farmhouse. Three or four of us were bedded down in a room over a shed. A German shell landed in the hay loft. There were no injuries but we promptly changed our quarters. Moved into a foxhole like a sensible G.I. should."

The diary of T/4 George Koskimaki, who had his radio positioned in the orchard, provided a brief record of the shelling:

Nov. 23—What a way to spend Thanksgiving! Jerry blew up our CP with heavy artillery. One explosion blew Bob Hayes out of the side of a barn. Hurt his foot a bit. We moved to a new CP that wasn't zeroed in.

Nov. 24—The artillery barrage must have been an inside job with civilian observers. . . .

Col. Thomas Sherburne of Division Artillery remembered the incident: "I will never forget when General McAuliffe held a meeting. German artillery was getting the HQ range. LTC Sidney Davis, Division Signal Officer, was complaining about not having enough wire for his communication nets. Just then a shell came in, hit the second floor of a barn next to our commanders meeting. The second floor bent down to the ground and a GI sleeping on that second floor slid down to the ground, jumped up and ran. That decided Colonel Davis. We moved out to a new location. I left our S-3 Elmer Kennedy there while I went to the new CP set-up. I came back. General Higgins and Kennedy were there, looking at a huge shell which had slid in on the wet ground and grass and lay there unexploded. We got our remaining equipment on jeeps, left that big shell. (Often wondered if it finally exploded—poor farmer, if it did!)"

Cpl. Jim Evans of Division Artillery remembered when the shell hit. "The Division Signal Supply was hit in a barn. A reel of wire landed in our orchard causing a few extra fox holes to be dug."

Capt. William G. Joe and his men of "D" Battery of the 81st AA and AT Battalion had supported 3rd and 1st Battalions of the 506th at Opheusden and later backed up the 327th in the same general area. After they were relieved, Joe moved his men into a two-story house in Slijk-Ewijk. An old man and his daughter occupied the house and moved into two rooms and the kitchen. The "Dog" Battery men slept in the attic and on the second floor.

The men had occupied the house two days when they were asked to move. Captain Joe related: "The next day a communications officer from Division showed up. He told me we must get out of the house because the Division CP had been shelled and they must move and this building was the one they wanted for the communication center. No way! My men just came off the line and they're resting. It's an unwritten law of first possession in the combat zone—period. Before you know it, he returned with Colonel Renfro. We had served in the old 327th at Camp Claiborne. We sat on the steps and smoked a cigarette. Well—he convinced me. I asked for time to make a reconnaissance for another place. Those Signal types were laying lines all through that building before we could move out."

Friend or Enemy?

The fact that the troops of the 101st seemed to be living in a goldfish bowl, with all daylight travel being "hazardous to one's health" due to the excellent observation the Germans had of the area on the island from their positions on the higher elevations of the north side of the Neder Rijn river hillsides, it was felt by many that they had observers calling in locations of prime targets in the Allied troop positions.

Capt. William Joe describes such an episode: "The roads and, of course, the dikes were elevated. The residential houses were set down on level with the farming area. There was one stretch of houses occupied by 506th small units. As normally occurs, not on the immediate front, our troops were washing and relaxing around the houses. This pastor or priest with the black frock and round black hat would ride his bicycle down the embankment on his way to give support to the various families still in houses behind our MLR and, as he passed the troopers, he would raise his hat in greeting. About 15 to 20 minutes later, the shells would begin to fall around the houses and vicinity. I understood this went on for a couple of days. I later heard the clergyman was either prevented from visiting his parishioners or he was taken in to G-2."

Another soldier, Pvt. William N. Chivvis of "I" Company of the 506th Regiment, had this recollection: "Near Dodewaard, three Dutch civilians became familiar with our positions. When the German attack came, the tree line once removed to our rear disappeared in a cloud of artillery smoke; I credit those civilians with furnishing incorrect information to the enemy."

The same incident must have been witnessed by PFC Leonard Schmidt, who recalled: "One day, two or three hours before the mortars set in on me, there were four Dutchmen in leather coats looking over the terrain and I couldn't figure out what they were up to. I inquired and someone said they were Dutch underground. I think they gave the Germans the exact coordinates on which our machine gun was situated. Other Americans said those Dutch gave the Germans false coordinates and all that happened was a huge barrage that hit a tree line that wasn't occupied. It disappeared completely with the shelling."

Line Crosser

The commanders of the units of the 101st, and particularly those of the artillery units, were anxious to position observers in strategic locations to call down artillery fire at opportune moments.

Capt. Joseph Perkins, S-2 officer for the 321st Glider Field Artillery Battalion, reported: "Lt. Francis Canham came to me and said, 'Captain, I've got a line-crosser at my OP up with the 506th on the dike. He has offered to take me back to his house in or near Renkum. I would like to set up an OP in his attic for a day. He says there is a lot of enemy traffic past his place.'

"I went direct to the Division G-2, as I didn't trust our wire net with this type of thing. He gave me the OK, so we set it up with the 506th to get Canham across and to pick him up 24 hours later. Nothing happened going over so we tuned in to his channel at dawn. By 1000 hours we had heard nothing, so I began to call him. Still nothing. It was a wreck of a day for me. The boat was sent back at the appointed time and he was waiting. His report was very complete on what he could see, but the controlled artillery fire was a washout. It seemed that a squad of Krauts moved into the bedroom below Canham and their voices were so plain he could not even open the net. The Krauts moved out at sundown. These were probably the night watch on the dikes. Canham, with his guide, then returned to the rendezvous on the river."

A British MP

As the elements of the 101st Division moved north to the island, the 326th Medical Company moved its hospital facilities to Nijmegen to be closer to the action. First Lieutenant Henry Barnes was in on the move and contrasts the area with that which they had been involved in for the past two weeks. He wrote: "The first night in this city, I slept in a hotel using a bed with white sheets. Unable to sleep because the bed was too soft, I went into the garden and slept in a slit trench. It seemed odd to be dug in in a city filled with civilians and British troops. We stayed two nights in a small basement sharing it with three or four British MPs. I remember one of the MPs in particular because he was so anxious while awaiting assignment to direct traffic on the bridge. And well he might because the bridge was shelled incessantly. The bridge was a long structure about a mile long with 'ack-ack' positions along both sides. At night it was bathed in a sea of ghostly light. The searchlights on each side of it were aimed in the direction of the German batteries, by the British for the purpose of making it difficult for the enemy to aim on to the bridge. I remember the day when the MP was leaving to go to the bridge to replace a wounded comrade. We wished him luck."

Troops were given an opportunity to return to the division rest area in Nijmegen from time to time for showers, haircuts, movies, and relaxation. They did run the risk of experiencing enemy shell fire en route to and from the island. On one such occasion, the trip was exciting enough to be recorded by T/4 George E. Koskimaki in his diary:

> October 21—While coming back from taking showers in Nijmegen, an 88mm shell landed fifty feet in front of our truck. It hit the road at an intersection and knocked the legs out from under an English MP who was directing traffic. A piece of shrapnel cut Art Frazier's arm. He was standing next to me as we stood looking forward over the cab of the truck.

First Lieutenant Henry Barnes was returning to Nijmegen from one of the 502nd aid stations near Elst on the afternoon of October 21. He wrote: "There was a lot of motor traffic over the Waal bridge and the MPs were busy moving things along. A shell came roaring in and exploded some fifty yards ahead of us. When we got there one MP was down, seriously wounded. We stopped the bleeding and splinted one leg, placed him on a litter and sped on toward the hospital housing my parent unit, the Medical Company. I didn't know the location of any British medical installation and this British MP was gravely wounded. As I drove up to the hospital, located in a residential area, and helped to unload him I recognized, with a shock, that it was the same MP who had worried so much about being stationed on the bridge. I felt suddenly very sad as I was afraid he was going to die. He was so covered with blood and my hands were dripping red despite the tourniquets."

Bombing of the Division Hospital

Though the division hospital was always well marked with a large Red Cross superimposed on a white circle, the hospital was hit twice by enemy bombers. In Normandy, the Château Columbierre was hit by two huge bombs on the night of June 9, 1944. The bombs were intended for Division Headquarters. Fortunately, the wounded had been evacuated to the beach earlier in the day, holding the bombing casualties to medical personnel only. In Holland, the forward hospital was hit in a school building in Nijmegen, south of the long bridge over the Waal River. The bombs were dropped by a high-flying jet, one of the first to make its appearance over the bridge site. Authorities believe the bombs were intended for the bridge but fell in the school area occupied by the hospital.

Several of the medical personnel and one of the paratroopers from a line company remembered the incident in their accounts.

T/5 Paul Nabours remembered the bombing incident this way: "We had moved up to Nijmegen and set up in a Catholic school. It was there I saw my first jet airplanes. One Sunday, a jet came over and started dropping A.P. bombs. One went through the roof of the school building but fortunately none of our people inside were hurt. Mass was being held in the church adjoining the school and several worshipers were injured. We weren't busy at the time so began treating and caring for civilians but after a short time orders came not to do anything for them so we had to turn people away. I have seriously questioned this incident in view of the hospitality of the Dutch people."

Capt. Willis McKee was more personally involved in the bombing incident. He wrote: "After several weeks, we moved to Nijmegen and set up in a school building. We were kept busy with many severely wounded. I was working a 12-hour shift— 6 P.M. to 6 A.M. and, one Sunday morning, Lts. Louis Shadegg and Everett Vogt, MAC officers, came by my room and invited me to go with them to a nearby Dutch hospital to take a shower. I dressed and went down to our headquarters office. Sammy Kaye's *Sunday Serenade* had just started on the Armed Forces radio network and I lay down on a cot to listen to it. Lou and Ev arrived and said, 'Come on, we're ready to go.' I responded, 'No, I want to listen to this program.' Despite their urgings, I refused to go with them. They went to the parking area to get their jeep. A lone, small German plane came over and dropped a bomb beside the jeep and both were killed. Shadegg was burned so severely that we identified him by the hunting knife that he wore in his boot. The building was damaged so we had to move into a monastery."

Capt. David V. Habif was also a surgeon with the same unit at the hospital. He wrote: "We were treating casualties in twelve-hour shifts. One morning while sleeping on a cot on the upper floor, a bomb was dropped in the schoolyard killing several soldiers in the motor pool area and injured others. The blast flipped my cot over but the drapes contained the flying glass."

Cpl. Chester Ostby from "B" Company of the 501st, had come down with flu while up on the island. He had been sent back to the division hospital for treatment. He wrote: "I was in the hospital when it was bombed. I had a case of flu and was able to walk about. I helped a nurse carry wounded to a basement but a few people were killed and all the windows were blown out. I went back to the front—flu and all."

Arriving on the scene shortly after the bombing, 1Lt. Henry Barnes was met by one of the company officers who led him around behind the hospital to a blackened and scorched area. Barnes said, "I immediately noticed the sweetish smell of death. There were two burned-out jeeps next to each other and near a burned out shell of a large Army truck.

"It seems a short time before I arrived, German planes bombed the hospital and the bombs landed in the back of the hospital on the jeeps and the truck. In the inferno, three Medical Company men were killed and six wounded. The officer put his arm around me and asked me, with tears in his eyes, if I would please identify the dead.

"There I was, on my knees, picking through the still warm blackened bones searching for dog tags. To my horror, I read the names of the other two MAC officers in our company. They had just been burned to death, while sitting miles behind the front getting ready to move off in a jeep.

"I sat back feeling so low. I was the only evacuation officer left from our company of four who started out in Normandy. For a medical company, normally the safest unit in the division, our casualties were mounting. We had lost 58 killed, wounded and missing in Normandy and our toll in Holland was now 19."

The Rescue

One of the most amazing rescue operations of World War II was the saving of a band of British paratroopers, downed airmen, escaped POWs, and some Dutch underground leaders by troopers of Company "E" of the 506th Parachute Infantry Regiment. The Screaming Eagles were aided by British airborne engineers and Dutch underground members. The daring rescue took place on the night of October 23, 1944.

In a letter he had written providing his recollections of the action, Col. Robert F. Sink,[133] commander of the 506th Parachute Infantry Regiment, described some of the actions: "During the airborne operation of the 1st British Airborne Division in Arnhem, Colonel Dobey became known as the 'Mad Colonel of Arnhem.' He told me the story of all the fighting they had in Arnhem and, after several days of terrific struggle, he had about six people left, many of whom, including himself, were wounded when they were finally cornered in a room in a building and there wasn't anything else to do but surrender. This he did for these six people and he was put in a hospital by the Germans. After several days in the hospital, Colonel Dobey walked out and made good his escape. He was picked up by the Dutch Underground, which was very good, indeed and had collected a flock of other British parachutists, none of whom had been captured. There was also a total of five American aviators (officers)

133. From a copy of a letter Col. Robert F. Sink wrote to a Lieutenant Van Horn on August 23, 1945. Copy sent by Cpl. Walter S. Gordon.

and about eight or ten Dutch civilians who were being sought by the Germans. Collected around this town then was a total of 140 people, most of whom were British parachutists and all of whom had a very healthy desire to get back across the Rhine."

Determined to prevent the men being captured by the Germans, the colonel promised the men that somehow he would bring help.

To make good his vow to get help, the British colonel had crawled through the German lines at night and then, under the eyes of Kraut sentries, swam the Neder Rijn. After reaching Screaming Eagle lines, he was quickly placed in contact with British headquarters.

When the British asked that the 101st aid in the rescue, the 506th was named as the unit to be involved. They were in the most suitable position on the line. First Lieutenant Fred T. Heyliger of "E" Company was given the task of planning and leading the rescue.

As told by Sgt. Donald Malarkey of "E" Company, extensive planning went into the operation as soon as the 101st was told they would be involved. He wrote: "In mid-October of 1944, I was taken to Division Headquarters by my company commander, 1Lt. Fred Heyliger, for a meeting with G-2, the purpose of which was unknown. We were escorted into a room that contained large wall maps and aerial photos. There were several British officers, together with our G-2 personnel, Lt. Heyliger and myself.

"At the time of the meeting, I was the sergeant for 2nd Platoon, having succeeded Bill Guarnere, who had been injured. Part of our platoon responsibility during the period included the night-time out-posting of an orchard and complex of farm buildings on the bank of the Rhine, due north of the island village of Randwijk. It was one of the few areas the Division occupied that had Rhine River concealment.

"I was asked if small British assault boats could be concealed in the orchard, so as not to be visible by the Germans across the Rhine or from the air. Also needed information on whether these boats could be brought in one night and used the following night. I responded to both questions in the affirmative and explained that there was a deep, high water overflow ditch that circled the south edge of the orchard. It was 6 to 7 feet deep and

8 to 10 feet across. The bordering fruit trees spanned the ditch with their limbs, blocking visibility from the air.

"Following the preliminary discussion, a somewhat disheveled red-bearded British colonel was brought into the room and introduced. It was explained that he had worked his way through German lines and swam the Rhine the night before into the Division sector. He related that he had been working with and aided by the Dutch underground. They had a plan to effect the escape of as many as 140 Allied soldiers, mostly British paratroopers, from German territory west of Arnhem. He laid out a detailed and elaborate plan that was to culminate in a river crossing through the 2nd Platoon sector a week later."

Sergeant Malarkey continued: "Dobey stated that all the paratroopers, airmen, escapees, etc. were secreted in various Dutch homes, barns and buildings, some as far as fifteen miles from the projected crossing point. They would move each night toward the Rhine, led primarily by Dutch women. The line of direction was to be identified by the firing each night, at midnight, of ten rounds from a British 40mm gun from atop the dike, across the orchard, into the high ground west of Arnhem.

"The British assault boats would be placed in the orchard ditch the night before the crossing, which would occur at 0100 hours, the following night signaled by a flashing red light. Two men from the 2nd Platoon, with rifles and tommy guns, would ride in each boat in the event German opposition was encountered."

The following Monday night was set as the time for the rescue attempt. Plans were for the 140 men to infiltrate through German lines and reach a designated area, a rough box four hundred yards long and five hundred yards wide on the bank of the Neder Rijn.

Further precautions called for machine gunners and riflemen from the 3rd Platoon to be positioned both east and west of the orchard on the banks of the Rhine for additional supporting fire. Also, as mentioned by Sergeant Malarkey, two machine-gun teams would accompany the rescue craft and set up positions on both flanks on the enemy side of the river, to ward off any German troops who might rush forward to interfere with the landing operation.

In the event that the Germans discovered the plot, Colonel Dobey was to call for massed artillery, mortar and machine-gun fire to "fence in" the box until the rescue was completed.

Planning the massed artillery barrage was Capt. Joseph Perkins, S-2 officer for the 321st Glider Field Artillery Battalion. He wrote: "I did the 'Box' barrage to protect the rescue mission of the 506th when they brought back the last of the British Airborne Division over the lower Rhine. Several artillery regiments, maybe a hundred pieces, were standing by for the code word, 'Oh Susannah' to fire the protecting barrage."

A 40mm Bofors gun crew, under the command of LTC X. B. Cox Jr. of the 81st Airborne Anti-Aircraft Battalion, was to fire the tracers due north, every hour on the hour, beginning at midnight.

To allay possible German suspicions, this procedure was practiced several nights—firing in different directions—prior to the rescue operations.

Sergeant Malarkey continued his story: "All personnel were to be positioned in the orchard before midnight, at which time the Bofors gun would be fired for the final time. Following this, a corps of British artillery would blast the high ground west of Arnhem with incendiaries which would provide background light for the boats making the crossing. There were 14 boats and each was to make one crossing. Then they were to be abandoned on the bank of the Rhine.

"Colonel Dobey was asked how that many soldiers could be moved in a week's time period, to a specific assembly point. He stated it would be done by Dutch women traveling at night by bicycle. German forces were apparently not very suspicious of the Dutch women.

"Driving back to our company area, I remarked to Lt. Heyliger that the plan seemed almost too perfect to have a chance. He said the British were exceptionally resourceful when they were cornered. The next week would determine the validity of that statement."

Cpl. Walter S. Gordon was one of the machine gunners involved in the flank operation. He wrote: "One day while positioned on the bank of the Rhine River, 1Lt. Fred Heyliger called a company formation and asked, or rather stated, he needed some men to accompany him on some sort of a mission. I don't recall him asking for any volunteers but rather pointed to a number of us and that was that. He required two machine gunners and a number of riflemen. PFC Francis J. Mellett was designated as one of the gunners and I was selected as the other. I recall we were later transported to a rear area and introduced to the canvas boats which were a part of the British equipment. They were fragile and had a plywood-like bottom. We were asked to familiarize ourselves with the operation of the boats by paddling about on a small pond."

All went well until forty-eight hours before the operation was to begin; then the Dutch informed Colonel Dobey that the Germans had ordered all able-bodied men in the village to report Monday morning to dig defenses.

For the British and Americans to appear for this detail would mean almost certain discovery and capture. Colonel Dobey decided, therefore, to set the rescue schedule ahead twenty-four hours. This was welcome news to the 140 men, some of whom were living, disguised as civilians, in the houses with German troops.

Colonel Sink[134] wrote: "The secret was so great on this deal that Colonel Cox, of our 81st AA-AT Battalion, who had been firing the Bofors gun for the several preceding nights, finally came and said, 'For God's sake, please tell me what the score is!' I don't know whether he was told or not."

Sergeant Malarkey continued his narrative: "Several nights before the crossing, I traversed the route with some of the British engineers, so they would be familiar with the terrain.

"The Bofors gun was fired each night, much to the puzzlement of both our own and the German forces. On the evening prior to the crossing, we escorted the British crews and boats so they could be placed in position. At 2300 hours on the appointed night, the personnel involved in the crossing worked their way into the orchard. They remained in the ditch to the river side of the orchard where the boats could be quietly skidded down the bank into the river. At 0030 the heavy concentration of British artillery shells firing at the high ground west of Arnhem began falling.

"So far, all the pieces of the British colonel's puzzle had fallen into place.

"At about 0100, Ed Joint, who was to be with me in one of the boats, and I were sitting with our backs against a tree on the edge of the orchard, looking intently across the Rhine. Ed remarked that he did not see how everything could work without a hitch. I said he might be right.

134. Sink letter to Van Horn.

"About two minutes later, Joint excitedly said, 'Look Sarge, a light!' The red light was flashing as planned. I yelled at the crew and we shoved the boat into the water. We were the first boat to cross.

"I was in the bow with my tommy gun, fully expecting that some kind of opposition would be encountered. I was crouched down, so that my eyes could just see over the bow. The fires in the distance provided a good background for any silhouette that appeared.

"About ten yards from the north bank of the Rhine, I saw figures milling in the water and above them, a huddled group. I jumped in the river and met a British sergeant. I told him we would take ten men in each boat that was to be in the crossing."

Colonel Sink[135] wrote: "Heyliger was in charge of fanning out his troops after he reached the other side, gathering in the fold, or inside the box, these people that were over there, corralling them toward the boats, putting them aboard, getting them back across the water, then gathering his men and getting them back, also."

Cpl. Walter Gordon wrote: "The idea was to establish two lateral outposts flanking the route which was to be used by the men rescued. The machine gun I manned was set up and riflemen were stationed nearby. We lay there quietly and guarded the front which had been assigned to us. I do not recall how long we were posted but eventually we were summoned back to the boats which had transported us over the river."

Colonel Sink went down to the river as soon as the boats took off for the north shore of the Rhine. There had been the firing of a burp gun, and a bunch of Nebelwerfers (Screaming Meemies) farther along the river sent shells hurtling toward the 506th command post down the river, some distance behind the dike.

S/Sgt. Robert J. Houston[136] wrote of an action taken by his unit of the 501st positioned farther to the east near Heteren. "Company 'H' sent a diversionary patrol across the river at the same time, and Lt. Douglas Wilcombe was killed during that patrol."

Sergeant Malarkey continued: "I brought ten British paratroopers, one British tanker and one American pilot in my boat.

135. Sink letter to Van Horn.
136. Houston, 78.

The most interesting one was a sergeant from the British 7th Armored Division, who had escaped from a German prison camp. He said, 'Sarge, I'm all through. My wife has been a widow five times now, and she is not going to be again.' He was from the famed 'Rats of Tobruk' and had been reported missing in action several times in Africa and for the last time on the continent."

Describing the trip back across the river as the last of the security force of machine gunners and riflemen returned, Cpl. Walter Gordon wrote: "In spite of the fact that we had been admonished to be quiet, we did get a bit zealous on our return and paddled like demons. Each time a paddle made contact with the wood frame of the boat, it had the sound of a kettle drum. I was astonished that we were not heard in Berlin. Not a shot was fired. We were scared as hell. I was damned glad to get back to the American side of the river. I never viewed a single British soldier or any party who had been rescued as they were whisked away prior to our returning."

"I got hold of the British brigadier (G. W. Lathbury) and Colonel Dobey and a couple other British officers who had been among the liberated and took them to my CP," said Colonel Sink. "The American officers had wanted to stay with the American troops until they saw what those Nebelwerfers had done to our CP. They then decided that perhaps it would be better for themselves to proceed with their British comrades back to the town of Nijmegen."

Sergeant Malarkey closed his account: "The next morning all hell broke loose at the orchard and the bank of the Rhine as heavy German artillery devastated much of the orchard, buildings and all of the boats."

No-Man's-Land

After the first few days of heavy fighting, Opheusden had become a dead town. No one lived there. It was a wasteland. Shell-shattered houses lay silent. Dead swine lay about the countryside, killed by stepping on the lethal Shu mines.

PFC George K. Mullins was sent on a mission to capture some prisoners. "We moved out with one rifle platoon, my machine gun squad, our platoon leader, a British artillery observer captain and PFC William J. Onstott from 'C' Company serving as his radio operator.

"We were south of Opheusden. After leaving the road we headed toward the railroad. We moved quietly down the ditch. Near the railroad tracks we spotted some fox holes. PFC Parker opened up with his machine gun while we fired our rifles. While we fired, keeping the enemy down in the holes, one of our men made a dash for the nearest hole and threw a grenade in it. We heard voices yelling 'Kamerade!' A white flag waved frantically from one of the holes. We moved in, taking the occupants as prisoners. They were ordered to help the wounded out of the holes. We started for the rear immediately as we had awakened everybody in the area.

"The enemy began raining artillery on us and the prisoners as they were being rushed up the ditch carrying their wounded.

"I turned my attention to some dugouts to our right. By this time the British captain was doing his thing with his artillery. This guy had to be the best. Out of three shells, he could put the third one in a particular fox hole. We moved in near the dugouts which were covered with railroad ties, a BAR fired a burst into the nearest one. I rushed in and threw a hand grenade down into the hole. It exploded. There was no sound—no moans or groans, no one yelled 'Kamerade!' I moved in, pausing long enough for my eyes to adjust to the darkness. I was almost bowled over by two German kids who rushed past me. While those two were taken care of topside, I investigated the back of the dugout. There lay their radio, all blown to bits, They had covered the grenade with the radio and it had absorbed the blast and left them without a scratch. We got the order to pull back. The artillery slacked off a bit as we had captured 'his eyes.' I took a good hard look at the faces of each of the prisoners. As usual, there was one 'SS' in each pack. No doubt this guy could kill his own mother without thinking twice.

"Returning to our lines on the south side of Opheusden, we paused for a few minutes. There, in a lawn, were buried 13 Germans, 3 Americans and 5 British soldiers. (I give the Germans credit for taking care of the dead.)

"As we arrived near our lines, we received another radio message ordering us to travel west along the large dike. Proceed west until we are contacted by the enemy. This didn't take long. A machine gun opened up in line with our column. Bullets cracked over our heads. Two riflemen were wounded. We had a brief skirmish and then pulled back to our line.

"Very soon our lieutenant showed up and asked for volunteers to go back to the German lines to get the other lieutenant, the British captain and radioman Onstott. They had been wounded. (Why those three stayed behind is a mystery.) Parker and I volunteered. From quite a distance, I could hear the captain yelling for all the voice that was in him. Parker immediately set up his machine gun in the road and laid down behind it, ready for action.

"What a sin—the lieutenant finally got the captain quieted down. He had stepped on a Shu mine. It had blown his foot off and the big muscle in his leg was peeled from the bone almost to his knee. It appeared that Bill Onstott had hit the ground on his hip with the mine blowing his leg almost in two, between the hip and knee. He was unconscious, but still breathing. The lieutenant was taking care of the captain. I gave Onstott morphine shots and took the backpack radio off him by cutting the harness. This being our first run-in with the foot mine plus the worries of war, especially myself—I didn't have it all together. It didn't register that under the gravel on either side of the road was a bed of foot mines. It was getting dark. Artillery shells began to fall in the area. I suppose the only reason the Germans didn't open up on us with their machine guns was that they wanted us to step on some more mines. What a dreary place!

"The captain hadn't lost his sense of humor yet. 'I'll be seeing London before you bloody Yanks do, that is for sure,' he yelled at us.

"The lieutenant said, 'We've got to call for help! Give me that radio.' Oh no, when removing the radio from Onstott's back, I had cut the phone cord. I hastened to splice the main wires together and carried it over to the lieutenant. He called company headquarters asking for all available medics. I was still kneeling beside Onstott when five medics arrived. One of them asked me to step back so he could pull Onstott up on the road. He stepped where I had been kneeling as he took hold of Onstott. A mine blew, taking half of his foot off and filled his face with gravel. If there was a hell on earth, this must have been the place.

"I never heard of the British captain since, although I have his beat-up field glasses that I retrieved from the slope of the dike. We loaded our wounded on the stretchers and headed back. Onstott died a few minutes later."

S/Sgt. Jack Williamson of "A" Company had worked with

the same British artillery observer captain earlier when "A" Company had been in danger of being overrun. Williamson's group was in position near a jam factory. He came upon the British officer while the observer was working with PFC George Mullins. Williamson wrote: "That same British forward observer captain was there with us again. He stepped on one of those Shu mines in Opheusden and lost a leg and some of the shrapnel got his left eyeball. He looked like he was near death. But, as they were carrying him back on a stretcher, he called to us, 'I say ole chaps, good hunting and cheerio!' Hell, I'm telling you—they're crazy! I guess the British artillery is the best. For sure, their forward observers had lots of guts."

After the British captain and the other wounded were returned to the lines of the 101st, placed on jeep ambulances and sent to the field hospital, PFC George Mullins went back to "C" Company. He closed his story with the following: "I returned the radio to company headquarters, then went back to the outpost. I tried to settle down for the night. Just to be in that foxhole and to know there wasn't a foot mine under my feet was a great feeling."

Sergeant Taylor's Patrol

The following notation is from the After-Action Report for the 506th Parachute Infantry Regiment for November 2, 1944:

> No change in unit dispositions. "F" Company sent twenty-two man combat patrol, under Lt. Thomas, across the railroad embankment. Their mission was to clear out any enemy in the dugouts and secure prisoners. They cleared about twenty dugouts and captured two enemy. This patrol suffered six casualties; two killed and four wounded. The patrol returned at 0300 hours.

The above action was carried out by what was left of 2nd Platoon led by replacement platoon leader 1Lt. Edward G. Thomas and the platoon sergeant, John H. Taylor. Taylor wrote: "One afternoon about 1600, Lt. Thomas came and told me we were gonna pull another combat patrol that night—the entire platoon or what was left of it—22 men. We went down to headquarters as a group—the five or six non-coms, to be briefed. We were to go over to the railroad, go over it and assault the enemy positions and do as much damage as we could and to bring back some prisoners. We decided to jump off about 0200. The temperature was about 40 and the night was clammy. The sector we were going to was about 1,000 yards south of the Arnhem railroad bridge, which had been destroyed. We carried two or three Thompson submachine guns, a BAR and M-1s and a bunch of concussion grenades. We moved through 'Easy' Company, which was about 400–500 yards back from the railroad. We stayed off the country lane road which was hit sporadically by mortar fire. The left side of the road we traveled had five or six ditches that you crossed with water from waist deep to neck level.

"We went in single file until we got to the first ditch and moved right and left forming a skirmish line. We eased into the water guiding on Lt. Thomas on the right and myself on the left instead of single filing through it. We continued on and went through the last ditch and this was about 25 yards from the railroad embankment. The grade was rather steep.

"We got to the bottom of the embankment and started up the slope before the enemy even heard us. They started throwing concussion grenades. We let out a yell and went over the railroad. A flare went off from a German position about fifty yards behind the track and I could see several men in the positions. With the dew and stuff, my feet went out from under me and I slid all the way to the bottom. I turned right. Clyde Jeffers had a phone and a wire he was trailing out as we went. He was beside me on my left. A burst of fire came from the embankment and Jeffers said, 'I'm hit in the arm!' I asked if he could make it back. Yes, he could.

"Lt. Thomas ran up near where I was and threw a grenade into a hole. I jumped down in it. It was a dugout into the side of the embankment and turned to the right. I fired a burst from the tommy gun and reached back in around the corner. I couldn't see but I felt a body. I pulled on it and it moved. I pulled some more and it started moving outward. I pulled a German soldier out of the hole, shoved him out and Lt. Thomas grabbed him. Before we left on the patrol, we agreed that once we got our hands on a prisoner—hold him and get him back to the company. Lt. Thomas got hold of him and took him back right then. This left me with the patrol. We checked out the dugout. Another flare went off. We knew we had to get those guys out of the hole so I worked my way out there and threw a grenade—

got rid of three of them and got another prisoner. We got all the dugouts pretty well checked and we had a signal when it was time to go back—I'd blow a whistle, which I did. My machine gun had jammed but I still had a grenade or two. I got together with a couple of the men. Homer Smith had been killed. We got Smitty back over the railroad. I figured it was time we got the hell out of there. We had been over there 20 to 30 minutes. We went down the sheltered side of the embankment. At the first ditch, we heard some splashing. We got down there and it was Dutch Ostrander. He had gone with us as radio operator from company HQ and had been hit by mortar fire. It had blown the radio off his back and shrapnel had gone up under his armpit so we had to pull Dutch out of the ditch and get him back. It was muddy and we slipped and slid. We got back to the house in the 'Easy' Company area where we had jumped off. We started counting heads—found we were missing Tommy Psar. I was pretty keyed up at the time. I decided Psar was nowhere around so I turned and headed back to get him and started running toward the railroad. I'd gone only a short distance when I heard noise behind me and here came Pat Casey, Marvin Crawford and Walt Puskar. We drew a little mortar fire and some MG fire from the flanks. I found Tommy sitting on the far side of the railroad beside a German hole and the minute I stooped and touched him, I knew he was dead. He had a large shrapnel hole in his back. I picked him up and we started down. I was going to carry him. It was so difficult to carry someone like that. I fell down with him just as I got to the road and Casey and the other boys—someone took a jacket off and we ran a rifle through each sleeve and wrapped it around and made a makeshift stretcher and we carried Tommy back. So we lost Homer Smith and Tommy Psar. Jeffers was wounded. Ostrander and Provenzano were wounded and a couple more who were on the MGs supporting us. We got back to the house. They had a jeep there to carry out our wounded and KIAs.

"We got the men together and sent them to the orchard to get into some dry clothes. We had our bedrolls in the orchard. It was nearing 0500 in the morning. Lt. Thomas and I were to report to S-2 at Battalion on the patrol. Gosh, it was cold riding back in the jeep as we were soaking wet. Colonel Strayer was back there. He gave us a cup of coffee and I think it was the best cup of coffee I ever had in my life. We were told to take off our wet clothes. Strayer threw a blanket around us. They called down to the company to get our bed rolls so we could get into some dry clothes. Just at the crack of dawn we made our way back to the company area. The guys had changed clothes and were sacked out.[137]

Enemy Patrol in the CP

When the 1st Battalion of the 506th Regiment was pulled back from Opheusden, it was positioned along the dikes to watch for German attempts to blow the dikes and flood out the Allied troops. S/Sgt. Charles A. Mitchell wrote: "After we were pulled back, a rumor, I feel sure, had it that the Krauts would flood the Island with six feet of water in twenty-four hours' time. It was decided that some units would take positions by outposts, occupied at night in foxholes with no visual exposure or movement at all come daylight."

Cpl. Henry Gogola wrote: "We were on forward outpost duty in a farmhouse from which we could see the blown-out bridge at Arnhem. It was the platoon CP and was also used as an artillery observation post. We had foxholes which were manned at night as listening posts to our front between us and the lower Rhine River.

"At that time, I had inherited the duties of phone and wireman. We had phones installed in the foxholes for the night so the men could keep in touch with the CP. What with artillery and mortar shells which were occasionally thrown our way, they had the uncanny knack of blowing some of the phone lines. I would have to go out and feel around for the wires and splice them together again. Talk about blind-man's bluff! On your hands and knees, feeling around for wires, every little noise making your stomach quiver and wanting to jump out of your shoes. But it had to be done. As a result of this I had very little, if any, sleep in 72 hours, which I know was not that uncommon. Several nights in a row crawling around like that can make you a little hyper. You tend to have a little difficulty sleeping anyway. That particular night, groggy but not sleepy, I had just finished checking the outposts, and with the new relief in place and the others sacked out in the basement we were quartered in. It was

137. Thomas and Taylor were awarded Silver Stars for their efforts.

a two-room affair with a wall between them and a doorway leading to either room. I was in the room away from the stairway. The others were sacked out in the room where the stairs led upward. PFC John Garrigan was on guard duty at the barn door overlooking the yard."

"The barn was a good size and was full of hay but the roof did have quite a few holes in it so the hay was wet," wrote John Garrigan. "The barn was connected to the house and we had run a rope from the barn door to the far end of the barn where you branched off; to the left you went down into a cold, damp cellar which had about eight stairs leading down into two rooms. The men used these rooms for sleeping. The first room with the stairs had a good sized area for sleeping five or six men. The other room was smaller but this is where the phone was located along with a couch and a few tables and chairs. This room had two windows about five feet off the floor and at ground level. The other room had one window. To the right, at the top of the stairs, you went into the kitchen where the side door was located.

"The particular spot for guard duty was not in the best location but to be anywhere else would mean you would have been a hundred feet further from the door and that was not a good idea so there I was with farm equipment piled five to six feet high on either side of me—not an ideal guard spot. The driveway ran alongside the barn to my right from the road."

Garrigan continued: "The time was early morning, some time in late October or early November. The moon was full and I was on duty at the 'B' Company 1st Platoon CP. It was in an area where we stayed in foxholes during the day and at night we just had guard duty at the door. The weather was rather cold on this particular morning and it was good to see the moon shine. For the past few weeks we had an awful lot of rain. 1Lt. Ed Long had taken out a patrol about an hour or so before I went on duty and now I was outside the barn just listening and looking when I heard footsteps coming down the driveway. The walkers did not sound like the regular (hobnailed) German boots so I felt as if it was Lt. Long and his patrol coming back to the CP. The German patrol did not make a sound in talking but their walk threw me off.

"Before I knew what was going on, the first soldier, a sergeant from an SS outfit, came around the corner and then the

second and third men until I had counted seventeen enemy soldiers. My first reaction was to fire but my decision was to hold
my fire and notify the boys who were asleep down in the cellar.
So with this thought in mind I just remained motionless while
the soldiers passed me by. I could have reached out and touched
all seventeen. The reason they did not see me was because I was
in the shadow of the barn and the obstacles beside me. When
the last soldier went by, I very slowly opened the barn door, put
my hand on the rope and walked back to the cellar.

"In the meantime, the Germans went in through the kitchen
door and now were breathing down my back just as I reached
the end of the rope. We had no lights at all so the Germans could
not see me go down the stairs, go into the room with the phone
where I wakened Sgt. (George) Puflett, telling him of the situation and he then put a call into our company CP for help, 'that
we have an enemy patrol in our barn!' Hank Gogola was awake
and so was Sgt. (Leonard) Mackey. We started to wake up the
rest of the men. I know we had three soldiers with us at that time
from an artillery outfit. They were using the building as an observation post."

Corporal Gogola continued his story. "When I heard footsteps
coming from upstairs, I thought it was the lieutenant coming
back. Instead it was Johnny coming down to tell me that a Kraut
patrol was in the yard milling around. We started trying to stir
up the others but it was too late. A tall shadowy figure had already come down carrying a hand-generated flashlight which
he kept pumping to keep it lit. I had put out the candles we had
lit before he came down so it was pitch black in the basement.
Johnny had come into the room I was in and I guess the Kraut
only saw the men sacked out.

" 'Hands up!' he shouted, still pumping away at the flashlight. In the meantime, Johnny kept moving back and forth between me and the doorway."

Two others were fully awake by this time.

"Sgt. Leonard Mackey stood at the bottom of the stairs as the
Kraut sergeant looked down and said 'Hande oop!' " wrote
S/Sgt. Charles Mitchell. "Leonard didn't know what to do but
freeze."

PFC Giles M. Thurman remembered, "My rifle was about ten
feet away and I could not reach it."

Gogola continued: "I had a P-38 pistol in my hand and stood

back from the doorway. Johnny moved in front of me as the Kraut shouted 'Hande oop!' a second time. I shoved Johnny away from me and yelled 'Hands up your ass!' as he turned toward me. I felt my hand jerk three times without realizing that I had shot at him. I couldn't miss as he was no more than three feet in front of me. He fell like a poled ox at my feet and I knelt down feeling for the pistol in his hand. I grabbed it and shouted out to the others who were awake now to hold their fire and to cover the stairway. The other Krauts had scattered as the shots were fired and were still around the yard. Suddenly, one of them fired his machine pistol. I felt the hot sting across my right temple. I fell to the floor. Talk about seeing a new galaxy of stars!"

Garrigan added: "Jose Almerez sprayed the top of the stairs with his Thompson sub. The next thing the Germans did was set fire to bunches of hay that they threw down the stairs. As soon as I saw this I figured this would be the end but with so much rain, the hay was wet and did not burn well.

"The next move they made was throwing hand grenades at the windows but we had enough sense to put some of the furniture and mattresses against the window openings. This was a great idea and by doing so we did not have a grenade go off in the basement but we certainly had enough go off outside as they would hit the barriers and bounce off."

At the 3rd Platoon CP, S/Sgt. G. A. Mitchell was awake. He wrote: "Early in the morning as I lay in the basement of our 3rd Platoon CP, I heard an urgent radio call, 'Come quickly, strong enemy patrol attacking our position.' Every man in 3rd Platoon was on the move in minutes.

"Dunning, with the .30 cal. machine gun, fired from the hip when we caught the Krauts leaving and he scored.

"When we reached 1st Platoon's farmhouse position, Dunning and I hit the ground at the door entrance to the house and shouted, 'Sound off or we open up!' John Garrigan called back, 'Hold it Mitch, Garrigan here!' "

"Ten minutes of enemy action and I heard Sergeant Mitchell yelling outside," wrote John Garrigan. "I knew then that we would make it. Sgt. Mitchell's 3rd Platoon cleaned out the area and once again we were able to relax. We took the body outside and cleaned up the rooms. The best part of the show was that no one was seriously hurt. Gogola did get grazed in the head. Thank God, that was it. Lucky again!"

After receiving first aid for his wound, Gogola returned to his platoon. They filled him in with what had happened and said they were glad to see him back. He ended his account. "Still without sleep to speak of, Lt. Ed Long left orders that I be relieved and ordered me to sack out for as long as I needed. I must have slept on and off for about eighteen hours."

The 506th Unit After-Action Report for November 12, 1944, reads:

> An enemy patrol estimated at 15 men attacked 1st Battalion at 0430. Attack repelled. One enemy killed. Unit identified as 21st SS Panzer, 11th Company.

The enemy did get back at the platoon. They remembered the location of the 1st Platoon CP. John Garrigan wrote: "The following night we received a terrible pounding from mortar shells. We stayed at this outpost for a couple more days and then we moved on."

Epilogue

Calm Before Another Storm

The last weeks of November on the island had been miserable with almost constant rain. There was a chill in the air. The men were cold. Clothes were never completely dry.

In mid-November indications that relief was in sight began to materialize. Advance parties from each unit left for France to prepare new quarters for the men.

The diary entries for T/4 George E. Koskimaki describe preparations for the move to France as the Holland campaign finally came to an end for the 101st Airborne Division:

> Nov. 25—More of the division left today. Living in a house in Slijk-Ewijk (Slicky-Wicky). Ohio State beat Michigan yesterday 18 to 14. We leave for France tomorrow.
>
> Nov. 26—Watched a Spitfire with motor trouble dive down. The pilot bailed out but his chute didn't open. Am writing from the division rest area (Nijmegen). We leave at 1400. Should be in Reims by 0700 tomorrow.

When the last troops pulled out on November 27, 1944, the 101st Division had spent seventy-two days in continuous contact with the enemy forces.

The division history, *Rendezvous with Destiny,*[138] describes the trip down Hell's Highway to the new post in France:

> Fall deepened into early winter, cold was added to dampness, and still the Division stayed on the Island. The hope for change got its first real encouragement in mid-November when units began to send advance parties to a new place no one had ever heard of before,

138. Rapport and Northwood, op. cit., 420.

Mourmelon-le-Grand, France. Finally, in late November, unit by unit, the Division pulled out.

The Dutch had not forgotten that the Airborne were the first to free them. As the trucks rolled back down the road "September 17" was what people shouted. The Island and all the miseries associated with it were soon left behind. Down the road to Uden, on to Veghel where the Dutch were already at work repairing their damaged buildings—"September 17" they yelled as they recognized the Screaming Eagles. Down through St. Oedenrode and Eindhoven, and September 17 became a memory—the Division was going to rest.

Koskimaki's diary made note of the arrival at the new post and a reunion with two old friends:

Nov. 27—Arrived at our new garrison in France (Mourmelon) at 0400. It is almost like Fort Bragg. Must go back to model soldering again. Chapman and Hickman are back with us. Both missed the Holland jump with appendectomies.

The new post of the 101st Division was twenty miles from the cathedral city of Reims. It had served as an artillery garrison for the French army. During the German occupation it had been used as a tank depot. The buildings were of a permanent type but were in disrepair. The men were happy to be out of the mud, and smoky fires could be burned to provide heat and comfort without drawing enemy fire from across a river.

Each battalion was given ten days to improve its situation, to bring its clothing and equipment needs to ready status. Equipment, weapons, and vehicles got a good overhauling. Athletic supplies were requisitioned and regimental football teams began preparations for intra-division competition. Boxing teams were organized. Replacements came in by the hundreds. Men who had spent long recovery periods in English hospitals returned to their old units. Others wounded in the early stages of the Holland campaign found their way back to the regiments and battalions.

The costs had been high again, just as in Normandy where 1,098 had been listed as killed. The KIAs numbered more than 858 in Holland; 2,151 were listed as wounded and 398 were counted as missing or captured during the campaign.

Less than a month after arrival in France, the 101st was

called on once more to do battle—this time to help stem the tide of the winter offensive in the Ardennes, the great Battle of the Bulge. Here the holding action and gallant stand of this great fighting division would give it the historic title of "The Battered Bastards of Bastogne."

Bibliography

Airborne Operations in World War II, ETO. USAF. Maxwell Air Force Base, Alabama, 1956.

Anonymous. "The Great Adventure." *The Royal Army Ordnance Corps Gazette,* January 1945.

Bollen, Hen. *Corridor naar de Ran*. Uitgeverij Terra, Zutphen, 1988.

Courtney, W. B. "Army in the Sky." *Colliers,* November 11, 1944.

Critchell, Laurence. *Four Stars of Hell*. Battery Press, Nashville.

Curreri, Joseph. "An Attack to Disaster." *New Breed,* 40–43+.

Curreri, Joseph. "The Clay Pigeon." *The American Legion,* May 1960.

Gilmore, L. J., and H. J. Lewis. *History of the 435th Troop Carrier Group*. Keys Printing Co., Greenville, SC, 1946.

Houston, Robert J. *D-Day to Bastogne*. Exposition Press, Smithtown, NY, 1980.

Katzander, PFC Howard. "Hell's Highway." *YANK,* October 8, 1944.

Korthals, Margry, Thuring and Voskuil. *September 1944*. Fibula-Van Dishoeck, Weesp, Holland, 1984.

Koskimaki, George E. *D-Day with the Screaming Eagles* (3rd ed). 101st Airborne Division Association, Sweetwater, TN, 1970.

McDonough, James L., and R. S. Gardner. *Sky Riders: History of the 327/401 Glider Infantry*. Battery Press, Nashville, TN, 1980.

Minick, Robert. *Kilogram: The Story of the 907th Glider Field Artillery Battalion*. Private Publication. Hobart, IN, 1979.

Perkins, Joseph K. *Mission Accomplished: A Story of the 321st Glider Field Artillery Battalion in World War II*. Salzburg, Austria, 1945.

Rapport, Leonard, and Arthur Northwood. *Rendezvous with Destiny* (3rd ed). 101st Airborne Division Association, Sweetwater, TN, 1948.

Spence, Harold. *Experiences of an Airborne Cipher Operator.* A Short Story. Birmingham, UK.

Wittebrood, Kees. *History of Zonhove.* Son, Holland, 1979.

Wolfe, Martin. *Green Light.* University of Pennsylvania Press, Philadelphia, 1989.

Documents

Airgood, Roger. *History of the 80th Troop Carrier Squadron.*

Higgins, BG Gerald J. *Tactical Operations of the 101st Airborne Division, Annex No. 4.*

Marshall, S. L. A. *Three Day Attack by 1st Battalion* (501st Parachute Infantry Regiment), 1944.

McCormack, Capt. George W. *History of the 81st Airborne Anti-aircraft and Anti-tank Battalion,* 1944.

Narrative of Market-Garden for 502nd Parachute Infantry Regiment.

Small Unit After-Action Report for 326th Airborne Engineer Battalion.

Small Unit After-Action Report for 326th Airborne Medical Company.

Small Unit After-Action Report for 327th Glider Infantry Regiment.

Unit After-Action Report for Holland, 506th, December 10, 1944, USNA #407.

Contributors

1Lt Roger Airgood (79 TCS)
T/5 Edward Albers (I/506)
1Lt Walter Amerman (B/506)
Cpl Lowell Anderson (B/907)
1Lt Alex Andros (H/506)
PFC Jack Applegate (HQ2/502)
S/Sgt John Bacon (H/501)
Cpl Thomas Bailey (HQ2/501)
T/5 Roderick Bain (E/506)
T/5 Albert S. Baker (C/377)
Mark Bando (501st Historian)
PFC Robert "Buck" Barger
  (326 Med)
1Lt Allen C. Barham (B/502)
Sgt John H. Barickman
  (HQ2/506)
1Lt Henry Barnes (326 Med)
S/Sgt Clive Barney (C/501)
PFC Luther E. Barrick (B/907)
T/5 Ray E. Barton (Med/501)
PFC James D. Bashline
  (H/501)
PFC Allen Bastina (F/327)
Sgt Wesley Bates (A/501)
PFC Carl D. Beck (H/501)
PFC Gerald J. Beckerman
  (B/501)
Roger Bell (British)
Dave Benfield (British)
PFC Wayne Bengel (E/501)
Cpl Bruce M. Beyer (HQ2/501)

S/Sgt Arthur Bittner
  (A/326 Eng)
1Lt Sumpter Blackmon (A/501)
Sgt Franklin "Ray" Blasingame
  (F/502)
Sgt John N. Boitano (B/506)
S/Sgt Michael A. Bokesch
  (HQ1/327)
1Sgt Gordon G. Bolles (H/506)
Cpl Courtney H. Boom
  (B/326 Eng)
1Lt Anthony Borrelli (A/506)
Cpl Jaap Bothe (Dutch Marines)
Sgt Robert M. Bowen (C/401)
Cpl John Braca (Div MP)
T/5 Glenn E. Braddock (PF/502)
T/5 Sam Brandenburg (B/907)
1Lt Guido Brassesco (82 TCS)
Sgt James E. Breier (H/501)
1Lt Eugene D. Brierre (C/501)
1Lt Robert B. Brewer (E/506)
Sgt Donald W. Brininstool
  (A/506)
Sgt Ottie Brock (C/81)
1Lt Ray I. Brock (HQ3/502)
Sgt Chester L. Brooks
  (HQ1/501)
Bill Brown (F/506 Historian)
Pvt Clyde O. Bruders (Sv/501)
1Lt Chester V. Buchanon
  (426QM)

1Sgt Marshall Buckeridge (C/501)

F/O George Buckley (Gli Pil)

PFC Robert Burgess (B/501)

PFC Laurence R. Burgoon (I/501)

S/Sgt Larry Bussler (75 TCG)

Cpl Matthew C. Butorayac (HQ2/502)

S/Sgt James F. Byrnes (D/377)

PFC James J. Cadden (C/506)

Sgt James S. Cain (A/501)

PFC James A. Calvin (C/501)

Pvt Albert P. Cappelli (I/506)

Capt Charles E. Carlsen (Sv/501)

Pvt Edward P. Carowick (B/326 Eng)

T/5 Frank J. Carpenter (C/501)

PFC Carl H. Cartledge (HQ/501)

Pvt John G. Cavaluzzo (D/501)

PFC Eugene Cavanagh (G/501)

Sgt Francis J. Chapman (C/377)

Sgt Robert R. Chapman (B/501)

PFC Lester Chaskins (B/907)

Sgt Michael Chester (PF/82)

Pvt William N. Chivvis (I/506)

T/Sgt Joseph Curreri (82 TCS)

Cpl Joe Choo (HQ2/506)

1Lt George A. Christensen (437 TCG)

PFC David Clark (Med A/506)

Cpl Herbert W. Clark (B/506)

Cpl Martin W. Clark (HQ3/506)

PFC Paul Clark (HQ1/401)

Sgt Stanley B. Clever (G/506)

T/5 Keith Clites (HQ3/506)

PFC Edward V. Colvin (H/502)

Pvt Lawrence T. Cormier (B/501)

S/Sgt Earl L. Cox (F/502)

Capt Lloyd Cox (HQ2/506)

LTC X. B. Cox Jr. (HQ/81)

PFC William K. Crews (Div MP)

Pvt. Arthur M. Crook (HQ/501)

Pvt Robert A. Crowe (HQ3/501)

S/Sgt E. A. Cunningham (HQ/327)

PFC Everett M. Daugherty (C/501)

PFC Lawrence H. Davidson (H/506)

S/Sgt Grayson A. Davis (C/401)

1Lt Gordon DeRamus Jr. (Pfdr/502)

Cpl Glen A. Derber (HQ2/501)

Pvt Henry A. DeSimone (E/501)

PFC Harry Dingman (I/506)

S/Sgt Levi W. Donnelly (HQ1/327)

Sgt George H. Dove (DivArty)

PFC George D. Doxzen (C/506)

PFC Kenneth O. Drake (D/81)

Cpl John Dumchock (DivArty)

Sgt. Thomas E. Earhart (C/502)

Sgt James D. Edgar (I/501)

Cpl James L. Evans (DivArty)

1Lt Charles M. Faith (Pfdr/501)

Pvt Patrick G. Fergus (F/502)

Sgt Michael Finn (I/501)

PFC Wilbur Fishel (I/506)

PFC Charles H. Fisher (HQ2/327)

1Lt Frank L. Fitter (HQ1/501)

1/Sgt F. G. Fitzgerald (C/377)

T/5 John E. Fitzgerald (HQ3/502)

PFC Thomas P. Fitzmaurice (H/506)

Cpl Eugene Flanagan (Sv/501)

Pvt James W. Flanagan (C/502)

PFC Robert A. Flory (B/506)

1Lt Robert Flynn (437 TCG)

2Lt David H. Forney (H/506)

T/5 P. A. Foutch (426 QM)

Sgt Willis H. Fowler (A/502)

Sgt Philip Fry (A/401)
PFC Herbert Fulsom (B/401)
1Lt David H. Galarneau (A/506)
Pvt William P. Galbraith
  (HQ3/506)
Pvt Jesse C. Garcia (G/501)
PFC Darrell W. Garner (B/81)
PFC John R. Garrigan (B/506)
1Lt Herbert L. Garris (D/377)
Sgt Lonnie Gavrock (I/506)
Pvt Jack L. Gehrs (Med/501)
Tom Giddings (British)
S/Sgt John L. Ghiardi
  (HQ2/501)
T/5 John Gibson (Med 3/506)
PFC Eldon Gingerich (G/506)
Capt Alphonse Gion (HQ/506)
Cpl Henry Gogola (B/506)
2Lt Wick Goist (HQ/377)
LTC David Gold (Div Surgeon)
Pvt Glen W. Goodwin (D/501)
Cpl Walter S. Gordon (E/506)
T/S Paul Goswick (Div Rcn)
PFC Devon Grahek (A/506)
Cpl Millard B. Greene (Div Sig)
Sgt Robert Greenhawk (D/501)
1Lt. Frank A. Gregg (E/501)
S/Sgt Claude S. Griffith (E/327)
S/Sgt Merville Grimes (G/506)
Sgt John W. Gring (Med/321)
PFC George Groh (A/327)
Cpl Robert L. Gryder (E/502)
S/Sgt William J. Guarnere
  (E/506)
Capt Alphonse G. Gueymard
  (B/81)
Capt David V. Habif (326 Med)
Cpl Joe Halderman (B/326 Eng)
T/5 Joe Haller Jr. (HQ1/501)
PFC Frank Halloran (B/326 Eng)
Capt Ian Hamilton (B/501)
Cpl Jack Hampton (D/501)
Capt Fred Hancock (C/502)

Maj Harold W. Hannah
  (Div HQ)
Pvt Gordon E. Hannigan
  (HQ/377)
PFC Emery C. Hansen (B/907)
1Lt William Hardie (HQ/377)
PFC Howard L. Harlan (Div Sig)
Capt John Harrell (DivArty)
PFC Alvin H. Harris (G/327)
PFC Joseph Harris (H/506)
PFC Johnnie Hart (B/377)
Pvt Duane K. Harvey (HQ1/501)
Capt Robert F. Harwick
  (HQ3/506)
1Lt Albert Hassenzahl (C/506)
S/Sgt Donald H. Hastings
  (C/327)
1Lt James Haslam (HQ/501)
Capt James J. Hatch (HQ1/502)
PFC Gerald J. Hauswirth
  (Div Sig)
2Lt Marshall Hays (C/501)
Kenneth Head (British Historian)
1Lt Clark Heggeness (H/506)
PFC Michael Heiberger (C/502)
T/5 Leonard F. Hicks (F/506)
F/O Edward L. Hillyard
  (435 TCG)
Sgt Willie R. Hiney (HQ1/401)
Sgt Albert W. Hoe (G/502)
PFC Charles W. Hogan (B/907)
Cpl Joseph J. Hogenmiller
  (F/506)
T/4 Thomas W. Holland (C/501)
Cpl Ray Hollenbeck (A/907)
PFC John Hopke (B/501)
Maj Sammie N. Homan
  (HQ1/501)
Pvt Harold Hoone (F/327)
PFC Lonnie G. Hoover
  (B/326 Eng)
S/Sgt Robert J. Houston (H/501)
Pvt. William J. Houston (D/501)

PFC Marion Hove (I/506)

Sgt Howard G. Howser
  (HQ1/502)

Pvt Bobby G. Hunter (D/501)

PFC Elroy Huwe (HQ/501)

S/Sgt John Hyatt (801 Ord)

Sgt Edward Ihlenfeldt (Div HQ)

Sgt Schuyler Jackson (HQ/502)

Pvt Robert W. James (E/501)

T/5 David Jackendoff (HQ2/502)

Cpl Matt Jemiolo (A/502)

Sgt Samuel C. Jermark (A/401)

PFC Robert Jessup (HQ/327)

Capt William G. Joc (D/81)

S/Sgt William John (C/327)

Sgt Thomas A. John (F/327)

Capt Barney J. Johnson (A/327)

Pvt Edward N. Johnson (H/506)

T/5 Eugene E. Johnson (H/506)

PFC Harry F. Johnson
  (HQ3/502)

Sgt Kenneth W. Johnson
  (Div Rcn)

Sgt Richard F. Johnson (C/502)

Pvt Gerald B. Johnston (C/502)

PFC Claude J. Jones (HQ2/506)

Capt Robert E. Jones (H/502)

PFC Norman A. Jorgenson
  (HQ2/506)

S/Sgt Edward Jurecko (D/501)

Sgt Robert J. Kane (B/377)

Capt Steve Karabinos (Div HQ)

Sgt Alvin H. Kargas (HQ3/327)

1/Sgt D. A. Keimer (Div MP)

T/5 Carl F. Kelley
  (Med/326 Eng)

Pvt William Kelly (Med/907)

PFC George A. Kempf (B/327)

T/4 James F. Kennedy (Div Sig)

1Lt William C. Kennedy (A/506)

S/Sgt Joseph Kenney (E/501)

Sgt Richard Ketsdever (I/501)

F/O Edward Keys (Gli Pil)

T/5 Gordon E. King (HQ2/506)

Pvt Ralph E. King (H/506)

Capt David Kingston (Med/501)

PFC Hugh A. Kiser (A/502)

T/4 Melvin Arthur Kitterman
  (Div Sig)

Capt Clifford G. Kjell
  (HQ1/327)

T/5 Richard L. Klein
  (HQ3/501)

PFC David Klinger (C/501)

F/O William Knickerbocker
  (435 TCG)

Sgt William H. Knight (C/506)

PFC Charles Kocourek (F/327)

Cpl Ernest Logan Koenig
  (Div Sig)

T/5 John W. Kolesar (HQ/377)

PFC Steve Koper (B/377)

T/4 George E. Koskimaki
  (Div Sig)

Cpl Steve Kovacs (HQ/506)

1Lt Walter Kron (D/81)

Cpl Chester Kubicki
  (A/326 Eng)

Pvt Lester Kuech (HQ1/501)

PFC Richard M. Ladd (HQ/502)

Pvt. Ruben LaMadrid (D/502)

S/Sgt Lawrence C. Lamb
  (D/501)

PFC Ernest A. Lambert (B/501)

Pvt William Lammers (D/502)

PFC Malcolm Landry (HQ/506)

T/5 Raymond Lappegaard
  (HQ3/501)

T/5 Charles M. Laden (Div Sig)

Pvt Frank Lasik (D/501)

T/Sgt Noah D. Lauten
  (HQ/377)

S/Sgt W. Thomas Leamon
  (C/401)

S/Sgt Thomas R. Leemon
  (801 Ord)

S/Sgt William A. Lemonds (801 Ord)

T/4 Mike Lewis (Div Sig)

Sgt. Robert Likam (C/326 Eng)

1/Sgt Carwood Lipton (E/506)

T/4 Frank J. Looney (HQ/81)

Pvt Moses Lopez (C/506)

S/Sgt Ernest A. Lowe (HQ1/327)

Sgt Joseph L. Ludwig (H/502)

PFC Lawrence C. Lutz (B/501)

Pvt Robert F. Mackey (G/506)

Sgt Jack MacLean (HQ2/506)

Sgt Patrick Macri (Div Sig)

PFC John MacNider (A/327)

Cpl Angelo M. Maione (E/327)

T/4 Gordon N. Majure (D/502)

Sgt Donald G. Malarkey (E/506)

S/Sgt Albert L. Mampre (Med2/506)

Cpl John Marohn (E/501)

PFC Robert Marohn (C/502)

T/Sgt Clifton Marshall (HQ/377)

Capt J. Roy Martin (HQ2/502)

PFC James H. Martin (G/506)

Pvt. Paul Z. Martinez (D/506)

Cpl Howard J. Matthews (F/502)

Sgt Clifton B. Maxwell (HQ/327)

T/5 Russell May (HQ/502)

F/O Weldon McBride (Gli Pil)

T/5 Charles McCallister (HQ2/506)

PFC James G. McCann (H/506)

PFC Nelson A. McFaul (A/506)

1Lt Joseph P. McGloin (85 TCS)

Capt Gerald McGlone (B/907)

Cpl Richard F. McGowan (I/501)

Capt Willis P. McKee (326 Med)

Sgt William McMahon (I/501)

PFC George R. McMillan (I/506)

S/Sgt John McMullen (H/501)

1Lt William McRae (HQ/377)

1Lt Werner T. Meier (IPW/501)

T/5 Oscar Mendoza (B/326 Eng)

Sgt Louis Merlano (A/502)

Pvt James Mielhus (HQ3/506)

PFC Clarence Milbrath (Div MP)

Cpl Daniel Miller (Div Sig)

Sgt Owen E. Miller (Med/506)

T/3 Paul R. Miller (Med/506)

Capt Walter L. Miller Jr. (C/327)

T/5 Jack E. Millman (G/327)

Pvt Frank P. Milner (Div Sig)

S/Sgt Charles A. Mitchell (B/506)

Sgt John J. Mitchell (Med/327)

Sgt Lionel C. Mitchell (HQ/502)

T/5 Harry T. Mole (HQ2/501)

S/Sgt Sol Molofsky (75 TCS)

PFC Barney Momcilovic (HQ1/501)

PFC James P. Monaghan (G/501)

1Lt Charles W. Moore (C/326 Eng)

PFC John B. Moore (Div Rcn)

LTC Ned B. Moore (Div HQ)

Capt Bill Morgan (E/501)

Sgt J. Herschel Morgan (HQ1/401)

Pvt. Tom Morrison (HQ/321)

Capt James C. Morton (HQ3/506)

Pvt Herman J. Moulliet (HQ1/506)

PFC George K. Mullins (C/327)

Pvt Wally Myers (C/502)

T/5 W. Paul Nabours (326 Med)

Cpl John Nasea (B/321)

T/5 E. Keith Natalle (326 Med)

PFC Julian Necikowski (DivArty)

PFC Norman A. Nelson (H/501)

PFC Forrest J. Nichols (B/502)

S/Sgt Roy W. Nickrent
(HQ1/502)
1Lt Thomas J. Niland (HQ2/327)
Pvt James W. Noreene (G/502)
Sgt Charles R. Norton (Div HQ)
PFC Robert J. Nuttall (Sv/501)
Sgt Joseph Nyeste (HQ1/327)
Pvt Harlan W. Oates (G/501)
T/5 John Obergoss (Med/506)
T/Sgt Robert O'Connell (9AF)
2Lt Robert P. O'Connell (D/501)
1/Sgt. Everett J. Oliver (A/401)
Pvt Albert J. Oliviera (D/81)
Capt Bill Osborne (D/501)
Cpl Chester E. Ostby (B/501)
Sgt Joseph P. O'Toole (C/81)
Sgt Ben L. Ottinger (B/401)
Cpl Cleon Overbay (C/401)
PFC John P. Oyach (HQ/907)
Pvt Bernie Palitz (C/377)
T/5 Frank Palys (HQ/506)
Sgt Arthur Parker (HQ/377)
Pvt Kenneth Parker (C/506)
PFC Emmert O. Parmley (F/502)
PFC Denis M. Parson (G/327)
1/Sgt Ted Patching (A/506)
S/Sgt Fred Patheiger (HQ/502)
Sgt Harold L. Paulson (C/501)
Sgt William J. Pekkanen (E/327)
Sgt Chester Pentz (B/502)
Capt Joseph K. Perkins
(HQ/321)
1Lt Herbert Perry (HQ/377)
PFC Arthur M. Peterson (F/506)
Capt Ivan G. Phillips (HQ/502)
Sgt Spencer O. Phillips (H/506)
PFC Willard W. Phillips (B/907)
Sgt John C. Piane (HQ1/401)
1Lt Ralph D. Pickens
(A-C/326 Eng)
Cpl Sam R. Pope (HQ2/501)
Sgt Joseph P. Powers (A/506)
Sgt Hugh E. Pritchard (D/506)

PFC W. C. Putney (HQ2/327)
Pvt Vorgie Pylant (A/506)
Capt William Pyne (C/506)
T/5 Paul J. Quaiver
(A/326 Eng)
PFC Samuel L. Raborn (E/501)
1Lt Robert Radmann
(50Med/Evac)
Helen Briggs Ramsey
(ARC 3/506)
Sgt Charles Randall (B/506)
Sgt Mike Ranney (E/506)
T/5 Loy Rasmussen (F/506)
1/Sgt Joe Reed (C/506)
Pvt Claude B. Reeves (HQ/377)
PFC Arthur Renner (HQ2/327)
Sgt Jack Reinhardt (B/326 Eng)
2Lt Donald E. Replogle (I/506)
Sgt Thomas M. Rice (C/501)
Cpl Donald J. Rich (G/327)
S/Sgt Robert C. Richards
(75 TCS)
Capt Marvin R. Richardson
(DivArty)
Cpl Henry R. Ritter (HQ3/506)
Cpl Charles J. Ritzler (D/501)
Capt Elvie B. Roberts
(HQ/501)
Cpl Rogie Roberts (B/81)
1Lt James A. Robinson
(HQ/377)
Cpl Dominick J. Rochetto
(C/377)
Sgt Willis F. Rohr (A/327)
Cpl George M. Rosie (HQ3/506)
PFC Harry Rosinski (G/327)
LTC Thomas W. Rouzie
(HQ/327)
Cpl Brownie Rusin (F/327)
T/4 Robert Ryals (HQ3/501)
Capt Bernard J. Ryan
(Med3/506)
Pvt Joe Rybale (503 PIR)

T/5 Robert G. Salley
(HQ326 Eng)
PFC Helmut Sambach (D/501)
PFC Paul E. Sanders (C/501)
1Lt Charles "Sandy" Santasiero
(I/506)
Cpl Peter Santini (HQ2/502)
Sgt Aloyse R. Schaefer (G/327)
Cpl Walter W. Schielke
(HQ2/327)
PFC Leonard T. Schmidt
(HQ3/506)
T/4 Robert A. Schmitz (Div HQ)
F/O Thornton C. Schofield
(75 TCS)
Sgt Russell Schwenk (F/506)
T/5 William Schwerin
(HQ3/501)
1Lt William G. Sefton
(HQ2/501)
Sgt Guy M. Sessions (C/501)
T/5 Frank Seymour (G/501)
1Lt Rex H. Shama (315 TCG)
Col Thomas L. Sherburne
(DivArty)
Cpl Jack Sherman (G/327)
Pvt Harry A. Sherrard
(B/326 Eng)
PFC James C. Sherriff (G/502)
Capt Charles Shettle (HQ2/506)
Cpl Charles Shoemaker (A/506)
Jean Showalter (Kin E/501)
Sgt James Shuler (I/506)
Sgt James Sirles (HQ/501)
T/4 Matthew Slifstein (HQ/502)
PFC Phillip Sluzar (HQ1/401)
Pvt David M. Smith (HQ/501)
PFC Fred T. Smith (B/506)
Pvt. Raymond D. Smith
(Pfdr/502)
Cpl Harold Spence
(Brit 1 Abn C)
PFC Bret Steele (HQ/377)

Cpl Frank V. Steh (F/327)
Pvt William H. Stephens (D/502)
Cpl C. E. Storeby (C/326 Eng)
PFC Donald B. Straith (A/506)
1Lt Robert Stroud (H/506)
PFC Charles Stultz (A/327)
1Lt Martin H. Stutman (C/81)
PFC Lloyd Summers (C/506)
F/O James A. Swanson
(305 TCG)
Capt Wallace A. Swanson
(A/502)
PFC Elton E. Taylor (HQ/327)
Pvt Henry G. Taylor (I/501)
Sgt John H. Taylor (F/506)
Cpl Malden Teal (C/506)
Cpl Dwayne L. Tedrick (D/506)
PFC Fred Terwilliger (A/502)
Pvt Donald E. Thoma (Div Sig)
Capt Eber H. Thomas (Sv/501)
Pvt John R. Thomas (C/501)
Capt Jack E. Thornton
(HQ3/501)
PFC Giles M. Thurman
(HQ1/506)
PFC Walter M. Tibbetts (B/377)
T/Sgt Harry M. Tinkcom
(81 TCS)
1Lt James W. Tolar (E/502)
Sgt Louis E. Truax (D/506)
PFC William E. True (F/506)
PFC Victor C. Truesdale
(HQ/321)
Sgt Eddie Turner (E/501)
T/5 Howard F. Turner (Div Sig)
Cpl Richard F. Turner (B/506)
T/4 Earl H. Tyndall Jr.
(HQ1/501)
Sgt Andy Uhlar (B/326 Eng)
S/Sgt John Urbank (G/501)
Cpl. Arie Van Dort
(HQ/326 Eng)
Sgt Joe Van Thiel (HQ/327)

Pvt Greg A. Vargas (B/377)
T/5 Edward R. Vetch (G/506)
S/Sgt Arnold J. Vincent (B/401)
Pvt Thomas R. Vella (Sig Co)
S/Sgt Charles Vess (Sv/501)
1Lt Kenneth L. Vyn (A/327)
Sgt J. Morris Wade (Div HQ)
Pvt Billy J. Waites (G/506)
S/Sgt Dallas F. Walker (HQ/327)
2Lt Jack Washichek (HQ/907)
PFC William Watson (B/907)
1Lt Darlyle M. Watters (81 TCS)
T/4 Dale G. Weaver
   (Med/326 Eng)
S/Sgt Robert R. Webb
   (HQ3/506)
Capt William W. Webb (Sv/327)
Sgt Elmer Weber (Div Rcn)
1Lt William Wedeking
   (HQ3/506)
Sgt Charles R. Weise (B/506)
PFC Paul West (A/401)
Sgt Allen L. Westphal (D/506)
S/Sgt Chester J. Wetsig
   (HQ3/501)
Cpl. James S. White (HQ3/501)
S/Sgt Maurice C. White (C/501)
T/5 Lowell E. "Tim" Whitesel
   (Sv/501)
T/5 George A. Whitfield
   (326Med)
Pvt Robert W. Wiatt (C/506)
PFC Fred A. Wilhelm (Pfdr/502)
PFC Robert Wilks (H/501)
PFC George E. Willey (D-E/501)
S/Sgt Jack L. Williamson
   (A/327)
Cpl Donald W. Wilson (B/501)
Pvt George F. Wilson
   (B/326 Eng)
Sgt Woodrow Wilson (426 QM)
1Lt George Woldt (Div Sig)
PFC Hilton I. Wolfe (DivArty)

Pvt Marvin C. Wolfe (I/501)
PFC Anthony Wysocki (Sv/501)
T/4 Gordon Yates (H/506)
PFC Harry G. Yaworski
   (B/326 Eng)
1Lt Harold E. Young
   (C/326 Eng)
Cpl Robert Young (HQ1/506)
Cpl Walter Zagol (HQ-F/502)
Cpl. John Zamanakos (Pfdr/502)
T/5 Herbert Zickuhr (326 Med)
Sgt. Gerald A. Zimmerman
   (Div Sig)
Pvt Emil Zorich (I/501)

Dutch Contributors

Joann v. Wely-Asselt
Andre van Bergeijk
Ernst and Rita van Bergeijk
Gerard van Boeckel
Micky Bokker
Abraham Bom
Alphonse Boxmeer
Peter van Breevoort
Geert v.d. Burgt
Pim Campman
Pierre and Hilde Cuypers
H.L.A. DeBeer
Mia v.d. Linden-deGreef
Fr. Arnold deGroot
Geurt and Coby deHartog
Helena Dowie
Johannes Evers
Miep Baer-Fast
Bernard Florissen
C. M. Van Gastel
John H. van Geffen
Adrian Goossens
Johannes J. van Gorkum
M.P.J. Goyaerts
A. J. van Hemme
Peter Hendrikx

Contributors 525

A.G.C. Hermens
J. A. Hey
Peter v.d. Heyden
Mary van Hoof
Josephine van Herpen-Hout
Mrs. G. van Houts
Jan Hurks
J. C. Jegerings
Gabriel v.d. Kaay
Peter Klompmaker
Frans Korte
Jan Kortmulder
Hans Kropman
Tonny Kuyper
Mrs. C. Boonman-Lammers
Joke van Hapert-Lathouwers
Willem Lavryssen
Mrs. Maria Leyts
Joop v.d. Linden
Rita van Loon
Joe Luyk
Albert Marinus
Jacoba Milovich
J. Meyer
Maryke Muller
Mike Nooijen
Herman van Ommeren
Willy F. J. van Ooyen
Lisa van Overveld
Pita van Overveld
A. P. Hoynck van Papendrecht
Fr. Hermen Peeters

J. W. Pieper
Mia Poos
P. Pouwels
Bert and Coby Pulles
Piet Pulles
Cornelius L. J. Rijken
Tony Rijkers
Family Roelofse
Christ van Rooy
Bert Sanders
Willem C. L. van Schaik
Johan Scheutjens
F. te Riet Ookgenaamd Scholten
A. van Sluiters
Cor H.E.G. Sprengers
Annie v.d. Steen
Willie Loedeman-Taken
H. Talen
Jan Tornga
Fr. Gerard Thuring
Joseph Verstappen
Jan Vervoort
Johan Vervoort
Theo v. Vroonhoven
J. v. Dongen v.d. Water
Hans Weimar
William van Wely
Tony Wernaart
Nellie Wijnen
Kees Wittebrood
John Wolfs
Nellie Zijlstra

Index

Please read on for a preview of
George E. Koskimaki's final book in the
Screaming Eagles chronicle

THE BATTERED BASTARDS OF BASTOGNE:

The 101st Airborne and the Battle of the Bulge, · December 19, 1944–January 17, 1945.

"The firefight had stalemated, with both sides digging in as darkness fell. We were told to expect a German armor attack at dawn. About 0400, a truckload of land mines arrived and I was designated to take a mine-laying party of one platoon out to 'mine the most logical avenues of armor approach.'

"I was supplied with a Belgian highway map and informed there was a combat patrol 'out there somewhere' ahead of me. What with the mines, engineer picks and shovels, plus normal combat equipment, the platoon sounded like a 5 and 10 cent store on the move, as we stumbled our way in the darkness. The Germans were firing one gun with shells that sounded like box cars coming through the air. One such landed a short distance away, spraying the area with clods of dirt as well as shrapnel. A voice behind me cried, 'Lieutenant, I'm hit, I'm hit!' I asked, 'Can you make it back yourself?' 'I think so,' he said. 'Then go back.' My last view of the casualty was a bulky shape making about six feet to the jump on one leg, toward the rear.

"A few hundred yards later, a skirmish broke out in the darkness somewhere ahead. The road map was being of no help whatsoever in determining routes of approach. In fact, I hadn't the foggiest idea as to exactly where we were. I called for the platoon sergeant, whom I'd met for the first time, before starting out with the mine-laying party. He was a chemical warfare tech sergeant, obviously brought aboard as a replacement. He didn't answer my summons, but a voice in the night explained his absence: 'He was hit and you sent him back!'

"It was wearing on toward dawn. I moved the platoon off to

the left from the direction of the skirmish ahead, found a flat piece of ground that might conceivably be of use to an approaching armored column, and said, 'Dig the mines in right here.' Within fifteen minutes, the eastern horizon was starting to pale. Now the trick was to get back through our own lines, wherever they might be in relation to our wanderings in the darkness.

"The trooper who had guided us out through the lines had long since dropped out of the party. Having veered from the original course to avoid the firing ahead, I could only head for Bizory by dead reckoning, with the skyline behind starting to silhouette us as we came in from the direction of the expected dawn attack. We would not be re-entering our lines at the point we left them.

"Concerned for the potential of disaster by 'friendly fire,' I preceded the group by some fifty yards, calling out warnings of our approach. I should have been yelling louder. A machine gunner opened up from maybe forty yards ahead, thereby provoking a career act of stupidity. Instead of hitting the ground, I stood there looking down the stream of tracers, which seemed to be passing on both sides of my face, and calling the gunner every abusive name I could recall, plus a few invented in the spirit of the moment. The fact that he stopped firing without hitting me or anyone in the group behind substantiates the adage—'God rides on the shoulders of the dumb.'

"I never did learn of any part the mines we laid might have played in the defense of Bastogne."